Canadian Women's Issues

Volume II
Bold Visions

Ruth Roach Pierson and
Marjorie Griffin Cohen

James Lorimer & Company, Publishers
Toronto, 1995

James Lorimer & Company Ltd. acknowledges with thanks the support of the Canada Council, the Ontario Arts Council and the Ontario Publishing Centre in the development of writing and publishing in Canada.

Canadian Cataloguing in Publication Data

Main entry under title:

Canadian women's issues

Includes bibliographical references and index.
ISBN 1-55028-429-0 (v. 2 : bound) ISBN 1-55028-428-2 (v. 2 : pbk.)
Contents: V. 2. Bold Visions

1. Feminism - Canada. 2. Women - Canada - Social conditions.
3. Women - Canada - Attitudes.
I. Pierson, Ruth Roach, 1938-   .
II. Cohen, Marjorie Griffin.

HQ1453.C36 1993 305.42'0971 C93-093812-7

James Lorimer & Company Ltd., Publishers
35 Britain Street
Toronto, Ontario
M5A 1R7

Printed and bound in Canada

Contents

Preface

For those who have been involved in the feminist movement for a long time, the shift to the right of North American politics is a signal that women's actions to bring about a more equitable society will not get easier. This two-volume work on feminism in Canada shows that women's efforts have been a progressive force in our society. As a result of women's determined efforts, the understanding of the dimensions of inequality has expanded and this, in turn, has forced important changes in social institutions. The period under consideration in these volumes represents the experiences of women in the process of developing and redeveloping feminist politics. Those of us who were part of the early development of feminist organizations were inspired by the awakening of a collective consciousness among women that social change was possible through action — if we acted together. We had a sense that we were experiencing something new in that we were going beyond dealing with injustice and inequality as individuals, limiting ourselves to criticism and resentment, or simply learning to "cope with it." The new feminism was an insurrection! We were inspired and strengthened by the conviction of being moral agents for change in the name of social justice. In writing this book we wanted to show how vital feminism has been to Canadian society and to tell the story of at least some of the issues women have confronted. We also wanted to show the various ways women began to understand what they needed to do, and how they related to each other and to the rest of society through political activism.

This is the second volume on the issues and actions of feminism in Canada covering the years from 1967 to 1994. The first volume included chapters on the women's movement in English Canada, the politics of the body, the politics of difference, social policy and social services, the law and the justice system, and culture and communications. Many of the progressive ideas of feminism that are currently being undermined by conservative politics are the focus of Volume II. This volume includes chapters on the politics of the household, paid work, education and training, economic policy, and the international and global dimensions of Canadian feminism.

Within each chapter we are interested in the complexities of issues within the context of the politics of the feminist movement. We explore, for example, the ways in which these issues have been understood in the process of making anti-racism an integral part of the women's movement. Similarly, we recognize the tension that class differences bring to political activism and the efforts undertaken, and still needed, to preserve the collective objectives of feminism.

In both volumes we have provided historical documents from the women's movement, in addition to an analysis of the issues and action, so that the rich diversity of feminist politics can be demonstrated through women's own voices. The documents sections include mostly unpublished items or those which would normally not be available in secondary sources. Most of what we have reproduced as documents has not come from published books, not because these were unimportant sources of information about feminist issues, but because they are more accessible through libraries and bookstores. We certainly recognize the significance of the work of other scholars and have referred to it, where appropriate, in the chapter texts and in the bibliography. The work of finding the documents for this project involved many people across the country over many years. While the documents of the history of the women's movement in Canada are extensive, much of the original material is still held by individuals or is in the files of various organizations across the nation. Our main task, in order to represent the diversity of feminist action and thought, was to find information.

Feminism has always been unpopular with the ruling élites in society and has invariably encountered resistance for its progressive ideas. But it has managed to change the way our society operates and the way in which people think about women. In the new reactionary climate, feminism's message is more unpopular than ever. We hope that by showing the ways in which women, so far, have confronted and overcome hostility to the objectives of feminism, new groups of activists will be strengthened in their determination to insist that our society can be better than it is.

Marjorie Griffin Cohen

Acknowledgements

The preparation of Volume Two: *Bold Visions* has benefited from the assistance of a great many individuals and institutions. As with Volume One: *Strong Voices*, we are especially grateful to all those who gave us permission to reprint, in whole or in part, their views and voices as documents in this book and who allowed themselves to be interviewed. The archives we thanked in Volume One for sharing their resources with us we would also like to thank again: the Canadian Women's Movement Archives; the Centre for Newfoundland Studies, Memorial University of Newfoundland; the Archives of the National Action Committee on the Status of Women; the Vancouver Status of Women Archives; the Victoria Status of Women Action Group Archives; the Women's Educational Resource Centre, Ontario Institute for Studies in Education; and the Archives of the Montreal Women's Centre.

We would also like to express our appreciation once again for the funding we received from: an Ontario Ministry of Education Transfer Grant to the Ontario Institute for Studies in Education; a Secretary of State Canadian Studies Program Grant; a Canadian Employment Work Study Grant; and Social Sciences and Humanities Research Council of Canada Small Scale Grants.

As before, a host of individuals helped us track down documents and verify information, among them Sandra Acker, Rosalie Bertell, Jenny Callahan, Muriel Duckworth, Nancy Forestell, Margot Francis, Monica Goulet, Margaret Hobbs, Madonna Larbi, Judy Morrison, Helene Moussa, Sylvia Novak, Dorothy Goldin Rosenberg, Darcian Smith, Donna Smyth, Gillian Thomas, and Esmeralda Thornhill. Special thanks are owed to Martha Beaudry, Nathlyn Jones, and Michelle Owen.

The contribution our freelance editor Beth McAuley has made to the preparation of this volume has been stupendous. We are greatly in her debt for her work as permissions editor, copy editor, and indexer. We also received much support and assistance from our Lorimer editor, Diane Young.

Volume Two is dedicated, as was Volume One, to all of the women in Canada who have made the women's movement possible. The royalties from Volume Two will also be donated to various Canadian women's groups.

Chapter 1

The Politics of the Domestic Sphere

Ruth Roach Pierson

One media view of feminism is that, as a movement, it speaks principally for professional career women. This view is reflected in the 1991 *Home-Maker's Magazine* article "Who's Home? Stay-At-Home Moms Struggle For Status." According to this article, to live the "feminist ideal" is to hold down "a $100,000-a-year position as vice-president of corporate finance with an investment firm on Toronto's big-league Bay Street" and thereby to have "it all: power, perks, prestige — even a secretary."[1] The main thrust of the *HomeMaker's* piece is to charge the feminist movement with ignoring the needs and desires of "stay-at-home moms" for the needs and ambitions of women in high-flying careers.

"The problem that has no name"

Such a charge is based on a very limited view of the more than twenty-year history of second-wave feminism. For, in fact, the issue of the oppression of women in the domestic sphere can be seen as the driving force of a number of major strains of the feminism resurgent in the 1960s and early 1970s. One of those strains was made up almost exclusively of white, university-educated, middle-class married women living in suburbia, and some working-class wives, who identified with the discontents articulated in Betty Friedan's classic *The Feminine Mystique.*[2] The concern with women's oppression within the home has tended to be class- or race-specific, and no work was more so than Friedan's 1963 bestseller.

Friedan brought into open discussion what she called "the problem that has no name." At the core of the problem was a medically undiagnosable malaise afflicting many middle-class, suburban housewives. The malaise was a complex compound of loneliness, boredom, feelings of inadequacy and inferiority, and a nagging fear of having wasted one's life. The women of whom Friedan spoke were not finding a sense of achievement or self-fulfilment in the daily round of domestic activities: getting the husband off to work and the children off to school, making the beds, tidying the house, baking bread, chauffering the children to after-school activities, preparing the evening meal, helping the children with their homework, and getting the children into bed. But the pop psychology of the day — "the feminine mystique" of women's maga-zines and advertisements geared to middle-class housewives —preached that normal women would find true fulfilment in housewifery and moth-erhood; and so, if they as wives and mothers were feeling unfulfilled, they could only conclude that there was something wrong with them. Friedan's solution for these women was threefold. First, they should organize their housework more efficiently, that is, not let it expand to fill the time available. Second, they should embark on the necessary training leading to the challenging careers for which their educations and class prepared them. And third, although less explicitly, but strongly at the level of subtext, they should hire other, less privileged and less formally educated women to do that part of the housework and childcare for which they themselves would no longer have time. The solution was, in other words, individualist and élitist, and also racist, given the pre-ponderance and ghettoization in domestic work of women from racially oppressed groups in North America.[3]

Although written by an American, Friedan's book circulated widely in Canada. Actually, some of its observations had been anticipated in *Chatelaine* and other Canadian women's magazines, as far back as the late 1950s, as one side of a debate over the proper role of middle-class married women in post–Second World War Canada.[4] On this side of the debate, commentators questioned the need for women's full-time devo-tion to home, pointing to the increasing tedium and mindlessness of housewifely chores in the middle-class household fully equipped with new-fangled appliances. These labour-saving devices were presented as freeing once housebound women to move out into paid employment or volunteer work on a grander scale. Commentators on the other side of the debate, however, pointed to the increasingly complex nature of running a modern home. Its great diversity of tasks and weighty respon-sibilities required, according to this view, a full-time homemaker who would be fulfilled through her efficient and creative management of the household. This was "the feminine mystique" side of the argument. Once motherhood was factored in, these commentators agreed that "a woman's place is in the home," fulfilling herself by fulfilling her prin-cipal responsibility to society: taking care of the children until they were grown.

And taking care of her husband and his needs, for his ultimate head-ship of the nuclear family was not challenged by either side in the 1950s/1960s debate. Those who portrayed the housewife/mother's role as complicated, absorbing, and worthy of a woman's life-long devotion based their argument on a belief in a man's right to have a housewife to care for him and a mother to tend his offspring. This "feminine mystique" side of the debate also did not challenge the priority of the husband's economic role. The privileges that priority in the workplace bestowed on men, whether in salaried or waged labour, were taken for granted: higher pay, greater access to jobs and to promotions, greater job security, better benefits. A few voices on the middle-class women's widening sphere side of the debate did call for "equal pay for equal work" and fought against sex discrimination in pensions and unemployment insurance coverage. But by and large, even those who advocated middle-class women's right to work for pay did not question the husband's right to head the family. Nor did they seek a holus-bolus dismantling of the ideology of separate spheres that underpinned men's privileged position in both home and workplace.[5]

The Doctrine of Separate Spheres

Inherited from the nineteenth-century Victorian era, the bourgeois gender ideology of separate spheres held that the sexes were predisposed by biology to operate optimally in distinct domains — men in the public realm of business, industry, and politics, women in the private realm of the home and charity. Character traits were parcelled out accordingly, entrepreneurial drive and ruthless competitiveness to men, compassion, delicacy, and nurturance to women.[6] Although perhaps only visible in retrospect, there were always "border cases" straddling the divide and giving evidence of the instability and artifice of the ideology.[7] Moreover, at various times in the nineteenth and twentieth centuries, middle-class women organized to push against their confinement to domesticity and socio-economic and political developments occurred, like wars, that necessitated a redrawing of the boundaries.[8] But each realignment was met with or followed by a backlash. In this way, the doctrine of separate spheres survived into the twentieth century, re-enshrined in new guises. Above all it served to rationalize a shifting but continuing sexual division of labour between women and men and the privileging of men in both the household and the workplace. In post–Second World War Canada, child psychology was at the forefront of the professional discourses, re-establishing the normative force of the divide between male breadwinner/dependent female child rearer. The father's role, in these discourses, was to be the provider, the mother's was to stay at home, changing the diapers and supervising the emotional/mental development of the child.

The doctrine of separate spheres has always been normative, establishing a standard of propriety acccording to which wives should stay at home while husbands go out to work. While very few working-class households have ever been able to achieve the ideal of the breadwinning husband, capable of supporting a dependent stay-at-home wife and their children, the doctrine of separate spheres corresponded to reality for many middle-class married women into the 1960s. The doctrine also corresponded to a real, structural division in both the working and the middle class insofar as mothers continued to be assigned major if not exclusive responsibility for child rearing. But while actual sex-typed public/private divisions existed, the doctrine's emphasis on separateness served the mystifying function of concealing the degree to which the public and private were interlocking and interdependent.

Another mystification that the doctrine of separate spheres performed was to mask the hierarchical nature of the relationship between the public and the private, presenting them as complementary. One of the major achievements of second-wave feminist theoretical analysis has been to interrogate the doctrine of separate spheres and thereby demystify it. First, feminist theorists have insisted on the interconnections between the public and the private. They have shown, for instance, that the state's non or inadequate provision of public childcare facilities has a direct effect on mothers' work load in the private sphere and on their freedom to access the public sphere of paid work. Second, feminist theorists have elucidated the degree to which the public has been privileged over the private. They have demonstrated, for instance, that men's ability to command more pay in the public sphere translates into unequal, not complementary, relations between husband and wife in the private sphere.

The debate in the 1950s and 1960s over the proper role for the middle-class wife reflected real contradictions in the middle-class married woman's position. On the one hand, the expanding service sector in both private industry and government increased the demand for women in white- and "pink"-collar jobs at the same time that a wife's wage packet or salary was increasingly needed for the couple to achieve middle-class status by being able, for instance, to buy a house of their own and furnish it with the latest in domestic technology. On the other hand, the construction of middle-class masculinity and, increasingly, respectable working-class masculinity, required the preservation of the public/private split as embodied in the ability of the husband to support a non-working wife. By the 1960s, the contradictions were intensifying between, on the one hand, a family's need for a double income to purchase the desired consumer durables and, on the other, the masculinist need for the status symbol of a dependent wife. In a context of excessively costly or inadequate childcare, these contradictions were being partially resolved through the growing trend for married women to work until the birth of the first of their children, stay out of the paid labour market during the children's early years, and re-enter only after the children were well launched in school.[9] Into the late 1960s, though, in the middle-income ranks as well as within the working class in single industry towns, the majority of married women with young children remained "stay-at-home moms."

"Why I Want a Wife"

In the sixties and seventies, wives were still expected to subordinate their needs and interests to those of their husbands. This expectation of subordination and subservience is what so infuriated a whole generation of university-educated, recently married wives and mothers. And it was anger at that unfair sexual arrangement, vented by Judy Syfers in "Why I Want a Wife," that helped swell the early ranks of second-wave radical feminists.[10] Appearing first in a New York Women's Liberation publication of 1971, Syfers' "Why I Want a Wife" (reproduced in the documents section of this chapter) was reprinted in abridged form, and often without any bibliographical data beyond authorship, in Canadian women's movement newsletters and consciousness-raising kits throughout the decade.[11] This piece became a classic because it resonated with the experience of so many young, middle-class women. Educated at co-educational colleges and universities that fostered the illusion of gender equality (female undergraduate students, for instance, competed for marks on an equal basis with male undergraduate students), such women found it a shock to graduate into marital relationships that were patently unequal. Their educations and the comfort of their middle-class upbringings gave them a sense of entitlement that was at odds with the role that was assigned to them in marriage. Some proportion of these young married women were working to put their husbands through the graduate or professional school training that was to secure the couple's middle-class to upper-middle-class income and position. But everyone knew that some men, once they were established in their well-paying professional jobs, "dumped" the wife who had made the sacrifices and replaced her with a "younger model." These women began to ask why it was their husbands, and not they themselves, who were entitled to have someone prepare their meals, type their papers, pick up after them, defer to their tastes, entertain their friends, and forgive them their sexual infidelities.

At the same time that these self-examinations of middle-class married women's confinement were taking place in consciousness-raising groups, other women were undertaking socio-economic and left-political analyses of housework and the housewife's role. These studies were necessitated by the degree to which the doctrine of separate spheres was entrenched in dominant schools of political economic thought. Both classic liberal and Marxian economic analyses so privileged the public over the private realm that neither paid much attention to the economic dimensions of the domestic sphere.[12] By and large what was understood as constituting "the economy" stopped at the door of the private residence. Nor did either school of economic theory attend much to the interconnections between the household and the wider economy.[13] The ideology of the separation of the public and the private — together with the liberal sanctification of the realm of privacy as beyond scrutiny — functioned fairly effectively to hide the world of the housewife and mother from public view. That realm was deemed worthy of study only to market researchers hired by advertisers and producers of domestic technologies and other household products. Of the many meanings attaching to the potent "the personal is political" slogan of early second-wave feminism, one important one was the demand that the veil of secrecy hiding the domestic sphere be torn aside to reveal the political economic nature of what went on inside the home.[14]

Analysing Housework

The early feminist studies of housewifery had both to analyse the nature of housework and to uncover its interconnections with the larger economy.[15] Many of these studies were socialist feminist in authorship and sought to work within a Marxist political economy framework. The struggle to apply Marxian concepts and categories to the analyses of the work performed by women in the home and its relation to industrial capitalism led to what came to be called "the domestic labour debate," to which a number of Canadian scholars made important contributions.[16] Marxist theoreticians engaging in the debate argued over such issues as whether or not the labour of housewives is productive, whether it produces "use value," "exchange value," "surplus value," or all three, and whether or not it constitutes a mode of production of its own. Over time the debate turned scholastic: the terminology became excessively cryptic, convoluted, and remote from the reality of women's lives.[17] Nonetheless, the debate served to unmask the intimate interconnections between the public realm of "production" and the private realm of "reproduction." The latter was understood to refer not only to generational reproduction but also to the daily replenishing of the body and soul of those who entered the public realm of production for pay. Molly Barber's 1985 poem "Shut Down Mode" compares "the reproduction of labour power" work of the housewife/mother with factory labour.[18]

These studies started from the premise that housework was oppressive and sought to figure out what made it so. One of the earliest Canadian analyses was done by Margaret Benston.[19] First published in 1969 and widely circulated in xeroxed copies thereafter, Benston's article "The Political Economy of Women's Liberation" analysed women's oppression as rooted in women's responsibility "for the production of simple use values in those activities associated with the home and family." Indeed having to bear responsibility for those tasks was Benston's definition of the category "women." Benston saw women's relegation to the tasks of home and family as oppressive for two major reasons: first, in an economy in which value was established monetarily, household labour was unpaid; and second, relegation to household labour effectively "denied [women] an active place in the market." In her examination of the links between household labour and the larger economy, Benston viewed capitalism as the system that did the relegating. And it was capitalism's relegation of women to housewifery that made women

CREDIT: Molly Barber, "Shut Down Mode", *This Magazine* 19, no. 3 (August 1985), 38.

Shut Down Mode

Molly Barber

Shut down my sister calls it,
comparing herself to a mine or a factory
or a nuclear plant. Maybe I'm thinking of meltdown.

No. Not meltdown, shut down,
When you extend the smallest amount
of energy possible,

When you only reproduce labour power
by feeding and cleaning and eating and sleeping
and being very kind in a quiet way.

Where you do the necessary but you do not produce
you occupy the time and space.
The trees and even frogs do this

In the winter. Shut down, the factories lay
off the workers, only those with the most
seniority stay, mine maintenance.

So the factory is peopled
with old men who maybe snooze and doze
and dream of spring.

Like the frogs and the trees,
Like my sister waiting for her next baby,
Like my sister, or Karen Quinlan, or sleeping
beauty, waiting for the prince.

Those also serve who only sit and wait.
This should have been engraved on my mother's
tombstone, but it wasn't,

For we could not admit that a life had been devoted
to the reproduction of labour power
and to being very kind in a quiet way.

*Domestic power can be as repetitive and lifelong as factory labour. And,
as expressed in this poem, women have coped by "shutting down" and
only giving the minimum required, laying themselves off from the job as
though their factory had closed.*

"remain a very convenient and elastic part of the industrial reserve army," that is, a cache of "unemployed" cheap labour that could be drawn into paid employment when the economy was booming and let go in times of economic recession and depression. Benston clearly saw interconnections between the public and the private; and, for her, women's path to liberation lay in women's ceasing to bear the principal responsibility for childcare and household labour and thereby gaining equal access to jobs and job stability outside the home.[20]

Other analyses sought to "unpack" the category "housework" and break it down into its component parts in order to reveal the oppressive nature of the labour itself.[21] Meg Luxton's study of three generations of working-class housewives in the northern Manitoba mining town of Flin Flon was one of the most systematic and thorough-going. Eventually published in book form,[22] shorter summaries of her findings appeared in magazines and periodicals, such as the *Canadian Dimension* article excerpted in the documents section of this chapter.[23] Because the terms "housework" and "housewife" themselves could obscure aspects of the work performed by women in the home, not the least of which was the labour of mothering, Luxton chose the more comprehensive label "domestic work." She broke down domestic work into four subcategories: 1) the housework itself, by which she meant "cooking, cleaning, and maintaining the house and the objects within it"; 2) "child bearing and rearing"; 3) "household management — orchestrating all household activities and co-ordinating the schedules of all household members"; and 4) "tension-managing — caring for the psycho-emotional needs of all the household members and the sexual needs of the husband."[24] Others would divide up the pie of domestic work differently, hiving off the work of shopping for clothes and food and other household essentials into a separate subcategory, for instance.[25]

Most studies agreed that the components of "housework" were many, diverse and often conflicting. The frequent tension between different aspects of domestic labour — between, for instance, the goals of housekeeping and the goals of mothering — made it oppressive. Many women who were both housewives and mothers experienced the incompatibility between child rearing and keeping a tidy house as a guilt-producing double bind. Feminist analysis brought to light another major contradiction facing housewives/mothers: while they experienced their multifaceted job as stressful and energy-draining, the public perceived their labour as light and trivial.

In her analysis of the relationship between domestic labour and the larger economy, Luxton related the perception of domestic labour as trivial to the changes in housework resulting from the expansion of industrial capitalism. Not only was the bulk of production moved out of the home, but it appeared that modern labour- and time-saving appliances had taken the *work* out of housework. The heavy drudgery of basic household tasks, like washing and ironing clothes, cooking, and cleaning house, was lightened and vastly reduced by "running water, electricity, flush toilets, cooking ranges, washers, dryers and vacuum cleaners."[26] Housework underwent an apparent "deskilling" and "despecialization" in conjunction with the introduction of these utilities and labour- and time-saving devices. Throwing clothes into an electric washer and dryer, in other words, did not appear to take the same degree of either physical strength or skill as did boiling clothes in tubs on top of wood-fired stoves and hanging them to dry on clothes-lines outdoors. No one, to put it another way, would have disparaged the work of our grandmothers and great-grandmothers as trivial. But what this perception of contemporary housework as trivial ignored, Luxton and others pointed out, was that the advertisers of domestic appliances and the "experts" in home economics, who made liberal use of the germ theory of disease, had greatly raised the standards of household cleanliness.[27] At the same time the "experts" in early childhood development were advocating an intensification of mothering as essential to a child's psychological health.

There were other ways, both feminist theorists and activists argued, in which these changes in domestic work did not necessarily make it less oppressive. One was the isolation of the housewife/mother in the privatized home, a point the author of the 1991 *HomeMaker's* article on "stay-at-home moms" hits upon as though making a new discovery. Also contributing to contemporary housework's oppressiveness, according to the feminist analysis, was its fragmentary and repetitive nature. Whereas in the past housework was organized on weekly and seasonal bases — that is, washday Monday, ironing Tuesday, top-to-bottom house cleaning in the spring, canning and preserving in the summer and fall — in the present the round of washing and drying clothes, going to the grocery store, and vacuuming the house could repeat itself daily. At the same time, in keeping with the decreased mental concentration these contemporary tasks seem to require, housewives/mothers are regarded as infinitely interruptible. Nor can their schedules be self-imposed, for, as Luxton's study revealed, the dependent housewife/mother's work is regulated by the work shifts of her husband. Finally, though much of the sheer physical drudgery has been removed, the overall 24-hour-a-day, 365-days-a-year responsibility for the smooth running of the household and the health and care of the children (and other household members) remains with the housewife/mother.

A further factor contributing to its trivialization, as Benston had argued and later analysts agreed, was the unpaid nature of women's domestic labour. In a market and money economy, the argument went, it was the lack of a monetary value assigned to the housewife's and mother's labour that led to its invisibility and devaluation. Non-payment helped housework take on the appearance of non-work. That classification of housework as non-work had entered official discourse was evident in the 1971 Canadian census question: "Do you work, or are you a housewife?"[28] To demonstrate that women's unpaid domestic labour has "real" money value, feminists sought to find out how much the various chores housewives/mothers perform for free would cost if the husband/father had to hire paid employees to do them. An example of this kind of calculation, though one that did not take mothering into acount, was reproduced in the 1974 booklet *Working Women in New-foundland.*[29]

Wages for Housework

One strategy that developed out of the focus on the unpaid nature of women's domestic labour was the "Wages for Housework" campaign. This was an international campaign that was led, insofar as it had leadership, by the authors of the widely read *The Power of Women and the Subversion of the Community*, Mariarosa Dalla Costa of Italy and Selma James of the USA.[30] By the mid-1970s, there was a dynamic Wages for Housework campaign in Canada. In 1973, Judy Ramirez was active in organizing the first Canadian tour for Selma James and Mariarosa Dalla Costa, documented on video tape by Francie Wyland. The tour culminated in a keynote address by James at the Montreal Feminist Symposium "where 800 women passed a resolution demanding wages for housework for all women from the State."[31] In 1975, Ramirez helped organize the Toronto Wages for Housework Committee, perhaps the largest and most active of the Canadian Wages for Housework Committees. It launched its Campaign for Wages for Housework with a May Day rally at Nathan Phillips Square. If working for no pay in the home is at the root of women's oppression and powerlessness in society, Wages for Housework supporters reasoned, then the way to liberate women was for the state to pay women an income for performing the socially necessary labour of housework and childcare. Such a state-paid income would liberate women simultaneously from impotent dependence on a wage-earning or salaried man and from the necessity of taking an outside-the-home job for the paltry wages usually paid women. As the Family Allowance scheme introduced in 1944 provided that the cheques be payable to mothers, Wages for Housework campaigners saw it as a recognition of the principle they were fighting for and as a first step, however inadequate, towards full wages for housework. Any threat to the scheme was to be resisted.[32] The Trudeau government's 1976 freeze on Family Allowance payments became the focus of protest in the May Day "mobile rally" organized that year by the Toronto Wages for Housework Committee.[33]

The Wages for Housework campaign had gained sufficient credibility in Canada by late 1977 that the New Democratic Party Federal Women's Organizer felt compelled to issue a policy statement denouncing it as "an obstacle to equality."[34] To begin with, Judy Wasylycia-Leis paid tribute to the campaign's success in exploding many of the myths regarding housework, such as the myth that housework "is the 'natural destiny' of women," the myth "that housewives 'do it for love,'" and the myth "that labour performed in the home is not really 'work.'" She also credited the campaign with helping to show how "the wageless condition of the housewife helps to sustain capitalism." But Wasylycia-Leis faulted the campaign on two major counts: namely, one, that the cost of a universal wages for housework program for all women would simply be too high; and, two, that implementation of such a program would lock women into the housewife role even more securely. The 1974 Newfoundland booklet on *Working Women* had made two similar arguments, namely that: one, "if the state paid [housewives] salaries, undoubtedly most of the money would be raised by taxing those who could least afford it"; and two, "it might also serve to reinforce the idea that women are primarily housewives..."[35] Instead Wasylycia-Leis called for the abolition of the role of housewife altogether. To that end, she argued, the party "should be demanding more socialized forms of child care and domestic work." Also crucial, in her view, was the proposal put forward at the 1976 Canadian Labour Congress convention, and rejected by the "wages for housework" committee within the CLC, that means be found "to encourage men to share the housework in order to open up more opportunities for women workers."[36]

Why Is Housework Women's Work?

This latter solution addressed a third question concerning the oppressiveness of domestic work for women. That is, beyond exploring the relationship of domestic labour to capitalism and investigating the oppressive components of domestic work, there was the gender question: Why is it almost exclusively women's work? Taking the long historical view, some argued that socio-economic developments led to this sexual division of labour. As production moved out of the home and as soon as men were able to earn a "family wage," that is, enough to support a dependent wife and children as well as the man himself, it made sense for the mother who bore and nursed the children to stay home and shoulder the domestic labour. Others argued that that explanation had too much of a "biology is destiny" ring to it.[37] Instead, they invoked the concept of patriarchy and patriarchal privilege to explain the male's sense of entitlement to having a wife/mother to service his needs and those of his offspring.[38] Contending that it was neither historically inevitable nor sociobiologically determined that women be saddled with the prime responsibility for housework and childcare, these feminists argued that a system of male power, not just capitalism, benefited from the public/private sexual division of labour. Within a social movement of women organizing to change the relations of power between the sexes, these women sought to change the behaviour of individual men.

However, many heterosexual women, committed to bringing the revolution home, learned to their dismay that getting male partners to share the housework was no easy task. One early, tongue-in-cheek account of the struggle, entitled "The Politics of Housework" by Pat

Mainardi,[39] found its way, like Syfers' "Why I Want a Wife," into many a consciousness-raising kit and women's liberation newsletter. Speaking from and to the position of a white woman university undergraduate, graduate student or recent graduate, the piece cleverly pinpointed many of the ways in which supposedly sympathetic, "progressive" men resisted, denied the resistance to, and weaseled out of sharing housework. Mainardi exposed the myriad evasive stratagems — ranging from pleading ignorance and ineptitude to claiming genetic inability — employed by the white male, accustomed to having the dirty work of household chores performed by someone else, when he was asked to do his share. One of the most successful ruses was for the man to demonstrate a higher level of tolerance for dirt and disorder and then, shrugging, to tell the woman that she simply had standards of cleanliness and order that he saw no need to uphold. All the while the man could count on the woman's having been conditioned to feel that poor housekeeping would reflect badly on her, not him, and therefore, in this war of wills, she would break down first and do the cleaning up.

"The Politics of Housework" is also a clear example of the race- and class-specific, if not to say racist as well as classist, character of some of the early second-wave feminist analyses of the politics of the domestic sphere. The piece betrays no recognition of the much greater risk that might be involved in this kind of individualistic struggle if the woman undertaking it were more economically vulnerable or socially marginal than a childless, college-educated, white woman. Mainardi herself could presumably move out and find reasonable employment and a place to live on her own with far less damage to her standard of living than a woman, for instance, who possessed few educational credentials, was encumbered with children, or belonged to a racially oppressed minority. Classism and racism are also apparent in the document's frequent analogizing between Blacks and women, and immigrants and women, as if there were no Black women or immigrant women and as if, historically in North America, the burden of housework has not fallen most heavily on women in socially subordinate groups.

Nonetheless, among many heterosexual feminists, there has been agreement that in each individual household the woman should struggle to get the man in her life not merely to "help with" but to "share" the housework on an equal basis. To discover what the allocation of household tasks was within a typical heterosexual couple, researchers carried out "time-budget" studies for which each member of the household kept a detailed account of how she/he spent her/his time within a 24-hour period. An 1976 analysis of data from Halifax and Vancouver concluded that, where both husband and wife were in the paid labour force, "[m]en clearly are still in the stage of 'helping' with the household maintenance and are not equally responsible with women for this part of the [couple's] total work load."[40] Moreover, it appeared that "the wife does most of the adapting" and that "men adapt minimally to the change

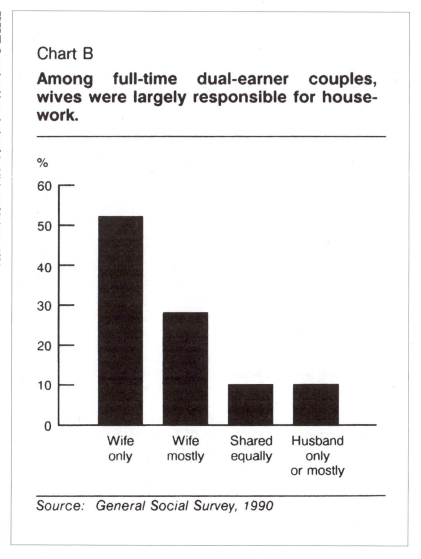

Chart B

Among full-time dual-earner couples, wives were largely responsible for housework.

Source: General Social Survey, 1990

The majority of women working for pay still have a greater share of responsibility for daily housework, while only 10 per cent of husbands in married couples share or assume most of the responsibility.

SOURCE: General Social Survey, 1990.
Taken from Kathleen Marshall, "Employed Parents and the Division of Housework," *Perspectives on Labour and Income* (Statistics Canada), 5, no. 3 (Autumn 1993), 23-30. Catalogue 75-001E.

in circumstances caused by their wives ceasing to be full-time house-wives and entering the labour force."[41] By the 1990s, the wife was still chief cook and bottle washer[42] even though now over 70 per cent of heterosexual couples with children aged eighteen or under formed dual-earner households as compared with 30 percent in 1967. A sexual division of tasks has persisted, with the man doing the bigger and outdoor jobs, the periodic (annual or seasonal) chores, and the woman doing the regular, unending (daily and weekly) ones. Drawing on Statistics Canada's 1990 General Social Survey (GSS) and defining housework as "meal preparation," "meal clean-up," "cleaning," and "laundry," Katherine Marshall argues that women are still "likely to assume primary responsibility for these routine tasks, which must be performed on a regular basis and which account for 78% of all housework."[43] Summarizing the GSS data, Marshall states that, while

> women employed full time have somewhat less responsibility for housework than do women with part-time jobs or those at home full time, ... the majority of wives who are employed full time continue to have all or most of the responsibility for daily household tasks.[44]

Furthermore, though the GSS did not gather information on responsibility for childcare, it recognized that "children in a household increase the amount of housework" and that "women are more likely to do the extra work" that children require.[45] "These women," Marshall concludes, "face the double burden of paid work and unpaid housework."[46]

As an increasing proportion of married women with children were drawn into the paid labour force, then, the overwhelming majority found they still bore the burden of responsibility for housework. While the home was a place of leisure and relaxation for the husband returning to it from his eight-hour day, for the wife it remained a site of labour, as she rushed around to throw together a meal after she came in from "work" and as she struggled to find time to do the cleaning in her "off" hours. One respondent to a survey by Ann Duffy, Nancy Mandell, and Norene Pupo on women, work, and family confessed

> that she often fantasizes about being single again, returning home after work able to enjoy silence, solitude and freedom from the domestic commitments that envelop her child-crowded life.[47]

The women's movement began to speak of women's "double day" of labour, for the increasing entry of women into the paid labour force was not matched, as we have seen, by an equivalent entry of men into unpaid domestic work. Nor was women's move into paid labour eased by society's or the state's provision of services to lighten the burden of housework borne by gainfully employed women. And if the housewife working outside the home for pay was also the mother of young children, then "double day" was something of a misnomer. The women's movement could have been speaking of the "triple day."

Childcare

By 1984, more than half of Canadian mothers of young children were gainfully employed. By 1990, "fully 70 per cent of families with children under 16 ... had mothers in the labour force. And 63 per cent of families with children under school age had a working mom."[48] In the end, only some aspects of the domestic labour problem allow for a solution on the basis of restructuring the relationship between the sexes in an individual couple within a privatized household. In the case of the question of who cares for the children, the mainstream feminist movement, while rejecting an appeal to the state to pay "wages for housework," has appealed to the state to provide childcare as a necessary precondition for women's social equality.

The conservative backlash against feminism in the early 1990s, however, persists in representing a mother's decision to work for pay or stay home with the kids as individualist and unmediated. This representation is a cruel distortion of the conflict-ridden situation facing most working mothers. A mother of young children who is working for pay out of economic necessity is hardly exercising "free choice." For many married mothers, their pay cheque is what keeps the family's collective head above water. In the case of the increasing number of sole-support mothers,[49] without the woman's income, the family unit would be dependent on the inadequate support of state welfare. Nevertheless, in the late years of the Mulroney regime the mainstream media carried a rash of advertisements and articles, such as the one from 1991 in *HomeMaker's Magazine* on "stay-at-home moms," that were dripping with nostalgia for a 1950s world of dependent, homemaker moms happily baking pies for hubby and the two kids in shiny, suburban kitchens.[50] This romanticized picture blots out the conflict and tension beneath the keeping-up-of-appearances surface of fifties suburbia. Even then that world was accessible only to the well-to-do middle class. And today the fantasy of that white, wonderbread world has become, for demographic and socio-economic reasons, so inaccessible to the vast majority that they could not "return" to it even if they wanted. The *HomeMaker's* article reproduced in the documents section, however, is steeped in the rhetoric of personal, individual choice. Most misleading is its claim, with respect to "stay-at-home-moms," that "20 years after the revolution for equality began, an increasing number of women are taking advantage of the single most valuable aspect of equality seeking — choice." The article implies that all mothers can choose to walk away from their jobs to stay at home with their children. The reality is that this option is only open to those women in stable relationships with securely employed and well-paid husbands. Some of these women are organizing groups, such as the

Ottawa-based Mothers Are Women (MAW) and the national Canadian Alliance for Home Managers (CAHM), and affiliating their organizations with the National Action Committee on the Status of Women (NAC) to resume the struggle for some of the goals of early second-wave feminism as yet unrealized. These include pensions for housewives and recognition by the Canadian census that work in the home is work.[51] But to suggest that all mothers who are fed up with "the overwhelming frustrations of inadequate child care" and "unfair wages" can simply throw over their jobs and go back home is a gross distortion. This line of reasoning misses the point that any semblance of "equality of choice" will only be achieved when the women's movement has succeeded in overcoming the almost insuperable difficulties to securing adequate childcare and decent wages for women.

Certainly the women's movement has also spoken the language of individual rights and individual choice. For instance, a strain of early radical feminism, embraced by young, unmarried women in the context of state- and society-sanctioned greater accessibility of birth control, held up a kind of flight from motherhood as the path to liberation.[52] To this day, most strains of feminism would support a woman's freedom to choose to become or not to become a mother and a woman's freedom of choice with respect to the question of abortion. But the broadly based women's movement recognized early on the importance of the fact that most women are socially located as mothers. Consequently, it addressed many of its earliest recommendations to changing societal structures so that the contradictions in women's social location as mothers could be resolved. To begin with, to support married women's right to enter gainful employment, early liberal feminists raised concern over the "empty nest syndrome," the feeling of uselessness many of those women felt who had, in the 1950s and 1960s, stayed at home and devoted themselves to housewifery and motherhood and then seemed to lose the focus of their lives after the last child left home.[53] This concern was voiced by the 1970 *Report* of the Royal Commission on the Status of Women. Speaking of women who had assumed the traditional role of wife and mother at a time when the average number of children per family was no more than two, the *Report* observed that "the rearing of children, the centre of their lives, is soon accomplished." Therefore, the *Report* reasoned, "the care of the family and a home ... is unlikely to take up the greatest part of [a woman's] time."[54] In fact, the "empty nest syndrome" mainly afflicted middle-class married women as few working-class women had had the leisure to devote themselves solely to their children.

Socialist feminists began drawing attention to the dilemma faced by less affluent women who must reconcile their work as mothers with their paid employment. This dilemma has acquired overriding importance as an increasing proportion of mothers from the working and middle classes have entered paid work outside the home. For that reason, the struggle to have child rearing recognized as a social responsibility, rather than the responsibility of the individual mother, has been a major focus of second-wave feminism.[55] Already in 1970, one of the Recommendations of the Royal Commission was for "a national Day-Care Act" and federal-provincial agreements to provide funds "on a cost-sharing basis for the building and running of day-care centres ... "[56] Since then the term "childcare" has replaced "daycare," and organized advocates across Canada have argued and agitated to gain public acceptance for the provision of "universal, affordable, quality" childcare.) Affiliated with the childcare committee of the National Action Committee on the Status of Women, these activists have worked tirelessly to put pressure on local, provincial, and federal governments to provide, not the childcare itself, but the *funding* for a childcare system that is community based, accountable to parents, and accessible to every child in Canada.[57]

But in its childcare campaign, the women's movement has repeatedly come up against the brick wall of government reluctance to institutionalize society's debt to the unpaid labour of Canada's mothers. As of 1992, there were approximately 2.8 million children in Canada aged twelve and under whose mothers were in the paid labour force. At the same time there were only 371,573 licensed childcare spaces, and only "144,617 of them subsidized to some degree."[58] According to Statistics Canada, for 68 per cent of children who do not have the luxury of stay-at-home moms (or dads), other childcare arrangements have had to be made.[59] In February 1992, the Conservative government of Prime Minister Brian Mulroney reneged on its eight-year-old promise to create a national daycare program. At the same time, it ended the universality of Family Allowance payments and continued to chip away at child benefits. The net result, according to the Caledon Institute of Social Policy, has been to increase the cost of parenthood, especially for those in lower- and middle-income brackets.

Domestic Labour, Immigration, and Racism

A small minority of working parents solve their childcare problems by hiring live-in nannies. The use of *paid* domestic help in the homes of the privileged also illustrates the close interconnections between the public (in the sense of state policy) and the private spheres. Historically, the Canadian government's immigration policy with respect to women has been geared towards filling a demand for paid domestic servants at the same time as the policy has been shaped by racism. Up until the 1930s, immigration officers looked to the British Isles as the preferred source of supply and after that to northern European countries, such as Finland.[60] The racist intent was to attract young women who would most easily assimilate to the Anglo-Saxon norm and preserve white dominance.

Another supply of domestic workers was provided by women descendants of those Blacks who were brought to Canada as slaves, or who came to Nova Scotia with the Loyalists, or who escaped along the underground railroad from slavery in the United States to settle in southern Ontario. Although the governments of the day expected paid domestic work to be but a transitional job for most immigrant white women, their expectations for Blacks were different. Canadian-born or immigrant, Black women were expected to enter domestic service as a life-time occupation. Indeed, until the Second World War, domestic service was one of the only paid jobs open to Black women in Canada.[61] Even after the Second World War, white householders in Nova Scotia felt they could call any number within the Black settlement of Birchtown if they were looking to hire a domestic worker.

Because Black women in Canada have always had to work hard for pay in one way or another, they have felt alienated by that strain of second-wave feminism that focused on the problems of the white, middle-class woman confined to dependent domesticity. For Black women, the struggle has not been to escape from the constraints of the doctrine of separate spheres but rather to struggle against the historical confinement to menial paid labour.[62] At the same time they have had to struggle against the multiple kinds of racist discrimination that impinge on the domestic sphere, such as racist discrimination in housing and the racist hostility their children have had to face in schools.

If racism has militated against non-whites having social intercourse with whites on an equal footing, it has encouraged intimate relations between whites and non-whites in which the latter retain a position of subservient subordination. Hiring Canadian-born Blacks for domestic work did not threaten the predominantly white composition of the population. During the Depression, when immigration was curtailed, domestic service was seen to some large extent as the solution to the problem of unemployment among young Canadian-born white women, particularly those from rural areas. It is only after the Second World War, when the demand for domestic servants could no longer be met either by Canadian-born Blacks or by white European immigrants, that Canada began to rely for its supply on women from Latin America and "Third World" countries, especially the Caribbean islands, the Philippines, and India. Despite this reliance, the racist barriers to immigration were not lifted to any significant degree. The "Caribbean Domestic Scheme" of 1955 granted landed immigrant status to a yearly quota (set in the hundreds) of carefully screened young, single West Indian women willing to come to Canada to work for at least one year as domestics.[63] But as many of these women, like their white European forerunners, opted out of domestic work after serving the mandatory year, the shortage continued, requiring the admission each year of more non-white women, some of whom sought to sponsor the immigration of other family members. To stem the influx of immigrants not desired as permanent residents,[64] Employment and Immigration turned in 1973 to a "temporary solution," allowing Caribbean and other "Third World" women into Canada on short-term employment visas to work as domestics under closely monitored conditions. Many still cherished the hope of eventually acquiring landed immigrant status and then of being able to bring their families to Canada. But as Savitri's story, reprinted in the documents ection of this chapter, indicates, the obstacles put in their way by Immigration have often been insurmountable.[65]

Governments' failure to implement policies to relieve the gruelling poverty to which thousands of mothers and children in Canadian society are consigned exposes the emptiness of official pronouncements on the sanctity of motherhood and the importance of children. An immigration policy that has facilitated the "temporary" entry to Canada of Third World mothers to work as nannies and also, in some cases, as household drudges in the homes of Canada's élite, at the same time denying entry to their own children, exposes even more dramatically not only the race- and class-specific character but the racism of an official rhetoric that speaks of the sacredness of the mother-child relationship. In 1983, Makeda Silvera broke the silence surrounding the experiences of such women with the publication of her interviews with West Indian domestic workers in Canada. In 1979, driven by the poverty and unemployment of her native Guyana, Savitri, a woman of East Indian descent, left her husband and four children to work as a domestic in Canada.[66] By the time Silvera spoke with Savitri in 1983, she was in her late forties and had not seen her family in four years. Though she has been sending them money and clothes as often as possible, she was by then desperate to receive landed immigrant status so she could bring her husband and children to join her in Canada. The Immigration officials' reluctance to increase Canada's non-white population by the admission of Savitri's children reveals blatant racism and, more specifically, a racist disregard for the maternal feelings of a non-white woman. Equally\ deplorable, Savitri's employers were willing to exploit her maternal and familial feelings in order to squeeze more work out of her. While white feminist analyses of housework uncovered the power differentials between men and women of the same class in relation to domestic labour, Silvera's work cast light on the political conflicts in the domestic sphere between women and women along the axes of race and class.[67]

Women concerned about the rights of immigrant domestic workers have organized and set up advocacy and information services. From its first days of existence, the Montreal Women's Centre was made aware of the crying need of women who had recently immigrated to Canada, often but not exclusively as domestics, for language and job training and for information about medical and other services essential to their own and their families' survival.[68] In 1979 a coalition of community, women's, and immigrant organizations in Toronto founded INTER-CEDE (International Coalition to End Domestics' Exploitation) as "an advocacy and counselling organization for domestic workers' rights." It also provides information and educational workshops to foreign domestic workers.[69] INTERCEDE can take credit for organizing, in 1981, the

CREDIT: O'Neill
COURTESY: Match International Centre, Ottawa

The federal government's Live-in Caregiver Program places greater immigration restrictions on domestic workers, over 70 per cent of whom come from the Philippines. The women who immigrate to Canada not only fill much-needed positions as domestic workers, but come with the hope and ambition for a better life.

first recorded demonstration of domestic workers in Canada. INTER-CEDE and sister organizations like the Committee for Domestic Workers' and Caregivers' Rights in Vancouver also deserve credit for helping to bring about changes in immigration law that allow foreign "domestic workers who have worked for two years to apply for immigrant status from within Canada."[70] But in April 1992, the Mulroney government's Live-in Caregiver Program introduced new, more restrictive immigration standards for foreigners who seek work in Canada as nannies or caregivers for the elderly or the disabled: "a worker must have a minimum grade 12 level education, must be able to speak either English or French, and must have six months of formal training in live-in care."[71] The new laws favour women, predominantly white, from European countries where such training programs exist, and discriminate against women, predominantly women of colour, from the "Third World" where they do not. For instance, the Philippines, which topped the list in the 1980s and early 1990s as the country of origin for most (up to 70 per cent) of Canada's foreign domestic workers, has no such programs. According to INTERCEDE, the new laws "create more barriers for women of colour and reinforce systemic racism in Canada's immigration policies." The impact of the new laws has been swift. "In the first eight months of 1992, only 2,343 domestic workers were allowed to enter Canada, over a 50 per cent reduction from 1991."[72]

From the Family to Families

Another major part of the domestic politics of feminism has been to contest the notion that there is a single, monolithic definition of "the family." Historically, a number of feminists have judged the institution of marriage to be oppressive of women.[73] Some unmarried, heterosexual, second-wave feminists put little faith in the effectiveness of the recommendation of the *Report* of the Royal Commission on the Status of Women in Canada that the provinces and territories "amend their law to recognize the concept of equal partnership in marriage."[74] Instead they opted for more casual, common-law arrangements. Other already married feminists sought in a variety of ways to equalize the relationship between themselves and their husbands. One way to resist subsumption under the identity of one's husband was to resume one's "maiden" name and thereby reclaim one's own identity. But, as discussed by Andrea Knight in 1975, statutory law in some provinces like New Brunswick put obstacles in the way of a formal name change by a married woman.[75] The marriage ritual itself became the object of much feminist criticism, particularly the wedding industry and the cultural hyperbolizing of the wedding ceremony as the high point, if not end point, of a woman's life. A 1984 poem by Erin Mouré captures the fear and disgust aroused in a young girl by the bodily contortions her wedding-bound babysitters underwent to make themselves attractive to their boyfriends.[76]

One of the major developments diversifying the face of "the Canadian family" has been the increase in single-parent families, over 80 per cent of which are headed by mothers. While in the past the death of a spouse was the main reason for single-parent families, today the main reason is separation or divorce. That sole-support mothers predominate among single-parent families is partly the result of mothers' getting custody of the children about 85 per cent of the time in cases of marriage breakdown. But another important reason is the growing trend among single women who become pregnant and keep their babies. In either case,

CREDIT: Erin Mouré, "The Wedding Party," *Domestic Fuel* (Toronto: House of Anansi Press, 1985). Reprinted with the permission of Stoddart Publishing Co. Limited.

Wedding Party

Erin Mouré

The women who babysat me in the 1960s,
I wonder who they are
with their bright nails & bubble hair, hardened
They never let us sleep,
blasted the hi-fi so loud into the phone,
one friend to another, yelling above the craze
They had boyfriends with cars, flames scrawled on the metal
Smoke cigarettes on my parents' sofa,
their high shoes & forbidden sweaters, acquiescence
to the male, their hope chest

Before all their weddings I watched them babysit,
the backs of their heads
ducked under the kitchen tap,
washing their hair colour
Their desires sent me out of my mind.
One way or another, the false clothes of
the wedding party
a lattice of future need
The possessions divided into gasoline & hairspray
the talk of modernity
With their heads soaked, rubbing red nails on the scalp,
bowed over, silent,
they scared me.
I didn't want to grow to fit their clothes.

*In the 1960s, marriage was the ultimate goal in life for many women.
But even then, some young women, as seen through the eyes of this poet,
made a firm choice not to grow up just to be married.*

except for a handful of professional women who earn high salaries and
can afford to pay for extensive, quality childcare, sole-support motherhood is a constant struggle to survive in a society still ordered according
to the male-headed, nuclear family norm. When only 5 per cent of
needed childcare spaces are subsidized, and then only partially, and
when women earn on average only two-thirds to three-quarters of what
men earn, it is no wonder that nearly half of sole-support mothers are
reduced to living on welfare and that mother-headed families are one of

the major sites of the increased impoverishment of women and children.[77]

But the discrepancy between the prescribed norm of "the family" — monogamous, heterosexual, nuclear, and male-headed — and the reality of women's lived experience is nowhere sharper than in the case of lesbian households. Here one also sees the inseparability of the public and the private, for when the male-headed, heterosexual, nuclear family is enshrined in law and public policy, the members of a jointly female-headed lesbian household encounter kinds of public discrimination that have serious implications for their "private" well-being. The heterosexism embedded in the justice system, in social legislation and social policy, as well as in the practices of public and private sector businesses can break up lesbian households. In a famous case of 1979, an Ontario lesbian mother won custody of her two children, but only on condition that she submit any prospective partner to the approval of the court. Since Judge Mahon had declared in handing down his judgment that "Homosexuality was a negative factor in the custody application," the mother could hardly have expected a favourable hearing in response to a request to live with her female lover. The partial victory of winning custody, albeit conditional, was owing to the credence the judge granted a child and family therapist who testified that the children "had a strong bond with the mother and the home she provided showed a lot of warmth and cohesiveness."[78]

Many other less fortunate lesbian mothers have lost custody of their children in separation and divorce cases.[79] "Wages Due Lesbians," which Francie Wyland helped form in 1975 in the same year as the Toronto Wages for Housework Committee was organized, "focussed much of its activity on the issue of lesbians and child custody" and "on the fight by more and more women for the power to choose to be lesbian without losing the possibility of having and keeping children."[80] What led many lesbians to give up the fight was the knowledge that they couldn't "afford to raise [their children] on 'women's wages' or welfare."[81] On International Women's Day, 1978, Wyland and Ellen Agger and other gay women from the Wages Due Lesbians and the Toronto Wages for Housework Committee founded the Lesbian Mothers' Defence Fund (LMDF), a support system which, in 1982, Thunder Bay feminists hailed as "exciting and energizing."[82] An Alberta LMDF was also founded in Calgary.[83] For nine years, LMDF Toronto provided financial help, "referrals to sympathetic lawyers and other professionals," peer counselling, and "personal and emotional support" to lesbians in custody struggles. In the last issue of the LMDF Newsletter *Grapevine* (Summer 1987), LMDF Toronto announced its closure. It was a matter of the members' "having run out of steam," not of there being no further need to struggle. Nonetheless, LMDF Toronto could point proudly to its having "helped many women keep or win custody of their children" and to having "helped begin the redefinition of 'family' so it will one day include us all."[84] But as Rachel Epstein has written in her study of lesbian parenting,

> The challenge lesbian parents pose to the traditional model of the nuclear family is undermined by the institutionalized homophobia and heterosexism embedded in the society and encountered in the behaviours of family, friends and institutions.[85]

Writing under a pseudonym "to protect my child, my career, and my lifestyle from our daughter's biological father, a man with a criminal past," Laura Barry speaks in 1994 of the fear she and her lesbian partner experience of being "outed" by their three-year-old daughter and of the hope that "as our little girl struggles to understand her type of family in this homophobic world, ... she will remain proud of her two moms ... "[86] Although Ontario, Quebec, and the Yukon have amended their Human Rights Codes to include sexual orientation as a prohibited ground of discrimination, the federal government continues to procrastinate on its promise to include sexual orientation in the Canadian Human Rights Act. Moreover, even in those provinces where sexual orientation is in the Human Rights Code, few women can afford the cost and risk of seeking redress before Human Rights Commissions.[87] So lesbians continue to face discrimination in many areas of the public sphere that impinge negatively on their private lives. For instance, lesbians who want to conceive and bear children encounter homophobia in clinics that provide the means for artificial insemination.[88] Lesbian couples who are "out" suffer discrimination in housing. Only occasionally are the spousal provisions in health insurance and other social benefit packages extended to lesbian partners. Rarely without a major union struggle have lesbian workers won the right to have their insurance coverage extended to their female partners as family members. In a hard fought case in 1985, Karen Andrews, a worker at a Toronto Public Library, was able, with the active support of her union, the Canadian Union of Public Employees, to use the leverage of her union contract clause prohibiting discrimination on the basis of sexual orientation to persuade CUMBA, the provider of dental and drug insurance to library personnel, to extend coverage to Andrews's lover Mary Trenholme and Mary's two teenage daughters. As the president of Andrews's union local argued, Karen, Mary, and Mary's two daughters form a family and therefore they "should be covered as a family."[89] In a similar 1986 case, the Vancouver Municipal and Regional Employees Union (VMREU) successfully negotiated the provision of spousal benefits to same-sex partners of clerical and support staff employed by the Vancouver School Board.[90] The federal government under Brian Mulroney, however, "threatened to deregister the Ontario pension plan if benefits were extended to same-sex couples."[91] In the summer of 1994, the NDP government in Ontario failed in its attempt to extend full family benefits to same-sex couples. The initiative split

MOTHERHOOD LESBIANISM and CHILD CUSTODY

FRANCIE WYLAND

"... We are demanding not only the power to choose to be lesbian without losing our children, or the possibility of having them. We are also demanding the power to be with those children *in a way that is not work*. And we will apologize to no one for rearing children who are -- like their mothers -- making a ferocious fight for the power to determine their own lives."

Francie Wyland

Published by Wages Due Lesbians (Toronto) and
Falling Wall Press, Bristol, England

Available :   *In Canada* from Wages Due Lesbians
             PO Box 38, Stn. 'E' Toronto M6H 4E1 Canada
  32 pp.   *In U.S.A.* from Women in Distribution
              PO Box 8858 Washington, D.C. 20003 U.S.A.
  $1.20   *Bulk Orders* from Falling Wall Press
              79 Richmond Rd. Bristol BS6 5EP, England

Wages Due Lesbians was founded in 1975 to give a voice to lesbians fighting for custody of their children.

the NDP provincial caucus and provoked powerful resistance, particularly from the Roman Catholic Church. The Archbishop of Toronto, Aloysius Ambrozic, issued a pastoral letter to 200 churches in the Metro area telling his more than one million parishioners that "Any attempt to promote a homosexual lifestyle as the equivalent of legal marriage must be vigorously opposed."[92]

Over the twenty-odd years of the recent feminist movement, with the steady increase of women in the paid labour force and the greater ease of divorce, the shape of households in Canada has changed. The male-headed, heterosexual, nuclear family of husband and wife, married for life, with two, three or four children, is no longer the statistical norm. This change has come about as a result not only of economic developments but also of feminists' experimentation with other kinds of households, like women-lead, "mothersharing" households, and non-profit housing co-operatives developed by women and for women. Gerda Wekerle has identified a host of initiatives by women to develop non-profit housing co-operatives, some by women's groups aiming to help other women, others by ad hoc groups of women seeking to create housing for themselves and others with similar needs. "One of the first non-profit, women-initiated housing cooperatives in Canada was Grandir en Ville in Quebec City, developed in 1981" by a group of sole-support mothers who took over a convent, slated for demolition.[93] The change in familial organization is also the result of feminists' efforts to win individual rights for women. These include the right to self-determination through economic independence; the right to live openly in same-sex relationships or in common-law heterosexual relationships; the right, even if married, to use one's own name; and the right to bear a child as a single woman without that child's bearing the burden of "illegitimacy." But as these rights have been granted more on the basis of individualism than on the basis of some vision of the just society, some of these gains have come at a high cost.[94] The extended family networks that women could once draw upon have been eroded by urbanism and social mobility. While women have won the right to stand as individuals in their own right, they have lost those protections they enjoyed, at least in theory, as dependent — albeit often exploited and even bused — wives and daughters. And neither the state nor corporate capital has been adequate to the task of supplying those eroded protections. Above all, the refusal of federal, provincial, and municipal governments to recognize through adequate funding society's collective responsibility for childcare has left the child the responsibility of the individual woman. Given the continuing gap between women's and men's pay, particularly in the case of non-white women, the increase in households headed by sole-support mothers has gone hand in hand with the increase in the so-called feminization of poverty.

But feminists do not welcome the conservative cry to restore so-called "family values." Feminists have fought long and hard to break down the barriers between the private and the public spheres; they are not keen to see them re-established. For instance, feminists have traced a link between the danger of woman battering and a woman's economic dependence on a man with whom she lives in isolation within the domestic sphere.[95] Claudette Bradshaw, executive director of Moncton Headstart, a New Brunswick anti-poverty and anti-abuse social agency, told federal politicians that abolishing family allowances would lead to an increase in wife abuse and a decrease in wives' ability to leave abusive relationships, because those "family allowance cheques, which are paid directly to mothers, are the only source of financial independence for thousands of women who are physically abused by their husbands."[96] The Conservative government of Brian Mulroney proceeded nonetheless with the elimination of family allowance payments, one of the oldest social programs in Canada. This move was in keeping with the goals of the powerful "family caucus" within the Tory party, a committee of thirty-five MPs with strong backing from cabinet ministers and the prime minister.

During the Mulroney years, according to the parliamentary bureau chief for *The Globe and Mail*, that influential caucus "scored victory after victory," the abolition of family allowances and the scrapping of the promised national daycare program being the most important. The caucus intended to entrench the "importance of family" in a proposed preamble to the Constitution, but the Conservatives were ousted from government before that could happen. That the definition of "the family" that the caucus held was a traditional and unitary one can be seen in the remarks of one of its members, according to whom, "a male and a female, living together to raise children, ... that's the only kind of family that ought to be defined." In the language of the family caucus, all other family forms are merely "alternate lifestyles."[97] Not surprisingly, the caucus was also staunchly opposed to the proposed amendment to the federal Human Rights Act that would prohibit discrimination against gays and lesbians. The family caucus shared many of the values of the anti-feminist women's organization REAL Women (the acronym standing for Realistic, Equal, Active, for Life). Since its founding in 1983, REAL Women has lobbied against many feminist causes, among them universal, state-subsidized childcare, equal pay for work of equal value, and rights for homosexuals.[98]

The stated goal of the family caucus was, as one of REAL Women's goals remains,[99] to give "women a greater opportunity to stay at home with their children."[100] Hence the early 1990s media flap over "June Cleaver-style moms back in fashion."[101] But that goal, even if desirable, is not realizable for the vast majority of adult women in today's society: single women, sole-support mothers, divorced women, women in relationships that require a double income, women seeking to escape from abusive partners. In a kind of conservative double speak, family caucus members denounced as "favouring the individual" the social legislation that had been designed to ease at least minimally women's participation in a labour market that is anything but a level playing field.[102] On the contrary, feminists have argued, it is precisely social legislation that can prevent consignment of all but a minority of women — those with husbands who are well-off, non-abusive and faithful for life — to an atomized society in which they must fend for themselves and their children as individuals on their own. In other words, the failure to implement such social policies as universal childcare or a guaranteed annual income and the erosion of existing social legislation, such as medicare and unemployment insurance, have helped consign increasing numbers of women and children to poverty. And stricter enforcement by the state of child support payments from divorced or separated fathers, some feminists argue, is not a good social solution. First, it ignores the history of damage to women of forced dependence on a possibly abusive man or on a man whose support might be at best erratic. Second, it helps perpetuate the male-breadwinner/dependent-female-housekeeper family as the norm, despite the fact that fewer and fewer people live in such households.

Feminists writing about the anti-feminist backlash in the English-speaking world remind us to beware of men talking about the restoration of "family values." As American historian Linda Gordon has observed, "[a]larms about the 'decline of the family' ... have been mainly backlashes against the increasing autonomy of women and children."[103] It is code, according to another analyst, for men lamenting the loss of "their sacred duty to own, control and enforce behaviour upon women."[104] Unmarried motherhood is a direct challenge to such men's sense of entitlement. It is also a challenge to heterosexist and racist notions of what constitutes a proper family. For this reason, perhaps, unmarried mothers remain so severely disadvantaged economically in addition to being still stigmatized as moral reprobates when reduced to dependence on welfare.

The intense interdependence of the private and public spheres remains central to feminist politics. The Western liberal individualism that evolved from the so-called Age of Enlightenment forward had men in mind and was predicated on what one academic feminist once called women's relegation to the "ontological basement."[105] What she meant was that men's embrace of the principle of individual equality of opportunity and of the right freely to enter as unencumbered individuals into the competitive marketplace of high politics and the public economy rested on the assumption that women would remain in the home, servicing the needs of men and their children. Women's allotted role was to make the home a "haven in a heartless world."[106] While individualism reigned supreme in the public sphere, "the family" of the private sphere was not reconstituted to consist of atomized individuals but rather resolidified as a corporate entity, hierarchically ordered from the headship of the father/husband down through the dependent mother/wife to the dependent children. But as women gained the vote and entered the paid labour market on an ever increasing scale, the corporatism of the family was eroded. This is a loss lamented by conservative men and those conservative women who are able and willing to risk making wifehood and motherhood their full-time career. The wife of former prime minister Mulroney is a classic example of the successful exercise of this option. For a majority of adult women, however, while the breaching of the barriers to the public sphere, above all entry into the paid labour market, has provided access to individualism, they have been left still carrying the burden of the "double," "triple," or "quadruple day."[107] With the exception of a few measures of social welfare legislation,[108] society has not been reordered to relieve women of the responsibility for the "ontological basement." Now that much of that minimal social legislation is being whittled away, many women and children are being left to suffer.

NOTES

1. Kathy English, "Who's Home? Stay-At-Home Moms Struggle For Status," *Homemaker's Magazine* 26, no. 3 (April 1991), 100–106, reprinted in the documents section of this chapter.
2. Betty Friedan, *The Feminine Mystique* (New York: W.W. Norton, 1963).
3. Evelyn Nakano Glenn, "From Servitude to Service Work: Historical Continuities in the Racial Division of Paid Reproductive Labor," *Signs: Journal of Women in Culture and Society* 18, no. 1 (Autumn 1992), 1–43.
4. Veronica Strong-Boag, "Working Wives and the Good Life: 1945–60," May 1992, revised under the title "Canada's Wage-Earning Wives and the Construction of the Middle Class, 1945–60," forthcoming in *The Journal of Canadian Studies*.
5. Veronica Strong-Boag, "Canada's Wage-Earning Wives ... "
6. For the most detailed account of the emergence in industrializing England of the bourgeois domestic ideology and doctrine of separate spheres, see Leonore Davidoff and Catherine Hall, *Family Fortunes: Men and Women of the English Middle Class, 1780–1850* (Chicago: The University of Chicago Press, 1987).
7. See Mary Poovey, *Uneven Developments: The Ideological Work of Gender in Mid-Victorian England* (Chicago: The University of Chicago Press, 1988).
8. See, for example, Ruth Roach Pierson, *"They're Still Women After All": The Second World War and Canadian Womanhood* (Toronto: McClelland & Stewart, 1986).
9. Sylvia Ostry, *The Female Worker in Canada* (Ottawa: Queen's Printer, 1968).
10. Judy Syfers, "Why I Want a Wife," *Notes From The Third Year: WOMEN'S LIBERATION (1971)*, 13–14.
11. For instance, a copy can be found in a "Consciousness-Raising Kit" prepared by the Toronto Women's Place, 1972, reprinted in the documents section. Copy at Canadian Women's Movement Archives (hereafter CWMA): file "Consciousness Raising."
12. According to Davidoff and Hall, "The world of production and the state has been systematically privileged as central to historical understanding." Davidoff and Hall, *Family Fortunes*, 29.
13. Joan Kelly, "The Doubled Vision of Feminist Theory," in *Women, History, and Theory: The Essays of Joan Kelly* (Chicago and London: The University of Chicago Press, 1984), 54, reprinted from *Feminist Studies* 5, no. 1 (Spring 1979).
14. Davidoff and Hall have argued, "Far from the market being separate from the family, the two were locked into a set of elaborate connections." Davidoff and Hall, *Family Fortunes*, 32.
15. For an example of a later work that benefitted from the earlier groundbreaking studies, see Natalie J. Sokoloff, *Between Money and Love: The Dialectics of Women's Home and Market Work*, forward by Elise Boulding (New York: Praeger Publishers, 1980).
16. For a collection of Canadian contributions to the domestic labour debate, see Bonnie Fox, ed., *Hidden in the Household: Women's Domestic Labour Under Capitalism* (Toronto: The Women's Press, 1980).

17. For an incisive and witty summary of some of the major contributions to this debate, see Eva Kaluzynska, "Wiping the Floor with Theory — A Survey of Writing on Housework," *Feminist Review* 6 (1980), 27–54.
18. Molly Barber, "Shut Down Mode," *This Magazine* 19, no. 3 (August 1985), 38, see poem reproduced on page 7.
19. See the special issue of *Canadian Women Studies/Les cahiers de la femme* 13, no. 2 (Winter 1993) on "Women in Science and Technology: The Legacy of Margaret Benston," especially Angela Miles, "Margaret Benston's 'Political Economy of Women's Liberation,'" 31–35.
20. Margaret Benston, "The Political Economy of Women's Liberation," *Monthly Review* 21 (September 1969), offprints of which circulated widely in North America in the early 1970s. New Hogtown Press were the publishers and distributors in Canada of a reprint of Benston's *The Political Economy of Women's Liberation* in pamphlet form. See also Mickey & John Rowntree, *More on the Political Economy of Women's Liberation* (Toronto: New Hogtown Press, 1974), 1–5, excerpted in the documents section of this chapter.
21. See, for example, Ann Oakley, *Housewife* (London: Penguin Books Ltd., 1974), and Ann Oakley, *The Sociology of Housework* (London: Martin Robertson, 1974).
22. Meg Luxton, *More Than a Labour of Love: Three Generations of Women's Work in the Home* (Toronto: The Women's Press, 1980).
23. Meg Luxton, "Housework," *Canadian Dimension* 12, no. 7 (December 1977), 35–38, excerpted in the documents section of this chapter.
24. Ibid.
25. See, for example, Veronica Strong-Boag, "Discovering the Home: The Last 150 Years of Domestic Work in Canada," in Paula Bourne, ed., *Paid and Unpaid Work* (Toronto: New Hogtown Press, 1985), 35–60.
26. Luxton, "Housework," 36, excerpted in the documents section of this chapter.
27. See, for example, Barbara Ehrenreich and Deirdre English, "Microbes and the Manufacture of Housework," chap. 5 in *For Her Own Good: 150 Years of the Experts' Advice to Women* (New York: 1978), 127–164.
28. Quoted in Elizabeth Batten, Dianna Gray, Carolyn Hallett, Albertha Lewis, and Jane Lewis, "Houseworkers," *Working Women in Newfoundland* (St. John's, Newfoundland: Women's Place, August 1974), 24, excerpted in the documents section of this chapter.
29. *Working Women in Newfoundland*, 25, excerpted in the documents section of this chapter.
30. Mariarosa Dalla Costa, "Women and the Subversion of the Community" [first pub. in Italy as "Donne e sovversione sociale," in *Potere femminile e sovversione sociale*, Marsilio, Padova, 1972], and Selma James, "A Woman's Place" [first pub. in the USA, February 1953, by Correspondence, a group organized around the publication of a workers' newspaper], in *The Power of Women and the Subversion of the Community*, with an Intro. by Selma James (Bristol: The Falling Wall Press, Ltd., 1972).
31. Curriculum Vitae of Judy Ramirez, n.d., in possession of Ruth Roach Pierson.
32. See "HANDS OFF THE FAMILY ALLOWANCE," *The Other Woman* 4, no. 2 (March/April 1976), 7, reprinted in the documents section of this chapter.
33. The rally "stopped at three locations including an immigrant shopping centre and a government housing project." "Wages for Housework Video Tapes," flyer of the Toronto Wages for Housework Committee, n.d., in the possession of Ruth Roach Pierson. See "HANDS OFF THE FAMILY ALLOWANCE," reprinted in the documents section of this chapter.
34. Judy Wasylycia-Leis, "WAGES FOR HOUSEWORK: AN OBSTACLE TO EQUALITY," New Democratic Party, Article No. 4, November 14, 1977. Copy at CWMA: file NDP-Federal. Reprinted in the documents section of this chapter.
35. *Working Women in Newfoundland*, 26, reprinted in the documents section.
36. Judy Wasylycia-Leis, "WAGES FOR HOUSEWORK: AN OBSTACLE TO EQUALITY," reprinted in the documents section of this chapter.
37. See Jane Humphries, "Class Struggle and the Persistence of the Working Class Family," *Cambridge Journal of Economics* 1 (September 1977); Hilary Land, "Family Wage," *Feminist Review* 6 (1980), 55–77; Michèle Barrett and Mary McIntosh, "The 'Family Wage': Some Problems for Socialists and Feminists," *Capital & Class* 11 (1980), 51–72; Johanna Brenner and Maria Remas, "Rethinking Women's Oppression," *New Left Review* 144 (March–April 1984), 33–71; and Jane Lewis, "The Debate on Sex and Class," *New Left Review* 149 (January–February 1985), 108–125.
38. Meg Luxton spoke of the "petty tyranny" that the husband's position as primary breadwinner and apparent "owner" of his wage could structure into marital relations.

The Politics of the Domestic Sphere   31

39. Derived from Pat Mainardi, "The Politics of Housework," in Leslie B. Tanner, ed., *Voices from Women's Liberation* (New York: New American Library, 1970), 336–342, or from Pat Mainardi, "The Politics of Housework," in Robin Morgan, ed., *Sisterhood is Powerful: An Anthology of Writings from the Women's Liberation Movement* (New York: Vintage Books, 1970), 447–453. Reprinted in the documents section of this chapter is the text from a xeroxed version that circulated in Canada and that included changes in language and lacked all bibliographic data including authorship. A copy has been filed under "Homemakers" in the CWMA and most probably comes from a 1970s consciousness-raising kit.

40. Susan Clark and Andrew S. Harvey, "The Sexual Division of Labour: The Use of Time," *Atlantis: A Women's Studies Journal* 2, no. 1 (Fall 1976), 64.

41. Ibid.

42. Jack Kapica, "Wife Still Chief Cook, Bottle Washer," *The Globe and Mail*, 21 December 1993, A1, A2.

43. Katherine Marshall, "Employed Parents and the Division of Housework," *Perspectives on Labour and Income* (Statistics Canada) 5, no. 3 (Autumn 1993), 24, excerpted in the documents section of this chapter.

44. Ibid., 30.

45. Ibid., 24, 26.

46. Ibid., 30

47. Ann Duffy, Nancy Mandell, and Norene Pupo, *Few Choices: Women, Work and Family* (Toronto: Garamond Press, 1989), 37.

48. Alanna Mitchell, "June Cleaver-style Moms Back in Fashion/Working Mothers Feel Guilty as Media Glorify 'Momism'," *The Globe and Mail*, 20 April 1992, A1, A5, reprinted in the documents section of this chapter.

49. "One in 10 Canadian families [is] headed by a single parent" and "[i]n 82% of those families, the single parent is a woman." "Counting Women In," *Encounter*, weekend magazine of *The London Free Press*, 9 March 1991, 5.

50. See Alanna Mitchell, "June Cleaver-style Moms Back in Fashion," reprinted in the documents section of this chapter.

51. See Maureen Kellerman, "Feminism and Women at Home," *The Womanist* 1, no. 4 (May/June 1989), 30–31; and Deborah Stacey, "Why the Hand that Rocks the Cradle is Rocking the Boat," *Herizons* 8, no. 3 (Fall 1994), 16–21. See the "Proposed Changes for '96 Census" reproduced in the documents section of this chapter.

52. See Jean Frances, "Kids — Pro and Con," from "Motherhood — Do We 'Need' It?," *Upstream* 2, no. 6 (July 1978), 9, reprinted in the documents sections of this chapter.

53. The 1974 booklet *Working Women in Newfoundland*, excerpted in the documents section below, made reference to the so-called "empty nest" syndrome: "After the children have grown up the older woman often feels that she is in a vacuum. She has invested her all in others and is left with very little."

54. Canada, Royal Commission on the Status of Women in Canada, *Report* (Ottawa: Information Canada, 1970), 227–228.

55. See the articles in Kathleen Gallagher Ross, ed., *Good Day Care: Fighting For It, Getting It, Keeping It* (Toronto: The Women's Press, 1978).

56. Canada, Royal Commission on the Status of Women in Canada, *Report*, 271.

57. See Marjorie Griffin Cohen, "Social Policy and Social Services," chap. 4 in Ruth Roach Pierson, Marjorie Griffin Cohen, Paula Bourne, and Philinda Masters, *Canadian Women's Issues*, Vol. I: *Strong Voices* (Toronto: James Lorimer & Company, Publishers, 1993), 277–282.

58. Laurie Monsebraaten, "Searching For a '90s Safety Net," *The Toronto Star*, 17 September 1994, A8.

59. Alanna Mitchell, "June Cleaver-style Moms Back in Fashion," reprinted in the documents section of this chapter.

60. Varpu Lindström-Best, "'I Won't Be a Slave!' — Finnish Domestics in Canada, 1911-30," in Jean Burnet, ed., *Looking Into My Sister's Eyes: An Exploration in Women's History* (Toronto: The Multicultural History Society of Ontario, 1986), 33–53.

61. Dionne Brand, "'We weren't allowed to go into factory work until Hitler started the war': The 1920s to the 1940s," in Peggy Bristow, co-ordinator, *'We're Rooted Here and They Can't Pull Us Up': Essays in African Canadian Women's History* (Toronto: University of Toronto Press, 1994), 171–191.

62. Dionne Brand, *No Burden to Carry: Narratives of Black Working Women in Ontario, 1920s to 1950s* (Toronto: Women's Press, 1991).

63. "… the Scheme was extended from 100 in 1955 to 200 in 1956 and to 280 by 1959 … Between 1955 and 1966, 2,940 domestics came to Canada on the Scheme." Agnes Calliste, "Canada's Immigration Policy and Domestics from the Caribbean: The Second

Domestic Scheme," in Jesse Vorst et al., eds., *Race, Class, Gender: Bonds and Barriers* (Toronto: Between the Lines Press, 1989), 144.
64. "Even more disturbing to the officials was the sponsoring by some women of their family members. Although the number of Caribbean applications was negligible compared to the influx of unskilled immigrants from Southern Europe, immigration officials complained that Caribbean immigrants were swelling the semi-skilled labour force through chain migration." Calliste, "Canada's Immigration Policy and Domestics from the Caribbean," 145.
65. Savitri's story is excerpted in the documents section below, from Makeda Silvera, *Silenced* (Toronto: William-Wallace Publishers, 1983). A second edition of this book has been published, with a new Introduction by the author. Makeda Silvera, *Silenced* (Toronto: Sister Vision/Black Women and Women of Colour Press, 1989).
66. Savitri's story from Silvera's *Silenced* is excerpted below.
67. S. Arat-Koc, "In the Privacy of our own Home: Foreign Domestic Workers as Solution to the Crisis in the Domestic Sphere in Canada," *Studies in Political Economy* 29 (Spring 1989), 33–58.
68. Mona Forrest, Interview by Ruth Roach Pierson, Montreal, March 11, 1991.
69. INTERCEDE holds monthly educational meetings at a community centre in downtown Toronto at which counselling and a legal clinic are available. And INTERCEDE's monthly newsletter, *Domestics' Cross-Cultural News*, carries information on a wide range of subjects of importance to immigrant domestic workers, from how to correspond with Immigration to what the childcare situation in Ontario is like. Its back page gives a list of important phone numbers, including those for the Canada Immigration Centre, the Immigrant Women's Job Placement Centre, the Immigrant Women's Health Centre, single mothers' and battered women's shelters, a variety of legal clinics and community legal services, and the Ontario Human Rights Commission.
70. Juliet A. Cuenco, "Domestic Workers in Canada: The Struggle for Recognition," *The Womanist* 12, no. 1 (Fall 1989), 40, reprinted in the documents section of this chapter.
71. Shela Larmour, "Canada Leaves Third World Domestic Workers Out in the Cold," *Match Newsletter*, Spring 1993, 1, reprinted in the documents section of this chapter.
72. Ibid.
73. For example, see the discussion of Mary Astell's *Some Reflections upon Marriage* (The Third Edition. London, 1706) in Florence M. Smith, Mary Astell (New York: Columbia University Press, 1916), 77–103. See also Emma Goldman, "Marriage and Love," in Alix Kates Shulman, ed., *Red Emma Speaks: An Emma Goldman Reader* (New York: Schocken Books, 1983), 204–213, and Barbara Taylor, *Eve and the New Jerusalem: Socialism and Feminism in the Nineteenth Century* (New York: Pantheon Books, 1983).
74. Canada, Royal Commission on the Status of Women in Canada, *Report*, 246.
75. Andrea Knight, "What's In A Name? A Rose By Any Other Name ... ," *Equal Times*, November 1975, 7, reprinted in the documents section of this chapter.
76. Erin Mouré, "Wedding Party," *Domestic Fuel* (Toronto: House of Anansi Press, 1985). See poem reprinted on page 22.
77. John F. Conway, *The Canadian Family in Crisis* (Toronto: James Lorimer & Company Ltd., Publishers, 1993).
78. "Lesbian Mother Wins Custody," *Kinesis*, February 1979, 3.
79. Ellen Agger, "Lesbians Fight to Keep Kids," *Body Politic*, December 1976/January 1977, 3, reprinted in the documents section of this chapter.
80. Curriculum Vitae of Francie Wyland, n.d., in the possession of Ruth Roach Pierson. See *Motherhood, Lesbianism and Child Custody* (Toronto: Wages Due Lesbians; Bristol, England: Falling Wall Press, 1977).
81. Ellen Agger, "Lesbians Fight to Keep Kids," reprinted in the documents section of this chapter.
82. Arja Lane, "Lesbian Mothers in Motion," *The Northern Woman Journal* 7, no. 4 (September 1982), 5, excerpted in the documents section of this chapter.
83. R.E.A.L. Women was incensed in 1985 that the Secretary of State's Women's Program had given a special project grant to the Calgary Lesbian Mothers' Defence Fund to help the latter set up a "'lesbian-gay workshop collective'" in order "'to become more effective and visible, thereby increasing the number of people we will be reaching.'" *reality* 3, no. 3 (1985), 1.
84. "Goodbye — and thanks — from the LMDF," *Grapevine (Newsletter of the Lesbian Mothers' Defence Fund)*, Summer 1987, 1. A note informed readers that "the Alberta LMDF is still active" and provided an address to write to. For a copy of a front page from Grapevine, see Paula Bourne, "Women, Law and the Justice System," chap. 5 in Pierson, Cohen, Bourne, and Masters, *Canadian Women's Issues*, Vol. I: *Strong Voices*, 344.

85. Rachel Epstein, "Breaking with Tradition," *Healthsharing* 14, no. 2 (Summer/Fall 1993), 21.
86. Laura Barry, "The Mouths of Babes: Lesbian Moms Take Us All One Step Forward," *XTRA!*, 21 January 1994, 27, reprinted in the documents section of this chapter.
87. See Bourne, "Women, Law and the Justice System," chap. 5 in Pierson, Cohen, Bourne, and Masters, *Canadian Women's Issues*, Vol. I: *Strong Voices*, 343–345.
88. Hence the need to resort to self-insemination procedures, as described in the document "Lesbian Conception," in the documents section of Chapter 2, "The Politics of the Body," in Pierson, Cohen, Bourne, and Masters, *Canadian Women's Issues*, Vol. I: *Strong Voices*, 143–144.
89. Gillian Rodgerson, "Lesbian Family Wins: Insurance Company Agrees to Cover Woman's Lover and Her Children," *The Body Politic*, December 1985, 21; Nancy Pollak, "Lesbian Family Wins Health Benefits," *Kinesis*, March 1986, 7.
90. Noreen Howes [Shanahan], "Lesbians Win Spousal Benefits," *Kinesis*, November 1986, 3, reprinted in the documents section of this chapter.
91. Michele Landsberg, "Time to End Cowardly Delay on Rights Issues," *The Toronto Star*, 22 January 1994, L1.
92. Julie Smyth, "Archbishop Assails Same-sex Benefits," *The Globe and Mail*, 30 May 1994, A5; Nicolaas Van Rijn, "Catholics Told: Fight Same-sex Benefits," *The Toronto Star*, 29 May 1994, A1, A16.
93. Gerda R. Wekerle, "Responding to Diversity: Housing Developed by and for Women," chap. 22 in Helalata C. Dandekar, ed., *Shelter, Women and Development: First and Third World Perspectives* (Ann Arbor, Michigan: George Wahr Publishig Co., 1993), 182.
94. For a fuller discussion of Western individualism as initially intended for men and predicated on continued relegation of women to the corporatism of the family, followed by women's increasing admission to individualism without sufficient compensation from society for the loss of former corporate protections, see Elizabeth Fox-Genovese, *Feminism Without Illusions: A Critique of Individualism* (Chapel Hill and London: The University of North Carolina Press, 1991).
95. According to Linda Gordon, "Lack of ability to support themselves and their children holds many women in abusive relationships ..." L. Gordon, *Heroes of Their Own Lives: The Politics and History of Family Violence — Boston 1880–1960* (New York: Viking, 1988), 113.
96. Geoffrey York, "Scrapping Baby Bonuses Seen as Fostering Wife Abuse: Poverty Activist Warns Government of Potential Danger," *The Globe and Mail*, 15 July 1992, A8.
97. Geoffrey York, "Tory Politicians Form Family Compact," *The Globe and Mail*, 3 June 1992, A1, A4.
98. For a fuller analysis of REAL Women, see Karen Dubinsky, *Lament For A Patriarchy Lost?* (Ottawa: Canadian Research Institute for the Advancement of Women, 1985).
99. "Realwomen of Canada: Position Papers" (Ottawa: realwomen, n.d.), flyer in the possession of Martha Beaudry.
100. York, "Tory Politicians Form Family Compact," A4.
101. Alanna Mitchell, "June Cleaver-style Moms Back in Fashion," reprinted in the documents section of this chapter.
102. Women enter the allegedly "free" labour market burdened with being assigned the chief reponsibility for childcare and facing the continuing segregation of paid labour along lines of sex and race, with women, particularly women from racial and ethnic minorities, concentrated in the lowest paying jobs.
103. Linda Gordon, *Heroes of Their Own Lives*, 73.
104. Margaret Anne Doody, "Women Beware Men," a review of *Backlash: The Undeclared War against Women*, by Susan Faludi, and of *The War Against Women*, by Marilyn French, in *London Review of Books* 14, no. 14 (23 July 1992), 8.
105. While this term entered common feminist parlance by the 1980s, and many of us in Canada believe it was coined by a Canadian, we have been unable to track down the source.
106. The phrase comes from a book on family history much criticized by feminists for its romanticization of the patriarchal, nuclear family. Christopher Lasch, *Haven in a Heartless World: The Family Beseiged* (New York: Basic Books, Inc., 1977).
107. "Double" hardly seems adequate when one takes into account, on top of paid labour, the unpaid domestic labour that may well comprise care of the elderly as well as childcare and housework.
108. Six months' paid maternity leave through Unemployment Insurance, for instance.

Documents: Chapter 1

The Politics of Housework

Stay-at-Home Moms
Toronto, 1991[1]

...Since the women's movement took wing, the home-based mom has been left behind in the nest. She's been practically invisible in the press and in studies regarding women's issues, while her sister who works for wages is profiled and interviewed on everything from day care to pay equity. As a result, she has felt at best overlooked; at worst criticized, disrespected and misunderstood.

But that's beginning to change. Today's psychologists and social workers are starting to notice her. Leaders of feminist organizations are applauding her. And she's saying, "How dare you ignore me all these years!" ...

Of course, choosing to stay at home is an option many women can't even consider. Fifteen per cent of the work force are single mothers, and in two-parent families, the escalating cost of living and relatively stagnant pay-cheques mean more women must work to pay the mortgage and put groceries on the table ...

Susan Thompson sits nursing her five-month-old daughter, Meredith, as she matter-of-factly describes the price and value she puts on motherhood. Two and a half years ago, after the birth of her son, Graham, the Oakville, Ont., woman walked away from a $100,000-a-year position as vice-president of corporate finance with an investment firm on Toronto's big-league Bay Street. An MBA graduate from York University, Thompson had it all: power, perks, prestige — even a secretary. But she opted for a job at half the salary and half the pressure after her son was born. Last fall, she quit that job, too, deciding she'd like to be a stay-at-home mom for awhile. "Five years ago, if anyone had told me I'd be doing this, I'd have said they were nuts, but becoming a mother has made me re-evaluate everything I once thought was important."

While Thompson lived the feminist ideal and believes in equality for all women, she's beginning to wonder whether the feminist agenda has done a disservice to women by not addressing the strong feelings of motherhood and the possible lifestyle changes they may provoke. "No one ever mentions the value of being a mother," she says.

1. Kathy English, "Who's Home? Stay-At-Home Moms Struggle For Status," *HomeMaker's Magazine*, 26, no. 3 (April 1991), 100–106.

Judy Rebick, president of the National Action Committee on the Status of Women, the largest women's organization in Canada, says: "A lot of women have talked about this to each other, but we need to start talking about it as part of the women's movement. In rejecting the exclusive role of women as mothers, we haven't paid enough attention to the importance of parenthood for women. Now, with the maturation of the women's movement, we can take on issues such as the new reproductive technologies and begin to pay more attention to mothering."

She stresses that the choice to opt out of the workforce for a time doesn't indicate a woman's abdication of the struggle for equality. "It's a personal choice when a woman decides to stay home, and it has nothing to do with feminism. If a woman supports equality for all women, and government action to create equality for all women, I have no problem with her making a choice to stay home. I have many friends who have chosen to stay at home because they want the delight of being with their babies." ...

"Why I Want a Wife"
1971[2]

I belong to that classification of people known as wives. I am A Wife. And, not altogether incidentally, I am a mother.

Not too long ago a male friend of mine appeared on the scene from the Midwest fresh from a recent divorce. He had one child, who is, of course, with his ex-wife. He is obviously looking for a new wife. As I thought about him while I was ironing one evening, it suddenly occurred to me that I, too, would like to have a wife. Why do I want a wife?

I would like to go back to school so that I can become economically independent, support myself, and, if need be, support those dependent upon me. I want a wife who will work and send me to school. And while I am going to school I want a wife to take care of my children. I want a wife to keep track of the children's doctor and dentist appointments. And to keep track of mine, too. I want a wife to make sure my children eat properly and are kept clean. I want a wife who will wash the children's clothes and keep them mended. I want a wife who is a good nurturant attendant to my children, arranges for their schooling, makes sure that they have an adequate social life with their peers, takes them to the park, the zoo, etc. I want a wife who takes care of the children when they are sick, a wife who arranges to be around when the children need special care, because, of course, I cannot miss classes at school. My wife must arrange to lose time at work and not lose the job. It may mean a small cut in my wife's income from time to time, but I guess I can tolerate that. Needless to say, my wife will arrange and pay for the care of the children while my wife is working.

2. Judy Syfers, originally published in *Notes From The Third Year: Women's Liberation* (1971), 13–14; reproduced here from a "Consciousness-Raising Kit" prepared by the Toronto Women's Place, 1972. Copy at the Canadian Women's Movement Archives (hereafter CWMA): file "Consciousness Raising."

I want a wife who will take care of *my* physical needs. I want a wife who will keep my house clean. A wife who will pick up after my children, a wife who will pick up after me. I want a wife who will keep my clothes clean, ironed, mended, replaced when need be, and who will see to it that my personal things are kept in their proper place so that I can find what I need the minute I need it. I want a wife who cooks the meals, a wife who is a *good* cook. I want a wife who will plan the menus, do the necessary grocery shopping, prepare the meals, serve them pleasantly, and then clean up while I do my studying. I want a wife who will care for me when I am sick and sympathize with my pain and loss of time from school. I want a wife to go along when our family takes a vacation so that someone can continue to care for me and my children when I need a rest and a change of scene.

I want a wife who will not bother me with rambling complaints about the duties of a wife. But I want a wife who will listen to me when I feel the need to explain a rather difficult point I have come across in the course of my studies. And I want a wife who will type my papers for me when I have written them.

I want a wife who will take care of the details of my social life. When my wife and I are invited out by my friends, I want a wife who will take care of the babysitting arrangements. When I meet people at school that I like and want to entertain, I want a wife who will have the house clean, prepare a special meal, serve it to me and my friends, and not interrupt when I talk about the things that interest me and my friends. I want a wife who will have arranged that the children are fed and ready for bed before my guests arrive so that the children do not bother us. I want a wife who takes care of the needs of my guests so that they feel comfortable, who makes sure that they have an ashtray, that they are passed the hor d'oeuvres, that they are offered a second helping of the food, that their wine glasses are replenished when necessary, that their coffee is served to them as they like it. And I want a wife who knows that sometimes I need a night out by myself.

I want a wife who is sensitive to my sexual needs, a wife who makes love passionately and eagerly when I feel like it, a wife who makes sure that I am satisfied. And, of course, I want a wife who will not demand sexual attention when I am not in the mood for it. I want a wife who assumes complete responsibility for birth control, because I do not want more children. I want a wife who will remain sexually faithful to me so that I do not have to clutter up my intellectual life with jealousies. And I want a wife who will understand that *my* sexual needs may entail more than strict adherence to monogamy. I must, after all, be able to relate to people as fully as possible.

If, by chance, I find another person more suitable as a wife than the wife I already have, I want the liberty to replace my present wife with another one. Naturally, I will expect a fresh, new life; my wife will take the children and be solely responsible for them so that I am left free.

When I am through with school and have acquired a job, I want my wife to quit working and remain at home so that my wife can more fully and completely take care of a wife's duties.

My God, who *wouldn't* want a wife?

Analysing Housework

"More on the Political Economy of Women's Liberation" Toronto, 1974[3]

In the September 1969 issue of Monthly Review there is an article by Margaret Benston on "The Political Economy of Women's Liberation." She defines women as "that group of people who are responsible for the production of simple use values in those activities associated with the home and family." Further, they are "denied an active place in the market" and "remain a very convenient and elastic part of the industrial reserve army." While agreeing with Benston's analysis of women's role in the home, we feel that the changing sex composition of the labor force since the Second World War belies her emphasis on women as house-workers, which minimizes their role as wage laborers.

In the United States in 1940, only about 1 in 4 women (14 years and over) were in the labor force, 1 in 10 mothers worked, and about 1 in 12 women (18 to 24 years old) were still in school. By 1968, almost 2 in 5 mothers worked, and more than 1 in 5 women (18-24 years) were still in school.[4] Rather than excluding women from the labor force, monopoly capitalism has increasingly drawn women out of the home and into the market. Between 1947 and 1968 the labor force participation rate for men in both civilian and military employment fell from 86.8 percent to 81.2 percent (reflecting longer schooling and earlier retirement), while that for women rose from 31.8 percent to 41.6 percent. This marked increase in the proportion of women working occurred while the proportion of adult women in school increased dramatically; for 18-24 year-olds, women in school increased from 9.9 percent in 1950 to 22.1 percent in 1967, and now exceeds the proportion of 18-24 year-old men who were in school in 1950, 20.1 percent. During the same period, 1950-1968, the percentage of women not in the labor force because they were "keeping house" fell from about 60 percent of women to less than 50 percent. In July 1969, there were 47,681,000 males (93.4 percent of the total) 20 to 64 years old in the total labor force, while there were

3. Mickey Rowntree and John Rowntree (Toronto: New Hogtown Press, Literature Committee, Toronto Women's Liberation, 1974), 1-5. "This material was reprinted from MONTHLY REVIEW, January 1970."
4. Unless otherwise noted, all calculations are derived from *Historical Statistics of the United States*, the *Statistical Abstract of the United States*, 1968 and 1969, and *Employment and Earnings*, Vol. 16, No. 2, August 1969. For working mothers, see U.S. Department of Labor, Women's Bureau, Leaflet 37, "Who Are the Working Mothers?" 1967.

25,807,000 females (48.1 percent) 20 to 64 years old in the total labor force and 25,810,000 females were not in the labor force because they were "keeping house."

It is difficult to treat women simply as unpaid producers of use-values in the home when more than two-fifths of them are in the labor force. (Only three-fourths of men are in the civilian labor force.) Only 28.1 percent of the civilian labor force in 1947, women were 37.1 percent in 1968. In April 1969, while women accounted for only 20 percent of employment in transportation and utilities and only 28 percent of the manufacturing workers, they were 39 percent of the wholesale and retail trade workers, 43 percent of the total government employees, 51 percent of the workers in finance, insurance, and real estate, and 54 percent of the service workers. Not only are women crucial members of the labor force, but the home is ceasing to provide them with a shelter from the imperatives of the market. The Department of Labor says that 90 percent of girls today will work some time in their lives.[5]

If the system needs to keep women in the home, as Benston says, then it is failing badly in meeting this need. Benston also suggests that one of the sources of the women's liberation movements may be the development of embryonic capitalized forms of home production which are freeing women to demand equality in work, pay, and status. Looking further for clues to the recent upsurge in the interest in the problems of women, perhaps we should look not just at the home and not just at the work place, but at the contradiction between women's role in one and the other. Women have been doing unpaid labor in the home for a very long time; this by itself is an unlikely source of women's discontent. Further, we argue that higher unemployment rates, lower wages, and unequal job opportunities for women are the results of the contradiction between women's cultural role and women as free wage-laborers.

In this society the father's family role is a market one, that of "provider." This role is compatible with his role as free wage-worker. But the mother's culturally defined role is a non-market one, the practical day-to-day care of children. While men can comfort themselves with the thought that "at least I'm providing for my family," working women fear that "I'm neglecting the children, too." As a result, women experience all the alienation faced by any worker under capitalism, face a conflict rather than a reinforcement of cultural values, and are not even financially rewarded for their discomfort.

To be treated equally as a free wage-worker requires equal cultural freedom to enter into the wage relation. But women do not enter into the market with the same cultural freedom as men. Men face lower unemployment rates than women. Women's role as mother contributes to this difference. Further, labor-market segmentation is exacerbated by the fact that men face conscription into the armed forces, so that the draft creates a relative labor shortage of male workers. From 1947 to 1962,

5. Reported in the San Francisco *Chronicle,* September 15, 1969.

when the armed forces averaged about two and a half million men, the yearly male unemployment rates averaged 4.6 percent, or only about 0.6 percent lower than the 5.2 percent for women during the same period. Since 1962 however, when the military averaged more than three million men, the male unemployment rate was only 3.83 percent, or about 1.67 percent lower than the 5.5 percent for women. Because they face the draft, men receive the "bonus" of lower unemployment rates. Furthermore, the typical work experience of women is to enter the labor market twice as many times as men do — once before they have children and once after the children are old enough to allow the mothers to return to work. In recent years almost half of the unemployed women are "re-entering the labor force." In July 1969, the percentage of those women who were unemployed by reason of "losing the last job," was approximately 37, or close to their proportion of the total labor force; on the other hand, of persons unemployed by reason of "re-entering the labor force," women outnumbered men by 2.2 times. Finally, since the "provider" role is the father's, mobility is largely determined by his job opportunities, not the mother's; thus, the woman in two-worker families bears disproportionately any unemployment burden involved in mobility. Thus, the higher unemployment rates faced by women, while not independent of "discrimination" are largely due to the fact that women, in their role as mother in the nuclear family, entr the labor market on different terms than do men. The "natural market forces" do the rest.

The median income of women workers is only about 60 percent of the median income of men workers. There is no doubt some truth in the businessman's explanation of this difference, that women do have absentee rates two to four times higher than men's and the job tenure of women is about half that of men (2.8 years vs 5.2 years).[6] It is the mother, not the father, who leaves the labor force to have children and then stay home from work when they need care. These factors entail more outlay for overtime and more frequent training of workers, adding to the costs of hiring women. Contributing to the lower median incomes of women are the facts that women are predominantly white-collar workers (about 60 percent of women workers), are relatively non-unionized (a situation made difficult to remedy due to low job tenure), have been competing with a rapidly expanding supply of women workers, and face some overt discrimination. In any case it is clear that, given women's conflict between rearing children and working, employers tend to hire women at jobs where training costs are relatively low and absenteeism is not costly.

Equal access to jobs outside the home, one of Benston's preconditions for women's liberation, will require that men and women become equally free of non-market norms of behavior. Perhaps the increasing

6. V.C. Perella, "Women and the Labor Force," *Monthly Labor Review*, February 1968, p. 9; H.R. Hamel, "Job Tenure of Workers, January 1966," *Monthly Labor Review*, January 1967, Special Labor Force Report, p. 31.

discontent among women is due to the rapid proletarianization of women who are facing a market which expresses the contradiction between the non-market norms of motherhood and the market norms of free wage labor. If women were to attain equal pay and if parents were to share the practical child-care responsibilities, the contradiction between the nuclear family and free wage labor under capitalism would become clear as employers turned from married to single workers because of their greater reliability and job tenure. Of course, as associates who agree that the emancipation of women requires, in addition to equality, the industrialization of house-work and the socialization of child-rearing, we can struggle for the abolition of both the nuclear family and capitalism. But it should be clear that capitalism itself is undermining the nuclear family as mothers become workers. (Currently, in any month, almost 40 percent of mothers with children under eighteen are in the labor force.)

Lastly, we believe the data call into question Benston's statement that "no one, man or woman, takes women's participation in the labor force very seriously." The three-fifths of women workers who are married and contributing to family income probably take it very seriously. The dramatic recruitment of women into the labor force since the Second World War and the concomitant increasing exploitation of family labor have been largely responsible for the spread of the "middle-class life style." The U.S. Department of Labor aptly summarizes the situation as of March 1967:

> Nearly half of all women 18 to 64 years of age work in any one month. About 3 out of 5 of these women are married and living with their husbands. Almost all of these wives contribute to family income. It is often the wife's earnings that raise family income above poverty levels. In other families the wife's contribution raises the family's income from low- to middle-income levels. In fact, it is at the middle-income level that the largest proportion of wives are in the labor force.

> There were 42.6 million husband-wife families in the United States in March 1967. In 15 million of these families, the wife was in the paid labor force. In the husband-wife families where the wife was an earner, the median family income in 1966 was $9,246 a year. In those families where the wife did not work, the median family income was $7,128.

> The likelihood of escaping poverty is much greater among husband-wife families when the wife is an earner than when she is not. Nearly 5 million husband-wife families had incomes of less than $3,000 in 1966. Only 5 percent of all husband-wife families fell into this income group when the

wife was in the paid labor force; 15 percent, when she was not.

An income of about $7,000 in 1966 dollars is considered a modest but adequate income for an urban family of four. Twenty-nine percent of all husband-wife families had incomes below this mark when the wife was a worker; 49 percent, when she was not.

The higher the annual family income (up to $15,000), the greater is the likelihood that the wife is in the labor force. The labor force participation of wives in March 1967 was lowest (13 percent) in families with 1966 incomes of less than $2,000, and the highest (53 percent) in families with incomes of $12,000 to $14,999.

Just how much do working wives contribute to family income? According to a study made by the Bureau of Labor Statistics, the median percent of family income in 1966 accounted for by the wife's earnings was 22.2 percent. However, when the wife worked full time year round, it was 36.8 percent.[7]

These data speak for themselves. The maintenance of the family's standard of living, and in many cases the avoidance of poverty, is now substantially dependent upon not one but two income earners. This is an irreversible process. Women's participation in wage labor can no longer be regarded as "transient." The time is past when women can go home again ...

"Housework"
Toronto, 1977[8]

According to the 1971 census, more than fifty percent of Canadian women work as fulltime housewives. While the percentage of married women in the labour force is steadily increasing, the occupation of housewife is still the largest single occupation for women. Even those women who are wage workers retain their domestic responsibilities; so the housewife experience is familiar to vast numbers of women.

Most people have a certain intimacy with housework for whether we do it ourselves or not, it impinges on our lives every day. Despite this familiarity, there is much that is not visible in our current notions about housewives and housework. What is most significant is that what housewives do, as part of their work, is much more than housework. To

7. U.S. Department of Labor, Women's Bureau, "Working Wives — Their Contribution to Family Income," December 1968.
8. Meg Luxton, *Canadian Dimension* 12, no.7 (December 1977), 35–38.

emphasize this point, I define the work that women do in their homes as 'domestic work' of which housework is only a part.

Of course, there are some situations where domestic work is not done by housewives. In some cases it is done by institutions or it can be bought, either by hiring a domestic servant or by using restaurants, laundries, hotels. In some cases men do it or groups of people in co-ops cooperate to do it together. While these alternatives exist, most domestic work is still done by women who are housewives.

"Do you work or are you a Housewife?"

By domestic work I mean: housework — cooking, cleaning, and maintaining the house and the objects within it; child bearing and rearing; household management — orchestrating all household activities and co-ordinating the schedules of all household members; tension-managing — caring for the psycho-emotional needs of all the household members and the sexual needs of the husband.

For capitalism, the underlying purpose of domestic work is the reproduction of labour power; that is, to ensure that the adult members of the household can, each day, show up for work, awake, fed, and relatively willing to work. It must also ensure that children are born and socialized so that eventually they too will begin to work.

It is only recently that what housewives do has been considered 'work'. The 'do you work or are you a housewife?' dichotomy flows out of the very contradictory nature of domestic work. Domestic work is done in the worker's home and it is unpaid. Thus it is unseen, privatized and apparently removed from the economic structure of industrial production. These aspects give it low status. At the same time it is unsupervised and its standards and schedules seem to be determined primarily by the woman who does it. This aspect provokes envy and a certain contempt from wage workers engaged in highly supervised routines that are completely beyond their control.

Finally, it also involves a 'labour of love' for the reproduction of labour power involves intense personal relationships. The workplace of the housewife is also the family home and the people she works for are her husband and children. As the family is one of the few places where people in capitalist society may find intimacy, affection and tenderness, it appears that a housewife's work must be less alienating and inhuman than most forms of wage work.

These various features of domestic work make it different from industrial work so that there are two apparently separate spheres of work: industrial wage work which produces goods and services and domestic unpaid work which reproduces people. There is, however, an intimate relationship between production and reproduction, and to understand either wage work or domestic work, we need to uncover the connections between them.

Domestic work reproduces human beings and a set of social relations, using the goods and services produced by industrial production. These human beings become the wage workers in production or the domestic workers in reproduction who produce the goods and services or transform them into a form suitable for consumption within the household. The relationship between these two spheres is extremely complex and requires extensive analysis if we are to fully understand it. In this article, I focus on the impact of wage work on domestic work and examine a few components of this relationship.

Housework is Changing

What is most significant in analyzing the connections between production and reproduction, is the fact that changes in domestic work do not emerge directly out of the needs of the household but instead reflect the requirements of industrial capitalism. Two trends have had particular impact on domestic labour.

Certain work has been removed from the home. While eliminating some work, this has also created new types of work. Women, for example, no longer grow their own food or make their own textiles or clothing. Food and clothing are mass produced and the housewife's task now involves shopping to purchase these items, and then transforming them into usable commodities for her household. Simultaneously, a variety of technical developments have introduced into the home a range of facilities and appliances which have drastically altered domestic work.

Running water, electricity, flush toilets, cooking ranges, washers, dryers and vacuum cleaners have all radically reduced the amount of labour involved in each of the operations of housework. This has not necessarily reduced the amount of time necessary for domestic work. For as the work involved in physical maintenance of the house decreased, other components of the work of reproduction gained in importance. The germ theory of disease and notions about standards of cleanliness, theories of early childhood development and the availability of new consumer products increased social expectations and created new standards of domestic labour. At the same time, the family car, TV and birth control have changed the nature of household social relations. The cumulative effect of all these changes has resulted in a complete restructuring of domestic work.

Certainly, housework has become less physically demanding. Much of the hard work and time consuming drudgery has been eliminated by labour- and time-saving devices. Not only has technology reorganized physical labour in the home, but the technology itself often does a more efficient job.

As a consequence the housewife requires less knowledge and skill as her work tends to become dull and repetitive. This component of domestic work forms part of the basis for the low esteem that many people have for domestic work and accordingly, for the women who do it. As each of the operations of housework has become less time consuming, the overall structure of housework and of the time required to do it, became more flexible.

These changes in the structure of housework did not result in a decrease in the amount of time necessary for domestic labour. Instead, the psycho-emotional components of domestic labour have steadily increased. Women spend increasing amounts of time and energy caring for their children. Tension-managing of this sort can be emotionally exhausting for the woman and the need to be constantly sensitive to other people's needs seriously impinges on her ability to care for her own personal needs and development. But this 'human' side of domestic work is also the most rewarding and satisfying part of a housewife's work. It is this part which gives meaning and worth to the rest of her work. It is also the blending of the work of tension-managing with the social and emotional relationships of the family which obscures the work aspect of a housewife's activities. The increased flexibility of housework means that it does not require intense concentration; it is repetitive and easily resumed if interrupted. These work characteristics are ideally suited to the spontaneous and unpredictable nature of psycho-social work. This flexibility also facilitates another important feature of women's work. It is her job to take the wage earned by her husband or by herself and use it to purchase those commodities necessary for the maintenance of the household members. While the wage imposes certain absolute limits, her skill and labour have the potential to maximize the household's standard of living. In times of economic inflation or recession, domestic work expands as the housewife increases her labour to absorb the household's loss of real income. For example, she shops more carefully, buys fewer 'convenience' foods, mends old clothes. If the real household income drops too low, for whatever reasons — the gap between the cost of living and his wages becomes too severe; he leaves her with dependent children; he is injured or ill or laid off and cannot get work — then she may be forced to take on wage work. When she does, she taks on a 'double burden' for her responsibility for domestic work continues in addition to the requirements of her new wage work.

"My Work is Regulated By His Work"

As a woman of 42 and the mother of 4 children told me:

> Lots of people say what a housewife does isn't work. Well, it is work, and it's just like men's work only it isn't paid and it isn't supervised. But I have things I have to do at certain times. The main difference is, my work is regulated by his work. And whatever I have to do is somehow always over-shadowed by the requirements of his work.

The most potent factor is that the existence of the family depends on his wages. If he misses work, even one shift, the household income declines. The primacy of his work is recognized and appreciated and domestic labour is structured to accommodate it. School attendance for children is also mandatory and domestic labour must be organized to take that into account as well. If the man is on shift work, the household is then operating around two, often contradictory, schedules. It is the woman's task to service each routine and to prevent the two from coming into conflict. Let me illustrate this with an example. A woman has four children; three attend school, one is still a toddler at home. Her husband works shifts and every third week is on graveyard (12am — 8am). She gets up at 7am, feeds the baby, then gets the three older children up, fed and off to school by 8:45am. Meanwhile her husband comes in from work and wants a meal; so once the children are fed, she prepares his dinner. Then he goes to bed and sleeps till about 6pm. During the day she must care for the toddler, do her housework, feed and visit with the other children who come home for lunch from 12 — 1:30pm and return again at 4pm. All of this occurs while 'daddy is sleeping' and the noise level must be restricted to prevent him from being disturbed. At 5pm she makes supper for the children and at 6pm she makes 'breakfast' for him. By 8:30pm when the children are in bed, he is rested and ready to socialize while she is tired and ready to sleep. Another woman in a similar situation described it to me this way:

> It totally disrupts my life, his shift work. I have to keep the kids quiet — I'm forever telling them to shut up — and I can't do my work because the noise wakes him. It makes my life very difficult.

The requirements of his work motivate hers in a variety of other ways as well. She must have a packed lunch ready when he leaves for work. She may have to wash and repair his work clothes periodically. Part of her job is to help him deal with the work-related tensions and anxieties that he brings home with him. Her work is profoundly affected by his but she has no control at all over his work and therefore in practice has very little control over the conditions limiting her work.

Two Jobs

The impact of wage work on domestic work is most immediately recognized when a housewife takes on wage work herself. While her wages increase the total income of the household, her new job increases household expenses. She may need more clothes for work; she may have to pay for child care and transportation. She has less time and energy available to exercise the 'buffer' aspect of domestic work and so will be forced to buy more prepared food, ready made clothes. Housework has to be squeezed into the available non-wage work time. Added to the emotional drain inherent in domestic labour is the fact that she acquires a new set of job-related tensions of her own.

Her domestic work now requires that she orchestrate three schedules all of which may be 'out of synch' with each other. The responsibilities of domestic work impinge on her wage work rather than his, so that for example if the children are sick, she must take time off to care for them. The demands of her domestic work frequently prevent her from participating in work related activities that occur after work hours. This is one reason why women find it difficult to become active in trade unions. Most significantly, she now experiences not only sex oppression but also exploitation as a wage worker. The sex stereotyping of women in the labour force traps women in low paid, insecure jobs, which reflect and reinforce women's oppression in society.

A Radicalizing Vanguard

What I have tried to show is that domestic work and wage work are intimately linked, are in fact two aspects of one social system. As a result, changes in one sphere have an impact on the other. Habitually, the left has tended to dismiss the political potential of housewives by arguing that the nature of housework makes housewives conservative, apolitical or unorganizable. More recently, as more and more married women with children enter the labour force, it is argued that housewives will disappear as a significant factor in the population. Housework will however continue to be done by women and thus working women will bear a double burden — doing both wage work and domestic work. Out of the pressures of this dynamic, these women will become politically explosive and may in fact form a radicalizing vanguard, but within the framework of the organized labour movement and flowing from their position as wage-earners, not from their position as domestic workers.

To evaluate the political potential of housewives, it is important to know what their working conditions are and to understand their relationship to capital. Those conditions and that relationship are far more complex than we have previously given them credit for. During the current attack on the working class, our major task is to help generate militant working class organizations willing to go beyond the historical role of the trade unions. This requires in part bridging the gap that currently exists between the work place and the home. It requires that we develop an analysis which acknowledges the critical role that women, as housewives, actually play and that we go from there to build strategies which draw on that potential source of energy and power.

Wages for Housework

"Houseworkers"
St. John's, Newfoundland, 1974[9]

"DO YOU WORK, OR ARE YOU A HOUSEWIFE?" ON THE CA-
NADIAN census you are either "occupied" or, like three-fourths of the
women in Newfoundland, a housewife. A housewife is unpaid and, in
the job world's view, unskilled, and therefore is officially categorized
as unoccupied. This is ridiculous when it is estimated that a housewife
with children under 6 years can spend approximately 2000 hours doing
her work. A Canadian study estimates that the contribution of housewives equals 11% of the gross national product. An American study puts
the figure as high as 21%, or one and one half billion dollars. A woman
working outside the home, no matter whether she is married or single,
still puts in about 4 hours a day on top of her 8 hours, doing housework,
for most women working outside the home usually don't earn enough
money to pay someone else to do their housework for them.

Housework today is generally not productive. Few women spin their
own wool, or grow all the vegetables their family eats. The housewife's
job is primarily a service occupation. She services workers who are
already in the labour force, and rears the next generation of workers.
These services are basic to the capitalist system. If houseworkers did not
do this, who would? The state? But at what cost? As soon as these
questions are asked, the importance of the housewife's role to the functioning of society becomes immediately apparent.

Work in the home has always been considered to be "women's work".
⟨In essence the housewife cares for other people, whether it is by keeping
their living quarters clean, feeding them, or caring for them when they
are sick. It is no coincidence that when women work outside the home
their jobs reflect the work women are expected to do in the home, and
which they are therefore supposed to be best at, e.g. nurse, teacher,
domestic, personal secretary. Nor is it coincidental that at their place of
work, women are always expected to "get the coffee" and otherwise
generally attend to the boss's needs. Housework is considered to be a
'natural' occupation for women. This is presumably an offshoot of the
'biology is destiny' idea: women have children, therefore they should
care for those children and therefore they should stay at home and also
care for the home while the man works. This idea obviously serves the
capital class, who gets two for the price of one — a worker, and a person
to service the worker for free who will work if she 'has to' and continue
to do her second job in the home as well.

While the nature of housework varies little between social classes,
the conditions do. A dishwasher can make life easier for the middle class

9. Elizabeth Batten, Dianna Gray, Carolyn Hallett, Albertha Lewis, and Jane Lewis, *Working
Women in Newfoundland* (St. John's, Newfoundland: Women's Place, August 1974), 24–26.
Copy in possession of Ruth Roach Pierson.

housewife, however washing dishes by hand is not so bad as washing clothes by hand. Many women are still ground down purely by their bad working conditions, and on top of this, many have the additional burden of too many children, or a husband who is uncaring or unfeeling.

Physical conditions are not the only concern of the housewife. The idea of wages for housework often provokes an emotionally antagonistic response along the lines of: "But it would take the love out of family life." The housewife has a very private relationship with the people she works for, her family, and any attempt to formalize that relationship would be difficult, and would involve many changes in thinking. When it was common to employ domestic servants, the latter also experienced much difficulty in obtaining decent working conditions and a living wage because employers refused to countenance anything resembling collective bargaining, or what they considered to be the intrusion of industrial practices, into the sanctity of home life.

All this considered, what is the capitalist ideal of the housewife? She is happy, supportive and efficient. She enjoys her roles, is a prop for husband and children, a shoulder to cry on and can make a meal out of a potato if necessary. She is never neurotic or snappy.

However, the stereotyped housewife, the cartoon-strip housewife, the housewife in many advertisements and TV shows, is none of these things. Certainly she accepts her role, but is often sick, always passive, and is usually too dumb to make her own decisions or understand her husband's work.

This ambiguity plus the greater ambiguity of doing work which somehow isn't work because you don't get paid for it, makes for many problems for the housewife. Many women may enjoy staying home, but often worry that they are not coming up to scratch, feel guilty if they put their children in daycare so that they can have some leisure time, because after all childcare is their responsibility, isn't it. Many women are just plain over-burdened by what is virtually a 24 hour job. After the children have grown up the older woman often feels that she is in a vacuum. She has invested her all in others and is left with very little.

There are ways to change the situation of the houseworker, a condition that many women find oppressive. If women are to fulfil their potential by furthering their education, joining the labour force, doing creative work in the home, working in the community, or whatever, they need money and time. To ensure that all women have these opportunities one method would be to pay houseworkers. This would also recognize the value of the work most women perform. However, if the state paid salaries, undoubtedly most of the money would be raised by taxing those who could least afford it. It might also serve to reinforce the idea that women are primarily housewives, and continue to keep women isolated in the home. Thus, pay for houseworkers, although it would be an immediate improvement of many women's lives, must only be a first step

**Time and Tasks
of an Average Housewife**

	Hours per week	Pay per hour
Nursemaid	44.5	2.00
Dietitian	1.2	5.00
Good Buyer	3.3	2.00
Cook	13.1	2.50
Dishwasher	6.2	2.00
Housekeeper	17.5	1.50
Laundress	5.9	2.00
Seamstress	1.3	2.50
Practical Nurse	.6	3.00
Maintenance Man	1.7	2.00
Gardener	2.3	1.50
Chauffeur	2.0	4.50
Total	99.6	$204.25

Adapted from *Changing Times*, a consumer magazine. These figures do not include a price for sexual activity, nor do they include a fee for the substantial executive talent involved in juggling a dozen or so jobs simultaneously.

in the process of abolishing privatised housework altogether. One even more immediate solution that some families have already adopted is to divide the household chores among husband, wife, and children, lifting sole responsibility for all of this work from the woman's shoulders.

There is no doubt that, no matter who does it, housework as it is now organized is inefficient. While work outside the home becomes more concentrated and inudstrialized, housework is still done in the smallest unit possible, the family, and no matter how many labour saving devices are introduced, this system remains the most inefficient method of supplying these essential services, because the same work must be done over and over again in every single household. The ultimate solution, which can only be achieved with destruction of the profit-oriented capitalist system, is to socialize various kinds of housework so that work now done by individual houseworkers would be done as part of the productive labour of society. Such facilities as free day-care centres and community laundries with full-time staff would free many women to do other useful work, while the few remaining unsocialized household chores would be the shared responsibility of all family members.

"Hands Off the Family Allowance"
Toronto, 1976[10]

No Increase in Baby Bonus

The $220,000,000 Baby Bonus increase we were all expecting has fallen victim to the government's "anti-inflation program". Why have they seen fit to make one of their biggest cutbacks from the pittance they give mothers? As always, we women are the ones expected to do without, to put ourselves last, and sacrifice "for the good of others". WHAT BETTER WAY FOR TRUDEAU TO LAUNCH HIS "LOWERED EXPECTATIONS WAY OF LIFE" THAN BY TAKING MONEY AWAY FROM MOTHERS, THE SYMBOLS OF SELF-DENIAL!

We Refuse to be a Good Example

We know it means EVEN MORE WORK, AND LESS FOR OURSELVES AND OUR CHILDREN. It also means we are more of a discipline on the men so many of us depend on. Nurses said "dedication won't pay the rent" and have fought for well-earned increases across the country. Teachers are refusing the blackmail of paying for cutbacks in education and are going on strike. All around us others are demanding their share of society's wealth which OUR UNPAID WORK IN THE HOME HELPS CREATE.

We Want Our Increase Too

And we need it more than most. Many of us are sole-support mothers and $36.00 a year per child — little as it is — does make a difference. Much more than anyone with a 10% surtax on their $30,000 salary can begin to imagine! And for those of us with husbands, the Family Allowance is often THE ONLY MONEY WE CAN CALL OUR OWN, the only recognition that we WORK in our homes.

Trudeau's cutbacks in Family Allowance represent a widespread effort to *make women pay for the present crisis*. On top of all the unpaid work we do in our homes, we are faced with:

-HIGHER PRICES which mean more work shopping for bargains and more time in the kitchen.

-A GROWING WAGE GAP between women and men in the paid labour force, and tougher policing of women on UIC.

-ELIMINATION OF GOVERNMENT-FUNDED SUBSIDIES (LIP, CYC, OFY) which provide wages for young people (many of whom are women) and sustain community services for children, old people, immigrants, etc.

-CUTBACKS IN DAYCARE SUBSIDIES which mean more work finding adequate childcare or looking after our children ourselves.

10. *The Other Woman* 4, no. 2 (March/April, 1976), 7.

-CUTBACKS IN SOCIAL SERVICES which jeopardize the wages of many women and throw the burden of the work back in the home.

-MORE HARDSHIPS FOR WOMEN ON FIXED INCOMES like the sick and the aged who are expected to live on next to nothing after a lifetime of hard work.

WE WOMEN ARE AN EASY TARGET BECAUSE WE ARE SO USED TO WORKING WITHOUT PAY IN OUR HOMES AND FOR LOW PAY OUTSIDE. But we don't intend to stay at the bottom. Let the government go after the banks and the corporations — they have more than us!

WE DEMAND

-the family allowance increase as scheduled.

-the removal of family allowance from taxable income.

A petition is being circulated to protest Family Allowance cutbacks. For copies and more information, contact Wages for Housework Committee, 745 Danforth Ave., Suite 301, Toronto, Ontario ...

"Wages for Housework: An Obstacle to Equality" Ottawa, 1977[11]

How much is a housewife worth? This question is the central issue of "wages for housework", a campaign which can only detract from the more desirable goal of abolishing the housewife role altogether.

"Wages for housework" is a movement to garner support for government-financed salaries to housewives. It challenges the unpaid work performed by women and argues that this is the root of women's position of powerlessness. State-paid incomes would recognize their worth to society rather than forcing them into dependence on their husbands.

The "wages for housework" campaign should be recognized, not for the solution it proposes, but for the assumptions it challenges. First, it dismisses as myths those assumptions which state that housework is the "natural destiny" of women, that housewives "do it for love", and that labour performed in the home is not really "work". It shows how society first restricts the choices available to women and then belittles and ignores the work they do.

The "wages for housework" movement also shows that the wageless condition of the housewife helps to sustain capitalism in two ways. First, housework and child care performed by women are a prerequisite to most men working the hours they do in the paid economy. Corporations depend on women's unpaid labour to get male workers to their jobs every day and to make sure that they don't arrive late, hungry, untidy and with a couple of kids under each arm.

Secondly, housewives sustain capitalism by being at its disposal whenever cheap labour is needed. Wages for housework is thus seen as a mechanism to give women the power to refuse dependence on men and to refuse the "liberation" of a second job at the lowest wages.

11. Judy Wasylycia-Leis, New Democratic Party, Article No. 4, November 14, 1977.

The "wages for housework" campaign may be performing an educational role. However, the concept itself is suspect. In practical terms, it is hard to imagine how such a concept could be implemented and where the money would come from.

Recently, the Ontario Status of Women Council estimated that there are 4.5 million housewives in Canada and that the average housewife should get a weekly wage of $204.25 for working a 100 hour week. If a programme only paid $1,000 per year to all women with children under 18 years of age at a tax rate of 100 per cent (one household salary dollar is taxed back for every dollar received in the labour force), the total cost of the programme, according to Gail Cook and Mary Eberts, would be $2.5 billion.

Aside from the tremendous cost of the programme, a universal plan for all women, as requested by the "Wages for Housework" campaign, raises other questions: Should government-financed salaries go to all housewives, regardless of family income level? Should labour force participants be taxed to support wages-for-housework services that other families perform themselves without payment or purchase from others? And finally should a public policy actually discourage labour force participation of women?

It is evident that any programme which provides monetary recognition for women working at home, encourages some women to drop out of the labour force or to reduce their hours of work in the labour force. It is a programme which makes for segregation, which puts the woman in the house even more and, therefore, must be rejected by the women's movement as a whole in this country.

A more progressive cry than "wages for housework" is the abolition of the housewife role. Housework should be shared by men — by everyone. As Simone de Beauvoir has stated "Society must change. Just as you don't pay someone for cleaning his teeth or his hands, so in the same way each one will have his own work, wash his own dishes, clean his own corner, make his own bed, and so on. Thus the very notion of housework will disappear."

At the 1976 Canadian Labour Congress convention, a proposal was presented that called for means to encourage men to share the housework in order to open up more opportunities for women workers. The "wages for housework" committee rejected that suggestion arguing that it is better for women to be paid for housework than to "be liberated at the minimum wage". Surely it would be more profitable to fight for equal job opportunities than for a measure which can only reinforce stereotyped roles.

Equality for women will not be achieved through wages for housework. Instead we should be demanding more socialized forms of child care and domestic work. We should be insisting that men and women share in this work, not justifying the "woman's place" by giving her the money to stay there.

Why is Housework Women's Work?

"The Politics of Housework"
Toronto, 1970s[12]

Housework. What? You say this is all trivial? Wonderful! That's what I thought. It seems perfectly reasonable. We both had careers, both had to work a couple of days a week to earn enough to live on so why shouldn't we share the housework? So I suggested it to my mate and he agreed — most men are too hip to turn you down flat. You're right, he said. It's only fair.

Then an interesting thing happened. I can only explain it by stating that we women have been brainwashed more than even we imagine. Probably too many years of seeing media-women coming over their shiny waxed floors or breaking down over their dirty shirt collars. Men have no such conditioning. They recognize the essential fact of housework right from the very beginning. Which is that it stinks.

Here's my list of dirty chores: buying groceries, carting them home and putting them away; cooking meals and washing dishes and pots; doing the laundry; digging out the place when things get out of control; washing floors. The list could go on but the sheer necessities are bad enough. All of us have to do these jobs, or get someone else to do them for us. The longer my husband contemplated these chores, the more repulsed he became, and so proceeded the change from the normally sweet considerate Dr. Jekyll into the crafty Mr. Hyde who would stop at nothing to avoid the horrors of — housework. As he felt himself backed into a corner laden with dirty dishes, brooms, mops and reeking garbage, his front teeth grew longer and pointier, his fingernails haggled and his eyes grew wild. Housework trivial? Not on your life! Just try to share the burden.

So ensued a dialogue that's been going on for several years. Here are some of the high points.

'I don't mind sharing the housework, but I don't do it very well. We should each do the things we're best at.'

Meaning: Unfortunately I'm no good at things like washing dishes or cooking. What I do best is a little light carpentry, changing light bulbs, moving furniture. (How often do you move furniture?)

Also meaning: Historically the lower classes (Blacks and women) have had hundreds of years doing menial jobs. It would be a waste of manpower to train someone else to do them now.

12. Derived from Pat Mainardi, "The Politics of Housework," in Leslie B. Tanner, ed., *Voices from Women's Liberation* (New York: New American Library, 1970), 336-342, or from Pat Mainardi, "The Politics of Housework," in Robin Morgan, ed., *Sisterhood is Powerful: An Anthology of Writings from the Women's Liberation Movement* (New York: Vintage Books, 1970), 447–453. This is copied from a xeroxed version that circulated in Canada. It included changes in language and lacked all bibliographic data including authorship. CWMA, file: Homemakers.

Also meaning: I don't like the dull stupid boring jobs, so you should do them.

'I don't mind sharing the work, but you'll have to show me how to do it.'

Meaning: I ask a lot of questions and you'll have to show me everything, everytime I do it because I don't remember so good. Also, don't try to sit down and read while I'm doing my jobs because I'm going to annoy hell out of you until it's easier to do them yourself.

'We used to be happy!' (Said whenever it was his turn to do something.)

Meaning: I used to be so happy.

Meaning: Life without housework is bliss. No quarrel here. Perfect agreement.

'We have different standards, and why should I have to work to your standards. That's unfair.'

Meaning: If I get bugged by the dirt and crap, I will say 'This place sure is a sty' or 'How can anyone live like this?' and wait for your reaction. I know that all women have a sore called guilt over a messy house or housework is ultimately my responsibility. If I rub this sore long and hard enough it'll bleed and you'll do the work. I can outwait you.

Also meaning: I can provoke innumerable scenes over the housework issue. Eventually, doing all the housework yourself will be less painful to you than trying to get me to do half.

'I've got nothing against sharing the housework, but you can't make me do it on your schedule.'

Meaning: Passive resistance. I'll do it when I damn well please, if at all. If my job is doing dishes, it's easier to do them once a week. If taking our laundry, once a month. If washing the floors, once a year. If you don't like it, do it yourself oftener, and then I won't do it at all.

'I hate it more than you. You don't mind it so much.'

Meaning: Housework is shitwork. It's the worst crap I've ever done. It's degrading and humiliating for someone of my intelligence to do it. But for someone of your intelligence ...

'Housework is too trivial to even talk about.'

Meaning: It's even more trivial to do. Housework is beneath my status. My purpose in life is to deal with matters of significance. Yours is to deal with matters of insignificance. You should do the housework.

'In animal societies, wolves, for example, the top animal is usually a male even where he is not chosen for brute strength but on the basis of cunning and intelligence. Isn't that interesting?'

Meaning: I have historical, psychological, anthropological and biological justification for keeping you down. How can you ask the top wolf to be equal?

'Women's Liberation isn't really a political movement.'
Meaning: The Revolution is coming too close to home.
Also meaning: I am only interested in how I am oppressed, not how I oppress others. Therefore, the war, the draft and the university are political. Women's Liberation is not.

'Man's accomplishments have always depended on getting help from other people, mostly women. What great man would have accomplished what he did if he had to do his own housework?'
Meaning: Oppression is built into the system and I as the white male receive the benefits of this system. I don't want to give them up.

Postscript

Participatory democracy begins at home. If you are planning to implement your politics there are certain things to remember.

1. He is feeling it more than you. He's losing some leisure and you're gaining it. The measure of your oppression is his resistance.

2. It is a traumatizing experience for someone who has always thought of himself as being against any oppression or exploitation of one human being by another to realize that in his daily life he has been accepting and implementing (and benefiting from) this exploitation; that his rationalization is little different from that of the racist who says "Niggers don't feel pain" (women don't mind doing the shitwork), and that the oldest form of oppression in history has been the oppression of 50% of the population by the other 50%.

3. Arm yourself with some knowledge of the psychology of oppressed peoples everywhere and a few facts about the animal kingdom. I admit playing top wolf or who runs the gorillas is silly but as a last resort men bring it up all the time. Talk about bees. If you feel really hostile bring up the sex life of spiders. After sex, she bites off his head.

The psychology of oppressed peoples is not silly. Blacks, women, and immigrants have all employed the same psychological mechanisms to survive. Admiring the oppressor, glorifying the oppressor, wanting to be like the oppressor, wanting the oppressor to like them.

4. Keep checking up. Periodically consider who's actually doing the jobs. These things have a way of backsliding so that a year later once again the woman is doing everything. Use timesheets if necessary. Also bear in mind what the worst jobs are, namely the ones that have to be done every day or several times a day. Also the ones that are dirty — it's more pleasant to pick up books, newspapers, etc., than to wash dishes. Alternate the bad jobs. It's the daily rigid grind that gets you down. Also make sure that you don't have the responsibility for the

housework with occasional help from him. 'I'll cook dinner for you tonight' implies that it's really your job and isn't he a nice guy to do some of it for you.

5. Most men had a bachelor life during which they did not starve or become encrusted with crud or buried under the litter. There is a taboo that says that women musn't strain themselves in the presence of men — we haul around fifty pounds of groceries if we have to but aren't allowed to open a jar if there is someone around to do it for us. The reverse side of the coin is that men aren't supposed to be able to take care of themselves without a woman. Both are excuses for making women do the housework.

6. Beware of the double whammy. He won't do the little things he always did because you're now a 'Liberated Woman', right? Of course, he won't do anything else either ...

I was just finishing this when my husband came in and asked what I was doing. Writing a paper on housework. Housework? he said. House-work? Oh my god how trivial can you get. A paper on housework.

"Employed Parents and the Division of Housework" Ottawa, 1993[13]

While the division of labour in the paid workforce has been given much attention, the division of labour at home has received less scrutiny. This issue is of particular concern to women because they have traditionally been responsible for housework, and now the majority of them are also facing the demands of a job outside the home. One of the central questions is how, in the midst of employment and parenting responsibilities, families manage domestic chores.

Results of Statistics Canada's 1990 General Social Survey (GSS)[14] show that dual-earner couples employed full time outside the home are the most likely to share responsibility for housework. Yet even for them, the allocation of household chores is far from equal. Sharing tends to be most common among younger, well-educated couples with few children. The likelihood of shared responsibility increases as the wife's income level rises. As well, the partners' satisfaction with several dimensions of their lives seems to be related to the way they divide responsibility for housework.

Most couples are dual-earners

The balancing of family and job obligations has become a challenge for more Canadian couples than ever before. In 1990, 71% of couples with

13. Katherine Marshall, *Perspectives on Labour and Income* (Statistics Canada), 5, no. 3 (autumn 1993), 23-30.
14. The General Social Survey (GSS) was established by Statistics Canada in 1985 to monitor changes in the living conditions and well-being of Canadians, and to provide information on various social issues of current or emerging interest. Data are collected annually from a random sample of households. Approximately 13,500 persons were interviewed in 1990. The target population consists of all persons aged 15 and over, except full-time residents of institutions and residents of the Yukon and the Northwest Territories ...

children aged 18 or younger in the household were dual-earners (both partners had at least some employment outside the home); by contrast, just over 20 years ago, only 30% of such families were dual-earners.[15]

In 1990, both the wife and the husband were employed full time in 51% of two-parent families. In 19% of two-parent families, the husband worked full-time, and the wife, part time ... Single-earner families, in which the husband was employed full time and the wife was at home full time, accounted for 27%.[16]

Traditional division of labour

The 1990 GSS showed that the assignment of housework tends to follow traditional patterns. For the purposes of this paper, housework refers to meal preparation, meal clean-up, and cleaning and laundry ... Women are likely to assume primary responsibility for these routine tasks, which must be performed on a regular basis and which account for 78% of all housework ... On the other hand, men tend to be responsible for repairs, maintenance, and outside work, tasks that must be accomplished less frequently ... Because the 1990 GSS did not ask direct questions about the responsibility for child care, this activity is not directly analysed in this article. However, the population studied consists only of couples with children at home, and it is generally accepted that children in a household increase the amount of housework.

The extent to which wives are responsible for housework varies with their employment status. As wives' involvement in the workforce increases, their responsibility for housework declines, but their husband's contribution does not increase enough to approach parity ... For example, 89% of wives who were not in the labour force were solely responsible for meal preparation; this compared with 86% of wives employed part time and 72% of those employed full time.

While husbands in full-time, dual-earner families were the most likely of all husbands to assume responsibility for domestic chores, the proportions who did so were relatively low. Meal clean-up was the task that these men most often shared (15%) or did on their own (16%). Slightly fewer shared (12%) or had sole responsibility (13%) for meal preparation. And although 13% of husbands shared the cleaning and laundry, these were the chores that they were least likely to do alone (7%).

There was almost no difference in the degree of responsibility for housework taken on by wives working part time and stay-at-home wives.

---

15. The 1967 information is based on unpublished data from the Survey of Consumer Finances, which refer to families with children under age 16.
16. The remaining 3 per cent consisted of dual-earners with the wife working full time and the husband part time or both working part time, and single-earners with the wife employed full time and the husband at home full time. Those respondents who did not state their employment status were also included in this residual category.

Full-time, Dual-earning parents

The division of housework by full-time dual-earners deserves particular attention, since half of couples with children aged 18 or younger now fall into this category. These parents generally have less time to devote to domestic chores than do those with other employment patterns. By definition, full-time dual-earners deviate from traditional gender roles because both partners share responsibility for paid work. Therefore, it may be reasonable to expect that they might also deviate from the traditional division of household labour by sharing responsibility for housework.

In reality, this was not the case. In most full-time, dual-earner families, the wife had primary responsibility for housework.[17] The majority (52%) of wives employed full time had all of the responsibility for daily housework, while 28% had most of this responsibility ... Only 10% of dual-earning couples shared responsibility for housework equally; in the remaining 10% of couples, the husband had all or most of the responsibility.

Who shares ... who doesn't?

Only a small minority of full-time, dual-earning couples had an egalitarian division of housework. What distinguishes these couples from those who do less sharing?

Several characteristics were associated with the likelihood that the husbands would assume greater responsibility for housework — or more precisely, that the wives would not be solely responsible ... For example, the younger the partners, the less likely was the wife to be solely responsible for housework. The proportion of full-time, dual-earner wives under age 35 who were responsible for all daily housework was 47%, compared with 69% among those aged 45 to 64. The trend was similar according to the husband's age.

The number of children in the household also had some bearing on the allocation of domestic responsibilities. The percentage of dual-earner wives with all responsibility for housework increased from 44% of those with one child at home to 83% of those with four or more children. This suggests that when there is additional housework, as is the case with several children at home, women are more likely to do the extra work required.

As well, dual-earner women in common-law unions were somewhat less likely than those in marriages to do all the housework. The wife had

---

17. A point system was used to determine responsibility for housework. Individuals scored a point each time they were acknowledged as having primary responsibility for meal preparation, meal clean-up, and cleaning and laundry. If responsibility for a chore was shared equally, each partner scored a point. Since daily housework consisted of three chores, the maximum score was three points. For example, "wife mostly" comprises scores of W=3 H=2; W=3 H=1; and W=2 H=1.

sole responsibility for housework in 46% of common-law unions, compared with 52% of marriages.

The educational attainment of both partners was also associated with the allocation of housework: the more educated the couple, the less likely was the wife to assume full responsibility for domestic chores. For instance, in 58% of households where the wife had less than high school graduation, she alone was responsible for daily housework; if she was a university graduate, the corresponding figure was 45%. The trend was similar according to the husband's level of education.

The relationship between domestic responsibility and income differed for wives and husbands. As the wife's income rose, the likelihood that she alone would be responsible for housework declined. By contrast, the higher the husband's income, the greater was the proportion of wives with all responsibility for housework.

Sharing and satisfaction

The way that full-time dual-earners divide housework appears to be associated with their satisfaction with several aspects of their lives: the allocation of household tasks, the time for other interests, and the balance between work and family.[18]

The majority of dual-earners indicated that they were satisfied with the allocation of housework in their homes. However, the most satisfaction was expressed by wives (98%) and husbands (97%) in households where housework was shared equally ... Not surprisingly, spouses with little responsibility for housework also reported high levels of satisfaction (94% or more) with this allocation of duties. On the other hand, lower levels of satisfaction were expressed by spouses who did all the housework: 75% of wives were were responsible for all the domestic chores and 88% of husbands who had most of the responsibility were satisfied with the arrangement.

A sizeable proportion of all full-time dual-earners felt that they did not have sufficient time to pursue other interests. Dual-earners' satisfaction with this aspect of their life, however, was also related to their partner's responsibility for housework. The highest satisfaction levels (at least 70%) were reported by spouses with little responsibility for domestic chores. By contrast, just 58% of wives who managed all the housework and 54% of husbands who assumed most responsibility for these tasks were satisfied with the time they had for other activities. Dual-earners who shared housework responsibility also tended to feel pressed for time, as only 58% of wives and 63% of husbands expressed satisfaction with their time for other interests.

The distribution of responsibility for housework did not affect the way dual-earner couples felt about the balance between their job and

---

18. Reports of satisfaction are difficult to interpret. Generally, it is more socially acceptable to be satisfied rather than dissatisfied with one's personal life. Therefore, reported levels of satisfaction may be exaggerated, depending on the nature of the question.

their family. Regardless of how housework was divided, approximately eight out of ten wives and husbands were satisfied with the balance ...

Childcare

"June Cleaver-Style Moms Back in Fashion"
Toronto, 1992[19]

A rosy celebration of the 1950s style mom who polished floors, kissed scraped knees and had a pot roast on the table by 6 p.m. is surfacing on several fronts across Canada, spurred by shifting social attitudes, advertising campaigns and some government policies.

The result, according to pollsters, trend-spotters and groups representing a diverse cross-section of women, is a guilt so intense it has wrapped many working mothers in a winding sheet of anxiety.

"I worry that my kids will say to me when they're grown up: 'How come you weren't at home?'" says Shelley Brook, a Toronto psychiatrist who works 3 days a week while a nanny cares for her 7-month-old twins, Max and Tamar.

Her two sisters-in-law stay at home with their children and one of them recently said to her: 'Gee, it will be interesting to see how our children turn out. They will have been raised so differently.' Such comments, she says, make her feel "really awful."

The problem for Canada's approximately two million working mothers is this: They are employed outside the home in greater numbers than ever, because they need the money or crave the satisfaction of a career, or both. But at the same time, they are being subtly — and unsubtly — told that their rightful place is at home taking care of the kids.

"In the 1950s, I remember, no decent, respectable mother went into the work force," says Gwendolyn Landolt, national vice-president of the group REAL Women. "By the 1980s, no respectable woman stayed home — they were called freeloaders and parasites."

Now, observers say, the pendulum is swinging back. "I don't think most of us are aware of the colossal change. We don't know how it's going to settle out," Mrs. Landolt says.

The numbers show that women are not deserting the work force in droves. Most simply cannot afford to and there is a question of whether the economy can afford to lose them.

The glorification of motherhood and domestic chores — dubbed "momism" by some — has begun to creep into popular literature, movies and advertisements.

The February issue of Chatelaine magazine, in an article under the headline "'Our families come first:' Why more mothers are choosing to stay at home," showed contented mother Diane Hamilton, 35, displaying her fussily dressed one-year-old daughter. Ms. Hamilton has given up

19. Alanna Mitchell, *The Globe and Mail*, 20 April 1992, A1, A5.

her high-powered advertising job to care for her daughter and bake cookies.

"Right now, what I'm doing seems far more valuable than working for money," she says.

Another headline in the article proclaims: "The careerist mother's glamourous image is tarnished." ...

A full-page advertisement in a Toronto newspaper this month pitched new homes with the line: "Featuring good old-fashioned country kitchens!" It appeared above a photograph of a grinning woman wearing an apron and fondly touching her daughter, who is sitting on a counter stirring something in a bowl.

Another home ad published in a community newspaper this month was even more overt, showing a father on his way to work while the mother stays at home.

Under the line "Welcome home to the values of yesterday" is a picture of a dad kissing his apron-clad wife goodbye at the door of their home. Her hair is rolled into a 1940s pompadour. Their daughter, sporting saddle shoes, hides behind her mother's stockinged legs.

Graham Denton, president of the Toronto market research firm Product Initiatives, says there is likely to be more of this type of portrayal of women in ads. He said research suggests the image holds tremendous appeal for many Canadians, in part the result of a return to traditional values and what he calls a "renaissance of personal responsibilities."

Rather than material goods, Canadians crave stability, he says, and to many that means mom ...

Between this longing for the security of the June Cleaver style-mom of the 1950s television show *Leave it to Beaver*, and the actual chucking of paid jobs for housework, falls the reality of most families' financial needs. Research shows that most of the 5.6 million Canadian women who work (compared with 6.7 million men, as of the end of February), are in no position to give up their incomes.

"Many of the women in the work force are not just there to buy makeup and nail polish," says Glenda Simms, president of the Canadian Advisory Council on the Status of Women, a federal agency.

Data collected by Statistics Canada show that the picture of a household with dad at work and mom home with the kids is no longer the statistical norm.

Fully 70 per cent of families with children under 16 in 1990 had mothers in the labour force. And 63 per cent of families with children under school age had a working mom. Since 1984, it has been more common for mothers with at least one child under three to work than to stay home.

Research by the Vanier Institute of the Family in Ottawa shows that the so-called "family wage" of the 1950s and early 1960s — a man's salary that could support him, a wife and children — has largely disappeared. Families have barely kept pace with inflation over the past decade, despite the fact that so many more women have entered the paid work force.

In fact, if women stopped working, the number of low-income families would rise by an estimated 62 per cent, the institute says.

Yet, for many Canadians, the anxiety over working continues to mount ...

Murray Philip, vice-president of Toronto-based Creative Research Groups Ltd., ... said his experience indicates that some women who joined the work force in the wake of women's liberation are having second thoughts.

The reason: They have taken up paid work outside the home, only to find that their unpaid work at home waits patiently for them to come in the front door.

"The husband may show attitudinal changes, but there is no sign of behavioural changes," Mr. Philip says. "Who gets stuck with two jobs?"

Some pressure to embrace motherhood roles also comes from government ...

While today's governments offer some measure to support working women, such as pay-equity programs and maternity leave, their ambivalence about women's paid work is apparent.

One obvious example of modern-day government trying to sell motherhood is Quebec, which has begun paying women cash bonuses to have babies. The more babies they have, the higher the bonus.

It appears to have worked. Almost half the babies born in Canada in 1990 were born in Quebec. And the increase in the number of babies born in that province in 1990 was almost double the increase for Canada as a whole.

But most of the pressures governments create for working mothers are more subtle. They chip away at support that would make working possible or easier, or embrace the assumption that women are available to provide caring services without pay ...

There is a broader question of the availability of out-of-home child care for working parents. The government's own figures showed that in 1990 the mothers of as many as three million children aged 12 and under were in the work force, up from 2.6 million in 1985 and 1.4 million in 1971.

But by 1990, the nation had just 321,000 licenced day-care spaces, up from 298,000 in 1985. Statscan reports that in 1990, Canada actually had 6-per-cent fewer licenced spaces for children under three than in the previous year — 47,000 in 1990, versus 50,212 in 1989.

Statscan figures also show that 68 per cent of children who are not cared for by their parents are looked after by babysitters ...

In February, the federal government killed its eight-year-old promise to create a national day-care program. It has also become much tougher for working parents to get a tax break or financial compensation for the expenses of raising children ...

"Proposed Changes for '96 Census"
Ottawa, 1994[20]

HOUSEHOLD, VOLUNTEER AND LABOUR MARKET ACTIVITIES

26. Last week (all seven days), how many hours did this person spend doing the following activities?

(a) Doing unpaid housework, yard work or home maintenance for members of this household, or others.
Some examples include: preparing meals, doing laundry, household planning, shopping and cutting the grass.

(b) Looking after one or more of this person's own children, or the children of others, without pay.
Some examples include: bathing or playing with young children, driving children to sports activities, helping them with homework, talking with teens about their problems.

(c) providing unpaid care or assistance to one or more seniors.
Some examples include: visiting seniors, talking with them on the telephone, helping them with shopping, banking or with taking medication, driving them to appointments or other activities.

(d) Providing unpaid care or assistance to persons other than children or seniors.
Some examples include: helping relatives with their banking, driving friends to appointments, house-sitting for neighbours.

27. Last week (all 7 days), how many hours did this person spend doing unpaid volunteer activities for a non-profit organization, religious organization, a charity or a community group?
Some examples include: organizing a special event, advocating for a cause, canvassing or fundraising, coaching or teaching, serving on a committee or on a board of directors.

"Kids — Pro and Con"
Ottawa, 1978[21]

This conversation was recorded recently at the UPSTREAM office ... One of the women is the single parent of two preschool-aged children, and the other is a career woman who, along with her partner, has decided not to have children. They prefer not to be identified. To make reading easier I have called them Susan and Linda.

Susan: You decided not to have kids at all, eh? Was it a conscious decision or did it just happen that way?

20. Statistics Canada, 1994, reproduced from Deborah Stacey, "Why the Hand That Rocks the Cradle is Rocking the Boat," *Herizons* 8, no. 3 (Fall 1994), 16–21.
21. Jean Frances, from "Motherhood — Do We 'Need' It?," *Upstream* 2, no. 6 (July 1978), 9.

Linda: So far it's been a conscious decision but it's not a forever decision. John agrees with it, he goes along with it, but I would have made the same decision if he weren't there.

Susan: If you made a conscious decision there must have been conscious reasons not to.

Linda: The main reason is that I'm trying to develop a career. I feel that having a child would inhibit my career in some way — delay it, or put a wrench into it for a while. That's what a lot of people tell me.

Susan: It's true!

Linda: One reaction I get from people when I give that reason is that it's a selfish reason. Because I'm a woman I'm expected to have children.

Susan: Do you think you're selfish?

Linda: On bad days I agree with them, bad days being days when I don't feel so strong, but generally I don't think it's selfish. I think it should be my right to have a career and develop my life ...

Susan: So you don't get particular people saying to you that you should have children?

Linda: The only person I could pin that on would be my own mother. And it's more that she wants a grandchild than that she wants me to have a child. The pressure that I feel is not that I should have a child, but that I'm wrong to have decided not to have one. There is a distinction between the two, and it gets back to that selfishness thing.

Susan: The whole thing that a woman is not supposed to be selfish for any reason.

Linda: It's part of our nature to be altruistic even to the extent of having children.

Susan: The whole motherhood mystique. Have you ever wanted to have a child?

Linda: No. I have friends who have children because they wanted the experience of carrying a child and childbirth and when they describe it there's a magical tone to the whole thing. I feel that it's a myth. I don't have that urge that seems to come to some people ...

Susan: ... Has anyone ever suggested that, instead of being selfish not to have a child, it's selfish to have one if you've already got a career and other things to take up your time? I think it's the very opposite of selfish not to bring a child into a situation where it would be resented.

Linda: Some women have said that, but I'm thinking of, for instance, co-workers and older people that do have families and they always laugh and say, "Well, you'll change your mind." They think it's just a phase. When I say that it's not a forever decision I don't mean I might change my mind next year; I'm 99.9 per cent sure. But I do allow for changes in my life, however improbable.

Susan: Have you ever considered sterilization?

Linda: Oh, yeah, I've considered that. I decided to postpone doing anything about it for a few years — until I'm thirty, if not before. People say that doctors won't sterilize a woman under thirty, anyway.

Susan: It's true. I knew a woman who had made a very firm decision at the age of about twenty-two or twenty-three not to have children. She started to make the rounds of the doctors and clinics and no one would touch her. I'm thinking seriously about it myself — I certainly don't want any more. I can barely manage as it is.

Linda: How do you survive?

Susan: That probably is the closest you could come to it. I survive; I get by. I'm on Family Allowance while I go to school, so my kids are in daycare. It's a hand-to-mouth existence that I sometimes feel really badly about. I mean, we get by — we're still alive — but we're so far below the poverty line we can't even see it when we look up. But once you've got kids you just do what you have to to survive. That's all there is to it. Now that I look back I realize that it was a very selfish thing for me to have done to have my first one.

Linda: Why do you say it was selfish?

Susan: In the end my reasons for going ahead with it were that I wanted the experience. I wasn't thinking of the child I was bringing into the world at all. I wasn't thinking in terms of, "That is a twenty-year commitment."

Linda: But in the end, your life is not that bad, nor is hers.

Susan: Things are the way they are, and we cope with things because we have to. If nothing else, I discovered in myself a strength I never thought I had. But if I had it to do over again — no, I wouldn't have kids.

Domestic Labour, Immigration, and Racism

I Don't Understand the Immigration: Savitri
Toronto, 1983[22]

...Savitri is in her late forties and is of East Indian descent. She is a plump woman who stands 5'3" tall. She wears her shoulder length hair which is showing signs of greying in a tight bun.

Savitri talks easily about her life, although at times, she seems nervous and anxious about her ability to express her feelings clearly. Her life seems complex, attending to her children's and husband's needs long distance — keeping the communication going between them — being mother, cook, and wash-maid to a Canadian family here, and struggling with the Immigration Department to review her files ...

Here is Savitri's story:

"Things were hard for us as a family"

I been in this country about five years now, working on the work permit as a domestic. I came here because life at home was rough and it was

22. Makeda Silvera, "Savitri," *Silenced* (Toronto: Williams-Wallace Publishers, 1983), 53–60.

easier for me to come up here and work than for my husband. I have a husband back in Guyana and four children. I have not seen them since I came up here in 1979. We write to each other and two times a year we talk on the phone.

Things were hard for us there as a family — my husband have a job back home, but sometimes when I was there things were slow, and he wouldn't have a job. He is a carpenter. So when I got the opportunity to come here on the work permit as a domestic, we all decided that it was the best thing for me to do. At least that way one of us would have a steady job and steady money coming in. I didn't expect to be here so long, though. I thought that I would be back home by now with my family, or else they would be up here with me, but as you see things didn't work out that way.

We try to write each other often, so we don't lose touch, and so I know what is going on with the children. My mother lives at the house with my husband, so that she can give a hand with the children to see that they don't lose their manners. I am glad I got the chance to come here because so far I have been able to send money home to my husband, even though it's not as much as I thought it would be, but it still helps to send the children to school. I miss them very much. This life is hard, really hard ...

"People who read this book can help"

Now my real problem is getting my landed and is this I want to talk about because I want to know if when people read this book they can help to do something about this matter.

I go into Immigration since February 1982, to find about this landed immigrancy business. They ask me to fill out an application and I fill it out, and I put down my husband and four children on the form. They ask me if my family would be eventually coming up and I tell them yes. They said they would get in touch with me, but after waiting months and months I didn't hear anything from them.

I went back down again in the month of July, and told them that I was taking a dressmaking course for my upgrading and that I had finished taking a St. John's Ambulance health care course. They write all that down in the files and said they would get in touch with me. Well, even in November 1982 I still didn't hear anything from them at all. So it was then that somebody from the Domestic Workers' Group gave me the name of a lady at a legal aid clinic to see. I went down and saw the lady and she took all the information and said she would write the Immigration for me and find out what was wrong. She heard back from them fast, for it was the middle of November that I get a phone call from her to come in to see her. When I went she said Immigration had no record of my application. That's what they say. I don't know what happened to it because I know that I went in to see them and they write it all up, all the information that I give them. The lady at the legal aid office was very nice to me, and she and another Black lady, I think she is a community worker, went down to Immigration with me and they give me another form to fill out. It was just like the first form that I did fill out, so I fill it out again and hand it back to the officer. Then they call me January 1983 and said that they look over my files and that I must come for an interview. I went in alone for the interview. That was the longest interview I ever had in my life.

"Immigration officer say we don't know how to take good advice"

The Immigration officer had me in his office for three hours asking me the same questions over and over again. Mostly he ask me about my husband and my children. He wanted to know first if I was going to bring up my family. I tell him yes, that I had put that down on the form. Then he ask me when was the last time I saw my husband. I tell him since I come up in 1979 I didn't see my husband, but that we write and talk on the phone. Then he ask me if I think my husband didn't have a girl back home. You know he just keep asking question like those. I was getting vexer by the minute. Bu I tried to keep cool, and answer him nice. He wanted to know if my children or my husband ever get in trouble with the law. I tell him no. Then he ask me why I didn't stay here and work in domestic work and try to save enough and then go home. He said it would cost me less if I did it that way instead of sending the whole family to come up. Then he tell me he was just giving me a little advice and don't usually give out that kind of advice but is because he think I am an "intelligent girl." I just sit there dumb. Then he tell me to go home and think about it until they call me in again.

They call me again in April 1993 and that time I see a different officer, who ask me the same thing about my husband. I say they was coming up, and he get rude, and say we people don't know how to take good advice and that is why we suffer so much. I didn't know what he was talking about and then I remember my meeting with the first officer, so maybe they got together and talk. He told me if I was going to be stubborn and not take good advice that it was my business, but that before they decide on my landed and my family that I have to get a job offer for my husband before he come into the country. So I leave the Immigration.

When I went home I told my employer about what the Immigration had said. I ask her if she could ask her husband if he could write a letter for my husband. Her husband run a cleaning company. You know, the ones that clean office and other work place in the night. For weeks I wait for an answer and didn't get any from her. So one night I approach her and ask her if she tell her husband. She pretend she had forgotten and said she would ask him right now. But I don't know, something was funny, and I just get the feeling that she did talk to him about it before. Both of them come in the kitchen where I was, and he said that he didn't need anybody else in his business and that if Immigration find out he was doing something like that they could get him in a lot of trouble.

He just kept talking like that for a long time, then he said he would do it because he really like me and the work I do. Then he said that he was going out of his way to do it, so I should also try to help him out too. Then both he and his wife stare at me. I ask him how he mean and he look at his wife. She said to me that he mean I could help him clean two nights a week. I couldn't say a word. It just numb me, for I work like a real race horse in that house and I didn't know that they would ask me to clean office at night on top of that, but I really wanted that letter for the Immigration so that my husband could come up, so I tell them yes I would do it. The husband said for me to come down to his office the next morning and his secretary would type the letter for me. I go down and got the letter and take it straight over to Immigration.

"From I have been here, I always work for my own bread"

I didn't hear anything from them after that, so I called them and they said that when they were ready to see me they would send a letter to me.

Well, three weeks ago I got a letter from them to come in. They say they checked out the letter and that it was o.k. but that now the problem was the children. They say they couldn't give the children landed, because they were big children. You know, that they were teenagers and that they were wondering what the children would do when they get here. The Immigration officer said again that his advice would be to let them stay in Guyana because the unemployment here was too high and they would come here and get frustrated and turn bad. He said I must take good advice and let them stay there with a relative and that my paper for me and my husband could come through quicker that way.

I couldn't sit still and listen to that, you know, because I come here five years ago and work my hands dry scrubbing other people floor and looking after their children, I didn't come here and thief or murder anybody so I didn't like the way he was talking to me, like I come here and beg the government to look after me ...

I couldn't sit quiet so I tell him that I want my children here with me, just like how he and his wife have their family with them, I tell him that we is not wild animal and that we know family life, too. Then I tell him good day and walk out of him office. So I don't hear anything since that, and is that I worried about now, for I don't know if they will hold all of that against me now.

But you know this time I couldn't sit quiet. I was trembling when I come out of the office. I even did expect a police or somebody to pick me up off the street and arrest me. All when I got home, I listen every time the doorbell ring to see Immigration officers coming for me to deport me. You know, they handle you like you is a piece of furniture. No respect at all.

But this thing really have me worrked and I wonder if anyone, like people with a say, who the Immigration will listen to, can help me. I don't understand the Immigration, I don't know why they want to keep me away from my children and husband. They just feel that we are going to be a burden to the government, which is not true. Look how long I work in this country. Away from my family, all this while and still they want me to stay away from them ...

"I don't want to die in this country"

After my papers come through, I want to stay here and work until I am about sixty-four years old and then I want to go back home. I don't wan't to die in this country, or be a old person in this country, things too lonely for old people here, it's not like back home where you have a lot of people to talk to; here they put you away in old people's home. I want to go back home to grow old and die. The dirt too cold here to be buried in. That is why I say that when I get my landed, I am going to rent a room — a furnished room. I don't want to spend out my money on expensive furniture because I don't plan to live here forever. I want one furnished room for I am going to save every penny I work here.

I just hope this paper come through soon. I don't know how much longer I can wait ...

"Domestic Workers in Canada: The Struggle, The Recognition"
Ottawa, 1989[23]

A domestic worker described how her employer angrily told her that she is "up against a Canadian with money" and threatened that "she could easily be deported."

These harsh words demonstrate just how vulnerable domestic workers are to abuse.

Women who do domestic work in Canada are mostly from the Third World. The Philippines tops the list as the country where most foreign domestic workers come from. In 1988 alone, Filipino domestic workers have reached approximately 10,000.

Given these two realities it was not surprising that Filipino domestic workers would come together to discuss their common concerns. The national dialogue on Filipino domestic workers, organized by the United Council of Filipino Association in Canada [UCFAC], was held last March during the International Women's Day Celebrations in Toronto.

During the Dialogue, the women workers, joined by others who support their issues, shared their common experiences and reaffirmed that organizing was vital to their recognition in society.

The women workers underscored the many reasons they were vulnerable. They cited that their two year temporary status in Canada, the lack of domestic workers' rights in provincial legislation, the wide

23. Juliet A. Cuenco, *The Womanist*, 2, no. 1 (Fall 1989), 40.

latitude of power exercised by immigration officers exacerbated by the lack of knowledge by domestic workers of their rights and of the bureaucratic system are contributing factors to their vulnerability.

In addition, where a domestic worker is a woman of color from another country, speaks a different language and has few friends and family, the potential for abuse is great. For Filipino domestic workers, their cultural value system has worked against them as women struggle for autonomy and dignity and adds another dimension to their potential for abuse. Values such as *utany na loob* (gratefulness), *pakikisama* (smooth interpersonal relations), and *hiya* (shame), contribute to a subservient mentality which can lead to exploitation.

While there are domestic workers who are happily employed because they have employers who are fair, reasonable and supportive, there are still many domestic workers who work under unjust conditions.

Many workers have reported violations of their employment contract, their common complaints are low pay and long working hours without extra pay for overtime ...

Others have not been given days off, deprived of telephone use and are only allowed to eat after everybody else in the family has finished their meals. Without friends or uninformed of support groups, domestic workers are isolated and suffer in silence. There was a case of a worker who had remained in the house of her employer for two weeks while her employers were away on holidays because they did not leave her the house key.

Nine serious cases of abuse against workers were reported. These involved physical abuse, sexual harassment and other forms of intimidation.

Foreign domestic workers have to meet the requirements of the Foreign Domestic Workers Program of the federal government and their rights as workers are covered by provincial employment standard legislation. Once accepted into the program, they work as live-in employees. Their status in Canada is temporary for two years. They hold a temporary working permit and are assessed each year, based on self-sufficiency criteria as interpreted by an immigration officer. A favorable assessment results in a placement's landed or immigrant status.

The employments standards code in each province varies in terms of protection of domestic workers' rights. UCFAC's study pointed out that discrimination is built right into the labor and employment laws of each province. The study compared provincial legislation which set out protection afforded to workers from Canada including minimum wage, maximum hours of work, overtime pay and the right to unionize. Some provinces set a different and lower minimum wage for domestic workers. In some provinces such as Alberta, domestic workers are not covered in legislation where other workers' rights are ensured.

Ontario, where the largest concentration of domestic workers are found has shown progress in protecting domestic workers. For example, after working a maximum 44 hours a week, domestic workers are entitled to overtime pay. (Most workers do not receive overtime pay either to maintain good relations or the employer gives them time off in lieu of pay which the legislation allows.)

Domestic workers find themselves in a Catch-22 situation. Generally paid very low wages, domestic workers have to demonstrate self-sufficiency in order to be able to stay in the country. Subject to the interpretation of an immigration officer, they have to convince them that they are financially secure (they must produce a bank deposit) and integrated into the community.

Domestic workers therefore often work as volunteers during the days that they are supposed to be off in order to prove that they are integrated into the community.

Their experience as good workers obviously counts as to whether they get to stay, and domestic workers are generally scared to displease their employers or even challenge employers for fear that they will be given a negative reference thereby jeopardizing their chances for permanent residence. Although release letters are no longer required (employers used to write a letter of release for change of employment) it is not uniformly followed across Canada. Such practice is a powerful tool for intimidation and further subjects a worker to subservience.

While performing a much needed service for Canadian families due to the increased labour force participation of women and current day care crisis, domestic workers continue to be unrecognized in Canadian society. Of course, the housework that they do is traditionally viewed as woman's work and is always undervalued, no matter what woman is doing it.

Over the last ten years domestic workers have been organizing across the country in an effort to profile their issues and increase the community's awareness to their exploitation.

INTERCEDE (Toronto organization for domestic workers' rights) is on the forefront of a continuing struggle for protection of domestic workers' rights. Its history includes the first recorded demonstration of domestic workers in Canada in 1981, resulting in some important changes in the Foreign Domestic Workers Program. One progressive step in favor of domestic workers has been to allow domestic workers who have worked for two years to apply for immigrant status from within Canada.

There are current attempts on the part of the federal government to examine the FDW program. There is a need for community consultation, and groups working on domestic workers' issues should bring their concerns to the attention of the government.

In the meantime, the struggle of domestic workers for recognition continues. Coordination of efforts and solidarity are needed to mount great pressure for change to benefit a marginalized and invisible sector of the Canadian population.

"Canada Leaves Third Work Domestic Workers Out in the Cold"
Ottawa, 1993[24]

Thousands of women come to Canada every year with dreams of a better economic future.

They come to work as live-in domestic workers, a job in high demand few Canadians want to do because it is low paying. At one time, most of these women were from the Caribbean, now over 70 per cent come from the Philippines. But with more restrictive immigration laws in effect since April, 1992, fewer women from the 'Third World' have been allowed to enter Canada as domestic workers.

Under the year-old Live-in Caregiver Program, a worker must have a minimum grade 12 level education, must be able to speak either English or French, and must have six months of formal training in live-in care. Job experience is not considered.

"They will create more barriers for women of colour and reinforce systemic racism in Canada's immigration policies," says Intercede, a Toronto-based organizaiton that started in 1979 as an advocacy and research group for domestic workers' rights. Interecede has since expanded to provide information, counselling and educational workshop to foreign domestic workers.

The new laws are favourable to European women, who have access to training programs. There are no such programs in the Philippines.

The impact of the Live-in Caregiver Program is already being felt. In the first eight months of 1992, only 2,343 domestic workers were allowed to enter Canada, over a 50 per cent reduction from 1991.

This leaves employment agencies scrambling to fill the demand. Since workers receive only minimum wage, families with more than one child prefer to hire live-ins to the more costly alternative of daycare.

Immigration Canada says the tighter restrictions are in place because most women want to leave domestic work as soon as they get landed immigrant status, and over 65 per cent of Canadian jobs require at least a grade 12 education. Under the old system, one of the requirements for women trying to get permanent resident status was to upgrade their education.

"Coming into the country with a grade 12 education doesn't necessarily mean anything," says Carol Salmon, a counsellor at Intercede. "These women come here with the mentality that they want to work, they don't want to just sit and accept money."

Many of the women who are successful in getting permanent resident status go into careers in computers, health care aid or early childhood education.

---

24. Sheila Larmour, *Match Newsletter*, Spring 1993, 1, 3, 6.

"Many want to get out of domestic work," says Salmon. "Many are working 15 to 16 hours a day, and some are lucky to make the minimum $643 a month for their work." ...

Domestic workers who enter Canada can do so only under "visitor's" status.

"It is this visitor's status, this temporary status, combined with mandatory live-in that makes foreign domestic workers vulnerable to abuse," according to Intercede.

Many women from poorer countries do not enforce their rights as workers because of the fear of threat of deportation. These women are subject to long working hours, unpaid overtime, and sometimes sexual or physical abuse.

Luz Ybanez worked 15-16 hours a day as a live-in domestic for 11 months and was paid $5,000, including plane fare. With Intercede's help, Ybanez registered a complaint with the Ministry of Labour and received a $2,700 settlement from her former employers.

According to Lorina Serafico, a representative of the Committee for Domestic Workers' and Caregivers' Rights in Vancouver, because traditionally "women's work" has been unpaid, domestic workers are denied the respect and material benefits that are given other workers for work of comparable value.

Although amendments to the *Labour Relations Act* now make it possible for domestic workers to form a union, there are no mechanisms in place to prevent an employer from simply hiring another worker, so domestic workers have little effective bargaining power. The government has recently set up a task force to look into the idea of collective bargaining, but so far unionization is "really only something in writing," according to Salmon.

A foreign domestic worker who comes to Canada leaves her family and friends behind, knowing she will probably not see them again until she gets her permanent status.

"She's often the one to come because there are no jobs there at home," says Salmon. "Many of these women are providers for their families, so a lot of their money goes back home."

Zeny Cabacoy sends half her earnings back to her children in the Philippines. They live with Cabacoy's father in Quezon City.

Recent changes in the immigration laws mean the families of women who become eligible for landed immigrant status after completing the requirements under the Live-in Caregiver Program will now be assessed at the same time as the women themselves. This one-time assessment will mean "all or nothing" for the domestic worker. If one member of her family does not pass the security and medical clearance, the whole family will not be accepted into Canada, and she will be sent back.

"The change is quite offensive," says Salmon. "She spends those years breaking her back and if her family doesn't pass, she gets sent back."

At the present time, the Women's Legal Education and Action Fund (LEAF) is looking at the ways that the Live-In Caregiver Program can be considered a violation of the Charter of Rights and Freedoms, as it may discriminate on the basis of race, colour, national and ethnic origin.

Despite the obstacles, many women feel the sacrifices are worthwhile.

"These women come here to have a better life, to be independent," says Salmon. "Many of them do."

From the Family to Families

"What's in a Name? A Rose By Any Other Name"
Fredericton, N.B., 1975[25]

What's in a name? A rose by any other name ... ? The whole question of one's name is becoming more of an issue for women. Generally, married women take their husbands' surname, a tradition which seems less valid as women pursue equality.

Under common law, the basis for our legal system, a woman is not compelled to change her name when marrying. The fact that the tradition is so firmly entrenched in our society, that many women think they must take their husband's name reflects the impact of attitudes. For many hundreds of years a woman was considered part of her husband's property, she had no status as an individual; first, she was property of her father, and bore his name, and when ownership was transferred to her husband, it became necessary to use his name so people would know who she belonged to.

Although many laws perpetuate the attitude of ownership (especially in the case of marital property), most women now consider it an expression of pride and love to take their husbands' name. On the other hand some of us have come to realize that there is greater pride in a sense of self, of being who we are, and are able to get strength from this without losing any respect for the marriage relationship. There is also no question that such traditions serve to hamper our struggle for equality under the law.

Tradition a Barrier

Tradition can work as a very real barrier to women wishing to revert back to the use of their maiden name. In view of interpretations of the law, tradition is actually more of a barrier than the law itself. Under common law a person could change his or her name at will, but the problems seem to arise when one considers statute law, the laws passed by provincial and federal legislature. Common law and statute law involve two very different methods. The change of name area falls under provincial jurisdiction and it is interesting to see how some of the provinces handle it.

25. Andrea Knight, *Equal Times*, November 1975, 7.

For instance, under New Brunswick Change of Name of Act, Section 2(1) "Subject to Part IV of the Health Act and Section 31 of the Adoption Act, no person shall change his name except under this Act, or except in the case of a change of surname to that of her husband by a woman upon her marriage, or except in the case of adoption of her maiden name by a woman upon the annulment or dissolution of her marriage." But Section 3(2) states "Any person except a married woman may make an application." ...

"Informal" Change

The interesting question is that of informal, opposed to formal change. Most people I have talked to feel that the statute law abrogates (cancels or repeals) the common law. However two additional factors must be taken into consideration. Besides the general assumption that it would require a strong authority and weighty submission to change the common law, most lawyers familiar with this area take that position that "Except when it is done fraudulently or for some other improper purpose, nothing in the law prohibits a person from adopting or assuming any name he or she desires." (Women's Bureau, Ontario, Ministry of Labour, Law and the Woman in Ontario, Revised 1972). Thus there seems to be no difference between the way the law views a change made under the Act and a change made in an informal manner, except in gaining recognition of this change. It is an additional and interesting point concerning married women who wish to return to the use of their maiden name, that one way the Act provides for recognition of the change is by allowing alteration of the birth certificate ... in most cases, of course, it is the woman's maiden name which appears on the birth certificate!! The other factor for consideration is that the only sanctions contained in the Act for changes made outside its procedures provide for penalties of a fine for persons who obtain the change through fraud or misrepresentation, or for persons who use a name after being refused permission to adopt it under the Act (Section 22). Thus, no mention at all is made in the Act in regard to penalties for informal change of name. So it would appear that the Change of Name Act was designed to assist people in making changes effective — by excluding married women the Act denies them access to such assistance for their common law right to change their name.

Amendments No Help

Amendments to the Act have recently been drafted in New Brunswick. Section 3 has been changed to include married women in eligibility, however Section 4(2) states that "where a married woman, who has taken the name of her husband upon the marriage, applies for a change of her surname, she shall apply for a change of the surname of her husband and the unmarried infant children of the marriage." (Section 4(1) makes the same provision for a married man applying for a change of surname.) However, this strengthens the argument that the law is concerning itself with a change of family name rather than a woman's right to return to the use of her maiden name. The purpose of such Amendments surely should be to clarify the situation. That, at present, does not seem to be the case. The one advantage for such lack of clarity is that it leaves room for discussion.

All this legal talk may seem confusing, and you might wonder why I am concerning myself with such involved discussion. But I must point out that my right to use my own name is important enough to me that I want to know where I stand under the law. As a result I decided to go ahead and initiate an "informal" change of name. What this entails is letting the change be known in the community as well as requesting the change on all pieces of identification. As yet I haven't encountered too many difficulties, which unfortunately is not the experience of others. If I was asked for a reason I answered that I was using my maiden name for all business and social purposes, that seemed to satisfy almost everyone. I received a new Social Insurance card promptly and encountered no opposition from my bank. There have been a few problems with my Medicare card, but more because of a misunderstanding of what I actually wanted, than opposition. Medicare did attempt to put me down as Mrs. Andrea Knight, but I pointed out the illogic of this and suggested they use Ms. I haven't received the card yet but I'll keep trying. Another change I haven't attempted is my Chargex card — I'm looking forward to that with relish ...

I can find no barrier to the slower, but effective method of allowing this name to be the one by which I am known in the community. My maiden name becomes my name by reputation. It would seem that under common law it is as legal as any other. It is my name and I am who I am. The question itself may seem petty but it is ultimately aimed toward a change of attitude. It is in no way a desire to slight my relationship with my husband but an attempt to deny a tradition which claims me merely as a part of someone else's identity.

"Lesbians Fight to Keep Kids"
Toronto, 1977[26]

Case One

A lesbian mother in the Toronto area is engaged in a court battle with her ex-husband for custody of two of her three children, now aged 15, 13 and 12 years. The former husband claims that the woman's lesbianism makes her unfit to raise the children.

The woman, whom we will call Mrs. Davis, must remain anonymous because of the risk of losing her home and her job.

Mrs. Davis was divorced in May 1976. Her husband retained custody of the children, who had been living with him since their parent's

26. Ellen Agger, *Body Politic*, December 1976/January 1977, 3.

separation in 1972. In June, after her 13-year-old daughter told Mrs. Davis that the man had been indecently assaulting her for several years, the two younger children joined their mother and her lover, with whom Mrs. Davis has been living for four years. Both women have had steady jobs for a number of years.

Because of the criminal charges pending against the husband, the court granted temporary custody to Mrs. Davis. Given the circumstances, her lesbianism did not bar her from obtaining custody. The outlook for permanent custody is now good.

But Mrs. Davis' situation is in many ways unusual. Every year in Canada hundreds of lesbian mothers lose their children. Most of these cases never reach the courtroom. To begin with, a woman must consider whether she can support herself and her children. Often she gives them up without a fight because she can't afford to raise them on 'women's wages' or welfare.

Even if she can and manages to gain access to an experienced lawyer, she can expect an ugly courtroom battle. She will have to answer many questions in court to satisfy the judge that she is indeed 'fit' to be a mother.

- Can she provide a more stable home environment than her husband or the Children's Aid Society can? If he is a convicted criminal, an alcoholic, or a drug-user, her chances are better.
- Did she take the children with her when she left her husband? Even if her circumstances were desperate, she is better off to have taken them with her. The courts prefer to leave children with the parent who has them.
- Does she have a stable relationship and a job?
- Has she organized openly in lesbian, women's, or gay organizations? This may mean to the court that she is 'crusading' for homosexuality.

The threat of losing their children prevents many lesbians from leaving marriages. Others, lesbian mothers trying to raise children without a man's higher wages, have to live with the continual dread of having their lesbianism becoming known, because a *custody decision is never final*. It can be challenged at any time until the child is 16 (in Ontario), particularly if the woman hid her lesbianism in the original case.

In the United States, lesbian mothers have won unconditional custody in fewer than a dozen cases. In Canada there has been only one such award. That was in Alberta in 1975. Sometimes the courts have given the children to their mother on the condition that she never associate with other lesbians or that she live apart from her lover. But more often than not, custody is given to the father.

The question of child custoy is a mounting concern, and not just for lesbian women. Increasingly, whether they are living with men or not, the price which women have to pay for refusing to stay in marriages is the loss of their children. Under the guise of equal rights, men are more often being awarded custody. The investment of women's lives in those children counts for less and less.

Now the courts look at the question of who has the greater financial resources and possibility of obtaining the services of a wife to raise the children. Men are much more likely to come up the winners. In the precedent-setting case in Alberta, the woman won because her husband was a drug-user, had an unstable job history, and *had no wife to look after the kids while he was at work.*

In the last few years, lesbian women in North America and England have begun fighting openly for the right to custody of their children. They are setting up defence funds, such as the one recently set up in Ottawa, to help each other cover court costs, publishing newsletters, and circulating information to lessen the isolation and vulnerability of fighting a case alone. But their scope has usually been limited to lesbian women only.

Toronto's Wages Due Lesbians, a group of lesbian women, is organizing to win wages for housework from the government for all women, so we will not be forced into the corners of poverty and hiding that now go along with being a lesbian and a mother. We are fighting against our disadvantage when we enter a courtroom fearful of being exposed or destined to lose because we haven't the means to provide a good home for our children.

On October 28, Wages Due Lesbians co-sponsored with women from the Community Homophile Association of Toronto a benefit for Mrs. Davis. We raised $300. The advertising for this benefit was as far-reaching as possible. We assumed that there are lesbian women everywhere, not just in the gay clubs and women's bars; we assumed that this benefit would be of interest to many women, not only lesbians and not only mothers, that we all have a stake in winning these cases, and not being punished when we step out of line as lesbians, as women who want to raise children on our own, as women who want to put our needs first for a change ...

The organizing of the benefit and the scope of publicity sought are part of the fight being waged by women to win the right to choose for ourselves our sexuality without facing the loss of our children. It is especially crucial now that we organize, as more of us are being pushed back into the closet or relationships with men just to survive.

Wages Due Lesbians is about to publish the first pamphlet on lesbian mothers and child custody available in North America. It can be ordered from Wages Due Lesbians ... and is entitled Motherhood, Lesbianism, and Child Custody. Any woman interested in sharing her experience or discussing the activities of WDL, should call [us] ...

"Lesbian Mothers in Motion"
Thunder Bay, September 1982[27]

Have any of you ever been threatened with the reality of losing custody of your children? With the rising rate of divorce in Canada, many parents have horrendous custody battles when the marriage dissolves and there are children involved in the separation.

In the past, women have usually been awarded custody of children of "broken marriages." Now, with changes in the Family Reform Act, fathers have a better chance of gaining custody of children. It seems that more and more consideration is being given to the whole question of responsible parenting when couples split up.

But the situation for lesbian mothers still remains archaic and riddled with patriarchal, capitalist attitudes and contradictory values which work to make the whole issue of child custody painful and expensive for women who are choosing to leave a marriage and pursue a lesbian lifestyle.

More and more women are choosing to be in relationships with women. We have more in common with each other, and therefore relating to each other is often easier, more creative and genuinely supportive. Lesbianism as a lifestyle is growing into something beautiful for women and children.

Still, lesbian mothers have a hell of a hard time gaining custody rights of their own children. Just because our sexual orientation switches to something other than male-defined, uncreative and physical violence masquerading as lust doesn't mean that we turn into irresponsible deviants. We are still the same human souls we were before making that decision to leave a lifestyle. A women doesn't ever forget her mothering skills once she's learned them through practice. And a women doesn't want to lose her children.

So, it's exciting and energizing to find out more about a positive support system being developed by lesbian mothers here in Canada by way of the "Lesbian Mothers Defence Fund" (LMDF). A Toronto office of the LMDF has been helping women and children for three years now, while the LMDF opened offices in Calgary and Vancouver just this year.

Two lesbians are cycling from Calgary to Newfoundland on a cycle tour to promote the development of the LMDF office in Calgary ... They ... spoke of the need for lesbian mothers to have a support system set up to help them through draining custody battles and personal prosecution, and of the need to provide financial assistance to those women faced with huge court costs as a result of those battles.

The Lesbian Mothers Defense Fund strives to provide these services to a very vulnerable group of women.

Isn't it incredible how human rights can be so easily taken away from those who don't fit into the right molds, by those who profit from our

27. Arja Lane, *The Northern Woman Journal* 7, no. 4 (September 1982), 5.

conformity? It amazes me how the practice of women loving women has been twisted into something threatening to our children. No one has yet explained the connection to me in a way that made human sense ...

Out of the Mouths of Babes — Keeping the "Special Family" Secret
Toronto, 1994[28]

My lesbian partner and I live in a very family-oriented, suburban community where there are many stay-at-home moms. I just happen to be one of those that must balance motherhood at home with a preschooler, with pursuing a writing career.

Politically incorrect or not, I use a pen name to keep myself in the closet, but, more importantly, to protect my child, my career and my lifestyle from our daughter's biological father, a man with a criminal past.

Since I have a child, I am often viewed as straight. And since I am not out in the community, I rather like the shield our daughter provides.

Occasionally my partner picks up our child from nursery school and, although eyebrows may be raised, so far none of the other moms have acted indifferent towards our daughter or to either of us. Even if they did, who is to say that it's not just a simple clash of personalities and not necessarily because we are lesbian moms.

Recently, the nursery school had a Christmas puppet show for the children and their parents. When our daughter walked in holding my partner's hand, she excitedly said, "I brought Dawn." The teacher, head tilted, eyed Dawn and replied, "Oh, that's great."

When the show ended, the teacher thanked all the moms, dads and "special friends" for sharing in the celebration. My partner was impressed that the teacher acknowledged her presence. In fact, we're quite certain that our family was well represented that morning.

Still, raising a child in these times is tough enough without worrying about our daughter innocently mentioning her at-home life. Ah, the wonder our three-year-old provides for her two moms. But it's equally incredible to think that at any time I may be outed by this same little person. What's that expression, "out of the mouths of babes."

What will happen when our daughter realizes that women have the option of loving either women or men? How will she react? So far, so good, but we sense the questions are just around the corner.

With our daughter's immense vocabulary it won't be long before she will want to share this new-found information at school. Will she be the one to teach the other preschoolers about the bees and the bees? And when will the phone ring with the other parents condemning this kind of honesty at such an early age? Are we supposed to hide our lifestyle from the child as something not to be proud of?

---

28. Laura Barry, "The Mouths of Babes: Lesbian Moms Take Us All One Step Forward," *XTRA!*, 21 January 1994, 27.

My partner and I are pleased to say that our daughter is a happy, well-adjusted child. Only last week she blurted out from the back seat of the car, "You and Dawn are my moms, right mom?" After I pulled myself back together, I could only reply, "Hmmm."

Her latest query concerns the need for a daddy for her dollies. When I heard this, my heart sank. It was time to explain that it's okay for a family not to have a daddy. Luckily we know a single mom with two kids to use as an example. Whew, I can breathe easy, that is, until the next question comes my way.

As our little girl struggles to understand her type of family in this homophobic world, I hope she will remain proud of her two moms who love her very much. I do not want her to sense my apprehension at being outed by her. After all, she wants to share her family with her friends.

All fears and apprehensions aside, our "special" family has become just one more stepping stone to a less homophobic society.

"Lesbians Win Spousal Benefits"
Vancouver, 1986[29]

For Krin Zook and Annette Clough a trip to the dentist, cavities or not, is a victory. Zook, an alternate education teacher with the Vancouver School Board, has recently won spousal health benefits for Clough, her lover of seven years.

The Vancouver Municipal and Regional Employees Union (VMREU) which represents Zook, has successfully negotiated benefits for gay and lesbian clerical and support staff employed by the Vancouver School Board. Equality provisions included with the benefit package give same sex partners access to medical, dental and other entitlement, such as compassionate leave, that were already available to heterosexual couples.

When Zook first applied to the school board last year for Clough's coverage, she was rejected on the grounds that the insurance company refused to insure same-sex couples. On further investigation, however, Zook discovered that the company processing school board claims, C.U.&C. Health Services Society, had no such discriminatory regulations and would, in fact, honour any request for same-sex coverage from any group or contract holder. Zook immediately filed a grievance with VMREU and asked the union to include in its contract demands a clause that provides access to benefits for the spouses of lesbian and gay employees.

She was astonished to see how easy it was to win support. "I used to do all the organising on my own," she said. "It was great to go to a union meeting and find other people so willing to work with me."

The same-sex benefits were soon won through negotiations with the school board. Zook attributes the success partly to the left-leaning Committee of Progressive Electors (COPE) which control all nine seats on

29. Noreen Howes [Shanahan], *Kinesis*, November 1986, 3.

the Vancouver School Board. "The union had good people and then there's the progressive attitude of the COPE trustees," she said.

Gudrun Landolf, staff representative for VMREU claims that there has been a general move within the union to win same-sex spousal coverage in all collective agreements. At the Vancouver Community College, for instance, the coverage was won two years ago. It was difficult to negotiate, partly because no gay or lesbian couples came forward, as in Zook's case. More recently, the Langara College Students Union has won same-sex benefits; once again negotiated by the VMREU. "Coverage wasn't difficult to achieve here," said Landolf "because another employer had already accepted this."

Gay activist David Carrell, who sits on the B.C. Federation of Labour human rights committee said: "All these things are possible if gays are persistent in demanding that their leadership push for these benefits." He hails the recent VMREU advances as a giant step forward. "It's not just symbolic. It means that your employer and your union are accepting a non-stereotype version of gay people as human beings."

Chapter 2

Paid Work

Marjorie Griffin Cohen

The feminist movement in the late 1960s and early 1970s focused much of its attention and activities on women's work because it could be used to generate opposition to male domination and privilege. The inequalities between men and women's work were well known to the women who encountered them every day, both in their unpaid work in the home and in their paid work in the labour force. Paid work became the focus for action initially because it is often easier to demonstrate inequalities in this type of work: differences in pay and occupational distribution are quantifiable and, therefore, make the inequalities between men and women more visible and convincing as arguments for change.

Inequalities are often obscured by what appears to be "natural" or is customary. Unequal work between men and women was long regarded as a normal feature of our culture. For example, in 1967 people were so used to jobs being defined as women's and men's jobs that it was not unusual for employers to specify in their advertisements that they wanted to hire a woman or a man, nor was it illegal. Paying women less than men was so commonplace that even minimum wage legislation in the late 1960s in Prince Edward Island, Nova Scotia, and Newfoundland permitted lower minimum wages for women than for men. The idea that men should be paid more money just because they were men was so ingrained in social norms that as late as 1968 an Ontario High Court judge was able to reject a policewoman's bid for equal pay with the justification that: "She is not being discriminated against by the fact that she received a different wage, different from male constables, for the fact of difference is in accord with every rule of economics, civilization, family life and common sense."[2]

These kinds of inequalities were usually justified as essential for the well-being and efficiency of the economy. Confining women to a small range of paid jobs made sense because, it was argued, women's biological make-up means they are specifically suited to work which is distinct

"Help Wanted Female" and "Help Wanted Male" advertisements such as these from the Vancouver Sun *in 1967 were legal and were typical of job advertisements all across the country. They very effectively excluded women from access to better paying jobs.*

from what men do.[3] The argument that women should be paid less than men for performing these jobs was usually justified by the assertions that either women's labour was less productive than men's or that they did not need the same pay as men because they were not responsible for the main family income, but merely supplemented it. As the economy changed and more women entered the labour force, these assumptions, which had long been challenged by feminists, increasingly came into conflict with the reality of working women's lives.[4]

Changing Patterns of Work

In the twenty-five years under consideration in this book, some characteristics of women's work have undergone dramatic changes, while other features have remained relatively static. The most dramatic change has been in the number of women who work for pay. The growth in the service sector of the economy has had profound implications for the lives of women because it has brought more women, and more married women, permanently into the labour force.[5] In 1968 about 37 per cent of all adult women were working for pay.[6] By 1991 the majority of women (about 58 per cent) were in the labour force at any time. (See Table 2-1.)

Over the period from 1968 to 1991, the biggest change occurred in the employment patterns of married women and women with small children. Not only did more married women enter the work force, but they also increasingly remained in paid employment even when they had small children. In the early days of the new feminist movement, married women's paid working patterns were usually described as "discontinuous" or less stable than men's because women tended to drop out of the labour force when they had children and to return when the children entered school. But this pattern changed dramatically. By the 1980s the majority of women with pre-school children were working for pay, and by 1991 over three-fourths of the women in Canada with school-aged children were employed.[8]

Table 2-1
Female Labour Force Participation Rates
1961–1991

Year	% of all women in labour force	women as % of total labour force
1961	29.5	27.3
1971	38.7	34.3
1981	51.0	40.6
1991	58.2	45.0

SOURCE: Statistics Canada, *Census 1961–1991*.

For most women, taking on a paid job doubled their workload because their responsibilities in the home did not diminish.[9] A woman working in a fish-processing plant in Nova Scotia noticed that the male co-workers did not seem as tired as the women. When the men went home they got more sleep because they didn't do the laundry, prepare the meals, or tend the children. Their time was free.[10] The "double ghetto" of women's work became an important theme for women's activism. Because women were primarily responsible for the household, men were advantaged in the workplace. Increasingly, women demanded that the structures of the workplace change to accommodate their different needs. Women wanted more flexible hours of work, adequate daycare for their children, transportation schemes that would accommodate their needs, and safe working environments. The sheer weight of numbers of women in the labour force meant that women's work needs could no longer be seen as marginal issues that applied to only a few people.

Women also wanted things to change in the home itself. Early studies confirmed what most married women knew; that is, when they took paid employment their husbands were not inclined to take on additional work in the home. In 1975 in Vancouver, a woman with children could count on an additional hour of housework a week from her husband when she took up full-time paid employment. By 1990, fifteen years later, a study of Hamilton families showed that husbands increased their housework only by an hour and a half when their wives worked for pay full time.[11]

The Wage Gap

As more women entered the labour force, their economic position, relative to that of men, did not always improve. Pay inequalities between men and women stubbornly resisted change, despite equal pay laws.[12] In every occupational category, in every age group, and at every level of education, women on average, still earned less than men. (See Table 2-2.) In her article in which she first named the "wage gap," Lynn McDonald documented how the difference in men's and women's wages had actually grown during the period from 1955–1973.[13] This statistical naming of the problem helped focus public attention on employers' exploitation of women. As McDonald put it, while the police in Canada actively pursued trivial thefts, which amounted to an average loss of $150, employers were able to get away with stealing thousands of dollars from women each year.

The Victoria Voice of Women's brief to the B.C. Minister of Labour in 1971 shows that women were paid less than men even when they did the same job.[14] Female elevator operators, sales persons, and office clerks received less pay than their male counterparts. But often, even women who had more experience and better training were paid less than men. So, for example, a practical nurse in B.C. earned less pay than an inexperienced male orderly, even though she was required to be licensed and hold a diploma from a Practical Nursing School and he had no

Table 2-2

**Earnings of women as a percentage
of those of men by occupation
1991***

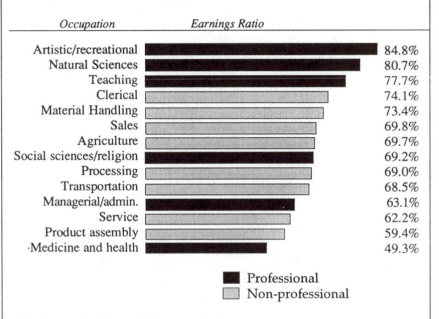

Occupation	Earnings Ratio
Artistic/recreational	84.8%
Natural Sciences	80.7%
Teaching	77.7%
Clerical	74.1%
Material Handling	73.4%
Sales	69.8%
Agriculture	69.7%
Social sciences/religion	69.2%
Processing	69.0%
Transportation	68.5%
Managerial/admin.	63.1%
Service	62.2%
Product assembly	59.4%
·Medicine and health	49.3%

■ Professional
☐ Non-professional

* Includes only full-time/full-year workers

SOURCE: Statistics Canada, *Women in the Workplace*, 2nd ed., March 1993, Table 3.4, p. 41. Catalogue 13–217.

specific qualifications set for his work.) Some trade union contracts actually negotiated different pay rates for men and women as was clear from the 1971 contracts negotiated by the United Fisherman and Allied Workers Union, the Retail Food and Drug Clerks Union, and the Canadian Food and Allied Workers.[15]

Since Lynn McDonald first wrote on the "wage gap," some indicators of women's wage performance have shown improvement, although the changes are rather small. In 1971, women earned 60 per cent of what men earned on average for full-time, full-year work (a figure which is unchanged from the biblical worth of a woman, calculated in Leviticus at three-fifths the value of a man), and twenty years later this figure improved only marginally to 67.7 per cent.[16] On average, in 1993 women still earned 30 per cent less than men. But even this modest narrowing in the percentage difference between men's and women's wages should not obscure the fact that in money terms, the gap is constantly widening.

Table 2-3

Earnings Ratio between Women and Men, 1967–1991

Year	Full-time/full-year workers Earnings ratio	All earners Earnings ratio
1967	58.4	46.1
1971	59.7	46.9
1976	59.1	46.7
1981	63.7	53.5
1986	65.8	57.4
1991	69.9	61.5

*Represents women's earnings as a percentage of those of men.

SOURCE: Statistics Canada, *Women in the Workplace*, 2nd ed., March 1993, Table 3.1, p. 40. Catalogue 13–217.

In 1971, women earned on average $3,538 less than men. Ten years later this figure had grown to $8,316 and in 1993 stood at $11,725.[17]

When we compare wage statistics for males and females, we usually compare them based on standard, or full-time, full-year work because that has been the more normal work situation for male workers. The point of doing this is to carefully compare analogous situations of male and female workers. However, as standard work becomes more elusive, this type of comparison may hide very real deteriorations in women's wages, particularly as women increasingly take on part-time or part-year work, paid work in the home, or contract work. Also, if the wages men receive are deteriorating, then the narrowing of the gap between male and female wages may not indicate improvements for women, but worse conditions for men. Comparing the incomes from work for all women and all men shows a substantially larger pay gap than exists when comparing just standard work. (See Table 2-3.)

Challenging Employers

The existence of equal pay laws has created the illusion that paying women less than men would be punished by law. Beginning with Ontario in 1951, Canadian jurisdictions throughout the 1950s and '60s gradually passed equal pay for equal work legislation.[18] Initially, these laws required that the jobs be identical for the pay to be equal, but since virtually every job could be considered different in some small way and employers used these minor differences to justify paying women less, the wording of the laws was changed. The changes specified that wages must be equal if the work was substantially the same, required similar skills, effort, and responsibilities, and was performed under similar working conditions.

Nevertheless, even this change to the wording did almost nothing to improve women's pay. Part of the problem was that the laws were not enforced. If any woman tried to bring a suit against her employer for unequal treatment, she soon learned the folly of this action. In 1975, Virginia Crabill, a woodworker/machine operator in Nova Scotia, objected to being paid less than the newly-hired man she was training and attempted to use the law to rectify a situation that was clearly illegal.[19] Ultimately, she lost her job, and after nine months of legal wrangling she was awarded only $363.00, the difference between her wages and her trainees' while she was employed. Women quickly learned that they had more to lose by pursuing equal pay for equal work cases than they could possibly gain. Time, stress, and job-loss were serious considerations, particularly when both the awards for "winning" and the chances of winning were so small. In Nova Scotia between 1972 and 1980, only 137 equal pay complaints were recorded and, of these, only 17 were successful.[20]

Despite the inadequacy of the laws, women actively pursued attempts to redress wage inequalities. Over this period of time, considerable effort was made by women's groups and trade unionists to change the wording of the law so that it would be more applicable to the real situations women were experiencing. But equally significant were women's attempts to act collectively to confront directly the wage practices of their employers. The attempts of women to organize in trade unions was bitterly fought by employers, and even when women did successfully organize, their unions were often destroyed by the employers when the women tried to negotiate their first contract. A common strategy for employers was to force a new and inexperienced union to strike in order to obtain the first contract. The employer, through the negotiating process, would often insist on wages and working conditions that were *worse* than those the workers had organized to oppose. This strategy would place the new union in a difficult situation. If it entered a strike without having time to build up funds or experience, it was bound to fail. If the union acquiesced, their members would certainly become disillusioned with what the union could achieve.

Feminist organizations were often enlisted as strike-support groups for women experiencing such tactics. In a bitter strike in 1972 against Dare Foods in Waterloo, Ontario, the women's movement publicized not only the miserable working conditions of the Dare cookie workers, 75 per cent of whom were women, but also backed the workers' boycott against Dare cookies.[21] Women around the province supported the boycott, although the pressure on Dare Foods was not sufficient to resolve the strike in the women workers' favour. But the memory of the strong-armed tactics of Dare has remained with many of us, and it is common,

Immigrant women in the garment industry have long fought for fair wages and better working conditions. In 1978, these Puretex Knitting workers won their strike demands for a more humane and respectful working environment.

even today, to see those feminists who remember still unable to buy or eat Dare cookies.

There have been many women's strikes and the story of each one in some way is unique and points to some distinct aspect of the unequal nature of women's work. The strikes almost always focused initially on inadequate and unequal wages, but often other issues became even more dominant — issues dealing with basic human rights or the plight of women who were specifically exploited because of their ethnicity, origin, or race. The inventive ways in which an employer could dominate women became evident in the Puretex strike in Toronto. Two hundred and twenty workers at the Puretex Knitting Company, most of whom were immigrants and all but twenty of whom were women, went on strike in November 1978.[22] The women wanted equal wages with the men, but this was not the issue that became the focus of public attention. People were appalled to learn that not only did the president of the company monitor the women's every movement with cameras as they worked at the cutting tables, sewing machines, and pressing machines, but he also used a camera to monitor their entry and exit from the washroom. Two years earlier, the union had filed a complaint with the Ontario Human Rights Commission about the discriminatory way the company used cameras, and, after the Commission abdicated its responsibility and dismissed the case, the workers went on strike.[23] Other unions and women's groups supported the women on the picket lines and by distributing leaflets at stores which sold Puretex clothing. After three months, the president agreed to remove the camera from the women's washroom door, and ultimately an arbitrator ordered the removal of the remaining eight cameras, calling them "seriously offensive in human terms."

It is not uncommon for immigrant women workers to have many experiences that are "seriously offensive in human terms." Their vulnerability, because of their difference, makes them easily exploited by unscrupulous employers. They often can find jobs only in manufacturing and agricultural industries that not only have poor wages and working conditions, but that the state has decided are inappropriate for the application of labour legislation, which is in force elsewhere. Kuldip Kaur Bains, in an interview in 1983, described the inhuman conditions immigrant farmworkers in B.C. experienced.[24] The workers lived in barns with no windows and no privacy. They were miserably paid and part of their salary was automatically deducted to pay for their rent. Even more serious was the danger they experienced. Normal health and safety standards that applied to workers in factories and offices did not apply to these farmworkers. They had no protection from chemicals that made them sick, and little recourse when they were overworked and underpaid.

Paid farmworkers in most provinces are excluded from basic labour legislation that sets standards for minimum wages, overtime pay, and vacations, and regulates hours of work. Some farmworkers are excluded from legislation that protects them when they try to unionize. Virtually none are protected by occupational health and safety laws.[25] Worst of all is the terrible danger to which these workers' children are exposed when they are left on their own because their parents are working and no childcare is provided by either the employer or the state. As Kaldip Kaur Bains explained, children have died under these circumstances. Farmworkers sometimes try to organize into unions, but the conditions of their work make this extremely difficult. Very few of the workers have permanent or long-term employment, but when they are working they can work as much as twelve hours a day, seven days a week. The hours are so long and the work so arduous that they have little time or energy for organizing. Also, they often live on the employers' property so union organizers have difficulty even reaching the workers. These barriers to organizing are virtually insurmountable for female farmworkers who also must cope with raising children in conditions of hardship.

Farmworkers and domestic workers share the distinction of having the least protection of all labourers in the work force and are the only two groups of workers for whom temporary work permits apply on a permanent basis. Not surprisingly, both groups are among the most exploited workers in this country. The exploitation of domestic workers who come to Canada on temporary work permits has long been visible to Canadians, yet little has been done to protect these workers. As the testimony of domestic workers show, the promises of wages, hours of employment, and living conditions often change once the worker has

CREDIT: National Film Board of Canada

Indian and Chinese farmworking women in British Columbia campaigned hard to help organize the Canadian Farmworkers Union, which came into existence on April 6, 1980. The hardships these women have endured and the militancy of their struggle for decent wages and working conditions are eloquently documented in the NFB film A Time To Rise *(1981).*

arrived in Canada.[26] Since these women have had no right to stay in Canada unless employed and can change employers only with great difficulty, they have little recourse when employers do not meet their obligations. Their vulnerability as workers, particularly since they are living with their employers, makes them unusually susceptible to sexual harassment.

Because more women with children are now part of the Canadian labour market and the provision of daycare has been so inadequate,[27] the trend away from live-in domestic help that began early in this century has now been reversed. Since the mid-1970s, temporary work permits have been issued to between 10,000 and 16,000 immigrant women a year as live-in domestic workers.[28] Various organizations have tried to improve the opportunities for these women to become permanent residents in Canada, and while some changes were made in 1981 so that women could apply for landed immigrant status if they met certain conditions, these changes did not benefit most women who came here as temporary domestic workers.[29] It is not simply coincidental that the workers who are given temporary work permits are female and are predominately women of colour. The normal protections that are provided for most workers do not apply to domestic workers, and only very recently did some provinces limit the work week of domestic workers in private homes. These women, because they are single employees working for a family, still do not have the right to organize in unions in many provinces.[30]

Women who clean outside private households appear to be in a superior position to those who work in isolated private households. Unfortunately, working collectively in offices does not necessarily provide better wages and working conditions, particularly when the employer does not hire workers directly, but hires contractors to provide the service. The practice of "contracting-out" work has become more prevalent as a way of evading costly fair labour practices and even governments are using this practice as a way of lowering costs for labour-intensive work. The people who do contract work as cleaners in office buildings are overwhelmingly immigrant women who often find that after years and years of work they are still working at the minimum wage. The case of the women who worked for the Ontario government in the mid-1970s demonstrates how the government, through contracting-out, kept women cleaners at the minimum wage.[31] When Portuguese women working for Modern Building Cleaning at government offices at Queen's Park formed a union, their employer was forced to raise their wages. This meant that when the government accepted new bids for the work, Modern Building Cleaning was not the lowest bid. The government took a lower bid, and the women, who would have made slightly more than the minimum wage through unionization with Modern Building Cleaning, were laid off. Many of them went to work for the new contractor under unionized conditions at the minimum wage.

The Ontario government was, in effect, preventing these women from forming a union. More recently, the federal government has subverted unionized workers by contracting out cleaning at many post offices.[32]

Trade Unions

Although legal changes are significant, being part of a trade union often brings improvements in pay and working conditions much more quickly than efforts to change the law. If labour legislation that applied elsewhere was applied to farmworkers and domestic workers, for example, these workers would then be in a much better situation to confront their employers. This is not to imply that the relationship between women and trade unions always has been a happy one. Historically, women have been considered difficult to organize, and although women were tolerated within the unions, few traditional unions did anything to accommodate women's different circumstances and different needs.[33] The sexist attitudes women encountered in the workplace were often duplicated within the unions to which they belonged.[34] Frequently, even unions whose membership was predominately female were controlled and run by men who neither knew about nor were receptive to women's concerns. While the male-dominated nature of trade unions was not the only reason women tended to be much less unionized than men, it certainly was significant in making the struggle to organize less attractive to women.[35]

Some unions, like the Canadian Textile and Chemical Union (CTCU) that organized the Puretex workers, were particularly sensitive to the conditions and needs of their members. This union not only understood the special circumstances of women's labour, but also the distinct kinds of difficulties immigrant women and women of colour experienced. Strong feminist union organizers such as Madeleine Parent and Laurell Ritchie worked within the CTCU to organize these women whom other unions had dismissed as not being worth the effort. CTCU organizers worked within the feminist movement to make the issues of minority women a focus for feminist action. One reason feminist organizers had influence in the CTCU, was because it was a Canadian union run by the people within the union itself.[36] Until fairly recently, the Canadian labour movement has been dominated by large, international (American) trade unions. Because these unions were often managed and controlled from outside the country, women in these unions in Canada had little power in determining either their own union activities or their own union officials. To many women in unorganized workplaces, the alternative Canadian unions were equally undemocratic. Women faced the choice of either creating their own unions or joining the more male-dominated unions and trying to work for reform through women's committees within these unions.

Two independent feminist unions that existed in British Columbia provide examples of unions that were formed specifically with feminist

Table 2-4

**Percentage of paid workers unionized by industry,
1980 & 1989**

	1980	*1989*
Agriculture		
Women	0.5	2.7
Men	0.4	1.6
Other Primary Industries		
Women	7.4	13.0
Men	38.2	38.3
Manufacturing		
Women	31.6	24.4
Men	47.3	41.3
Construction		
Women	3.9	4.4
Men	63.3	61.4
Transportation/communication/		
other utilities		
Women	48.3	48.2
Men	54.6	55.4
Trade		
Women	7.2	10.2
Men	10.3	12.6
Finance		
Women	2.6	3.9
Men	2.4	3.5
Service Industries		
Women	25.3	35.9
Men	22.6	32.4
Public administration		
Women	67.2	76.3
Men	68.1	81.2
Total		
Women	23.9	29.4
Men	37.3	38.0

SOURCE: Statistics Canada, *Women in the Workplace*, 2nd ed., March 1993,
Table 4.4, p. 48. Catalogue 13–217.

principles in mind.[37] These were The Association of University and
College Employees (AUCE) and the Service, Office and Retail Workers
Union of Canada (SORWUC), both formed in 1972.[38] These unions not
only took on the employers in restaurants, banks, and offices who had
never before experienced the power of unions but also confronted the
traditional union establishment in the form of the Canadian Labour
Congress and the B.C. Federation of Labour over organizing jurisdictions. Since existing unions already had "rights" to organize in certain

sectors, the emergence of feminist unions that infringed on these rights created difficulties within the existing labour movement.[39] These difficulties were never resolved and, ultimately, AUCE and SORWUC did not survive as independent feminist unions.

Nevertheless, even within the traditionally male-dominated trade unions, change did occur as women within the union movement itself fought hard to ensure that they not only had a voice but that the structures and objectives of the labour organizations changed.[40] Initially, these initiatives were greeted by male trade unionists with little enthusiasm, but as the composition of the labour force changed, it became exceedingly practical for them to try to meet women's needs. With the restructuring of the economy and the decline in the proportion of the labour force working at manufacturing jobs[41] (the traditional source of trade union membership), it became increasingly important, if the trade union movement was to retain its strength, for jobs in expanding sectors to be organized. These were mainly women's jobs in the rapidly growing service sector, which now accounts for about 70 per cent of all Canadian workers, including those working for all governments. So while women continue to be less unionized than men, increases in union membership has been coming mainly from women. (See Table 2-4.)

As a result of women's growing importance to the trade union movement, issues such as pay equity and employment equity, maternity and parental leave, and daycare have become more central to the negotiating demands of some unions. In the past, it was not unusual for these issues to be raised in contract negotiations with the employers, although they were usually dropped in the bargaining process in favour of issues male trade unionists found more important. Now equal pay demands are the central issue in many strikes, as was evident in the strike of the federal public sector workers in 1991. The Conservative government's 1991 budget imposed a wage freeze that would have meant that if some women made any progress on pay equity, other workers would lose their jobs. The public sector workers, most of whom were low-paid female workers, were enraged by the federal government's hypocrisy with regard to equal pay issues: although the government boasted about its excellent pay equity policies, it would give no money to implement these policies. As will be seen in Chapter 4 on economic policy in this volume, budget decisions can be even more dramatic than legislation in shaping the conditions of women's work. The public certainly supported the strike of government workers, but Parliament, in very short order, legislated them back to work without meeting their demands. Government workers were deemed essential workers and, therefore, denied the right to strike.

Denying workers the right to strike takes away their only real power to act collectively. This issue has become a woman's issue because in most cases this prohibition against striking occurs in jobs where women predominate, particularly in the caring industries. It would seem reasonable that if the state took away the workers' right to strike for better pay and working conditions, that some other measures would be put in place to ensure that the workers were treated fairly. One might expect that these workers would have the best wages and working conditions as an example of goodwill between the public sector employers and their workers. In fact, workers in these industries are rarely well paid. Hospital workers in the late 1960s, for example, were paid wages which were below the poverty line.[42] In Ontario, only defiance on the part of workers — defiance of the male local union negotiators and defiance of the law that forbids them from striking — brought public attention to the working conditions of hospital housekeepers, food handlers, nursing assistants, and laboratory technicians. The 1981 Canadian Union of Public Employees' (CUPE) strike in Ontario hospitals was unprecedented, as were the reprisals in its aftermath: thirty-four workers were fired, another 3,400 were suspended, some for as long as a year, and three union leaders, including CUPE president Grace Hartman, were jailed for contempt of court for supporting the workers' strike.[43]

Jailing union leaders has usually not produced the effect governments desire, since these leaders tend to become celebrated for their courage and defiance. Nevertheless, governments continue to use the courts to punish workers in the public sector who have been denied the right to strike. The strike of the United Nurses of Alberta (UNA) in 1988 was no less bitter than the Toronto CUPE strike in 1981. Strikers were charged with contempt of court and the union itself was charged with criminal contempt and fined $250,000 for the nineteen-day strike involving 11,000 nurses.[44]

Unlike other types of strikes, the strikes of public sector workers directly affect the delivery of a service to people, not employers' profits. Consequently, any withdrawal of services is extremely difficult for workers whose whole worklife is devoted to caring and serving. So when workers withdraw their labour, such as the four hundred home support workers in B.C. who went on strike in 1990 protesting pay rates as low as $5.10 per hour, it was the elderly, the disabled, and the chronically ill who suffered and were directly affected by the government's unwillingness to pay these workers decent wages.[45] Employers also can point to this withdrawal of services as evidence of callousness on the part of workers and, frequently, as was evident in the 1992 B.C. health workers' strike, demonstrate just how damaging this can be to patients by blaming patients' deaths on the strike. The implication is always that workers who strike are more interested in money than the people in their care. This kind of blackmail has been used repeatedly against women who are supposed to undertake their paid jobs because of dedication to people, not because of self-interest.

Women's work, whether in the home, the hospital, or the daycare centre, is supposed to be a labour of love. When women demand a living wage, they are deemed selfish. Women who are forced to strike in the caring industries are acutely aware of the hardships they impose on those for whom they care. Daycare workers, for example, realize that the families of the children they work for simply cannot afford to pay them more, since often they are the working poor themselves.[46] But these workers, whose wages are amongst the lowest of any in Canada, are forced to strike to gain the attention of the governments who are responsible for their wages.[47] Unfortunately, dramatizing the low pay of women workers has not brought necessary changes. A study of daycare workers' wages in 1985 sparked an uproar when it revealed that the women who cared for children in Canada earned 30 per cent less than people who cared for animals in zoos. This revelation was shocking, but it produced no improvements for daycare workers. Neither the appalling inadequacy of facilities for children nor the miserable working conditions of those caring for them has swayed the government in its decision to cancel plans for a national childcare program. According to a 1992 survey, not only do daycare workers' wages remain less than zoo keepers', but they have even declined in recent years and now approach poverty level.[48]

Pay Equity

In the struggle to improve women's wages, the fact that women generally do not do the same jobs as men means that when comparisons are made, employers can rate women's work as less valuable than men's work. For many years it had been obvious to feminists and trade unionists that while collective action was necessary to reduce the discrimination against women, this action would not be effective as long as laws protected employers when they paid women less than men. There needed to be some mechanism in the law so that different types of jobs could be compared. The wage issue that provoked a strike at Canadian Kenworth in Burnaby, B.C., in 1980 was typical of the type of problem new legislation needed to address. When women data processing workers were included in the bargaining unit, the employer insisted that they receive less pay than the male workers' starting rate, and less, in fact, than the wages paid to unskilled summer students on the assembly line.[49] The "traditional hierarchical structure" was always upheld by politicians as too difficult to challenge or as equivalent to solving "the world's problems," as Mel Couvelier, the Mayor of Saanich, B.C., saw it in 1981.[50]

The kind of legislation that would be necessary to compare different kinds of jobs was not a new issue and had been the subject of much discussion throughout the twentieth century. As early as 1919 in the Treaty of Versailles, the principle of equal pay for work of equal value was included, but the most significant international declaration was made by the International Labour Organization (ILO) Convention 100.[51] Passed in 1951, the declaration provided for "equal remuneration for men and women workers for work of equal value." Canada did not sign this declaration until 1973 because, while this country wanted to be seen

This 1981 IWD photograph graphically shows the cost for women of unequal wages. Even today pay equity legislation is limited in Canada, with only Ontario applying its laws to both the public and private sectors.

as supporting the principle, no provincial jurisdiction was prepared to bring in legislation to make it effective until that time. The first juris-diction to use the "equal pay for work of equal value" language was Quebec in 1975. The Canadian Human Rights Act of 1977 also included similar language. Both of these legislative initiatives on equal pay for work of equal value corrected the existing legislation by raising the principle of comparing different types of work on the basis of skill, effort, responsibility, and working conditions. Once these initiatives were adopted, the new legislation could compare and evaluate jobs as diverse as grounds keeper and secretary.

The major problem with this legislation, however, was that it was "complaints based." That is, employers had to change their employment practices only if an employee filed a complaint with a human rights commission against an employer and the employer was found to have discriminated against a woman.[52] This complaints-based system required a great deal of stamina, effort, and time from any individual pursuing a case. As a result, not many cases, at least relative to the degree of discrimination in the labour force, were initiated. It certainly was in the employers' interest to maintain discriminatory pay practices until they specifically encountered a complaint, since their chances of being charged were small.

The corrective to this complaints-based model was the system that became termed "proactive legislation." This would require employers to examine their employment practices and make changes so that women's work, even when jobs were different, would be as equally valued as men's if skill, effort, responsibility, and working conditions were comparable. The onus would be on the employer, not the employee, to initiate change. So far, after years and years of pressure from women's groups and trade unions, five provinces have instituted proactive equal pay legislation: Manitoba (1985), Ontario (1987), Nova Scotia (1988), Prince Edward Island (1988), and New Brunswick (1989). This legislation is referred to as "pay equity" legislation to distinguish it from "equal pay for equal work" and "equal pay for work of equal value" legislation.[53] Of the five provinces, only Ontario's legislation includes employers outside the public sector. The other provinces have been much more conservative and, in response to employers' demands, have applied pay equity legislation only to the work that falls under the public sector. But even the far-reaching legislation introduced in Ontario is controversial, and its effectiveness is questioned because of its design and complexity. The main complaint is that it is based on a complex system of job evaluation plans that are extremely costly to administer, with the result being a burgeoning industry for equity consultants and relatively little money actually going to women themselves. While the criticism of this legislation is too detailed to be discussed here, it should be emphasized that the political process through which the legislation was developed was one of compromise between what women demanded and what employers did not want to happen. The result is a strange mixture of accommodations, the impact of which may only really be understood after the legislation has been in place for some time.[54]

Employment Equity

Not all women have seen the equal pay issue as the most pressing equality issue. For women who do not have access to jobs or who work at jobs that would have no chance of being compared with those of males (such as domestic cleaners), the issue of who is hired for specific jobs is more fundamental and urgent than the level of pay itself. Immigrants, ethnic minorities, the disabled, and people of colour have long stressed the need for changes in legislation that would prohibit discriminatory hiring practices.[55] But in Canada equal pay legislation has been publicly more amenable to pressure for change than has been legislation that would eliminate job segregation by sex, race, or colour. In the United States, for example, affirmative action legislation that requires employers to adhere to quotas or goals in hiring women and racial and ethnic minorities has been in effect for at least twenty-five years.[56] In Canada it is still resisted by employers even more strenuously than pay equity

CREDIT: Sandy Shreve, *Bewildered Rituals* (Vancouver: Polestar Press Ltd., 1992.) Reprinted with the permission of the publisher.

Spring Cleaning

Sandy Shreve

weeding the files I pretend
the cabinet into a plot of land
as if through this thinning
it will blossom
and everyone who walks in
will admire my new bouquet
lean into each drawer
and breathe deeply the scent
of sorted papers, no longer
ragged edges crammed in every
which way and poised to slash
at skin in vengeance
but petal soft and quivering
to the gentle nudge
of noses seeking fragrance
instead of sneezing dust
now billowing up as I shred
pile after pile of paper
bound for some recycling bin
and bound to come back to me
again in more superfluous copies
to be stuffed and wedged and jammed
into the space I've created
for flowers

legislation. A workforce that is balanced by gender, race, colour, and physical difference is very threatening to employers. While employers may comply, albeit with strenuous objections, to interference in their pay practices, they will stand firm against any encroachments on their perceived right to hire whom they please.

One of the more static features of women's paid work in Canada has been the relatively unchanging nature of women's confinement to a small number of occupations. There has been an illusion of substantial change, but women are still overwhelmingly confined to clerical work, sales, and service occupations.[57] (See Table 2-5.) With the huge increases in women's employment since the 1960s, there has been considerable attention paid to the increased diversity of women's work, creating the perception in the public mind that women are now widely engaged in work that not long ago was the sole preserve of men. While women have moved into professions that were once mostly male, most notably as medical doctors, lawyers, and accountants, these incursions into male-dominated professions have been fairly limited to a class of well-educated, relatively highly paid women. Some changes, particularly the increase in the proportion of women in management positions, are not quite as impressive as might appear by simply looking at the figures. While women were much more likely to be managers in 1991 than ten years earlier, this change probably has more to do with occupational re-definitions than genuine increases in the number of women in administrative positions.[58] The percentage decreases in women working at clerical and service occupations seem to mirror their proportional increases in managerial and administrative jobs. In other occupational classes the gendered division of labour has remained virtually unchanged: if women are on road crews, they direct traffic, not the building of the roads, and if they work for the railroad, they are more likely to clean the cars than do anything else. And if women do succeed in moving ahead, it's because of the fight they've had to put up.

These occupational ghettos have certainly been challenged by women and these challenges have taken a variety of forms. Sometimes unions have been supportive of women's attempts to enter the male work world, as in the case of the Steelworkers campaign at Stelco in Hamilton, Ontario, and reform has taken place within an organization without legal intervention.[59] While legislation that has focused on breaking down occupational barriers has been ineffective in Canada, anti-discrimination legislation has been used by women to pursue gross discriminatory treatment. One of the most dramatic cases of this was the case women brought against CN Rail for its consistent refusal to hire women for blue-collar jobs. Women like Katie Curtin who applied for relatively unskilled jobs with CN were routinely turned away because they were deemed to lack the qualifications necessary for the jobs.[60] What became clear was that the requisite qualifications were not really necessary for doing the work, but were designed to keep women out of the jobs. This case was taken to the Human Rights Commission. Ultimately, the Commission ruled in August 1984 that CN did indeed discriminate against women, and it ordered CN to increase women's participation in blue-collar jobs to a level equal to women's participation in these types of jobs in the labour force in general.

The intransigence of employers sabotaged hopes that voluntary affirmative action programs could be effective in changing the composition of the labour force.[61] In response to the blatantly discriminatory labour force experience of women and other minority groups, a Royal Commission on Equality in Employment was established with Judge Rosalie Abella as the sole commissioner. The report of this Commission in 1984 recommended detailed changes including recommendations for legislation that would require employers to implement employment eq-

Table 2-5

Distribution of employment, by occupation, 1981 and 1991

Occupation	1981			1991		
	Women	Men	Women as % of employment	Women	Men	Women as % of employment
Managerial	5.4	9.9	27.4%	12.0	14.7	40.4%
Natural sciences	1.4	5.2	15.6	1.6	5.9	18.1
Social sciences	1.8	1.6	42.6	2.9	1.9	56.2
Teaching	5.8	3.0	56.7	6.4	2.9	64.7
Doctors/dentists*	0.3	0.8	18.3	0.4	0.8	26.9
Nursing/health*	8.9	1.1	85.1	9.3	1.1	87.0
Artistic	1.4	1.4	39.5	1.7	2.0	41.9
Clerical	34.3	6.4	78.4	29.3	5.8	80.8
Sales	10.1	10.4	39.5	9.8	9.5	46.1
Service	18.3	10.1	55.0	16.1	10.5	56.6
Primary	2.9	8.4	18.9	2.4	6.9	22.2
Manufacturing	7.3	20.5	19.4	5.0	17.4	19.1
Construction	0.2	10.0	1.4	0.3	9.4	2.1
Transport equip.	0.6	5.9	6.1	0.7	6.1	8.7
Material handling	1.8	5.2	18.9	1.5	4.8	20.7
Total	100.0	100.0		100.0	100.0	
Total (000s)	4,445	6,556		5,589	6,751	

*Figures are for 1982

SOURCE: Statistics Canada, *Women in the Workplace*, 2nd ed., March 1993, Table 1.12, p. 23. Catalogue 13–217.

uity, collect data on minority groups and women, and provide for a way to enforce the legislation.[62] While the Commission had been appointed by a Liberal government, the Progressive Conservative candidate for prime minister, Brian Mulroney, promised that employment equity legislation would be passed by his government, if elected. In what can only be described as a cynical move, his government did indeed pass employment equity legislation. But the only requirement of the legislation was that employers in the federal jurisdiction report each year on the employment status of groups designated as disadvantaged. The penalty involved for not reporting would be a fine on the employer, but there would be no penalty if the employer continued to discriminate against women, Native peoples, the disabled, or visibly different employees.[63] The federal Employment Equity Act does not require that employers change their employment practices, merely that they report on their labour force each year.[64]

As work undertaken by the National Action Committee on the Status of Women has shown, the mere requirement that employers' file data on employees each year does not improve working conditions for women and other disadvantaged groups. The five-year experience with the Employment Equity Act has meant that women in industries covered by this legislation such as the banks and the CBC, are virtually at a stand-still relative to men. The disabled, Native peoples, and people of colour have experienced deteriorating conditions in some circumstances.[65]

Workplace Pressures and Work Deterioration

Many of the problems that women encounter as workers seem timeless, and although some problems may disappear for a while, they tend to resurface as employers face new economic pressures and respond by finding new ways to cut their labour costs. For example, working conditions once associated with the rise of industrial capitalism in the nineteenth century are now being revived. Particularly significant is the increase in manufacturing production being performed in the home by women, who obtain their work through subcontractors working on behalf of the clothing firms. Encouraging "home work" is an effective way for employers to circumvent both trade unions and labour legislation. As a result, women receive a fraction of what they might earn were they working in a factory. In Toronto the increase in home work in the clothing industry has been dramatic, and it is estimated that now more than 4,000 people sew designer label clothing in their homes, sometimes earning as little as $4.00 for an Alfred Sung jacket that sells for $375.00.[66] The large unionized garment factory is rapidly disappearing: in Ontario only 23 per cent of garment factories employ more than twenty people, with 43 per cent operating with fewer than four workers.[67] Appallingly low wages is certainly one consequence of shifting manufacturing employment from the factory to the home, with some garment

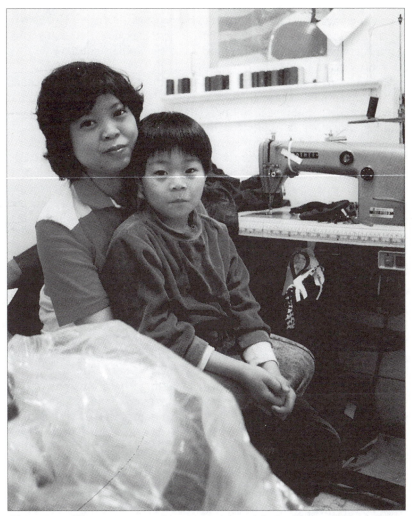

Chau Yuet-Sheung is an ardent organizer with the Homeworkers Association, which strives to protect the rights and wages of home workers in the garment industry. In Ontario alone, there are as many as 4,000 home workers, most of who earn less than the minimum wage and receive no benefits from their employers.

workers making as little as $3.50 an hour and most making $5.58 an hour, in a province where the minimum wage is $6.70 an hour.[68] Home work is not confined to the garment industry; it is also increasing for women involved in "telecommuting." This kind of employment is often attractive to women with young children because they can work at home now that technological changes permit various types of clerical work to be performed off the traditional worksite. However, since these workers, like their counterparts in the garment industry, are not covered by labour legislation, they too are likely to experience the exploitation that seems inevitable when workers are isolated from each other and have neither the protection of the law nor a union.

Changes in technology are continually re-organizing the way that work is performed. These changes are not new. During the last quarter of the twentieth century, many new inventions eliminated the work of humans altogether or redirected it. But what is new is the speed of change and the elimination of forms of work that historically provided the means for women to enter the paid labour force. In the early part of this century, one of the major new jobs for women was the position of telephone operator. This was an especially viable occupation for women in smaller communities. With new telecommunications, however, the positions were eliminated. As Heather Menzies's article shows, the closing of local switchboard offices transformed not just the workers' lives but also the lives of their entire community.[69] Similarly, the automation of banking has eliminated all but a small proportion of the jobs women used to hold as tellers in banks, and the advent of the personal computer has meant that the most traditional form of women's work in an industrial society — clerical work — is becoming less significant.[70] Factories are, in many cases, becoming workerless as robots perform many of the tasks workers used to do. In Northern Telecom's Brampton plant, robots now do 85 per cent percent of the circuit-board assembly, something which has historically been women's work.[71] And in garment factories most of the pattern-making and cutting is performed by operatorless machines with the sewing being transferred to individuals working in their own homes. But probably most significant is the way that technology has changed the location of work and the power of the employer. Because of easier communication and cheaper transportation systems, entire companies can easily relocate to take advantage of cheaper wage rates or more favourable business climates in other countries.[72] This mobility puts increasing pressure on workers to accept home work and contract work that result in a deterioration of wages and other conditions.

Piece work is another example of a method of paying, which in earlier periods was the focus of many struggles for women in the clothing industries and which is now being revived by employers. Rather than paying workers for the time they work, employers pay for each individual piece of work produced. Usually associated with nineteenth-century working conditions, it is a brutal pay scheme that pits workers against one another, forces their wages down, and causes them physical harm. It is now staging a comeback as employers who face an increasingly competitive market force concessions from their workers. The women involved in any type of home work are usually paid by the piece, but increasingly, hourly wages in many factories are also being replaced by piece rates.

Table 2-6 Part-time Employment 1984, 1991 (% of total employment)		
Females	1984	1991
15-24	35.0	43.4
25+	22.7	21.4
all ages	25.6	25.6
Males		
15-24	26.8	33.3
25+	3.1	3.9
all ages	7.6	8.1
All workers	**15.3**	**16.4**

SOURCES: Statistics Canada, Unpublished Data, Reference # SOC62 & #SIC61.

Part-time work and job-sharing have been frequently viewed as ways that work can be organized to accommodate women's special needs. For many women, working part-time was the only way to earn an income while children were small and paid childcare was either not available or too expensive. But part-time work seldom lived up to its promise of combining the joys of motherhood with the joys of earning money. As a Vancouver study in the 1970s showed, usually part-time work was underpaid, uninteresting, and routine.[73] Women predominate among part-time workers, accounting for over 70 per cent of all part-time workers. And while the proportion of women who work part-time has remained relatively stable over the past decade, this statistic may mask a more dramatic trend in the increase in this non-standard work form. (See Table 2-6.) Over 43 per cent of all young women in the labour force do not have full-time jobs. This increase in non-standard work forms since the mid-1980s for women in this age group is substantial and may indicate a long-lasting trend.

Job-sharing is a new form of work that holds considerably more promise than regular part-time employment. The idea is that two people with similar qualifications apply for a job together and each performs certain aspects of it at different times. In this way parents, for example, might share a paid job and child rearing. However, as the National Union of Provincial Government Employees paper states, job-sharing, unless it is carefully constructed, can be both exploitative and damaging to trade union goals.[74] People working at shared jobs often find that the employer expects as much from each job sharer, as he would from a full-time worker — particularly if the job sharers are professionals. This means that in many cases individuals receive part-time pay for working hours that are almost full time. Many employers have found job sharing a convenient way of reducing the full-time workforce without substantially reducing the amount of work received. Job-sharing makes sense for many people in a variety of circumstances, but before it can be a reasonable option for large numbers of people, it must be designed to improve, rather than worsen, people's working conditions.

Workplace Hazards

Sexual harassment appears to have been one of the persistent forms of workplace hazards for women: women have always been vulnerable as employees to the sexually aggressive acts of employers and co-workers. But now that feminists have focused on this issue, women employees have named this type of behaviour and no longer allow themselves to be blamed for its occurrence. As a result of the courageous actions of some women who have pursued this issue in court, the problem can be addressed openly in workplaces. Bonnie Robichaud's decade-long struggle with the Department of National Defence was crucial for other women who had experienced harassment on the job.[75] In her case, sexual harassment took the form of unwanted sexual advances from her supervisor, but it can take other forms too. When women began to look at other employment practices, they realized that what the employer saw as normal conditions of the job were degrading for women and, in fact, constituted harassment. If food servers were required to wear sexually provocative costumes, they were being harassed.[76] If male co-workers were hostile, violent, and created difficult working conditions, women were being harassed.[77] As a result of women's naming the problem and challenging men in court, employers have become more conscious of their obligation to create a safe environment for their female employees. Employers have not made these changes voluntarily. It was only after an employer was named in a court case for knowing of a harassing situation but doing nothing to protect the worker that changes began to happen. Even so, sexual harassment has not been eradicated from the workplace.

Other hazards for women workers are considerable. While the violence against women in the home has become more visible to society, there has been less focus on the violence women can expect in the workplace. Just getting to and from work can be life-threatening.[78] Traditionally women's jobs, in comparison with those men do, are seen to be safe. The most direct fatalities from jobs in Canada are those associated with fishing, forestry, and mining: these are the things men do and many die doing them. The work women do is less likely to produce fatal accidents, but many do work in conditions which, over time, can cause serious health problems or even death. Some of the traditional work women have done is now linked to serious diseases, such as lung cancer as a result of exposure to dust and lint in textile factories.[79] And with technological changes in the workplace, new illnesses are being recognized as women are constantly exposed to computer display terminals. Often women's complaints are dismissed because they arise from accumulated stress and seem vague — headaches, backaches, upset stomachs — but these symptoms are no less real.[80]

The most recent workplace injury to receive considerable attention is repetitive strain injury, which is commonplace among workers who constantly perform the same muscle movements during the course of their work. Supermarket checkout clerks, data processors, and fish plant workers are particularly prone to this type of injury. For years employers denied that this was a real health problem because there was usually nothing specific to see, other than swollen joints on arms. But this has been one area in which considerably hard work on the part of unions has forced employers to recognize the seriousness of the problem — employers have had to redesign work stations to provide frequent rest breaks for their employees so that the effects of repetitive strain injury could be minimized. Some unions, such as the United Fishermen and Allied Workers Union (UFAWU) in B.C., have successfully negotiated with the employers to change the configuration of work stations to avoid injury. Only after evidence from a study commissioned by the union demonstrated conclusively that the repetitive strain injuries women suffered were a result of their work on the fish processing lines, did the companies agree to change.

Another complaint, which has been long known but which is only recently being taken seriously, is the problem of air quality in the office place. Many women work in inner offices in buildings where they have neither access to natural light nor windows that open. Often these buildings have poor air quality and are labeled "sick buildings," and the people working in them develop serious health problems that intensify over time. No compensation is offered to women who have to take sick leave or even quit their jobs because of these problems.

Similarly, the quality of air on planes has been known to be a result of the deliberate policy on the part of airlines to reduce costs by reducing oxygen in certain sections of the plane during flights. Flight attendants, many of whom suffer from headaches, dizziness, burning eyes, and fatigue, recently demanded a federal investigation into the low levels of oxygen, despite their employers' denial that this was the problem. The flight attendants noted that their symptoms have improved immediately whenever their complaints have been met with increases in the oxygen levels.[81]

Think Like a Weightlifter, Think Like a Woman

Kate Braid

First day on the job and the foreman orders
in a voice like a chainsaw,
Hoist those timbers
by hand to the second floor.
Crane's broken down.

I keep my mouth shut
with difficulty, knowing
how much a six by six timber
twelve feet long and fresh
from the Fraser River, knowing
how much it weighs.

Lorne, my partner, says nothing,
addresses the modest mountain of timbers
towering over our heads, smelling
sweetly nostalgic for forest.

Weighing in with the wood he faces,
with a belly like a great swelling bole,
he shakes off my motion to help and
bends as if to pick up a penny,
scoops up the timber and packs it, 50 feet,
to lean against the damp grey sides
of the concrete core.
When he doesn't look back,
it's my turn.

And now, because I need this job, and
because it's the first day and because
every eye is watching The Girl,
I bend my knees as the book says,
think like a weightlifter, take the beam
by its middle and order my body
to lift.

CREDIT: Kate Braid, "Think Like a Weightlifter, Think Like a Woman," *Covering Rough Ground* (Vancouver: Polestar Press Ltd., 1991). Reprinted with the permission of the publisher.

Reluctantly, the great tree, sweating pitch,
parts with its peers with a sucking sound,
and the beam and I sway to the designated spot,
I drop it. Repeat.

Alone, I carry beams to Lorne
who alone heaves them with the slightest grunt
to the labourer who bends from the second floor
with a hurry-up call,
Faster! Faster!

No. I will never be a carpenter, I think, *never
able to work like these men.* Then
Lorne falters.
Without thinking I reach up my two arms beside him
and push with all my might.
The beam flies to the second floor and mindless,
I turn to fetch him another.

Without a word
Lorne follows me back to the pile,
lifts one end and helps me
carry the next timber to the wall.
Without a word we both push it up,
continue this path together
find a rhythm, a pace
that feels more like dancing.

Lorne says, *You walk different.* Yes.
For on this day I am suddenly
much, much stronger, a woman with the strength
of two.

Conclusion

A survey of the issues of women's work over the twenty-five years in this collection undoubtedly highlights the difficulties women encountered as they increasingly took paid jobs and increasingly objected to the inferior position planned for them by their employers, the government, and their male co-workers. Focusing on difficulties does produce a kind of negativity that in many respects gives a false picture of the changes in this period. As a woman who was beginning a working life in the late 1960s, I am acutely conscious of how much better it is to be a working woman now than it was in 1967. In 1967 an employer could say he didn't want to hire you because he wanted a man for the job. He would not dare do this now. When I was teaching at York University as a teaching assistant in the mid-1970s, it was considered natural by my department chair that I receive less pay for my work than the male teaching assistants, something which now seems quite unnatural. Tremendous gains have been made by women themselves because they were able to be critical of the way things were and were able to change them. There is, of course, much that still needs to be done and as economic policy changes to accommodate the interests of international business, there is a very real danger of a regression in women's employment conditions. (See Chapter 4, "Feminism's Effect on Economic Policy.") But in many ways the thinking about what is fair and just has changed in very substantial ways. These are changes that could not have occurred without conflict, grief, and real pain for many women. Nor would they have occurred without the concerted effort of women working together in women's groups and in trade unions to ensure that employers understood the power of women's collective action.

NOTES

1. Canada, Royal Commission on the Status of Women in Canada, *Report* (Ottawa: Information Canada, 1970), 77. See also the letter from the Waitresses' Action Committee, May 1977, reprinted in the documents section of this chapter, for the ways in which women's work can command lower minimum wages even when the language in the legislation is gender neutral.
2. *Beckett v. City of Sault Ste Marie Police Commissioners et al.* (1968), 67 D.L.R. (2nd) 294. Cited by Linda Silver Dranoff in *Women in Canadian Law* (Toronto: Fitzhenry & Whiteside, 1977), 74.
3. For a discussion of the biological arguments used to justify a division of labour by sex, see Pat Armstrong and Hugh Armstrong, "Biological Determinism," in *The Double Ghetto: Canadian Women & Their Segregated Work*, 3rd ed. (Toronto: McClelland & Stewart, 1994), 131–155.
4. For an excellent overview of women's work in Canada see, Paul Phillips and Erin Phillips, *Women & Work: Inequality in the Canadian Labour Market*, rev. ed. (Toronto: James Lorimer, 1993).
5. The service sector includes all industries except manufacturing, construction, mining, agriculture, fishing, and forestry.
6. Statistics Canada, *Women in Canada: A Statistical Report*, 2nd ed. (Ottawa: 1990).

7. See for example: The Royal Commission on the Status of Women in Canada *Report*, 56; Armstrong and Armstrong, *The Double Ghetto*, 3rd ed.; Gail Cook, ed., *Opportunities for Choice* (Ottawa: Information Canada, 1976).
8. Statistics Canada, *Women in Canada*, 80, Tables 4 & 5; Statistics Canada, *The Labour Force, Annual Averages* (Ottawa: 1991).
9. For a discussion of the implications of the dual workload for women, Armstrong and Armstrong, *The Double Ghetto*, 3rd ed.
10. See "Fisheries Workers," *Working Women in Newfoundland* (St. John's, Newfoundland: Women's Place, 1974), excerpted in the documents section of this chapter.
11. For details of these studies, see the references in Armstrong and Armstrong, *The Double Ghetto*, 3rd ed., 80.
12. See, for example, the pamphlet "How Far Can You Go As a Woman in Banking?" that discusses female bank employees' wages and jobs relative to male bank employees, distributed in 1973 by the Ontario Committee on the Status of Women to women in banks, reprinted in the documents section of this chapter.
13. Lynn McDonald, "Wages of Work: A Widening Gap Between Women and Men," *Canadian Forum*, May 1975, reprinted in Marylee Stephenson, ed., *Women in Canada*, rev. ed. (Don Mills: General Publishing, 1977).
14. Victoria Voice of Women, "Discrimination Against Women in the British Columbia Labour Force," Brief submitted to the Honourable James Chabot, Minister of Labour, Province of British Columbia, December 1971, excerpted in the documents section of this chapter.
15. Ibid.
16. "Women's Wages Edging Up But Real Gains Still Not Seen," from the Canadian Press, in *The Globe and Mail*, 28 January 1992, A5, reprinted in the documents section of this chapter.
17. *Women in Canada: A Statistical Report* (Statistics Canada: Ottawa, 1990), 100, Table 31; Alan Freeman, "Wage Gap Between the Sexes Shrinking," *The Globe and Mail*, 15 January 1993.
18. Dranoff, *Women in Canadian Law*, 73.
19. "Trying to Get Your Just Deserts Under Equal Pay Legislation in Nova Scotia," *Equal Value* 3 (n.d.), reprinted in the documents section of this chapter.
20. *Equal Value* 2 (n.d.). Copy at CWMA, file: Equal Pay #2.
21. "Solidarity With Our Striking Sisters," *Windsor Woman* 1, no. 7 (September 1972), 1, reprinted in documents section.
22. Canadian Textile and Chemical Union, "Appeal from the Strikers at Puretex Knitting Co., Toronto," December 15, 1978 and "Scioperare!," one of the Puretex songs written by Puretex women on the picket line, reprinted in the documents section of this chapter.
23. Sue Vohanka, "Getting Organized ... in the CCU," in Maureen Fitzgerald, Connie Guberman and Margie Wolfe, eds., *Still Ain't Satisfied: Canadian Feminism Today* (Toronto: The Women's Press, 1982) 141–151; Maureen O'Hara, "Puretex Workers Strike for Human Rights and Equal Pay," *Upstream*, January 1979.
24. "Three Children Died Last Year," an interview with Kuldip Kaur Bains, interviewed and translated by Prabha Kholsa, *Currents* (Winter 1983/84), 14, reprinted in the documents section of this chapter. This article originally appeared in *Women of Colour* special issue of *Fireweed: A Feminist Quarterly*, Issue 16 (Spring 1983), 44–46.
25. Erma Stultz, "Organizing the Unorganized Farmworkers in Ontario," in *Working People and Hard Times*, Robert Argle, Charlene Gannage, D.W. Livingstone, eds. (Toronto: Garamond, 1987), 293; Judy Cavanagh, "The Plight of Women Farmworkers," *Resources for Feminist Research/Documentation sur la recherche feministe*, 2, no. 1 (March 1982), 6.
26. Household Workers Association, "Household Workers Demand Protection Under the Law," *Communiqu'ELLES* 13, no. 6 (November 1987), 12–16, excerpted in the documents section of this chapter. See also, Silvera Makeda, *Silenced: Talks with working class West Indian Women about their lives and struggles as Domestic Workers in Canada* (Toronto: Williams-Wallace Publishers Inc., 1983).
27. For a discussion of the inadequacy of public childcare, see Marjorie Griffin Cohen, "Social Policy and Social Services," Chapter 4 of R.R. Pierson, Marjorie Griffin Cohen, Paula Bourne, and Philinda Masters, *Canadian Women's Issues*, Vol. I: *Strong Voices* (Toronto: James Lorimer & Company, 1993), 277–282.
28. Sedef Arat-Koc, "Importing Housewives: Non-Citizen Domestic Workers and the Crisis of the Domestic Sphere in Canada," Meg Luxton, Harriet Rosenberg, Sedef Arat-Koc, in *Through the Kitchen Window: The Politics of Home and Family*, 2nd ed. (Toronto: Garamond Press, 1990), 83.

29. "Domestic Workers Need Your Support," circular from the International Coalition to End Domestics' Exploitation (INTERCEDE), August 1981, reprinted in the documents section of this chapter.
30. Sedef Arat-Koc, "Importing Housewives," 88. The amendments to the Ontario Labour Relations Act of 1993 gave domestic workers the right to organize, although separate legislation was being considered for agricultural workers. See Julie White, *Sisters & Solidarity: Women and Unions in Canada* (Toronto: Thompson Educational Publishing, 1993), 202, and Mary Cornish and Lynn Spink, *Organizing Unions* (Toronto: Second Story Press, 1994), 27–30.
31. Marjorie Cohen, Letter to the Editor, *The Globe and Mail*, 19 April 1976, reprinted in the documents section of this chapter.
32. For a discussion of the ways in which the unions responded see White, *Sisters & Solidarity*, 194–199.
33. Julie White, *Women and Unions* (Ottawa: Canadian Advisory Council on the Status of Women, 1980); Ruth Frager, "No Proper Deal: Women Workers and the Canadian Labour Movement, 1870–1940," in Linda Briskin and Linda Yantz, eds., *Union Women* (Toronto: Women's Educational Press, 1983); Ruth A. Frager, *Sweatshop Strife: Class, Ethnicity, and Gender in the Jewish Labour Movement of Toronto 1900–1939* (Toronto: University of Toronto Press, 1992), especially Chapter 5; Cornish and Spink, *Organizing Unions*, Chapter 1.
34. Carl J. Cuneo, "Trade Union Leadership: Sexism and Affirmative Action," in Linda Briskin and Patricia McDermott, eds., *Women Challenging Unions: Feminism, Democracy, and Militancy* (Toronto: University of Toronto Press, 1993), 109–136.
35. For a discussion of the reasons so few women were organized, see Laurell Ritchie, "So Many Unorganized," *Resources for Feminist Research/Documentation sur la recherche feministe* 10, no. 2 (July 1981); White, *Sisters & Solidarity*, Chapter 6.
36. The CTCU was affiliated with the Confederation of Canadian Unions (CCU) until it merged with the Canadian Auto Workers in 1993 and thereby became affiliated with the Canadian Labour Congress (CLC).
37. See "Union Run by Women," *The Other Woman*, April/May 1973, 14, and "Support Restaurant Workers' Right to Organize," SORWUC Local 1, Flyer, n.d., reprinted in the documents section of this chapter.
38. Jackie Ainsworth et al., "Getting Organized ... in the Feminist Unions," in Fitzgerald, Guberman and Wolfe, *Still Ain't Satisfied*, 132–140.
39. Maureen Fitzgerald, "Wither the Feminist Unions? SORWUC, AUCE and the CLC," *Resources for Feminist Research/Documentation sur la recherche feministe* 10, no. 2 (July 1981); Esther Shannon, "SORWUC: A Union for Working Women," *Upstream* 2, no. 3 (April 1978). For a discussion of the difficulties in organizing bank workers see Patricia Baker, "Reflections on Life Stories: Women's Bank Union Activism," in Briskin and McDermott, eds., *Women Challenging Unions*, 62–86.
40. For a discussion of women's activism as union staff members, see Jane Stinson and Penni Richmond, "Women Working for Unions: Female Staff and the Politics of Transformation," in Briskin and McDermott, eds., *Women Challenging Unions*, 137–156.
41. Some industries in the manufacturing sector are experiencing dramatic decreases in unionization. For example, in the garment industry, whose workforce is primarily female, the rate of unionization has dropped from 80 per cent thirty years ago to only 20 per cent in the 1990s. See, Armine Yalnizyan, "From the DEW Line: The Experience of Canadian Garment Workers," in Briskin and McDermott, eds., *Women Challenging Unions*, 284–303.
42. Jerry P. White, *Hospital Strike: Women, Unions and Public Sector Conflict* (Toronto: Thompson Educational Publishing, 1990), 41.
43. Ibid., 3.
44. Rebecca Priegert Coulter, "Alberta Nurses and the 'Illegal' Strike of 1988," in Briskin and McDermott, eds., *Women Challenging Unions*, 44–61.
45. White, *Sisters and Solidarity*, 85.
46. Rita Chudnovsky, "Pay Equity and Childcare: A Two-sided Problem," *Just Wages* 2, no. 2 (1992).
47. Penny Lane and Jamie Kass, "Play Fair with Daycare," in Jennifer Penny, eds., *Hard Earned Wages: Women Fighting for Better Work* (Toronto: The Women's Press, 1983).
48. Geoffrey York, "Child-care Pay Near Poverty Level, Survey Shows Zoo Workers in Higher Salary Scale" *The Globe and Mail*, 23 April 1992, A1, A2, reprinted in the documents section of this chapter.
49. See the letter reprinted in the documents section of this chapter from Rosemary Brown, M.L.A., June 19, 1980, to the president of Canadian Kenworth. See also press release June 4, 1980, "Strike Issue at Canadian Kenworth," issued by the Canadian

Association of Industrial Mechanical and Allied Workers, and press release June 4, 1980, Vancouver Status of Women, copies at the Vancouver Status of Women archives.

50. Letter from Pamela Blackstone, Status of Women Action Group, to Mel Couvelier, June 27, 1981, reprinted in the documents section of this chapter. Mel Couvelier was later a minister in the provincial Social Credit government.

51. Debra J. Lewis, *Just Give Us the Money* (Vancouver: Women's Research Centre, 1988), 24.

52. Patricia McDermott, "Pay Equity in Canada: Assessing the Commitment to Reducing the Wage Gap," in Judy Fudge and Patricia McDermott, eds., *Just Wages: A Feminist Assessment of Pay Equity* (Toronto: University of Toronto Press, 1991), 21.

53. See Government of Manitoba, "The Facts on Pay Equity," *Pay Equity*, n.d. reprinted in the documents section of this chapter.

54. For a discussion of the compromise in Ontario and the problems with implementation of the legislation see Part II and Part III in Fudge and McDermott, eds., *Just Wages*. In the same book, Debra Lewis's "Pay Equity and the State's Agenda" gives a convincing analysis of "pay equity" as procedural reform that will do little to actually change wage structures.

55. For facts about employment for women with disabilities see the DisAbled Women's Network, "Dawn Toronto Fact Sheet on Employment," n.d., reprinted in the documents section of this chapter.

56. Lorna R. Marsden, "The Importance of Studying Affirmative Action," *Canadian Woman Studies/les cahiers de la femme* 6, no. 4 (Winter 1985), 11.

57. Patrica Connelly and Martha MacDonald found, in their examination of 1986 census data, that female occupational concentration actually increased between 1971 and 1986. In 1971, 55 per cent of all employed women were in clerical, sales, and service occupations, compared with 58.1 per cent in 1986. 1986 Census of Canada, *Women and the Labour Force*, 1990, 22.

58. Catherine Shea, "Changes in Women's Occupations," *Social Trends* (Ottawa: Statistics Canada, Autumn 1990).

59. Jeannette Easson, Debbie Field, Joanne Santucck, "Working Steel," in Jennifer Penny, ed., *Hard Earned Wages* (Toronto: The Women's Press, 1983), 191–218; also White, *Sisters & Solidarity*, 83.

60. See Richard Fidler, "Women in Railway Trades? Why Not? How Kate Curtin Won Her Battle with CN," *Socialist Voice*, 30 April 1979, reprinted in the documents section of this chapter. See also, "1 in 4 Hired Must Be A Woman, CN Ordered," *The Toronto Star*, 23 August 1984, A1, A8.

61. For a summary of the results of voluntary affirmative action programs in Canada, see Mona Kornberg, "Employment Equity: The Quiet Revolution?" *Canadian Woman Studies/les cahiers de la femme* 6, no. 4 (Winter 1985), 17.

62. Canada, Commission on Equality in Employment, *Report* (Ottawa, 1984), 255ff.

63. For a critique of this legislation, see my article "Employment Equity is not Affirmative Action," *Canadian Woman Studies/les cahiers de la femme* 6, no. 4 (Winter 1985), 23–25.

64. The House of Commons of Canada, "Bill C-62, An Act Respecting Employment Equity," First Reading, 1985, excerpted in the documents section of this chapter.

65. For a detailed examination of the effect of the Employment Equity Act on women in banks see Phebe-Jane Poole, *Employment Equity and the Banks: Year II Report*, 4 vols.: *Women; Disabled Persons; Visible Minorities; Aboriginal Persons* (Ottawa: Canadian Centre for Policy Alternatives and the National Action Committee on the Status of Women, 1990). See also, "'Justice Works': Response of The National Action Committee on the Status of Women to 'Working Towards Equality,' Ontario Discussion Paper on Employment Equity Legislation," February 1992, 4–6, reprinted in documents section of this chapter.

66. Virginia Galt, "$375 Jacket Stitched for $4, Conference Told. Protection for Home Workers Promised as Union Seeks End to 'Exploitation'," *The Globe and Mail*, 2 October 1992, A1, A8, reprinted in the documents section of this chapter.

67. Yalnizyan, "From the Dew Line," in Briskin and McDermott, eds., *Women Challenging Unions*, 287.

68. James Rusk, "Garment Trade Conditions Protested," *The Globe and Mail*, 15 February 1994, A16.

69. Heather Menzies, "Women's Work is Nearly Done," *This Magazine* 8, no. 1 (April 1984), 32–36, excerpted in the documents section of this chapter.

70. For a discussion of the impact of technology, see Heather Menzies, *Fast Forward and Out of Control* (Toronto: McClelland and Stewart, 1989); Marcy Cohen and Margaret White, *Taking Control of Our Future: Clerical Workers and the New Technology* (Van-

couver: Women's Skill Development Society, 1987); Phillips and Phillips, "Technology, Free Trade and Economic Restructuring," *Women & Work*, 96–113.
71. Phillips and Phillips, *Women & Work*, 99
72. These issues will be discussed more fully in Chapter 4 of this volume.
73. Status of Women Council of B.C., *An Investigation of Part-Time Work for Women*, May 1973, 6, excerpted in the documents section of this chapter.
74. National Union of Provincial Government Employees, *National Union Policy on Job-Sharing*, 1–2, adopted at the 7th National Convention, March 1988, excerpted in the documents section of this chapter.
75. Ellen Adelberg, "Sexual Harassment: We've Only Just Begun," *Breaking the Silence* 3, no. 3 (Spring 1985), 10–12, excerpted in the documents section of this chapter.
76. Chris Morris, The Canadian Press, "Sex Exploitation Claimed," in *The Ottawa Citizen*, 16 May 1981, 60, excerpted in the documents section of this chapter.
77. Leslee Nicholson, "A Powerful Statement on Workplace Sexism," *OPSEU News*, 31 January 1990, reprinted in the documents section of this chapter. This article was written in response to the debate that followed the Montreal Massacre of whether or not this was an act of a "madman" or the ultimate manifestation of the violence faced by women on a daily basis.
78. See letters between Grace McCarthy and Sylvia Weldon, April and June 1976, Vancouver Status of Women archives.
79. Judy Wasylycia-Leis, "Occupational Health Standards Needed for Women Too," Article #7, New Democratic Party, February 8, 1978, 2–4, excerpted in the documents section of this chapter.
80. Marcy Cohen and Margaret White, "Introduction," *Playing With Our Health: Hazards in the Automated Office* (Burnaby, B.C.: Women's Skills, 1986), reprinted in the documents section of this chapter.
81. Virginia Galt, "Attendants Complain About Air on Planes," *The Globe and Mail*, 2 February 1994, reprinted in the documents section of this chapter.

Documents: Chapter 2

Working Differences

Waitresses' Action Committee
Toronto, 1977[1]
Waitresses' Action Committee
Toronto, Ontario
May 1977

Dear Sisters and Friends,

In their effort to save (and increase) profits, the tourist industry has lobbied the Ontario government into thinking about lowering the minimum wage of servers of alcohol. They would do this by leaving our wage at $2.50 an hour, when they increase the minimum wage of other workers to $3.00. But before they go on thinking, let them hear what we have to say!

We know that we waitresses would be hardest hit, because thousands of us work for minimum wage and the lowest tips on the scale. We're organizing this protest so we can take the signed petitions to the Minister of Labour, and tell her we want more money, not less!

What can you do?
- Sign the petition and show it to your workmates, family and friends
- Circulate the petition anywhere and everywhere, but especially among waitresses
- Get your group or organization to endorse the petition

For more information, copies of the petition, or the brief we have sent to the government, write to the Waitresses' Action Committee at the above address ...

Yours,
Ellen Agger for the
Waitresses' Action Committee

P.S. Don't forget to mail back the signed petitions!

---

1. From Marjorie Cohen's files to be deposited with the Canadian Women's Movement Archives, Ottawa (hereafter CWMA).

"Fisheries Workers"
Newfoundland, 1974[2]

Women's Place

"I work in a fish plant on the night shift. I start work at 6 p.m. and finish at 3:30 a.m. I reach home about 4 o'clock feeling cold, miserable, and dirty. I take my boots off at the door and put them outside in the back garden to air. I then remove the rest of my clothing, wash myself, and get a cup of tea before collapsing into bed. I try to make as little noise as I possibly can because if I wake my son, who is 2, then that means I get no sleep at all that night. At 8 a.m. the next morning, or rather the same morning, I get up to start my chores, which means washing and ironing, preparing meals, bathing and dressing my son, washing dishes and floors, taking lip from my husband, and doing whatever else I can manage. This goes on until 4:30, and again it's time for me to get into my fish plant clothes and go off to work.

"There is one thing that I've noticed since I've been working at the fish plant, and that is that the male fish plant workers never seem to be as tense and as tired as the women. From what I've learned from talking to both male and female plant workers, there is a very good reason for this, and that is that the men, when they go home, get more sleep and don't have the responsibility that the women do. They don't have to go home and dig their way out of a mountain of laundry and ironing, nor do they have to care for children. They are simply free after work.

"I find that there is a lot of tension in a fish plant or at least the ones I've worked in. We are given production sheets to keep a record of what work we do, and if for any reason we stop work, that must also be written in. For instance, sometimes we have to wait for block pans for 15 or more minutes. We must write this down, and then have a signature from our forelady verifying that what we have written is correct. According to the management, you have to get a 60% average, and if you go below that, then you are standing on pretty thin ice, and had better get a move on. I'd been hearing talk about a bonus to be paid you for doing so much fish, but it seems that nobody ever got a bonus except one girl. She got something like 72¢ and had it taken back from her. The first time I started work I was scanning over the production sheet when it was given to me, and noticed the word bonus. Of course I got pretty excited because I worked in a fish plant before for about 2 years, and I knew I was very speedy when it came to packing fish, so I thought I could make extra money. I asked a female worker about this and she said that to her knowledge or anybody else's, nobody had ever received bonus money."

---

2. *Working Women in Newfoundland* (St. John's, Newfoundland: Women's Place, 1974), 23. Booklet in possession of Ruth Roach Pierson.

The Wage Gap

"How Far Can You Go as a Woman in Banking?"
Toronto, 1973[3]

The Manpower Utilization in Canadian Chartered Banks, published last year for the Royal Commission on the Status of Women in Canada, revealed that the position of women in Canadian chartered banks in 1968 was strikingly inferior to that of men. Consider the following.

did you know that ...

Women in Banks	*Men in Banks*
89.7% earn less than $5,000/year	72.3% earn more than $5,000/year
56.5% earn less than $4,000/year	7.2% earn less than $4,000/year
2 earn more than $15,000/year	about 900 earn more than $15,000/year
17 earn more than $10,000/year	5,483 earn more than $10,000/year
1 senior executive	326 senior executives
29 branch managers	about 5,900 branch managers
about 53,000 employed	about 30,000 employed
(64% total employees)	(36% total employees)

Since these statistics were compiled, some banks have made efforts to improve this situation. However, the progress has been too slow. The reality is that for women, getting promotions, training and salary raises depends for the most part on the attitudes of branch managers and individual employees (yes, you!). To see how your branch measures up

ask yourself ...

Yes	*No*	
[ ]	[ ]	When you were interviewed for your job, were you asked questions that probably would not be asked of men, such as intention to marry, have children, spouse's occupation and income and likelihood of transfer, etc?
[ ]	[ ]	If a job applicant were clearly a "little bit" pregnant would she be turned away?
[ ]	[ ]	If a well-qualified man applied for a teller's job, would he be turned away?

3. Ontario Committee on the Status of Women, Fair Employment Practices Committee, Pamphlet, 1973. From Marjorie Cohen's files to be deposited with CWMA.

[   ]   [   ]   When female and male employees hold essentially
                  the same jobs, are there differences in salaries and
                  titles?

[   ]   [   ]   Are there any differences in retirement plans,
                  pensions, life and health insurance plans for female
                  and male employees?

[   ]   [   ]   Are men more likely to be asked to join training
                  programs than women?

[   ]   [   ]   Is your immediate superior the only one you can
                  approach if you feel you have encountered sex
                  discrimination on the part of your employer?

If you have answered yes,

WE ENCOURAGE YOU TO ...

-Discuss these issues with other employees.
-Make your branch management aware of your concern with
 inequality.
-Explore opportunities for your own advancement.
-Share your ideas and concerns with us by sending us the attached
 form ...

"Discrimination Against Women in the British Columbia Labour Force" Victoria, B.C., December 1971[4]

The status of women report was written for the rest of Canada. It
does not apply to British Columbia.

                              –James Chabot (August 2, 1971)

Economic discrimination against women is alive and well and living
in B.C.

                              –Victoria Voice of Women

---

4. Brief submitted to the Honourable James Chabot, Minister of Labour, Province of British
Columbia by the Victoria Voice of Women, December 1971. Copy at Status of Women Action
Group (hereafter SWAG).

I. Economic discrimination against women within Government Service

...

Annual Salary Range of Employees of B.C. Govt Depts — 1970

Department	Under $6,000		$6,000-$12,000		Over $12,000	
	male	female	male	female	male	female
Labour	31%	91%	53%	9%	16%	—
Attorney General	43.1	88.3	51.5	12.1	5.1	0.2%
Education	34.4	77.1	44.75	21.6	20.79	1.3
MunicipalAffairs	34.78	87.5	47.8	12.5	17	—
Travel Industry	59.3	99	33.3	1	7.4	—
Pub. Health Serv.	54.8	72.66	34.29	26.9	10.88	0.4
HospitalIns. Serv.	23.4	84.7	60.9	14.3	15.6	1
Social Welfare	48.8	76	47	23.7	4.1	0.25
Finance	32.77	89	56.5	11	10.7	—

Source: Public Accounts of B.C. — Year ending March 31, 1970

It is obvious that discrimination exists under the auspices of the Government itself. We can infer, therefore, that upward mobility within the Provincial Government Service is open only to men, and that over 70% of the female employees in every department studied are locked into low paying jobs with no real opportunities for advancement. It would appear that while the Government speaks of the principle of equal opportunities for all its citizens, it condones and profits from this policy of economic apartheid.

II. Economic discrimination against women in Industry

...

Comparison of Selected Occupations in B.C. — 1970

(From statistics compiled by the Dept. of Industrial Development, Trade and Commerce.)

Office Workers	Average Monthly Rate	Predominant Range
Clerk Jr., Male	$418	$313–471
Clerk Intermediate, Male	537	404–660
Clerk Senior, Male	674	541–810
Clerk Jr., Female	360	300–416
Clerk Intermediate, Female	447	368–537
Clerk Senior, Female	501	407–621

Note — that the Intermediate level male office clerk receives more than the Senior level female office clerk. Thus, even when a woman takes on added responsibility in the performance of her job she does not receive appropriate remuneration in comparison with her male counterparts ...

Hospitals	Average Monthly Rate	Predominant Range
Nursing Services		
Practical Nurse	$444	$429–449
Nursing Aide	400	386–416
Orderly, Experienced, Male	553	525–576
Orderly, Inexperienced, Male	501	487–553
...		
Dietary and Housekeeping		
Cook, Male	572	510–647
Cook, Female	475	414–544
Assistant Cook, Male	542	515–595

Note — In spite of the fact that Practical Nurse is defined "as one who is in possession of a diploma of a recognized Practical Nurse School and/or has a valid B.C. Practical Nurse License", while an Orderly is required to have no prior training, the inexperienced male orderly earns far more than the Practical Nurse.

...

III. Economic Discrimination through Union Contracts

...

The following discriminatory contracts were negotiated through the B.C. Mediation Commission.

1. Atlin Fisheries Ltd. with Fisheries Association of B.C. and B.C. Provincial Council United Fisherman and Allied Workers Union.

Fresh fish — Wage Increases		
	Effective Apr 16, 1971	*Apr 16, 1972*
Base rate		
Female	$2.69	$2.89
Male	3.61	3.87
Skilled rate		
Female	2.94	3.16
Male	3.90	4.19

...

4. Canada Safeway Ltd. et al, with Retail Food and Drug Clerks Union, Local 1518.

Wage increases	*Apr. 19/71*	*Apr. 17/72*
Male clerk full time	$4.45	$4.85
Female clerk full time	3.85	4.30

Source: Vol. 4, No. 9.

5. Nalley's Ltd. Vancouver, and Canadian Food and Allied Workers, Local 341.

Wage increases	*Aug. 16/71*	*Aug. 16/72*
Factory help, Female	$2.50	$2.75
Factory help, Male	3.05	3.30

Source: Vol. 4, No. 9.

"Women's Wages Edging Up, But Real Gains Still Not Seen" Ottawa, January 1992[5]

Women who work full time have crept closer to earning what men do, but it is still not clear that women are making real gains.

Full-time female workers earned 67.6 per cent of what men did in 1990 — $24,923 compared with $36,863, Statistics Canada reported yesterday. That is up from 65.8 per cent in 1989.

Women's wages have never been closer to men's earnings — 25 years ago women made 58.4 per cent of what men did. But the figures do not necessarily mean that women are taking even tiny steps forward, labour experts said.

The main reasons:

- More women have lower-paid part-time jobs or work from their homes — jobs that were not taken into account in the statistics.

5. From The Canadian Press, in *The Globe and Mail*, 28 January 1992, A5.

- Women may be catching up only as men fare worse.

"We're not looking at women at the bottom of the labour market; we're looking at women who are lucky enough to have full-time jobs," said Judy Fudge, who heads the employment committee of the National Action Committee on the Status of Women.

Women made 59.9 per cent of what men did in 1990 when part-time and temporary wage earners are considered. But Statistics Canada says comparing full-time workers more accurately reflects the male-female wage gap.

Ms. Fudge said even full-time women workers are not necessarily getting paid much more — the wage gap is narrowing because the average male wage is falling.

Men earned 6.9 per cent less in 1990 than 15 years earlier in real terms, Statscan figures show. Women's earnings rose 6.4 per cent in the same period.

Jeffrey Reitz, a University of Toronto industrial relations professor, said a U.S. study showed that only some women are making gains. Those in traditionally male jobs are earning more, but that is offset by large numbers of women entering the work force and vying for traditionally female occupations where real wages have fallen, Prof. Reitz said.

The Statscan figures also show:

- Women with university degrees earned 72.8 per cent of what similarly educated men did. Women with Grade 8 or less made 62.4 per cent of what men in the same group did.
- Women's earnings were 87.6 per cent of men's in the 15-to-24 age group, but 61.9 per cent for those aged 45 to 54.
- Wages of women who had never married were 89.8 per cent of those of men in the same category; married women's wages were 62.6 per cent of those of married men.

Challenging Employers

Women's Work: Underpaid and Undervalued
Nova Scotia, n.d.[6]

Virginia Crabill
September 1975 — May 1976
"A Nine Month Struggle"

The Case

During the spring and summer of 1975, Virginia Crabill worked as a woodworker-machine operator in a small company, Lunenburg County. She was paid $2.25 per hour. In September 1975 a man was hired to

---

6. "Trying to Get Your Just Deserts Under Equal Pay Legislation in Nova Scotia," *Equal Value* 3, n.d. Copy at CWMA, file: Equal Pay #2.

work along side her. She trained him to do his job and he was paid $3.25 per hour.

The Job

He took lumber from one pile and put it into a planer; she took the lumber out of the planer and put it in another pile.

Virginia had more work experience, more training and had trained him to do his job. But, because she was a woman, she was paid $1.00 less an hour.

In September 1975 she asked for an increase in her rate of wages. Her employer stalled for several weeks and eventually refused.

Labour Standards and Virginia Crabill

In November 1975 Virginia filed a complaint under the equal pay legislation in Nova Scotia.

Step 1: The Complaint

Virginia's first problem was trying to get Labour Standards to investigate her complaint.

At first they were not interested. It took two phone calls to get Labour Standards to do a preliminary investigation. The first investigation was simply a phone call to the company. They said that there was no discrimination. Labour Standards told Virginia there was no case.

Virginia was angry and demanded a more thorough investigation or she would go to the press. The Officer said goodbye. Later, the Director of Labour Standards called her and then agreed to look at the complaint again.

Step 2: The Investigation

A trip to the workplace was made. Virginia was not allowed into the plant to see or hear what was being said. She waited all day in the car in the parking lot. Finally, the Labour Standards Officer returned and asked if she wanted to pursue the case.

What was there to lose? She had quit her job because of the discrimination. She was not likely to be rehired because of her complaint. But the issue and the wages were important.

Step 3: The Outcome

It was determined by the investigation that Virginia's job was equal to her male colleague's. Labour Standards tried to get a settlement, but the Company refused. A Labour Standards Tribunal was set up to hear the case in April 1976.

Virginia was advised to get a lawyer. She went to legal aid.

The Company went to MacInnes Hallet and Wilson, a well-established Halifax firm of lawyers.

One day before the hearing, the company agreed to negotiate a settlement. The Tribunal was cancelled. In May, Virginia received $363.00. This represented the difference between her and her male colleague's rate of pay, while they were doing the same job ...

"Solidarity With Our Striking Sisters"
Windsor, Ontario, September 1972[7]

Two weeks ago, four representatives from Local Union 173, International Union of United Brewery, Flour, Cereal, Soft Drink & Distillery Workers in Waterloo, Ont., visited Windsor for two days to explain what is happening with regard to their legal strike against Dare Foods Ltd. in Kitchener. The representatives have been on strike with 340 other members of the union, since May 29. Seventy-five percent of the Dare workers are women.

Theirs has been a long and bitter struggle. The issues are: better wages, plus equal wages for women employees, hours of work (the day-shift must work 42 1/2 hrs. per wk.), fair share of the payment of health & welfare coverage by the company, and improved working conditions.

Their plea to the citizens of Windsor is, "PLEASE DO NOT BUY DARE COOKIES."

The women spoke to as many people as possible during their short stay in Windsor. As far as their working conditions are concerned, these can only be described as appalling. In the baking area of the plant, temperatures reach as high as 130 degrees. There are no exhaust fans in this area and Mr. Dare refused to install any. Speed-ups in production are enforced whenever management chooses and this, plus the intensive heat, has resulted in several employees fainting or becoming unable to work on the packing belts every week.

As well, female workers must stand at all times; even if there is a pause in production, no sitting is permitted in the working areas.

Also, female workers must raise their hand and ask permission to go to the washroom. They must ask a half-hour before they wish to go and on many occasions their supervisors refuse such permission when the half-hour has been reached. The workers' lunch breaks have not been fixed (time or length) and are subject to the company's production requirements. Another complaint is that the foreladies and foremen have insensitive and abusive attitudes. Family emergencies are often disregarded. Illnesses and deaths in the worker's family are treated with suspicion, and emergency calls to workers from relatives have been ignored by the company at times.

Shortly after the strike was called, the Dare Company hired the services of Canadian Driver Pool — they're the people who, for a very high fee, will "help solve the problems of big business." In other words, they are strike-breakers. When they arrived on the scene the strikers tried

7. *Windsor Woman* 1, no. 7 (September 1972), 1. Copy at CWMA.

to force them away. Fights broke out. The cops arrived. Stiff injunctions were handed down against the strikers and have been enforced meticulously. On the other hand, the activities of Canadian Driver Pool are of questionable legality and certainly the tactics of Dare (intimidation of striking employees — phone calls at home, etc.) are not legal. But in these instances the people in the great halls of justice look the other way ...

Immigrant Women on Strike
Toronto, December 15, 1978[8]
Greetings:

Two hundred and twenty (220) workers at Puretex Knitting Co. in Toronto, members of our union, have been on lawful strike since November 13, 1978. Two hundred (200) of the strikers are women. This is their first strike.

They are demanding:

1. REMOVAL OF CLOSED CIRCUIT TV CAMERAS FROM THE WORK PLACE. Gary Satok, President of the company, sits at his desk and monitors women workers from nine TV screens, one of which is beamed on the women's washroom door;
2. 40¢ an hour across the board increase in Year 1 and 40¢ an hour across the board increase in Year 2 of a two year collective agreement. The majority earn $3.60 to $3.75 an hour for sewing machine, pressing and other operations;
3. MORE WELFARE BENEFITS. The Company now only pays the major part of Government Hospitalization (OHIP).
4. STRONGER SENIORITY RIGHTS. Protection against layoffs and retraining of seniority workers into other skills;
5. A BETTER GRIEVANCE PROCEDURE

Our members are fighting back against low wages and unfair treatment that are too often the lot of women workers, especially those of foreign origin, which is the case here.

After over one month on picketlines, we are appealing for your support. You could help by (1) sending financial donations to the Canadian Textile and Chemical Union at the above address; (2) going to department stores where you may find men's sweaters with the labels shown on the accompanying leaflet and telling the Department Manager what you think of the inhuman treatment by Puretex Knitting Co. of the women who make the sweaters.

We would be happy to hear from you and will report any news on the picketline.

Yours fraternally,

Madeleine Parent   Maria Iori, President
Secretary Treasurer   Local 560, C.T.C.U.

---

8. "Appeal from the Strikers at Puretex Knitting Co., Toronto" Canadian Textile and Chemical Union, Toronto, 1978. Copy at CWMA, file: Canadian Textile and Chemical Union.

Puretex Song
Toronto, 1978[9]

SCIOPERARE!

Dacci l'aumento, Signor Padrone	Give us an increase, Signor Padrone
Se no faccaimo rivoluzione	Or we shall now have to rebel
Siamo sdeganto a scioperare	We are outraged enough to strike
Perche diritti non ci vuoi dare	You won't give us what is our right
Tu ti profitti di noi operai	You have profited from our labour
Siamo emigranti per lavorare	We emigrated so we could work
Con questi soldi che ci vuoi dare	The pennies you offered aren't enough
Non ci possiamo accontentare	We can't possibly live on that
Noi Italiani forte e potenti	We immigrants strong and powerful
Non ci arrendiamo proprio per niente	Won't give in for so little
So che tu pensi che noi soffriamo	So when you think that we suffer
Invece noi ci divertiamo	Instead we entertain ourselves
41 ore dobbiamo fare	We have to work 41 hours
E con le bosse dietro a pusciare	Always the bosses pushing us harder
Noi lavoriamo a timework	We work by the hour
Ma lavoriamo pui delle piecework	But it's more like piecework
Viene la bossa e ci domanda	Here comes the boss to ask how long
Quando ci vuole a fare 1 bundle	Before a bundle can be finished
A 5 minuti ce la portato	Within five minutes, sure enough
E lo vorrebero gia impaccato	She wants it finished, packed and bundled
Se tu sei duro e prepotente	If you're hard-headed and don't give a
Non ci importa proprio per niente	damn
Ma noi italiani intelligenti	It's not the end of the world for us
Siamo uniti e resistenti	We are intelligent, immigrant workers
	And we'll endure, strong and united
Il nostro progresso vogliamo fare	We want to make some progress
Ma le telecamare devone levare	But the cameras must come down
Noi non vogliamo, Signor Padrone	We do not like it, Signore Padrone
Che i tuoi ridono sopra di noi	When you and your friends laugh at us
Noi non siamo Sophia Loren	We are not Sophia Loren
Noi Italiani lavoratori	We immigrant workers in this factory
Ti abbiamo fatto tanto furore	We work for you and make you rich
IL NOSTRO PROGRESSO	WE WANT SOME PROGRESS IN
VOGLIAMO FARE	OUR CONTRACT
E CONTINUAMO A SCIOPERARE!	SO, IN THE MEANTIME, ON WITH
	THE STRIKE!

9. Puretex Songs. These songs were written by Puretex women on the picket line. The free translation doesn't give the rhyming contained in Italian. Copy at CWMA, file: Canadian Textile and Chemical Union.

Profiles of Working-Class Indian Women
Fraser Valley, B.C., 1983[10]

"THREE CHILDREN DIED LAST YEAR"

Most of the farmwork in British Columbia is concentrated in the Fraser and Okanagan Valleys and is done by immigrant workers. In Greater Vancouver, the majority of farmworkers are primarily Indian or Chinese. There is also a small percentage of working class whites. Farmwork is seasonal, and consequently, a large proportion of the workforce is migratory. Some, like the Quebecois workers, travel to the Okanagan Valley every summer to pick fruit. Due to inadequate housing, they usually have to resort to tenting. Many of the farmworkers in the Fraser Valley live a great distance away in the interior of British Columbia. They are accommodated in converted sheds or barns. It is estimated that the majority of the 10,000 farmworkers in British Columbia are girls and women between the ages of 8 and 70 years old. Kuldip Kaur Bains, who is interviewed below, is sixty-three years old, a grandmother and a worker.

We come down to this farm about March-April, and we live here the whole summer till the end of August, beginning of September.

This is the third year we have come to this farm: me, my husband, my daughter-in-law and her two children. My son works at the saw mill in Williams Lake. That is where we live. And my daughter-in-law comes later when the children have finished school.

We live in this barn here, that has been converted so that it can now accommodate five families. It's been divided up into five sections, but as you can see, it's all rough work with an unfinished plywood ceiling and the walls are bare gyproc. Nothing has been painted or anything. And there aren't enough light bulbs and there are no windows. We have two bunk beds next to each other with a small table. We keep our clothes and other things under the beds.

In the area outside the bedroom we have two fridges which we all share and five gas plates — one for each family. The washrooms are outside, around the back and there is no light there either. There are no showers and we wash ourselves by carrying water in buckets. There are two toilets and two small divided areas where we clean ourselves.

We have to make a living, so we just learn to accept these things. It is very difficult for me to get any other work. I'm old and I don't speak English, so this is the only work I can get. We get up early in the morning, make some breakfast and lunch to take with us to the fields. We don't come back here until the evening.

The work is hard and back-breaking. But only us Indians do it. Nobody else will. And we get paid so little. For example, if we pick

10. "Three Children Died Last Year," an interview with Kuldip Kaur Bains, interviewed and translated by Prabha Kholsa, *Currents* (Winter 1983/84), 14. Copy at the Vancouver Status of Women (hereafter VSW). Originally appeared in *Women of Colour*, special issue, *Fireweed: A Feminist Quarterly*, Issue 16 (Spring 1983), 44–46.

raspberries we get $2.50 for one flat which weighs 16 1/2 lbs. It takes a lot of picking to fill one flat and towards the end of the season it takes even longer. But we don't get the whole $2.50 because the farmer deducts money for allowing us to stay here in his barn. So what we get to keep for ourselves is something like one dollar out of every $2.50.

When we are picking broccoli and cauliflower, we use sharp knives and quite often people get hurt. But there is no first aid on the farm and they usually don't take us to hospital unless it's very serious. So most of us carry bandages with us. Many of us have rashes. People say it's from the pesticides we use on the vegetables and fruits, but the farmer is not doing anything about it.

It's also dangerous for our children. Some of the older children work with their parents but the younger ones stay with their mothers in the field. Three children died last year, because no one was looking after them. They were just playing by themselves.

Because of all these problems, I joined the Canadian Farmworkers Union. They said that if we are all united we will be able to get better money for our work and also be covered by the Workers' Compensation Board. We don't get many of the benefits that other workers get. After all, aren't we like other people? We do the work like everyone else and we should get these things. How would they eat if we were not doing this work?

"Household Workers Demand Protection Under the Law" Montreal, 1987[11]

For over ten years now, the Household Workers Association (Association du personnel domestique) has defended the rights of women who work in private homes. When this organization was founded in 1975, household workers had no protection under Québec law; even though there were many women working in this occupation, Québec society seemed to be completely ignoring them.

In 1980, following years of lobbying and publicity by the Household Workers Association, some categories of household workers were included under minimum wage laws, through Bill 126: cleaners and cooks. However, at the same time the law explicitly excluded household workers who take care of a child (or children), an adult(s), or an elderly or handicapped person as well as cleaning and cooking ...

The Household Workers Association would like to remind Québécers that most domestic workers are excluded from coverage by the Minimum Wage Law.

In effect, Chapter 2 of Bill 126 states that the law does not apply to "workers whose principle function is to care for a child, an ill person, a handicapped person, or an elderly person."

There are approximately 35,000 household workers in Québec and most of them must take care of children or adults as part of their jobs.

11. Household Workers Association, *Communiqu'ELLES* 13, no. 6 (November 1987), 12–16.

Most of these domestic workers receive less than the minimum wage because the law does not force employers to pay them more.

THE ABUSE OF HOUSEHOLD WORKERS

During a press conference held September 30, the Household Workers Association reported on 26 cases of abuse of domestic workers, cases of clear exploitation of women workers reported to the Association by the women themselves. Note that the names have been changed to protect the anonymity of the women involved ...

ANITA

Anita works in the home of a family. She is in Québec on a temporary work permit. She looks after the children and does the housework, the cooking, the washing, the ironing, etc.

When her employers left on vacation, they "loaned" her to their friends for two weeks. Anita did not agree with this decision that she would do the housework for another family, but her employer told her that she did not have the right to a paid vacation and that he would not permit her to remain in the family home while the family was absent.

Since she was not covered by Bill 126 because she took care of the children, Anita had no choice but to work for the other family for two weeks. This woman was "rented out", like you would rent a car during a trip to another country ...

CECILIA

Cecilia had just obtained her landed immigrant status here. She informed her employer of this fact and was fired.

She was not able to make a complaint to the Minimum Wage Commission for being fired for insufficient reasons and for the absence of notice because she took care of the children and was thus excluded from protection by Bill 126 ...

GABRIELLE

Gabrielle made a verbal contract with her employer to the effect that during her employment as a domestic, including the care of children, regular deductions would be taken from her pay (tax, unemployment insurance, pension, etc.). When she left this post, she discovered that the deductions had never been sent to the government. The employer complained that she did not have enough money to pay "all that". However, she and her husband were both engineers, and both working ...

ISABELLA

Isabella works from 7AM to 9PM, from Monday to Friday. On Saturday her hours are even longer. She lives with her employers and receives $400 a month. Her work? All the cleaning and taking care of two children. She does not receive an annual vacation and has only one day off a week — and this is not even guaranteed! With her salary of $1.28 an hour and her awful working conditions, Isabella cannot even lay a complaint with the Minimum Wage Commission because she takes care of the children ... AND ALL THIS IS LEGAL ...

KATHLEEN

Here on a diplomatic passport, Kathleen works as a domestic-guardian in the home of a staff member of a consulate. When she arrived in Québec, her employer refused to give her her passport; he said it belonged to him.

Her working conditions deteriorated very quickly, and became much too heavy for her: taking care of three very young children, doing all the cooking, the washing, the ironing, looking after the garden during the summer and removing the snow in the winter.

She contacted the Association for help in obtaining a temporary work permit so that she could look for another position. But in order to do this, she had to go to the Immigration Department with her passport, which her employer continued to refuse to give to her, stating that if he did, he would not be repaid for her plane fare to Canada ($1,000).

Kathleen earned only $250 a month, which she used to support her two children who were still living in her country of origin. It is evident that she did not have the money to repay her employer for her plane fare to Canada.

Cases of household workers exploited by embassies and consulates are not rare. The Canadian government hesitates to intervene in these diplomatic questions. Thus, on Canadian soil, human rights guaranteed by the Charter of Rights and Freedoms are ignored ...

THERESE

When the first child was born, her employer paid her $160 a week. After the birth of the second, her salary rose to $170. When the third child arrived, her employer refused to give her a raise. While her workload tripled, her salary rose just $10 ...

VIOLETTE

Violette is from Europe, and is in Canada on a temporary work permit. She receives $150 a week for 45 hours of work as a domestic worker. She also cares for the children. After one year of work, Violette came to the Association because she was unable to cope any longer. She works more than 20 hours overtime every week without an increase in pay, and the husband thinks nothing of walking naked in front of her when he leaves the shower, without even offering an excuse. She must deal with all the whims of the child she looks after, and when she actually could have some time off, she is forced to remain in the house when the family goes to the country. She must guard the house, like a guard-dog ...

"Domestic Workers Need Your Support!"
Toronto, 1981[12]

Dear friends,

As you are probably aware, every year the federal government has to "import" about 10,000 temporary workers — mostly from Third World countries — to do live-in domestic work. This is because the wages are kept too low, and the hours too long, to attract Canadians or permanent residents to do the work. The only way the Employment & Immigration Commission can meet the great demand for live-in domestics is by bringing in women who have no rights either to do different kinds of work or to stay in Canada permanently, and by closing their eyes to the countless non-status women who have little choice but to do domestic work.

As a result of initiatives by domestic workers, supported by organizations such as INTERCEDE of Toronto, the Montreal Household Workers' Association, the Ottawa-Carleton Immigrant Services Organization, and Labour Advocacy and Research Association of Vancouver, the Immigration Minister, Lloyd Axworthy, has been forced to admit that the temporary work permit system is unjust and has promised changes.

His public statements led us to believe that the point system would be revised so that women presently working in Canada as temporary domestic workers, as well as women wishing to come to Canada as domestics, could get landed status.

His private actions are a different story. He has made changes that are making things worse than ever. In order to apply, a woman now needs a certificate from a homemakers' or nannies' school as well as job experience — qualifications that West Indians and Filipinos, who make up the vast majority of temporary domestics, do not have. In other words, Mr. Axworthy's promised improvements mean that a select group of nannies from the U.K. and northern Europe will get landed status, while black and Asian women continue to be as little more than, as one domestic worker put it, "sophisticated slaves".

The Minister needs to be told that slavery days are over, and to do this your help is needed. Please write a letter to Mr. Axworthy, saying that all domestic workers, whether on temporary work permits or without status, should be able to apply for landed status on a point system that recognizes both the demand for domestic workers in Canada, as well as their work experience ...

The domestic workers have already gotten hundreds of letters signed, but we need thousands more to let the Minister know that the Canadian public will no longer tolerate racist immigration policies.

---

12. International Coalition to End Domestics' Exploitation (INTERCEDE), Circular, August 1981. From Marjorie Cohen's files to be deposited with CWMA.

As the slogan of the domestic workers in Toronto goes, "If we're good enough to work here, we're good enough to stay". Thank you for your support.
Yours truly
Frances Gregory
Coordinator, INTERCEDE

Contracting Out
Toronto, April 19, 1976[13]
April 7, 1976
Editor
Globe and Mail

Dear Sir:
[The recent revelation of fraud associated with Federal Government contracts for building cleaning is just one example of the kind of abuse which follows from Government contracting out of essential, labour-intensive work. The Government contracts out work in order to reduce costs. It is unable to hire workers directly at artificially low wages because of certain laws the Government itself has established to ensure that labour is not exploited. But by accepting the lowest bid for a contract the Government encourages (even forces) the subcontractor to engage in abusive and illegal employment practices.]

The Ontario Committee on the Status of Women met with Margaret Scrivener, Ontario Minister of Government Services, in February to discuss the problems of Government subcontracting in the cleaning industry in the province. Our recommendations were that the Government phase out subcontracting in building cleaning as quickly as possible and that in the time necessary to implement this, fair-employment guidelines should be included in all new contracts.

These included, among other things, establishment of wage guidelines which would pay employees the same wage as that paid to employees hired directly by the Government in similar work. Also, it would require that the subcontractor strictly adhere to the Employment Standards Act and the Human Rights Code in regard to equal pay and sex discrimination. The case of the Portuguese cleaning staff at Queen's Park was used to illustrate the problems in the present system.

The Minster's response to our description of the case of these women was that they were not forced to remain in their jobs and could find work elsewhere if conditions were intolerable. From the Minister's response we feel it is unlikely that there will be any change in either the Minister's or the Government's attitude toward improving the deplorable conditions that currently exist.

---

13. Marjorie Cohen, Letter to the Editor, *The Globe and Mail*, 19 April 1976. The editor of *The Globe and Mail* did not print the first paragraph. From Marjorie Cohen's files to be deposited with the CWMA.

Surely it is not unreasonable to suggest that the Government require subcontractors to adhere to its own laws on equal pay and sex discrimination. Yet the Ontario Government is unwilling to enforce this. If the Government is committed to the principle of a fair wage, it is clear that this can best be achieved, at lowest cost, through direct hiring of building cleaners by the Government itself. Contracting out of this work is unnecessary and almost certainly leads to abuse.
Sincerely,
Marjorie Cohen
for the Ontario Committee on the Status of Women
Toronto

Trade Unions

"Union Run By Women"
Toronto, 1973[14]

THE SERVICE, OFFICE AND RETAIL WORKERS' UNION OF CANADA [SORWUC] WAS FORMED IN VANCOUVER OCT. 22, 1972 BY WOMEN WHO WORK IN THOSE INDUSTRIES. THE UNION IS ESPECIALLY CONCERNED WITH THE NEEDS OF WOMEN WORKERS WHO ARE THE MAJORITY OF EMPLOYEES IN THESE OCCUPATIONS AND ARE MOSTLY NOT UNIONIZED.

OBJECTIVES — FROM OUR CONSTITUTION:

1. SORWUC believes that everyone who works should earn enough to provide a decent living for her/himself and her/his family.
2. The union will bargain collectively on behalf of its members to bring about fair wage standards, to reduce the differences between the lowest and the highest rates, and to assure equal pay for comparable work for all, regardless of sex, age, marital status, race, religion or national origin.
3. The union will strive to improve working conditions of members, to maximize the opportunities for personal fulfillment in the work situation of all members, and to reduce working hours and eliminate overtime.
4. The union will work to ensure job security for all members and to end discrimination in hiring and promotion.
5. Within the community, the union will work for the establishment of political and social equality, for free parent controlled child care centres, for community control of schools, for community health services, against price and rent increases which erode the gains made through collective bargaining.

14. *The Other Woman*, April/May 1973, 14. Copy at CWMA.

6. The union will encourage unionization of unorganized workers and will charter local unions, maintaining at all times the principles of local autonomy and democracy within the national union and its local unions ...

"Support Restaurant Workers' Right to Organize" Vancouver, n.d.[15]

Only about 2% of restaurants in the Vancouver area are organized. That means that most restaurant workers make minimum wage or not much more. We have no job security. People are fired without cause and we have no grievance procedure — no right to appeal any management decision. Management arbitrarily changes our hours.

At Muckamuck we were forced to strike because the owners refused to negotiate with us. Rather than recognize the union and sign a collective agreement, they attempted to break the union by firing people. There were 21 people working at Muckamuck when we joined the union. By the time we took our strike vote, eight people had been fired or forced to quit.

Your support is essential to us. Every customer who crosses the picket line encourages the owners to hold out a little longer. Every customer who respects the line encourages the owners to recognize the union and come back to the bargaining table.

As service workers, we need the support of customers in order to win basic rights on the job.

If you would like to make a donation to the strike fund, or help in other ways, or if you would like further information, please contact us at:

1114 — 207 West Hastings Street Vancouver
Service, Office, & Retail Workers Union of Canada
Local 1
PLEASE DON'T CROSS OUR PICKET LINE

"Child-care Pay Near Poverty Level, Survey Shows Zoo Workers in Higher Salary Scale" April 23, 1992[16]

OTTAWA — The wages of Canadian child-care workers, already worse than those of animal workers in zoos, have continued to decline in recent years and are now approaching the poverty level, a national survey has found.

The survey of 7,200 child-care workers found that the average wage is less than $7 an hour in some provinces, and that their pay after inflation is taken into account has dropped by 4.5 per cent over the past seven years.

15. Service, Office & Retail Workers Union of Canada (SORWUC) Local 1, Flyer, n.d.
16. Geoffrey York, *The Globe and Mail*, 23 April 1992, A1, A2.

Child-care "teachers" (those who are in charge of a group of children, often with staff supervisory duties as well) have a national average wage of $18,498 annually, the survey found.

"It's another demonstration of the chronic underfunding of child care in Canada," said Sylvia Fanjoy, executive director of the Canadian Child Day Care Federation. "The situation cannot be allowed to get any worse. These people are dedicated and well trained, and we cannot ask them to continue making these kind of sacrifices to keep child care going in this country."

Despite their low wages, child-care workers are relatively well educated, the survey found. Two-thirds have a post-secondary certificate, diploma or degree. By comparison, only 41 per cent of the national labour force has a similar education.

The survey also concluded that the day-care sector is still a "female job ghetto." An overwhelming 98 per cent of child-care workers are women.

In 1985, an uproar was sparked by a similar national survey which found that the wages of child-care workers were 30 per cent below the wages of animal-care workers and farmhands.

This year, the researchers made a different comparison. They looked at warehouse workers and prison guards, and found that both categories of workers are much better paid than child-care workers.

For example, the average warehouse worker earns 58 per cent more than the average child-care worker, according to Statistics Canada figures obtained by the researchers ...

The survey found a wide discrepancy in the wages of child-care workers in difference provinces. The average hourly wage was as low as $6.03 in Newfoundland and $6.76 in Alberta, and as high as $11.51 in Ontario.

It also found that the average wage for unionized staff was 33 per cent higher than the wage of non-unionized staff. And it found that the wages in non-profit child-care centres were significantly higher than the wages in profit-making commercial centres.

"It's an illustration of what a patchwork system of child care we have in Canada," Ms. Fanjoy said. "There are no national regulations, the salaries differ so widely, and the education standards vary so widely. It points out a strong need for federal leadership on the issue."

Earlier this year, Health Minister Benoît Bouchard announced that the government has cancelled its long-standing promise to create a national child-care program.

Pay Equity

Equal Pay for Work of Equal Value
Burnaby, B.C., June 19, 1980[17]

Robert Buckner
President
Canadian Kenworth
Station E, P.O. Box 4458
Ottawa, K15 5B4

Dear Mr. Buckner:

Re: Strike at Canadian Kenworth and Paccar of Canada, Burnaby (B.C.)

I am writing in support of the workers at the Kenworth plant and the workers at the Paccar of Canada warehouse, located in my constituency of Burnaby-Edmonds, who have been on strike since May 21, 1980.

From what I understand this strike is over one of the most basic demands of the women's movement — that of equal pay for work of equal value.

Your company spokesman Ed Blouin is quoted as saying that raising the women's wages to equal that of plant workers "is not a major economic issue" for the company, "I guess you could say it was a matter of principle." And yet the rates offered to women data processors (with two years experience before you will hire them) are a base rate of $7.07 an hour, compared to the rates you offer to unskilled summer students on the assembly line of $8.17 an hour. I would like an explanation of the "principle" involved.

There are ample statistics which prove that women in Canadian society are poor, are supporting families, are single parents, are penalized by discriminatory practices, are often the "last hired" and the "first fired" during times of growing unemployment.

For you to make a decision to deny the value of the labour contribution which these women make to the success of your operation and to condemn them to inferior wages seems to me to be a lack of principle.

Yours truly:
Rosemary Brown M.L.A.
Burnaby-Edmonds

17. Letter from Rosemary Brown. Copy at VSW.

Opposing Wage Discrimination
Victoria, B.C., June 27, 1981[18]

Mr. Mel Couvelier,
Mayor of Saanich,
Saanich Municipal Hall,
770 Vernon, Saanich, B.C.

Dear Mr. Couvelier:
I write on behalf of the Status of Women Action Group with regard to comments on the CUPE strike attributed to you in this week's Monday Magazine.

I, along with many other local working women, am shocked and angry at the ignorance and sexism revealed by your remarks. We are told that for women to seek equal pay for work of equal value and an end to discrimination in the workplace is "emotionalism" and "irrelevant". We are told we are threatening the "traditional hierarchical structure" and "historical relativity" of the workplace in seeking wage parity. This jargon translates as a noxious attempt to justify the continuation of discrimination.

While you admit such change is "something the world needs", you go on to say you "cannot solve the world's problems". No-one is asking you to "solve the world's problems". The CUPE workers are asking only for what is fair and just, and you are using gross hyperbole in your efforts to invalidate their demands.

You express your fear for the "ripple effect" it would create ... that women in the region would "get emotional about this equal value issue and demand substantial wage increases". Well they should.

You have conveniently managed to forget, however, that the majority of Victoria's working women are clustered in low-paying, non-unionized job ghettos. They have little bargaining power. Thus, your precious status quo — maintained at the expense of women — remains unthreatened.

You also provide the ridiculous excuse that the "tax-payers will not stand for this". We have, I might point out, seen the tax-payers (50% of whom are women) tolerate constant outrageous wage demands, including the settlement the male CUPE workers received ($3.15/hour — exactly what they demanded) ... not to mention the recently-negotiated settlement the province's doctors received.

We can only conclude that, because these demands come from women, they are not being taken seriously. Your accusation of "emotionalism" and "irrelevance" is infuriating. It is hardly emotionalism for women to expect a fair living wage, to enable us to keep abreast of inflation and obtain a comfortable standard of living ...

18. Letter from Pamela L. Blackstone. Copy at SWAG.

Wake up, Mr. Couvelier, it is 1981 ... It is neither "emotionalism" nor "irrelevant" that these striking workers seek wage parity with the male outside workers. It directly affects their lives and their future. Women, whether you like it or not, have the right to full, equal participation in the economic life of Canada, and the right to the same human dignity males have enjoyed for so long. SWAG supports the CUPE strikers and deplores your inexcusable ignorance and sexism.

Angrily,
Pamela L. Blackstone,
Corr. Co-ordinator, SWAG.

"The Facts on Pay Equity"
Manitoba, n.d.[19]

1. What is Pay Equity?

Pay equity is a system which bases wages on the value of the work performed regardless of gender. Its goal is to eliminate gender discrimination from the wage setting process. It means that women performing jobs of equal value to those performed by men in the same establishment will be entitled to receive equal pay.

2. Is Pay Equity different than Equal Pay for Equal Work?

Yes. Equal Pay for Equal Work requires the same pay for the same or substantially the same job. Thus, a telephone installer is entitled to the same wage whether the job is done by a man or a woman.

Pay equity allows comparisons to be made between different kinds of jobs being done for the same employer. Overall, if the two jobs involve levels of skills, effort, responsibility and working conditions that can be fairly considered equivalent, both jobs should pay the same. For example, consider a general maintenance worker and a secretary, a forester and a home economist, or a police training director and a director of nurses. In each of these three sets of occupations, the two jobs are quite different. But when the job requirements are analyzed, they could well be of the same value. If the secretary, home economist and director of nursing make lower salaries than the general maintenance worker, the forester and the police training director respectively, pay equity would require the salaries in these "women's" jobs to be increased.

3. Why is Pay Equity Necessary?

Pay equity is necessary to reduce the wage gap between men and women. On average, women only earn 66¢ for every $1.00 men earn.

19. Government of Manitoba, *Pay Equity*, n.d. Copy at CWMA, file: Equal Pay #2.

Only a small part of this wage gap can be narrowed through equal pay for equal work laws which cover the situation where men and women do the same work. The reason is that by and large, women and men in Manitoba do <u>different</u> kinds of work. An estimated 70% of employed women work in traditional "women's jobs" which are often undervalued and underpaid.

Pay Equity will address this problem by requiring fair comparisons between different kinds of jobs and appropriate salary increases.

4. Why are "women's jobs" undervalued and underpaid?

A combination of factors is responsible.

First, there is evidence that the undervaluing of women's work is a phenomena that has existed throughout history and still persists in most, if not all countries today. Anthropologist Margaret Mead found that ... there are villages in which men fish and women weave, and ones in which women fish and men weave. But in either village, the work done by the men is valued higher than the work done by women.

Secondly, when women began to move into the paid labour force in increasing numbers, the jobs open to them often involved the same or similar kinds of work women in the home traditionally performed, such as caring for children, teaching, tending the sick, serving food and other service work. This kind of work was done by women at home, without any pay and often without proper recognition of its value. The labour market perpetuated this discriminatory attitude, so that low pay for women was considered justified.

Thirdly, it was not very long ago that it was perfectly legal to deliberately exclude women from "men's jobs". Remember the "Help Wanted Female" and "Help Wanted Male" ads in local newspapers? The deliberate exclusion of women from access to better paying men's jobs resulted in the overcrowding of women into the traditionally female jobs, which may well have played a role in depressing women's wages.

Finally, reasons for the undervaluing of women's work can be traced to a time when women were thought to work for "pin money" rather than for a living. In fact in today's society a growing number of women are solely responsible to support themselves and their children. As well, the two income family has now become the norm in our society. Most married women now work outside the home, and that second income is vitally necessary to provide their families with an adequate standard of living.

Employment Equity

Employment Equity for Women With Disabilities
Toronto, n.d.[20]

...

* American statistics from 1981 show an astonishing earnings spread of $8,000 between disabled men and women. The percentage of people working full-time that year was pegged at: non-disabled men, 61.4%; disabled men, 22.3%; non-disabled women, 32.7%; and disabled women, 7.4%.
  Although Canadian statistics are not nearly as comprehensive, a 1984 Winnipeg report entitled "Social Needs Assessment of the Physically Disabled", showed an unemployment rate of 74% for disabled women in contrast to an unemployment rate of 60% for disabled men, with 66% of women surveyed living on annual incomes of less than $5,000.
* What kind of occupations do women with disabilities most often end up in? A U.S. 1982 population survey which studied the occupational categories of women with disabilities aged 16-64 who were not in institutions found that: 25.4% worked as clerical type workers (about one third less than non-disabled women workers); one in three were service workers (one and half times higher than non-disabled women). Disabled women were twice as likely as non-disabled women to be self-employed.
* Part-time work is a preferable alternative to some women with disabilities because it better accommodates attendant care schedules and fatigue problems. This type of work remains out of reach however, because individuals would no longer be entitled to benefits associated with social assistance such as drug and hospitalization costs as well as U.I.C. and C.P.P. associated with full-time work. Government and private industry must recognize that part-time employment in some cases may be necessary and preferable.
* The lack of opportunities and the tendency towards stereotyped occupations begins at the earliest stages in the school system with lower educational expectations for young girls with disabilities. There appears to be growing evidence that disabled women have a higher rate of illiteracy than other groups of our society.
* Women who use wheelchairs may find career counsellors suggesting that they work as secretaries since they are "already sitting down". Because women have often been placed in positions where physical attraction is a key component, women with dis-

20. DisAbled Women's Network, "DAWN Toronto Fact Sheet on Employment," n.d. Copy at CWMA, file: DAWN.

abilities who are not attractive in the traditionally accepted fashion miss out on these "career opportunities".

* Many women with disabilities are unable to work for employment services targeted for and run by women because of the physical inaccessibility of these services. Women with disabilities who wish to use these services are unable to do so for the same reasons. Such services must be provided with the funds to make their facilities accessible to women from all walks of life including those with or without disabilities.

* The concept of employment equity is still seen as a non-disabled women's issue — more effort needs to be made to include women with disabilities as rightful members of the women's movement.

"Women in Railway Trades? Why Not? How Katie Curtin Won Her Battle With CN" Montreal, 1979[21]

"There's a place for women at CN," says a sign at CN Rail's personnel office in Montreal. It shows women driving trucks and working in the yards.

But they'll have to fight every inch of the way to get those jobs, says Katie Curtin ...

One day in early March a CN official who had been sitting on Curtin's file for two months said he had just discovered she was not qualified for a job because she had no welding experience. She had been told this was not necessary. He said he would look into it.

Curtin was called in for another interview, and asked again why she wanted to work at CN. Finally, an interview was arranged with the foreman at the yards.

There she was asked to pick up a brake shoe that weighted a least 25 pounds. "I picked it up easily with two hands. He then said to pick it up with one hand. I was unable to do this because I couldn't get a proper grip on it."

Back at the yard office, the foreman and other officials subjected Curtin to "a sexist barrage the likes of which I had never before seen."

"How do you think you can do that work if you can't even pick up the brake shoe?"

"The other women here are not working out ... One got a spine injury from the work. None of them are doing any work right now."

"How can you expect to do the work if you aren't capable of it. You are smaller and feminine." ...

... They said that a woman who works in a job like this is not really a woman, and things like that.

21. Richard Fidler, *Socialist Voice*, 30 April 1979. Copy at CWMA: file, Non-Traditional Jobs Clippings.

"And they also said they were in favor of CN requiring tests of physical strength and welding experience — which the company is introducing now simply to exclude women.

"It was pretty discouraging."

Katie Curtin doesn't discourage easily, however. On March 23, together with other women from Action Travail Femmes, she went to a public meeting where Marc Lalonde, the federal minister responsible for the status of women, was speaking about all the great things the Liberal government had done for women.

Confronting Lalonde, Curtin described her experience with CN, a government-owned corporation. She was warmly applauded by the audience, mainly women.

Lalonde said she should take her case to the Human Rights Commission. Curtin replied that it took months or years for such bodies to make decisions on these cases. (In fact, Curtin is still waiting for the Quebec Human Rights Commission to rule on her dismissal from a job with the Olympics in 1976, when she was fired for her political views.)

"The government has to take real measures to ensure that women get integrated into those jobs that are traditionally male, such as establishing quotas for the hiring of women," Curtin told Lalonde.

The minister lamely replied that U.S. officials had told him that quotas had not worked in the States. Curtin pointed out in reply that several thousand American women had been hired as coal miners following the establishment of quotas by the companies.

This exchange was given wide coverage in the news media, both in Montreal and cross country. A couple of days later Curtin was phoned by CN and told she would be given a job later that week. She began work in the yards on April 3.

"After my ordeal with CN management," she told *Socialist Voice* recently, "I had braced myself for a difficult first few weeks on the job.

"I needn't have worried. I found it an exhilarating experience. All my co-workers have been very friendly and helpful, from day one. And I've met with no hostility.

"Many have told me they support the right of women to have these types of jobs, and have asked me when there will be more women coming."

Katie Curtin emphasizes something else, too. "The reason I got my job," she says "was not just that I fought for it, but because of the pressure of the women's movement on the employers, and the help I got from Action Travail Femmes. But if women are to make real progress in this field, the unions too must take up this issue — by fighting for affirmative action and job hiring quotas for women and oppressed minorities.

"It's in their interests — the interests of all working people — to see that women are no longer confined to low-paying job ghettos."

"Bill C-62, An Act Respecting Employment Equity" Ottawa, 1985[22]

...

PURPOSE

2. The purpose of this Act is to achieve equality in the work place so that no person shall be denied employment opportunities or benefits for reasons unrelated to ability and, in the fulfilment of that goal, to ameliorate the conditions of disadvantage in employment experienced by women, aboriginal peoples, persons with disabilities and persons who are, because of their race or colour, in a visible minority in Canada by giving effect to the principle that employment equity means more than treating persons in the same way but also requires special measures and the accommodation of differences.

...

EMPLOYMENT EQUITY

4. An employer shall implement employment equity by
(a) identifying and eliminating each of the employer's employment practices, not otherwise authorized by a law, that results in employment barriers against persons in designated groups; and
(b) instituting such positive policies and practices and making such reasonable accommodation as will ensure that persons in designated groups achieve a degree of representation in the various positions of employment with the employer that is proportionate to their representation
(i) in the work force, or
(ii) in those segments of the work force that are identifiable by qualification, eligibility or geography and from which the employer may reasonably be expected to draw or promote employees.

REPORTS

5. (1) On or before June 1, 1988 and on or before June 1 of each year thereafter, every employer shall file with the Minister a report in respect of the immediately preceding calendar year containing information in accordance with prescribed instruction indicating, in the form and manner prescribed,
(a) the industrial sector in which employees of the employer are employed, the location of the employer and employees, the number of all employees of the employer and the number of persons in designated groups so employed;

---

22. House of Commons of Canada, First Reading, 1985.

(b) the occupational groups of the employer and the degree of representation of persons in designated groups in each occupational group;

(c) the salary ranges of employees and the degree of representation of persons in designated groups in each range and prescribed subdivision thereof; and

(d) the number of employees hired, promoted and terminated and the degree of representation in those numbers of persons in designated groups.

(2) A report under subsection (1) shall, in prescribed manner, be certified as to the accuracy of the information contained therein and the certificate shall be signed by the employer or, where the employer is a corporation, by a prescribed person on behalf of the corporation and under its seal.

6. An employer who fails to comply with section 5 is guilty of an offence and liable on summary conviction to a fine not exceeding fifty thousand dollars.

7. The Minister shall in each year prepare a consolidation of the reports received in that year under section 5 and shall, as soon as possible thereafter but not later than the end of that year, cause the consolidation, together with such analysis thereof as the Minister may wish to make, to be laid before each House of Parliament.

8. Each report filed with the Minister under section 5 shall be available for public inspection at such places as may be designated by the Minister and any person may, on payment of the prescribed fee, obtain from the Minister a copy of the report ...

"Do Women Really Need Employment Equity?"
Toronto, February 1992[23]

In the public discourse on employment equity, there is a great deal of mythology. The suggestion is that white women have really made it and do not need mandatory employment equity measures. Few women, it is argued, "want to work in non-traditional jobs and why implement mandatory employment equity just to move educated white women into management positions? Really what white women need is pay equity. Employment equity is for minorities and people with disabilities who really face discrimination. Maybe we need mandatory measures for these groups but surely we have reached a stage in society where women are advancing."

---

23. "'Justice Works': Response of the National Action Committee on the Status of Women to 'Working Toward Equality,' Ontario's Discussion Paper on Employment Equity," February 1992, 4–6.

Common sense might tell you that after twenty years of the women's movement this should be true. Unfortunately, it is not, as the annual federal reports clearly show.

Women are still only 4% of apprentices in the skilled trades. Can it be true that only a few women want trades jobs when most women who have these high paying relatively secure unionized positions wouldn't trade them for the world? The reality is that there is no effort being made to encourage women to train in non-traditional jobs. Most-retraining programs for women are geared to the traditional, mostly low-paid, occupations. Nor is any effort being made to overcome the sexual harassment, intimidation and isolation which still are faced by women who do enter male-dominated occupations or workplaces.

Transforming male or white-dominated work sites so they are workable for women is a central issue for employment equity. Indeed the culture of the workplace and its impact on the designated group is a very little studied issue but one which in our experience has tremendous impact on the ability of women, minorities, aboriginal people and people with disabilities to fully function in the workplace. Our discussions with women tell us that harassment, whether sexual, racial, homophobic, class-based or against people with disabilities is one of the most difficult aspects of their work. Even if women are hired, the climate in a workplace can ensure that they will not stay.

Employment equity plans are not just to move women into non-traditional jobs. In most of the occupational groups, a greater proportion of the female workforce than that of the male is found in the lowest salary quarter. For example, at the Canadian Broadcasting Corporation, 53% of all women working full-time in all middle management positions were in the lowest salary quarter compared with 40.4% of all men. Furthermore, the number of women in this low salary quarter increased from 1987 to 1990 by 23 while the number of men decreased by 35. This even occurred in the largely female occupational group at the Bank of Nova Scotia. In 1990, over 72% of all women working full-time in the clerical jobs were in the lowest salary quarter compared with 48% of all men.

The large percentage of the female workforce in the lowest salary quarter in management and professional occupations raises the question of how jobs have been classified for employment equity purposes. Have women actually been promoted and hired into management and professional work or have their job titles just been changed? For example have 'clerical' occupations simply been retitled to 'administration' for classification as middle management without any change in salary levels or decision-making responsibility? Why are 86% of all women in middle management positions at the Bank of Nova Scotia in the lowest salary quarter compared with only 40% of all men? The Employment Equity Commission should carefully examine its proposal for data collection to ensure that such distortions cannot take place.

Finally, promoting more women into management positions is critically important to ensuring more equality in the workplace. However, at the three companies examined there were actual decreases from 1987 to 1990 in the representation rates of women promoted in some occupational groups. For example, at the Bank of Nova Scotia, the representation rate of women promoted in upper level management positions decreased by 1.3%. Furthermore, the actual number of women promoted decreased from two to one. Therefore, in 1990, one of the eight women upper-level managers was promoted. Even within the largely female clerical occupations, the representation rate of women promoted declined by 7.1% from 93.9% in 1987 to 86.8% in 1990. The number of women promoted in this occupational group decreased by 393 while the number of men promoted increased by 91.

While companies are responding to pressure on this issue, their efforts are minimal, usually resulting in a token number of women in the boardroom, thus creating the appearance of change without affecting fundamental shifts in the overall structure.

But we are in a recession

We know that you will hear arguments that employers cannot afford effective employment equity measures in this time of economic hardship. On the contrary, we would argue, employment equity is more required in these times. Over the last thirty years major changes have occurred in family status. In 1962, 64% of families were headed by a sole male wage earner, by 1990 the figure was reduced to only 13%. While 15% of families are now headed by a female sole wage earner, the majority of families require two incomes to survive. Women are becoming poor at a much faster rate than men. When parents are poor, children are poor. Employment equity is a critical measure to solve child poverty.

The groups designated by employment equity measures are disproportionately poor, unemployed and marginalized in our society. Even during boom periods these groups suffer more economic deprivation. If we permit discrimination to intensify during periods of economic crises, many in these groups will become permanently marginalized thus leading to increased racism, violence against women and dependence on social assistance. If we do not go forward with measures like employment equity, we will go backwards.

Moreover it is not fair that those who are disadvantaged should suffer the worst effects of a recession. It is no more tragic for a forty year old skilled tradesman who has worked for good wages all his life to be laid off than it is for a young black woman who has her first good job.

Workplace Pressures and Work Deterioration

Protection for Home Workers
Toronto, 1992[24]

What's an Alfred Sung jacket that sells for $375 worth to the person who actually stitched it together? A grand total of $4.

This news from union officials fighting to "end the exploitation of home workers" drew shocked gasps yesterday from a conference in Toronto organized by the Ontario Federation of Labour and attended by several provincial cabinet ministers.

They were told that home-based garment workers earn less than the province's minimum wage of $6 an hour to produce clothing bearing such prestigious designer labels as Alfred Sung, Lida Baday, Linda Lundstrom, Jones New York and Peanut Power children's wear. According to the International Ladies Garment Workers Union, a Baday gown that retails for $400 fetches only $10 for the worker who does the sewing.

Flanked by other members of the New Democratic Party cabinet and caucus, Labour Minister Robert Mackenzie promised to change the Employment Standards Act to increase protection for home-based workers.

He also said the province will create a task force to study a broader approach to collective bargaining that could make it easier for unions to organize home workers and then represent them in some form of industry-wide negotiations.

A home worker, asking that her name not be used, told the meeting she is one of those who earn less than the minimum wage for producing designer clothes. Because she is considered self-employed, she receives no benefits, such as vacation pay, unemployment insurance or Canada Pension Plan contributions. "I do not have any protection. Sometimes I cannot get paid."

Alex Dagg, manager of the garment workers' union, said that by law, manufacturers are supposed to register any home workers, ensure their pay rate for piecework amounts to the minimum wage, and make CPP and unemployment insurance contributions on their behalf.

But few comply, she said. There are as many as 4,000 home workers in the garment industry in Ontario, but only about 70 are registered.

The OFL has asked the government to enforce existing laws and to rescind the regulation that currently exempts home workers from the standards covering hours of work, overtime pay and statutory holidays.

The federation also wants the government to include home workers involved in data entry, clerical and other "telecommuting work" in any new employment-standards protections.

---

24. Virginia Galt, "$375 Jacket Stitched for $4, Conference Told. Protection for Home Workers Promised as Union Seeks End to 'Exploitation'," *The Globe and Mail*, 2 October 1992, A1, A8.

Because the garment work is heavily subcontracted, the federation also has asked the government to "ensure that firms at the top of the subcontracting pyramid have joint liability for the provision of minimum employment standards."

Mr. Mackenzie said he would not go into detail about the government's proposed amendments to the Employment Standards Act, but promised that most of labour's concerns would be met.

In addition to lobbying members of all three Ontario political parties yesterday, the OFL endorsed the "clean clothes campaign" launched yesterday by a group called the Coalition for Fair Wages and Working Conditions for Home Workers.

The postcard campaign urges major retailers, such as the Hudson's Bay Co., Dylex Ltd. and T. Eaton Co., to buy only from garment manufacturers "who agree to ensure that all workers are paid fair wages, work in decent conditions and who comply, at a minimum, with the standards as set out in the Employment Standards Act."

Neither the retailers nor the designers mentioned at yesterday's meeting had an immediate response. However, the president of Etac Sales Ltd., which holds the licence to sell Alfred Sung clothing, said the labour campaign is misleading and unfair.

"They are talking about the exception rather than the rule," said Alfred Chan, explaining that the bulk of garments made in Canada are produced in factories.

Etac factories produce Alfred Sung clothes, he said, but some work does go to other factories that may, in turn, have it done by home workers — and he doesn't know what they're paid.

Mr. Chan said his company lost money last year. "We as a company can produce our goods either in the Orient or Canada or Mexico. We have chosen to do a portion of our production in Canada in order to help the unemployment rate."

"Women's Work is Nearly Done"
Ste. Agathe, Quebec, 1984[25]

... the forty-one women who ran the local telephone switchboard aren't there anymore. The telephone exchange has been shut down; closed due to automation.

For as long as the women could remember, that switchboard had been central to the community and to their lives. All local people, many of whom had grown up together, were a microcosm of the northern Laurentian town as they sat side by side in front of the old cord switchboard. Their deft fingers plugging and unplugging wires, they relayed the traffic of local gossip, births, deaths and business affairs.

For thirty-five years, Rollande Labonté was one of those women. A warm-hearted person with laugh lines fanning out from her eyes and

25. Heather Menzies, *This Magazine* 8, no. 1 (April 1984), 32-36. Copy at Women's Education and Referral Centre.

hair in a perpetual chaos of curls, she remembers calls from people whose kitchen clocks had stopped or from people who wanted to go off on hunting trips but didn't trust their alarm clocks to get them up at 4:30 in the morning; so if the operator wasn't too busy and didn't mind, could she maybe phone ... ? Mlle. Labonté and the others were happy to comply; it was their idea of providing good service — 'service with a smile' they called it, as if they had coined the phrase ...

Then one hot Saturday afternoon in July 1980, an operator from Sorel phoned through asking: 'Is it true, you're going to close?' The women hadn't heard a thing, ...

On Monday morning, there was a memo on the noticeboard. It was true. Ste. Agathe was to close; details would follow.

'It was unbelievable at first; after seventy years in Ste. Agathe!' Mlle. Labonté recalled. The implications began to sink in. 'It wasn't so bad for me, I'm single and I own my own home. But many of the other women, the family budget depends on their paycheque. Some had just bought cars or a house. Why didn't they tell us sooner? I can't believe the company made its plans just a few months ahead. It must have been planning this for a couple of years, at least.' Her voice is bitter. 'They played us like a yo-yo.'

For nearly four months, the women were left in the dark, not knowing whether there were jobs elsewhere or what benefits they were entitled to. For most of them, being a telephone operator right there in Ste. Agathe had been the only work they'd done since they were school girls and got hired on for the summer. Jacques Goudreau, Bell Canada's general manager of operator services for the Quebec region, explained in an interview that the delay in dealing with the redundant Ste. Agathe operators was due to internal corporate logistics. Very simply the final budget for the closure hadn't been approved yet ...

The Communications Workers of Canada have one of the better technological change clauses in the country. Yet for the women of Ste. Agathe it was cold comfort. With their regular union rep. still on maternity leave and her replacement still green, the women didn't realize that the company's obligation to transfer and to do so by seniority applied only for being transferred to another job as a telephone operator. By the time some of the women found out, the handful of job openings in Montreal and elsewhere had been snapped up — suspiciously by younger women with little seniority. But then, most of the older married women were tied to Ste. Agathe. Even if their husbands' work was seasonal or paid little more than their wives', there was the pride of being the main bread winner, and one didn't threaten that ...

The company followed its budget plan to the end. They held a farewell luncheon for the women which took place in the Bell offices, half empty of furniture and equipment by then. Sandwiches and coffee were served. Then, in a parting gesture, each women was given a rose. A plastic rose. A 15-cent plastic rose. It was their final humiliation.

Part-Time Workers
Vancouver, 1973[26]

...Many women tend to think that there are many exciting, interesting part-time jobs available, but this, in fact, is simply not the case. Moreover, these jobs, where they do exist, carry little responsibility or potential for further advancement.

During this study, we did not encounter any employer who would place a part-time employee in a position of responsibility as a decision-maker, or in any managerial capacity. It is even rare to find part time people working directly under those who are themselves in decision-making positions. Thus, secretaries to executives, administrative assistants and so forth are all full-time positions.

When questioned about this practice employers state, either explicitly or implicitly, that a woman who is serious enough to want a position of responsibility must also be serious enough to work full time. Thus willingness to work long hours indicates seriousness of intent, and this in turn implies commitment to the job. Reverse this line of reasoning and it is clear why employers think that if a woman says she wants to work fewer hours, she is also saying that she does not want to commit herself to the job, and is therefore not "serious" enough to be given a responsible position.

The consequence of this practice is that part-time jobs are usually low paying. Except in rare instances (such as when a professional woman works part time), a woman could not live on her part-time earnings, let alone support a family, unless her income were substantially supplemented by insurance monies, child support, maintenance, etc. Part-time work is, therefore, not a viable alternative to living on welfare, nor is it financially feasible for many single parents who need a lighter work load in order to cope more successfully with heavy family responsibilities.

Job-Sharing
1988[27]

...

Background

While the number of job-sharing arrangements appears small so far, many cases may exist without being recognized and can therefore have the effect of undermining the number of full-time positions and the negotiated provisions of the collective agreement.

90 per cent of employees who wish to enter a job-sharing arrangement are women. The reasons that women workers want to enter job-sharing

---

26. Status of Women Council of B.C., *An Investigation of Part-Time Work for Women*, May 1973, 6. Copy at VSW.
27. National Union of Provincial Government Employees, *National Union Policy on Job Sharing*, 1–2, Adopted at the 7th National Convention, March 1988.

are varied. Many wish to spend more time with their young children; others want to balance work with their efforts to achieve higher education; some simply wish to have more time for other interests.

The problem for far too many women is that they are forced to consider job-sharing because their family responsibilities are heavy and they have to bear these responsibilities without adequate support and assistance.

National Union members are committed to the development of childcare policy and programs which will provide quality childcare for Canadian children and which will permit Canadian women to enjoy full rights to full-time employment.

The National Union is also alert to the right-wing promotion of job-sharing and the motives that inspire it. The National Union rejects the encouragement of job-sharing as a method of

- reducing unemployment figures
- reducing the number of full-time positions
- undermining the contract language of negotiated collective agreements
- reinforcing the regressive view that women are not full-fledged participants in the work force
- reinforcing the regressive view that "women belong in the home".

In addition to the concerns of National Union members about the pressures women are under because of responsibilities for their families, members are concerned that women do not have adequate access to programs of job-training or educational leave. Women should not have to job-share in order to improve their skills and education.

Both men and women who are in high-stress positions are vulnerable to the "burnout" syndrome and may feel that job-sharing is their only option. Collective agreements which provide adequately for stress leave will help employees in high-stress positions and prevent situations in which employers use the technique of job-sharing as a substitute for adequate levels of staffing.

In short, the establishment of a National Union policy on job-sharing is not aimed at promoting job-sharing among National Union members. Its purpose is to ensure that members who seek job-sharing as a way to maintain their links with the workplace while they meet their other needs, will not be undermining the role of the union in maintaining full-time positions and negotiated collective agreement language ...

Workplace Hazards

"Sexual Harassment: We've Only Just Begun"
Ottawa, 1985[28]

In 1979, while she was on probation as a lead hand cleaner at the Canadian Forces Base in North Bay, Bonnie Robichaud was asked by her supervisor to perform sexual acts with him. The acts included masturbation, fellatio, fondling of his penis and attempted sexual intercourse (apparently he couldn't achieve an erection). Bonnie, married and a mother of 5, claims that she felt intimidated by Dennis Brennan (her supervisor) into performing the sexual acts because he threatened to discipline her and sabotage her attempt to pass probation for the lead hand position, if she refused. As soon as her probation was over, she filed a complaint with the Canadian Human Rights Commission alleging sexual harassment, discrimination and intimidation.

For a long period after filing the human rights complaint, Bonnie was disciplined as a result of written complaints about her work. Five of the complaints were from Brennan. They resulted in a demotion, as well as social and physical isolation from other workers.

Five years later, the case seems far from finished. After filing her complaint, Bonnie's allegations were investigated by staff of the Human Rights Commission, and found to be substantiated. A tribunal was appointed in 1981 to do a formal inquiry and its decision was released in June of 1982. Richard Abbot, a law professor, found the allegations to be unsubstantiated, largely because he judged that the sexual acts described by Bonnie (and flatly denied by Dennis Brennan), could only have been carried out with her consent.

Bonnie immediately appealed the tribunal decision and a review tribunal was appointed. It ruled in February of 1983 that Bonnie had a valid sexual harassment complaint. Review tribunal members were then to hear arguments to establish the amount of damages. Before that happened, Brennan appealed the review tribunal's decision to the Federal Court of Appeal. After two court hearings, one in May of 1984 and another in November of that year, Bonnie Robichaud is still anxiously awaiting the Federal Court of Appeal judges' decision.

As Constance Backhouse and Leah Cohen documented so well in The Secret Oppression (1978), unwanted sexual attention in the workplace happens to almost every woman at some point in her life, be she a cleaner, secretary, middle manager or professional. Yet a 1983 CROP poll (the first national poll on the subject of sexual harassment), revealed that while about 1.5 million Canadians believe they have been sexually harassed, few have ever reported the incidents, and even fewer of the harassers have been disciplined.

---

28. Ellen Adelberg, *Breaking the Silence* 3, no. 3 (Spring 1985), 10–12. Copy at CWMA.

Given Bonnie Robichaud's experience, one can easily underst. why few women bother to report unwelcome sexual contact, let alone a boss's pat on the bottom or co-worker's lewd talk about women. Backhouse and Cohen's book, and other recent writing on the subject, demonstrates clearly that sexual harassment is most commonly treated as a joke by men, or else as a "fact of life" — after all now, men will be men, and girls will be girls won't they? ...

We have all made some gains as a result of Bonnie's bravery and tenacity. Her claim of discriminatory treatment based on sex was the first of its kind investigated and upheld by the Canadian Human Rights Commission. Shortly afterward, the Canada Human Rights Act was amended to include sexual harassment as a form of discrimination ... However, there are many important questions we need to ask ourselves as a result of Bonnie's experience. For one, is the Human Rights Commission complaint route a worthwhile avenue? Since 1978, nine sexual harassment cases have been heard by the Canadian Human Rights Commission. One was dismissed, the rest were upheld. The largest settlement received by a complainant was $5,000; some were as little as $500. Many of the women were forced to quit or otherwise lost their jobs; all of the women suffered personal grief and trauma impossible to measure in dollar terms. In Bonnie's case, after five years she has yet to receive a cent of compensation for the wages she lost as a result of her demotion from lead hand cleaner.

Another problem with human rights complaints is that they must be submitted on an individual basis. This means that each woman who suffers sexual harassment must decide on her own to lay a complaint, quite possibly leaving herself open to job dismissal, and other forms of non-sexual harassment. Another obvious problem with human rights complaints is the length of time they take to be settled ...

Sex Exploitation in the Workplace
Fredericton, N.B., 1981[29]

A demand by a local club owner that his waitresses work in scanty uniforms has placed the issue of sex exploitation in the workplace smack in the lap of the New Brunswick Human Rights Commission.

The commission is inquiring into a complaint of sex discrimination filed by two cocktail waitresses fired from their jobs for refusing to sport the brief, leg-revealing uniforms ordered by David Kileel, owner of Tiffany's Cabaret.

Marianne Doherty, 24, and Cindy Meehan, 22, both of Fredericton, consider their firing unjust.

They describe the uniforms as humiliating and an invitation to sexual harassment on the job.

"I'm really mad about it," Doherty says.

29. Chris Morris, The Canadian Press, "Sex Exploitation Claimed," in *The Ottawa Citizen*, 16 May 1981, 60.

"I think its a great injustice that we were subjected to something that I think should not happen in 1981 ... I think it reflects an archaic attitude towards women in general, using us as sex objects to sell a commodity."

The brown, tuxedo-style outfits feature short pants that just cover the top of the thigh, a long-sleeved jacket with tails and a vest with a scooped neck and bow tie.

Doherty says too much flesh was exposed when the waitresses bent over in the short pants.

Kileel is standing firm in what he considers his right as an employer to insist waitresses don uniforms of his choice.

He maintains the outfits are not indecent or undignified.

"I think the uniform is fine and I've had nothing but compliments from customers who frequently visit Tiffany's," he says.

But Kileel has had a petition signed by about 100 men and women supporting the Doherty-Meehan complaint that the outfits are degrading to the female sex.

Joy McShane, a founding member of the *ad hoc* committee which gathered the petition, says the group would like to see the "demeaning" uniforms eliminated and waitresses given a choice of another outfit.

McShane, who also works at the local rape crisis centre, says the uniforms simply invite trouble for the waitresses wearing them.

"It leaves the women wide open to sexual advances and harassment."

Meehan and Doherty wore the uniforms on a trial basis for three nights before deciding they were too uncomfortable and humiliating.

During the test, Doherty says even regular customers "looked at us in a different, unpleasant light."

"I felt everybody was looking at me like I was on display," Meehan adds.

"I felt very, very uncomfortable."

Kileel says sexual overtures and personal remarks are well-known hazards of being a cocktail waitress.

"It's really unfair for the girls to say ... that I was trying to exploit sex at Tiffany's," he says.

"I believe any girl who works in a lounge, whether she's in a dress or a uniform is going to get remarks from customers visiting any liquor establishment, and if she doesn't know how to handle these customers or how to accept these remarks, she shouldn't be working in this kind of establishment."

Workplace Sexism
Halifax, N.S., December 1989[30]

I've been a tradeswoman working among 1,500 men at the Halifax dockyard for the past eight years of my life.

---

30. Leslee Nicholson, "A Powerful Statement on Workplace Sexism," *OPSEU News*, 31 January 1990.

Learning to be a machinist wasn't the hardest thing I've ever done. The greatest challenge was, and still is, facing the fact there are dozens of my co-workers who hate my guts and they don't even know me.

They know nothing about who I am, my beliefs, my thoughts. And yet they despise me. Why? Because I am a woman.

They say I'm taking away the job of some family man in an area of high unemployment. They say that I'm "degrading" the trade. Their sense of self-worth is mostly derived from the idea that they do a "man's job." So a woman successfully performing the same work has the effect of a pin near a balloon.

They hate me because I'm a woman and I've dared to enter their domain. And that to me is the hardest hate to deal with.

If someone dismisses me because of something I do or say — I can live with that, I can learn from that. Reconciliation is a possibility.

But there is nothing on God's green earth I can do about the hate some feel for me simply and only because I'm a woman.

This hate is manifested every single day. Every time I go to work I can count on meeting someone who has a problem with my just being there. I live with comments, jokes, gestures, and in extreme instances, violence.

I was struck by a co-worker during my second year. No witnesses. He made sure.

I've been harassed for months on end by an obscene phone caller, who among other things, can tell me the particulars of the job I was working on that day.

We have seven tradeswomen scattered throughout the dockyard. Each one of us has called upon union intervention at least twice to get harassers off our backs. Even then we do it with great reluctance and only when we can't stand it another minute. You can always count on the guy's friends harassing you twice as bad for awhile, to teach you a lesson about blowing the whistle.

There's hate and violence everywhere in our society. But I don't think you can even begin to compare the experience of men to women in this regard. It would be like comparing a rain shower with a monsoon.

Sexual Harassment: "Emergency Resolution" Burnaby, B.C., December 20, 1984[31]

...

Emergency Resolution 2

WHEREAS the first case to come before the new Human Rights Council of B.C. has now been heard; and

WHEREAS the complainant, Andrea Fields, alleged sexual harassment by her supervisor at Willie's Rendezvous Restaurant, in the form

---

31. B.C. Federation of Labour, *Sisterhood* 8, no. 19 (December 20, 1984), 1–2.

of attempts to hug, kiss, pinch and grab her, and writing of crude and offensive notes; and

WHEREAS she resisted and was subsequently fired; and

WHEREAS the Chair of the Council ruled against the complainant on the grounds that it was in the nature of the supervisor to "warmly greet his staff" and that he was a "compulsive writer of notes" and thus his behaviour did not constitute sexual harassment; and

WHEREAS this decision proves the Council has no commitment to or understanding of human rights issues; now

THEREFORE BE IT RESOLVED that the B.C. Federation of Labour publicly condemn in the strongest possible terms the decision of the Chair of the Human Rights Council in the case of Andrea Fields versus Willie's Rendezvous Restaurant, and call on the Minister of Labour to reverse this decision; and

BE IT FURTHER RESOLVED that the B.C. Federation of Labour call for the resignation of the Chair of the Human Rights Council on the grounds that he is incompetent to decide human rights issues in the light of precedents established by Human Rights Tribunals across Canada; and

BE IT FINALLY RESOLVED that the B.C. Federation of Labour demand the reinstatement of the previous Human Rights Code, Commission and Branch, and support human rights groups fighting this decision and working toward returning human rights protection to B.C.

Occupational Health Hazards for Women
Ottawa, 1978[32]

...In 1913, the Inspector of Factories for Ontario described the situation facing laundry workers in this way: "Standing the whole day, their exhausted bodies had to contend with an atmosphere vitiated by gas and other impurities, which had continued to accumulate during the whole day, and the workers then inhale it at a time when the body is fatigued by a full day's work."

Very little has changed since 1913. Today 62 per cent of all launderers and dry cleaners are women and these women still experience constant exposure to chemicals and solvents which can lead to scaling skin, cancer, and spontaneous abortion. Similarly, laboratory workers, hospital employees, and dental assistants are exposed to radiation, anaesthetic gases, mercury and toxic chemicals which, according to U.S. and European studies, are linked to cancer, leukaemia, liver damage, central nervous system changes and congenital abnormalities in children.

More and more research is being conducted on the relationship between lung diseases and employment in the mining sector. However, very little has been said about the hazards that face women who work

32. Judy Wasylycia-Leis, "Occupational Health Standards Needed for Women Too," Article #7, New Democratic Party, February 8, 1978, 2–4. Copy at CWMA, file: NDP Federal.

in the textile and clothing industries. Earlier this year, Elmina S. died after having worked for over 40 years in a shirt factory. She died of a lung disease caused, one would suspect, by years of breathing in lint and dust. This disease was discovered just months before she was to retire. There was no Workers' Compensation, no inquiry, no attempt to analyze the effects of such an environment on a woman's health with a view to correcting the situation for all other employees.

Even more neglected than the dangers facing garment workers are the health hazards found in offices. Denise D. had a job of answering the telephone for a northern Ontario company. She was allowed no lunch breaks and, thus, had to spit out or swallow her food when the phone rang. She also developed a persistent ear infection as a result of poor ventilation on the job. Because this infection forced her to miss several days on the job, she was fired at a moments notice despite the fact that a medical report had identified the source of the problem ...

Hazards in the Automated Office
Burnaby, B.C., 1986[33]

Anne, a clerical worker, complains that she developed a rash on her face when she started working on the computer. At first she blames the computer but then quickly retreats — "No, maybe it was something else". It wasn't her nerves but she wasn't sure it was the computer either. When computers were first introduced Anne and her co-workers had raised their concerns about the health hazards of VDTs. The company responded by bringing in a doctor who reported that the computers were absolutely safe. He wouldn't lie, would he? Anne lacks the necessary information to refute the doctor's claim.

Mary, another clerical worker in the same company, slowly, reluctantly, and painfully describes how her health problems have worsened since she started working on a computer terminal. Almost two years ago Mary was transferred from working on an accounting machine to a video display terminal where she now spends ninety per cent of her time inputting data at a very high speed. About six months after working at the computer terminal, she started experiencing muscle spasms. She's fine as long as she keeps working but as soon as she relaxes, she gets spasms in her back, a sharp pain down the side of her face, her temple starts to throb, and her stomach gets upset. She now spends most of her weekends and holidays in bed.

What is Mary doing about all this? She is not trying to find different work — she is a single mother who has been with the company for twenty-two years and is afraid to quit in times of such high unemployment. Nor does she express any open anger toward the company for the way her work has been reorganized — she used to have more variety in her job. Instead, she has been encouraged to see her muscle spasms as

33. Marcy Cohen and Margaret White, "Introduction," *Playing With Our Health: Hazards in the Automated Office* (Burnaby, B.C.: Women's Skills, 1986).

her own individual problem. Mary is taking a stress management course that is teaching her relaxation techniques and she is going to a chiropractor. It hasn't really worked yet but maybe ... Because of company cutbacks Mary was reluctant to admit the severity of her health problems. Instead, she feels that she has to keep coping if she wants her job. Her work could be organized differently — hourly rest breaks, job rotation, and good ergonomic conditions could help reduce the health hazards of working with VDTs. However, Mary had no union protection or health and safety committee to support her ...

"Attendants Complain About Air on Planes"
February 1994[34]

Flight attendants are suffering from dizziness, burning eyes, headaches and sudden fatigue because of poor on-board air quality, says the Canadian Union Public Employees, which wants a federal investigation.

In a statement to be released today, CUPE says 70 per cent of 291 flight attendants who participated in a national survey reported health problems they attribute to poor air quality. Passengers are affected as well, the union says.

"All of a sudden, a passenger will get a really strong headache and they don't realize it is because of the air," said CUPE representative Frances Pelletier, a long-time flight attendant.

The Air Transport Association of Canada, representing the industry, has rejected the union's complaints as "pure garbage."

Gordon Sinclair, president of the association, also denies CUPE's allegation that the industry had "pressured" the previous Progressive Conservative government into squelching plans for a comprehensive study of air quality on Canadian aircraft — although plans for such an investigation were dropped in 1992 after Transport Department officials heard representations from the industry.

Yesterday, CUPE asked Liberal Transport Minister Douglas Young to revive plans for such a study, saying poor air quality poses a serious health and safety risk to airline employees and the travelling public.

In pressing its request, CUPE cited a 1990 advisory by the Transportation Safety Board that said it had "received numerous complaints" from flight attendants and passengers about the poor quality of cabin air.

The advisory, signed by W.T. Tucker, the board's director of safety programs, warned that poor air quality could affect the ability of flight attendants to carry out their safety-related duties. He recommended further investigation.

Mr. Tucker said then — and CUPE says now — that the air-quality problems were caused partly by airliners flying at higher altitudes and turning off air-circulation equipment to save on fuel costs.

Mr. Sinclair of the industry association said yesterday that the carriers are not flying at higher altitudes and that they are not turning off the "air

34. Virginia Galt, *The Globe and Mail*, 2 February 1994.

packs." Turning off the air-circulation equipment would result in "negligible savings," he said.

However, Ms. Pelletier of CUPE said the air-circulation equipment is frequently shut off or turned down on long flights and is turned back on only if passengers complain.

As a result, flight attendants are sometimes forced to take whiffs from oxygen canisters so they can continue doing their jobs, she said.

The problems that the surveyed flight attendants reported having experienced one or more times in the past six months include heart palpitations, ringing ears, sinus pain, respiratory pain, dizziness, headaches, shortness of breath, burning eyes and nausea.

Ms. Pelletier said the flight attendants know the problems are related to poor air quality because "after we go up to the cockpit and ask for more air, the symptoms go away." ...

Chapter 3

Education and Training

Ruth Roach Pierson

If education is about changing and developing consciousness, then education has been at the heart of the women's movement. Certainly in the politics of second-wave feminism, education has been seen as a necessary first step towards collective action for progressive social change. Insofar as most feminisms prefer peaceful evolutionary process over violent revolutionary change, and democratic organizing and protest over individual or collective acts of violence, the women's movement has put great faith in the potential of education and moral suasion to change attitudes and to disabuse people of false and stereotypical notions about women. Feminists have turned to educational tools — to argument, to the marshalling of evidence, and to storytelling — as the means of changing the minds and winning over the hearts of the public and the powerful to the justice of the feminist cause. Even the consciousness-raising groups (CR) of the early days of the second wave can be seen as educational — as providing a kind of feminist adult education. Moreover, as CR was originally conceived, the individual's raised consciousness was to be the beginning, not the end, of the process. Carried out in groups, consciousness raising was itself a communal enterprise. In addition, its ultimate purpose was to motivate the individual to move out from the small group towards collective social action.

Formal Education

One of the first social institutions feminists sought to change through collective action was the existing educational system. Beginning with the Royal Commission on the Status of Women, feminists have spilled much ink and expended much energy to expose the ways in which existing educational institutions contribute to the subordination of women. Yet, their belief in the liberatory potential of formal education has rarely wavered. Feminists' attitudes toward formal education have in fact been double-edged. As Linda Briskin and Rebecca Coulter have written, "Feminism recognizes education both as a site for struggle and as a tool for change-making."[1] On the one side are the scathing critiques levelled at existing educational structures and practices; on the other side are the struggles for girls and women to attain equal access with boys and men to such institutions. The equal access approach has often had an affirmative action orientation. Criticism and pressure for change have been directed towards gaining equal access for girls and women to particular educational institutions, to certain programs of study and training, and to positions as educators and educational administrators. Following immediately upon the struggle for equal admission and job equity has come the struggle to reform the substance of education — curriculum content — and the ways in which that content is delivered. These last two arenas of struggle represent in many senses the more difficult and more radical attack on the existing educational system. The feminist agenda with respect to content has aimed to revolutionize the foundations of knowledge while the feminist agenda with respect to methods has attempted to create a new feminist pedagogy. From these struggles, feminists have learned many things. We have learned that neither equal access nor a revolution in knowledge nor teaching practice can be achieved without major structural changes in the educational system. The system's structures have, however, proved extremely resistant to feminist challenge. We have also learned that questions of access, content, practice, and structure are complexly intertwined. The initial feminist challenge tended all too frequently to treat women as an undifferentiated category and gender as a category that could be isolated from class, race, sexuality, and bodily ability. And while white, able-bodied, heterosexual, and middle-class feminists succeeded, however minimally, in institutionalizing our agendas, we have been slow to respond to the demands for change in access, content, practice, and structure to meet the educational needs of more marginalized girls and women.

Access

The Royal Commission revealed the extent to which women were second-class citizens within the educational system. Briefs presented to and research produced for the Commission exposed women's unequal access to the higher levels of academic training as well as to the higher levels of educational administration. While women's percentage of total undergraduate enrolment had climbed from the 1920s to 1970, women's proportion of the enrolment in graduate schools had declined steeply over the same period.[2] As teachers within the school system, women were concentrated in the elementary grades. As school administrators, women were vastly underrepresented in school principalships, even of elementary schools. Moreover, within colleges and universities, women were almost totally absent from the ranks of associate and full professors and formed only a tiny minority of the assistant professors. At the same time, although few records have been kept of this important component of Canada's post-secondary teaching staff, haphazard evidence would seem to indicate that women were overrepresented among the part-time and sessional lecturers who carry a large part of the teaching load at many community colleges. Women were also overrepresented within the temporary teaching staff of many degree-granting universities. For years, "marriage bars" operated to exclude academic women married to other academics from full-time, tenure-stream university appointments — informal agreements, even formal terms and conditions of employment, contained so-called anti-nepotism clauses which forbade the hiring of spouses within the same department, sometimes within the same university. The "spouses" affected were almost always wives who, although kept from regular academic jobs, formed a conveniently captive labour force on which the university or the nearby community college could draw to fill temporary teaching posts.

Women teachers organized within teacher federations have lobbied and bargained hard for women's improved access to administrative positions within school systems.[3] Although women teachers, particularly since the 1960s, have won formal equality in pay and benefits with their male counterparts,[4] equal representation in positions of educational leadership still eludes women. As Ruth Rees concluded in her study for the Canadian Education Association,

> the research shows quite clearly that men manage and administer our school systems — at school boards, at secondary schools (where a majority of the teachers are male), at junior high schools (which have about equal proportions of male and female teachers), *and* in the elementary panel, in spite of the large majority of women there as teachers. Men dominate the line positions within education, those positions of authority in and out of schools, with supervisory duties — those in the CEO positions, as superintendents, supervisors, and as principals and department heads.[5]

At the university level, the last twenty years have seen a small increase in the number of women advancing into administration, a few rising even to the height of university president. Currently there are eight women presidents among the eighty-eight member universities of the Association of Universities and Colleges of Canada.[6] The assumption has been that the two sides of the feminist educational struggle were joined; in other words, that increasing women's presence among educational decision-makers would further the feminist revolution in educational content and structure. At this point, the jury is still out on the validity of that supposition.

Over the last twenty-five years, the gender structure of higher education has dramatically changed, as more and more women have gone on to university. Women have accounted for a large proportion of the increase in university enrolments since the 1960s. The trend towards

Percentage of Full-Time Women University Teachers in Canada for the years 1960-61 and 1990-91				
Year	Full Professor	Associate Professor	Assistant Professor	Rank Below Assistant Professor
1960-61	4	10	12	24
1990-91	8	20	33	50

SOURCE: Compiled by Carmen Armenti from Statistics Canada (1993). *Teachers in Universities: 1990-91.* Ottawa: Minister of Industry, Science and Technology. (Cat. No. 81-241.) Modified from Table 1 "Number of Full-Time University Teachers by Rank, Sex and Region, Selected Years, 1960-61 to 1990-91."

After thirty years of feminist education and activism, women remain underrepresented in the professorial ranks of Canadian universities.

increasing accessibility of post-secondary education for women was discernible by the mid-1970s.[7] According to Statistics Canada, in 1967–68 women constituted 34.2 per cent of university undergraduate students and 19.3 per cent of graduate students, while by 1992–93 women constituted 53.5 per cent of undergraduate enrolment and 42.2 per cent of graduate enrolment.[8] Women have also made dramatic inroads into professional schools that were once bastions of male privilege, particularly medical schools and law schools (as compared with 13.8 per cent in 1967–68, in 1992–93 women constituted 45.4 per cent of medical students[9] and in 1991 women formed 48 per cent of first-year law students).[10] But engineering schools have proved more resistant to "feminization."[11] Long before the mass murder of fourteen young women at the École polytechnique in Montreal in December 1989, feminists linked the serious underrepresentation of women in engineering schools to the blatant misogyny of engineering students' rituals and publications.[12] As of January 1993, women constituted only 16.3 per cent of engineering students at the Bachelor of Science level, 16.5 per cent at the master's level and a mere 9.9 per cent at the doctoral level. In mathematics and the physical sciences, women have fared slightly better: women constituted 29.1 per cent of the total students in these B.Sc. programs, 25.2 per cent of those in Master of Science programs, and 17.2 per cent of those in doctoral programs. And in the agricultural and biological sciences, women are in the majority at the undergraduate level: women constitute 59 per cent of those in B.Sc. programs, 47.1 per cent of those in M.Sc. programs, and 31.7 per cent of those in doctoral programs.[13]

Meanwhile, the ratio of female-to-male university teachers in under-graduate and graduate departments and professional schools, particularly in the higher ranks of associate to full professor, has remained low, even where the student bodies have acquired a fairly even distribution of women and men.[14] According to 1991–92 data, women constitute 35.4 per cent of the professorate at the assistant professor level, 20.5 per cent at the associate professor level, and a mere 8.8 per cent at the full professor level.[15] In the agricultural and biological sciences, women represent 17.7 per cent of total faculty; in applied sciences, mathematics, and the physical sciences, 6.7 per cent; and in engineering, 3.1 per cent.[16]

Structures and Attitudes

Early on, feminists came to realize that access to education was affected by a range of attitudes and practices that were hidden or unexamined as well as by social and economic structures apparently unrelated to edu-cation. At first, feminist scholarship uncovered the ways in which teach-ers' responsiveness to pupils, from kindergarteners right through post-graduate students, varied according to gender.[17] In co-educational settings, boys and later men were found to command more of the teacher's attention: males were called on more frequently and they were more often awarded with approval for what they had to say.[18] A boy's solving of a mathematics problem might be regarded as clever, while a girl's, merely "rule-following."[19] Boys and young men who achieved academically were seen to be properly ambitious; girls and young women, to be overachievers.

Later studies have highlighted the fact that not all girls are treated equally, that a teacher's attitude towards and expectations of a pupil or student are often affected by the teacher's race and class in relation to the pupil's or student's.[20] Moreover, more recent educational research has moved beyond the assumption that the teacher and classroom activi-ties are alone responsible for reproducing class, race, or gender relations. That approach, as Roxana Ng has written, "overlooks the fact that power dynamics, based on one's race, gender, ability, and other characteristics, operate in mundane, taken-for-granted, and 'common sense' ways."[21] Instead, attention is being given to what some researchers call *regimes* of gender, race and class, produced and maintained by a whole panoply of societal institutions and practices.[22] The power relations that inhere, for example, in divisions of labour by sex, race, and class, in commer-cialized sports,[23] in the control of the media, and in much of popular culture are not left outside the classroom door as the teacher and the pupils or students enter. Nor can these power relations be dismantled merely by changes in classroom attitudes and practices.

The structure of universities and post-graduate professional schools puts obstacles in the educational path of women with family responsi-bilities and of financially strapped women reliant on outside work for pay. The basic structure has been organized on a male model, that is, in such a way as to accommodate the career path of a single, middle-class male unencumbered by family or work obligations. By and large, mainstream university and post-graduate education has been set up for the student who could attend on a full-time basis. It is the education of women, overwhelmingly more often than that of men, that is interrupted or cut short by the birth of children and the responsibilities of child rearing. And it is women, more than men, who have flocked to those educational programs that offer the possibility of formal education on a part-time basis and the opportunity to make up for educational opportunities foregone in the past.

Some feminists have argued that the accessibility of education is affected by women's different "ways of knowing."[24] Certain of these feminists accept, in order to re-evaluate, the old division of rationality as a male characteristic, intuitive reasoning as a female characteristic, arguing that these differences are not biologically but rather culturally determined. A few of these so-called "cultural" feminists have argued that abstraction is a more "male" way of reasoning, as women are used to perceiving the world in "context-dependent" ways. But even feminists utterly committed to the notion that brain power is gender free recognize that gender experience can affect the ways in which we learn. To take a not-so-extreme example, a large proportion of girls and young women enter the formal educational environment after having been or while being sexually abused by men in positions of fatherly trust and authority over them. Until recently, few educational theorists would have inquired into the impact such a violation might have on a young person's ability to speak up in class or to listen with any degree of trust to the words of authority figures, such as male teachers.[25] Researchers began to refer to the "chilly climate" that faced girls and women in educational institutions.[26] Documented instances of campus and date rape, to say nothing of the so-called Montreal Massacre of December 1989, challenged the picture of college, university, and professional school life as protected and ivory tower.[27]

Maths and Sciences

In a world of increasingly complex technology and dependence on the artificial intelligence of computers, feminists have recognized that the lower accessibility of mathematics and science education to girls presents a serious problem.[28] What has come to be called "math anxiety" in teenage girls has been of deep concern to feminists.[29] One explanation for math anxiety was based on a belief in biological determinism. It pointed to differences between the brain's left and right hemispheres, spatial abilities being associated with the right, verbal abilities with the left, and then argued that the right brain is more dominant in males, the left brain in females.[30] As feminists feared, the response of some educators was to propose remedial verbal skills training for boys.

CREDIT: Margie Bruun-Meyer

Feminist education has opened doors for young women in the male-dominated professions and non-traditional occupations. Young high school women are being encouraged to get their "hands dirty" and explore the world of technology.

Most feminists, however, have argued that the reasons girls and young women resist maths and sciences are cultural and social, not biological. They have pointed to the importance of the association of maths and sciences with the male domain and, consequently, to a loss of femininity as the price paid by girls and women who excel in them.[31] In addition, it is significant that mathematics and the natural sciences have been taught in terms of work environments and machinery with which boys are more likely to be familiar than girls. In physics, for instance, the principles of mechanics and propulsion tended to be taught in terms of car motors and guns. Some 1960s and 1970s mathematics textbooks surveyed depicted girls and women as less capable of solving arithmetic problems than boys and men.[32] More recently, with the advent of the computer age, studies have revealed "a boy centred 'computer culture' growing up in schools or within classrooms." According to one 1980s' study of eighteen Ontario elementary schools, boys used aggressive strategies and even downright sabotage to dominate computer use. Commenting on the behaviour of her male classmates, one girl remarked: "'When it comes to computers, they are sharks.'"[33] And not to be overlooked is the fact that many of the math- and science-based occupations and professions have been openly inhospitable to women.[34]

Curriculum Content

The question of access blends into the question of curriculum content. In the early phases of the new feminism, feminists were concerned with the limited range of "role models" to which girls and young women in school would be introduced. White feminist researchers examined textbooks for sex-role stereotyping and the imaging of women. These researchers interpreted sex-role stereotyping as an important factor in perpetuating stereotypes and believed that in curriculum materials it had the power to undermine girls' and women's confidence to act outside the confines of a narrowly defined femininity. They found elementary school readers cast the adult female characters predominantly as housewives/mothers while male adult characters appeared in a wide variety of roles.[35] Young white girls tended to be depicted as dutiful, middle-class daughters who smile, help their mother with the baking, and play with dolls and kittens. In contrast, white boys were shown going camping, building tree-houses, and exploring caves.[36] As the Royal Commission on the Status of Women in Canada reported in 1970:

> Even in arithmetic textbooks there are examples of sex-typing. In one series of books for Grades 3 to 8, questions such as the following are asked: "A girl can type about 48 words per minute. She has to type 2,468 words. Can she do this in 45 minutes?" or "A girl spent one-quarter of an hour sewing and one-quarter of an hour reading. What number of hours did she spend sewing and reading?"[37]

Moreover, as protagonists in stories, males vastly outnumbered females. In the Ginn 360 series being phased into New Brunswick elementary schools in 1975, Lois Camponi and Paulette Gallant found that "58.7 percent of the characters even mentioned in the eleven texts [they] studied are male, as opposed to 21.08 percent female." Furthermore, they continued, if one considered "the numbers of males and females used as main characters this discrepancy becomes even larger."[38] A study of the school readers used in the North York system in 1975 came up with similar results.[39] Also of concern to feminist critics was the sex-stereo-typing of emotions. In the New Brunswick texts studied by Camponi and Gallant, fear was missing from the male emotional register while ever present in that of females. At the same time, Camponi and Gallant drolly observed, the pronounced sex-stereotyping of apparel in the texts' illustrations "would lead one to wonder if the apron were a secondary sex characteristic," it was so commonly found on females, both animal and human.[40] Combining her feminist concerns with a concern with Canadian content, Priscilla Galloway examined the mandatory senior literature courses taught in eight Ontario secondary schools in the late 1970s and found them "sexist," "un-Canadian," and "outdated."[41] As Briskin and Coulter acknowledge,

> the work done by classroom teachers, school boards, ministries of education, and teacher federations to eliminate sex-role stereotyp-ing ... has drawn attention to sexism in education and in society.[42]

Feminists went to work producing texts that counteracted sex-role stereotyping. In 1978, sociologist Lorna Marsden identified three ap-proaches in these remedial texts. In one, the goal was to erase the differences between boys and girls. In a second, the emphasis was on giving equal representation to girls and boys. In a third, the focus was on showing women in other than housewifely and maternal roles.[43] As an example of the third approach, in 1975 the Education Group of the Newfoundland Status of Women Council had published a booklet of photographs and biographical sketches of women working in the prov-ince in a range of jobs not traditionally held by women, such as biologist deep sea diver, taxi driver, fisherwoman, surgeon, garbage collector, and lawyer.[44]

But by the second half of the 1980s, reliance on role models and role modelling had come under criticism for its tendency to individualize solutions to problems that are systemic. Catherine Overall critiqued the very concept of the role model for its implication that "the model herself is (artificially) playing a role," while her "real" self is hidden behind the assumed part. Also misleading, Overall argued, is the way that celebrat-ing the exceptional woman who has broken through patriarchal barriers to achieve success in a traditionally male dominated field can give "the impression that sexual inequality is at an end, or on its way out."[45] As

Jane Gaskell, Arlene McLaren, and Myra Novogrodsky point out, any remedial program that sets up a "deficit model" by focusing "on what is wrong with girls (or women, or minorities or poor families)" and ignores the larger social and political structures, serves to entrench the notion of the inferiority of girls or women, or minorities, or the poor. Their advice is to beware of approaches that set up successful white men as "the model of achievement," for then, in comparison, most women, members of racially oppressed minorities, and the poor will appear not to "measure up."[46] Still, we cannot rule out the possibly empowering effect of exposure to members of one's own social group who occupy leadership positions. The sight of a woman standing at a lectern or wearing the uniform of a firefighter may give a girl the sense of entitlement she needs. Certainly members of racially oppressed minorities lobby to have the teaching staffs in schools more closely reflect the racial composition of the classroom. The Organization of Parents of Black Children in Toronto, for instance, has expressed concern at the "lack of Black teachers as role-models in the system."[47] Here the need is also to have persons in positions of authority who understand what it is like to deal with racism on a daily basis, just a white women have felt a need to have women in positions of power who have a firsthand, everyday understanding of the workings of sexism.

In the textbooks for older grades, the problem was not so much sex-role stereotyping as the nearly total absence of women. Ignoring the dynamic interdependence of the public and the private spheres and granting historical or social or political significance only to "leaders" at the level of prime ministers and military generals, most texts in the social sciences — history, sociology, and political science — represented to female readers a world from which members of their sex were almost totally excluded. In some cases, this eclipsing of women would seem to have been the result of wilful ignorance.[48]

In other cases, however, women's near invisibility has been the result of the application of criteria of significance that ignore or undervalue women and women's activities. In field after field, feminists have exposed the sex bias (later called gender bias) in what passes for knowledge. These knowledges, feminists revealed, were by and large created by men for men, and most often by élite men for an audience of other élite men, that is, for men in positions of economic, political, social, and cultural power. In the creation of these knowledges, whether in the field of philosophy, economics, psychology, history, or sociology, man was the measure of things, men's experiences and men's interests the yardstick of significance. Neither sex bias nor gender bias seemed an adequate term. Feminists began to speak and write of the male-centredness, or androcentrism, and eventually phallocentrism of these knowledges. The male-centred character of the production, content, distribution, and preservation of these bodies of knowledge was astounding. Through vast stretches of learning and culture, women's experiences and perspectives were deeply subordinated or obliterated altogether. The examples are legion.

Continuing today in some political science, philosophy, and educational theory courses, the pre-French Revolution thinker Jean-Jacques Rousseau is routinely taught, while the political and educational theory of Mary Wollstonecraft, author of *The Vindication of the Rights of Woman* (1792), is ignored. In music composition and theory, attention is paid to Felix Mendelssohn but not to his sister Fanny Mendelssohn Hensel.[49] In English literature, Daniel Defoe's *Robinson Crusoe* has been traditionally celebrated as the first novel in the English language, while Aphra Behn's thirteen novels, written thirty years earlier, are rarely mentioned.[50] Nor is it common to include one of Aphra Behn's seventeen plays, all of which were produced during her lifetime, in courses on Restoration Drama.[51] Even in Marxist economics and political science, Karl Marx, Friedrich Engels, and Vladimir Lenin are *de rigueur*, but Rosa Luxembourg seldom receives a passing remark.

As contemporary feminists delved into the past to uncover women's lost history, it was discovered that the exclusion of women happened in two phases. During their lifetimes, a few fortunate, determined, usually highly placed women may have succeeded in breaking through the obstacles to their participation in the culture and creation of knowledge in their day. But after their deaths, the custodians of knowledge and culture, almost universally male — that is, the editors of and contributors to encyclopaedias, the compilers of dictionaries of national biography, the keepers of the repositories of documents and artifacts, the writers of the historical accounts — tended to let such exceptional women drop out of the record. Or they tended to record the achievements of such women while representing their personal characters in disparaging terms.[52] Male centredness seemed an insufficient explanation for women's near disappearance from, or disfigured representation within, the cultural historical record. The term "patriarchy" was appropriated to convey the systemic barriers to women's contributions to knowledge creation during their lifetimes and the systemic exclusions of women from the cultural record after their deaths. In the production and preservation of knowledge and culture, feminists argued, there were deeply entrenched structures operating to ensure male dominance. The term "misogyny" provided a framework for comprehending the extent to which hostility or mistrust of women seeped into the few recorded accounts of exceptional women, presenting them as tarts, twisted spinsters, or shrews.

Among the suppressions feminists discovered was a long tradition of feminist and proto-feminist social and cultural criticism, and, in the nineteenth and twentieth centuries, organized feminism. Formal education in history, philosophy, political science, and literature did not inform girls or young women of this long feminist tradition. White feminists of the 1970s and 1980s discovered they had foremothers, who in their time and place had grappled with many of the same issues that their contemporary feminist descendants were raising. Second-wave white feminists were amazed to learn, for instance, that as recently as 1942, the historian and social critic Mary Ritter Beard had critiqued the *Encyclopaedia Britannica* for its androcentric bias. She had questioned the objectivity of the decision of the compilers of the prestigious compendium of knowledge to include an entry on pig sticking, a locally specific but male activity, while omitting one on bread making, a much more widespread but usually female activity.[53] Like Virginia Woolf in her reclaimed 1929 classic *A Room of One's Own*,[54] white, middle-class feminists were amazed to discover how many learned tomes had been written on "woman" by men who presented women as their mental, moral, and physical inferiors. But sadly, white feminists' rediscovery of a white feminist tradition perpetrated similar suppressions and distortions.

An enormous outpouring of books and articles has resulted from the scholarly efforts of feminists, placed within and outside the academy, to redress these wrongs and set the record straight. For example, sociologist Dorothy Smith critiqued the processes of knowledge construction in mainstream sociology that marginalized women's lives. She wrote of the need to have a sociology for women that started from women's experience.[55] Aided in part by the recentness of the founding and development of their professional society,[56] women sociologists and anthropologists have made notable gains in the last twenty-five years. According to sociologist Margrit Eichler, female participation in the annual meetings of the Canadian Sociology and Anthropology Association (CSAA) "has been steadily increasing from around 11 per cent in the first five years (1965–1969) to around 42 per cent" in the years 1985 to 1989.[57] In the field of psychology, Paula Caplan has addressed and contested some of the common psychological theories that are disparaging of women. In the *The Myth of Women's Masochism*, Caplan refutes the Freudian association of masochism with females and femininity;[58] and in *Don't Blame Mother: Mending the Mother-Daughter Relationship*, Caplan takes issue with the all-too-frequent psychotherapeutic tendency to mother blame.[59]

Countless feminist historians have been actively engaged in the project of restoring women to history and history to women. A sense of one's own history is a crucial component of one's sense of identity, feminist women's historians have maintained. And conventional history in the main deprived women of that important component of identity formation. Even so-called "women worthies," women such as Nellie McClung, Flora MacDonald Denison, and Thérèse Casgrain, needed to be unearthed and examined in terms of what their lives revealed about the societies in which they lived. Unfortunately, the first books and articles reclaiming Canadian women pioneers and women's rights activists overlooked or gave no more than passing mention to Black women trail blazers such as Mary Ann Shadd Cary. Yet, as well as being an abolitionist, Shadd Cary was the first woman publisher and editor of a Canadian newspaper (the *Provincial Freeman* between 1853 and 1859) and one of the earliest Canadian women to write articles on women's rights.[60]

Through arduous digging in the archives or the collection of oral histories, feminist historians uncovered the contributions women had made to the development of the Canadian economy, state, and society. For example, Sylvia Van Kirk restored women, in particular aboriginal women, to the history of the Western Canadian fur trade;[61] Joan Sangster restored women to the history of the Canadian left;[62] Marjorie Griffin Cohen restored women to the economic development of nineteenth-century Ontario;[63] Lynne Marks restored working-class women to the history of the Salvation Army;[64] and I restored women to Canada's history of the Second World War.[65] The everyday lives of ordinary women, consigned to oblivion by the histories of "high" politics and macro-economics, were recovered and given voice in the words of the women themselves, as in Eliane Leslau Silverman's *The Last Best West: Women on the Alberta Frontier 1880–1930,*[66] Margaret Conrad's, Toni Laidlaw's, and Donna Smyth's *No Place Like Home: Diaries and Letters of Nova Scotia Women 1771–1938,*[67] and Dionne Brand's *No Burden to Carry: Narratives of Black Working Women in Ontario 1920s to 1950s.*[68]

By granting importance to women's experiences and women's perspectives, this rewriting of history, as in the rewriting of sociology and the other social sciences, involved a rethinking of the criteria of significance. For instance, the politics of birth control and human reproduction[69] and likewise the politics of rape and heterosexual conflict[70] were deemed as worthy of historical study as the politics of parliamentary elections and military strategy. Similarly, significance was granted to the everyday activities of ordinary women — working informally to survive in cities,[71] labouring in factories,[72] immigrating to a new land,[73] teaching in schools.[74]

In feminism's attempt to shift the paradigms, women came smack up against the sexism embedded in the gendered structures of language. Women face a different set of problems in every language. In English, the struggle has been to dislodge the masculine pronouns (he, his) and words with clearly masculine referents, such as man, mankind, and son, from their position as ostensible universals.[75] Feminists have argued that in formulations like "man is the measure of all things," "for all mankind," and "in all our sons command," the signifier signifies the male of the species, not all humans, humankind, or daughters as well as sons. Feminists have advocated the use of inclusive language in place of false universals. In the Canadian national anthem, for instance, the offending phrase "in all our sons command" could be reformulated simply as "in all of us command." The feminist contention is that the continued use of masculine forms as allegedly encompassing both men and women actually works to perpetuate not only women's exclusion but the symbolic subordination of the female to the male. But as Margrit Eichler has shown, not only is it sexist to use sex-specific language for generic purposes, as in the above examples, it is also sexist to use generic language for sex-specific purposes. Thus, to speak of the French Revolution as having granted universal suffrage, as many history books have done, is to obscure the fact that it was not universal but manhood suffrage from which women were excluded. At the same time, using generic terms such as "parents" to refer to those responsible for the care of small children, when in fact it is almost exclusively women to whom childcare is relegated, renders the work of mothers invisible.[76] Feminists have made some progress in our attempts to uproot sexism from language, but we have also met with obdurate resistance. A recent decision of the Vatican is a powerful example. As originally submitted, the English translation of th new universal catechism of the Roman Catholic Church employed gender-neutral language. But when the translation was officially unveiled in May 1994, the inclusive language had been scrapped and "humanity" was once again represented by "man."[77]

Women's Studies

Across the disciplines, the labour required to remedy the misrepresentations of women, to fill in the empty spaces, to give voice to the hitherto silent, and to rescue the forgotten from oblivion was and remains prodigious. The multifaceted and complex work of rediscovery, reclamation, reformulation, and rehabilitation helped give birth to the multidisciplinary field of women's studies. But its birth was also a response, in colleges and universities across Canada, to the demands voiced by women students, touched by feminism, for an education relevant to their lives. Frequently quoted by feminist students and faculty alike is the advice poet Adrienne Rich gave to a group of women university students in 1977:

> ... you cannot afford to think of being here to *receive* an education; you will do much better to think of yourselves as being here to *claim* one.[78]

Starting in the early 1970s, and often not without struggle, women in community colleges and universities across Canada began mounting courses on "Images of Women in Literature," "Women in History," and "Women in Sociology," as well as cross-disciplinary women's studies courses. The women's studies course Greta Hofmann Nemiroff helped organize at Montreal's Concordia University in 1970 might well have been the first one offered for credit in Canada.[79] Advocates often had a tough time establishing the legitimacy of such courses, as is clear from Helga E. Jacobson's 1973 account of "Organising Women's Studies at the University of British Columbia."[80] While hard to believe in the face of today's explosion of women's studies literature, curriculum materials had to be scrounged in those early days. Gradually women's studies programs gained academic approval: the one at the University of Toronto was founded in 1971;[81] the one at Simon Fraser University in British Columbia in 1975; and the one at the University of New Brunswick in 1986.[82] Mount St. Vincent University in Halifax introduced its first women's studies courses in 1973, a women's studies program in 1984, and a women's studies department in 1987.[83] Already in 1977, Centennial College hosted a Conference on Women's Studies in the Community Colleges.[84] And as early 1978, an article in *Branching Out* by Christa van Daele reported on threats to existing women's studies programs coming from budget cuts and pressures to meet "academic standards." The article also documents early cases of "burn out" among the women designing and offering the women's studies courses.[85] The massive innovation that the first women's studies courses and programs entailed was largely enacted by women graduate students and untenured and sessional faculty who, despite their insecure positions, took on the extra work out of enthusiastic commitment to the cause. This established a pattern that has persisted into the present: inadequate institutional support, above all inadequate staffing, for women's studies programs. A big debate developed, as the van Daele article indicates, over whether one should put one's efforts into the separatist approach of women's studies or into the attempt to integrate the new and rediscovered knowledge about and by women into existing courses, departments, and programs. That many feminist teachers tried to operate on both the separatist and the integrationist fronts also led to overextension and early burn out. But few white feminist faculty denied the value of a separate women's studies focus, program, or department. This institutionalization of women's studies, no matter how meagre, provided a place of refuge and a source of support for women faculty members who, isolated as the only women or only feminists in traditional and unregenerate departments, could not on their own have achieved the critical mass necessary to launch new courses or reform old ones.

Despite opposition and in the face of persistent institutional underfunding, women's studies has flourished and become institutionalized. The Canadian Women's Studies Association/Association canadienne des études sur les femmes (CWSA/ACEF) was founded in 1982 and quickly gained status as one of the Learned Societies.[86] Five federally-funded chairs in women's studies were established in 1985: one in the Atlantic provinces at Mount Saint Vincent University in Halifax; one in Quebec at Laval; one joint chair in Ontario at the University of Ottawa and Carleton University; one joint chair in the prairie region at the University of Manitoba and the University of Winnipeg; and one in British Columbia at Simon Fraser University. The massive Canadian women's studies research project co-ordinated by Margrit Eichler found that between forty-four and forty-six of the fifty-nine main universities examined had women's studies programs in 1988.[87] Project researchers located a total of 892 professors who identified themselves as having taught at least one women's/feminist studies course at the university level, including seventy-three persons no longer in the university system, 107 part-time lecturers, "as well as full-time and part-time professors who once taught but no longer teach women's/feminist studies courses."[88] In 1991, York University received approval from the Ontario Council of Graduate Studies for Canada's first Ph.D. program in women's studies, which was launched in January 1992.[89] But as Beth Westfall (now Davies) indicates, although Simon Fraser University in British Columbia and Athabasca University in Alberta offer women's studies courses by correspondence and Memorial University of Newfoundland "has offered women's studies through a combination of print, video and teleconferencing," on the whole universities and colleges have not made women's studies easily available or sufficiently relevant to rural women.[90] And as Martha Colquhoun's account from Manitoba indicates, women's studies in high schools have not fared very well.[91]

The revolution in knowledge, which the creation of women's studies represents, has led inevitably to the revolutionary act of attacking the "canon." Variously understood as a core curriculum or a list of great books that all educated persons should have read, the term canon itself carries connotations of the officially sanctioned if not of sanctity.[92] In the field of education, feminism has been at its most subversive in challenging the sacred, carved-in-stone character of the canon. These texts, when taken altogether, are thought to constitute "Western civilization." But as feminist scholarship has revealed, the selection ignores women's contributions to culture and women's perspectives on what is of importance. "When you read or hear about 'great issues,' 'major texts,' 'the mainstream of Western thought,' you are hearing about what men, above all white men, in their male subjectivity, have decided is important,"[93] Adrienne Rich warned her audience of women students in 1977. Compounding the injustice of their androcentricity, these canonical works, feminist analysts have argued, parade the élite male point of view as universally valid, as speaking for and to everyone. The canon is the repository of an élite culture that, generalizing from the experience of a very small group of men, has grandiosely claimed to identify what constitutes the essence of humanity. It has been the feminist determination to recover women's voices and perspectives that has exposed as fraudulent the canon's claim to be a collective history. As Elizabeth Fox-Genovese has written, "much of the revolt against the canon has been fuelled by the refusal to accept someone else's autobiography as our own, and by the insistence that — whatever the world may say — our own autobiography matters."[94]

But from a feminist perspective, even more serious than the silencing of women's voices and the obscuring of women's points of view is the harm the canon can do, if taught uncritically, to women's self-image and sense of identity. As Fox-Genovese has pointed out, many of the canonical texts carry strong "traces of the anxiety that informed these men's determination to keep women in their male-defined place."[95] The canonical tradition includes many texts that posit the idea that the arena for the exercise of the highest reason, the purest piety, the strongest minds, the greatest proximity to the divine is accessible only to men. For example, no matter how violently the heroes of the French Revolution disagreed amongst themselves, the principal leaders "agreed on the necessity of women's subservience to men"[96] and their absence from political decision-making. Freud depicted women, given the domesticated position to which civilization consigned them, as deficient in a sense of justice and as the natural, inescapable enemies of civilization.[97] The implicit or explicit conviction that women need to be kept subordinate crosses over frequently to misogynistic fear and hatred of women, as in Nietzsche's "go to women, but do not forget the whip."[98] Feminist educators have argued that such texts can have the same effect as psychological abuse when they are taught without gender analysis and historical contextualization — that is, when they are taught as repositories of the eternal verities. Taught uncritically, such texts can contribute to a continuum of conditions that encourage women "to feel inadequate to certain tasks, to feel powerless — to lack faith in themselves."[99]

The canon can also undermine self-esteem by racial silencings and racist disfigurings. Racist texts, taught without contextualization within the history of racisms, colonialisms, and imperialisms, can cause serious psychological pain. The extraordinary condemnation of their race and culture to which aboriginal girls and boys were exposed at residential schools, however, goes far beyond exclusion from or misrepresentation in the canon. Vicki Wilson, a founding member of the Aboriginal Women's Council of Saskatchewan, spoke at a conference in 1989 on being hauled off to such a school in the back of a truck. On the journey she and the other children were given no toilet breaks and had only a tarp over their heads to protect them from the rain. At the school they were beaten for speaking in their native tongue, especially to other members of their family. They were forced to accept an alien religion and told that their own was pagan and wrong.[100] Elizabeth Bear writes of the physical, emotional, and verbal abuse she had to endure repeatedly in the mission school she was forced to attend between 1958 and 1968.[101]

For a long time women's studies, dominated as it was by white, middle-class teachers and academics, tended to speak and write, as I have mostly done up to this point, of girls and women as undifferentiated categories. That is, the developing field of women's studies often concerned itself with gender in such a way as to obscure the inextricable intermeshing of gender with race, ethnicity, class, bodily ability, and sexual orientation. Indeed, white Western feminists, including white Euro-Canadian feminists, developed a feminist canon that privileged the writings and voices of élite white women just as the dominant canon privileged those of élite white men. Throughout most of the seventies,

dominant spokeswomen among white Western feminists
of gender oppression as receiving less of a hearing than
oppression; indeed, they saw a need for women to imitate t
and racially oppressed in demanding studies relevant to the
following passage from the oft-quoted Rich lecture to won
in 1977 on "Claiming an Education" makes this idea clear:

> Black and other minority peoples have for some time recognized
> that their racial and ethnic experience was not accounted for in the
> studies broadly labelled human; and that even the sciences can be
> racist. For many reasons, it has been more difficult for women to
> comprehend our exclusion, and to realize that even the sciences
> can be sexist.[102]

What this passage does not address is the fact that half of the "Black
and other minority peoples" are women.[103] It took over a decade or more
for the predominantly white women who struggled to develop the curriculum material, to secure approval for courses, and to launch the
women's studies programs to listen to and eventually hear the pained
voices of discontent of those girls and women who saw no representation
of their worlds of experience reflected in what we had put together.
Carmen Henry's account of the racism she experienced in a women's
studies course at a Canadian University in the late 1980s is only one of
many statements of sadness and rage addressed to white feminists that
"you had bypassed my whole story and made it only a footnote in your
texts."[104] The long-time and persistent exclusion of non-white women's
realities from women's studies courses is a sad commentary on the
difficulties persons suffering one kind of oppression have in recognizing
the oppression of others, particularly if they are complicit in that oppression. But as white women had clamoured at the gates of traditional
knowledge for inclusion of women and for attention to gender, so
women suffering oppressions along axes of sexual orientation, ethnicity,
race, disability, and class began to make their demands heard for voice
and fair representation in women's studies courses.

Among the first to demand and receive a hearing were white lesbians,
perhaps because their spokeswomen could often draw on advantages of
both race and class. In provinces and institutions where making one's
same-sex sexual orientation known was protected by human rights
codes, lesbian educators began to develop strategies for "coming out"
to pupils and students. Whether "out" or not, lesbian teachers also
worked out strategies for dealing with lesbian issues in women's studies
courses.[105] The gay and lesbian struggle to throw off societal stigmati-
zation and discrimination has gone hand and hand with a tremendous
flowering of lesbian creativity as well as recovery of "lesbian" voices
from the past.[106] Given how severely silenced women's same-sex experiences have been in written history, some lesbian writers have ingen-

iously combined archival research with imaginative recreation to fashion historical novels and short stories that evoke a past of women loving women.[107] Sociologist Madiha Didi Khayatt has researched how lesbian teachers managed to survive in the school systems of Ontario by "passing" as heterosexuals and by other means of accommodating the prevailing norms before the passage into law of Bill 7.[108] Towards the end of the 1980s, Sharon Stone, later joined by Gary Kinsman, Ellen Long, Steven Maynard, and Becki Ross, helped John Hunter develop lesbian/gay studies courses at Ryerson Polytechnical University in Toronto.[109]

Feminists of colour, particularly African Canadian feminists, have been at the forefront of the struggle against racism in education. It took six years between proposal and acceptance before "the first ever accredited university course on Black Women was offered in Canada" as part of the 1988–89 academic program at Concordia University's Simone de Beauvoir Institute: Esmeralda Thornhills' "Black Women: The Missing Pages from Canadian Women's Studies."[110] As a result of campaigns to overcome the invisibility of people of colour in Canadian scholarship, including feminist Canadian scholarship, some white feminist educators began revising course syllabi to incorporate studies by and about women outside the dominant racial and class groups. As a result of the anti-racist struggle of women of colour over access to resources for the production and dissemination of knowledge, particularly the publishing of books and periodicals, feminist journals and presses began to make space for the voices of women from other than the white majority. Readers can be introduced, for instance, to the experiences and perspectives of African-Caribbean-Canadian women through the poetry and prose of Dionne Brand, to the complex history of generations of women and men of Chinese descent in British Columbia through the Sky Lee's many-layered novel *Disappearing Moon Cafe,*[111] to the pain and triumphs and the spirit of resistance of First Nations peoples in the poems, short stories, and novels of Lee Maracle. Through reading this new outpouring of interviews, first-person accounts, poetry, short stories, novels, and sociological and historical research, white feminists could learn about the oppression suffered by women whose sisterhood had only too often been asserted in theory and denied in practice. Perhaps more important, readers could learn about the achievements of women from racially oppressed groups and about their immense strength, courage, and dignity in the face of systemic racism. In an interviw published in the academic periodical *Resources for Feminist Research,* four young refugee and immigrant women of colour speak of the racism endemic in Canadian officialdom, media, and classrooms.[112]

But the remedial steps taken by white feminist educators have been halting. White feminists have criticized male academics for failing to incorporate gender as a category of analysis and resting satisfied with devoting at most one week or one session of their courses to women.

TO GAIN PERSPECTIVE ON WOMEN'S PLACE
IN HISTORY WE MUST FIRST LOOK
<u>EXTENSIVELY</u> AT MEN IN HISTORY. THEN,
IN MARCH...

But not infrequently, white feminist teachers have done precisely the same thing, preserving the dominance of white women's reality by assigning at best only one week or one session to issues of racial or cultural difference. As Linda Carty has argued, a women's studies that does not address the relation of white feminism to racism and imperialism, that does not critique Eurocentrism in Canadian feminism, has become part of the problem insofar as "it does not engage the real problematic of race, power, and subjugation."[113]

In a society in which Black male youths run a considerably greater risk of being arrested or even shot and killed by police than white male youths, mothers of Black children are understandably deeply concerned by the perpetuation of racist images and the absence of positive images of Black people in school texts. Though Carty and others have exhorted, "white feminists can and should teach race,"[114] it has been women of African descent who have led the struggle to introduce education in the schools that is anti-racist as well as being anti-sexist. Enid Lee developed the widely used *Letters to Marcia: A Teacher's Guide to Anti-Racist Education*;[115] Dionne Brand co-authored *Rivers Have Sources, Trees Have Roots*, an oral record of people's experiences with racism in Canada;[116] and Makeda Silvera put together *Growing Up Black: A Resource Manual for Black Youth* with chapters on, among other topics, "Career Planning" and "Sexuality."[117] A chapter on "Your Rights as a Black Youth" has advice on how to be not passive or aggressive but firmly and respectfully assertive when stopped by the police on a false charge of car theft.

Feminist Pedagogy

Many feminist educators were not content with changing curriculum content. Inspired by a resurgent feminism, they were committed to changing the very methods of teaching and learning in the classroom. The term "feminist pedagogy" began to be bandied about in higher education, and those of us who regarded ourselves as feminists tried to introduce a feminist ethos into our university classrooms. Because feminism addresses social injustice and works for progressive social change, feminist pedagogy joined the ranks of other liberatory pedagogies.[118]

Those of us who were feminist teachers, often privileged by race and class, assumed we could revolutionize the classroom environment by abiding by some of the salient principles of second-wave white feminism. For example, building on the feminist axiom "the personal is political," feminist teachers encouraged students to bring their own experience into the classroom. Attempts were made to translate the early movement's emphasis on non-hierarchical organizing and the bonds of sisterhood into pedagogical practice. We sought to reduce if not eliminate the distance between teacher and student, particularly woman teacher and woman student, and thus achieve a sisterly and non-hierarchical egalitarianism. The thinking went: if we treat students like equals, they will be equals. Another tenet of second-wave feminism that exercised considerable sway was the cultural feminist celebration of a women's specificity. The hallmark of this female specificity was maternal nurturance associated with women's reproductive capacity and the fate of most women to be mothers. In their role as university professors as well as elementary school teachers, many women believed they should treat their pupils and students, especially the girls and young women among them, with a maternally nurturant caring.

We soon found that an uncritical adherence to these principles was fraught with contradictions. Serious problems arose when these principles were applied with *naïveté* as well as with obliviousness to differences of class, race, and sexual preference. Reviewing the articles they selected for the 1992 *Canadian Journal of Education* special issue on feminist pedagogy, Briskin and Coulter found these problems to cluster under five thematic headings: nurturance, experience, safety, power, and resistance.

Nurturance: A set of maternalist assumptions, insufficiently critiqued, has continued to prevail in much thinking and writing on feminist pedagogy. As early as the mid-1980s, philosopher Kathryn Morgan gave the label "The Paradox of the Bearded Mother" to the contradictions facing the feminist teacher expected to provide nurturant support (indeed a form of unconditional love) to her symbolic daughters and at the same time offer critical evaluation and advice.[119] Casting female teachers as mothers not only undermines their authority as critical thinkers, but also, Kathleen Martindale argues, obscures the work of teaching, that is, the fact that the classroom is a workplace. Moreover it buys into the bourgeois (i.e., class specific) "fantasy of nurturing motherhood."[120]

Experience: As Briskin and Coulter remind us:

> Recovering, naming, and theorizing women's experience has been central to developing new knowledge, making the curriculum more relevant to women, and re-visioning research.[121]

Bluma Litner, Amy Rossiter, and Marilyn Taylor recommend encouraging students to narrate their experiences in the classroom and "affirming the commonality of experience between students and teachers."[122] But as others have pointed out, these practices can have the effect of insisting on commonality and thereby further marginalizing, silencing, or ostracizing the different. Moreover, as Sherene Razack has argued, the expectation that one should air one's own experiences in the public space of the classroom is an assumption rooted in privilege.[123] As she herself confesses, "I had [when a student], and still have, a very unfeminist lack of faith in experiential learning in classrooms where the imbalances so clearly increase the risks taken by minorities."[124] Meanwhile, as Ann Manicom discusses, the need felt by some women to "validate experience" and to claim women's experience as an unproblematic source of authentic knowledge is being challenged by feminist postmodern epistemologists who critique the unproblematized assertion that "women are the only 'authentic chroniclers' of their own experiences, that women are the best knowers of their world."[125] These critics remind us that our personal narratives "are threaded through with theory, with hegemonic discourse, and with dominant ideologies."[126]

Safety: The model of a nurturant feminist classroom fostered a belief in the ability of the feminist teacher to create a "safe" classroom. "Safety" was understood to mean that one could embark on politicizing the personal by speaking of it in class without suffering ridicule, condemnation, or any other adverse consequences. But all too often, the model of safety assumed homogeneity. Feeling safe for some students came to mean never having one's account or point of view disagreed with. To ensure such safety required the suppression of conflict and contradiction. In this way, safety was equated with comfort, particularly in the case of students disturbed by readings or comments that opened up their social privilege to critical examination. In other words, an education that challenged or questioned one's sense of well-being in the world rather than confirming it was regarded as "unsafe." Feminist teachers critical of comfort as an educational goal refer with approval to bell hooks's development of a more confrontational style of pedagogy.[127] At the same time, feminist teachers continue to try to make classrooms "safe" for discussion of topics, such as child sexual abuse, that might cause considerable pain to individual class members by giving them the option, for instance, of absenting themselves from class when that topic is on the agenda and doing a written assignment instead.[128]

Power: All of the trouble sites in feminist pedagogy are riddled with questions of power. Feminist teachers soon learned the *naïveté* of assuming we could create, in the feminist classroom, an egalitarian oasis within the hierarchical structures of the educational system. To not deny but openly acknowledge the power differentials between students and teachers has been recognized as a more realistic approach. Power, as Martindale succinctly puts it, "can't be wished away."[129] But while women teachers have sometimes had difficulty conceding the power invested in their position, they have also encountered challenges when they have claimed the power of authority and expertise. Particularly in higher education, this power is more easily granted to men than to women teachers. The problem is often exacerbated when the university teacher is a racial minority woman. For Homa Hoodfar, it is not as a mother but as an Iranian Muslim woman who is critical of many anthropological and feminist approaches to so-called Third World women that her authority and knowledge are easily questioned. As Hoodfar has explained:

My acknowledging the inequalities in power relations between students and teachers is seen not as an attempt to point out institutionalized inequalities but as my not being confident as a teacher or as compensation for my lack of knowledge.[130]

Roxana Ng, who identifies herself as "a feminist and member of a racial minority," has analyzed "how gender and race relations interact to undermine the authority and credibility of minority faculty members."[131] Ng arrives at the conclusion that the criticisms made of her teaching have had less to do with her competence as a teacher than with who she is. Meanwhile, the power exercised by students in the classroom and the power relations between and among students have been largely ignored by feminist pedagogical theorists, to the detriment of women teachers. The teacher is not solely responsible for the power dynamics in the classroom or capable of eliminating the differentials in power and privilege that students bring there. Further complicating the power dynamics are the psychosexual dynamics often at play at subliminal levels, between teachers and students and between and among students. These areas of pedagogy are desperately in need of more study.

Resistance: Feminist teachers have for a long time confronted the problem of the resistance to feminist perspectives that comes from not only male but also female students. But some of that is a class- and race-specific resistance, in the words of Dawn H. Currie, "to the domination of feminism by privileged women." Certainly, student challenges and protests do not, Currie concedes, "make feminist teaching easy." But, she astutely observes, they provide at least one answer to "the neglected question 'who shall educate the educators?'"[132] Like the mainstream women's movement in general,[133] women's studies and feminist pedagogy in Canada have shown considerable resistance to addressing the issue of difference. In 1991, Linda Carty wrote that the systematic exclusion of women of colour in women's studies courses across the country, "even when they may be physically present in the classroom," had the devastating effect of negating their existence. Paraphrasing Audre Lorde's "It is axiomatic that if we do not define ourselves we will be defined by others for their use and to our detriment," Annette Henry argues in 1993 with respect to all levels of schooling that "at this critical time in Canadian race relations, [the necessity for] Black self-representation is axiomatic."[134] That the curriculum of women's studies courses and the priorities of feminist teachers are beginning to change is a sign of progress. Some white feminist teachers have begun to develop "anti-racist feminist pedagogy."[135] But as Razack argues, until feminism addresses institutional racism and campaigns to make "the faculty and the student population ... both more racially diverse than they are currently," the problems of exclusion, tokenism, misappropriation, and misrepresentation will remain.[136] Similarly, Mary Bryson and Suzanne de Castell write of the deeply embedded resistances to opening the classroom to a diversity of sexual identities. In a women's stuies course they co-taught, they implemented "queer pedagogy," described as "a radical form of educative praxis" designed to interrupt the production of white heterosexual dominance as "normal." But at the end of the day, they still found subordinate identities remained marginal, and "lesbian identity," in particular, remained fixed and monolithic.[137]

Job Training/Language Training

While those enjoying the middle-class privilege of higher education have concentrated on issues of theory and pedagogy, other women have focused on overcoming discrimination against women in vocational education and training. The issue of girls and women's access to job training has been one of decisive importance to the women's movement goal of greater economic independence and equality for women. As Nancy Jackson has written,

> Patterns of education and training in the twentieth century have channelled women into a narrow range of occupations in the service, clerical and public sectors, while creating barriers to entry in the vast majority of industrial occupations where males predominate.[138]

Barriers to training were and are a bread-and-butter, often near life-and-death issue, because non-access to training is part of the pattern of women's ghettoization in low-paying, low-status female-typed jobs. Non-access to re-training or upgrading acts as a barrier to re-entry into the paid labour market for older women. Non-access to language as well as job training contributes to immigrant women's vulnerability to exploitation.

Throughout second-wave feminism, the blatant discrimination against women in employment-oriented courses has been the target of feminist advocacy and activism. With the acceleration of women's activism, community, provincial, and national organizations have emerged to tackle these problems. Federal training initiatives have frequently been the object of criticism and human rights complaints. Feminist critics have argued not only that women get a smaller slice of the training pie, but that the training offered women is often limited to courses sex-typed female. For instance, in 1982, the Montreal-based Action Travail des Femmes filed a complaint before the Canadian Human Rights Commission against the Minister of Employment and Immigration, accusing the Canada Employment and Immigration Commission (CEIC) "of training policies which operate to exclude women from training courses which have been, and still are, reserved for men." Their brief itemized the obstacles placed by CEIC in the path of women seeking access to trades training, such as welding courses: that is, systematic discouragement by counsellors from registering in such courses, and the scheduling of the courses at night when it would be most difficult for women with family responsibilities to attend.[139]

The Canadian Congress for Learning Opportunities for Women began in 1972 as an ad hoc committee of the Canadian Association of Adult Education (CAAE). The idea was

to form a small national committee that would facilitate communications between women across the country concerned about women's educational needs and provide support to women developing programs for women.[140]

Members researched the learning needs of women. The resulting report by Janet Willis was a turning point culminating in the Banff, 1979, decision to leave the shelter of the CAAE and found the Canadian Congress for Learning Opportunities for Women/Congrès canadien pour la promotion des études chez la femme (CCLOW/CCPEF). As its name signals, CCLOW/CCPEF aims to increase women's life-long ability to acquire new knowledge and skills. Working within a broad understanding of its educational mission, CCLOW/CCPEF has promoted research into, and conferences on, all kinds of women's learning activities. To fulfil its aims, CCLOW/CCPEF functions by means of networks. Individual members and member organizations support local networks which come together to form a larger network in every province and territory. Each provincial and territorial network sends its co-ordinator to serve on the board of directors, the national network. These networks function to implement programs, to lobby governments and institutions to increase women's learning opportunities, and for the purpose of sharing information about, and assessments of, educational programs and lobbying efforts.

From the beginning, a major focus of CCLOW/CCPEF's activities has been on extending the scope of the vocational and skills training available for women. CCLOW/CCPEF is acutely conscious of the extent to which women are frequently ineligible for federal job training initiatives because they cannot satisfy the criteria. Experienced adult educators in CCLOW/CCPEF were aware of the special difficulties mature women face when seeking to re-enter the paid labour force. While these women have acquired considerable life experience, they may lack confidence because of a lack of recent school or work experience. CCLOW/CCPEF members are also acutely aware of the extent to which the lack of child care acts as a barrier to women learners.[141] In 1983/84, CCLOW/CCPEF carried out a research project to determine the impact of the 1982 National Training Act on women's access to training. The research showed that, throughout Canada, both the number of women trainees and the proportion of women trainees had declined in all areas of institutional and industrial training.[142] One of CCLOW/CCPEF's principal recommendations resulting from the study was:

> That bridging programs be established — i.e., programs that take women from where they are now to where they need to be to access training programs, e.g., re-entry programs, pre-trades, pre-tech, ABE (Adult Basic Education) programs, and that support services for women be established to compliment these programs, i.e., child care, part-time programmes, supportive counselling, etc.[143]

In 1983 CCLOW Regina developed and in 1985 implemented, in conjunction with the Regina Plains Community College, the Bridging Program for Women. Open to all women, it was "particularly committed to serving":

- women with disabilities
- native women
- women re-entering the workforce
- women whose jobs are disappearing because of technological change
- young women who have not yet joined the workforce[144]

In 1987, CCLOW Newfoundland, in association with the St. John's branch of the provincial Association for Adult Education, initiated the bridging program WISE (Women Interested in Successful Employment). Like Regina's Bridging Program for Women, the WISE program aimed to allow "women to develop personal awareness, upgrade academic skills, explore a wide range of occupational choices, and establish realistic, long-term goals for themselves" and sought to remove barriers to women's participation by providing "financial assistance equal to the provincial minimum wage rate, financial support for child care, and transportation services for children (and participants when possible)." Two years into the program, WISE participants testified to the importance of such a program to their lives.[145] In the winter 1993/94 issue of CCLOW/CCPEF's quarterly *Women's Education des femmes*, current Executive Director Aisla Thomson expressed outrage at the fact the Regina Bridging Program for Women, the demonstration project developed by CCLOW in 1983, had, in 1993, been opened to men on unemployment insurance benefits.[146]

Since its research on the results of the National Training Act of 1982, as government job training initiatives have come and gone, CCLOW/CCPEF has continued to monitor the training situation for women. CCLOW/CCPEF supported the brief presented to federal cabinet ministers in 1985 by thirty-seven women representing forty immigrant and visible minority women's groups across Canada. They spoke for "the most disadvantaged immigrant women" in Canada and drew connections between their lack of fluency in English or French and the fact that, as compared with one-fifth of Canadian-born women,

> one-third of immigrant women work in the non-unionized under-belly of the labour market where they toil as chamber maids, building cleaners, domestics, waitresses, sewing machine operators and so on.[147]

Their first four recommendations concerned language training. The very first was for immigrant women's increased access to adequate training in English or French as a second language (ESL – FSL). The second was for language training in the workplace, the third for language training at the community level for immigrant women who lack literacy skills, and the fourth was for increased access to language training for immigrant women at home either by providing daycare or increasing the delivery of language training by radio and television. Recommendations six through nine concerned access to job training and recognition of training and degrees from other countries.[148]

But when the federal government introduced the new Canadian Jobs Strategy (CJS) at the end of June 1985, the executive director of CCLOW/CCPEF at the time, Susan McCrae Vander Voet, wrote that there was no indication in the new job creation program that women would "receive a proportion of training funds comparable to our numbers in the workforce."[149] She could see only one of the six program areas as potentially beneficial to women, the re-entry portion of the Job Entry program. A major thrust of the CJS was to promote the involvement of employers in training. As Terry Dance, chairperson of the Community Outreach Department at George Brown College in Toronto, and Susan Witter, associate dean of Continuing and Developmental Education at Fraser Valley College in British Columbia, forcefully demonstrated in 1988, "privatization of training as a systemic trend" was "detrimental to women." Particularly to undereducated women who had hardly any opportunity to receive "employer-sponsored training."[150]

Indeed, workplace apprenticeship programs can disadvantage women in a variety of ways. First, female-typed trades, such as hairdressing, make up but a tiny percentage of total apprenticeships available. Second, training programs like Ontario's Women in Trades, Technology, and Operations have focused on channelling women into formerly male-typed trades such as those of plumber, carpenter, and electrician that are disappearing in the "new economic order." Third, harassment is a serious problem. The climate in many male-dominated places of work and training is extremely hostile to women, particularly in a recessionary period when they are seen as taking "men's" jobs. Moreover, an apprenticeship, by definition, only exists if an employer is willing to take on a person to be trained. There is thus a basic power imbalance between the employer who has condescended to offer training and the trainee who brings nothing to the relationship but her/his raw potential and willingness to learn. That power imbalance is further tilted in favour of the employer, who is usually white and male, when the apprentice is a woman, who might also be a member of a racially oppressed minority group. Fourth, systemic barriers are erected against many immigrant women. Among these are eligibility requirements that demand equivalency in education where such education was not available in the woman's home country and when "bridging" programs are not available in Canada.[151]

Despite organized women's efforts, the training situation for women has not improved over the years. "We have witnessed the amount of dollars allocated to training decline steadily," Aisla Thomson's editorial in the Winter 1993/94 *Women's Education des femmes* laments. "We have protested the sharp decrease in the number of women receiving training, literacy instruction, and upgrading."[152] But as Pat Armstrong reminded women at a workshop organized by the Centre for Research on Work and Society at York University in the summer of 1993, in a series of questions and answers she devised to test one's "knowledge of the connections between training, education and employment for women," education and training are not a cure-all for rising unemployment.[153]

Community Outreach

The efforts of feminists to educate the public on issues of importance to women are far too numerous to list, but here are a few examples. Much educational work has been done to bring the issue of violence against women before the public as a serious social concern to the entire nation. But women have not been content to leave it at that. Action has been taken to educate women on how to defend ourselves against violent sexist attack. Nadya Burton, of the Montreal Assault Prevention Centre, writes of teaching and learning self-defence as an important corollary to counselling for rape, assault, and incest survivors. She also understands education in assault prevention as an effective means of moving from "the notion of women as powerless victims" to seeing women as capable of taking power and inventing "new ways of using power to protect ourselves."[154]

In the case of lesbophobia, lesbians have exerted great effort to educate the heterosexual world about heterosexism, homophobia, and the rights of homosexuals. For example, feeling under specially strong homophobic attack as the result of an appearance by Ken Campbell in Northern Ontario in 1986, members of the recently founded Pink Triangle North in Timmins circulated a flyer seeking support for gays and lesbians. The unprecedented attack on homosexuals in their area gave rise to the "enormous need" for the creation of their group, whose main purpose, members saw, was to be educational. "We have a long battle

CREDIT: John Mahoney   COURTESY: *The Montreal Gazette*

Ethel Ingham (left) and Elizabeth Adam (centre) practise self-defence techniques with instructor Patricia Kearns at ContActivity, a social group for seniors in Montreal. The course was one of many offered by the Montreal Assault Prevention Centre during International Women's Week in 1991.

ahead in educating the public about equality and rights of Gays/Lesbians," the flyer explained.[155] This educational work has been taken up by the Lesbian Issues Committee of the National Action Committee on the Status of Women (NAC). It has prepared a flyer designed to teach heterosexual feminists how to support lesbian feminists.[156] The flyer's message takes as axiomatic the notion developed by lesbian feminists that heterosexual feminists need to recognize their own sexuality as a matter of social conditioning and choice and as conferring social privilege.

Lesbian feminists have been joined by feminists with disabilities and feminists of colour in the project of educating their more privileged sisters. The DisAbled Women's Network (DAWN) has produced a series of fact sheets to inform able-bodied women about ableism and the extraordinary difficulties differently-abled women face in a range of situations, including in the women's movement itself.[157] Anti-racist educational work, as in the contributions by Himani Bannerji and Linda Carty to *Unsettling Relations: The University as a Site of Feminist Struggles*,[158] has recently been put on the agenda of the National Action

ANTI-RACISM

The women of colour within the executive of NAC wrote this short guide in response to the expressed need for a brief summary for activists on how to raise their consciousness of and complement their education in anti-racism organizational change.

WHAT IS RACISM?

- It is a way in which power is distributed and exercised in society (as in organizations, for example);

- where such power maintains and promotes the values of the dominant group (such as white European);

- and such power is based on race, culture, language, colour of skin and other physical features, that belong to the dominant groups.

- "...The ideas or actions of a person, the goals or practices of an institution and the symbols, myths or structure of a society are racist if (a) imaginary or real differences of race are accentuated; (b) these differences are assumed and considered in terms of superior, inferior; and (c) these are used to justify inequity, exclusion or domination." (Franz Fanon)

WHAT IS ANTI-RACISM?

- anti-racism is an active process of identifying and eliminating racism by changing systems, organizational structures, policies and practices and attitudes, so that power is redistributed and shared equitably.

HOW CAN WE MAKE ANTI-RACISM ORGANIZATIONAL CHANGE IN NAC?

Anti-racism organizational change seeks to eliminate racist systems and values by deliberately making changes to advance equality through:

- the composition of the membership and leadership;

- the organizational policies and processes;

- staff hiring and administration practices;

- outreach and mobilization;

- work styles;

- individual behaviors and attitudes, etc.

HOW CAN CHANGE IN SYSTEMS, STRUCTURES, ORGANIZATIONS BE BROUGHT ABOUT?

- through affirmative action in leadership positions, in hiring practices, in appointments;

- through changes in policies and policy implementation that recognize and address racism, and that respect and value diverse racial and cultural experiences;

- through the integration of an anti-racism perspective in all aspects of an organization's plans, activities, outreach, etc.;

- through continuing anti-racism education.

Anti-racism education is as important as non-sexist education to promote equality among all women. Anti-racist awareness can come from anti-racist curricula as well as grassroots materials such as this poster produced by NAC.

▼▼▼▼▼▼▼▼▼▼▼▼▼▼▼▼▼▼▼▼▼▼▼▼▼▼▼

NATIONAL ACTION COMMITTEE ON THE STATUS OF WOMEN
Annual General Meeting, June 10-13, 1994

ANTI-RACISM ORGANIZATIONAL CHANGE ...

- is threatening

- is taking risks

- is challenging

- is a continuing struggle!

- anti-racism questions and shatters myths, stereotypes and attitudes.

▼▼▼▼▼▼▼▼▼▼▼▼▼▼▼▼▼▼▼▼▼▼▼▼▼

AVOID	REPLACE WITH
1. **Guilt and self-blame:** "I want to apologize for my ancestors", "I wish I could change history"	An acknowledgement of your privilege and a resolve to learn more about racism. Start questioning your assumptions
2. **Referring to other forms of oppression,** lesbophobia or ableism, as a means of avoiding dealing with racism or trivializing it.	An understanding of racism, lesbophobia, ableism, of their interconnectedness, of how they compound each other, and of how they are different from one another.
3. **Denial and self-justification:** "If what I said was racist, that was not my intention".	Listening to what has been named as racist, and being honest about your reaction, and about what and how you were thinking. Realizing that the impact of racism cannot be denied.
4. **Silence or avoiding the issue:** "I would rather not say anything, because I will be accused of being racist"	Open and honest discussion, in order to put issues on the table and learn. Confronting the issue is better than letting it fester.
5. **Compartmentalization:** "Our organization is dealing with racism, we have an anti-racism committee"	Integrating anti-racism into all processes of thinking and acting within the organization and on a personal level.
6. **Being patronizing:** "I am sorry you feel offended by my comments" or "The one thing you can say about this organization is that we are very tolerant."	"I am sorry I offended you" shows you are taking responsibility for a racist comment or action. Tolerance is not based on equality but in fact on, unequal relations.
7. **Generalizations:** Assuming that there are no class or political and work style differences among women of colour.	Understanding that these differences exist among women.
8. **Tokenism:** For example, including a woman of colour as a member of a work committee, but not expecting her to work, or to have any say in the process and decisions.	Genuine participation and readiness to change traditional ways of working.

▲▲▲▲▲▲▲▲▲▲▲▲▲▲▲▲▲▲▲▲▲▲▲▲▲▲▲

design, layout and typesetting by ARTCETERA

Committee on the Status of Women. Women of colour on the NAC executive developed a flyer on anti-racism. Their aim was to set out, as briefly and concisely as possible, what racism and anti-racism are and how changes to promote anti-racism in systems, structures, and organizations, including NAC, can be brought about. The flyer was approved by the entire NAC Executive Committee and distributed to all members attending the 1994 Annual General Meeting.[159]

And one final example comes from the Canadian Research Institute for the Advancement of Women (CRIAW). In the spring of 1994, CRIAW received funding from Multiculturalism and Citizenship Canada to document how "organizational structures," including CRIAW's own, "can facilitate or hinder inclusiveness and diversity."[160] The project, which will result in the production of a handbook, embodies the tri-partite mandate of CRIAW, set out in its statement of purpose shortly after its founding in April 1976: (1 — research) to promote and itself carry out research on women's experience; (2 — policy) to ensure that policy affecting women be based on sound research; and (3 — education) to make the results of sound research on women as widely available as possible. But the project also embodies the new commitment on the part of CRIAW to link feminism with anti-racism. But the struggle to join anti-racism to the mainstream feminist movement is not easy. As Monica Goulet indicated in her banquet speech at the fall 1993 CRIAW Conference in St. John's, Newfoundland, she knew that her election as an aboriginal woman to the presidency of an organization sometimes criticized as "white elitist" had not occurred without protest.[161] In her message to CRIAW members in the Summer 1994 *Newsletter*, Goulet stressed her conviction that:

Strengthening the links between anti-racism and feminism is a development which can only make the women's movement more dynamic and unified.[162]

However, by September 1994, Goulet felt compelled to resign as CRIAW president in the face of the continuing reluctance on the part of some staff and board members to address the racism inherent in resistance to inclusion.[163] Despite her resignation, Goulet takes hope from the increasing numbers of aboriginal women, women of colour, Black women, minority women, and white women who are willing to challenge the inequalities in the women's movement.[164] Clearly, as this chapter has demonstrated, "strengthening the links between anti-racism and feminism" is the only path which can lead toward realization of the liberating and transformative vision originally embraced by the creators of women's studies and the advocates of feminist pedagogy.

NOTES

1. Linda Briskin and Rebecca Priegert Coulter, "Feminist Pedagogy: Challenging the Normative," Introduction to the Special Issue on Feminist Pedagogy, *Canadian Journal of Education* 17, no. 3 (Summer 1992), 249.
2. Canada, The Royal Commission on the Status of Women in Canada, *Report* (Ottawa: Information Canada, 1970), 168. Women garnered 21.4 per cent of the total master degrees and licences granted in 1930–31 and 15.2 per cent of the total doctorates earned in that academic year. In 1966–67, women received 20.6 per cent of the master degrees and licences and a mere 7.6 per cent of the doctorates. Ibid., 170.
3. See Avebury Research and Consulting Ltd., "The Status of Women Teachers in Ontario High Schools," *Women's Education des femmes* 4, no. 4 (Summer 1986), 34–37, excerpted in the documents section of this chapter.
4. Sandra Gaskell, "The Problems and Professionalism of Women Elementary Public School Teachers in Ontario: 1944–1954" (Ed.D. thesis, University of Toronto, 1989).
5. Ruth Rees, *Women and Men in Education: A National Survey of Gender Distribution in School Systems* (Toronto: Canadian Education Association, 1990), 90.
6. Information provided by Tara Kingswood of the Association of Universities and Colleges of Canada, 27 June 1994.
7. Edward Harvey, "Accessibility to Post-secondary Education — Some Gains, Some Losses," *University Affairs*, October 1977, 10, reproduced in the documents section of this chapter. Copy at the Women's Educational Resource Centre at OISE (hereafter WERC).
8. Statistics Canada data obtained from Tara Kingswood of the Association of Universities and Colleges of Canada, FAX of 16 June 1994.
9. Ibid.
10. Canada, Department of Justice, Research and Development Directorate, "Survey of Students at Ten Law Schools in Canada," working paper, prepared by Colin Meredith, with the assistance of Chantal Paquette, March 1992, vi, 8.
11. See, *inter alia*, Association of Universities and Colleges of Canada/Association des Universités et Colleges du Canada, "Despite Gains, Women Still Under-Represented in Engineering and Applied Sciences," *communiqué*, 22 February 1990, reproduced in the documents section of this chapter.
12. For a discussion of the Montreal Massacre, see Ruth Roach Pierson, "The Politics of the Body," chap. 2 in Ruth Roach Pierson, Marjorie Griffin Cohen, Paula Bourne, and Philinda Masters, *Canadian Women's Issues,* Vol I: *Strong Voices* (Toronto: James Lorimer & Company, Publishers, 1993), 115, 168–172, and for graphic examples of the sort of misogyny that was not uncommon in engineering school publications, see the documents section of that chapter.
13. Data collected by Tara Kingswood of the Association of Universities and Colleges of Canada, FAX of 16 June 1994. The statistics are from Statistics Canada, Census Data, citing the Report of the National Advisory Board on Science and Technology entitled: "Winning with Women in Trades, Technology, Science and Engineering," January 1993, and made available by the Canadian Association for Women in Science.
14. Sandra Acker, "Women Academics in Britain and Canada," *Women's Education des femmes* 9, no. 3 (Spring 1992), 16–20.
15. Statistics Canada data obtained from Tara Kingswood of the Association of Universities and Colleges of Canada, FAX of 16 June 1994.
16. Data collected by Tara Kingswood of the Association of Universities and Colleges of Canada, FAX of 16 June 1994. The statistics are from Statistics Canada, Census Data, citing the Report of the National Advisory Board on Science and Technology entitled: "Winning with Women in Trades, Technology, Science and Engineering," January 1993, and made available by the Canadian Association for Women in Science.
17. Barbara Houston, "Should Public Education be Gender-free?," in Greta Nemiroff, ed., *Women and Men* (Fitzhenry and Whiteside, 1987), 136–139.
18. Elizabeth Sarah, Marion Scott, and Dale Spender, "The Education of Feminists: The Case for Single-Sex Schools," in Dale Spender and Elizabeth Sarah, eds., *Learning to Lose: Sexism and Education*, rev. ed. (London: The Women's Press, 1988), 58–61.
19. Sue Askew and Carol Ross, *Boys Don't Cry: Boys and Sexism in Education* (Milton Keynes, UK, Philadelphia: Open University Press, 1988), 27, drawing on R. Walden and V. Walkerdine, *Girls and Mathematics: From Primary to Secondary Schooling,* Bedford Way Papers, No. 24, (University of London, Institute of Education, 1985).

20. Linda Grant, "Race and the Schooling of Young Girls," in J. Wrigley, ed., *Education and Gender Equality* (London: Falmer Press, 1992), 91–113.

21. Roxana Ng, "'A Woman out of Control': Deconstructing Sexism and Racism in the University," *Canadian Journal of Education* 18, no. 3 (Summer 1993), 193.

22. For a discussion of gender regimes, see Sandra Kessler, Dean Ashenden, Bob Connell and Gary Dowsett, "Gender Relations in Secondary Schooling," in Madeleine Arnot and Gaby Weiner, eds., *Gender and the Politics of Schooling* (London: Hutchinson for the Open University, 1987), 223–236. For the reproduction of gender and class hierarchies, see Susan Russell, "The Hidden Curriculum of School: Reproducing Gender and Class Hierarchies," in Roberta Hamilton and Michèle Barrett, eds., *The Politics of Diversity* (London: Book Centre Inc., 1986), 343–360.

23. Helen Lenskyj, *Out of Bounds: Women, Sport & Sexuality* (Toronto: Women's Press, 1986).

24. Mary Field Belecky, Blythe McVicker Clinchy, Nancy Rule Goldberger, and Jill Mattuck Tarule, *Women's Ways of Knowing: The Development of Self, Voice, and Mind* (New York: Basic Books, 1986).

25. Anne-Louise Brookes, *Feminist Pedagogy: An Autobiographical Approach* (Halifax: Fernwood Publishing, 1992).

26. The term was coined by Roberta M. Hall and Bernice R. Sandler, *The Classroom Climate: A Chilly One for Women?* (Washington, D.C.: Project on the Status and Education of Women, Association of American Colleges, 1982).

27. See Ruth Roach Pierson, "The Politics of the Body," chap. 2 in Pierson, Cohen, Bourne, and Masters, *Canadian Women's Issues*, Vol. I: *Strong Voices*, 115, 168–169.

28. Jan Ferguson, "Alice in the Laboratory," Science Council of Canada, *Bulletin of Science Education*, June 1981, 4, reprinted in the documents section of this chapter. Copy at WERC.

29. Sheila Tobias, *Overcoming Math Anxiety* (Boston: Houghton Mifflin Company, 1978).

30. Sheila Tobias, "Right- and Wrongheadedness: Is There a Nonmathematical Mind?," chap. 4 in *Overcoming Math Anxiety*, 101–127.

31. In one study, "even third-grade children perceive math to be in the male domain." Sally L. Boswell, "The Influence of Sex-Role Stereotyping on Women's Attitudes and Achievement in Mathematics," in Susan F. Chipman, Lorelei R. Brush, and Donna M. Wilson, eds., *Women and Mathematics: Balancing the Equation* (Hillsdale, NJ, and London: Lawrence Erlbaum Associates, Publishers, 1985), 197. See also in the same book, Jane M. Armstrong, "A National Assessment of Participation and Achievement of Women in Mathematics," 59–94.

32. Tobias, *Overcoming Math Anxiety*, 84–89.

33. Sandra Acker and Keith Oatley, "Gender Issues in Education for Science and Technology: Current Situation and Prospects for Change," *Canadian Journal of Education* 18, no. 3 (Summer 1993), 258–259, citing H. Carmichael, J. Burnett, W. Higginson, B. Moore, and P. Pollard, *Computers, Children and Classrooms: A Multisite Evaluation of the Creative Use of Microcomputers by Elementary School Children* (Toronto: Ontario Ministry of Education, 1985).

34. For the misogynistic practices of some Canadian schools of engineering, see Ruth Roach Pierson, "The Politics of the Body," chap. 2 in Pierson, Cohen, Bourne, and Masters, *Canadian Women's Issues*, Vol. I: *Strong Voices*, 114, 169–172.

35. Royal Commission on the Status of Women in Canada, *Report*, 174.

36. Elena Gianini Belotti, *Little Girls: Social Conditioning and Its Effects on the Stereotyped Role of Women during Infancy*, with an Introduction by Margaret Drabble (London: Writers and Readers Publishing Cooperative, 1975), 89–90.

37. Royal Commission on the Status of Women, *Report*, 174–175.

38. Lois Camponi and Paulette Gallant, "N.B. Girls Learn to be Invisible: New Textbooks Still Sexist," *Equal Times, Fredericton's First Women's Newspaper*, August 1975, 1, excerpted in the documents section of this chapter. Copy at the Canadian Women's Movement Archives, Ottawa (hereafter CWMA).

39. Ad Hoc Committee Respecting the Status of Women in the North York System, Interim Report No. 2, *The Rape of Children's Minds*, June 1975, 17, excerpted in the documents section of this chapter. Copy at WERC.

40. Camponi and Gallant, "N.B. Girls Learn To Be Invisible," 1.

41. Priscilla Galloway, *"What's Wrong With High School English? ... It's Sexist — Un-Canadian — Outdated* (Toronto: OISE Press, 1980).

42. Briskin and Coulter, "Feminist Pedagogy: Challenging the Normative," 249.

43. Lorna Marsden, remarks made at the "Landmark Conference on Sex-Role Stereotyping and Women's Studies," in *Dimensions: Ontario Education* 12, no. 2 (Winter 1979), 6–7. Copy at WERC.
44. The Education Group of the Newfoundland Status of Women Council, *This Is Our Work: Some Newfoundland Women Talk About Their Careers* (St. John's: Newfoundland Status of Women Council, 1975).
45. Catherine Overall, "Role Models: A Critique," in Kathleen Storrie, ed., *Women: Isolation and Bonding* (Toronto: Methuen, 1987), 184.
46. Jane Gaskell, Arlene McLaren, and Myra Novogrodsky, *Claiming an Education: Feminism and Canadian Schools* (Toronto: Our Schools/Ourselves Education Foundation, 1989), 16.
47. Toronto, Board of Education, *The Education of Black Students in Toronto Schools* (1988), 6–7, quoted by Annette Henry, "Missing: Black Self-Representations in Canadian Educational Research," *Canadian Journal of Education* 18, no. 3 (Summer 1993), 213.
48. Until recently on the Circular 14 list of texts recommended for use in Ontario secondary schools, a book on the Russian Revolution proposed that students, "in order to experience history," "assume the identity of a person who lived through the time period." The text then went on to explain that because "many of the events that follow — though certainly not all of them — are seen through the eyes of male characters, ... some girls may find it convenient to develop and work through a male identity." D.A. Hurst, *The Russian Revolution* (Toronto: Academic Press, 1981), 1. Did the author not know that many historians, Trotsky among them, have credited women's storming of the Winter Palace with the triggering of the March 1917 revolution? Had the author not heard of Alexandra Kollontai, who sat as the Commissar of Social Welfare in the first Bolshevik government formed after the November revolution?
49. Eugene Gates, "The Woman Composer Question: Four Case Studies from the Romantic Era" (Ph.D. thesis, University of Toronto, 1992), 78–112.
50. See, for example, Aphra Behn, *Oroonoko or, The Royal Slave* (1688; reprint New York and London: W.W. Norton & Company, 1973). See also Dale Spender, *Mothers of the Novel* (London and New York: Pandora, 1986), 47–66.
51. Angeline Goreau, *Reconstructing Aphra: A Social Biography of Aphra Behn* (New York: Dial Press, 1980); Angeline Goreau, "Aphra Behn: A Scandal to Modesty," in Dale Spender, ed., *Feminist Theorists: Three Centuries of Women's Intellectual Traditions* (London: The Women's Press, 1986), 8–27.
52. See Dale Spender, *Women of Ideas and What Men Have Done to Them: From Aphra Behn to Adrienne Rich* (London: Routledge & Kegan Paul, 1982).
53. Mary Beard et al., "A Study of the *Encyclopaedia Britannica* in Relation to Its Treatment of Women," submitted November 15, 1942, reprinted in Ann J. Lane, ed., *Mary Ritter Beard: A Source Book* (New York: Schocken Books, 1977), 215–224.
54. Virginia Woolf, *A Room of One's Own* (London: The Hogarth Press, 1929), 48.
55. Dorothy Smith, "A Sociology for Women," in Julia Sherman and Evelyn Torton Beck, eds., *The Prism of Sex: Essays in the Sociology of Knowledge* (Madison: University of Wisconsin Press, 1979), 135–187.
56. The Canadian Sociology and Anthropology Association (CSAA) came into being in 1965 and developed in tandem with the rise and spread of the women's movement.
57. Margrit Eichler, "The Unfinished Transformation: Women and Feminist Approaches in Sociology and Anthropology," in W.K. Carroll, L. Christiansen-Ruffman, R.F. Currie, and D. Harrison, eds., *Fragile Truths: Twenty-Five Years of Sociology and Anthropology in Canada* (Ottawa: Carleton University Press, 1992), 72.
58. Paula Caplan, *The Myth of Women's Masochism* (New York: E.P. Dutton, 1985).
59. Paula Caplan, *Don't Blame Mother: Mending the Mother-Daughter Relationship* (New York: Harper & Row, 1989).
60. Peggy Bristow, Dionne Brand, Linda Carty, Afua P. Cooper, Sylvia Hamilton, and Adrienne Shadd, "Introduction," and Adrienne Shadd, "The Lord Seemed to Say 'Go'": Women and the Underground Railroad Movement," in *'We're Rooted Here and They Can't Pull Us Up': Essays in African Canadian Women's History* (Toronto: University of Toronto Press, 1994).
61. Sylvia Van Kirk, *"Many Tender Ties": Women in Fur-Trade Society in Western Canada, 1670–1870* (Winnipeg: Watson & Dwyer Publishing Ltd., 1980).
62. Joan Sangster, *Dreams of Equality: Women on the Canadian Left, 1920–1950* (Toronto: McClelland & Stewart, 1989).
63. Marjorie Griffin Cohen, *Women's Work, Markets, and Economic Development in Nineteenth-Century Ontario* (Toronto: University of Toronto Press, 1988).
64. Lynne Marks, "The 'Hallelujah Lasses': Working-Class Women in the Salvation Army in English Canada, 1882–92," in Franca Iacovetta and Mariana Valverde, eds.,

Gender Conflicts: New Essays in Women's History (Toronto: University of Toronto Press, 1992), 67–117.

65. Ruth Roach Pierson, *"They're Still Women After All"* : *The Second World War and Canadian Womanhood* (Toronto: McClelland & Stewart, 1986).

66. Eliane Leslau Silverman, *The Last Best West: Women on the Alberta Frontier* (Montreal and London: Eden Press, 1984).

67. Margaret Conrad, Toni Laidlaw, and Donna Smyth, *No Place Like Home: Diaries and Letters of Nova Scotia Women 1771–1938* (Halifax: Formac Publishing Company Ltd., 1988).

68. Dionne Brand, *No Burden to Carry: Narratives of Black Working Women in Ontario 1920s to 1950s* (Toronto: Women's Press, 1991).

69. Angus McLaren and Arlene Tigar McLaren, *The Bedroom and the State: The Changing Practices and Politics of Contraception and Abortion in Canada, 1880–1980* (Toronto: McClelland & Stewart, 1986).

70. Karen Dubinsky, *Improper Advances: Rape and Heterosexual Conflict in Ontario, 1880–1929* (Chicago and London: University of Chicago Press, 1993).

71. Bettina Bradbury, "Pigs, Cows and Boarders: Non-Wage Forms of Survival Among Montreal Families, 1861–1891," *Labour/Le Travail*, no. 14 (Fall 1989), 9–46.

72. Susan Mann Trofimenkoff, "One Hundred and Two Muffled Voices: Canada's Industrial Women in the 1880's," *Atlantis: A Women's Studies Journal* 3, no. 1 (Fall 1977), 66–82.

73. Marilyn Barber, "The Women Ontario Welcomed: Immigrant Domestics for Ontario Homes, 1870–1930," *Ontario History* 72, no. 3 (September 1980), 148–172.

74. Marta Danylewycz and Alison Prentice, "Teachers' Work: Changing Patterns and Perceptions in the Emerging School Systems of Nineteenth and Early Twentieth Century Central Canada," *Labour/Le Travail*, no. 17 (Spring 1986), 58–80.

75. See, for example, Alette Olin Hill, *Mother Tongue, Father Time* (Bloomington and Indianapolis: Indiana University Press, 1986).

76. Margrit Eichler, *Nonsexist Research Methods: A Practical Guide* (Boston: Allen & Unwin, 1988), 48–64.

77. Alan Cowell, "End Talk of Women Priests, Pope Says," *The Globe and Mail*, 31 May 1994, A1, A15.

78. Adrienne Rich, "Claiming an Education" (1977), in Adrienne Rich, *On Lies, Secrets, and Silence: Selected Prose 1966–1978* (New York: W.W. Norton & Company; Toronto: George J. McLeod Ltd., 1979), 231.

79. For a description of that course, see Susan McCrae Vander Voet, "Interview: Greta Hofmann Nemiroff," *Women's Education des femmes* 4, no. 3 (Spring 1986), 24–26, excerpted in the documents section of this chapter.

80. Helga E. Jacobson, "Organising Women's Studies at the University of British Columbia" (paper presented at the Canadian Sociological and Anthropological Conference, Kingston, Ontario, 27–31 May 1973), later published in *Canadian Newsletter for Research on Women* 11, no. 3 (1973), 19–24, excerpted in the documents section of this chapter. See also Concordia University, "Why Women's Studies?" in *Arts and Science: Women's Studies*, pamphlet, 1978–79, excerpted in the documents section of this chapter.

81. Bonnie Ward, "Women in the Twentieth Century: A Student's Critique," and James Blyth, "A Male Student's View," enclosed in a packet of information on the women's course offered through Interdisciplinary Studies at the University of Toronto, prepared by Ruth McEwan, Coordinator, Women: Oppression and Liberation, c/o Interdisciplinary Studies at the University of Toronto, 1971–72, excerpted in the documents section of this chapter.

82. Judith Grant, "The Women's Studies Programme at the University of New Brunswick: One Student's Perspective," *Women's Education des femmes* 7, no. 2 (1989), 26, reprinted in the documents section of this chapter.

83. Mount St. Vincent University, "Why Women's Studies?" in pamphlet, n.d., excerpted in the documents section of this chapter. Copy at WERC.

84. Marion Colby, *Centennial College Report on Conference on Women's Studies in the Community Colleges, Toronto, Ontario, February 1977* (Scarborough, Ontario: Centennial College, March 1977).

85. Christa van Daele, "Women's Studies: Time for a Grass Roots Revival," *Branching Out* 5, no. 1 (1978), 8–11, excerpted in the documents section of this chapter.

86. See Frances Early, "Anglophone Coordinator's Report," *CWSA/ACEF Newsletter* 1, no. 1 (Autumn 1982), 1–2, reprinted in the documents section of this chapter.

87. Rosonna Tite with the assistance of Margaret Malone, "Our Universities' Best-Kept Secret: Women's Studies in Canada," *Atlantis* 16, no. 1 (Fall 1990), 25–39.

88. Margrit Eichler, "On Charming Princes and Reviews: Response to Brodribb and Pujol's Review Essay 'The Canadian Women's Studies Project: Inside Looking In?'" *Resources for Feminist Research/Documentation sur la recherche féministe* (RFR/DRF) 21, nos. 1 & 2 (Spring/Summer 1992), 3. See the "Reports of the Canadian Women's Studies Project," *Atlantis* 16, no. 1 (Fall 1990).
89. York University, Faculty of Graduate Studies, "Proposal for an M.A./Ph.D. Programme in Women's Studies," October 1989, excerpted in the documents section of this chapter. Document provided by Thelma McCormack, first director of the Graduate Programme in Women's Studies at York University.
90. Beth Westfall [Davies], "The University, Women's Studies, and Rural Women: Some Thoughts on Feminist Pedagogy and Rural Outreach," *Women's Education des femmes* 7, no. 1 (1989), 23–26, excerpted in the documents section of this chapter. See also Joanne Prindiville and Cathryn Boak, "From the Straight Shore to the Labrador: Women's Studies as a Distance Education Course," *Women's Education des femmes* 5, no. 4 (Summer 1987), 6–11.
91. Martha Colquhoun, "The Story of an Orphaned Curriculum: Women's Studies in Manitoba High Schools," *Women's Education des femmes* 2, no. 3 (March 1984), 10–13, excerpted in the documents section of this chapter.
92. According to one of its major definitions, the "canon" refers to those books of the Bible officially recognized by the Church as genuinely biblical. There is disagreement between the Roman Catholic Church and various other Christian churches as to the composition of "the canon."
93. Rich, "Claiming an Education" (1977), 232.
94. Elizabeth Fox-Genovese, *Feminism Without Illusions: A Critique of Individualism* (Chapel Hill & London: The University of North Carolina Press, 1991), 182.
95. Ibid., 176.
96. Ibid., 179.
97. Sigmund Freud, *Civilization and Its Discontents* (New York: W.W. Norton, 1961).
98. Quoted in Fox-Genovese, *Feminism Without Illusions*, 175.
99. Isaiah Smithson, "Introduction: Investigating Gender, Power, and Pedagogy," in Susan L. Gabriel and Isaiah Smithson, eds., *Gender in the Classroom* (Urbana and Chicago: University of Illinois Press, 1990), 6.
100. Priscilla Settee, "Fighting Racism — At Home," *The Womanist* 2, no. 1 (Fall 1989), 38.
101. Elizabeth Bear, "Dealing with Residential School: The Healing Process of an Adult Child," *Women's Education des femmes* 9, no. 4 (Summer 1992), 20–21, reprinted in the documents section of this chapter.
102. Rich, "Claiming an Education" (1977), 232.
103. See Gloria T. Hull, Patricia Bell Scott, and Barbara Smith, eds., *All the Women Are White, All the Blacks Are Men, But Some of Us are Brave* (Old Westbury, NY: The Feminist Press, 1982).
104. Carmen Henry, "Racism in Women's Studies," *The Womanist* 1, no. 4 (May/June 1989), 17, excerpted in the documents section of this chapter.
105. See Nancy Adamson, "Lesbian Issues in Women's Studies Courses," *RFR/DRF* The Lesbian Issue, 12, no. 1 (March 1983), 5–6, excerpted in the documents section of this chapter. See also for the USA, Sarah-Hope Parmeter and Irene Reti, eds., *The Lesbian in Front of the Classroom: Writings by Lesbian Teachers* (Santa Cruz, CA: HerBooks, 1988).
106. See Philinda Masters, "Women, Culture and Communications," chap. 6 in Pierson, Cohen, Bourne, and Masters, *Canadian Women's Issues*, Vol. I: *Strong Voices*, 394–417, for a fuller discussion of this flowering.
107. See, for example, Daphne Marlatt, *Ana Historic: A Novel* (Toronto: Coach House Press, 1988), and Ingrid MacDonald, *Catherine, Catherine: Lesbian Short Stories* (Toronto: Women's Press, 1991).
108. Madiha Didi Khayatt, *Lesbian Teachers: An Invisible Presence* (Albany, NY: State University of New York Press, 1992). See Paula Bourne, "Women, Law and the Justice System," chap. 5 in Pierson, Cohen, Bourne, and Masters, *Canadian Women's Issues*, Vol. I: *Strong Voices*, 321–393, for more information about Ontario's Bill 7.
109. Becki Ross and Gary Kinsman, telephone conversations with author, November 3, 1994.
110. Esmeralda Thornhill, "Black Women's Studies in Teaching Related to Women: Help or Hinderance to Universal Sisterhood?" and Esmeralda Thornhill, "Black Women: The Missing Pages from Canadian Women's Studies," *The Womanist* 1, no. 1 (September/October 1988), 13, reprinted in the documents section of this chapter. "Black Women's Studies in Teaching Related to Women ... " is an abstract of a longer piece published in

Women of Colour, special issue of *Fireweed* 16 (Spring 1983), 77–83, and reprinted in *The Issue is - Ism: Women of Colour Speak Out* (Toronto: Sistervision Press, 1989).

111. Sky Lee, *Disappearing Moon Cafe* (Vancouver/Toronto: Douglas & McIntyre, 1990).

112. Debbie Douglas, "Young Black Women Speak!," *Immigrant Women,* special issue of *RFR/DRF* 16, no. 1 (1987), 17–18, reprinted in the documents section of this chapter.

113. Linda Carty, "Women's Studies in Canada: A Discourse and Praxis of Exclusion," *RFR/DRF* 20, nos. 3/4 (Fall/Winter 1991), 12–13.

114. Carty, "Women's Studies in Canada: A Discourse and Praxis of Exclusion," 15.

115. Enid Lee, *Letters to Marcia: A Teacher's Guide to Anti-Racist Education* (Toronto: Cross Cultural Communication Centre, 1985).

116. Dionne Brand and Krisantha Sri Bhaggiyadatta, *Rivers Have Sources, Trees Have Roots: Speaking of Racism* (Toronto: Cross Cultural Communication Centre, 1986).

117. Makeda Silvera, *Growing Up Black: A Resource Manual for Black Youth* (Toronto: Sister Vision Press, 1989).

118. Linda Briskin, *Feminist Pedagogy: Teaching and Learning Liberation, Feminist Perspectives,* no. 19 (Ottawa: Canadian Research Institute for the Advancement of Women, 1990); Briskin and Coulter, "Introduction — Feminist Pedagogy: Challenging the Normative," 251.

119. Kathryn Pauly Morgan, "The Paradox of the Bearded Mother: The Role of Authority in Feminist Pedagogy" (1987, 46–49, in the possession of Ruth Roach Pierson); Kathryn Morgan, "The Perils and Paradoxes of Feminist Pedagogy," *RFR/DRF* 16, no. 3 (September 1987), 50.

120. Kathleen Martindale, "Theorizing Autobiography and Materialist Feminist Pedagogy," *Canadian Journal of Education* 17, no. 3 (Summer 1992), 321–340.

121. Briskin and Coulter, "Introduction — Feminist Pedagogy: Challenging the Normative," 254.

122. Briskin and Coulter, "Introduction — Feminist Pedagogy," paraphrasing Bluma Litner, Amy Rossiter, and Marilyn Taylor, "The Equitable Inclusion of Women in Higher Education: Some Consequences for Teaching," *Canadian Journal of Education* 17, 3 (Summer 1992), 295.

123. Sherene Razack, "Story-telling for Social Change," *Gender and Education* 5, no. 1 (1993), 55–69.

124. Sherene Razack, "Issues of Difference in Women's Studies: A Personal Reflection," *RFR/DRF* 20, nos. 3/4 (Fall/Winter 1991), 45.

125. Ann Manicom, "Feminist Pedagogy: Transformations, Standpoints, and Politics," *Canadian Journal of Education* 17, no. 3 (Summer 1992), 372. Manicom, cites Mary Field Belecky, Blythe McVicker Clinchy, Nancy Rule Goldberger, and Jill Mattuck Tarule, *Women's Ways of Knowing: The Development of Self, Voice, and Mind* (New York: Basic Books, 1986) as among those making the claim that women's experience is an unproblematic source of authentic knowledge.

126. Ann Manicom, "Feminist Pedagogy: Transformations, Standpoints, and Politics," 373, drawing on such studies as The Personal Narratives Group, eds., *Interpreting Women's Lives* (Bloomington: Indiana University Press, 1989).

127. Martindale,"Theorizing Autobiography ...," 335, citing bell hooks, *Talking Back: Thinking Feminist, Thinking Black* (Boston: South End Press, 1989), 53.

128. Discussion with Nancy Forestell, 22 June 1994.

129. Martindale, "Theorizing Autobiography," 330.

130. Homa Hoodfar, "Feminist Anthropology and Critical Pedagogy: The Anthropology of Classrooms' Excluded Voices," *Canadian Journal of Education* 17, no. 3 (Summer 1992), 311.

131. Roxana Ng, "'A Woman Out of Control': Deconstructing Sexism and Racism in the University," 190.

132. Dawn H. Currie, "Subject-ivity in the Classroom: Feminism Meets Academe," *Canadian Journal of Education* 17, no. 3 (Summer 1992), 358.

133. See Ruth Roach Pierson, "The Mainstream Women's Movement and the Politics of Difference," chap. 3 in Pierson, Cohen, Bourne and Masters, *Canadian Women's Issues,* Vol. I: *Strong Voices,* 186–214.

134. Annette Henry, "Missing: Black Self-Representations in Canadian Educational Research," *Canadian Journal of Education* 18, no. 3 (Summer 1993), 206, 217. The Audre Lorde quotation is from *Sister Outsider* (Trumansburg, NY: The Crossing Press, 1984), 45.

135. Lorna Weir, "Anti-Racist Feminist Pedagogy, Self-Observed," *RFR/DRF* 20, nos. 3/4 (Fall/Winter 1991), 19–26.

136. Razack, "Issues of Difference in Women's Studies," 45.

137. Mary Bryson and Suzanne de Castell, "Queer Pedagogy: Praxis Makes Im/Perfect," *Canadian Journal of Education* 18, no. 3 (Summer 1993), 285–305. See also in the same issue, Linda Eyre, "Compulsory Heterosexuality in a University Classroom," 273–284.
138. Nancy S. Jackson, "Skill Training in Transition: Implications for Women," in Jane Gaskell and Arlene McLaren, eds., *Women and Education: A Canadian Perspective* (Calgary, Alberta: Detselig Enterprises Ltd., 1987), 359.
139. Carole Wallace, "Systemic Discrimination and the Provision of Training Programs to Women," *Women's Education des femmes* 2, no. 1 (September 1983), 13–15, excerpted in the documents section of this chapter.
140. Lynn Fogwill, "CCLOW Journey," *Women's Education des femmes* 7, no. 2 (1989), 7.
141. Linda MacDonald and Patricia Morris, "Lack of Child Care A Barrier to Women Learners," *Women's Education des femmes* 4, no. 4 (Summer 1986), 5–9.
142. "Women and The National Training Act: Executive Summary of CCLOW's Research Project," *Women's Education des femmes* 2, no. 4 (June 1984), 15.
143. Ibid., 16.
144. "The Bridging Program for Women: A CCLOW Model that Works," *Women's Education des femmes* 5, no. 1 (Fall 1986), 36.
145. Sylvia Ash, Helen King, Dorothy Robbins, Gladys Watson and WISE Participants, "Women Interested in Successful Employment: Perspectives on a Bridging Program," *Women's Education des femmes* 7, no. 2 (1989), 30–33, excerpted in the documents section of this chapter.
146. Aisla Thomson, Editorial "Training for Whom?," *Women's Education des femmes* 10, nos. 3/4 (Winter 1993/94), 2, reprinted in the documents section of this chapter.
147. "Excerpt from a Brief, presented by the IMMIGRANT AND VISIBLE MINORITY WOMEN at a meeting in Ottawa, June 3, 1985," *Women's Education des femmes* 4, no. 1 (Fall 1985), 32.
148. See "Consultation Meeting with the Federal Ministers," Ottawa, 1–3 June 1985, excerpted in the documents section of Marjorie Griffin Cohen, "The Canadian Women's Movement," chap. 1 in *Canadian Women's Issues*, Vol. 1: *Strong Voices*, 75–77.
149. Susan McCrae Vander Voet, Editorial, *Women's Education des femmes* 4, no. 1 (Fall 1985), 3.
150. Terry Dance and Susan Witter, "The Privatization of Training: Women Pay the Cost," *Women's Education des femmes* 6, no. 1 (Winter 1988), 8–14.
151. Information gained in conversation with Jenny Callahan, Anti-Racism Organizational Change Consultant, Ontario Anti-Racism Secretariat, Ministry of Citizenship, 24 July 1994.
152. Thomson, "Training for Whom?", 2, reprinted in the documents section of this chapter.
153. Pat Armstrong, "Good Jobs, Bad Jobs, No Jobs: A Not-So-Trivial Pursuit," *Women's Education des Femmes* 10, nos. 3/4 (Winter 1993/94), 46–49, reproduced in the documents section of this chapter.
154. Nadya Burton, "Tools Not Rules: Challenging Traditional Power Dynamics as Assault Prevention," *Women's Education des femmes* 10, no. 1 (Winter 1992/93), 10–12, reprinted in the documents section of this chapter.
155. Flyer, sent out by Pink Triangle North, Box 2311, Timmins, Ontario, P4N 8E7, received by NAC, 4 September 1986. NAC Archives: File: September 1986 Journal.
156. "Do You Know a Lesbian?" 1992 flyer prepared by the Lesbian Issues Committee, NAC, based on an article by Helen Fallding originally published in the *OptiMst*, Whitehorse, Yukon, 1991, reprinted in the documents section of this chapter.
157. For examples of these fact sheets, see Pierson, Cohen, Bourne, and Masters, *Canadian Women's Issues*, Vol. I: *Strong Voices*, 131–132, 166; and "Employment Equity for Women with Disabilities" in the documents section of Marjorie Griffin Cohen, "Paid Work," chap. 2 in this volume.
158. Linda Carty, "Black Women in Academia: A Statement from the Periphery, " and Himani Bannerji, "But Who Speaks for Us? Experience and Agency in Conventional Feminist Paradigms," in H. Bannerji L. Carty, Kari Dehli, Susan Heald, and Kate McKenna, *Unsettling Relations: The University as a Site of Feminist Struggles* (Toronto: The Women's Press, 1991).
159. Fely Villasin, telephone conversation with author, 5 July 1994. The Theme of the 1994 NAC AGM was "International Perspectives: Women and Global Solidarity."
160. See "New CRIAW Research Project," *Canadian Research Institute for the Advancement of Women Newsletter* 14, no. 4 (Summer 1994), 3, reproduced in the documents section of this chapter.

161. Monica Goulet, "Moving Towards an Anti-Racist Feminism" (banquet speech at the CRIAW Conference, St. John's, Newfoundland, November 1993), excerpted in the documents section of this chapter.

162. She was specifically referring to a joint meeting CRIAW had had with CCLOW to explore ways the two organizations could work together to combat racism and sexism. Monica Goulet, "President's Message," *CRIAW Newsletter* 14, no. 4 (Summer 1994), 1.

163. Monica Goulet, letter of resignation from presidency of CRIAW, 1 September 1994, reproduced in the documents section of this chapter.

164. Monica Goulet, telephone conversations with the author, November 1994 and January 1995.

Documents: Chapter 3

Access

"The Status of Women Teachers in Ontario High Schools"
Toronto, Summer 1986[1]

In 1976, the newly-formed Task Force on the Status of Women was mandated by the Ontario Secondary School Teachers' Federation (OSSTF) to study the reasons for the underrepresentation of women in positions of added responsibility within boards and the Federation, and to recommend remedial action. To carry out its mandate, the Task Force sought to expand its data base by commissioning a comprehensive province-wide survey about the position of women Federation members. The survey was designed to identify:

- the employment status of women relative to men;
- the attitudes of women and men teachers concerning the competence of women to teach;
- the attitudes of women and men teachers concerning women's promotability;
- the attitudes of women and men administrators concerning women's competence and promotability;
- the attitudes of women and men teachers and administrators toward the academic achievement and career aspirations of male and female students.

The major conclusions of the 1976 report were that women generally perceived themselves and were perceived by male peers and decision-makers to be less promotable than men and had, in fact, received fewer promotions than their representation among teachers and their qualifications warranted.

In addition, the study found that the factors outlined above were related to each other and to age, marital status, responsibility for housework and child care and, in general, to attitudes about appropriate male and female roles. In other words, most women and men teachers in 1976 held somewhat traditional attitudes about themselves and their colleagues that were reflected in their career histories and in their current behaviours, priorities and aspirations.

1. Avebury Research and Consulting Ltd., *Women's Education des femmes* 4, no. 4 (Summer 1986), 34–37.

In the 1976 review, it was recommended that such a wide ranging and complex problem should be dealt with on as many fronts as possible, since each factor interacted with virtually all others. Specific actions recommended were:

- awareness training and counselling for both men and women;
- identification and tracking of women with potential;
- an Affirmative Action perspective in negotiations and relations with Boards of Education;
- the creation of non-stereotyped learning environments.

Ten years later, the Status of Women Committee has resurveyed the Federation membership to determine what changes have occurred in women's employment status and in attitudes towards the notion of women seeking positions of added responsibility. The survey, reported here, also examined attitudes toward students and explored other issues in more depth than in the original study (e.g., eligibility for pension, willingness to use workplace child care arrangements).

As in the previous study, the present study used a "process of career development" framework for describing the factors that indicate who may or may not achieve positions of added responsibility. This process includes the following factors:

- Family Responsibilities — refers to the obligations other than financial, for which people are directly or psychologically responsible within the family. Breaks in years of service for maternity and child care are included in this category.

- Career Commitment ("Paying the Price") — refers to the degree of importance attached to one's career and the willingness to undertake activities (gaining extra qualifications, taking on extra work responsibilities) which enhance promotability.

- Formal Qualifications — refers to the years of service and the accumulation of formal, Ministry-required education necessary for performing a given job.

- Job Performance — refers to the level of competence and the degree of innovation shown by teachers in the classroom, in the opinion both of the teachers themselves, and of their supervisors.

- Promotion — refers, first, to the encouragement that committed, qualified and competent teachers receive to apply for promotion; second, to the number of applications teachers make for promotion; and third, to the number of times that qualified teachers who have applied for promotion are selected for positions of added responsibility.

* Attitudes — refers to how women teachers feel about their ability to advance in their careers, and how promotable they are perceived to be by male peers and, especially, by those who make decisions about their career aspirations.

FINDINGS AND RECOMMENDATIONS

The 1976 survey demonstrated that the gender of a teacher had a profound effect on each phase of the career development process, with fewer women attaining positions of added responsibility. Since the first survey, considerable effort has gone into addressing the concerns raised in that report. Some of the notable changes since the report was published include:

* Status of Women programs sponsored by OSSTF and other organizations;
* increased concern in the Ontario Ministry of Education for women's professional status.

These efforts are, in part, responsible for the positive and significant changes in how women teachers now view their careers. The following list summarizes the changes which increase the likelihood of career advancement for women.

* The aspirations of women teachers are higher.
* Women are more prepared to "pay the price" for advancement. They are increasing their formal qualifications and their level of activities within schools, Boards and the Federation. Overall, their careers are of more importance to them than in 1976.
* Women have more confidence in their effectiveness in fulfilling key administrative functions.
* Women receive more encouragement from superiors to apply for promotions.
* Women apply for promotions more often and are more often successful than they were in 1976.

When the difference in age group between OSSTF women and men is taken into account, there is little or no difference between them in level of qualification or experience. Because male teachers, as a group, are older than female teachers (43% of women but 62% of men are over 40 years old) they have, on the average, more experience.

While women's progress from 1976 to the present has been substantial across the province, further OSSTF support is needed to address some key areas of concern where men continue to have an advantage in 1985:

- Women are slightly less qualified than men to apply for Vice-Principal positions.
- Women evaluate themselves as somewhat less innovative than men.
- Women consider themselves to be somewhat less effective than men in administering schools and disciplining students.
- Although there has been improvement since 1976, women continue to receive less encouragement to apply for promotion and remain less likely to apply for promotion.

By far the greatest advantage men teachers have over women is that women continue to have major responsibility for home and child care tasks. In consequence, women have more concerns about the negative effect promotions can have on their ability to perform these essential and largely unshared responsibilities. It appears that some of the capable young women respondents will hesitate to consider advancement unless and until administrative jobs are restructured to allow for both a successful career and responsible parenting.

In addition, the necessity of taking maternity and child care leave to fulfill parenting obligations has a negative effect both on women's career advancement and on their eligibility for pensions in their later years ...

Another important finding is that, although women's opinions about their promotability have improved markedly since 1976 and the assessments by male administrators of women's promotability have also improved, the perceptions of these decision-makers have not kept pace with women's present attitudes, level of qualifications and degree of career commitment. Until male administrators are able to view women and men teachers as equally capable and promotable, women's low representation in positions of added responsibility will continue.

Women in 1985 are undertaking those aspects of the promotion process which are under their control. Their demonstrated career commitment must now be met by a reciprocal willingness on the part of their superiors to encourage them to qualify for and apply for senior positions, and to appoint them to these positions in proportion to their representation in the Federation ...

Sex Differences in Post-Secondary Education
Ottawa, 1977[2]

Sex Differences

The most significant findings of this analysis are those relating to sex. The proportion of females to males has grown in all programs except terminal college programs. Of the more dramatic gains by women in specific fields some, such as architecture and dentistry, are based on small sample numbers and should be treated with caution. In fields such as commerce and law the considerable growth in the proportion of women is manifest.

However, it should be noted that women still constitute less than 25 per cent of the total enrolment in law, less than 20 per cent in commerce. In overall terms the data suggest that women, as a group, have made greater proportional gains over time than students with fathers having lower levels of educational attainment, although the proportion of the latter is larger in all five program areas and all fields of study except nursing.

Table 1 compares the proportion of males to females in the five major subdivisions of post-secondary study for two time periods. College transfer programs are community college programs, such as the CEGEP in Quebec, which can lead to continued university study. The other four categories are self-explanatory. As may be seen from the table, the proportion of females to males has increased in all categories except terminal college programs, where the proportion of females to males has declined between 1968-69 and 1974-75 by 5.6 per cent. The greatest increase in the proportion of females has been in college transfer programs (+14.3%); followed by undergraduate programs (+9.6%), professional programs (+7.6%), and post-graduate programs (+6.3%). In 1974-75 women still constituted less than 50 per cent of the enrolment in all programs with the exception of terminal college programs and were most underrepresented in professional programs followed by post-graduate programs.

Table 2 provides more detail on the proportion of males to females in specific fields of study. In 1974-75 women comprised more than 50 per cent of the enrolment in three fields: nursing, education and pharmacy in diminishing order of magnitude. The greatest increases in the proportion of female enrolment were found in law (+15.1%), agriculture (+14.0%), commerce (+12.2%), dentistry (+11.9%), pharmacy (+9.8%) and architecture (+9.7%). Lesser gains have been recorded in the proportion of females in education (+4.3%), medicine (+2.6%), nursing (+2.2%) and engineering (+1.7%). The proportion of females in arts and science has declined by -1.5 per cent. Although women have made gains

2. Edward Harvey, "Accessibility to Post-secondary Education — Some Gains, Some Losses," *University Affairs*, October 1977, 10. Copy at the Women's Educational Resource Centre (hereafter WERC).

over the six year period, in a majority of fields there are still three to four times as many men as women ...

TABLE 1
TOTAL POST-SECONDARY ENROLMENT BY SEX AND PROGRAM: 1968-69 AND 1974-75 COMPARED

	1968-69			1974-75		
	Male	Female	Totals	Male	Female	Totals
	%	%	N	%	%	N
College transfer	70.1	29.9	29,147	55.8	44.2	69,408
College terminal	41.9	58.1	79,333	47.5	52.5	114,135
Undergraduate	64.0	36.0	212,122	54.4	45.6	224,516
Professional	84.7	15.3	12,255	77.1	22.9	16,680
Postgraduate	70.9	29.1	19,192	64.6	35.4	27,313

TABLE 2
UNDERGRADUATE AND PROFESSIONAL ENROLMENT BY SEX AND PROGRAM: 1968-69 AND 1974-75 COMPARED

	1968-69			1974-75		
	Male	Female	Totals	Male	Female	Totals
	%	%	N	%	%	N
Arts & Sciences	60.6	39.4	124,802	62.1	37.9	170,863
Education	41.2	58.8	22,565	36.9	63.1	34,864
Engineering	98.5	1.5	19,564	96.8	3.2	15,333
Commerce	92.7	7.3	17,427	80.5	19.5	22,174
Architecture	90.7	9.3	2,356	81.0	19.0	1,529
Agriculture	89.5	10.5	4,249	75.5	24.5	2,988
Nursing	4.5	95.5	4,037	2.1	97.9	5,190
Pharmacy	53.8	46.2	2,239	44.0	56.0	2,689
Medicine	74.5	25.5	5,773	71.9	28.1	6,136
Dentistry	95.5	4.5	1,756	83.6	16.4	1,973
Law	93.1	6.9	4,726	78.0	22.0	8,162
Other	53.8	46.2	15,001	44.0	56.0	6,023

"Despite Gains, Women Still Under-Represented in Engineering and Applied Sciences"
Ottawa, February 1990[3]

...Figures published by the AUCC today [February 22, 1990] in the 1990 edition of Trends: The Canadian University in Profile, the Association's annual statistical handbook, show that:

- The number of women enroled in engineering and applied sciences jumped 679 per cent (to 5,216 from 670) at the undergraduate level in the fifteen years from 1972-73 to 1987-88 and 638 per cent (to 760 from 103) at the graduate level.

- Even so, the proportion of women among engineering and applied sciences students is only 13 per cent at the undergraduate level (5,216 out of 38, 952) and 12 per cent at the graduate level (760 out of 6,127).

- The situation is similar in mathematics and the physical sciences where women account for only 27 per cent of students (7,080 out of 25,476) at the undergraduate level and about 20 per cent (1,198 out of 5,857) at the graduate level.

UNDERGRADUATE ENROLMENT
FULL-TIME BY SEX AND FIELD, 1987-88

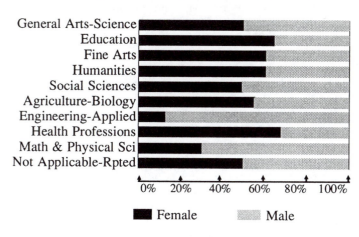

Source: AUCC

3. Association of Universities and Colleges of Canada/Association des Universités et Collèges du Canada, *communiqué*, 22 February 1990, 1–2.

Maths and Sciences

"Alice in the Laboratory"
June 1981[4]

"The time has come," the Walrus said,
"To talk of many things:
Of shoes — and ships — and sealing wax —
Of cabbages — and kings
And why the sea is boiling hot —
And whether pigs have wings."
(Lewis Carroll, *Through the Looking Glass*)

The Walrus and the Carpenter must be two of the most original and engaging scientific collaborators of all time. While we may doubt their ethical taste (they eat their experimental subjects), we cannot question the fact that they were engaged in a serious scientific discussion, for science is the systematic probing of the world around us. Whether we poke at subcellular pieces with an electron microscope or prod the interstellar sky with a laser beam, the essence of the inquiry is the same as testing the feel of sand sliding between our fingers.

But where was Alice? When the science of sealing wax was being discussed was she home dusting the dresser, or polishing her patent leather shoes? Whatever the answer, studies show that she was very unlikely to be found in a senior mathematics or physics class, and only slightly more likely to be in a chemistry lab. Girls begin to drop math and science courses as early as grade ten when these subjects become optional. What this means, of course, is that at 15 or younger Alice has decided that she will never become an engineer, dentist, chemist, ornithologist, doctor, microbiologist, oceanographer, pharmacist, crystallographer, or ecologist. She has eliminated at least 50 per cent of her professional career choices. Oh well, you say, Alice wants to be a secretary anyway. But one day soon Alice will show up for work to be confronted by a green eyed monster called a word processor that doesn't take coffee breaks, sick days, vacation pay, or maternity leave and never makes a mistake. Stiff competition. Microelectronic technology will certainly open new and interesting jobs, but these jobs will require a basic broth of technological skills — a dash of electronics, a pinch of physics ... perhaps a soupçon of mathematics.

Books have been written on the subject of why girls avoid math and science. From the time they are born, girls live within the confines of the female stereotype. They are taught to see the world as a place to be cleaned up and organized rather than messed up and explored. They are taught to be cautious, unadventurous and sweet. Rarely are they encour-

4. Jan Ferguson, Science Council of Canada, *Bulletin of Science Education*, June 1981, 4. Copy at WERC.

aged to play soccer, talk back and argue, or worry about how to support themselves. A majority of girls still believe that marriage and mother-hood will be their life's work, while Statistics Canada reports that in 1976 nearly 45 per cent of married women were working outside their homes.

It's time for Alice to start arguing about pigs' wings and cabbages, and possibly even queens.

Curriculum Content

"N.B. Girls Learn to be Invisible: New Textbook Still Sexist" Fredericton, N.B., August 1975[5]

> He clapped his hands to summon a servant, and immediately the door of his room opened.
>
> His wife stepped in.
> "What does the master of the house desire?" said she.
> "Thank you," said Charlie. "Where's Mother?"
>
> But Mother Beaver had run back to the boat, rowed across the pond as fast as she could, and had flapjacks and maple syrup ready on the table when the men got home.

A relic from days gone by? A conspiracy to put down women? No, these are excerpts from the new Ginn 360 series of text books currently being phased into New Brunswick elementary schools. This colourful new series is very modern in its approach. Bright little faces of many different hues smile out from its pages. But most of them are male. Why shouldn't they be smiling? Of the total characters illustrated 71.6 percent are male as opposed to 28.3 percent female. This is to be expected when one considers that 58.7 percent of the characters even mentioned in the eleven texts studied are male; as opposed to 21.08 percent female. The animal kingdom carries a similar imbalance where we find almost three times as many males as females (6.91:2.61).

Males Have Monopoly on Adventure

Any one using these books as an indicator would have to assume that two-thirds of the world population is male. When one considers the numbers of males and females used as main characters this discrepancy becomes even larger.

It seems that males have a monopoly on adventure and we see them in a large variety of occupations ranging from fireman and air-sea

5. Lois Camponi and Paulette Gallant, *Equal Times: Fredericton's First Women's Newspaper*, August 1975, 1, 3. Copy at the Canadian Women's Movement Archives, Ottawa (hereafter CWMA).

rescuer to businessman and farmers, 152 in all. Women are much more limited in their scope, restricted to occupations such as housewife, mother, store clerk, teacher, secretary and of course fairy, witch and princess, a total of 41.

If one breaks the jobs down into categories, the variance is readily apparent: 86 percent of the professional workers in the series are male (as compared to 13.8 percent female) and even the nonprofessionals are overwhelmingly male (86.0 percent:14 percent) ...

Males Denied Emotions

But occupations are not the only criteria. Children also take cues from the activities of others. Here too, there is a definite imbalance. Males engage in all kinds of exciting activities. They explore, fight monsters, save helpless females, they play ball, climb trees and swim. They're very creative and solve problem after problem in the most ingenious ways, inventing new machines, building things, learning new skills and carrying out scientific experimentation.

Fear is an emotion they are allowed to feel, but it must never be revealed to the outside world. Very few emotions are allowed to males, in fact, and the few instances in which a father shows tenderness toward his own children stand out as noteworthy.

Females, on the other hand, while allowed to show their feelings, play such a minor role in the stories that only one emotion really stands out — fear. It seems that almost every time a girl leaves the familiar terrain of her home, she finds herself in difficulty and in need of rescue (by some brave and clever male of course!).

The females are far too busy practicing for their adult roles: cooking, cleaning, and serving (usually for one or more males). True, the males in the series must also perform chores of various sorts, but theirs tend to be of a generative nature: they teach others how to do things, they build things (boats, dog-houses) and they learn new and interesting skills. Girls, on the other hand, perform duties of a dull, routine nature often involving some personal sacrifice. Even in those chores which should be creative, such as nurturing of the young, they are generally restricted to the negative aspects such as scolding. "Mother seemed unusually grumpy today."

Females Primp Perpetually

While the males show no interest in personal appearance, the females in the series spend a good deal of their time and energy primping. Even the female animals frequently appear in dresses, and of course, that most indispensible article of feminine apparel: aprons. A study of the illustrations would lead one to wonder if the apron were a secondary sex characteristic, it is so commonly found ...

The females do a lot of watching. They watch the boys play, they watch their fathers solve problems, and they even watch the boys work.

Mostly, however, they practice the art of invisibility, that gentle art of remaining unobtrusively in the background, stepping forward now and again to offer refreshments.

Boys Do Things; Girls Watch

The message is clear. Boys do things, girls watch, boys solve problems, girls watch (and offer praise), girls get into trouble, boys save them. While boys are encouraged to be bold and adventuresome, to prepare themselves for skilled and interesting occupations, girls are being told in subtle (and not-so-subtle) ways that their place is in the home, that they need only be trained as mothers, that appearance, not intelligence, is the key to success. The message has undertones as well: girls and women are not as smart as boys and men; girls are not as capable as boys. Hence the notion so often expressed by boys that girls are useless creatures, inferior to boys in every way.

"This is a nice dog," Lucy said. "It's almost as good as having a girl next door."

"It's not almost as good as having a girl next door," William said. "It's better."

Is this the message we want to convey to our children? We think not. Liberation is not only for women, but for all humans. People should be freed from sex-role stereotyping, freed to develop to their full potential, rather than constricted to some preconceived notion of what they SHOULD be. Children of elementary school age need balanced models to identify with if they are to reach full personal development. Girls must feel that they, too, can make a contribution to the world, just as boys need encouragement if they are to discover the total joy of adhulthood.

The argument is often made that the textbooks are only painting a picture of the way things are. If that is true, where are the one-parent families? Where are the women who in reality make up one-third of the work force? In fact the books are far from a reflection of real life. Boys are given the highest of goals to aspire to — how many astronauts or presidents do you know? Rarely, however, are girl's expectations raised beyond variations on the wife and mother role. Even if the stories did present a true picture of life, which they definitely do not, it would be better to help children aspire to a better world, rather than to limit them to the confines of stereotypes ...

Sexism and Stereotyping in School Readers
North York, Ontario 1975[6]

NUMBER OF PAGES					
	CC*	HRW	N	G	Total
Total Pages	1,179	1,129	1,220	1,496	4,975
Male Oriented	492	437	617	910	2,456
Female Oriented	60	62	148	94	364
Boy Centred	119	213	310	258	900
Girl Centred	32	41	84	51	208

*CC = Copp Clark   HRW = Holt, Rinehart & Winston
N = Nelson   G = Ginn.

CHARACTERS					
	CC	HRW	N	G	Total
Boys in boy-centred stories	42	35	55	86	218
Girls in girl-centred stories	23	8	16	9	56

CHARACTER PLACEMENT						
	ADULT Female	ADULT Male	CHILD Female	CHILD Male	NON-Human	NON-Human
Primary	68	243	185	474	42	239
Secondary	54	100	54	27	—	—
Background	174	122	30	18	—	—

MAIN CHARACTERS – approximate ratio				
	CC	HRW	N	G
Male to Female	3:1	6:1	4:1	5:1
Page ration, Male to Female	4:1	5:1	3:1	4:1

6. Vicki Wright, Ad Hoc Committee Respecting the Status of Women in the North York System, Interim Report No. 2, *The Rape of Children's Minds*, June 1975, 17. Copy at WERC.

OCCUPATIONS	
For Men	139
For Women	14

Sex Role Stereotyping in Children's Books
Toronto, 1978[7]

...As teachers we face each day in an unremitting fashion groups of young people who are absorbing our culture before our very eyes. We may want vast and deep changes in our culture and society, but somehow these changes have to come about because of our day-to-day activities. We can think about role models, reinforcement of new attitudes and beliefs; we can fight the stereotypes about women and men which can become prejudices and lead to discrimination. But how? ...

In educational literature, I want to suggest that three categories, or approaches are being taken by modern authors wanting to enlarge the boundaries of roles available to women. I label these categories, for descriptive purposes, the "neutered approach", the "school of polite revenge", and the "brave new world" approach. Each is an attempt to present new opportunities or options to women and each has serious limitations, in my view. In facing the problem of stereotyping, we must first come to grips with the messages that are being offered us about this problem of social change.

In the first approach, the "neutered approach", an attempt is made to mingle male and female almost to the point of androgyny. For example, in some children's books the children play interchangeably at games, wear interchangeable clothes, have interchangeable adventures and deal interchangeably with success and failure. It is as if sex differences did not exist.

Such an approach usually excludes anything to do with life past age twelve because puberty, reproduction and the obvious sex differences in the adult life of our society are far too difficult to portray with such values in mind. While the attempt to suggest that sex should not limit behaviour is there, I suggest to you that this commits a sin of omission. The fact is, that our society does make sex differences central to social organization, and androgyny is nothing more than a theoretical game. It is beginning to create a new stereotype — that is, ignoring the facts — that is just as dangerous as that we are trying to change. Reproduction and all that that entails, is a fact.

The second approach, which I call the school of polite revenge, advocates the radical separation of males and females and female domi-

7. Lorna Marsden, remarks made at the "Landmark Conference on Sex-Role Stereotyping and Women's Studies," in *Dimensions: Ontario Education* 12, no. 2 (Winter 1979), 6–7. Copy at WERC.

nance. In children's stories it ranges from a mild challenge to male supremacy in stories such as *Margie Becomes a Lumberjack* to stories in which the world appears to be populated entirely by women who run the whole show with great success and happiness all around.

Again the facts of reproduction and of our social surroundings disappear in this fantasy — sins of omission, revisited.

The third approach, which you can tell I advocate since I've put it third and last, attempts to redefine the roles of women and men in what I think of as a realistic way. Girls and boys alike find they can cope with stress, success and failure, criticism and praise, etc. My major criticism of this literature is that it usually doesn't go far enough. It leaves vague the transition from childhood to adulthood and often does not come to grips with the question of how a girl is to express her femaleness while stretching the boundaries of her opportunities as wide as those of boys in the work world and the community, and, reciprocally, how a boy is to express his maleness while expanding his roles to include those traditionally thought of as women's roles ...

Women's Studies

Women's Studies for Credit
Montreal, 1986[8]

Greta Hofmann Nemiroff is a feminist educator and Director of the New School, Dawson College, in Montreal. She is a feminist writer and has been Quebec Director of CCLOW for several years. She is interviewed here, for WEDF, by Susan McCrae Vander Voet, an independent consultant and former Executive Director of CCLOW.

Susan: How did you come to be interested in teaching women's studies?

Greta: When I was an English student, I always found myself writing papers on women characters and authors. As a teacher of English at Concordia in about 1968, I made sure to include material on women. But it wasn't really until another friend, a philosophy teacher and I got together to try and discuss some papers we were writing, between the demands of our three babies, that we realized we needed to be writing about ourselves, as women.

This led to the first women's studies course at Concordia in 1970, which might also have been the first formal course offered for credit in Canada. We decided to hold it in the evening in order to attract older women, as well as the younger university students.

Susan: Did you notice any difference between the older and younger women in the course?

8. Susan McCrae Vander Voet, "Interview: Greta Hofmann Nemiroff," *Women's Education des femmes* 4, no. 3 (Spring 1986), 24–25.

Greta: Oh, yes. Some of the older women had a much better sense of the material, because they had lived the reality of women's lives. Many of them were trying to return to work after raising families, or had found themselves alone with their children, either as widows, or separated, after many years of marriage. Many of them could see that marriage wasn't a guarantee of security.

The younger women, though, who hadn't experienced as much, would deny the problems initially. They were still ready to buy the myths about women, and believed in individual power. So they didn't develop a systemic sense of women's problems as readily.

Susan: How long have you been teaching women's studies?

Greta: A group of students decided they wanted to study some historical material on women, so I gave them some de Beauvoir to read. They were to write about what interested them in the chapter being discussed each week. At one point in the book, de Beauvoir makes just passing mention of virginity, and that week, seven out of ten students wrote about virginity. So we stopped right there and began extensive discussions about virginity as a male construct which served male interests. This evolved into a course on women's bodies and body images which has had a number of spinoffs in the school and in my own writing.

One year, a young man wanted to be involved in the course. The women did not feel they would be as free to discuss the issues with him present, so a separate part of the course was set up for young men, with both groups getting together for a time at the end. The young men discovered that the materials available on men's sexuality and roles was dismal. As a result of this experience, I was encouraged to edit a book of materials on women and men.

Susan: What do you feel are the most essential ingredients for young women's education?

Greta: It is critical to help them separate out what is a given and what is not, in their identity as women, and to develop a collective consciousness which will lead to collective action. They need to understand the relativity of gender identity. As Margaret Meade observed years ago, in every society, women and men do different kinds of work and, although the actual work they are responsible for varies from one society to another, the constant is that, whatever work women do, it is valued less than men's work.

It is important that they learn to trust their own instincts and to validate one another's experience of the world as women, compared with how women are described by society. And in this regard, they need to explore who has the power to define their reality. We also discuss race and culture in this context.

The objectives of this kind of education are to help them identify where they stand as individuals on a variety of issues; to examine the choices they have in their own lives; to assist them to develop a public stand in order to be consistent with their own values. The objective for young men is to sensitize them to women, and to turn them into feminists as well ...

"Organising Women's Studies at the University of British Columbia"
University of British Columbia, May 1973[9]

A course in Women's Studies will be offered for the first time at the University of British Columbia in the academic year 1973-74. This paper is concerned with some problems relating to content and organisation which emerged during the process of establishing the course at the university. The problems can be interpreted in the context of three different areas: establishing the legitimacy of the subject matter, the bureaucratic process involved, and the status of women in the university ...

For those of us involved in establishing the content of the course and calling it "Women's Studies," the aim is twofold. First to argue that the disciplines as presently constituted do not adequately allow for a framework for asking about and understanding the roles and experiences of women as a legitimate area in itself. We will explain how and why this has come about and what the omission means. Second we will work towards the creation of analytical frameworks that genuinely include women and at the same time suggest the areas in which we still need further information. This argument for Women's Studies as a legitimate area of study in its own right must be seen in the context of the arguments frequently presented against it. That is that within disciplines women are automatically included because the concern is with "people" (for example in History, Sociology, Anthropology, Economics, etc.). In this connection it can be argued that "people" generally means the public world of men and that women are included only in the sense that they are subsumed under this heading. What we want to establish is a basis for understanding and interpreting the roles and experiences of women in their own right, which will lead to a full understanding of the worlds of both men and women. The issue of legitimacy of the subject matter concerns the right to ask questions that relate specifically to women and incorporate the answers in the framework of interpretation which is proper to the disciplines involved.

In relation to the bureaucratic process the problems of organisation I want to discuss are concerned with introducing a curriculum innovation and with the ways in which questions were raised about both the course and course content. The way in which the right of the course to exist was questioned reflects the particular subject matter and the status of women in the university.

In order to come into being the course had to be considered by altogether eleven different committees. These were two in each department (Anthropology & Sociology are one department), the Arts Faculty

9. Helga E. Jacobson, paper presented at the Canadian Sociological and Anthropological Conference, Kingston, Ontario, May 27th — 31st, 1973, 1-4.

curriculum committee, and the Arts Faculty as a whole; the Senate curriculum committee, the Senate New Programmes committee, and the Senate itself. This is simply due process at UBC and the Women's Studies course was only treated differently in the kind of issues that were raised around its right to exist and the kind of questions that were asked concerning the course. It is worth noting that the brief which was presented initially in justification of the course remained substantively unchanged at the end of the process.

As is generally the case with curriculum innovations, a brief has to be presented justifying the course in terms of its content. What struck me repeatedly as differentiating the Women's Studies course from others going through the same process were the terms in which justification was required of us. There was considerable concern not with the content of the course but with personnel. The focus of interest was not on what was to be taught but on who had the right to teach and learn, e.g., would men be allowed to teach and take it. Issues of qualifications were raised not in relation to content of the course, requisite preparation or experience, but with respect to formal qualifications, i.e., whether or not we had Ph.D.'s. Where content was raised as an issue for discussion it took the form of questioning as to whether there was anything to teach in terms of availability of material and the right to existence of a separate area called "Women's Studies." The right to existence of the course was always measured against the idea that women are automatically included in all disciplines and subject matter and therefore there is no need for a special focus or area of study ...

In discussing the personnel of the course, that is the right both to teach and take it, the recurrent question in every committee was would men be <u>allowed</u> to do either. I stress "allowed" because this seems to me to take the course out of the normal framework of consideration. We were essentially being asked if we would give permission in these terms. In the normal course of events it is assumed simply that those qualified to teach will take or be allocated the responsibility for doing so by the department and those interested in learning will register. In addition, the implication that the course was one for women, taught by women, and indeed solely about women, suggests that our focus would simply be "women's concerns" and whatever this perception means it was clearly not seen as in any sense a legitimate enterprise within the university curriculum.

What this mode of questioning suggests is that the course was seen simply as a political move to include women in the university. While it is correct that women are under-represented in many ways and at many levels, the aim in setting up the course was not simply to manoeuvre for our inclusion. Clearly, in discussing aspects of the situation of women some of the needs for change will be shown and argued for socially and academically, this, as has already been shown, is by no means the sole or even the principal aim of the course. Since we saw the course as being aimed at increasing knowledge and understanding we also saw this as a task that did not define participation by sex. There is no reason in principle why men cannot equally share this task. In practice, however, it is the political situation which defines the process of organising the course, and the interest in it, and this does relate to the status of women. The question of participation raised the issue of legitimacy of the subject matter against a background in which the claims for it were not validated and reasons for offering a basis for greater knowledge and better understanding were not recognised. Given this background, then, it is not surprising to find that women have a greater interest in filling the gaps both as teachers and students, nor that women are the organisers of the move for recognition and validation of the subject matter ...

"Why Women's Studies?"
Concordia University, Montreal, 1978[10]

Women's Studies is a new academic field which takes woman as its primary object of study. The programme is based on the recognition that the systematic study of women has been neglected by all academic disciplines, history, philosophy, sociology, psychology, etc. Only recently have academic communities become aware of this neglect and started to accept the responsibility of rectifying this lack of knowledge of half the human species, partly by developing Women's Studies programmes.

The academic matter of this programme comes from two sources. Firstly there is a great deal of earlier writings about women and their position scattered in various social, political and philosophical journals. These reports are being gathered and evaluated to see what knowledge they can give us of women's historical past and to see what revisions in our presently accepted knowledge are necessary. Secondly, generated by this new consciousness, much recent research has been stimulated in sociology, psychology, anthropology, psychiatry, and other disciplines.

The Women's Studies Programme incorporates these two approaches — to gather and to create knowledge, evaluate it as a part of a total pattern developed by different disciplines, and to produce a more accurate and more comprehensive view of women in society.

Women's Studies is an area in which almost every discipline contributes and, for this reason, is an interdisciplinary programme. Most courses offered within it are directly related to a particular discipline. The programme is designed for students who wish to combine Women's Studies with a discipline such as sociology, psychology, history, political science, literature, religion, etc ...

---

10. Concordia University, Pamphlet, *Arts and Science, Women's Studies*, 1978–79.

Women's Studies at University: A Female Student's View
Toronto, 1972[11]

In September 1972, two hundred people, primarily women, signed up for the University of Toronto's new interdisciplinary course on "Women in the Twentieth Century". Divided into seven sections, the course proposed to emphasize different dimensions of this currently "hot" subject, depending on the resources and particular concerns of the two women responsible for each of the sections. These would include: women in history, women and literature, feminism and Marxism, women and economics, women and film, and women in the Third World. A brief autobiographical sketch of these women indicated which would be their specific concerns, but this was accompanied by a warning that responsibility for the direction of the course was a collective affair, between teachers and students. Academic credentials of the teachers were veiled; their experiences in the women's liberation movement were not.

My elected section proposed to study women in history and literature. Forty people, including two or three men, appeared the first Wednesday evening, and were advised to register in other sections if possible, to make for a more workable group. Within six weeks a stable core of a dozen or so appeared regularly. Some students participated in several sessions before they could clearly identify the teachers. We were called to join the Texpack workers on strike (chiefly women workers) as we were handed our course material. There were more and more indications that this was not the average university survey course, content Women. By Christmas, auditors, students, and teachers were preparing to spend the holidays researching and organizing the material for the second term. Contradictions began to fly with knitting needles and crochet hooks, and shawls and scarves emerged in the denunciation of capitalist, male-chauvinist society. Marx's "Wage, Labour, and Capital" was effective course material, on a par with students' descriptions of self-induced abortions, or their guilt and confusion associated with experiences of sexual feelings as women for women.

Energy was generated out of this process for monthly public meetings, a women's festival, plans to publish student projects, launching a women's press, video-taping people's changing consciousness. Course notes were shared with housewives, house-mates, and husbands.

11. Bonnie Ward, "Women in the Twentieth Century: A Student's Critique," enclosed in a packet of information on the women's course offered through Interdisciplinary Studies at the University of Toronto, prepared by Ruth McEwan, Coordinator, Women: Oppression and Liberation, c/o Interdisciplinary Studies at the University of Toronto, 1971–72.

Women's Studies at University: A Male Student's View
Toronto, 1972[12]

...When I returned to university in the fall of 1971, for my final year of a dismal and boring four years, I was confronted with the problem of choosing a "non-technical elective" to "complement" the engineering courses I was taking. My primary concern was finding a course that interested me, one that I would enjoy, one that would not bog me down with a lot of studying and assignments, and one that was as far removed from engineering and the physical sciences as possible. I had just about decided to take an introductory physiology course, as the lesser of a number of evils when I happened to notice a poster advertising a women's course ...

Eventually the group jelled through and people relaxed. Discussions became more spontaneous and I could feel myself becoming more relaxed and felt willing to take more of a role in the classes. It was interesting and encouraging to me that while the women in the group were very pro women's liberation they were not particularly anti-men.

The relaxing of the group led to a new situation. We tended to become side-tracked very easily and discussions often strayed from the initial topic under discussion to a situation where people would start to talk about their person, situation or topics only vaguely related to the original topic under consideration. This was very frustrating for a number of people as they felt that the course was not accomplishing what it set out to do, in that it was not covering all the prescribed readings ...

I found these digressions from the topics of discussion both interesting and informative. I had never been in a situation where women expressed their feelings in such a manner. It was apparent to me that these women wanted the same things from their lives that most men wanted from theirs. They want a chance to use their skills and ability to fulfil their potential; not to be held back by the stigma of being someone's wife, a mother to my children or too lady-like. In short, they want the same things I want. Another important thing I learned was that, contrary to what my mother had taught me, women were not holier than thou and were not to be placed on a pedestal and worshipped. Women can be just as base, common and vulgar as men. I found that women were not all wives, mothers, or other such stereotypes but just common, run-of-the-mill people. I also realized that my role as a man in our society was not all it's chalked up to be and there is a need not only for the liberation of women but also the liberation of men ...

---

12. James Blyth, "A Male Student's View," enclosed in a packet of information on the women's course offered through Interdisciplinary Studies at the University of Toronto, prepared by Ruth McEwan, Coordinator, Women: Oppression and Liberation, c/o Interdisciplinary Studies at the University of Toronto, 1971–72.

"The Women's Studies Programme at the University of New Brunswick: One Student's Perspective"
University of New Brunswick, 1989[13]

Women's Studies Programmes have significantly increased in number and expanded in content at many university campuses across Canada in the past two decades. At the University of New Brunswick this multi-dimensional and interdisciplinary programme was implemented in 1986 with an initial enrolment of two students. The Programme is now completing its third year. There are, at present, 16 students within this Women's Studies Minor, with six graduating this year.

The programme requires a student to accumulate 24 credit hours for a Minor focus within various disciplines. The students are provided with a varied and diverse examination of the lives of women throughout history and within contemporary society through the following perspectives and disciplines: Psychology, Sociology, History, Literature, Political Science, Anthropology and English, plus two core courses that examine the basic feminist theories inherent in Women's Studies. The Minor Programme succeeds in providing a comprehensive approach within the various disciplines, thus giving the students a more balanced understanding of women in society.

The Women's Studies Minor may be the catalyst for change in the lives of many women students. The Programme entails a consciousness-raising aspect that unveils the invisible and silenced portions of the lives of women. Such knowledge succeeds in empowering women and helps them to understand the fairness and injustice in our patriarchal society. The revelations gained from the knowledge within the Women's Studies courses help in expanding the lives of the students and enriching them immeasurably. The integration of the Women's Studies Programme at the University of New Brunswick is a focus long overdue. That it has been implemented and termed a success attests to the tenacity and hard work of the feminist scholars at this University. The Programme has succeeded, and will continue to succeed, in providing its students with a knowledge of, and for, women that is unparalleled in other university courses.

"Why Women's Studies?"
Mount St. Vincent University, Halifax, n.d.[14]

Why is it important to have Women's Studies? Aren't women people, too? Can't women be studied simply as part of the human group?

Ideally, this should be the case. However, traditionally, most academic disciplines have either slighted or ignored the role and contribution of women to society. Women's Studies seeks to correct this situation by studying the historical and contemporary situation of women from a cross-cultural interdisciplinary perspective. If you are interested in any

---

13. Judith Grant, *Women's Education des femmes* 7, no. 2 (1989), 26.
14. Mount St. Vincent University, Pamphlet, n.d. Copy at WERC.

of the following questions and their answers, you will want to be involved in Women's Studies:

* Are women always the subordinate sex? What is the nature of female power and male dominance in our own society? In non-Western Societies?

* What have the lives of women been like in former eras?

* How have philosophy and religion influenced women's perceptions of themselves and their struggle for equal rights?

* Who are the major thinkers and activists who have influenced the women's rights movements of the 19th and 20th centuries?

* How have political and religious changes affected women's lives?

* What kinds of political, economic, social, ethical and religious problems are women facing in the world today?

* Do the sexes differ in their psychological reactions to people and events? How much are we influenced by our biology? Do the sexes have equal potential for acquiring the knowledge and skills necessary for a variety of occupations?

* What does real equality between the sexes mean? What are women doing to achieve equality?

* What are the bases of present gender arrangements in our society? What might gender arrangements be like in the future? ...

"Women's Studies: Time for a Grass Roots Revival" Toronto, 1978[15]

... Women's Studies at the University of Toronto, for three fast-paced years, drew from a broad popular base, enjoyed political connections with other groups in the city, and provided a public forum for much of the feminist discussion going on in Toronto. It was a two-way relationship of the most dynamic kind: the teaching group provided a ready focus and target that put it in the publice eye, and the public, in turn, fed energy and expertise back into the programme.

The three year pitch of sustained excitement ended as abruptly as it began. Women's Studies, along with other interdisciplinary courses designed in 1971, was scheduled for evaluation at the end of the three-year period. That had been a term of the original mandate. At evaluation time, the course did not fare well. University budget cuts left only

15. Christa van Daele, *Branching Out* 5, no. 1 (1978), 8–11.

enough money for modest salaries, and a switch to a new location disoriented the programme. Enrollments dropped. Mutterings that there was no longer a women's studies constituency began to be heard. One thing aggravated another; the drop in enrollments was not cheering, and the teaching collective that had founded the core course was beginning to register a degree of exhaustion. Demoralization ensued; by 1976, a Women's Studies was lost in yet another political shuffle. This time, the programme was moved to New College, with four highly committed members of the original group of 13 now left. The rest had moved on to other things, or dropped out because of increasing exhaustion. In very short order — December 1976 — three of the group of four received notice, suddenly and dramatically, that their teaching contracts had not been renewed. Although the letters didn't specifically say so, the three instructors, all of whom were still in the process of completing their graduate work, were later led to understand that a full PhD constituted the appropriate criteria for staying on. Only Kay Armatage, who had completed her degree, was invited to re-apply. It was clearly the end of an era.

During this period, an equally significant trend emerged. This was the push for academic respectability, seriousness of course content, and a growing awareness of the all-important 'standards' issue that was to characterize the struggle for the programme's survival in the especially formal university environment of the University of Toronto. At U of T, the pressure to bring standards 'in line' with existing academic standards came from two directions: the administrators of the colleges who hosted the programme, and the tenured faculty women who had begun to offer a number of the Women's Studies courses under the auspices of their own department as the original teaching collective was in the process of disbanding. These women owed their mainstay appointments to the traditionally organized arts and science departments of the university. As successive budget cuts and decreasing enrollment took their toll, the rationale for tightening up course requirements and guaranteeing impressive research and teaching credentials of the faculty presented itself as a strategy for survival ... the survival strategy of women's studies, to the surprise of no one in particular, has changed with the times. It has become co-operative rather than confrontative, exploring for support and for assurances of survival the traditional avenues that the university offers.

The York Experience

In 1975, York University, with a totally different kind of ambience — more fluid, interdisciplinary, and American-patterned rather than British — became the site for a somewhat less flamboyant initiation of Women's Studies, long after the first collective phase at U of T had cooled into history ...

The Women's Studies courses themselves, though on first glance extensive, are not without attendant problems at York. For one thing, there is no *department* of Women's Studies as such, and course offerings are largely dependent on what departments choose to offer. A course can thus be added or withdrawn at a given department's discretion, making continuity and structure in the Women's Studies programme exceedingly problematic ... A second and more immediate difficulty that bodes ill for future developments is the pressing problem of the lack of job security for the part-time women instructors, who teach on contract only. The tenured female faculty members I spoke to at York emphasized the "absolutely inpsirational" role that younger part-timers play in the Women's Studies curriculum. Without the "fresh blood" of the younger women, some of whom teach the key introductory course or the politicizing and contemporary courses, much of the excitement and strength of the programme would doubtlessly evaporate. The prospect of losing them — and the courses that they teach — is a saddening one.

The False Alternatives: Ghettos and Integration

To develop the complications just one step further, let's look at two things: (i) budgets (ii) the prevailing conflicting philosophies on the subject of Women's Studies in the university setting. The first is relatively straightforward: budget cuts are in immediate threat at both universities. At York, sociology professor Judy Posner predicted tough times ahead. A way of bracing for future programme cuts, she said, "would be to make cuts ourselves ... to make sure that there is no duplication of courses." In addition to the almost certain loss of some of the part-time instructors, other course cuts might conceivably occur in an economically precarious future. At U of T, official predictions about the future of Women's Studies seemed obscurely worded, at best. When I queried the Dean of Arts and Sciences about the status of Women's Studies in days to come, he prepared a cautious and elaborately qualified reply. It was his hope, he said, that Women's Studies would eventually — when he could not say — "do itself out of business." What he was really hoping for, he said, was "an integration of the women's studies material into the mainstream." It would not do, he added, to continue to foster an image of Women's Studies as "a ghetto group." ...

    In the past few years, the undesirability of a continuing separate Women's Studies branch has also emerged as a dissenting opinion, albeit a minority opinion, among the ranks of feminist academics themselves. Ann Marie Ambert, a sociologist at York, has become an outspoken critic of a separate Women's Studies curriculum. Although Ambert agrees that Women's Studies as a separate area of research can constitute a step in the right direction, she qualifies her view rather heavily. "Unfortunately," she adds in a personal addendum to the Report on the Status of Women's Studies at the Graduate Level, "women's studies also serve the function of segregating the new perspective and empirical material from the mainstream of sociology ... In many ways, women's studies contribute to reinforce our sexual division of labour — and of status (for women's studies are not given much prestige by many of our peers)." Margrit Eichler, a sociologist at the Ontario Institute for Studies in Education, elaborates on the guilt-appeasing and status-quo maintaining dimension to the problem: as long as a token Women's Studies branch exists off in the corner somewhere, she says, "departments will rest secure in the knowledge that they have one ... course on women and that, therefore, nothing needs to be changed."

The much rued notion of the dangers of a ghetto group, of course, means different things to different people. For the already uneasy and somewhat unconvinced university administrators, it may prove highly convenient to find allies in the camps of the women academics themselves; here, they could conceivably argue, is *feminist* support for the integration-into-the-mainstream idea. One can well imagine, in the troubled times to come, Women's Studies expediently phased out from above without any compensating *enforced* integration of Women's Studies material into the mainstream ...

Evidently, then, ambitious feminist academics who yearn for a piece of the pie — or, in these times, for the right to simple survival — have not escaped the series of depressing binds that they have always found themselves in. With an eye on integration, they can 'approach' the men, but not without tact, caution, and patience; they can integrate the material into their own courses till the cows come home, but receive little respect or remuneration for their efforts; or they can teach their material under the confining Women's Studies label, and suffer the isolation, tokenism, and low-prestige repercussions that Amber and Eichler raise. Or, of course, they can put their shoulder to the wheel and do all three. Many choose to do exactly that: enter the chilling spectre of Superwoman once more ...

"Canadian Women's Studies Association/Association canadienne des études sur les femmes"
Vancouver, 1982[16]

Dear Members,

I am very pleased to inform you that since June 1982, our numbers have more than doubled: we now have 121 individual memberships in CWSA/ACEF! And I have every indication that this figure may have doubled again by June 1983, when we gather in Vancouver for our annual meeting. I think it is also significant that we have nine institutional members. I have been impressed, too, with the generosity of

16. Frances Early, "Anglophone Coordinator's Report," Canadian Women's Studies Association/Association canadienne des études sur les femmes *Newsletter* 1, no. 1 (Autumn 1982), 1–2.

individuals who have made founding donations well above the $5 membership fee.

I and the other members of the executive are actively seeking a francophone coordinator for CWSA/ACEF. No one has stepped forward yet, but we have established valuable contacts with francophone women who have already joined CWSA/ACEF. At present, approximately 15 per cent of our membership is francophone. I feel confident that more francophone women will join as they become aware of our existence. I urge CWSA/ACEF members to lend a hand in helping us find a francophone coordinator. We will welcome your suggestions in this important matter. (The French version of this newsletter will appear shortly; it is now being translated.)

On another front, Nikki Strong-Boag and Susan Jackel have been busy since June preparing an excellent, well-rounded program for us at the upcoming Learned Societies Conference at U.B.C. in Vancouver. CWSA/ACEF will be participating at the Learneds this year in conjunction with the Canadian Studies Association and the Canadian Association of Adult Learners. These sessions will take place over two days, June 4 and 5; the registration fee will be $10 per day. The agenda includes panel discussions on Women as Adult Learners; Funding for Women's Studies Research, "Women and the Canadian Economy"; and Women's Studies Program Building. There will also be a session "Feminism and Nationalism in Canada" (please see CALL FOR PAPERS blurb in this newsletter). Various social activities — a Banquet, a Wine and Cheese party, etc. — are in the works, too. The annual business meeting of CWSA/ACEF will take place on the evening of June 4 ...

In closing, I wish to leave in your minds the sense I have that an incredible energy and creativity and purpose exists in all of us. I am looking forward to hearing from you all. We have made a promising start — onward!

With best wishes,

Frances Early

"Proposal for an M.A./Ph.D. Programme in Women's Studies" Toronto, October 1989[17]

a) INTRODUCTION

The year 1990 marks the twentieth anniversary of the Report of the Royal Commission on the Status of Women. Its recommendations for education were modest and focussed primarily on the elimination of discriminatory barriers so that women might enjoy the same educational opportunities as men. However, it also anticipated the new and rapid developments in what we now refer to as Women's Studies.

In the two decades that followed the Report, the most significant development occurred in universities where scholars, chiefly women,

17. York University, Faculty of Graduate Studies, Proposal, October 1989, 1–5.

were reexamining existing curricula, university organization, research methodologies and knowledge. Their well-documented findings of gender biases led eventually to the introduction of new courses, undergraduate and graduate, within disciplines. Many of these courses critiqued and "corrected" the biases; others, however, went further to establish the foundations of a new paradigm within which there were several theoretical directions.

Women's Studies, as it now exists, represents a paradigmatic shift that has provided new insights about women's experience and has been demonstrably productive. The quality of research and publication in Women's Studies moved very quickly to a high level of professional standards.

Administratively, the next step in the development of this new area of focus was the introduction of Women's Studies undergraduate degree options, usually interdisciplinary. At the graduate level, some concentration in Women's Studies was permitted but restrained within traditional discipline boundaries. These new courses and programme options reflected the emergence of a new scholarship in almost all disciplines, based on feminist perspectives.

The proposal presented here for a graduate programme in Women's Studies is a response to these developments and a commitment to further knowledge both for its own sake and for its relevance to the larger issues of gender change in our social structure. It is based on the commitment to excellence, and innovation stated in The York University Five Year Plan. It does not duplicate any existing graduate programmes within the Ontario system and will provide an opportunity for students to engage in advanced study in an area many have begun as undergraduates. It will also enhance the richness and diversity of our offerings to all graduate students at York and neighbouring universities, and will draw its enrollments from universities across Canada and among Visa students from abroad. While it is difficult to assess with any precision the marketability of a doctoral degree in Women's Studies, it is not inconsiderable given the growth of undergraduate courses and programmes across Canada and the need for qualified faculty ...

i) Objectives

The objectives of the programme are, first, to recognzie and give coherence to a body of knowledge that is now widely dispersed and constrained by separate disciplinary frameworks and their methodologies. Women's Studies is intended to unify that knowledge within its own theoretical frameworks, and to develop and to equip students with methodologies appropriate to the development and evaluation of knowledge. Like any other developing branch of knowledge, Women's Studies has reached the stage where it is necessary to systematize and deepen the field in some orderly way.

Second, the proposal acknowledges a relatively new branch of knowledge that has been developing in the shadows of established disciplines. It provides a basis for setting a research agenda and seeking research funds as a body of knowledge in its own right. In addition it provides an opportunity to referee and publish scholarly work of high quality which either does not appear in discipline-based journals or must justify itself as a contribution to a discipline.

A third objective of the proposal is to define Women's Studies as a field and to strengthen its unique perspective and methodologies. Here, as elsewhere, the whole is greater than the sum of its parts. The current situation is "parts"; that is, Women's Studies courses are scattered throughout the university and do not offer an organized/integrated body of knowledge or interdisciplinary forum to students. The situation is counterproductive for leading-edge research and is an inaccurate representation of the progress in the field. Graduate students enrolled in discipline-based programmes are often dependent for access to Women's Studies courses on the generosity of Graduate Directors who may have other curriculum priorities. At best, graduate women within disciplines sense the inadequacy of their training, the irrelevance of at least some of the disciplinary requirements, and would prefer the more comprehensive perspective. In short, the proposal is a step in the direction of rationalization for the student and for the system without the restrictive ethos of bureaucratic structures and at a marginal cost. It follows in the tradition of programmes such as Social and Political Thought, Environmental Studies and Interdisciplinary Studies, all of which broke new ground in knowledge building.

Student demand has been a major consideration in the proposal; some of the demand has been generated by undergraduate programmes in Women's Studies; some is the result of public sector initiatives, specifically federal and provincial government agencies whose clients are women. The demand has also come from the private sector whose services or goods produced are directed increasingly to women. Finally, it comes from the professions — law, medicine, psychiatry, social work — where a new interest has been developing with respect to gender problems of equity. All of these groups — students, public and private sector organizations, professionals — are looking for a more holistic pattern of information and theory than a single discipline, whether in the Humanities or the Social Sciences, can offer.

Both men and women are interested. But bearing in mind that the structure of universities and methods of instruction in the past have been developed to accommodate male students, it is our intention to provide an intellectual environment which is conducive to women scholars and compatible with their interests and needs. The content of courses, and the patterns of advising will be sensitive to the lifestyles of women in Canada, including women who are in mid-career, re-entering the labour force after a period of child-rearing, or returning to university with a new professional interest. The guiding principle is the creation of a learning environment designed to maximize the participation of women as far as is feasible.

Finally, the proposal represents a mission or action-oriented approach to the utilization of knowledge. Women's Studies has developed parallel to the women's movement in Canada and to new social policies in both the public and private sector designed to redress gender inequities and to empower women as a group. From the Canada Council to hospital practices, from family policies to Canada's approach to aid to developing countries, from economic organization to inter-personal therapies, women have a growing input, which, to be effective, must also be well informed. Thus the traditional distinction betwen basic and applied knowledge is replaced here by a continuum.

In summary, then, the objectives of this programme are to provide an environment for serious scholars to pursue a new and developing branch of knowledge which is focussed on gender; to further the integration of this knowledge at an abstract theoretical level, and to relate the development of the programme to changes in social life. The cost is minimal — the potential considerable, and it sets the pace for other universities in Canada and Ontario ...

iii) Fields on Which the Programme will Focus

Because this programme draws widely from the humanities, social sciences, environmental studies, fine arts and law, it is not possible to divide it into fields. However, the programme does recognize five separate but overlapping components which constitute the new interdisciplinary scholarship.

Women's History
Feminist Theory
Women and Culture
Research Methodology
Public Policy
...In addition, all M.A. and Ph.D. candidates will participate in a non-credit seminar organized by faculty members, in which students can collectively discuss new work in the field, analyze current work, and maintain an overview that might not be so apparent in specific courses.

iv) Special Matters and Innovative Features

...But the proposed M.A. and Ph.D. programme in Women's Studies goes beyond a new organization of knowledge or a new degree. It provides a unique environment for learning and research that will train students to apply feminist perspectives to social, economic, and political decisions that have become part of Canada's public agenda and the curricula offerings of other Universities in Canada and elsewhere ...

"The University, Women's Studies, and Rural Women"
Brandon University, Manitoba, 1989[18]

...If Canadian universities have, to some extent at least, accepted the challenge of feminist scholarship, how well have they addressed the particular needs of that doubly excluded group, rural women? Half the population of Canada lives in towns under 100,000; in the Prairies, nearly 25% of the population live on farms. Many of the conditions on which women's studies programs are predicated do not apply to rural women.

Of particular significance to farm women who are seeking self-ful-filment is a sense of disloyalty to their men, who are also seen as excluded and unheard in Canadian society. Rural women do not in general accept their right to pursue self-development; the level of consciousness and confidence assumed in the women's studies class-room is less firmly established among them. Because rural society as a whole is endangered rural women are inclined to identify with their men, who are both oppressors and oppressed. There is ambivalence about the Canadian women's movement among the very sector of society which, at the beginning of the century, could be said to have given it birth.

A rural woman who does identify with the women's movement finds herself without the physical, psychological and academic supports that would make it possible for her to pursue women's studies. The forum to exchange ideas, voice experience, foster growth does not exist outside the urban setting. A farm woman cannot assume that childcare is available to her, nor transportation to school, nor the physical space to read, discuss and process new ideas. She does not have the access to library resources that her urban sisters enjoy. Most important of all she is alone. She cannot share that sense of strength and solidarity that women feel when they come together to discover the commonality of their experience.

What have the universities done to address the needs of rural women? Very little. A handful of institutions have made women's studies courses available to isolated non-urban students. In British Columbia, Simon Fraser University offers women's studies courses by correspondence, as does Athabasca University in Alberta. Carleton University has devel-oped a "talking head" video version of an introductory course in women's studies. In Newfoundland, Memorial University has offered women's studies through a combination of print, video and teleconfer-encing. Some other universities have sporadically made women's studies courses available off-campus.

There are, however, serious discrepancies between distance education technology and the objectives of women's studies courses. The devel-opment of the capacity to transmit information to remote locations has

18. Beth Westfall [Davies], "The University, Women's Studies, and Rural Women: Some Thoughts on Feminist Pedagogy and Rural Outreach," *Women's Education des femmes* 7, no. 1 (1989), 24–26.

revolutionized post-secondary education and made it available to people who previously had no access to university courses. What it does not permit, without significant modification, is the collaboration of the students in the learning process as equal partners with each other and the instructor.

The print medium is, of course, fundamental to any academic course. Reading is a vital part of developing the cognitive framework within which one's personal experience assumes meaning. Video presentation can be a stimulating way to transmit information and challenge patterns of thinking. What neither of these technologies permit is interaction; they cannot be made responsive. Consequently, they reinforce the old learning hierarchies: "I must learn what the experts say about my experience" is only a small step forward from "My experience is not valid here." This "banking" methodology whereby information is deposited by the teacher into the essentially passive learners is completely incompatible with feminist pedagogy.

A further difficulty with the distance delivery of women's studies courses is the lack of any provision for the affective impact of the material and its relation to personal experience. Eruptions of pain, anger and grief are a common inevitable component of women's studies. Women must be permitted to process the rediscovery of their suppressed experience and to deal with the emotive explosion this often produces. Anger and pain are unlikely to be converted into constructive energy when they are confronted alone. Women experiencing emotional release in a supportive group of their peers feel cleansed and strengthened by the experience. Women facing pain alone will avoid it, and turn their anger against themselves.

In Atlantic Canada, attempts have been made to use teleconferencing networks to link women in isolated locations with each other and with the instructor. Clearly, there are advantages to this. The telephone is a communication tool that most women are comfortable with. There is the possibility of making students responsible for segments of the curriculum, breaking down the teacher-learner hierarchy. Some interaction is possible between all participants who are therefore able to collaborate more actively in the learning process ...

The role of the universities, and women's studies programs in particular, among rural women must be examined carefully. Are we offering a new tyranny of the experts, which will serve further to alienate women from their own experience and stifle their voices? Are we imposing another alien value system on rural women which no more reflects their reality than did the one it replaces?

The universities do have a responsibility to teach rural women not what their experience is or what it means but how to tap into that experience and find ways of expressing it. Feminism has become in many ways as elitist and exclusionary as the patriarchal system it seeks to replace by reflecting the reality and the consciousness of a segment of society sufficiently privileged and secure to question current social and academic structures. Feminist educators should use their strength to develop ways in which rural women can also be empowered to reclaim their own history. By reaching out to rural women, university-based feminism can provide assistance in community development, in organization, in building networks. Rather than interpreting experience for rural women, the universities should be assisting them to build the supports they need to rediscover and articulate their own reality.

Women Studies in Manitoba High Schools
Manitoba, 1984[19]

Women's studies in Manitoba schools died when the human rights thrust of the 70's — those wonderful years when it seemed that at last we might all stay our hunger at the first sitting — took a terrible turn to the right, to privatization, self-interest, the "Me" generation. The economic recession has forcefully reminded us that concern for human right's issues is a function of the size of the pie, not the size of the heart.

In Manitoba there was never a large number of schools offering courses in women's studies — perhaps six at best — but the materials developed for use in those courses and the mere fact of their existence sparked other teachers to include modules, or units, on women's studies in such regular courses as language, arts, literature, social studies, even general business and economics. A few dedicated, determined feminists such as Maxine Hamilton at Kildonan East Regional Secondary School have integrated topics for women's studies into their programs, but generally with the pressure of heavier workloads and the preoccupation with job security, the impetus has been lost.

The Manitoba Department of Education no longer has a full-time or even half-time consultant for women's programs. Because of her own commitment, Grace Parasuik, who previously held the position, has carried the responsibilities of women's studies consultant into her new position as special assistant to the Deputy Minister, but her workload is heavy and time pressure severe. She hopes to find someone already on staff with the necessary commitment and time to assume responsibility for women's programs, but cut-backs in the Department make it impossible to hire someone for the job.

Ten years ago, Department of Education priorities were such that a full-time consultant, Heather Henderson, was available to work with teachers in the field and to develop the material resources necessary to support women's studies programs in the schools.

Ten years ago, the first women's studies courses were introduced in Manitoba. By looking back to 1974, we perhaps can gain some insight into the changes brought about by a decade.

Since I know best my own experience, it is that I will review.

As a full-time counsellor at a large urban high school, I was struck by how often academic difficulties, anger and depression, aggression and delinquency were caused by the students' not being aware of remedy or recourse to societally inflicted harsh or unfair treatment ...

Gradually, the full weight of a basic fact of human rights forced me to re-examine the service I provided students in the school: *THAT HUMAN RIGHTS — THE RIGHTS OF THE INDIVIDUAL IN SOCIETY — MEAN NOTHING UNLESS THE INDIVIDUAL (1) IS AWARE OF HIS OR HER RIGHTS AND (2) HAS THE MEANS TO DEFEND THEM.*

I began to think that maybe instead of dealing with students individually after the fact, it might make more sense to offer a course informing students of their rights as students, members of families, consumers, employees, sexual beings, and as women, and making them aware of the agencies and organizations in our society whose purpose was to protect those rights.

I had been particularly concerned by a case of incest that had lead an honour student ... to become so divided from herself that she became almost totally dysfunctional. Why had this bright, sensible young woman acquiesced to something so foreign to her conscience that it destroyed her? Because, I was finally to decide, like the other students she did not know her rights, did not realize that she had the right to say no, that there were resources available to her ...

I got permission to offer a six-week module on women's rights in society. I called it "Women Now — Women Then" and stressed with the head of the English Department the strong literary flavour it would have. Students discovered our Manitoba heroes, Nellie McClung, Margaret Laurence and Gabrielle Roy, but they also read Mother Was Not A Person, Vaginal Politics, Women and Madness, The Descent of Woman, The Second Sex, The Female Eunuch and Against Our Will. They read the poetry of Plath, Rich, Piercy, Atwood, Clifton, Sexton, and Griffin. More important they listened to, interacted with speakers like June Menzies, Chris Lane, Heather Bishop.

When I transferred to another more traditional (but closer to home) high school in the division, I wanted to take my course with me, but there the course would have to be a full-semester credit course. Even then it seemed unlikely that I would gain approval for its inclusion in the program of studies.

At the time, the Department of Education was offering grants for innovative programs in the area of curriculum development. It was an opportunity to get funding to purchase teaching materials ... and to legitimize the course by securing the Department's stamp of approval.

With help from the newly appointed Women's Studies Consultant, Heather Henderson, ... my proposal to develop a curriculum together with a supportive kit of materials ... was one of a handful of finalists in the screening process ...

I taught the course for six years. In that time a number of other women teachers developed and taught courses or units of courses on women's studies. Sara Berger, Heather Henderson and Linda McDowell worked to develop a kit containing a wealth of contemporary and historical material about women. Under a succession of women's studies consultants ... Manitoba developed a great deal of top-notch resource materials ...

Unfortunately, just at the point that a storehouse of materials was available to teachers, a number of influences served to check the progress of women's studies. Most important, the handful of dedicated feminists who were the driving force behind women's studies courses moved into positions which forced them to leave behind the course they had propelled through the second half of the seventies.

I like to think that the momentum, the driving force, has not been lost: that in a myriad of ways women's studies lives in the raised consciousness of all teachers ...

"Dealing with Residential School: The Healing Process of an Adult Child"
Pukatawagan, Manitoba, 1992[20]

I was sent to residential school in 1958 when I was six, and would continue to return every September until 1968. During that ten years, I was with my parents for twenty months. That's less than two years. The only reason I was able to get away from Guy Indian Residential School was because I was expelled for my bad behaviour.

Please read my story with the understanding that I am now an adult using healthy corrective resources in my healing process. Also visualize my experiences as the child that I was. My intentions are to help you understand me. I have had to include the past with my present experiences as part of my history that needs to be healed and I have to deal with the four aspects of my being — physical, emotional, mental, and spiritual — and how they were affected by violence throughout my life.

My first year at the residental school included myself and two hundred other girls. There was absolutely no room for taking care of an individual's needs. I would experience feeling lonely and abandoned by everyone.

I really missed my family and wanted to be with them. I would often cry and be told by the nuns that I "should not cry," that crying made me "a weak person." I would witness other girls going through the same experience and some would be punished for their crying. I would see them getting the' strap on their hands and told that they now had reason to cry.

My PHYSICAL SELF would be hurt so many times throughout the years. I cannot even begin to tell how many times. I learned to ignore the physical punishments that caused my physical pain. As I would be

20. Elizabeth Bear, *Women's Education des femmes* 9, no. 4 (Summer 1992), 20–21.

getting strapped I learned how to take myself away. I would stare straight ahead and imagine I was in the forest collecting flowers or watching a mother deer taking care of her fawn, her baby. This was my survival skill to deal with physical pain.

My EMOTIONAL SELF was then affected and I learned NOT to cry. Later in my adult life I would still not cry and for that I was emotionally crippled and would convince people that I was tough. I would not let anyone know that my feelings were hurt either by their actions or words but I would then hurt them back with my actions or words and mostly in words because I knew that it would have a longer lasting effect on them.

Now, how did I know that? I experienced physical, emotional and verbal abuse repeatedly in the residential school system and I learned this as a child; as an adult I used it in a negative manner because I was hurting inside.

I was in grade four when I learned how to spell and do arithmetic every day. It was almost a ritual and this is how my arithmetic class started. The nun would say "Everyone, recite and spell Arithmetic," so we would say outloud "A red Indian thought he might eat tobacco in church." Eating or chewing tobacco was dirty, and doing it in church was being disrespectful, was the message.

My MENTAL SELF was affected by this as I perceived this message to mean I was dirty, I was disrespectful, because I was an Indian.

The constant reminder that I was in residential school because I was an Indian and I was to learn to be a civilized person and not be a savage like my ancestors, affected the way I thought about myself.

Geography and History classes were used to continue this reminder. I hated both classes but I also tried hard to forget. I would do colourful maps, draw animals, children playing around their mothers and other people sitting around the campfire. I never did believe what I read in the History books.

For all my years at the residential school, I had Catechism classes and did my daily prayers every morning and every night. When I talk about my SPIRITUAL SELF it has nothing to do with religion. My spiritual self is my spirit to feel, to understand, to relate, to experience and to be my self.

My spirit was deadened by all the pain I endured as a child.

As a university student, I began my healing process to deal with the "Mission School Syndrome": I turned my negativism into positive energy. My healing process has been remembering my childhood and adolescent years and being aware of my behaviours and feelings. It hasn't been an easy process, remembering is very painful and learning to accept the positive and negative experiences is very hard.

Today, I share my experiences with openness and no regrets. I accept all experiences as part of my lifelong learning process.

Education is also part of learning and I know that in order for an individual to be an effective member in society and to be able to survive in the mainstream workforce, one has to have a good, acceptable education level.

It is my desire and intent to use my skills to help my people.

I am a Canadian Native Woman and proud of my culture.

"Racism in Women's Studies"
Toronto, Ontario, 1989[21]

Let me first ask, what are women's studies courses made of? Are we non-white women part of it? If yes, then why are our experiences left out, or made marginal content in the new herstory books.

Women's studies came about when women realized that their own historical perspective and experience had been left out of their education. Women's studies was to be the arena where the neglect and misrepresentation of women were to be counteracted. This was to be the place where women could come together and share collectively their herstory.

Black women have been among their white sisters, marching and negotiating for equality for women in the women's movement, yet they are still not recognized as equal in women's studies courses. Is this racist?

Racism is an ideology that propagates white supremacy, whose function is to justify inferior treatment for racially distinct groups. Is the women's studies curriculum contributing to this ideology? Is there a dominant group who have the power to oppress? You bet. Furthermore, non-white women have fewer resources to resist the oppression. One resource we do have and are using constantly is anger. Black women have been complaining for years about racism in their education. Although some people have been listening, little, if anything constructive has been done to alleviate the problem. This is why we show our anger. It is our only power and if we fail to use it positively we have no hope of achieving equality.

Black women crave knowledge, we want to read and learn about the lives, struggles and achievements of other black women. That is why we venture into women's studies courses, hoping that our thirst will be quenched. It is yet to happen. I speak from personal experience in a women's studies course.

As a past women's studies student, I can honestly say that at times, I felt marginal and neglected by the feminist movement. Although I shared the classroom with my white sisters, we did not share the same experience and realities. Hence, I was forced to be only an observer during their realm of reasoning.

I barely existed with my sisters and continued to learn "herstory" which was not much different from "history".

21. Carmen Henry, *The Womanist* 1, no. 4 (May/June 1989), 17.

I felt enraged and saddened that you had bypassed my whole story and made it only a footnote in your texts.

When you did give me a small skit to play in the curriculum — you paid close attention to me and observed me under your microscope along with all the other non-white sisters.

I was only called upon to clarify and answer ignorant questions that you could not find answers to in your text books. Only then was I allowed to speak about my plight as a non-white woman.

As racism slowly began to emerge in our conversation, it was quickly compared to gender and class oppression and again, the arena in which sexual liberation is addressed.

Do you know, that my oppression is not one or two-fold? My reality is subjugated not only by gender and class, but by race. When I am seen, I am seen as a Black woman. Note: Black comes first!

I was the only Black woman in this course and the term paper was to find a woman's group that Betty Friedan's book **The Feminine Mystique** didn't address. I thought that Friedan's concept was not addressing the plight of the domestic workers who had to leave their country to work in Canada under sometimes harsh conditions.

My views and arguments were very strong on this subject, so I did very thorough research, taking my holidays and sick days off to write this paper. When I got my marks, I was very thrilled. I had done previous papers for this professor and my marks ranged from B to C+. But this time I got an A. Wow! I was asked to see the professor. I expected praise in front of this class of 35 people. However, my excitement was short-lived. Within minutes, the professor accused me of plagiarism!

She told me I was not capable of writing this paper and must have paid someone to do it. I was furious! Instead of going on to work from my class that night I went home and I complained to everyone who would listen. Then I started crying. For days I couldn't stop.

I complained to the Dean of the department and was told that as long as I wasn't charged with plagiarism he couldn't do anything. Since then, March of 1988, I have had a problem writing.

It wasn't until I was asked to speak at the "Forum: Equity and Access for Black, Asian and Native Women at York", in January, 1989, that I regained some confidence in my writing skill.

I suffered emotional stress because of this allegation, although I am healing now. Forewarned about feminist courses, I decided to venture forth, and I came out with wounded pride. I couldn't believe a woman would do this to another woman after studying the struggle women have endured to achieve anything. I re-enact the scenario many times in my mind to project how this could have been avoided. I thought, "Why didn't she ask to see my research notes, if she was in doubt about my writing ability?" I didn't want to believe that this had happened because I was Black.

It is time women writers and others who are involved in curriculum development stop pussyfooting around and confront racism, ethnocentrism, classism and limited treatment of Black women in their works. Our white sisters have to address the real issues of the economic racial oppression among non-white women.

In doing so, course offerings on Black women and other women of colour must be added to the curriculum of women's studies. In the curriculum, there should be a theoretical perspective of non-white women, which would take us out of the margin and place us at the centre of the analysis, giving us the same status as our white sisters. [So, what is it we women of colour are really looking for?] We are looking for women's studies courses that reflect the importance of cultural, racial and social class variables ...

"Lesbian Issues in Women's Studies Courses" Toronto, March 1983[22]

...A crucial element in any early discussion of lesbianism is to provide an atmosphere in which students feel that they can honestly state their concerns, fears, stereotypes and questions. I try to combine consciousness-raising techniques with more traditional academic approaches in these discussions. Starting from their own experiences and fears, students can then examine those in the light of lots of new information. By the end of the class they have often thrown out many stereotypes, and can leave the classroom thinking lesbians are people just like anyone else. It is important not to condemn homophobic students as being 'bad people', but rather to try and expose the ways in which our society encourages homophobia and then get the students themselves to question that. The best way I have found to do that is to start from our own personal experiences with lesbianism. The start of a discussion on lesbians looks something like the following:

Nancy:I thought we'd begin our discussion of lesbians by looking at some of our society's stereotypes about lesbians. What are some that you've heard? You don't have to believe them, we just want to list them right now.

Class: Lesbians look like men. They are unattractive. They are lesbians because they can't get a man. You have to be careful around them — they try to seduce you. They are aggressive and loud. They are big women and they always wear men's clothes. Mostly they think about sex and they sleep with lots of women but they don't have many long-standing relationships. They hate men. They had overbearing (weak) fathers (mothers). Lesbians decide whether they will be the man or the woman in a relationship and then play that role. They don't like children.

22. Nancy Adamson, from "Lesbians and Teaching," *Resources for Feminist Research/Documentation sur la recherche féministe*, The Lesbian Issue, 12, no. 1 (March 1983), 5–6.

Nancy:The sex researchers tell us that about one in ten women is a lesbian. That means there are probably one (or two) lesbians in this room. If we had to identify them, do you think the stereotypes would help us to do that?

Class:No. Probably not. In a few cases, maybe. No, they're about stereotypes not about real women.

(Lots of nervous laughter and furtive glances around the room at each other.)

Nancy:We can test the stereotypes by looking at a real live lesbian. I am a lesbian and have been for about ten years and I don't think you would have identified me from those stereotypes. I don't hate men. I don't wear men's clothes. I do like children. I am not going to try to seduce you.

Coming out to my classes as a lesbian is my own personal choice. I judged that I had little to lose by coming out to my students, and since I feel comfortable it is a positive experience for all of us. Many women cannot make that choice (even if they would like to) for fear of losing their jobs, alienating workmates, losing custody of their children and many other reasons. It is not necessary, however, for the discussion leader to be a lesbian or be out as a lesbian. As long as she is sensitive to these issues she can be effective in helping to unmask the extensive homophobia in our society and help students change how they think ...

"Black Women's Studies in Teaching Related to Women: Help or Hinderance to Universal Sisterhood?" Montreal, 1988[23]

How many students of Women's Studies can identify with female pioneers of colour who have marked milestones in the History of women and humankind?

Women of Colour have played out key roles, have blazed important trails and have laid down bridges on which many of us today intrepidly tread. Yet much of today's Teaching related to Women, colourblindly ignores, omits, or simply fails to acknowledge such realities. Black women and other Women of Colour remain invisible. And so, Black Women's Studies is a positive response to the neglect of Black Women by today's Women's Studies and Teaching related to Women which clearly exclude — especially in their philosophical underpinnings — Women of Colour.

Women's Studies aspires to complete and correct the record by grafting on to present knowledge, knowledge about Women — ALL WOMEN. Consequently, Women's Studies must break with traditional approach, traditional content, and traditional values, and go **beyond** the proverbial cosmetic cover-up or lip service, in order to become more

23. Esmeralda Thornhill, *The Womanist* 1, no. 1 (September/October 1988), 13. This article is an abstract of a paper presented to the First International Conference on Research and Teaching Related to Women, 1982. The paper became the pilot for the course, "Black Women: The Missing Pages."

relevant to Black Women and not merely appear as a fight in which white women are fighting for the right to oppress Black Women equally with white men.

Through a progressive social movement like Women's Studies and Teaching related to Women, Sisterhood can become a real worldwide possibility, provided such educational initiatives do not remain short-sighted, tunnel-visioned, or colourblind. For the struggle for equality of Women (with a capital "W"), must be waged not only within the ranks of the fight against sexism, but also on the broader field of the war on racism.

Black women already share a past far different from that of white women, checkered as it is with a long history of "non-traditional" roles. And although multiple issues the world over are truly common denominators, the point remains that **it is the order of priorities that differs** when it comes to Black Women — whether they be the marginated Black Women in North America, or Women of Colour in the underdeveloped and oppressed countries of the world. Therefore, it becomes primordial for Teaching related to Women, Women's Studies and the Women's Movement to begin to address seriously issues of economic and racial oppression in order to be equally relevant to Black Women and other Women of Colour.

Black Women's Studies is a necessary component and an essential dimension to any Teaching related to Women. Black Women's Studies should be omnipresent and ubiquitous, pervading and permeating any Women's Studies program.

From a methodological viewpoint, in order to realize fully a program of Teaching related to Women, I posit that Women's Studies:

1. Can no longer remain colourblind to Black women.

2. Can no longer subscribe to the "Addendum Syndrome", "footnoting and appendixing" Black Women.

3. Can no longer exclude the active involvement of Black Women from **decisional** levels and **blueprint** stages.

4. Can no longer ETHICALLY continue being accomplices in the "Conspiracy of Silence on Racism".

The first ever international coming together of Women to discuss Teaching and Research related to Women must mean that from the outset WE BELIEVE we share a common concern, a common commitment and a common goal. If we Educators in the area of Teaching related to Women and Women's Studies are really the progressive activists and committed professionals we profess to be, if we consider ourselves true Members of the International Community of the Concerned, if we believe that we ARE indeed universally Sisters in Struggle, then we can do no less than "Agitate! Agitate! Agitate!" until Black Women's Studies assumes its rightful place in Teaching related to Women as a help to universal sisterhood.

"Black Women: The Missing Pages From Canadian Women's Studies"
Montreal, September 1988[24]

"This is a survey course, intended to introduce students to the experience of Black women in Canada as a triply oppressed group. The course will begin by examining the matrifocal role of Black Women during slavery and end with some consideration of the reasons behind the neglect of Black Women's issues by the current Women's Movement. Topics studied will include the politics of immigration, education, employment, human rights, culture and relationships. Prevalent negative stereotypes and pervading myths derived from slavery will be analyzed and re-evaluated, as will the influence of African traditions via slavery on such literary genres as slave narratives, biographical memoirs, letters and folk proverbs.

The combined intellectual (theoretical) and experiential (practical) approach of this course will offer a unique perspective which will provide an important link and much needed insight into the contributions of Black Women to the Canadian and Québec experience. At the same time the course will strive to improve and upgrade not only the image of Blacks in Canada, but also the links of communication, solidarity and sisterhood among Canadian women in struggle.

The foregoing description accompanies the course WMNS 398 c/2 **Black Women: The Missing Pages from Canadian Women's Studies**, the first ever accredited university course on Black Women offered in Canada.

This three (3) credit ground-breaking course is being offered by Concordia University's Simone de Beauvoir Institute as part of its 1988-89 Academic Programme and it is complemented by another follow-up three (3) credit course scheduled for January 1989, WMNS s/4, **Women of Colour Speak Out! Confrontation and Collaboration: Issues and Implications for Canadian Women's Studies**.

It was in 1982, immediately following the first International Conference on Teaching and Research Related to Women, that, under the aegis of the Congress of Black Women of Canada, the idea for a formalized course on Black Women's Studies was first proposed to Concordia University by Jane Kouka-Ganga and Esmeralda Thornhill. The University responded by offering during the summer of 1983, in what turned out to be a "one-shot deal", **Black Women: The Missing Pages ...** Despite unmitigated success and manifest popularity, it is only now — five years later — that Black Women's Studies is being "mainstreamed" into the Regular Academic Curriculum.

Interestingly enough, before the end of August, University authorities were reporting that student registration for both components, **Black Women ...** and **Women of Colour ...**, was already complete and closed.

24. Esmeralda Thornhill, *The Womanist* 1, no. 1 (September/October 1988), 13.

"Young Black Women Speak!"
Toronto, 1987[25]

Rosalie:I came to Canada from Jamaica ten years ago. I was 11 then. When I hear about how wonderful Canada is, I think back to my first year here. While in grade six at a west Toronto elementary school, I got into a fight with a white student. He called me a nigger one day at recess and I beat him up. I was the one who got in trouble with the principal. This was my welcome to Canada!

Marcia: The first thing I remember about Canada is watching the lights from the airplane. That was nice. My second memory isn't as pleasant. My mother was here and after six years had sent for us. Once we got to the immigration officer, my mother was told that we could not remain here. She was told that she had to apply for landed immigrant status for us while we were out of the country. The officer suggested that we all go to the States and apply from there. I don't know where he expected my mother to get the money from. Anyways we got the whole thing sorted out. We were allowed to stay but we could not go to school until we got our visa. I missed a whole year of school. That is why I'm nineteen and still in grade 12.

Shakela: My experience is similar to yours Marcia. My family applied for refugee status a few years ago. We were given the runaround but our application was finally accepted. To work my parents had to get a special permit from immigration. They must renew it every so often. Imagine we still have not received the official visa yet. Whenever I go out looking for work I have to explain my situation. Getting work is hard enough when you're not white, but it's worse when you're not a Canadian citizen.

Marcia: The first thing I always get asked when I'm looking for work is whether or not I'm eligible to work in Canada.

Rosalie:I know. You always have to prove that you're eligible.

Shakela: An immigrant always has to show more identification. You always have to carry your passport. Citizens just have to carry a card (citizenship card) or birth certificate.

Erin:I don't have as much problems now as I did when I first came here. I was born in Britain and my accent was constantly questioned. White people acted as if they did not know that Britain had Blacks. I got into many a fight in elementary and senior public schools. I haven't had much discrimination in job hunting. That could be because I'm just starting to look for full-time work.

Rosalie: What really bugs me is that after all the hassle you end up not getting the job. All this proving eligibility makes me feel like a criminal.

Marcia: It makes me feel as if I don't belong. I feel left out.

25. Debbie Douglas, *Immigrant Women*, special issue of *Resources for Feminist Research/Documentation sur la recherche féministe* 16, no. 1 (1987), 17–18.

Shakela: Sometimes I'm glad that I'm here but all the hassles are frustrating and sometimes not worth it.

Marcia: All that hassle and it's cold too. (laugh)

Shakela: Going to the immigration office is a hassle. You never get through on one day. It's appointment after appointment. You get treated like you're nothing.

Erin: They treat us as if you're nothing or like a criminal. Whenever someone who isn't white gets in trouble the police starts talking about deportation. You constantly have to watch your back.

Rosalie: What really gets me is the way the television and newspaper report the news. Whenever a white person commits a crime, all they tell you is whether or not that person was female or male, the colour of their eyes and hair and their weight and height. Once they think it's a Black person however, they stress his colour and sometimes even go as far as to say which island he's from. No wonder so many people think that all Blacks are criminals.

Marcia: You would think the schools would be doing something to educate white students about other people. But they're not. It's just as bad in the schools as it is out here.

Erin:I know. That's what I was saying before. The kids laughed at the way I spoke and the teachers didn't say anything.

Marcia: You're singled out a lot because you're Black. I spent three years at a school where there were seven hundred students and only three of us were Black. I always felt that I was singled out.

Shakela: Ya! No one would talk to me.

Marcia: Whenever the teacher asked me a question everyone would turn around and watch me. They were all waiting to hear my answer. I always felt as if I was weird or something. It took me a long time to feel comfortable. Teachers always made me feel as if I couldn't speak English.

Rosalie:I know. I had a very heavy Jamaican accent. The teacher would always ask me to repeat myself. This would make the other students laugh. I always got asked what language I spoke. I failed my English class because I did not participate in class discussions.

Shakela: Whenever I answered a question in class, the other students would laugh and I would be told that I spoke like a "Paki." You know the first time I heard that word was in elementary school.

Erin: Teachers never seem to realize what is going on. Instead of dealing with the problems, they say that you have a learning disability and they put you in a basic-level school.

Marcia: There must be something Blacks can do to stop teachers sending Black students to dead-end schools. Our parents don't know what the differences in levels are. By the time they find out it's too late.

Erin:I made sure that I went to a school that I knew had a good academic program. Dealing with discrimination is difficult but you have to have a way to cope. If you don't, you start believing what they think about you because you're Black. Young Black people need to get together more to talk.

Marcia: You're right. There must be something we can do!

Job Training/Language Training

"Systemic Discrimination and the Provision of Training Programs to Women"
Montreal, 1983[26]

In filing a complaint before the Canadian Human Rights Commission against the Minister of Employment and Immigration in July 1982, ACTION TRAVAIL DES FEMMES (A.T.F.) accused the Commission of training policies which operate to exclude women from training courses which have been, and still are, reserved for men. The Ministry's refusal to provide a welding course to 15 Montreal women was cited as an example of an overall policy not to make trades training accessible to women.

The evidence that such policies exist is to be found firstly in the Ministry's own statistics. Of 48 courses designated by C.E.I.C. as non-traditional and supposedly the object of the policy known as "priority to women" since 1977, only three trades courses — cook, butcher and business administration (finances) — had substantial (at least 20%) female enrolment in 1981-82. It is interesting to note that these three courses are offered during the day. The other 48 courses mostly offered from 4 p.m. to 10 p.m. had a total enrolment of 3, 274, including only 11 (3%) women. Needless to say, courses such as clerk-typist and sewing machine operator are composed totally of women. Such courses are also generally offered during the day.

According to a study published in 1980 by the Canadian Advisory Council on the Status of Women, women are underrepresented in institutional training programs subsidized by C.E.I.C. In 1980-81, women were 48% of the unemployed while they comprised only 32% of C.E.I.C. institutional trainees.

These statistics are the inevitable result of the implementation of Commission policies.

Women who register with Canada Manpower and who seek information on retraining programs are systematically oriented towards courses such as typing, bookkeeping and keypunch operator. Since September 1980, 744 women have come to A.T.F. for employment counselling; 63% of these women have previously registered with Canada Employment and Immigration. To date we have never encountered a woman who has been informed about trades training by a C.E.I.C. counsellor although many women have been encouraged to enroll for secretarial training. No written material is available in C.E.I.C. offices in Quebec

26. Carole Wallace, *Women's Education des femmes* 2, no. 1 (September 1983), 13–15.

on the so-called "priority to women" in trades courses and many counsellors with whom we have dealt are unaware of this policy.

Women who find out about trades training are systematically discouraged from registering for such courses by C.E.I.C. counsellors. Between January 1981 and January 1983, we referred 41 women for specific trades courses in which there was supposedly priority given to women. In 29 cases we were obliged to intervene directly in order to assure that the women be registered. In 2 cases, counsellors did not know of the existence of such a policy, in 2 others they insisted that women must undergo aptitude testing before being allowed access to trades training, in another case a woman was told that she had no right to a retraining course because she had been absent from the labour market for five years in order to be with her young children.

Several individual women managed to pressure counsellors without our help, but reported back to us that there had ben considerable scepticism about their career choices ...

The majority of trade courses are offered at night from 4 p.m. to 10 p.m. The impact on women who have family responsibilities is obvious especially in the case of women who head families, C.E.I.C. statistics indicate that 4 times as many women as men trainees are likely to be divorced or separated. Courses offered at night when schools and daycares are closed are inaccessible to women who have children given that C.E.I.C. offers only $20.00 per week in childcare for the first child and $15.00 for each subsequent child. Many women who have been interested in trades training have been deterred by the impossibility of finding reliable childcare (including suppers) for $20.00 for 40 hours a week ...

"Women Interested in Successful Employment: Perspectives on a Bridging Program"
St. John's, Newfoundland[27]

...The WISE program was initiated in November 1987 by CCLOW-Newfoundland in co-operation with the Association for Lifelong Learning (St. John's branch of the Newfoundland and Labrador Association for Adult Education). It is an innovative bridging program offering flexible learning, counselling, and self-development and was established to assist women who are seeking to enter or re-enter the work force and women who want or need to re-direct their career paths or develop skills or career decision-making. Since its inception, the program has received enthusiastic response from participants and from over 500 women in the community who have expressed interest in joining. This article profiles the program from several perspectives, presenting the voices of women who have been involved in different ways — as participants, staff, and volunteers.

---

27. Sylvia Ash, Helen King, Dorothy Robbins, Gladys Watson and WISE Participants, *Women's Education des femmes* 7, no. 2 (1989), 30–33.

PARTICIPANTS

WISE participants have different reasons for coming to the program but they share many experiences.

For several years, I worked in a cafeteria. I always wanted to go back to school, but my husband told me that I was too old to go back. Now, here I am back at school. I'm forty and I'm just going to get older anyhow. I'm hoping to do office work which a lot of people don't want to do, but to me it will be a change from working in the cafeteria ...

My husband died recently and suddenly I'm faced with the responsibilities of a home, a car and two children. I feel scared about all the things I have to take over. I thought, how in the world does a woman earn a man's wage? I had done office work. I had worked in a nursery school. I had worked selling real estate. But what do I have to offer an employer so that I can earn a wage that my family can live on? So that's why I'm here — to gain some confidence and to develop what areas I can ...

Over and over again, participants express surprise at finding a program that is so flexible, that gives them the opportunity to explore different options and does not tie them to a particular job or trade before they know what their education and employment possibilities are. Access to support services such as child care and transportation is also considered extremely important. Several participants have said that when they first heard about the program they could not believe it was true, it was so perfectly suited to their situation.

THE BRIDGING PROGRAM MODEL

WISE offers an individualized approach to training, needs assessment, and skill development in an environment designed to reduce the barriers to women's participation. It encompasses the development of problem-solving and goal-setting skills, and the development of support systems to facilitate the transition to further training and/or successful employment.

The most innovative aspects of the WISE project are the bridging and flexibility of the training process. The project design incorporates learning modules, transferrable skills, computer assisted learning, contract learning, and small group learning. The program includes: individual assessment, individual counselling, individual and group career exploration, voactional planning, pre-technical and trades bridging, work observation stations, some academic upgrading, and introduction to computer operations. All modules and components, with the exception of the work observation stations, are located on one site and are supplemented by support and advocacy. Participants receive financial assistance equal to the provincial minimum wage rate, financial support for child care, and transportation services for children (and participants when possible). The staff team includes a co-ordinator, a counsellor, two instructors, an administrative assistant, and a van driver. The van driver provides transportation for participants' children from the WISE program to and from their respective schools and daycare programs.

Despite the fact that WISE has advertised only twice in the local newspaper and has the financial capacity to accommodate only twenty-five women at a time, over five hundred women have attended the WISE information sessions. Applicants attend an initial counselling session where an assessment is completed. The selection of appropriate candidates is determined by the counsellor and co-ordinator. WISE has had four intakes of participants since February 1988 when the program began. In the first intake, there were twenty-six women from diversified employment-related and economic backgrounds ranging in ages from nineteen to forty-seven; from this initial group, twelve women entered the job market and twelve women entered training programs.

When participants have been selected, they meet individually with the counsellor to sign a contract and set a tentative time frame for program attendance so that child care and other arrangements can be set up. All new participants attend a two-week orientation phase which includes not only a general introduction to the program, but also sessions with guest speakers and a workshop on math and science. Following orientation, participants finalize their contract with the program by choosing which combination of program components they will take and the length of time they will assign to each.

"I have been involved in other adult education entry and re-entry programs where the goals were to train people in skill areas for direct entry into the workforce," says Sylvia Ash, WISE instructor. "The philosophy was that if a person had the required educational prerequisites, she could acquire the skills necessary to enter the workforce and should not have any barriers in doing so. But since other factors often impinge on a person's life, skill training alone does not always result in successful employment, neither does it provide vocational planning, exposure to employment, or other training options. The WISE bridging program recognizes and addresses the individual needs of adult learners and, in particular, the unique learning needs of women. It approaches the learning needs of women 'where they are'."

For many participants, increased self-confidence is the most immediate benefit of the program and staff play a major role in creating a positive environment.

The instructors are great. They're helpful. They're terrific. A lot of us haven't been in school for years. It's difficult at this stage to go back and have somebody lecture to you. You don't want that. The instructors at WISE don't teach us in a student/teacher relationship which is great. It's very casual.

Participants also emphasize the importance of the relationship with others in the program: how valuable it is to be part of the group and to know that others share similar experiences and challenges.

I remember getting up in the morning and not knowing what to do and feeling so isolated. You feel that you can't go out and tell anybody how you feel because they won't really understand. Then when you get in here you realize that everybody has felt like that ...

The program components participants identify as most valuable are job search and computer training ...

... There is a need not only to document the success of briding programs for women's education and training, but to advocate for government policy and funding that fosters the development of bridging programs for women across the country. As one WISE participant suggested: *The whole mentality has got to change. Everyone's mentality has go to change when it comes to the subject of educating women.*

"Training for Whom?"
Toronto, 1993[28]

ATTENTION
MEN AND WOMEN
ON
UNEMPLOYMENT INSURANCE
The Bridging Program is offering a computer software training to men and women receiving unemployment insurance. Register NOW by calling the Bridging Program for Women.

Taken from an ad appearing in the
Regina Sun, *November 14/93*

Wait a minute. The Bridging Program for *Women* — the demonstration project developed by CCLOW in 1983 to provide women with the necessary supports, lifeskills, and options for going on to futher education, jobs, and better lives — is offering training to *men*?!

Since the introduction of the National Training Act in 1982, CCLOW has monitored the situation of women's training in Canada. We have witnessed the amount of dollars allocated to training decline steadily. We have protested the sharp decrease in the number of women receiving training, literacy instruction, and upgrading. We have advocated for pay and employment equity, and for greater access for women to trades and technology. More recently we have watched the erosion of social pro-

---

28. Aisla Thomson, Editorial, *Women's Education des femmes* 10, nos. 3/4 (Winter 1993/94), 2.

grams and the dramatic shift in the direction of government policy and a re-definition of the "most in need".

Now our fears around the backlash against women and the competition for scarce dollars have come to pass. Women's programming has been deemed expendable: a frill in a healthy economy, a loadstone in a recession.

The Bridging Program for Women is a successful model of training that has been adapted and applied to a range of situations including pre-trades and pre-technology training for women. Women Interested in Successful Employment (WISE) operates in two communities in Newfoundland and has a long waiting list of women wanting to access its services. The purpose of the bridging program model was to compensate for the situational, systemic, and dispositional barriers that women face, with the ultimate goal of making women economically self-sufficient.

The shift in the focus of training to those who are recently unemployed and still receiving unemployment insurance benefits has had a detrimental effect on marginalized people in Canada, especially women. Training dollars are being directed towards those in society who have the greatest potential to "make it"; that is, people who have skills, who have university degrees or training, people who have already had the advantages of work experience. This change in focus has meant that re-entrants and new entrants to the labour force, immigrants, persons with disabilities, the undereducated, and the underemployed are disregarded.

It is exactly those people that bridging programs were designed to serve. Bridging programs for women recognize that women need positive, supportive, safe, and women-centred programming and environments in which to develop their full potential. Adding men to the program will negate the very principles and premises upon which the bridging program is based. Furthermore, courses dealing with technology must be woman-positive and for women only.

If the full human resource potential of women is going to be realized, then the necessary supports and enabling structures and policies must be put into place. This is necessary in both public institutions and the private sector. Employers must be encouraged to place more emphasis on on-the-job training for women, and to train women as much for their potential as their current skill level. Training for women must be viewed as an investment rather than a risk.

As demonstrated through the articles in this special issue on women's training in Canada, there is still a long way to go before the need for bridging programs and woman-positive programming disappears. Despite gains we have made in terms of legislation around pay and employment equity, there is still work to be done to ensure equity in education and training.

"Good Jobs, Bad Jobs, No Jobs: a Not-So-Trivial Pursuit" Toronto, 1993/94[29]

Test your knowledge of the connections between training, education and employment for women! [Answers follow.]

1. Statistics Canada's Employment/Population Ratio refers to the percentage of the population aged 15 and over that has some paid employment.

a) Which of the following was the only male group to have their employment/population ratio rise between 1982-1992?
Men whose highest formal education level was:
[] 0-8 years
[] high school graduation
[] some post-secondary education
[] a post-secondary certificate or diploma
[] university

b) Among females, which was the only group to see their unemployment rate decrease between 1987-1992?
Women whose highest formal education level was:
[] 0-8 years
[] high school graduation
[] some post-secondary education
[] a post-secondary certificate or diploma
[] university

2. Between 1987 and 1992, which showed the largest percentage increase?
[] the number of unemployed women
[] the number of unemployed women with post-secondary education

3. In 1990-91, the media reported a drop in the wage gap between women and men.

a) Which group experienced the largest *decrease* in the wage gap?
Women whose highest formal education level was:
[] 0-8 years
[] high school graduation
[] some post-secondary education
[] a post-secondary certificate or diploma
[] university

29. Pat Armstrong, *Women's Education des femmes* 10 nos. 3/4 (Winter 1993/94), 46–49. This questionnaire was originally part of a presentation by Pat Armstrong at a workshop organized by the Centre for Research on Work and Society, York University, Toronto, on June 18, 1993.

b) Which group of women was the only group to experience an *increase* in the wage gap?
Women whose highest formal education level was:
[] 0-8 years
[] high school graduation
[] some post-secondary education
[] a post-secondary certificate or diploma
[] university

4. a) Which group had the largest percentage increase in part-time work from 1991 to 1992?
[] males 15-24 years of age
[] males 24-44 years of age
[] males 45+ years of age
[] females 15-24 years of age
[] females 24-44 years of age
[] females 45+ years of age

b) What proportion of women employed part-time in 1992 worked part-time because they did not want full-time work?

[] 1/4	[] 1/2
[] 1/3	[] 3/4

5. Who is more likely to have more than one paid job?

[] men   [] women

6. Between 1985 and 1990, the number of people with paid work increased by nearly two million. What proportion of this two million did *not* get full-time, full-year work?

[] 10%	[] 20%	[] 30%
[] 40%	[] 50%	

7. New jobs have been appearing more frequently in small businesses than in large businesses.

a) Which firms are more likely to provide training?
[] small firms   [] large firms

b) Which firms have higher wages?
[] small firms   [] large firms

c) Which workers are more likely to be permanently laid off?
[] in small firms   [] in large firms

8. There has been a great deal of discussion of the separation of work into good jobs and bad jobs.

a) Which worker is most likely to have the longest work week?
[] the least formal education
[] the most formal education

b) Which worker is most likely to work on temporary contract?
[] the least formal education
[] the most formal education

c) The number of management jobs increased significantly between 1986 and 1991. Where was the larger percentage increase in jobs?
[] senior management
[] sales

Answers

1. a) Men who graduated from high school had a 0.9 percent proportionate increase in employment.

b) Women who graduated from high school had a 0.7 percent decrease in unemployment.

All other groups had a decrease in employment. Women with post-secondary certificates or diplomas had a decrease in employment almost equal to that of women with grade 8 or less.

2. Between 1987 and 1992, the total number of women unemployed increased by 21.4 percent; the number of women with post-secondary education who were unemployed increased by 74.3 percent. Rising unemployment rates cannot be blamed on a poorly-trained workforce.

3. a) Women with grade 8 or less had the largest decrease in the wage gap (from earning 62.4 percent to earning 66.9 percent of comparable men's wages).

b) Women who attended university had an increase in the wage gap (from earning 72.8 percent to earning 71.7 percent of comparable men's wages).

The drop in the wage gap between women with the lowest level of education may be due to a decrease in the wages of male workers.

4. a) All groups of males had larger increases in part-time work than comparable groups of females, but males aged 25-44 showed the largest increase in part-time work (up 10 percent).

Although part-time work is still done primarily by women, it is rapidly increasing for men. Moreover, hours of paid work are decreasing for both full- and part-time workers and both sexes.

b) 1/3 of women employed part-time did so because they did not want full-time work. They gave school and personal reasons. Two-thirds of women working part-time are not doing so by choice. As well, women who say they prefer to work part-time may not really have a choice if they have no one else to look after children or other dependents.

5. More men than women have more than one paid job, but the number of women holding multiple jobs has increased while the number of men with more than one job has decreased.

This suggests that there is less work available for men and reflects the high number of women with only part-time work.

6. Approximately fifty percent of the two million did not get full-time, full-year work. According to the Economic Council of Canada, non-standard (part-time, short-term, temporary, "self-employed") work accounted for 44 percent of job growth in the 1980s.

7. a) Large firms are more likely not to provide training. Six percent of small firms (20 or less workers) provide training, while 11-15 percent of medium-sized firms and 22 percent of large firms do.

b) Large firms pay 21 percent more than small firms.

c) Workers are more likely to be permanently laid off if they are employed by a small firm.

8. a) Workers with the most formal education were twice as likely to have the longest work week.

b) Workers with the most formal education were more likely to be on temporary contract.

c) The actual number of senior managers decreased by 5,000 between 1986 and 1991, while the number of sales managers grew by 37,000. These sales managers work mostly in small boutiques and small businesses.

Conclusions

Lack of education and training cannot explain rising unemployment, nor can unemployment (and under-employment) be solved with more education and training.

We are experiencing a feminization of the labour force. Men's jobs are becoming more like women's jobs, i.e., less pay, more part-time work.

Job growth is occurring in so-called "bad jobs": part-time and temporary jobs, jobs in small businesses which are likely not to provide training, have lower wages and less job security.

The growth of the global economy means that decisions affecting employment can be made anywhere. The solution to unemployment is not more training but a stronger government at the federal and provincial levels which can act as a buffer between workers and international capital. The Canadian government must form an economic policy that is directed at changing jobs rather than people.

Community Outreach

"Tools Not Rules: Challenging Traditional Power Dynamics as Assault Prevention"
Montreal, 1992/93[30]

I've been involved with the Montreal Assault Prevention Centre for over two years and it's still strange to me that people gloss over the word prevention in our name, regularly confusing us with the Montreal Sexual Assault Centre. It is as though, hearing the word assault, people automatically think "crisis centre," "counselling." ...

It is precisely this not so little word — prevention — which defines our work and informs all our ideas and approaches to assault. It is because of this word, this not so simple idea, that I was drawn to work here. The Montreal Assault Prevention Centre does precisely that, attempts to prevent assault. We offer unique prevention programs for many groups who are particularly vulnerable: women, children, elderly people, those with intellectual or physical disabilities.

Assault prevention is a radical idea. I worked for years in a rape crisis centre, helping women heal from the painful trauma of assault — everything from street harassment to ongoing incest and rape ... What is radical about rape crisis centres is the fervent belief that if only we could expose the truth — that men have power and women are victimized by the misuse of that power — then the whole patriarchal system we call society would *have* to change. If only we could get everyone to see the world as it is, a revolution would be inevitable.

Perhaps not all centres would share this analysis, but encouraging women to talk about the pain and trauma of violence is in itself a revolutionary project. Fighting to change blame-the-victim attitudes and helping women battle the medical and legal-justice systems were radical ideas when rape crisis centres came into being, and these continue to be the day-to-day, invaluable services the centres provide. However, as an individual counsellor struggling through the daily pain of helping survivors to heal, I felt we had a parallel mission: to generate social change, to limit or stop sexual violence altogether. And we fough for this change ... by educating, by exposing the reality of injustice and inequality.

But we were stuck within the confines of the very system we were seeking to change. We accepted, perhaps too uncritically, the notion of women as powerless victims. For to say that we *could* fight back, that we *could* take power and not let ourselves be victims, seemed to suggest that we were also responsible when we *did not* fight back, or *could not* get away. I stumbled over that one, and there was an uncomfortable silence around these questions at the rape crisis centre ...

When I moved to Montreal, I came across almost by accident the Montreal Assault Prevention Centre. Here we do say, quite comfortably, that there is almost always something you can do to prevent or stop an aggressive situation. Here we teach women, children, and others to fight back; to stand and confront aggressors; to yell, make a scene; to use instinct and awareness to get out of dangerous situations; to kick and punch; to do what is necessary to get to safety. We teach those who are traditionally disempowered *to take some power*. Power is not something men have in the absence of women; power is a relation between people or between groups. In assault situations we are one side of a power dynamic, not hapless victims.

I do not want to imply that the notion of prevention is simple or unproblematic. Prevention based on rules governing our behaviour, which keep us fearful and still skill-less when facing an aggressor, is not empowering. Rather, empowering prevention is grounded in the notion of developing tools, instincts, awareness, confidence, verbal skills, assertiveness, and physical manoeuvres. These tools are varied, adaptable, and flexible; they improve the quality of our lives, they give us choices and freedoms we may never have felt before.

So when we say that women and others vulnerable to assault can fight back, we are changing the parameters of the debate. We are not accepting as immutable the notion that men are *powerful*, women power*less*. Women can take power, can invent new ways of using power to protect ourselves, and can challenge old ideas of power-over as the only power dynamic possible. Perhaps it is for this reason that the word prevention gets ignored so often. Because in believing we can prevent assault, we are throwing off the notion that men and other groups have exclusive access to power; we are stepping out of the structure which keeps us believing in our own oppression.

Which is not to blame the victim. Most of us have never learned to take power, to kick, yell, fight back, say *no*. Many of us have no idea how to do so. And once we learn, perhaps we will carry with us a sad sense of not having learned earlier, of having missed opportunities to stop some of the violence in our lives. But at least we are ready for the next time.

"Do You Know a Lesbian?"
Whitehorse, Yukon, 1991; Toronto, Ontario, 1992[31]

As women's organizations and other progressive groups endeavour to address the diversity of the Canadian community and seek to open themselves to a broad range of concerns, a frequently invisible minority speaks out. We are lesbians. We are in most of your organizations and many of your families. We are your daughters, your sisters, your friends and your mothers. You know us and love us, whether you realize it or not. We struggle alongside you, often on issues that touch your lives far more than they touch ours. As we have supported you, it is time for you to support us.

31. Flyer prepared by the Lesbian Issues Committee of NAC, 1992, based on an article by Helen Fallding originally published in the *OptiMst*, Whitehorse, Yukon, 1991.

1. Use the word lesbian often. Use it in conversations with lesbians (it will make us feel less invisible), use it in front of other progressive people (it will teach them to use it), and use it in front of people who you imagine will drop dead when they hear it (it's time they got used to the idea).

2. Think about your own sexuality. Examine how you became heterosexual — because there is as much or as little "cause" for that as there is a "cause" for another woman being a lesbian. Much homophobia is rooted in people's discomfort with their own feelings for people of the same sex. Get past that and you'll be emotionally ready to be an ally.

3. Don't always claim heterosexual privilege by making it clear you are straight. Try casting doubt in people's minds about your own sexual orientation every once in a while. Make it clear that it would be no insult to mistake you for a lesbian. Refer to past relationships with women, if you've had any. Refer to lesbian friends (using their names only if they're comfortable with that). Talk about how any issue under discussion might affect lesbians. If all of this starts people asking you point blank if you are a lesbian, think of creative answers that teach people something.

4. Don't assume anyone is exclusively heterosexual. Use inclusive language if you are asking someone whether she has any new romantic interests. If she gets offended, help her to look at why she considers it an insult. If your friend is in fact a lesbian, your choice of words will be a sign to her that you are someone she can talk to.

5. Remember that we're as diverse as you are. We wear Levi's and we wear pearls. We come in every shape, size, disability, race, colour and age. We are rich and we are poor. We speak every language.

6. Don't require that your lesbian and gay friends behave or look like heterosexuals in order to be accepted in your social circle or organization. Welcome the flaming queen or the butch lesbian. For some of us our appearance is a part of our culture and a strategy to affirm our right to be whoever we are.

7. Don't assume your kids will grow up to be heterosexual, and don't assume your heterosexual friends will all remain that way. Try to make sure there are lesbians and gay men in your children's lives. Let the people you care about know that whomever they chose to love, you will celebrate with them.

8. Openly acknowledge the contributions of lesbians to the feminist movement and to local women's organizations. Make it clear that women's services are there to offer assistance to lesbians as well as heterosexual women. Make sure this is true in practice by including training about homophobia for staff members. If funding bodies balk, fight this discriminatory policy and make it known to your community that it exists — don't roll over and play dead.

9. Support us in our political struggles as we have supported you in yours. Write to the Justice Minister and demand Human Rights Act and

Charter protection for lesbians and gay men, and send copies to the leaders of the Opposition. Insist that we be given the same social and employment benefits as heterosexuals.

It has often been said about the women's movement that at its most basic, it is about choice, the right of women to choose who they wish to be. Ask yourself this: is there any choice more fundamental than the choice of whom to love?

Documenting Inclusiveness and Diversity
Ottawa, Summer 1994[32]

This spring CRIAW received funding from Multiculturalism and Citizenship Canada to carry out this exciting and promising project. Through this project we hope to gain a better understanding of how the decision making structures and communication strategies of various women's organizations can facilitate or hinder their ability to become inclusive and diverse.

More specifically the objectives of the project are:

1)To see if some organizations have been more successful than others in including certain groups;

2)To document how the structures of an organization can influence its capacity to become inclusive;

3)To examine and compare the various materials used by organizations to reach out and communicate with a more diverse audience;

4)To revise our own communication strategies, more specifically our newsletter, with the objective of communicating with a more diverse audience;

5)To integrate this information into CRIAW's own restructuring.

By inclusive and diverse we mean the participation of racial minority and immigrant women, disabled women, native women, poor women, francophone women and lesbians.

This project is being overseen by an advisory board composed of Caroline Andrew, Roxana Ng, Martha Muzychka, Bo Miedema, Monique Hébert and Noga Gayle. This committee (with the exception of Noga Gayle who was unable to attend) met on the weekend of May 13 and 14 to determine the parameters of the study and to design the interview structure to be used by the research assistants.

Interviews will be carried out with women's groups as well as with individuals who have had various experiences as members of women's groups. We will contact women's groups who work at the national level, provincial level or local level. It is important to note that this project is a documentation and not an evaluation. In our report and handbook we

32. "New CRIAW Research Project: A Documentation of How Organizational Structures Can Facilitate or Hinder Inclusiveness," *Canadian Research Institute for the Advancement of Women Newsletter* 14, no. 4 (Summer 1994), 3.

will not be describing the specific structures of the interviewed groups. Using the gathered information we will develop models of structures such as the collective model, the board model, etc. This project will begin this summer and will hopefully be finished by the end of this year.

"Moving Towards An Anti-Racist Feminism"
St. John's, Newfoundland, November 1993[33]

Our annual conferences are evolving and becoming places where CRIAW's goal of bridging the gaps between academic and grassroots-community research is reflected in who participates in this event. As an active participant in last year's conference on Anti-racism & Feminism: Making the Links, I was inspired by some of the speakers. As I listened to what these women had to say, I was struck by their forthrightness and strength. Often I was moved to tears or heady joy, and ultimately I was inspired and renewed to continue my involvement in an anti-racist women's movement.

Although there was a public mood of celebration, there was also an underlying dissatisfaction being voiced at the conference. There was even criticism that CRIAW was a white elitist organization. I did not then, nor do I now, feel compelled to defend CRIAW's record.

I can, however, share some information on how I came to be involved. In 1991, when I was acclaimed as Saskatchewan representative, I was recruited primarily because the board was trying to become more multicultural in its composition. I did not know the person who nominated me. My name was recommended to her by a friend. I came on the eighteen-member Board, at a time when the only other woman of Aboriginal ancestry was completing her three-year term.

Some board members were genuinely interested and warmly welcomed me. Others exhibited a patronizing, tolerant attitude toward me. I quickly realized that CRIAW was reflective of the Canadian population. They have limited knowledge about how racism and sexism intertwine to create another level of disadvantage for women of colour. Simply by nature of CRIAW's overwhelmingly white board composition, there was less commitment to addressing the issues of race. Racism had not affected their daily lives so they felt little drive to incorporate it as a critical concern. The realization that any commitment to eradicating sexism and racism in Canada must also include eradicating racism within the feminist movement has not yet permeated the fabric of CRIAW. Unfortunately, this failure probably characterizes most women's organizations.

If you will reflect back on the appointment of Sunera Thobani as president of NAC, you will clearly recall the heated public outcry (by some white women) that Sunera was an immigrant, not a Canadian, that she was not aware of the problems that Canadian women faced, and was therefore an ill-suited candidate to represent their interests.

---

33. Monica Goulet, banquet speech at the CRIAW Conference.

My heart went out to Sunera, and I was disgusted with the women who voiced their racism on national television. I was also extremely irate with the network for producing a clearly biased, anti-immigrant piece of propaganda and allowing these racist viewpoints to go unchallenged during that broadcast.

When I tell you that my heart went out to Sunera, it did so because I had experienced similar racism. When I was asked to allow my name to stand for president-elect of CRIAW last November, I initially declined. Having been a board member for only a year, I felt I did not have enough experience. When I received yet another more pressing phone call to reconsider, I agreed to let my name stand. Between phone calls, I talked with friends who encouraged me to run for the position. As a woman of Aboriginal ancestry, I have always struggled with the imprint on my psyche that tells me I am not good enough, not smart enough, not capable enough for the task at hand. My family and friends then remind me to stop this negative thinking. I was not borm with a scar on my soul. It is the result of years and years of oppression. Chief Poundmaker, a Cree chief, once prophesied, "You who fought so well ... will have to fight the toughest battle — yourselves — and the belief that we are less than they are, because it is not true."

Ironically, at the board meeting preceding last year's conference on Anti-racism & Feminism, I discovered that my nomination had been a topic of "hot controversy." In my absence, there had been heated debate about the politics of the nominating committee. In fact, a few people resigned from the board. I have been provided with various interpretations of what transpired and why. There was even a petition circulated so that my nomination could not be overturned. I was assured by some board members that there had been problems with the nominating procedure for a long time and that my nomination as president-elect had been unanimously approved by the board in the end. For me, this is the clearest example of racism that I have personally experienced as a CRIAW board member.

In light of this experience, some of you may wonder why I would choose to stay. It is because **I have a right to be here**. Women of Aboriginal ancestry have only recently begun to claim positions of leadership in the mainstream feminist movement. There have been a lot of negative stereotypes perpetuated about us in some of the 'unenlightened' feminist research ...

... we continue in the struggle to free ourselves from those lies which we have been taught about ourselves. Those lies we have been taught about each other. We must not be afraid to speak out about our experiences of discrimination within the women's movement. Pretending and not naming or challenging injustice, in whatever form it may strike, only creates isolation and a sense of hopelessness.

Inclusion is no longer a polite request served up on a plate to "middle-class darlings" who are content with token representation. We have not survived years of oppression in a system of partriarchy only to be relegated to similar status in a movement that identifies itself as a women's movement.

We can no longer afford to call ourselves the Canadian Research Institute for the Advancement of Women if only a select group can advance, if we don't really mean all women, if we don't support research that will liberate and empower all women.

As does any organization, ours must change. There are still policies and practices in place which continue to prevent the meaningful participation of marginalized women. The CRIAW board is now comprised of three women of Aboriginal ancestry, two Black women, one Chinese woman, and twelve European women. While that is an improvement from last year, we still do not have full representation. As your new president, I will do my utmost to help bring about that change. Let us work with a renewed sense of passion and commitment as we formulate a more cohesive feminism for the 1990s!

Letter of Resignation from Presidency of CRIAW
Ottawa, September 1, 1994[34]

As the beginning of a new school year creates cause for reflection on goals and commitments, I find myself thinking and feeling absolutely unmotivated about yet another CRIAW meeting.

Life is so precious and so is the energy provided with which to live it in a full and satisfying manner. Generally, if I am in an organization that is truly committed to creating positive change for those it deems to serve, then I am motivated and excited about meetings. Having served on CRIAW in a volunteer capacity for a number of years now, I feel I have an "insiders" perspective on the organization.

I have talked at length, and after much reflection on how CRIAW might change to become more inclusive, I know that I may as well be "talking to the wind" — but then, on the other hand, I think the wind would at least hear me.

The reason why so many Aboriginal women leave CRIAW is because it is not a comfortable place to be nor does it act as a vehicle to truly address our concerns. I believe this is the case for "other" racial and ethnic minority women.

My life and energy are to be used wisely in the pursuit of social justice. CRIAW is not an organizatin in which this can happen.

PEACE AND JUSTICE
MONICA GOULET

---

34. Monica Goulet, "President's Letter of Resignation."

Chapter 4

Feminism's Effect on Economic Policy

Marjorie Griffin Cohen

The feminist slogan "the personal is political" of the 1960s was an attempt to identify the everyday life of women as a sphere of political activity. This stress on personal experience was both powerful and revolutionary. Feminists insisted that the "political" involved not only governments, wars, finance, and elections — that is, all the things normally identified as part of the male political arena — but also involved power between people, and most significantly, power between men and women. Women were encouraged to examine the power politics of their most intimate experiences and to understand how these politics shaped their lives and perpetuated their subordination.

The best part of this approach was its inclusive nature: any woman's experience could be expressed and heard.[1] And women did find strength and did gain insight through discussing husbands, sexual experiences, children, childbirth, housework, jobs, money or lack of it, and relationships with other women. They discovered that their experiences were not always unique and that much of what seemed personal, private, and theirs alone, was common to other women's lives. This realization was important. If what was distressing and destructive in any individual woman's life was not simply the result of individual mistakes and failings, then something more systematic might be identifiable and something more public might occur to change circumstances for all women.

By the circuitous route of "the personal is political," feminists approached the structural constraints that acted as a straight-jacket on the possibilities for liberation. I do not mean to imply that this was necessarily a linear route, because the identification of systemic barriers was always in the background of women's analysis of why they faced obstacles to freedom. But it took time before concerted political activity in the arenas normally the preserve of men — and particularly that of economic policy — became the focus of feminist collective action.

Economics, both in the theoretical and the practical sense, has developed over the centuries in an exceedingly narrow way.[2] When women tried to question the logic of existing economic policies, they were challenging not only the vested interest of class and gender in maintaining hierarchies, but they were also challenging all of the wisdom and power of an ideology which was part of the collective unconscious of the society. The fundamental nature of Western industrial society is its organization around the profit motive and the practice of placing a value on all human activity through the mechanism of "the market." "The market" is the term used for the buying and selling that not only places a value on things, including labour, but also is the mechanism through which decisions about what to make or provide and who gets these products or services are determined. These decisions, of course, are based on what is most profitable. So, for example, when the market produces forty different kinds of aspirin, pays baseball players as much as $7.5 million a season, and rewards David Letterman a whopping $15 million a year for talking late at night, the assumption is that this is what people "demand," as reflected through their buying decisions on the market.

When women questioned the logic of a system that, in the name of efficiency and profitability, places enormous value on the inconsequential, frivolous, and often harmful, they were accused of being economically unsophisticated. The myth that the market will, except under unusual circumstances, truly sort out people's needs and desires, has been elevated to a belief of almost religious proportions. And like all religions, it is supported by intricate doctrine, although in this case the doctrine has been deemed a science. The "scientific" nature of economic analysis has become a powerful defence against criticism, because anything not confined to the hermetically sealed logic of the discipline could be dismissed as unscientific, unrealistic, and impractical.

Almost any demands women made on the political and economic system were juxtaposed against "economic reality." Politicians and their supporters in the business community[3] would often express sympathy with women's calls for a more equitable way of distributing wealth; the elimination of poverty; the protection of the environment; the provision of decent care for children, the old, and the sick; and enough jobs for all who wanted them. They too wanted to be identified with human values, but they repeatedly insisted that these values could only really be met if the capitalist business structure of Canada was truly healthy and truly comfortable with the economic environment in the country, and if that structure was given sufficient support to maintain its profitability so that businessmen would continue to invest in Canada. The assumption was that when the business economy flourished, then all people would benefit because not only would more jobs be created but also more wealth would be generated, more taxes paid, and government could then afford more humane programs. This became known as the "trickle-down theory" of economic policy which was, in essence, a belief that making the élite richer would ultimately improve the lot of the rest of us.[4]

As the "trickle-down theory" took hold and all too obviously shifted priorities even further away from those that women found valuable, feminist political action focusing on economic issues became more pronounced. Women began to criticize government budgets, tax policy, and the move toward free trade and privatization, but they met with strong resistance. These were not deemed women's issues in the first place, but even more significant was the idea that the policies were not discriminatory, because they were assumed to have universal, not gendered or class, implications. The language of economic policy, after all, was certainly gender neutral, but this supposed gender neutrality made women's experiences invisible.[5] Women's task was both to show that the consequences for women and other groups was never a part of the analysis of the effects of specific economic policy and that the impact on women was often distinct.[6] While the effects on certain industries of a new tax or trade policy would be endlessly studied, no comparable analysis would be done to see what it might mean for women, immigrants, aboriginal people, people in different areas of the country, and people with different income levels. If it was good for business, it was good enough for all.

Analysing the potential impact of policy initiatives was not an easy task. The constraints of insufficient money and time made the preparation of proper analyses to distribute among women and the development of convincing briefs to government for public airing difficult. More serious was the need to confront the vested interests of the economic élite in perpetuating the values of the market system. The negative effects of economic policy on women were not simply an oversight — something that needed to be identified in order to be corrected — they were an inherent feature of the system and permitted it to function as it did.

Throughout most of the 1970s, women's confrontation with the federal government over national economic policy was muted. While economic expansion and increased demand for women's labour generally characterized this period, the relatively optimistic economic conditions were not solely responsible for this subdued attention to economic matters. For many women's groups, simply dealing with the more overt forms of discrimination was all-consuming. But also, there was frequently a sense that women should concentrate their energies on clearly defined women's issues and should not spread their meagre resources thinly by taking up causes which, while worthy, were the focus of other progressive groups. This was the argument, for example, put forward at a annual meeting of the National Action Committee on the Status of

Women (NAC) when the Liberal government's wage and price control policy was being debated.[7] I do not mean to imply that women neglected economic issues altogether — collectively, they did confront economic constraints during the course of their daily lives, particularly in their worksites and through social service networks.[8] It was through these kinds of experiences that the significance of overall economic policy (or what economists refer to as macro-economic policy) became apparent. Women might spend years, for example, struggling for legal changes related to equal pay, but ultimately achieving equal pay legislation could be subverted by economic policies that were eliminating jobs altogether.

Community Development and Planning

At the local level, women began to examine the ways in which economic planning and development within their communities should change so that women's experiences could be part of the process. By the middle of the 1970s, the deficiencies of traditional types of economic development became the topic of community discussions when new economic initiatives were proposed, and women began to demand that their needs be considered. This occurred in cities, in single-industry towns, in remote areas, and in rural communities.

Single Industry Towns
Women in single industry towns are particularly disadvantaged by the very nature of the develoment process. In the resource-extracting industries in the northern parts of the country, the work of exploiting oil, gas, timber, and minerals is male work. In an attempt to attract a male workforce to these remote and physically demanding areas of the country, the employers were concerned with the well-being of the workers and generally paid them well. But, as women pointed out, not planning for the needs of others in the community created hardships with which women had to cope.[9]

Industries which focused on resource-extraction created peculiar economic circumstances, such as "boom and bust" economic cycles, poor job opportunities for women, and poor or non-existent social service deliveries. Unlike the southern parts of the country, where economic expansion was more diversified and women were increasingly part of the paid labour force, the opportunities for women to earn a living in the north were extraordinarily constrained.[10] Employers blatantly discriminated against women in the hiring process in these traditionally male industries. In addition, because poor planning had failed to provide the normal service institutions which existed in other areas of the country, even the traditional jobs which women held elsewhere were not widely available in the north. If women were lucky, they might find part-time work at the minimum wage at the local grocery store, but even these types of jobs, as unsatisfactory as they were, were limited.

The development of projects like gas pipelines either greatly expanded existing communities in a very short time, or created entirely new ones. The problems of "boom and bust" created strains on communities and families of workers. Women at the Alaska Pipeline Hearings demanded not only that these community needs be part of the construction planning, but that the provincial government become involved in helping to meet those needs. Specifically, they called for increased funding for the local organizations that would have to carry the extra workload; for increased provision of mental health services, alcohol treatment services, and emergency shelters for women and children in trouble; and for decent and affordable housing and recreation spaces. The conditions characterized by an extremely harsh climate, the often lengthy periods of isolation, and the "ethic of the hard working, hard drinking worker in the north,"[11] required more than leaving the social aspects of the development project to chance. The pace of development was simply too fast, and it clearly demanded concerted planning to meet all people's needs.

As women's groups gained more experience discussing development issues with each other, and as research projects proceeded, other questions about the nature of development itself began to surface. Demands for improved access to jobs and improved community services continued to be a significant part of the political action of women, but eventually, the entire structure of the exploitation of resources was called into question. The economic strategy of taking as much out of the land or sea as quickly as possible was condemned not only because of the short-term nature of the benefits to the people in these communities, but also because of the real damage to the environment of this type of development.[12] The export nature of the resource economy was unsatisfactory as a development process because it encouraged an over-exploitation of the natural resources and yet never managed to provide a basis for a self-sustaining local economy.[13]

From the northern regions to the fishing communities of Atlantic Canada, the effects of almost total reliance on extraction of resources for export left the local economies in poor shape. Very high rates of unemployment have been problems that simply will not go away with even greater attempts to exploit natural resources. Because there is little planning to integrate this resource extraction with other aspects of economic development, a healthy economy that provides opportunities for all who need to work simply never develops.

At the local and provincial levels, women's groups pursued two distinct approaches to this problem. In Newfoundland, for example, the Hibernia oil exploration project raised the possibility of thousands of jobs being created. But, as the Provincial Advisory Council on the Status of Women of Newfoundland and Labrador pointed out in its 1991 brief to the provincial government, these jobs would not be available to women.[14] The council did not reject the Hibernia mega project as a way

Herring "popping" provides about four to six weeks of work each spring for women in this industry. Popping is work which requires breaking the heads off the herring and, if it is female, squeezing out the roe. The whole process is a very wasteful use of high-protein food source since only the roe is eaten and the rest of the fish is used for fertilizer. This work is being mechanized so immigrant and Native women who worked in this industry, sometimes for as long as thirty-five years, are losing their jobs.

to develop the economy, but rather it wanted the government to put initiatives in place that would provide better opportunities for women within the mega project itself. In addition, the council urged the government to create a climate that encouraged diversification of the provincial economy, rather than dependence on oil for growth and development. The idea put forward was to link the mega development project to other industries in the communities so that the people within the community could supply services, knowledge, and manufactured items to be used in the oil project.

In the case of the Hibernia project, some token gestures were made towards women's concerns, and women were allowed into the apprenticeship programs with the understanding that they would eventually find regular jobs with Hibernia. But as Patricia Frangos's story in the *Newsletter* of Women in Trades and Technology shows, this progression to regular employment did not occur for most of the women involved.[15] Of the forty-seven women trained, only nine found regular employment.

Community Economic Development
Other groups rejected altogether the idea of "mega projects" and resource extraction for export as a solution to development. Instead, there

was a call for women to generate community economic development (CED) schemes that would be controlled by and planned for people within the community.[16] Usually the focus for the economic activity would be to provide for local needs in small scale goods or services industries, but CED could involve larger-scale industries that met consumption needs outside the local community as well. Attempts were made to encourage women's co-operatives, to create credit unions to provide the funding the commercial banks would not usually give to businesses initiated by women and to help women develop skills to start their own work projects.[17] None of these initiatives by themselves was presented as a single solution to economic development. As Philinda Masters writes in her article on "Feminist Credit Unions," although establishing a credit union was not a comprehensive political strategy, it was a way to begin to provide what women needed — money.[18]

Community economic development strategies were important because they initiated a way for women to think about economic issues. The promise was that action could occur at the community level, and women were imbued with the sense that they could be effective in changing their economic surroundings and their lives. This was in juxtaposition to the dominant notion that the type of development that was occurring in the economy was inevitable: ideas about taking charge locally challenged the notions that development needs to always be organized, planned and directed by the interests of large, international business organizations.

Sometimes the projects of community economic development initiatives were supported by state financing of one sort or another. But even if they were, they were almost always underfunded. The self-exploitation which could occur under these circumstances made some women cynical about the collaboration between the state and feminist projects aimed at community economic development. Kathleen Donovan's letter to the editor of *Canadian Dimension* expresses just such frustration with the working conditions of the feminist projects where she had been employed. To her, CED was just a new version of "the old labour of love," where women are deflected from the "class nature of the economic crisis, and which camouflages the massive restructuring of industry which is occurring in our society today."[19] Donovan's letter describes her oppressive experiences as an employee of a woman's organization that was funded by a government grant, but many women who were encouraged by governments to become "self-employed" also experienced oppressive working conditions, and they also recognized how unlikely it was that an individual could develop her own business which would provide a decent income. While governments often touted the successes of women entrepreneurs and their relatively low bankruptcy rates (compared with men's), the reality was that the average self-employed woman would earn considerably less than the employed woman, and even when the wages of those working part-time were included for comparison. Working for oneself not only meant a low income but also excessive hours of work and often poor working conditions. While self-employment was distinct from CED and tended to glorify the potential of the individual, its appeal to women in areas of high unemployment was understandable.

Urban Planning

At the same time that women in resource communities began acting to change the dynamics of the "boom and bust" economies of the north, women in urban areas began to understand how the economics of the city and city planning constrained their economic lives and often prevented them from doing various kinds of work. In urban areas women were more commonly working outside the home, but the transportation systems which had been designed to meet male needs, for example, did not meet those of women. Suburban areas had been designed with cars as the main source of transportation, but in moderate- or low-income families, the men usually owned the car and if public transportation was not available at convenient times, women could not work. Since suburbs are typically low-density areas, conventional public transportation is usually not frequent.

Within cities, women's transportation needs were often distinct from men's. Gerde Wekerle, writing in *The Status of Women News* in 1979, argued that transit stops and fare structures were designed to encourage people who have choices between cars and public transportation to use public transportation. For this reason they focused on attracting rush-hour users.[20] The fare structure, which did not permit multiple stops, punished women who were more likely to shop or drop and pick up children as they travelled. Also, the location of bus stops did not consider the transit patterns of women — they were usually blocks from supermarket entrances or were located at spots which were dangerous because of their isolation, such as at the edge of large parking lots.

It is very rare that women get a chance to design their own transportation systems, but this is exactly what the Status of Women Council of Whitehorse did in the mid 1970s.[21] The small size and low density of Whitehorse meant that more traditional forms of urban transportation, such as regular bus services, did not exist until the creation of the Yukon Women's Mini-bus Society. This bus service was designed to meet women's scheduling needs — the passengers' as well as the bus drivers', most of whom were women. This flexible and inexpensive service was an enormous success and developed into a well-functioning public transit system, which not only met women's needs but also those of the whole community.

Agricultural Issues

Growing food in Canada is a special challenge that has been met, successfully, in the past by organizing farming in ways which are distinct

Women farmers, such as Bev Morrow, a member of Women of Unifarm in Alberta, understand the implications of losing control of their family farms to corporate farms. Women farmers have organized through groups such as Women for the Survival of Agriculture and the National Farmers Union to raise women's issues in the struggles to save family farms.

from the ways it is organized in smaller and warmer countries. Canada's harsh climate, tremendous distances, and relatively small population have produced challenges in the growing of food itself and in getting it to the people who consume it. To meet these challenges, many relatively small farm units, made up mainly of families, have come together to develop an agricultural infrastructure that works. Because this country is colder than most and the growing season is considerably shorter than it is in many parts of the United States, special measures have been taken in Canada to manage the supply of agricultural products. Also, because our major food export — wheat — is grown in the centre of the country, special transportation schemes have had to be devised to lower the cost of transportation. Supply management schemes in dairy and poultry products, high tariffs on imported fruits and vegetables during the summer months, and cheaper transportation rates have all been rational solutions to difficult problems for agriculture, solutions which have made it possible for agriculture to continue in this country.

For women in the farming community the changes in economic policy and international trade relations in agriculture have had profound implications for them and their families. As Nettie Wiebe, former Women's President of the National Farmers Union (NFU), argues, the very measures which permitted farming to exist in Canada are now being challenged by international trade agreements.[22] The replacement of family farms by large corporate farms has meant that the kinds of economic policies that supported relatively small family farms were not the kinds of policies that the large corporate farms favoured. As these groups became more powerful, particularly on the international scene, their interests became paramount.

The shift from family farming to corporate farming affects women farmers throughout the world and as women confront the internationalization of food production, they recognize all of the dangers inherent in this process. For women in poor countries, the shift from food production for local consumption to food production for exports threatens women's very ability to feed their families. Stories abound of how areas that were once self-sufficient in the provision of food, largely through women's efforts, became dependent on food imports as their lands were converted to growing products for export. To international agencies, which dictate the terms on which poor countries can receive loans, shifting to production for export becomes a requirement for receiving these loans. Marilyn Waring gives an example of what happens as production for food is replaced by production for exports:

> In Belize in Central America, more and more land was put into sugar cane. More and more men took jobs in the sugar industry, and more and more small holdings were planted with cane. Local food production steadily declined. In one year alone, consumption of local maize and rice declined 15 percent, and wheat imports rose 62 percent. Soon there was a national shortage of staple foods. "In the old days," says Maya Indian villager, Dona Ettelvina, "we were poor but there was plenty of food. Now, we have money but nothing to eat." ... The sugar cash that has replaced food belongs to men, yet their incomes have not risen enough to pull families out of poverty.[23]

The promise, when converting agriculture for local consumption to agriculture for exports, is that the increased income from the exports will enable people to buy more cheaply the food they used to grow for their own consumption or for sale on the domestic market. This promise rarely materializes in poor countries or even large, wealthy ones like Canada. For poor countries, the failure of international markets to buy whatever they export can, and often does, result in the need to borrow simply to feed people in the country. As a result of abandoning food production for subsistence, many poor countries have become hopelessly indebted to the banks of larger, wealthier countries and are increasingly obliged to continue the programs which got them into difficulties in the first place in order to have foreign currency to repay their debts.

In the 1980s and 1990s, female agricultural workers in Canada have recognized the common interests they have with their counterparts in poorer countries. The Women and Food Production Conference held in Guelph, Ontario, in 1984 brought together 120 women from around the world to discuss the problems of "the international influence of the transnational corporation in the international flow of capital and of food."[24] The increased competition from large corporate farms has affected farm families in Canada just as drastically as it has women in poor countries.[25] In 1991 there were half as many family farms in Canada as in 1971.[26] As some farmers went bankrupt or were forced to sell to avoid bankruptcy, their neighbours frequently took on huge debts in order to keep their own holdings on a scale large enough to combat the competition from large corporate farms. The results were frequently disastrous for both the families and the environment. Increased farm size meant more work for families, who were usually working both on the farm and at paid work off it. Often, it also meant the abandonment of farm practices which, because they were time consuming, had helped preserve the land.[27]

Throughout this period women farmers organized through groups like Women for the Survival of Agriculture, Concerned Farm Women of Ontario, and the National Farmers Union to raise women's issues in the struggle to save the family farm. Even more traditional organizations, such as L'Association des Fermières de l'Ontario (the Ontario Association of Farmers' Wives, founded in 1937), shifted their focus. Groups such as these evolved from social clubs which promoted kitchen handicrafts and recipe exchanges to organizations that offered courses in municipal politics, law and business in order to strengthen women's understanding of the forces affecting family farms.[28] Since the signing of the Free Trade Agreement (FTA) and the North American Free Trade Agreement (NAFTA) the consequences of the internationalization of food production have become even more pronounced. Particularly important has been the patenting legislation that gives international firms, such as Cargill, monopoly rights over living organisms. This raises the threat of giant international firms patenting seeds and requiring farmers to pay royalties for the use of the seeds they save for planting from each harvest. For farmers in poor countries, the royalty requirements are devastating and may remove from these people their very ability to feed themselves. The new trading rules are distinctly biased toward fostering international agra-industry and do not benefit individual women farmers, whether in industrialized and wealthy countries like Canada, or in poor countries like Mexico or India. The new trade agreements have designed rules to benefit the highly capital and energy intensive agricultural industries in countries where its production at most involves only single-digit proportions of the labour force. These rules are a disaster for countries where huge proportions of the population rely on farming for their subsistence.[29]

Economic Restructuring

Economic restructuring is a relatively new term which implies not only economic change but also the development of entirely new economics structures within ongoing systems. The term itself receives widespread use, particularly in the media, and is associated with another relatively new term, "globalization."[30] Economic restructuring is a seductive term because it appears benign and implies an inevitability imposed by some type of external force over which people have no control: its presentation as a universal force makes "restructuring" appear apolitical and, in conjunction with this, gender, race and class neutral. For the public, the term has specific implications which are associated with economic hardship, unemployment and all of the economic policies that are designed to encourage business investment decisions. It is also associated with the redesign of social policies to accommodate the demands of business groups for lower taxes. Economic hardship and unemployment are certainly not new phenomena, nor is dramatic economic change. But "restructuring" has distinct connotations related to public policy changes that are a departure from those which are normally used in times of economic crisis. One commentator put it this way:

> Sometime in the late 1970s and early 1980s, discussion of the "recession" metamorphosed into discussion of "economic restructuring." This was not just a change of rhetoric. It was, rather, a shorthand for some enduring changes in our way of life in Canada. Recession had implied that we were living through a temporary hiccup in an otherwise sound economy. Restructuring implies something more fundamental: a change in people's relationship to wage work and the concomitant alteration of a pattern of life centred on full employment of men in permanent jobs supported by women's dual roles.[31]

The reference to change in people's relationship to waged work relates to the shift in government priorities away from full employment as one of the major goals of economic policy and a shift in the expectation of individuals of achieving a standard form of work in adult life.[32] Although Canadian governments have never been entirely committed to full employment, they did in the past, at least, usually mention it as a goal that they were working toward.[33] The goal was economic stability: everyone who wanted a job could have one. In the post–Second World War period, as governments took more responsibility for the smooth functioning of the economy, this became the expectation of normal times. But with increases in international competition, governments have been persuaded otherwise. Full employment is not one of the goals of the business community, and business has been influential in convincing governments that it is no longer realistic to expect that full employment could be achieved. Business dislikes full employment because it tends

Canada Post has responded to the demands of "economic restructuring" by cutting wage costs through privatization and technological change. Since it has become a profit-making corporation, Canada Post has eliminated many manual sorting jobs (such as the manual flat sorting done by these Stoney Creek Plant workers in Hamilton, Ontario); has increased contracting-out work to low-wage, non-unionized firms; and has privatized its postal outlets.

to raise wages as employers compete with each other to hire workers. However, with fairly high levels of unemployment, workers compete with each other for jobs and wages can be kept from rising. Recessionary periods when unemployment is high can be beneficial for business and reducing unemployment isn't in its interests. This is probably best illustrated by reading the business sections of newspapers where often it is difficult to tell the good news from the bad. Take for example Terence Corcoran's article "Recession Isn't the Problem, It's the Solution" in *The Globe and Mail*.[34] For people without jobs, a recession is certainly not a solution to their problems. This is where the conflict exists: between those who need jobs to exist and those who need high levels of unemployment to keep wages down.

In modern societies, we, as individuals, are dependent on the proper functioning of the system to be able to provide for ourselves. While we are conscious of the control that we can have as individuals over our own lives, we nonetheless recognize that even getting the right education and being in the right place at the right time may not be enough to ensure our employability if the system is operating at a level that requires that many people not work and that many others are underemployed.[35] Eliminating unemployment is crucial for women, not only because of their need to work but also because it is only in times of high employment that women have a chance to eliminate wage and hiring discrimination. High levels of unemployment undermine all attempts to bring equity into the workforce, particularly because as the number of employees in workplaces decrease, the initiation of employment equity schemes becomes pointless. The good news, then, for employers is that when unemployment is high they can avoid the costly employment equity requirements of law simply by not hiring new people and refusing to give wage increases to all workers.

The Macdonald Commission
The economic depression of the early 1980s was the catalyst for thinking about economic change and public policy at the national level. Between 1982 and 1984, Canada experienced the highest unemployment rates since the Great Depression of the 1930s. In a typically Canadian response, the government of the day (a Liberal government with Pierre Trudeau as prime minister) instituted a royal commission — the Royal Commission on the Economic Union and Development Prospects for Canada (widely known as the Macdonald Commission) — to canvas Canadians and develop a coherent economic policy.

The Commission travelled throughout Canada holding public hearings about major economic problems and what direction people wanted the government to take in developing national goals and policies. Not surprisingly, unemployment was identified as the primary problem in most areas of the country, and many innovative and interesting proposals were suggested as ways of dealing with economic and social issues and of redefining national goals.[36] The brief presented in B.C. by Women Against the Budget reflected the sentiment increasingly voiced by women's groups: economic policy not only excludes women but is also detrimental to their interests.[37] With specific reference to develoment projects in northern B.C., the brief showed how economic planning consistently ignored women's involvement in society and excluded women from the decision-making process. Women Against the Budget demanded that women be more than marginal players in determining economic objectives, and seeing that these objectives were implemented was a consistent theme in the presentations made by other women's groups.[38]

The Commission generated a great deal of enthusiasm and hope for changes in policy approaches. Unfortunately, the progressive ideas voiced by women and other popular sector organizations were almost totally ignored, while the research of professional economists, which was undertaken separately from the work of the public hearings, and the ideas espoused by business groups were adopted as the position of the Commission's final *Report*.[39] This *Report*, which was published in 1985, was not simply a document buried in government archives, as are many government enquiries, but became the active plan for the Conservative government's economic and social policy. It continues to guide the economic policy formation of the Liberal government elected in the fall of 1993.

Some of the ideas which were raised in the *Report* were considered as workable strategies for the first time. Most notable were those dealing with free trade, constitutional reform, and changes in social policy, including reform of unemployment insurance and the social welfare system. Women's groups were immediately aware of the dangers of these recommendations. Once again, women's ideas were not taken into account when policy objectives were formulated, and the policies which were favourably received by government would almost certainly retard or reverse the progress women had been making during the previous twenty years.[40]

The Free Trade Agreement (FTA)

In the campaign against free trade in the late eighties and early nineties, the women's movement established itself as an effective and serious critic of economic policy in Canada.[41] For the first time economic issues that were not known to people in this country received publicity and became part of the public debate because of the actions of women. Free trade had been raised at various points in Canada's earlier history as a viable option for dealings with the United States, but it was the Liberals in the 1984 election that revived the subject (which hadn't been seriously considered since 1911) and made it a political option once again. At that time Brian Mulroney was adamantly against free trade, saying: "Don't talk to me about free trade. That issue was decided in 1911. Free trade is a danger to Canadian sovereignty. You'll hear no more of it from me."

Yet we did hear considerably more about it from him. During the early years of the Mulroney administration (1984–1985), the Macdonald Commission published its *Report*. Its most prominent and distinctive feature was its advocacy for a free trade initiative with the United States. Although the Mulroney government had previously rejected free trade, pressure from the international business community, particularly as organized through the Business Council on National Issues, was sufficiently strong that the Conservative government heartily endorsed these recommendations of a Commission set up by the Liberals.[42]

What was unexpected was the adamant opposition to free trade that emerged from virtually all popular sectors.[43] The government had recognized that public discussion of this issue would likely lead to serious opposition and the development of coalitions against it, so it did all in its power to "keep Canadians in the dark" about free trade. However, despite the government's efforts to stifle public discussion, coalitions developed in unprecedented ways and people and groups which had never worked together before began to identify their common interests in opposition to free trade. The first anti-free trade group was initiated in Toronto by Laurell Ritchie, a trade unionist who was then on the NAC executive and involved in its employment and economy committee. In November 1985, Laurell Ritchie organized a meeting of representatives of women's, labour, Native, agricultural, cultural, senior, poverty, and religious groups to discuss how free trade would harm their constituencies and to find ways to stop the process. This bringing together of groups, which previously had often had little in common and sometimes had been on different sides of public policy issues, was only possible because NAC was considered neutral territory. Even labour groups that had been at odds with one another for decades were able to meet together on NAC's premises and under NAC's auspices. This group became known as the Coalition Against Free Trade, and it and NAC ultimately joined the nationally organized group against free trade called the Pro-Canada Network.[44]

The initial task of all the groups was to understand what the implications of free trade would mean for the people they represented. I began writing on this issue sometime in the mid-1980s when the Liberals first raised it as a political possibility. At that time I had been working with immigrant women's groups in establishing language and skills training centres in Toronto. Since I was also on the NAC executive, I was able to see the connection for women and to make this issue one of NAC's own. It seemed clear to me that any free trade agreement with the U.S. would immediately jeopardize work for immigrant women in the manufacturing sector, because they tended to be concentrated in the most vulnerable manufacturing industries such as clothing, textiles, food processing and electronics.[45] Loss of manufacturing employment seemed an obvious consequence of free trade, and one which even the Macdonald Commission *Report* recognized as one of the negative consequences of such a deal,[46] but as we began to learn more about what free trade would include, it became obvious that more than just women's jobs in manufacturing were at stake.

One of the most significant contributions that women's analyses gave to the discussion of free trade was an understanding of what it would mean for services. The service sector includes everything that is not counted as resources (fishing, forestry, mining), agriculture, manufacturing, and construction, and accounts for almost 70 per cent of the labour force. It covers diverse activities that range from daycare and house cleaning to financial services and communications. In short, it is a substantial proportion of the Canadian economy and since the majority of women employed in Canada, or in any other industrialized country for that matter, work in service industries, the implications for both the jobs in this sector and the provision of services themselves were significant. Until the FTA, most trade agreements focused on tariff reduction, or the elimination of export and import taxes on things. But this trade agreement went much further than that and included, for the first time in any major trade agreement, a comprehensive treatment of services. When NAC raised the issue of services, many groups that would not normally have dealt with trade issues (such as nurses, teachers, daycare advocates, and data processors) began to analyse the FTA and to understand how negative its impact would be. This understanding became significant politically.[47]

NAC spent a great deal of effort providing information to women's groups and supporting their initiatives to extend the analysis of the FTA so that women could understand what it would mean for their communities, jobs, and daily lives.[48] Executive members spoke at rallies throughout the country, prepared briefs that were presented at parliamentary committees, and distributed pamphlets that outlined the FTA and how it would affect women.[49] Often women's groups or even individual women like Marilyn Corbeil, a teacher in North York, Ontario, would share these materials with colleagues and friends. Through these actions, women's opposition to free trade grew.[50]

Raising the ways in which the FTA would adversely affect social services had an important influence on the way the public viewed the trade deal. When the government first raised the issue of free trade, the vast majority of people, when polled, said that they approved of it. By the time of the 1988 election, the majority of people were opposed to it. When people had a chance to learn about free trade, they understood that it was about more than trade.[51] While the public was concerned about the possibility of job loss, the most important issue for most was the ability for Canada to maintain sovereignty over its economic and social programs. It was obvious that the logic of free trade would jeopardize Canada's ability to provide adequate social programs, and the most serious threat to social programs was the increased competition with low-waged sectors in the U.S. Those of us against the FTA argued that business interests in Canada would either shift production to these areas in the U.S., or would try to reduce their own costs by reducing both wages and taxes. Along with this, we predicted that Canadian business would argue it was overtaxed compared with American corporations and would initiate a campaign towards downsizing Canada's social safety net. The pitch, we anticipated, would be that Canada could no longer afford the level of social programs it had and that radical changes would be necessary.

The government and business tried to reassure people and accused NAC of scaremongering. The extent to which those in favour of free trade began to attack the position of womens' groups is probably a fairly good indication of how effective our message had been. The Minister Responsible for the Status of Women, Barbara McDougall, countered NAC's position by taking to the airwaves to assure women that free trade would be good for them. Groups that worked closely with government to promote free trade, such as the C.D. Howe Institute, did their own special studies to show how free trade would benefit women and came to the conclusion that women were being manipulated by people who were using the FTA for other political objectives.[52] The new phrase

The 1989 Free Trade Agreement had a dramatic effect on women's work in manufacturing industries. Many corporations, particularly in Ontario and Quebec, shifted their factories to Mexico or low-wage U.S. states. At the Sunbeam Appliance factory in Ontario, women who had been employed by the company for 15 to 20 years were laid off. If factories didn't close under FTA, the workers who were lucky enough to keep their jobs usually faced lower wages and deteriorating working conditions.

"gender gap" emerged to describe women's opposition to free trade and their tendency to be firmer in their opposition than men. Free trade was the major issue in the 1988 election. The Conservative government did not receive the majority of the votes, but because those opposed to free trade split their votes between the Liberals and the New Democratic Party, the Conservatives under Brian Mulroney's leadership won. Despite widespread opposition, the FTA went into effect in January 1989. The Conservatives used their victory in the election as justification for not only proceeding with the FTA but also for beginning discussions on including Mexico in the trading arrangement.

Women's experiences with the FTA proved that our predictions about it were not exaggerated, and if anything, occurred with greater speed than had been predicted. Job losses for women in manufacturing dropped 16.5 per cent from the time free trade went into effect until 1993. The biggest losses, in terms of the number of jobs, were in the clothing and electrical products industries, although the percentage of losses were highest in industries that were more typically employers of males, such as in primary metals, furniture, and leather. In traditionally female industries, like clothing, the losses have been devastating, as has been the downward pressure on wages and working conditions.[53] Between 1988 and 1992, female employment in clothing dropped 23 per cent and wages had fallen from 65 per cent of the average manufacturing wage in 1980 to 58 per cent of the average manufacturing wage in 1992. Production in the clothing industry decreased in Canada, indicating that firms either shifted production to low-wage sections of the U.S. or Mexico, or went out of business. There is evidence to suggest that a great deal of what is still being produced in Canada is now being produced under different and much worse conditions. In the clothing industry, in particular, there has been a considerable increase in the number of women who do contract work in their homes for wages below the minimum set by law and under conditions that are not monitored by labour standards.[54] Altogether there has been a substantial rise in non-standard forms of work. Particularly significant has been the rise of part-time and temporary employment. While Canada lost 458,000 full-time jobs betwen 1990 and 1992, 126,000 part-time jobs were created. In 1992 alone there were 125,000 fewer full-time jobs for women; at the same time there was an increase of 69,000 part-time jobs. (Women account for 71 per cent of all part-time workers.)[55] This change in the nature of new jobs appears to have the worst effect on young women entering the workforce. Now over 43 per cent of the young women in the workforce are working part-time, compared with about one-third of young men, indicating that the availability of full-time work for young women has declined substantially since before the FTA.[56] The effects of the FTA have not been confined to employment, but are also evident in changes to social programs, which are discussed below.

North American Free Trade Agreement (NAFTA)

During the campaign against the FTA, many of us predicted that very low-wage countries like Mexico would be added to the agreement in the future, and we pointed out how damaging this would be for Canada. The government ridiculed us and depicted those of us who raised this issue as radicals with overstimulated imaginations who were trying to frighten people into believing the worst about free trade. Yet this idea had been clearly articulated by U.S. President Ronald Reagan. Once Mulroney's government was in power the rhetoric changed and, indeed, free trade with Mexico became a reality. Those of us who worried about and campaigned against the impending North America Free Trade Agreement (NAFTA) between Canada, the U.S., and Mexico were accused of even worse motives. That is, our fears were depicted as merely dog-in-the-manger attitudes which were less than charitable to Mexico.[57] But our fears about the deal were shared with many others, both in Mexico and in the U.S. Critics of the agreement recognized that as corporations' freedom to move between countries increased, while labour was required to remain in its home country, production would shift to take advantage of poor working conditions and lax corporate and environmental laws. The repressive nature of political life in Mexico has meant that its business climate is seen as "favourable" by North American businesses. But the increase in foreign investment in that country has not brought prosperity for most Mexicans, as has been promised. Since the Mexican government embraced open markets and foreign investment in the mid-1980s, the standard of living for the majority of Mexicans has decreased. As the article in *Briarpatch* shows, prices for basic food rose dramatically while wage rates were frozen.[58] This meant that for most Mexicans the standard of living dropped by about a half since the introduction of economic reforms. The extent to which some Mexicans fear NAFTA is best illustrated by the uprising of peasant farmer in the state of Chiapas on January 1, 1994, the day NAFTA came into force. The people were protesting what they characterized as "the death certificate for the indigenous people of Mexico."[59]

In contrast with the FTA, NAFTA has afforded opportunities for women in Canada to make links with women in Mexico and the U.S. This did not happen under the campaign against FTA because feminists in the U.S., while sympathetic to Canadian women's concerns, did not feel the same need to put energy and resources into this issue, since it would not affect them as adversely as it would us. However, with NAFTA, women in the U.S. became concerned about the capital shifts and the concomitant loss of American jobs. Through such organizations as Mujer a Mujer (Woman to Woman), Mujeres en Accion Sindical (Women in Union Action), Labour Notes, and NAC, women's concerns in all three countries became more focused on the consequences of capital mobility throughout the hemisphere. NAFTA was going to affect women in each country differently; nevertheless, these organizations recognized that there were common interests among women in limiting the strength and mobility of capital.[60]

Unfortunately, NAFTA did not generate the same level and intensity of public debate as occurred around the FTA.[61] There are a variety of reasons for this, but probably most significant is that the Liberal Party this time around was not opposing the agreement during the election (as it had during the 1988 election), but was promising to renegotiate some of its more offensive features once elected. Also, there appeared to be a general perception (at least through the media) that this was not substantially different from the FTA, and since the FTA existed and would continue to exist, it would not make sense for Canada to be excluded from a trade pact between Mexico and the U.S.[62] This actually became the crux of the government and business argument for entering NAFTA, since there clearly was nothing Canada could gain by entering into a trade agreement with Mexico. But pundits like Jeffrey Simpson of *The Globe and Mail* argued that if Canada was excluded from this deal, the U.S. would have a tremendous advantage and would be the hub of trade activity around which Canada and Mexico would behave as spokes.[63] Therefore, any country wishing to service the entire North American market would locate in the U.S. and trade from there.

However, NAFTA is substantially different from the FTA in that it goes much further in limiting the rights of nations to control international business. In areas such as intellectual property rights, energy, textiles and clothing, and public services, this agreement is much more dangerous than the FTA.[64] For women, the issues in most cases are similar to those raised during the FTA debate, as one can see from the publication of the Ontario Women's Directorate and the discussion of NAFTA in the *NAC Voters Guide*.[65] But there is increasing concern for the implications of trade liberalization on the democratic rights of women and other political minorities.[66] It seems that just as women have figured out how to be significant politically and have gained some inroads into the political process within Canada (as we did, for example, during the debate around the Charlottetown Accord) the locus of power has shifted. With these new free trade agreements, many of the decisions that most seriously affect Canada are no longer subject to debate within this country, but rather, are decided at the international level by institutions to which we have no access and whose members are individuals not even elected by the people. So even though we are much better represented in our legislatures, we may, in reality, be participating even less in the democratic process, because real decision-making power continues to elude us.

While NAC and other organizations worked against NAFTA, the public debate never gained the momentum needed to prevent its ratification. NAFTA was not a logical outgrowth of trading patterns that needed to be regularized through trade law; rather, it was a creation of an entirely new policy to foster economic relations between two countries which were as far removed in economic terms as they were in space. Existing trade between Canada and Mexico is minimal. Of all the things Canada imports, only a little over 1 per cent comes from Mexico, and exports to Mexico account for about 0.5 per cent. It is much more likely that with free trade, manufacturing firms and certain types of service production will leave Canada and locate in Mexico at an accelerated rate. When Canadian or international firms can sell in the Canadian market without being located here, they will relocate their production sites to wherever they will have a cost advantage.

The economic future under NAFTA looks bleak, but this does not mean that political options do not exist. The positive news is that women throughout this hemisphere are beginning to discuss economic issues and by acting together are finding ways to combat the might of international corporations. Organizations such as NAC, through its Future of Women's Work program,[67] and Oxfam, through its project on "Women of the Americas Changing the Terms of Trade," may be able to bring about a common understanding among women and to change the terms of the debate in the future. Women working on this issue and others involved in the debate recognize that more needs to be done to counter the ideology of free trade and to establish clear political objectives and possibilities for changing the ideological framework of international trade agreements. The major opposition to the ideal that economic "might makes right" comes from the poorer countries in this world — such as India, Brazil, and Mexico. Perhaps it will be through women's international alliances, then, that the vision of these people for a fairer deal can become the basis for new principles of future trading agreements.

Budget and Taxation Issues

Often dramatic changes to economic policy have occurred through budgetary measures, rather than through extensive debate on economic principles. Because these program changes involved considerable technical detail, which was both difficult to understand and even more problematic to explain simply enough so that the media would take an interest, they were not usually used as political rallying points. In recent years budget and taxation issues have been the focus of feminist discussion and action primarily because of the enormous emphasis placed by government and business interests on the public debt as the major economic problem that Canada faces. This was promoted by Finance Minister Michael Wilson immediately after the free trade election of 1988 as a means of beginning the campaign toward two new initiatives: the reform of the tax system to ease the tax burden of the wealthy, and the reduction of the proportion of government revenues spent on social programs.

Taxes

Women's protests against taxes have usually been because of increases in taxes for people with smaller incomes (where women tend to be concentrated) while taxes of the more wealthy have decreased. But there are also specific incidences of taxes that seem to apply specifically to women which have been seen as unfair.

Ever since modern governments have begun raising substantial revenues through taxation, it has generally been conceded that the tax burden should correspond to people's ability to pay. The first income tax was introduced in Great Britain during the Napoleonic Wars. Before this most taxes were on consumption, and taxes on consumption (other than on luxuries) were considered inherently unfair because they invariably meant that poorer people would pay a higher proportion of their income in tax than the wealthy. So a tax on bread, for example, was enough to cause a riot because it would be much more onerous to the poor than the rich. The introduction of a progressive tax base through the income tax was an important advance for the underprivileged in society since it established the ability-to-pay principle by recognizing that the wealthy could afford to pay a larger proportion of their income in tax than could the poor. When taxes are graduated so that the wealthy pay a larger proportion of their income in tax, it is known as a progressive tax, which is distinct from a "flat tax" in which everyone would pay the same percentage of their income in tax.[68]

For most of this century the idea of the ability-to-pay principle remained an important feature of Canadian taxation,[69] although in recent years, particularly with the introduction of the GST, there has been serious erosion of the principle. The Mulroney government introduced major changes to the Canadian tax system which skewed the system in favour of the wealthy. Incursions into the ability-to-pay principle was justified by the ideas of an American economist, Arthur Laffer. Laffer popularized the notion that high marginal tax rates[70] on the wealthy were unwise because they would cause that class to evade taxes, reduce their investments, or work less. This was a fairly persuasive argument to the government, and as a result, Canada, which had ten federal income tax brackets until 1988, reduced the top brackets considerably and narrowed them so that there were only three. The objective in the tax changes instituted by Mulroney's government has been to ease the tax burden for corporations and the wealthy and to increase it for almost everyone else. The new "simplified" system, which the Conservative government introduced, is virtually a flat tax: the bottom rate is 17 per cent, but most people fall in the middle range, which is taxed at 26 per cent and is not substantially different from the 29 per cent tax for the top income earners. According to the National Council of Welfare, the income taxes of the average working poor family increased 44 per cent under the Conservatives, while those of the typical middle-class family increased only 10 per cent. The rich fared best — their income taxes dropped by 6 per cent. For women, who are more represented among the lower income earners than the higher ones, this has meant an increased tax burden. At the same time as taxes on individuals have increased, taxes on corporations account for a smaller proportion of the national income than ever. As was pointed out by Mel Hurtig at the Senate's hearings on the Goods and Services Tax, or GST, the vast maority of bank tellers in Canada, including those with the lowest salaries, paid a far higher rate of tax throughout the entire 1980s than did the banks which employed them.

While changes to the income tax system made the whole tax system less progressive than it had been, the most significant change was the introduction of the Goods and Services Tax. The GST is an extremely unpopular tax that was introduced by Michael Wilson, then minister of finance, in the 1989 budget. As I explained in my article in *Feminist Action*, women found this tax to be particularly unfair because, as a tax on consumption, it would increase the tax burden on the poor, who usually spend everything they receive.[71] The distinct feature of the GST was that it was not just another sales tax on things, which is something people in every province but Alberta were used to paying, but it extended the sales tax to include services. This meant that very basic items like rent and hydro would be taxed. Although basic groceries were not included in the GST, various types of prepared and take-out foods were. This was particularly hard for very poor people who live in rented rooms with no kitchens and who by necessity are forced to pay a tax on food. NAC's brief to the government estimated that familes with incomes of less than $15,000 a year would spend 74 per cent of their earnings on taxable items in contrast to families with incomes over $50,000 that would spend about 49 per cent of their income on taxable items. Some women were particularly incensed that even necessities such as sanitary napkins were being included in this tax and tried to rally women's support for having this item exempted as a necessity.[72] Neither this nor other protests, such as that against taxing reading materials, produced exemptions. In its 1994 election, the Liberal government campaigned against the GST, saying they would replace it with another tax. However, at this stage it would appear that any new tax would be a variation on the GST and would be just as regressive, in that it would affect lower income individuals more than wealthier ones.

As the Ontario Fair Tax Commission pointed out, because women earn much less than men, fairness in the tax system can't be determined simply by looking at special features that apply specifically to males or females. In fact, "nothing in the letter of the law singles out either men or women for special treatment."[73] Rather, because women on average earn less than men, the outcomes of elements of the tax that affect economic relations are not gender neutral. Also, because women tend to earn less than men, they are less able to take advantage of various subsidies that are delivered through the tax system.

Women's groups have long argued that tax deductions through the income tax scheme favour the wealthy. Tax deductions for expenses associated with owning one's own business, for example, mean that lawyers and doctors can deduct items like meals and entertainment and car expenses as legitimate business expenses, while working people whose only income is a salary cannot. Also, a tax deduction, such as the child or spousal tax deduction, has a much more positive effect on reducing the tax obligations of the wealthy than it does on those with smaller incomes.[74] As a result of these effects of tax deductions, the usual position of feminist and anti-poverty groups has been to campaign to have tax deductions eliminated and replaced by refundable tax credits that would go to the lowest income earners. A refundable tax child credit scheme was initiated in the late 1970s to assist families with incomes of less than $18,000 a year, in recognition of the inability of the existing child tax deduction system to do much to help those who were poor. But there were problems with this scheme, as women's groups noted. First, many of the poorest parents did not file income tax returns (they had too little income), and because one had to file in order to receive the credit, they often missed out on receiving this money. But more startling was the practice that was instituted by several provincial governments, most notably Quebec and Manitoba, of deducting from a family's welfare cheques the $200 it would receive from this credit The poor were no better off with this federal government initiative because their provincial governments were pocketing this money.[75]

Feminists have not been united on all tax issues, and the most contentious issue has probably been tax deductions. As noted above, tax deductions favour those with high incomes, and, as a result, women's groups have not campaigned for them. The exception was the case of Elizabeth Symes, a feminist lawyer in Toronto, who tried to deduct the cost of childcare for her two children as a business expense, rather than as a basic childcare deduction. Her argument was that childcare burdens fall disproportionately on women, and because self-employed women must hire nannies to care for their children while the women carry out their businesses, a nanny's salary should be part of a business deduction. Elizabeth Symes had long been associated with the feminist movement and her case was argued by Mary Eberts, a lawyer who had been closely identified with the feminist legal advocacy group Women's Legal Education and Action Fund (LEAF). This was one instance where a tax deduction was seen as a feminist issue.[76] But many feminist groups did not support this action and viewed it as a contradiction to feminist approaches to childcare and taxation. NAC, for example, felt that this undermined its call for universal public childcare at affordable prices, because granting such deductions to business women would cost considerably more than providing childcare spaces in public centres. Also, it undermined the principle of equity in that it gave greater tax advantages to higher-income women than it would give to lower-income women. The first ruling on this issue was found in favour of Elizabeth Symes's claim and was hailed in the press as "a victory for women".[77] Ultimately, this decision was overturned by the Supreme Court of Canada, with dissenting opinions coming from women justices.

It isn't possible here to raise all of the intricacies of tax law that have affected women disporportionately, but one which persists and defies considerable feminist attempts at change is the way in which child support payments are taxed. Once again, the law is not written in gendered terms, but because most recipients of child support payments are women while most contributors are men, this law benefits men at women's expense. The issue is, once again, a tax deduction. In this case, the person paying child support (usually the father) is able to claim the full amount of this support as a tax deduction. At the same time, the person receiving this support payment (the mother) must declare this as income on her tax returns. In 1992, Suzanne Thibodeau took Revenue Canada to court for taxing her child support payments: 30 per cent of what she received for her children's support was paid to the government in taxes.[78] In no other country are child support payments taxed. The usual justification for this is that fathers are more inclined to live up to their support obligations if they can get tax relief for doing so. The problem, though, is that the mothers who raise the children then have less money on which to do it.

Budgets and Implications for Social Reform

As women's analysis of the economy developed, the ways in which the various pieces of economic policy fit together became more obvious. Taxation and budget issues were not discrete, but were part of the general ideology that supported free trade and privatization. Governments usually have wanted to discuss each policy item as though it was not related to other policy items. Take, for example, the redesign of the tax system and social programs, which governments have discussed as though they were not a logical outcome of free trade.

The focus on the deficit was another example of how governments attempted to shift attention away from the consequences of specific policy initiatives, such as free trade and inflation fighting. Rather than focus on job loss and decreased social assistance, a great deal of attention was placed on the inability of Canada's people and governments to afford the social programs that had been initiated in more prosperous times. These social programs, it was argued, were the problem — the reason the debt was so large. As "debt mania" took over, governments outdid each other in pointing the finger at culprits — usually they were the poor and unemployed who, once again, as is common in economic hard times when governments want scapegoats, were accused of fraud, laziness, and unnecessary dependency on the state.[79]

Women's groups wanted to show that it was not the poor who were responsible for the economic woes of Canada, but that economic hard times were the result of misguided economic policy.[80] In a nation-wide attempt to mobilize against the first free trade budget in 1989, NAC initiated a campaign called "Get the Budget on Track."[81] The national campaign was a specific event in which people from all over the country boarded trains bound for Ottawa where a rally was held to protest not only the drastic cutbacks to VIA Rail but also the cutbacks to all of the other programs that the government claimed needed to be reduced because the deficit was too large.

The association between the deficit and excessive spending on social programs has been successful as a publicity strategy for governments, and it has allowed them to abandon certain responsibilities. There is no doubt that there is a problem with the federal debt, since interest payments on it amount to over one-third of government revenues.[82] But it has not been too much spending on social programs that has caused the debt to grow, rather it has been because of very specific government policies. During the late 1980s, when certain parts of the economy (particularly Ontario) were said to be "overheated," the federal government began a deliberate high-interest-rate policy in order to combat inflation. The idea was that with high interest rates, people would postpone buying things for which they had to borrow money, such as cars and houses. But the problem with this strategy was that when interest rates are high, governments too must pay high rates to borrow money. And since the government already had a large debt, the cost of this debt grew very rapidly. At the same time, the government instituted free trade and the GST, two measures which resulted in lower government revenues. Free trade resulted in many corporations either closing altogether or laying off workers, and this meant that since fewer people had jobs and fewer people were paying taxes, there was less money for governments. Also, the GST had a discouraging effect on the economy and, rather than generating the income expected for government, it brought in $4 billion a year less than the tax it replaced. It also discouraged people from spending, which in turn had a further effect on employment, since one person's expenditure is another person's income. So while the debt and the deficit [83] are a problem, they are a problem of the government's own making; they were not created by excessive social spending.

The successful targeting of the deficit as the country's major economic problem has enabled successive governments to proceed with a massive shift in the direction of social policy. The plan for these changes were outlined in 1985 with the publication of the *Report* of the Macdonald Commission, initiated by the Conservative government, and appear to be the foundation for the social reforms initiated by the Liberal government elected in 1993. The list of changes that occurred while Brian Mulroney was in power is extensive: the family allowance was cancelled; seniors' benefits were reduced; unemployment insurance was cut back; transfer payments to the provinces for health and (post-secondary) education were seriously eroded; CBC, Air Canada, Via Rail, the Post Office, and social housing programs experienced either privatization or substantial funding cuts; and foreign aid, funding of social advocacy groups, and farm programs were either eliminated or substantially reduced.

The only difference between the approach of the Conservative government and Chrétien's Liberals is that now there is greater emphasis on persuading people that improved efficiency will mean that the poorer will be better serviced.[84] This was a message that the Conservatives tried to get across, but as people believed less and less of what that government said, it was not something people were ready to accept. Even when the Conservatives considered giving people what they wanted, there was a twist, and the objectives that people demanded were subverted in some perverse way. The best example of this is the proposal in the Macdonald Commission's *Report* that Canada institute a Guaranteed Annual Income, or, as it is called in the *Report*, a "Universal Income Security Program." As Jean Swanson shows in her article "Co-opting the Guaranteed Annual Income," the idea of a minimal income which would keep people from extreme poverty is a good one, and one which had long been on the agenda of the poor.[85] However, when business groups began advocating it, there was reason for suspicion. When the Macdonald Commission made its recommendations, the form this so-called "safety-net" took would, in effect, worsen the position of the poorest in society. As Jean Swanson reports, its recommendations were to eliminate almost all social programs and replace them with only one which would be targeted at the very poorest. Since the primary objective is to reduce government expenditures, rolling all or almost all social programs into one tax-based scheme will certainly not be able to meet all of the objectives that existing programs do.

The overhaul of social programs that have been initiated by the Liberal government will most likely take the form of moving more closely to the model described in the Macdonald Commission's *Report*. The impact of further cuts to social programs and their elimination (as in the case of the family allowance) will probably have the effect of making more women poor, because it is often the provision of these programs which keeps people on the margin of poverty from actually slipping into it.[86]

The driving philosophy behind the Macdonald Commission's *Report* was the belief that the less government was involved in the economy, the better the economy would function. This philosophy coincided with that of the Conservative Party and the results were fairly dramatic nation-wide.[87] Privatization of publicly owned industries and the deregulation of many sectors was an objective that was enthusiastically pursued. For women, the possibility of achieving objectives other than those tied solely to profit became more remote. The example of what happened

COURTESY: Mary Otto Grieshaber and Margaret McRae

Women in rural areas organized a nation-wide campaign called "Rural Dignity" to prevent the closure of rural post offices. These stickers, pointing out that most rural postmasters were women, were materials prepared by women in Aggassiz, B.C., to support their 1986 petition campaign against post office closures and privatization.

in the post office was one of the most dramatic changes that affected not only the people employed, but entire communities in rural areas. In an attempt to "rationalize" services so that the post office could become profit oriented, thousands of rural post offices were closed and many others were privatized. This was a particularly significant issue for women in rural areas not only because close to 80 per cent of rural postal workers were women, but also because it was the post office which was the main form of communication and contact between people in communities. Rural Dignity was a group organized originally by women in the Maritimes to work against post office privatization. It staged a nation-wide campaign which was extremely successful in linking rural women throughout the country in this political work.[88] But despite the considerable negative publicity to the government and overwhelming public support for maintaining local post offices, huge numbers were eliminated altogether and those which remained were privatized.

Since the first free trade agreement with the United States, unemployment rates have soared and the economy has restructured in ways that do not promise improvements in the foreseeable future. The prediction even by governments that want to be optimistic is that unemployment will remain above 10 per cent well into the next century. At the same time there has been considerable harassment of the unemployed themselves. This has been a recurring feature of any economic downturn as governments attempt to deflect criticisms from their own ineffectiveness and shift the burden of responsibility onto individuals. As Laurell Ritchie pointed out in her brief for NAC on changes to unemployment insurance in 1989, the problem is not with the scheme, but with the lack of jobs.[89] Whenever the unemployed are under attack because they are costing more money, proposals are made to redesign the scheme so that fewer people can receive money. While in the past women used to be specifically named as people whose benefits should be reduced or eliminated, governments today cannot and do not specifically target any gender, racial, or minority group. Nevertheless, through their design of the program changes, they do affect some groups more than others. Women, for example, tend to be more involved in part-time work than men, so when the unemployment insurance scheme is redesigned to greatly reduce the ability of part-time workers to participate, it is women who are most affected. Laurell Ritchie's main point, however, is that eliminating or reducing benefits to the unemployed does not solve the problem of unemployment and that specific government policies need to be designed to this end.

Conclusions

Through dealing with the "macho economics"[90] rampant in Canada, the feminist movement has forced many issues to be raised in new ways. There is still much resistance to a feminist approach to understanding the economy, although women's assertiveness in policy debates over free trade, budgets, and development issues means that we are a force which is ignored only at great political risk. Today, women recognize that all of these economic policy issues are as significantly women's issues as are those more readily identifiable with our causes. Whatever measures we need changed in our society ultimately have some link with economic reality: the way in which the most powerful forces in society view and manipulate the economy has implications for us which go beyond our role as workers or consumers. Women have a stake in how our economy is defined, not just because we need jobs and social programs to meet our needs, but also because how the economy works defines who we are as people who live together in a common land. If our economic policy lauds greed and the ideology of the survival of the fittest, women and other minorities will be confined to the margins of society, and, at best, only do well when we are as aggressive and ruthless as those in power. This is not the vision that has motivated a feminist critique of the economy or feminist action on economic issues.

NOTES

1. For an interesting analysis of the problems of "the personal is political," see bell hooks, "Feminist Politicization: A Comment," chap. 15 in *Talking Back: Thinking Feminist Thinking Black* (Toronto: Between the Lines, 1988), 105–111.
2. Many feminist critiques of classical economics exist. See, for example, Nancy Folbre, *Who Pays for the Kids? Gender and the Structures of Constraint* (New York: Routledge, 1994); Marilyn Waring, *If Women Counted: A New Feminist Economics* (San Francisco: Harper & Row, 1988); Marjorie Cohen, "The Problems of Studying 'Economic Man'," in Angela Miles and Geraldine Finn, eds., *Feminism in Canada* (Montreal: Black Rose, 1989); Isabelle Sawhill, "Economic Perspectives on the Family," in *The Economics of Women and Work* (New York: Penguin, 1980); Martha Macdonald, "Economics and Feminism: The Dismal Science?," *Studies in Political Economy* 15 (Fall 1984); Michele A. Pujol, *Feminism and Ant-Feminism in Early Economic Thought* (Brookfield, Vermont: Edward Elgar, 1992).
3. It is probably not politically insignificant that business is commonly referred to as a "community" while labour and women's groups are either referred to as "movements" or depicted as representing "special interests."
4. The decision by the Ontario government to forgive a $7.6 million loan to Chrysler Canada Ltd. in 1994 in addition to a loan of $30 million it had forgiven in 1993 is an example of the mechanisms through which the "trickle down" system works. In order to convince Chrysler to train workers and set up a third shift on its production line, the government gave this money to the company, despite the company's record profits and bonuses of 100 per cent of salary awarded to its top executives (*The Globe and Mail*, 8 March 1994).
5. This is a consistent theme among feminist analysts of public policy. See, for example, Martha MacDonald, "Becoming Visible: Women and the Economy," in Geraldine Finn, ed., *Limited Edition: Voices of Women, Voices of Feminism* (Halifax: Fernwood, 1993), 157–170; Thelma McCormack, *Politics and the Hidden Injuries of Gender: Feminism and the Making of the Welfare State* (Ottawa: CRIAW/CREF, July 1991); Dorothy Smith, "Feminist Reflections on Political Economy," in M. Patricia Connelly and Pat Armstrong, eds., *Feminism in Action: Studies in Political Economy* (Toronto: Canadian Scholars' Press, 1992), 1–21.
6. For a further discussion of this issue, see Isabelle Bakker, "Through a Feminist Lens: Macroeconomic Restructuring in Canada" (paper presented at Economic Equality Workshop sponsored by Status of Women Canada, Ottawa, November 1993).
7. See Marjorie Griffin Cohen, "The Canadian Women's Movement and Its Efforts to Influence the Canadian Economy," in Constance Backhouse and David F. Flaherty, eds., *Challenging Times: The Women's Movement in Canada and the United States* (Montreal and Kingston: McGill–Queen's University Press, 1992.) Some of the reluctance of NAC to confront the government of the time was also related to the close ties some officers of the organization had with the Liberal Party.
8. See Marjorie Griffin Cohen, "Social Policy and Social Services," chap. 4 in Ruth Roach Pierson, Marjorie Griffin Cohen, Paula Bourne, and Philinda Masters, *Canadian Women's Issues*, Volume I: *Strong Voices* (Toronto: James Lorimer & Company, 1993), 264–320; and "Paid Work," chap. 2 in this volume.
9. See Diana Ellis and Sharon McGowan, *Women and Economic Development*, Handbook, Vancouver, 1980, excerpted in the documents section of this chapter.
10. This was repeatedly pointed out in studies by women on their experiences in northern single-industry communities. See, for example, *Northern B.C. Women's Task force Report on Single Industry Towns* (Vancouver: Women's Research Centre, 1977), and Meg Luxton, *More Than a Labour of Love: Three Generations of Women's Work in the Home* (Toronto: The Women's Press, 1980).
11. See, "Economic Development: Women Speak Out at the Pipeline Hearings," *Aspen* 2, no. 3 (1980), 6, 8, excerpted in the documents section of this chapter.
12. See, for example, Michelle Swenarchuk, "NAFTA and the Environment," *The Canadian Forum*, January/February 1993,13–14.
13. See, for example, Martha Macdonald and Patricia Connelly, "Class and Gender in Fishing Communities in Nova Scotia," *Studies in Political Economy* 30 (Autumn 1989), 61–87.
14. Martha Muzychka, with Kay Anonsen and Wendy Williams, "A Response to the Government of Newfoundland and Labrador's Consultation Paper on a Strategic Eco-

nomic Plan for Newfoundland and Labrador" (The Provincial Advisory Council on the Status of Women, Newfoundland and Labrador, November 14, 1991), excerpted in the documents section of this chapter.

15. See, Patricia Frangos, "All Training and No Jobs: Women Trained for Hibernia Project Denied Placements," Women in Trades, Technology, Operations & Blue Collar Work, *WITT National Newsletter* 3, no. 2 (Fall/Winter 1993), 17, reprinted in the documents section of this chapter.

16. See Melanie Conn, "Women's Worker Co-operatives Needed, Vancouver Organizer Says," *Worker Co-ops* (Winter 1985), 16–17.

17. See the letter from Mary Hassard and Marcia McVea announcing the opening of the Metro Toronto Women's Credit Union, Toronto, October 1974, reprinted in the documents section of this chapter.

18. Philinda Masters, "Feminist Credit Unions," *The Other Woman* 4, no. 3 (May/June 1976), reprinted in the documents section of this chapter; see also the the letter from Hassard and McVea, reprinted in the documents section of this chapter.

19. Kathleen Donovan, "Feminist Economics a Fantasy," Letter to the Editor, *Canadian Dimension* (December/January 1986/1987), 2, 45, reprinted in the documents section of this chapter.

20. Gerda Wekerle, "Urban Planning: Making it Work for Women," *Status of Women News* 6, no. 1 (Winter 1979/80), 2–4, 11, excerpted in the documents section of this chapter.

21. Wendy Lawrence, "Transportation: An Innovative Approach in Whitehorse," *Status of Women News* 6, no. 1 (Winter 1979/80), 8, reprinted in the documents section of this chapter.

22. Nettie Wiebe, "What Happened in Agriculture in the Last Ten Years?," *The Womanist* 3, no. 2 (Fall 1992), 15, reprinted in the documents section of this chapter.

23. Waring, *If Women Counted: A New Feminist Economics*, 240.

24. Laura Sundberg, "Rural Canadian and Third World Women Come Together," *Herizons* 2, no. 5 (September 1984), 9.

25. For more information on this issue see Marjorie Griffin Cohen, "The Canadian Women's Movement," chap. 1 in Pierson, Cohen, Bourne, and Masters, *Canadian Women's Issues*, Volume I: *Strong Voices*, 1–97.

26. Wiebe, "What Happened in Agriculture in the Last Ten Years," 15.

27. Gene Jamieson, "Farming No Picnic," *The Manitoba Women's Newspaper*, 2, no. 1 (April/May 1981), 7, reprinted in the documents section of Marjorie Griffin Cohen, "The Canadian Women's Movement," chap. 1 in Pierson, Cohen, Bourne, and Masters, *Canadian Women's Issues*, Vol. I: *Strong Voices*, 73–74.

28. "Rural Image: Rural Women," *The Manitoba Women's Newspaper*, 2, no. 1 (April/May 1981), 6.

29. For a further discussion of these issues, see my paper entitled "Democracy and Trade Agreements: Challenges for Disadvantaged Women, Minorities and States," in Patrick Boyer and Daniel Drache, eds., *Do Nation States Have a Future?* (Montreal and Kingston: McGill-Queen's Press, forthcoming).

30. Globalization refers to the dramatic increase in the mobility of capital and the increase in the international organization of production. Through this process it becomes imperative for more stationary factors of production (labour, land, natural resources) to become internationally competitive. This usually involves either increases in productivity or reductions in prices to these factors. For a further discussion of globalization in the Canadian context, see Robert Chodos, Rae Murphy, Eric Hamovitch, *Canada and the Global Economy: Alternatives to the Corporate Strategy for Globalization* (Toronto: James Lorimer, 1993), and James Laxer, *False God: How the Globalization Myth Has Impoverished Canada* (Toronto: Lester, 1993). For some recent publications on women and globalization see, for example, Lourdes Beneria, "Gender and the Global Economy," in Arthur MacEwan and William Tabb, eds., *Instability and Change in the World Economy* (New York: Monthly Review, 1989); Swasti Mitter, *Common Fare Common Bond: Women in the Global Economy* (London: Pluto Press, 1986); V. Spike Peterson and Anne Sisson Runyan, *Global Gender Issues* (Oxford: Westview Press, 1993).

31. Suzanne Mackenzie, "Neglected Spaces in Peripheral Places: Homeworkers and the Creation of a New Economic Centre," in *Cahiers de Geographie du Québec* 31, no. 83 (1987), cited in Sandra Harder, *Economic Restructuring in Canada: Developing a Gender-Sensitive Analytic Framework* (Ottawa: Status of Women Canada, June 1992), 7.

32. Standard work refers to full-time, full-year work with remuneration close to the average industrial wage and regular employee benefits.

33. Ramesh Mishra, *The Welfare State in Capitalist Society* (Toronto: University of Toronto Press, 1990), 17.

34. Terence Corcoran, "Recession Isn't The Problem, It's The Solution," *The Globe and Mail*, 14 February 1991.
35. Marjorie Griffin Cohen, *Women and Economic Structures: A Feminist Perspective on the Canadian Economy* (Ottawa: Canadian Centre for Policy Alternatives, June 1991).
36. See Daniel Drache and Duncan Cameron, *The Other Macdonald Report* (Toronto: James Lorimer & Co., 1985) for excerpts from the popular sector's briefs to the Macdonald Commission.
37. Women Against the Budget, *Brief to the Royal Commission on the Economic Union and Development Prospects for Canada* (September 1983).
38. See, for example, NAC's brief to the Commission in Drache and Cameron, *The Other Macdonald Report.*
39. Canada, *Report of the Royal Commission on the Economic Union and Development Prospects for Canada* (Ottawa: August 1985).
40. See, for example, my analysis of the report of the Macdonald Commission written for NAC and published as "Weakest to the Wall," *Policy Options* (December 1985).
41. For a political analysis of women's involvement in the anti-free trade campaign see Sylvia Bashevkin, "Free Trade and Canadian Feminism: The Case of the National Action Committee on the Status of Women," *Canadian Public Policy* 15, no. 4 (1989), 353–375; Jill Vickers, Pauline Rankin, Christine Appelle, *Politics As If Women Mattered: A Political Analysis of the National Action Committee on the Status of Women* (Toronto: University of Toronto, 1993), 272–274.
42. For a discussion of the role of the Business Council on National Issues, see David Langille, "The Business Council on National Issues and the Canadian State," *Studies in Political Economy* 24 (1988); Linda McQuaig, *The Quick and the Dead: Brian Mulroney, Big Business and the Seduction of Canada* (Toronto: Viking, 1991).
43. The popular sector refers to organized groups that are outside government, political parties, and business, but that represent people's interests through political actions, which attempt to influence those in positions of power in both the public and private sectors.
44. For a discussion of the Pro-Canada Network (which later became Action Canada Network) see Peter Bleyer, "Coalitions of Social Movements as Agencies for Social Change: The Action Canada Network," in William K. Carroll, ed., *Organizing Dissent: Contemporary Social Movements in Theory and Practice* (Toronto: Garamond Press, 1992), 102–117.
45. I wrote a fair amount about free trade during the time the issue was politically controversial. Much of what follows is based on my writings, some of which are listed here: Marjorie Griffin Cohen, *Free Trade and the Future of Women's Work: Manufacturing and Service Industries* (Toronto: Garamond Press, 1987); "Americanizing Services," in Ed Finn, ed., *The Facts on Free Trade* (Toronto: James Lorimer & Co., 1988); "Services: The Vanishing Opportunity," in Duncan Cameron, ed., *The Free Trade Deal* (Toronto: James Lorimer & Co., 1988); "Women and Free Trade," in Duncan Cameron, ed., *The Free Trade Debates* (Toronto: James Lorimer & Co., 1986); "The Lunacy of Free Trade," in Jim Sinclair, ed., *Crossing the Line: Canada and Free Trade with Mexico* (Vancouver: New Star, 1992); "Exports, Unemployment and Regional Inequality: Economic Policy and Trade Theory," in Drache and M. Gerther, *The New Era of Global Competition: State Policy and Market Power* (Montreal: McGill-Queen's, 1991).
46. The Macdonald Commission report recognized that certain industries where women were concentrated would suffer under free trade. but saw this as an opportunity for women to "leave low wage declining sectors of employment for expanding ones." The *Report of the Royal Commission on the Economic Union and Development Prospects for Canada*, 629.
47. See, for example, the article by Ellen Adelberg written early in the anti-free trade campaign, "Danger to Women: Free Trade Ahead," *Breaking the Silence* 5, no. 1 (September 1986), 21–22, 33, reprinted in the documents section of this chapter.
48. See, Cathy Crowe and Roger Hollander, "Free Trade: Its Effects Upon Women, the Health Care System, and the Arms Industry," in *Nurses for Social Responsibility Newsletter* 3, no. 1 (February 1988), 1–2 and "The Free Trade Agreement and the Garment Industry," a statement by Alvarine Aldridge in National Organization of Immigrant and Visible Minority Women of Canada, *Ontario Region Newsletter* 1, no. 3 (Fall 1987/Winter 1988), 1–2, both reprinted in the documents section of this chapter.
49. See the pamphlet by NAC, *What Every Woman Needs to Know About Free Trade* (Toronto 1988), reproduced in the documents section of this chapter.
50. See Marilyn Corbeil's response to a NAC free trade survey in a letter to Marjorie Cohen, May 2, 1989, and the response to NAC's free trade survey from the Antigonish Women's Resource Centre, May 15, 1989, both reprinted in the documents section of this chapter.

51. See, for example, Leonard Shifrin, "Free Trade in Social Programs," *Perception* 12, no. 1 (Winter 1988), 27–29.
52. Katie Macmillan, "Women and Free Trade," *C.D. Howe Institute Trade Monitor*, no. 5 (May 1988), 1, 10–11, excerpted in the documents section of this chapter.
53. Information on the effect of the FTA on the clothing industry comes from Leah Vosko, "Shrink, Cut ... Dye? NAFTA and Women's Work in the Canadian Clothing Industry," (M.A. thesis, Simon Fraser University, 1994).
54. Belinda Leach, "Flexible Work, Precarious Future: Some Lessons From the Canadian Clothing Industry," *Canadian Review of Sociology and Anthropology* 30, no. 1 (1993), 64–77.
55. Pat Armstrong, "The Feminization of the Labour Force: Harmonizing down in a Global Economy" (paper presented at the North-South Institute conference on Structural Change and Gender Relations in the Era of Globalization, Toronto, September 30, 1993).
56. In 1984, in contrast, 35 per cent of young women in the labour force were employed in part-time work. See Table VI in Marjorie Griffin Cohen, "The Implications of Economic Restructuring for Women: The Canadian Situation" (presented at the Canada in Transition conference at the Autonomous University in Mexico City, November 27, 1992), reprinted in Isabelle Bakker, ed., *The Strategic Silence: Gender and Economic Policy* (London: Zed Books, 1994).
57. Michael Hart, then a Canadian trade official, refered to opponents of the new deal as "the nationalists and professional worriers" who were against "business and global realists." Linda Diebel, "Free Trade Deal May be Altered in Mexico Talks, Top Officials Say," *The Toronto Star*, 20 October 1990, A3.
58. Vicki J. Northcott [Victoria Jean Weatherspoon], "Women in the Maquiladoras," *Briarpatch* 20, no. 7 (September 1991), 29–31, excerpted in the documents section of this chapter.
59. Shawn McCarthy, "NAFTA Drives Poor Farmers From Land, Critics Charge," *The Toronto Star*, 4 January 1994.
60. See, for example, the "Women's Plan of Action," the statement endorsed by 100 Women from Central America, Canada and the US and issued at the First Trinational Working Women's Conference on Economic Integration and Free Trade, Organized by Mujer a Mujer and Mujeres en Accion Sindical and co-sponsored by NAC and Labour Notes, and held in Valle De Bravo, Toluca, Mexico, 8 February 1992, reprinted in the documents section of this chapter.
61. This does not mean that Canadians accepted NAFTA. According to a Financial Post-COMPAS public opinion survey, only 11 per cent of Canadians believed that there was anything to be gained by NAFTA. Alan Toulin, "Canadians Give Thumbs-down to NAFTA," *Financial Post*, 22 June 1992.
62. For examples of analyses that favour NAFTA, see: Steven Globerman and Michael Walker, *Assessing NAFTA: A Trinational Analysis* (Vancouver: The Fraser Institute, 1993); Stephen J. Randall with Herman Konrad and Sheldon Silverman, eds., *North America Without Borders: Integrating Canada, the United States, and Mexico* (Calgary: University of Calgary Press, 1992); Rob Dobell and Michael Neufeld, *Beyond NAFTA: The Western Hemisphere Interface* (Lantzville, B.C.: Oolichan Books, 1993).
63. Jeffrey Simpson, "Why Canada Must Be Involved in the U.S.-Mexico Free-Trade Deal," *The Globe and Mail*, 6 September 1990.
64. For further information about the negative effects of NAFTA, see the following: Leah Vosko, "Shrink, Cut ... Dye? NAFTA and Women's Work in the Canadian Clothing Industry"; Bruce Campbell, *"Free Trade": Destroyer of Jobs: An Examination of Canadian Job Loss Under the FTA and NAFTA* (Ottawa: Canadian Centre for Policy Alternatives, October 1993); Canadian Centre for Policy Alternatives, *Which Way for the Americas: Analysis of NAFTA Proposals and the Impact on Canada* (Ottawa: CCPA, November 1992); Ecumenical Coalition for Economic Justice, *Intellectual Property Rights in NAFTA* (Toronto: ECEJ, October 1993); Canadian Environmental Law Association, *Environmental Implications of Trade Agreements* (Toronto: Ontario Ministry of Environment and Energy, 1993); Ian Robinson, *North American Trade as if Democracy Mattered* (Ottawa and Washington, D.C.: CCPA and International Labor Rights Education and Research Fund, 1993); Jim Stanford, *Estimating the Effects of North American Free Trade: A Three-Country General Equilibrium Model with "Real-World" Assumptions* (Ottawa: CCPA, September 1993); Canadian Environmental Law Association, *NAFTA and Water Exports* (Toronto: Ontario Ministry of Intergovernmental Affairs, 1993).
65. Ontario Women's Directorate, "The North American Free Trade Agreement: Implications for Women" (Toronto: OWD, 1993); Huguette Leger and Judy Rebick, *NAC Voters' Guide* (Hull: Voyageur Publishing, 1993), 23–30.

66. For a fuller discussion of the limits of free trade to democracy, see Cohen, "Democracy and Trade Agreements: Challenges for Disadvantaged Women, Minorities and States."

67. Lorraine Michael, "Women Creating Alternatives," *Action Dossier* 39 (Autumn 1993), 39–41

68. Much of this discussion of taxes comes from a brief I prepared for NAC, "Why the Goods and Services Tax will be Harmful to Women" (presented to the House of Commons Standing Committee on Finance, Regarding Standing Order 108(2), An Examination of the Goods and Services Tax — Technical Paper, Vancouver, October 2, 1989); information also comes from my publication *Women and Economic Structures: A Canadian Perspective on the Canadian Economy.*

69. The federal income tax was introduced in Canada in 1917 as the Income War Tax Act. For an interesting discussion of the differences in treatment of spousal taxation between countries, see Louise Dulude, "Taxation of the Spouses: A Comparison of Canadian, American, British, French and Swedish Law," *Osgoode Hall Law Journal* 23, no. 1 (Spring 1985), 67–129.

70. A marginal tax rate is the amount that is charged on the last dollar of income earned. This is distinct from the average tax rate, which is the total taxes paid as a percentage of total income earned. When someone, for example, complains about a 50 per cent marginal tax, it does not mean they pay 50 per cent of their income in taxes. Rather, income at a relatively low level is taxed at a low rate, but as people earn more, the additional income above a certain amount is taxed at a higher rate. The average tax rate, then, is considerably lower than is the marginal tax rate.

71. See Marjorie Griffin Cohen, "Why the GST will be Harmful to Women," *Feminist Action* 4, no. 2 (December 1989), reprinted in the documents section of this chapter. See also, the brief I prepared for NAC, "Why the Goods and Services Tax Will be Harmful to Women" presented to the House of Commons Standing Committee on Finance; and "Women and the GST," *The Womanist* 2, no. 1 (Fall 1989).

72. See the letter dated 5 March 1991 from Jacqueline Burnett and Sheridan Glenn, which they sent to 160 publications in Ontario, reprinted in the documents section of this chapter.

73. Government of Ontario, *Fair Taxation in a Changing World: Highlights, Report of the Ontario Fair Tax Commission* (Toronto: University of Toronto Press, 1993), 28.

74. For another argument against tax deductions, see "What's Wrong with Tax Deductions for Daycare?," *Action Daycare Newsletter* (Fall 1982), reprinted in the documents section of this chapter.

75. See "Does Your Child Tax Credit Belong to You?" *Upstream* 3, no. 4 (March/April 1979), 5, reprinted in the documents section of this chapter.

76. See Deborah Wilson, "Nanny's Salary Valid Deduction, Court Rules," *The Globe and Mail*, 12 May 1989, A13, reprinted in the documents section of this chapter.

77. Peter Howell and Catherine Dunphy, "Tax-cut Ruling a Victory for Women, Lawyer Says," *The Toronto Star*, 12 May 1989.

78. See Mijin Kim, "Sexist Tax Strikes Again," *Kinesis*, October 1992, 3–4, reprinted in the documents section of this chapter.

79. The crackdown against welfare fraud in B.C., Ontario, and Quebec is a good example of this, although as shown by Peter Small's article "Crackdown on Welfare Fraud Called Pre-election Gimmick," *The Toronto Star*, 30 March 1994, there is actually very little fraud and little money recovered from these actions. Rather, it is more government bravado of being tough in times of economic restraint.

80. See, for example, "Women Meet Michael Wilson," *Alberta Status of Women Action Committee Newsletter* 6, no. 2 (March 1985), 8–9, reprinted in the documents section of this chapter.

81. See the letter from Lynn Kaye, Tony Clarke and Tom McGrath dated 24 May 1989, and The Canadian Press, "Nurses Fight Ottawa Over Trade, Budget," in *The Toronto Star*, 6 August 1989, both reprinted in the documents section of this chapter.

82. Provinces do not have such high debt charges. In B.C., for example, less than 6 per cent of government revenues are devoted to debt payments. The figure is about 12 per cent in Ontario.

83. The deficit is the difference between what the government earns and what it spends each year when spending is greater than income. The debt is the accumulation of the deficits.

84. See National Action Committee on the Status of Women, Flyer, "Liberals Condemn Women to Greater Inequality," February 1994, and Dawn Black, Letter to Women, April 18, 1989, both reprinted in the documents section of this chapter.

85. Jean Swanson, "Co-opting the Guaranteed Annual Income," *Kinesis*, September 1986, 14, reprinted in the documents section of this section.

86. Marjorie Griffin Cohen, "A Good Idea Goes Bad: Guaranteed Income or Guaranteed Poverty," *This Magazine* 21, no. 2 (May/June 1987).
87. See Trudy Richardson, "While Some Progress is Being Made in Alberta, Privatization is a Looming Problem," *Feminist Action*, October 1985, 11, excerpted in the documents section of this chapter.
88. See Mary Otto Grieshaber and Margaret McRae, Postal Petition in B.C., June 1987, excerpted in the documents section of this chapter.
89. See Laurell Ritchie, "The Problem is Still Jobs ... Not Unemployment Insurance, A Brief to the Legislative Committee on Bill C-21: An Act to Amend the Unemployment Insurance Act and the Employment and Immigration Department and Commission Act" (presented by NAC, August 1989), excerpted in the documents section of this chapter.
90. Macho economics refers to the Rambo-like way in which markets behave with all human objectives subsumed under the dictates of what is good for the market. Marjorie Cohen, "Undressing Macho Economics," *Our Times* 5, no. 4 (June 1986).

Documents: Chapter 4

Community Development and Planning

Women and Economic Development
Vancouver, 1980[1]

What is economic development?

The term economic development usually refers to the creation or expansion of the economy of a community, region or country. The process of economic development occurs in many ways, and can be a huge undertaking involving thousands of people and billions of dollars or it can be a smaller and more local development.

In Canada, the large supply of natural resources such as coal, gas, oil and timber means that economic development often involves the exploitation of those resources.

The exploitation of a resource affects the economy of an area and people's lives in many ways. New towns may be created to house workers who are needed to extract the resource, or existing settlements experience an influx of new people who come to work. Pipelines, raillines or highways may be built to ship the resource out, changing the lives of people who live on their routes.

The extraction of primary resources such as gas and coal is an important aspect of Canada's economy, but economic development also includes the development of secondary industry and expansion or creation of ports or other transportation facilities. The damming of rivers to give hydroelectric power is another important part of Canada's economic development.

Why does economic development happen?

Economic development usually takes place because corporations see the development of a specific location or resource as a way to make money. Governments usually encourage corporations to undertake development projects, and sometimes even solicit their interest in poorer areas of the country.

Who benefits from economic development?

Very simply, the first priority of any economic development is to create profit. This gives economic power to the company or organization re-

1. Diana Ellis and Sharon McGowan, *Women and Economic Development*, Handbook, which was produced as part of an animation project on this topic in conjunction with the NFB Film "No Life For A Woman," Vancouver, 1980.

sponsible for the development. However, depending on the nature and size of the project, the development process can also offer benefits to people living in the area, such as employment ...

How are communities affected by an economic development project?
Industrial and resource development greatly changes the social and economic environment of a community or region. The population increases rapidly as new workers arrive, often with their families. Local businesses and economic activities may expand if the demand for their goods and services increases. Sometimes employment opportunities are made available to local people as well.

In general, this economic growth is not accompanied by a concern for the human needs in the area being developed. To date in Canada, much of the economic development has involved the creation of boom-towns or single-industry towns. These are created to house workers who are needed to extract or process a resource. The only reasons these towns exist is because a company is exploiting a resource in the area. In 1972 there were over 800 single industry towns in Canada with a total population of over 2 million people.

The well-being of the workers who live in a single industry town is a concern of the company, but usually only insofar as it affects their productivity. The needs of the rest of the people who make up the community — women and children — are rarely seen or provided for.

As a result, the women and families living in towns or areas created or expanded through economic development face particular hardships due to inadequate planning. For example, existing medical, dental and counselling services are often not planned to meet the needs of an increased population. In fact, sometimes there are no support services. Neighbourhoods, schools and homes are poorly designed, and built quickly and cheaply with little thought about the needs of the people who will be using them and living in them. Often there are no community centres and recreational facilities are inadequate.

Many of the development projects that involve the extraction or processing of a natural resource such as gas create problems of transiency in communities. A large labour force is needed to build a pipeline to transport gas, but once it is built relatively few people are needed to maintain it. For a short period workers will flood into a community, but once the project is finished, most will leave. This 'boom and bust' development puts a strain on the services and social fabric of even the most stable community.

Many serious problems occur because of the rapid change in a community as new people, money and a whole new way of life engulf a community. Wife-battering, high rates of alcoholism and child abuse, drug abuse, juvenile delinquency and family breakdown are just some of the results of economic development that doesn't take human needs into account ...

Community Research From Women's Perspective

In 1976 and 1977, women in northern British Columbia organized the Northern B.C. Woman's Task Force on Single-Industry Resource Communities. The Task Force involved women living in the single-industry towns of Kitimat, Fraser Lake and Mackenzie, B.C., in describing what life in these towns was like for themselves and their families.

The women outlined the difficulty of maintaining their family in a community where women had no say in the planning. They pointed out that their communities were designed mainly for employed male workers, and this made it hard for them to meet their own and their children's needs. Among issues raised in their report were housing, transportation, shopping, health care, employment, childcare and social needs. Some of the concerns women had about these issues were:

- Homes designed without consideration of family needs for space, storage and recreation. Such faulty design was especially noticeable in northern areas where cold weather forces children to be indoors much of the year, and when shift work requires the father to sleep in the day when small children are up and about.

- Discriminatory hiring practices and inadequate childcare facilities that meant women could seldom work outside the home.

- Town planning that did not cater to children's needs, demonstrated in the lack of safe places for children to play outdoors and poorly located schools.

- A lack of crisis and support counselling services for women and their families.

- Few, if any, places outside the home other than the bar, coffee shop or ice rink where women could meet for social and recreation activities.

- The lack of an adequate public transportation system and spreadout physical layout of the towns which made it difficult for women and children to get about and do shopping, transport children and themselves unless the family had two cars.

Women Speak Out at the Pipeline Hearings
Prince George, B.C., 1980[2]

Delegates from the Fort Nelson Women's Centre, the Women's Research Centre and the Yukon Status of Women Council appeared at the hearings on the proposal for the construction of the Alaska Highway Gas Pipeline Project in December in Fort Nelson. These women spoke to the Northern Pipeline Agency on the effects that it seems likely the pipeline will have on their lives and the lives of their families. They also spoke on what they expected the companies and governments involved to do to reduce this impact ...

What do women have to do with pipelines?

... The pipeline, although years away from being built, or even approved to be built by the government, is already starting to have an effect on life in these communities. Speculators have moved in, housing prices are soaring, the cost of living rises steadily. Furthermore, women are concerned about progress. Development based on the extraction of natural resources in order to satisfy the requirements of industrial and economic growth in the south, does not come without change to the communities in which it is centred. This change affects the lives of women and gives them definite perspectives on economic development. "Women are concerned with the human element of development — about what it will do to their children, their homes and community. Women are the ones who end up coping with the results and effects of development decisions usually made by men."

The private world of women

Women are "also concerned about what they knew was their invisibility to pipeline decision makers. The world of women is generally the private world of the home, the family and the community. (This is especially true in single-industry resource-based towns where it is so difficult for women to find paid work.) The work that women undertake in maintaining the family is seldom acknowledged or considered as serious work in the public world of commerce and development. Women's groups in Fort Nelson and Whitehorse wanted to be sure that women living in their communities had the opportunity to be heard and to have their lives and work made visible."

Need for social services

Fort Nelson is already lagging in basic social services, such as a transit system, mental health services and adequate medical services. With the influx of pipeline workers, the strain on those services will be further aggravated. The women maintain that the "governments and corporations, which will benefit from pipeline construction, have a responsibil-

2. From "Economic Development: Women Speak Out at the Pipeline Hearings," *Aspen* 2, no. 3 (1980), 6, 8. Copy at Canadian Women's Movement Archives (hereafter CWMA).

ity to mitigate against the negative impact of that development project, and should start by improving present services immediately and by establishing other services that have been identified as necessary." This should be done before construction on the pipeline begins.

Housing is the major issue that women in both Fort Nelson and Whitehorse spoke for. Housing is going up very rapidly, and much of it is inadequately constructed. Homes need to be built properly to withstand northern climates. They must be built with adequate space for children to play in for the long northern winters. Women are concerned about the high cost of housing and the lack of moderately sized and priced housing for families or young couples to purchase. Without adequate housing to purchase, workers and their families will be less likely to develop community roots and become a part of the life of the area.

Another area of concern is mental health services and support services "to help women deal with the proven negative effects of isolation and climate" of which depression, loneliness and cabin fever are specific elements. To date, Fort Nelson has only had periodic visits from a travelling psychologist or psychiatrist. The excessive use of alcohol, product of the "ethic of the hard working, hard drinking worker in the north" also figures in the need for improved social services.

More than anything else, the women spoke of their concern over the effect of rapid developments on their families. When men are away for long periods of time working in the bush, there are added strains on the family. Few services are available to meet the crisis and special needs of the children. Men are concerned about the safety of their children and the access their children will have to what public facilities exist when the pipeline construction workers arrive. "Family needs are part of community needs and the scenarios women painted of their family life need to be part of what planners look at when they design the plans around economic development initiatives in a particular area. These concerns should be taken into account when plans are drawn up for company housing, work camps, employment and training and general community impacts."

"A Response to a Strategic Economic Plan for Newfoundland and Labrador" November 1991[3]

1.1 Barriers to Women's Employment in Non-Traditional Fields

Many of the proposed jobs and prospects for development outlined in the **Consultation Paper** target the diversification of existing or potential resource industries such as mining, forestry and oil development work

3. Researched and written by Martha Muzychka, with Kay Anonsen and Wendy Williams, "A Response to the Government of Newfoundland and Labrador's Consultation Paper on a Strategic Economic Plan for Newfoundland and Labrador," submitted by the Provincial Advisory Council on the Status of Women, Newfoundland and Labrador, November 14, 1991.

(construction and production). It is important for the provincial government to realize that these areas have traditionally been identified as men's work, and that is has been difficult for women to be trained and hired in these fields.

The Advisory Council is especially concerned that the Hibernia development, which promises "65,000 person-years of direct and indirect employment," will not provide significant numbers of women with jobs. Our concern arises from the experiences of women entering non-traditional trades and jobs in other areas. As a result women's lack of presence in the oil industry can be linked to the generally minor presence women have in many industrial and male-dominated professions.

But the low participation rates of women in the oil industry can also be linked with the reluctance of oil companies to recruit, train and hire women aggressively, and the lack of penalties imposed for failing to meet government targets, quotas and guidelines. In both contexts, specific barriers exist which prevent women from accessing the employment opportunities which come from offshore oil development. These are:

1) Women do not have access to flexible, affordable daycare.
2) Women have to leave home and family to work on the rigs.
3) Women don't have qualifications to work in the industry.
4) Women do not have the same access to training and apprenticeship programs as men do.
5) Women's employment interests are not considered when planning recruitment campaigns.
6) Women who work in non-traditional trades face sexual harassment, lack support for their choice of career in their workplaces, and are not valued for their contributions to the workplace.
7) Employment equity policies lack substance and commitment to improving women's participation rates.

The Council recommends:
1) That the provincial government establish a policy regarding flexible work time for employees, especially single parents and people in two worker families. This is essential for full utilization of the province's human resources.
2) That the provincial government implement employment equity laws for the private sector.
3) That the provincial government provide affordable, flexible, and quality daycare for the families of this province.
4) That the provincial government provide relevant and accessible non-traditional training programs for women and that these training programs include support networks.

1.2 Small Business Initiatives

During a recent research mission to Norway and Scotland, we learned that there was a need to diversify business development. The experience in Scotland has been that the solution to long-term employment lies in looking at the natural resources of the area as opposed to relying solely on oil related mega industries. It is essential to promote more understanding of how the oil industry works.

We were told not to underestimate the spin-off impacts in small business development as a route to help women take advantage of the benefits associated with offshore oil development. Distribution, hotel/catering projects, transportation, financial services, supply services, and administrative supports can be sources of work and self-employment for women.

Communities experienced an expansion in these areas because of the demand by oil companies. This is obviously an area of growth and it seems clear that small businesses which offer supports or provide services needed by the oil companies can be developed. Infrastructure, in particular, is a very important focus.

Scottish researchers cited the misperception of the oil industry as very sophisticated and oriented primarily to high technology. Some businesses thought they didn't have the resources to supply the oil industry's needs. While there is a tendency sometimes to use supplies from satellite plants of a national company, Norway's success in exploiting the multiplier or spin-off effects lies in that country's determination to use and develop local resources, businesses and expertise.

Research in Norway and Scotland showed there is also a need to invest in businesses with a maritime focus. The traditional shipbuilding industry was one which was transformed to provide services in building oil rigs. Such companies include Aker Stord and Kvaerner-Rosenberg. Shipyards and manufacturers were adjusted to meet new construction demands and they were able to take advantage of an already skilled workforce. However, during down times, there has been some effort to look for contracts which can use the shipbuilding skills of the workforce.

The Council recommends:
1) That the provincial government acknowledge and include women's traditional skills and industry (i.e., cottage industries) in its development planning.
2) That the provincial government work closely with the Women's Enterprise Bureau to ensure government support of small business includes those operated by women...

"All Training and No Jobs: Women Trained for Hibernia Project Denied Placements" Newfoundland, 1993[4]

There are currently nine women working in construction on Hibernia project Bull Arm site. Of the forty-seven women trained as rebar apprentices, only a few have been slotted into cage manufacturing only, while male apprentices with the same training are being offered varied employment opportunities. Three days after the CBC was approached with this story, two female apprentice rebar workers were called to work. A female gritblaster/spray painter was called one week later. Patricia Frangos was trained as a Rebar Apprentice for the Hibernia project. Here is her story.

On June 1, 1993, I completed a Rebar Apprentice Training program. This training was put in place for the Hibernia project. I felt very honoured to be chosen as one of the fifty women trainees. There was no doubt in my mind that I would obtain employment at the Bull Arm site and work on the massive Gravity Base Structure.

Well, it is five months later and I, along with forty-seven other women, am fighting strongly for these "should have been" positions. Federal funding was granted to put necessary training programs (such as mine) together for the Hibernia project. The unions agreed that women should partake in the training (and 50 were chosen in the Rebar area) and subsequent employment at the Bull Arm site. To date I have not secured any employment at Bull Arm.

In October, 1991, I completed a training program with the Labourers Union (Local 506) in Ontario. The program was called Cement Finisher Apprentice. It advertised cement finishing as a dying art and in demand. This program was also federally funded and women were encouraged to be part of it. Myself and two other females completed this program and awaited our 2 1/2 year apprenticeship which we were told would be a possibility on completion. There would be no apprenticeship for us, the reason being the economic recession.

Months later the union approached us again to follow up with another program. Advanced Cement Finishing. All three of us declined (needless to say, the earlier program had not gone over well with all three of us). Interestingly enough, federal funding was not approved for the new program.

I feel very cheated by the unions in both of those situations. I also feel the construction industry should never have been placed outside the guidelines of the Federal Contractors Program. I believe women have been used and in the worst possible way. I took on these programs very ignorant to the "non-traditional" world of work. I admit I did very well in the courses but apparently not well enough to "cut it" in the so-called man's world. I firmly believe that someone should be held accountable

4. Patricia Frangos, Women in Trades, Technology, Operations & Blue Collar Work, *WITT National Newsletter* 3, no. 2 (Fall/Winter 1993), 17.

for exploiting women in this manner. As I'm sure you agree, the exploitation of women and abuse of federal funds must stop. There must be accountability so that women receive jobs after training.

Women's Worker Co-operatives
Vancouver, 1985[5]

Economic Options for Women, an innovative Vancouver-based project, was formed in February '85 with a mandate to promote community economic development and, particularly, worker co-operatives for women ...

Some reasons for starting women's worker co-ops are the same as for co-ops in general: chronic unemployment or unstable employment; dissatisfaction with the traditional, hierarchical employment structure; and, commitment to co-op philosphy — democratic control, surplus-sharing, and education for members.

However, women also have special needs which may be satisfied more fully through their own co-operatives. Women's worker co-ops provide the opportunity for access to business skills such as marketing, financing, budgeting, and bookkeeping. Women's co-ops devise different methods for building business expertise: taking courses, hiring consultants, and learning by trial and error ...

Production is another important area for skill development. A number of women's co-ops are in non-traditional trades such as printing and construction. A member in a women's co-op has much greater access to all aspects of the trade than does a sole tradeswoman in a traditional operation. In more traditional areas, such as food preparation and sewing, members of a women's co-op may have access to new aspects of production including equipment purchase and design ...

Women's co-ops also provide the opportunity to integrate new responsibilities as a worker/owner with family responsibilities. Many have developed creative systems for childcare, from on-site facilities with rotating supervision to flexible work-hours geared to children's needs. There's also recognition in women's co-ops that members may experience family pressure as they gain confidence and new independence.

Women often say their main reason for working in a women's co-op is that they find it easier to take on the challenge of operating a business from a familiar, socially-comfortable base. To gain this social cohesion some mixed co-ops, such as Wild West Organic Harvest, have evolved into women's co-ops ...

For the individual woman, the co-op is often a way out of social isolation as well as a chance for economic survival. Also, connections are made between women in co-ops and the women's community. Some women's co-ops have been initiated through the support or outright sponsorship of a women's centre or organization. Other women's co-ops

5. Melanie Conn, "Women's Worker Co-operatives Needed, Vancouver Organizer Says," *Worker Co-ops* (Winter 1985), 16–17.

support women's issues. For example, Press Gang prints materials for women's groups and publishes feminist books. Some co-ops contribute a percentage of their profits to women's groups; Plane Jane Construction provided carpentry services at reduced rates to women's groups with limited budgets.

In a more general way, women's co-ops interact with the women's community providing services and products that women want to purchase. Women of different cultural backgrounds formed a co-op in England to produce multicultural toys and games; a number of cities support women's co-op bookstores. Of course, the financial viability of women's co-ops will always require markets beyond the identified women's community.

Some of the particular problems that women's co-ops confront have been outlined: lack of business expertise, the need for confidence-building and support with family responsibilities. Access to capital is another significant problem for women with low or fixed incomes ...

In Canada, specific programs for financing women's co-ops do not exist. One solution lies with financial institutions known to have a commitment to the needs of women, such as the Ottawa Women's Credit Union and CCEC Credit Union in Vancouver. Financing for women's co-ops may also come from community development corporations. Also, women's groups are beginning to organize endowment funds to raise venture capital for women's enterprises.

... We hope to catalyze women's co-op businesses by continuing to hold educational workshops, and by providing development and business assistance. We are also preparing a directory for women to use in their planning. We want to hear from women working in co-ops so that we can exchange and share experiences ...

Metro Toronto Women's Credit Union Ltd.
Toronto, October 1975[6]

Dear Sisters:

A group of Toronto women concerned with the state of women's credit have been working for the past ten months on forming a credit union and we have formally incorporated as the Metro Toronto Women's Credit Union. We are the only credit union in Canada set up to serve the needs of women.

A credit union is a non-profit financial cooperative formed by a group of people to save their money together and provide loans to members who need them. It is owned and controlled by its members, and operated by a Board of Directors and Credit and Supervisory Committees elected by the members at annual meetings. Savings in a credit union are insured, so a member will never lose her money.

---

6. Open Letter from Mary Hassard and Marcia McVea, October 1975. Copy at CWMA, file: Metro Toronto Women's Credit Union.

Becoming a member entails opening a 'share account' of $5 or more, and joining the Women's Information Centre. The government requires that credit union members belong to a common group or organization and WIC has agreed to participate. This is more or less a formality and we will be looking for other women's groups interested in participating in the membership bond.

Credit Unions differ from banks in that the profits are returned to the members at the end of each year in the form of dividends and interest rebates. Banks' profits are returned to the shareholders, not to the customers ...

In sisterhood,
Mary Hassard & Marcia McVea
for the METRO TORONTO WOMEN'S CREDIT UNION LIMITED

"Feminist Credit Union"
Toronto, 1976[7]

A feminist credit union will give women a bit more money, a bit more access to money, both individually and as a group. By putting our money in a credit union and using it for women, we will make the most of our limited resources. But this will not give "rich", middle-class women a larger share of the pie, because we are operating outside the pie. No matter what, women have very little money and pooling it doesn't make us rich or give us access to real wealth or real power.

For that reason, a feminist credit union can't be considered a political strategy — it is not The Answer to women's powerlessness. It is also not a centre for organizing around women's issues. It is a holding tank for resources, in the monetary sense, to be used by the movement when needed.

But that's not to say that a women's credit union doesn't have worthy goals. Something that provides a much-needed service is always valid. And while the sole purpose is not to provide easy credit or combat credit discrimination, it certainly helps a woman who's in a bind. It's also better to pool our money for our own benefit than not to.

The idea for the Metro Toronto Women's Credit Union came into being several years ago when it was agreed that projects within the women's movement should not have to rely on government grants and unpaid labour for their existence. A structure that would provide a way to pool our money and redistribute it among women was needed, and a credit union for women seemed the most suitable.

Eventually it is hoped that the credit union can provide money for educational loans (particularly for women who want training in the trades), the funds to buy a building to house women's projects and food and housing co-ops. These long-range goals are not unrealistic (the credit union movement in Quebec has managed it) but in the meantime the

7. Philinda Masters, *The Other Woman* 4, no. 3 (May/June 1976), 4–5. An unpublished copy of this piece is in the CWMA, file: Metro Toronto Women's Credit Union.

credit union relies on granting small personal loans until it can increase its assets substantially.

But as useful as it is, one credit union in one city is not enough. In terms of giving women the economic base to begin controlling our own lives, its is a drop in the bucket. What is needed is an organized movement of autonomous women's credit unions across Canada. Women with some financial backing will be in a much better position to demand changes.

"Feminist Economics a Fantasy"
Prince Albert, Saskatchewan, 1986/87[8]

I am hearing more and more these days about feminists and other groups taking up the government's schemes for 'job creation' or 'community development' and calling it something else, cushioning it in words like 'collective' or 'feminist economics' and implying that it is a great benefit to individuals and communities. I am seeing peace and solidarity groups here in Saskatchewan using welfare recipients on workfare grant schemes to run their offices and projects. I am seeing feminists take up and promote programs under the Canadian Jobs Strategy which undermine unionized public services and which replace institutionalized training through tech. schools. Leftists are fulfilling the government's notions of job creation and training and seem to see nothing wrong with it. To me it is submission to the widescale onslaught turning our country into a low wage, unskilled and non-unionized society with drastically lowered standards of living and diminished worker's power.

I was shocked to read the article by Dorothy Smith in Canadian Dimension 20 #5. Perhaps if she had mentioned one word regarding a long-term strategy or goal for these community development projects, such as contributing to organizing skill development aimed at gaining more grassroots control, or accomplishing the building of examples of what work could be like under socialism, I would not have been so amazed. Instead, community development is described as a "collective initiative for sustained job creation", jobs which, presumably, we are to except at low or even *no wages*, under some new form of accounting. Spare me! Being recognized for my work might help build my self-esteem, but it won't pay the rent! Or am I supposed to live in a dormatory with ten other women living off the 'informal economy' and work in sweat shops sewing children's clothes in a 'non-heirarchical' manner?? There are people talking about the way the conditions of the Third World are coming home, but they aren't advocating putting down the red carpet for it!! I am not ready to accept the eternal entrapment of women in poverty.

8.Kathleen Donovan, Letter to the Editor, *Canadian Dimension* (December/January 1986/1987) 2, 45.

Neither am I ready to accept that needed public services like women's centres and rape crisis services must depend on the success of accompanying small businesses for their existence.

I've already had my experience working for a feminist organization funded under a Canadian Employment grant and found it to be the most oppressive work situation I have ever experienced. Not only were we to reveal openly our disagreement with management in 'collective' forums, we were not to think in those terms but to work as 'sisters', involving huge expectations for volunteer labour after hours. I would be very surprised to find that everyone in the 19 projects referred to in the article is working for the same wage. If so, perhaps there is something to be said for everyone working their butts off equally for a pittance. But a solution to the economic crisis or of women's poverty, it is not! As for 'non-dollar considerations', forget it! I guess I'm a selfish, greedy, old fashioned worker with no morals, but this whole thing sounds to me like something some women who have never been poor would come up with, or, maybe (again), middle-class feminism.

It never ceases to amaze me the contortions the state under capitalism puts us through and into which we often enter innocently, wanting to do good. Must we get back to the basics again? This is a class society and needs to be changed. I'm not sure how to contribute to this, but at least design your strategies to accomplish this end. Going along with the manipulations of the state and even saying it is beneficial to women or progressive actually scares me. Feminism is being twisted to fit the designs of the state, and saying that we care more about other things than money sounds like a new version of the old 'labour of love'. I think this is a feminist fantasy which deflects from the class nature of the economic crisis, and which camouflages the massive restructuring of industry occurring in our society today. Feminists like Chudnovsky appear to be leading the way in designing creative ways of adjusting to the state's design for the future. I'm sure Flora MacDonald, et al, would love it. I think it is deadly.

In solidarity,
Kathleen Donovan
Prince Albert, Sask.

"Urban Planning: Making it Work for Women Toronto, 1979[9]

Canadian cities are planned by men for men. Not only are there few women in the planning profession (less that 10% in Canada and those mainly in junior positions), but when we look at how houses are designed, how neighbourhoods are laid out, how transportation systems are organized — they are still planned as *if* most women were in the home full-time and as if the predominant family were the nuclear family...

9. Gerda Wekerle, *Status of Women News* 6, no.1 (Winter 1979/80), 2–4, 11.

This article focuses on two aspects of urban planning — transportation and zoning — neither of which have traditionally been defined as "women's issues", for, unlike daycare or equal pay, they seem to apply equally to everyone in the city. But I will argue that women are particularly disadvantaged by the way transportation and zoning are currently organized, and that changes are essential if women's opportunities in the urban environment are to increase.

Transportation

... Compared with men, women are transportation disadvantaged. In a car-oriented society, fewer women than men own and drive cars. When we look at all the licensed drivers in Ontario, for example, only 40% are women and not all of those have access to a car. Because women, and especially elderly women and women heads of families, are disproportionately represented among the poorest groups living in metropolitan areas, they cannot afford cars now and will be increasingly less able to do so as gasoline prices rise. We can also anticipate that many of the families with two cars will be forced to give at least one up — usually the wife's car.

Women are heavily dependent on public transportation and this dependence is increasing. In transportation studies conducted in cities across North America, twice and three times as many female workers as male workers used public transit to get to work. In Toronto, the T.T.C. found that 57% of the heaviest transit users are women.

Women's heavy reliance on transit has wide-ranging implications for all aspects of their lives. It affects their ability to take paid work and the extent of the job search area in which they can look for work. Women in the paid labour force operate under extreme time constraints because they are also responsible for housework and childcare. As a result, they try to reduce commuting time and distance to work and this either limits their choice of jobs or makes them a captive labour market for low paying local jobs. It also means that women often cannot take jobs in the new industrial parks and offices in the suburbs where new jobs are created because there is no public transportation.

Sometimes whole areas of a city are transportation disadvantaged. One of these is the Jane-Finch area of Downsview, a suburb of Toronto, where there is no weekend or evening bus service even though many residents are shift workers, and many elderly and single parents living in the area cannot afford cars.

Transportation systems are designed primarily to carry workers to and from their jobs during peak commuting hours, and to service business and industry. Planners assume that people have a choice between transit and an automobile and must, therefore, be lured out of their cars by improved rush hour services such as express buses and advertising campaigns which emphasize the amount of money to be saved by taking transit to work... There is no attempt to make the transit system more convenient for those captive riders who have no choice but to use public transit for all their daily needs at all hours of the day and night. For example, women and the elderly must use transit for shopping, yet often bus stops are located a block or more away from supermarket entrances or on the edge of the vast parking lot of a regional shopping centre.

Women are known to make "multiple trips", i.e. they try to combine shopping and household errands with their journey to and from work. Yet fare structures penalize them for such "stopovers". Mothers are generally responsible for taking children to childcare centers and picking them up. This usually involves two additional daily transit trips, often in a direction away from the mother's place of work. The transportation models which are used to predict demand for service and regulate bus scheduling don't take into account these ways in which women's travel patterns differ significantly from men's and, since women are not defined as a separate user group, their needs are not taken into account when priorities are set.

What is needed?

1) Greater attention to the needs of the "transportation disadvantaged" — the poor, elderly, handicapped, children, and women who are now the captive users of the system. This requires a recognition that the population with no access to cars is increasing and that a higher priority must be placed on access by public transit to all essential services such as hospitals, social services, shopping, and cultural and recreational facilities.

2) Because Canadian cities are predominantly low density and often cannot support even conventional bus routes, more attention must be given to developing alternative forms of flexible transit systems. After a short trial period, Toronto eliminated its dial-a-bus routes on the grounds that the cost per trip was too high compared with regular buses. Almost 2/3 of the users of dial-a-bus were women. The cost accounting did not include the social benefits to families and the community of increasing mobility for a substantial segment of the population, not did it document the costs of eliminating it. We might ask how many women could no longer be employed, had to buy a car, or became housebound when the service was discontinued?..

"Transportation: An Innovative Approach in Whitehorse" Yukon, 1979[10]

When a group of concerned women got together in Whitehorse to establish a Status of Women Council in 1973, one of the things they found themselves talking about was "cabin fever", that emotional downturn people suffer after being housebound for weeks on end. The severe

---

10. Prepared by Wendy Lawrence from information by Natalia Boland, Assistant Transit Manager, Whitehorse, *Status of Women News* 6, no. 1 (Winter 1979/80), 8.

winter weather in the northern city was taking its toll, especially on homemakers, who were cut off from friends and basic services. Even shopping for everyday needs became difficult.

Fortunately, the women had an idea: by organizing transportation they could offer a solution to their own problems and contribute to the community in other ways. Within a year they formed the Yukon Women's Mini-bus Society, and thanks to a grant from the Company of Young Canadians, began research in order to propose a local bus service.

Given their lack of experience with transportation planning, the women had quite a task ahead of them. The 14,600 inhabitants of Whitehorse are spread out over a large area around the city centre, so, to draw up schedules, the Mini-bus Society members drove around the routes they had developed and timed these runs repeatedly. They also sought support from major Whitehorse organizations which then backed their submission to city officials. It was accepted. The Women's Mini-bus Society was to provide transportation for an 18-month trial period, under contract to the municipal government. Financing came from all three levels of government: Transport Canada contributed $80,000 to purchase buses, while the municipal and territorial governments agreed to split the cost of covering the projected operating deficit. By February of 1976, four new buses were on the road.

The Women's Mini-bus Society set up a system operating from 7 a.m. to 7 p.m. week-days. Except for three official stops downtown, the vehicles stop on request. Each bus seats 16, and one bus has a wheelchair lift for disabled passengers. Fares are 50¢ for adults, 25¢ for children or senior citizens, and the longest run travels over 10 miles in 45 minutes. Success was immediate.

In its first three months, the bus service carried 25,000 passengers - an average of 11 passengers per vehicle hour. This exceeded expectations, and compares favourably with transport services in communities of a similar size. In 1977, the system won the approval of an evaluation committee, which recommended that the City Council establish an independent Transit Commission to provide such a service on a permanent basis. On July 1, 1978, the new Transit Commission took over the system from the Women's Mini-bus Society.

The general structure designed by the Whitehorse women remains, however. Because the work patterns and needs of women were initially taken into consideration, most of the drivers are women. The 15 drivers work anywhere from four to 24 hours a week. (Some work four hours a day, some divide a week between them, and still others are on call to run a spare vehicle if necessary.) While there are problems in scheduling this amount of shift work, there are also advantages: more job opportunities, alert drivers, and low costs.

The bus service has continued to adapt to the needs of the growing city. To meet the passenger load of almost 900 users a day, the Transit System has had to add vehicles and alter routes. It is now awaiting the arrival of four new 25-passenger buses purchased with a grant from the Urban Transit Assistance Program.

Whitehorse women have reason to be proud when they see their original idea transformed into a functioning public transit system.

"What Happened in Agriculture in the Last Ten Years?" Ottawa, 1992[11]

This has been an unkind decade for food producers in Canada. The farming community took a sharp turn for the worse a decade ago and has been travelling rapidly downhill ever since.

Farmers have had hostile weather conditions, including a series of drought years during the mid-eighties. But the outdoor weather has been relatively benign compared to the political climate farmers have had to contend with during this period.

The overriding objective of the federal government since 1984 has been to make agriculture more "competitive" in a global marketplace. Underlying this directive is the assumption that growing food must be treated like any other business in a capitalist economy where fewer people producing more products for lower prices is deemed to be more efficient and competitive. Predictably, restructuring agriculture to achieve this goal is having drastic consequences for farming people.

Throughout the term of this government, farm people have been promised that becoming more "self-reliant, competitive and market oriented" ... will make them more prosperous and keep the industry viable. The possibility of selling more foodstuffs into the international market is toted as a great opportunity. Those who don't share this enthusiasm for the liberalized global market and the further industrialization and concentration of food production are discounted as nostalgic, unrealistic and non-adaptive.

The federal government has pushed this competitive model of agriculture on every front. Internationally, it entered into the Canada–U.S. Free Trade Agreement, which undermines the possibility of having a domestic food policy. For example, with the border open to U.S. baked goods, Canadian millers demanded Canadian milled wheat be supplied to them at U.S. price which was about half the Canadian domestic price at the time. (Significantly, consumers did not enjoy any drop in the price of bread while wheat farmers suffered that financial loss.)

Meanwhile, the milling industry has had to "adapt" by rationalizing and merging with multinational corporations. Much the same has occurred in many other food sectors. The North American Free Trade Agreement (NAFTA) and the General Agreement on Tariffs and Trade (GATT) will lead to more of the same in larger measure.

In its determination to be globally competitive, the federal government has systematically undermined any means farmers have in place to get a fair price for their products, supply domestic food needs, take care of the land and maintain rural communities. Farmer controlled

11. Nettie Wiebe, *The Womanist* 3, no. 2 (Fall 1992), 15.

marketing boards are under attack. The benefits of orderly collective marketing bodies such as the Canadian Wheat Board, are being tossed into the jaws of corporate alligators, whose appetite for ever cheaper raw products is insatiable.

As the farming community struggles with both farmgate prices that do not meet the costs of producing food, and debts with attendant high interest bills, the federal government continues to teach us lessons in adaptation and self-reliance. Hundreds of miles of rail lines are abandoned so that the cost of transporting grains is transferred to farmers. Farmers have just been handed the bill for agricultural research with the passing of check-off legislation (Bill C-54) this September. Federal responsibility for crop insurance and other farm income programs have been handed off to the provinces. The list could go on for pages.

Periodically, like the landlord who has evicted a tenant in a winter storm tossing her a blanket through the window, the federal government has delivered ad hoc aid to farmers. Despite the publicity and gratitude attending these hand-outs, they have, in fact, not changed the overall position of farmers a great deal.

The 1991 Census tells the story in numbers. Canada had about half as many family farms in 1991 as in 1971. Even more alarming is the fact that the rate of losses had increased sharply during the last five years. Twenty-six percent of the farms were lost in the period from 1986-1991.

A look at the income decline on farms explains why family farms are not surviving. It is no longer possible to make a living growing food for prices which multinational corporations deem competitive. Indeed, the 1991 figures reveal that the surviving farm families earned more income from off-farm jobs than from farm sales.

Instead of applying a tourniquet to stop this bleeding of people from the land, government policies continue to open new wounds.

By now, many farming communities are anemic beyond recovery. If these policies continue, Canada will be left with a small number of large commercial farms producing most of the product, a smattering of "hobby" farms reliant on urban employment and very few vibrant rural communities. And Canadian consumers will become increasingly dependent on imported food.

"Restructuring: The Free Trade Agreement (FTA) to Women: Free Trade Ahead"
Ottawa, 1986[12]

Do not turn this page because you are sure you won't understand any article that discusses free trade. You will, I can assure you. Also, please

12. Ellen Adelberg, *Breaking the Silence* 5, no. 1 (September 1986), 21–22, 33. Copy at CWMA. The vigorous debate surrounding the economic impact of the Canadian/U.S. Free Trade Deal frequently ignored the negative implications of free trade for women. Yet, as the author of the following extract showed, women stood to lose more than men. The information presented was based on a speech made by Marjorie Cohen, a feminist economist, whose public lectures and writings brought the detrimental impact of free trade on women to national attention.

do not turn the page because you are tired of seeing those two ubiquitous words every time you open your daily newspaper. Articles in the newspaper never discuss what free trade might really mean for women. This article does.

If you have heard about free trade, but only in the mainstream media, you are likely to be wondering what all the hubbub is about. After all, what would be wrong with having unrestricted access to American-made products which, no matter what they are, are often cheaper and come in more colours and varieties than do Canadian-made goods? And why should we not expand our markets for Canadian-made goods to the millions and millions of consumers who live down south of the border? What could we possibly lose in such a deal?

Nothing, claims Brian Mulroney. Lots, claims Marjorie Cohen (a feminist economist at York University and a vice president of the National Action Committee on the Status of Women). According to Cohen, if we are women, and work in a service sector or manufacturing industry, or rely on welfare payments to live, we could be hit hard by free trade. But wait a minute, you say, Brian Mulroney is a politician. If Cohen is right, why would Mulroney risk alienating thousands of voters by moving towards a policy which could have disastrous results? If you have a healthy dose of neuroticism bordering on paranoia, you may think Brian is part of the ultimate male plot, conspiring with his cronies to permanently impoverish and disempower women. If you are less prone to rashness, you may simply think Brian is not too bright, and misguided by his trusted and well-read business advisors.

In order to understand why Cohen's concerns should be weighted seriously, it is necessary to weave our way through the seeming confusion of today's Canadian economy. No easy task, although it was one which was attempted last winter by the Ottawa chapter of Organized Working Women. It was during a series of four lectures which this group held that I chanced upon hearing Cohen speak about the clearly negative implications of free trade for women, and thus became a convert in the rally against it. I want to state that I am not an economist; however, none of us have to feel that we need a degree in economics to understand what free trade is, or why it is just not going to do us any good.

To begin with, let's look at the type of production Canada has relied upon throughout its existence to furnish economic prosperity. Without a doubt, harvesting natural resources has always been our ticket to maintaining and increasing the general standard of living in Canada. We have never had a very strong manufacturing sector, although in recent years the service sector (where, by the way, the majority of women in the work force are employed), has expanded at a great rate.

Canada is, and has always been, extremely dependent on trade to sustain economic growth. In fact, we are more dependent on trade than any other country in the western world. The catch is, our trade surplus is due to the export of natural resources, which employs only about 6 per cent of Canadian workers. When times are good in other countries, primarily the United States, and demand for our resources is high, we are able to spend lots of money to import most of the manufactured goods that are sold here. When times are bad, and nobody wants our wood, iron ore or oil, what happens to Canadian industry? Tied as we are to expecting revenues for these resources from other countries, primarily the United States, and lacking a strong manufacturing sector to provide us with goods to substitute for the ones we import, we suffer the same economic recession as the other countries upon which we depend.

This being the case, and with unemployment still hovering around the 10 per cent mark in Canada, what route might we logically take to reduce unemployment and increase everyone's level of prosperity? Economists such as Cohen, Mel Watkins of the University of Toronto, and Sam Gindin of the United Auto Workers all argue that we need to develop our own industries which could produce the goods we now import, and that we need to process our resources before shipping them out. This would result in jobs and a healthier Canadian economy. These strategies need to be accompanied, not by liberalized trade agreements, but if anything, by continued import restrictions in order to protect our fledgling industries.

Why then, you logically ask, are the Tories up on their high horse about negotiating a free trade agreement with the United States? What are they hoping to accomplish? If we can assume that they have used the Macdonald report on the economic prospects of Canada as their rationale, they would be expecting free trade to result in a "radical restructuring" of the Canadian economy, leading to huge economies of scale in our manufacturing sector, which would allow us to compete on an international scale as finished-goods producers. As Marjorie Cohen pointed out in her talk, theological expressions seem to constitute a good deal of the verbiage used by Macdonald and other free trade defendants when they are questioned about the value of the concept. "Faith" in the market system is one underlying precept; "belief" in the new era of prosperity that a more integrated world capitalist economy can bring is another.

But what, you may say, in practical terms might free trade bring? In the short term, even its staunchest defenders agree, free trade is likely to herald an era of plant closures in Canada for those which simply cannot compete with more efficient manufacturers south of the border. But in the long term, they argue, some of our industries will thrive on their access to new markets in the United States and will grow as job creators and revenue producers. We are told to believe that, perhaps ten or twenty years down the road, Canada will ultimately benefit from liberalized trade with the United States.

Aside from the spectre of immediate job loss for thousands of Canadians, there is a flip side to this scenario, which, for women, is likely to be nothing short of disastrous. First of all, women tend to work in the weakest sectors of our manufacturing industries and therefore are the most likely to lose their jobs in the short run due to still competition in the United States. A tracking study done in the mid-1970s by the government, during a period of unprecedented increase in imports, showed that women who lost their jobs at that time remained unemployed longer than men, and ultimately found worse-paying jobs than did the men who were laid off.

Macdonald, indicating some sensitivity to this situation, suggested that the government should provide some form of "adjustment assistance" to women to move into the new "high wage" industries that he has faith will flourish under free trade. However, he stressed, women must be "suitably adaptable" in the new era; that is, we must be willing to be retrained and relocated to wherever these new industries will be found. Women with dependents, and possibly attached to higher-wage-earning spouses, will not find such a transition easy to make.

Secondly, let's look at women who work in the service sector of our economy (that is in occupations such as clerical, waitressing, or hospital workers). After all, it is a significant employer today, as noted earlier. According to Mulroney, the Canadian government does not want to include free trade in services in the trade talks with Washington. However, it is well known that the United States is extremely interested in developing free trade agreements in services with us, as well as with any other countries which might be willing partners. In fact, it has already negotiated such an agreement with Israel.

Free trade in services is extremely important to the United States these days because it has lost a significant number of manufacturing jobs to third world countries. About 70 per cent of the American labour force is currently employed in the service industries. Should free trade in services occur, it is likely that even more women in Canada will be forced to work in the traditionally low-paying, non-unionized, dead-end jobs that the service sector provides; only in this case, more and more of the employers will be American, and more and more, the employment standards will be in the United States, where "right to work" laws at no minimum wage exist in some of the southern states.

And what about the women who comprise the majority of workers in the public services? In the United States, privatization of such services is being actively encouraged. Non-unionized employers, with a tendency to hire part-time workers for less wages and benefits than full-time workers, could be given free licence to compete in the public sector if privatization were given free reign here. Clearly the strength of our public service unions, which have achieved impressive wage gains for women, would be severely threatened.

There is another, and perhaps more dire threat to women who work in the service sector, regardless of whether or not free trade in services is negotiated. That threat is embodied in the American wish to make everyone play on a level playing field (this is literally the language of Washington, as Mel Watkins points out). Are we talking about National Football League franchises or exchanging goods? Neither; we are talking about the need perceived in the United States for its free trading partners to reduce any unfair advantages industries may receive in the other country (Canada, in this case) due to government policies, programs and subsidies. Such unfair advantages might be considered in Washington as government-sponsored maternity leave benefits which constitute two-thirds of women's salaries here, but only 50 per cent of women's salaries in the United States. Even Canadian medicare plans are seen in America as an unfair subsidy to our workers. While our welfare state is no doubt inadequate, do we really want to replace it with the American model, replete with its thousands of homeless citizens?

Last but not least, what about the potential effects of free trade on women who live either alone or as mothers on social assistance? There is no question that welfare and pension benefits in this country are outrageously inadequate, but they are certainly unlikely to improve if we align ourselves more closely with America, home of Reaganomics and social welfare budget-slashing. Higher social assistance payments in Canada than in the United States may well be perceived as yet another unfair government subsidy — for complex reasons only economists could fathom ...

"Free Trade: Its Effects Upon Women, the Health Care System, and the Arms Industry"
Toronto, 1988[13]

Free Trade and Health Care

Two factors which reduce the quality of care for patients and reduce protection and benefits for health care workers are "contracting out" and "privatization". These trends, which have begun to occur in Canada, are greatly advanced in Reagan's America.

Contracting out various types of jobs in order to cut costs results in lower wages and benefits, the loss of full-time jobs to part-time ones, deteriorating working conditions and a consequent loss of morale and productivity.

Free Trade competition demands will accelerate the contracting out phenomenon and encourage other cost-saving schemes such as the introduction of patient classification systems in hospitals. These systems, which allocate nursing time according to various illnesses have been used to cut "costly" nursing services by reducing full-time nursing staff to supervisory staff only and by cutting most nursing positions to part-time and temporary ones. Access to public funding that is now restricted to non-profit operators will likely be broadened under the agreement.

13. Cathy Crowe and Roger Hollander, *Nurses for Social Responsibility Newsletter* 3, no. 1 (February 1988), 1–2.

This will ensure rapid privatization such as has already occurred in the U.S. where conglomerates are taking over the care of the chronically ill and the elderly (as well as child care). As with contracting out, privatization reduces the quality of service because it wrings more work from health care employees for lower wages, benefits and working conditions.

Free Trade and the Arms Race

In a general sense, Canada's newly trade-driven economy will be intricately tied up with and dependent upon the U.S. economy, far beyond what it is today. The potential for U.S. economic retaliation against *independent* Canadian policy on peace and arms reduction will render such independence virtually suicidal. We will be, in effect, the 51st U.S. state, the only one with no political representation.

More specifically, when it comes to American potential to interpret the subsidization of impoverished regions as "unfair competition", there is one exception: military production. The likely effect will be the introduction of new arms production facilities, and corporations such as General Electric who already engage in significant military production, will be encouraged to accelerate in this direction.

What Can Be Done to Stop Free Trade?

Since the Mulroney government holds a massive Parliamentary majority and has the power to impose Free Trade, the only way to stop it at present is to develop a huge grassroots movement. The focus of this movement, which is already growing rapidly, is an attempt to force an election on the Free Trade issue. The National Action Committee on the Status of Women (NAC) is taking a prominent role in this activity. We believe nurses and nursing organizations should be in the forefront. To this end, individual nurses and nursing students must pressure their organizations to become active in this struggle.

"The Free Trade Agreement and the Garment Industry" Ontario, 1988[14]

... I am a single mother and have three dependent children. I depend on my job to provide my living.

The industry is already weakened by off-shore competition and is listed as one of the weakest Canadian industries by the MacDonald Commission on free trade. Free trade will only put the future of the clothing industry as a major industrial employer at stake.

The Canadian clothing industry is currently protected by high tariff barriers from American garments. The tariff is on the average about 22 percent, varying on the type of garment and its fabric composition. Currently, because of these tariffs, only ten percent of Canadian clothing

14. Statement made by Alvarine Aldridge, factory worker at G.H. Sportswear Ltd., during a meeting with Barbara McDougall, Minister Responsible for the Status of Women. Reported in National Organization of Immigrant and Visible Minority Women of Canada *Ontario Region Newsletter* 1, no. 3 (Fall 1987/Winter 1988), 1-2.

imports come from the United States. A free trade deal will mean an increased volume of American imports that will not seriously compete with offshore imports, but will provide further competition for our domestic production.

There are a number of reasons why the Canadian clothing industry cannot compete with the American industry on an equal footing. Probably the most important factor is the abundant supply of cheap labour in the Southern United States, providing cheaper garment production to Canadian manufacturers who want to serve the American market as well as the Canadian market from the south.

Phasing out the high tariff barriers in the clothing industry will have a disastrous effect on the working lives of Canadian garment workers. Thousands of immigrant women will lose the only employment they have known while in Canada. We are estimating that 20,000 – 25,000 jobs will be lost in Ontario alone.

Job retraining has never been successful for the typical middle-aged immigrant woman, who will be the dislocated worker if this free trade deal is approved. Women have always been under-represented in government training programs, making up less than 20 percent of the participants. Immigrant women, speaking English as a second language, make up even less proportion of participants in training programs than Canadian-born women. The dislocation and effects on our lives will be massive.

The few garment jobs that will remain in Canada will be subject to significantly increased downward pressure on wages and working conditions, in order to remain competitive with the American industry.

We are urging the federal government to cancel the free trade deal as the only just solution to the disastrous effects the deal will have on the standard of living of immigrant women workers in the clothing industry. Free trade will increase women's unemployment, decrease the ability of women to pursue better working conditions and to further increase the wage gap between men and women.

On a personal level, I have just received notice from my employer that the company has been put up for sale. The owner has said that the operation cannot compete with offshore competition and that on the onset of free trade with the U.S. means further competition for him.

The Americans benefit from longer production runs which is highly important in the lower-end of garment production. The factory will be closing in the spring. Some of my fellow garment workers have also received notice that their factory will not continue to be open. The owner makes baby clothes, and he applied for a $100,000 bank loan to improve his capital base. His loan was refused on the basis that the bank manager did not have sufficient confidence in his industry to survive with free trade.

500 garment workers have already lost their jobs in Toronto in the last two months. There are more on the horizon. The manufacturers are

also united with us in opposing the free trade deal. We are worried, and I am not sure where I will be able to get another job in the spring when my factory closes down.

I need a job where I can provide a decent living for my family. The garment industry, although not the highest paid jobs around, does pay an industrial wage. Service jobs are much lower paid, with little or no benefits. How will I and thousands of others like me survive?

"What Every Woman Needs to Know about Free Trade" Toronto, 1988[15]

The Gender Gap

Across the country, polls show a larger "gender gap" on the issue of free trade. More women than men are against the free trade deal. This is because it will affect every issue women of this country are concerned about including employment, wages and conditions of work, education, day care, health care, the environment, consumer protection and prices, and peace issues.

Free Trade is more than the removal of tariff barriers. It would mean a much closer integration of the economic and social systems of the United States and Canada.

The supposed reason for entering into the agreement in the first place was to counteract U.S. protectionism. The United States was using its trade laws to challenge the Canadian way of managing the economy - arguing that a wide range of Canadian practices are "unfair" subsidies to export industries. The intent of negotiating the agreement was to ensure that U.S. trade legislation could not be used to retaliate against Canadian exports.

The tragedy is that the agreement did not deal with the issue of how an "unfair subsidy" would be defined. And the promised exemption from U.S. trade laws never materialized. As a result, Canada would be undertaking a whole range of changes which would dramatically affect our way of life, without any guarantees of access to the U.S. market for Canadian industries.

The free trade deal is packaged in two parts: The Canada/U.S. Free Trade Agreement and Bill C-130, the federal government's legislation to change Canadian Laws. The commitments in the Free Trade Agreement itself will require other changes, beyond these contained in the Bill C-130 legislation. All of these changes will be devastating to women, should they eventually come into place.

Jobs

Manufacturing: Women's employment in manufacturing is concentrated in industries where jobs are most at risk: textiles, clothing, food

15. Pamphlet, National Action Committee on the Status of Women.

processing, electrical and electronic products, and other consumer goods. These are often characterized as "sunset" industries, not deserving to survive. Yet textiles and clothing, for example, are the largest industrial employers in Canada and account for 7% of our total national income.

The women who will be particularly affected by job losses in manufacturing are immigrants, women of colour, older women, disabled women, and women with low levels of formal education.

While new and better jobs are promised there is little real evidence that this will occur. Where women have moved out of manufacturing jobs in recent years, they have tended to find work only in low-paying, unorganized, and part-time work in the service sector.

Services: The majority of women work in the service sector (84%), where jobs will be threatened as restrictions on the provision of services from outside the country are removed. Just about every type of service can be traded internationally, including banking, data processing, telecommunications, computer services, and culture. The removal of the current restrictions on data processing, for example, will eliminate many clerical jobs which will shift to low-wage states in the U.S. Also, in the Free Trade Agreement, there is no "country-of-origin" provision for services. This means that much of our data processing could also occur in low-wage countries and be imported into Canada via the U.S. Almost one-third of all women in the labour force now hold clerical jobs.

The Free Trade Agreement also lays the groundwork for the privatization of public services. This will result in the loss of many women's jobs in areas of work which are among the better paid in Canada.

Agriculture: According to the National Farmers Union, almost half of the production from family farms in Canada is the result of women's labour. Women's work in agriculture is jeopardized because so many of our agricultural industries are at risk under free trade. With increased competition with U.S. agribusiness, Canadian farmers will lose access to our own domestic market. Canadian grain growers, fruit and vegetable farmers, the dairy industry, the grapes and wine industry, the horticulture industry, and poultry and egg production are particularly threatened by free trade.

Wages and Working Conditions: Under Free Trade, women and men would also have lower wages and poorer working conditions. With increased U.S. competition here, Canadian firms would be forced to cut costs by lowering wages, ignoring health and safety standards, and fighting legislative protection which ensures equal rights and equal pay for women. They will do this because their major competitors will be companies located in U.S. states with low or no minimum wage, poor labour legislation and very low levels of unionization ...

Social Services

Our social services (such as health care, daycare and unemployment insurance), could also be endangered by free trade. U.S. firms can challenge any public program they feel is an unfair subsidy to business. In the past, the U.S. has challenged aspects of the unemployment insurance system, the national railroads, and regional development schemes. Particularly troubling is the Free Trade Agreement's provision for on-going negotiations over the next five to seven years on the definition of "unfair" subsidies.

In addition to the problem of subsidies, the free trade deal provides "right of establishment" and "right of national treatment" to U.S. companies in 299 different service categories. This means that U.S. firms may freely do business here and receive treatment "no less favourable than that accorded to Canadian service enterprises."

The prospect of U.S. firms taking over our service sector is only half the tale. Canadian businesses can be expected to apply pressure on all levels of government to lower the taxes that support our social programs — all in the name of becoming more competitive.

Health Care: Canada and the U.S. have radically different ways of providing health care. In Canada it is publicly supported while in the U.S. it is run by private enterprise.

Under free trade, U.S. businesses will be free to come in and manage (and/or own) our hospitals, nursing homes, homes for the disabled; our halfway houses, and community health clinics; our ambulance services, medical labs, X-ray labs, and even our blood banks.

A few hospitals in Canada are already run by such private U.S. management firms. They cut costs by using "patient classification systems." These are computer programs which determine the type and amount of nursing care necessary. As a result, the full-time nursing staff is cut to a minimum, and the part-time nurses are expected to follow the computer printout with regard to time and care for each patient ...

Day Care: Under the investment chapter of the free trade deal, private U.S. day care corporations could claim access to public funds for establishing centres here. They would be allowed to compete for such funding on an equal basis with our own non-profit day care centres. This could lead to a preponderance of "for-profit" care delivery in Canada. Private day care companies usually pay lower wages to their workers and have lower standards for care giving.

New Social Programs: Under free trade it would be virtually impossible to set up new publicly provided services, as Canada did in the 1960's with Medicare with agreement from the provinces. For example, many Canadian women feel that we should be moving toward things like public auto insurance and public dental coverage. Under free trade,

Canada would first have to get approval for such programs from the U.S., and then our governments would have to financially compensate for U.S. insurance firms for losses they would experience under such new programs. Obviously, no province could ever afford this.

Education: Free trade gives U.S. private educational firms rights of national treatment and access to public funds for training programs. This means that our local training program for women through our community colleges, vocational schools, trade schools, schools of art and performance, and business colleges will have to compete with big U.S. private firms for public funding ...

The Consumer

Those in favour of free trade usually claim that the Canadian consumer will be better off as a result of the deal. The claim deserves careful examination.

Duty-Free Goods: Canadian authorities have admitted that under free trade there will still be the normal limits on the amount of duty-free purchases tourists can make across the border.

Taxes: Under free trade, the Canadian government will lose more than $2 billion a year by not collecting tariffs. The government plans to recover this loss by extending the federal sales tax to include not only manufactured items, but taxes on all goods (except food) and taxes on all services. This may mean that every time we ride the bus, make a banking transaction, and have our hair cut, we will have to pay a tax on the service.

Prices: The recent changes which Canada has been forced to make in our drug patent legislation are a direct result of the government's push for free trade and pressure from U.S. drug firms. This resulted in higher prices for Canadians and this is a forerunner to what will happen to prices for many items under free trade.

While the elimination of tariffs would seem to suggest lower prices, the Federal Finance Department's own studies acknowledge that there is no control over whether savings will be passed on to consumers or be kept in the pockets of suppliers and retailers. Prices can be kept lower when there are domestic producers who compete with importers — otherwise importers can charge whatever they want. This happened in the Canadian shoe industry when tariffs and quotas were removed and import prices increased by as much as 26%.

Pesticides and Food Additives: For decades, Canadian women have been leaders in changing attitudes and practices with regard to harmful additives in our foods. Ironically, the Free Trade Agreement commits

Canada to "work toward equivalent methods" for use of chemical substances such as herbicides, pesticides, growth hormones and steroids.

As a result of this "harmonization" under free trade, Canada will have to adopt the far more lax U.S. approach towards regulating chemical substances based on a "risk/benefit" analysis. This means that if the economic benefit in using a chemical substance outweighs the health risk, then that is the deciding factor for licensing the product.

U.S. "factory" farms make extensive use of hormones and antibiotics to speed growth and counter the disease-ridden conditions in which they confine farm animals. These additives are a danger to human health.

Energy: Under free trade, the Canadian government is committing itself to a one-price policy on oil and gas and energy exports. This means that it can't impose a policy whereby Canadian consumers buy energy at lower prices than those charged to U.S. consumers.

Equally important, the Free Trade Agreement obliges Canada to share our energy - even in times of shortages. The Agreement guarantees U.S. buyers the same proportion of Canada's energy resources that they now receive. In the case of some resources, such as oil, the U.S. uses more Canadian oil than Canadians do and we will be locked into this, even where there is not enough oil for our own use.

The Environment

Canadian women are increasingly concerned about our environment and the need for environmental protection. All governments in Canada, including the federal and all provincial governments, have endorsed the need to integrate environmental protection with economic planning and policy. However, the free trade deal will seriously erode governments' ability to take such measures.

Acid Rain: The acid rain which is destroying our lakes and forests is caused by the sulphur dioxide emissions released from smokestacks of industries relying on coal for fuel. Under free trade, government subsidies to help Canadian industries cut acid rain pollution may be seen as unfair trading practices. "Harmonizing" standards will likely mean that Canada will have to accept the lower U.S. standard for emissions control of acid gas pollution.

Water: The trade agreement does not allow Canada to limit exports of natural resources on the basis of shortages, unless restrictions are also placed on Canadian consumption. In addition, it does not permit export restrictions for the purpose of protecting the environment.

Every Canadian resource is subject to the provisions of the Free Trade Agreement. THERE IS NO EXCLUSION FOR WATER. Where the agreement intends to exclude an item, as in the case of logs, it explicitly states this ...

Forests: What little reforestation is carried out in Canada is heavily subsidized by the government. The U.S. lumber industry regards reforestation grants as "unfair" trade practices and subsidies to Canadian lumber exports. Because of the Softwood Lumber deal, the B.C. government has already agreed to end its replanting subsidies to the forest industry.

Another casualty of free trade will be our prospects for adding to Canada's parkland and wilderness areas. Unimpeded development in the oil, gas, mining, and lumber industries will have a tremendous impact on our wilderness areas, on aboriginal hunting grounds, and on areas that support traditional ways of life.

Peace Issues

The trade deal will reduce the possibility for an independent Canadian voice on peace and security issues like the U.S. "Star Wars" initiative. Women are in the forefront of the peace movement and are concerned about the potential use of our resources and labour for military purposes under free trade.

Militarization of Regional Development: The ostensible objective of entering the free trade agreement was to eliminate the ability of U.S. firms to challenge Canadian policy, such as regional development schemes, as unfair subsidies to trade. The agreement failed to achieve this. Most government subsidies to poor regions can still be challenged. But there is one exception. If any government subsidy is "sensitive to the defence of the country," it will be permissible. The result may well mean the increased focus on military industries in the economies of poorer sections of this country.

Militarization of jobs: Building weapons is not the answer to Canadian unemployment, but as thousands of jobs are lost in other sectors, this is one area where the free trade deal allows governments to subsidize and intervene as much as they wish. Already in Quebec, female employment levels are down as textile companies relocate to low-wage states in the U.S., and the defence-related industries expand.

Our Way of Life

The Canada/U.S. Free Trade Agreement is not simply about tariff reduction and trade, as the proponents of the Agreement would have us believe. It is about how much control Canadian will have over our future.

Women have long recognized that we need the modifying influence of public policy to correct the most discriminatory and unjust features of the market system. Market forces alone cannot provide us with sufficient jobs and eliminate the grossly unfair ways women and minority groups are treated.

Our experience is that justice and fairness have to be imposed on business. Yet the move toward free trade is an attempt to return to a greater reliance on the workings of the international market to determine our economic and social policies. Once we embark on the free-trade route our ability to establish priorities, other than those dictated by profit-making and the private market mechanism, will be relinquished.

Trade is important for Canada. We are a great trading nation and will continue to be one. But the main issue now is the role of trade policy: it should serve economic and social goals — not determine them.

Teachers Respond to a Free Trade Survey
Scarborough, Ontario 1989[16]

...

Dear Marjorie:

I'm not sure if my experience is of value, but here is what I did at my school, an elementary, North York school with a staff of 18.

I analysed the pamphlet, underlined key phrases that I thought could affect my staff members. Then I circulated the pamphlet with a covering letter, asking each teacher to carefully read it.

Much discussion ensued during lunch hours ... on the topic of free trade and its potential harm for Canadians, especially women. The majority of those who shared their opinions indicated opposition to free trade and this grew as time passed. Our staff is ... mostly 35-40 year old women with young families. (Very busy.) Many people expressed confusion about this issue and were grateful for the information and the chance to discuss the whole matter ...
Sincerely,
Marilyn Corbeil

Antigonish Women's Centre Responds to NAC's Free Trade Survey
Antigonish, N.S., 1989[17]

NAC'S "WOMEN AND FREE TRADE ACTION" QUESTIONNAIRE:
Please mark any sections you wish to be treated confidentially with an asterisk (*).
1. Please indicate the level of activity of your group in anti-free trade activity.

    Very active
    Moderately active
    No action
       1. Moderately active

---

16. Letter from Marilyn Corbeil to Marjorie Cohen, May 2, 1989. In possession of Marjorie Cohen.
17. Letter from Antigonish Women's Resource Centre, Antigonish, N.S., in response to NAC's "Women and Free Trade Action" Questionnaire, May 15, 1989. The Centre's responses follow each question. In possession of Marjorie Cohen.

2. When did your group become aware of free trade as a women's issue? How did you learn of the effect on women?

> *2. We became aware of free trade as a women's issue through the Women's Action Coalition of Nova Scotia. Our council representative informed us of the WACNS and NAC activities around the issue. A few of our members also attended a workshop on Free Trade at a conference in Sydney, N.S. sponsored by Women Unlimited.*

3. Did your group help form or join a coalition against free trade? If yes, please indicate which one.

> *3. We formed an ad hoc committee of concerned citizens in Antigonish to work on the free trade issue.*

4. Please indicate the ways in which your group participated in coalition efforts.

Check those which apply:
a. sent delegate to meetings
b. helped plan events
c. financial contribution
d. contributed office staff, mailing, or other in-kind resources
e. publicized coalition events
f. participated in events and activities
g. provided speakers for events
h. other (please specify)

> *4.a. sent delegate to meetings*
> *b. helped plan events*
> *d. contributed office staff, mailing, or other in-kind resources*
> *e. publicized coalition events*
> *f. participated in events and activities*

5. Were there specific difficulties you experienced, as women, in being part of these coalitions? Please give details.

> *5. No.*

6. Did your group do anything to inform your members or other women about the effect of free trade on women?

7. If you answered "yes" to question 6, please indicate the form this took. That is, did you hold workshops or seminars; provide information about it through mailings to members; hold public forums? Where possible, please give dates, location for events and titles and copies of articles and information pieces.

> *6. & 7. Yes. We, the AWRC, sponsored an information evening and invited Marion Mathieson to speak about*

how free trade would affect women. The workshop took place in early spring, 1988. During the same evening Hall Linbland talked about how free trade would affect the fisheries, John Rovers looked at agriculture and Hugh McLean gave an overview of the agreement.

We helped organize a free trade debate which took place in June 1988. Gwen Wolfe, N.S. Federation of Labour, Murray Coolican, Public Affairs International, and Wayne Easter, National Farmer's Union participated.

We participated in Women Vote Day, November 5, 1988, by meeting with women on the street and passing out information sheets "Free Trade is a Women's Issue".

8. Did your group generate a specific analysis of the effect of free trade on those issues of specific concern to your membership or region? If you did, please indicate titles of papers or briefs and indicate how it was distributed.

  8. No.

9. Did your group present briefs on free trade to local, provincial or federal government bodies? If you did, please indicate where and when, authors of the briefs and provide copies if possible.

  9. [No response.]

10. Was your group responsible for media attention on free trade? What form did this take? Please provide copies of written material if possible.

  10. Local papers covered all the above activities. The local radio station, CJFX, covered the discussions with the politicians.

11. Are you responding for
   a) yourself?
   b) your organization?

  11. b) our organization.

12. Please feel free to add any other information or comments.

  12. [No response.]

"Women and Free Trade"
May 1988[18]

Public opinion surveys have revealed a "gender gap" in Canadian attitudes toward free trade. Women appear less likely than men to support

---

18. Katie Macmillan, *C.D. Howe Institute Trade Monitor*, no. 5 (May 1988), 1, 10–11.

the Canada-U.S. Free Trade Agreement or to consider free trade a positive step for Canada.

Opponents of free trade and some women's groups maintain this gender gap indicates that Canadian women feel they will be worse off under free trade. They argue that free trade will create special problems for female employment and retard progress toward economic and social objectives that are important to women.

Economic analyses, however, do not support the contention that free trade's impact on women will be either substantial or negative. Any changes in women's employment and incomes, although not expected to be significant, will be positive. Real incomes will rise due to the lower prices that will result from reductions in trade barriers. Employment opportunities for males and females will also increase. Women workers could gain even more than men, since the female labour force is already heavily concentrated in the services sector, which is where the bulk of the new jobs generated by free trade probably will occur ...

Conclusion

Free trade offers Canadian women a chance to improve their economic standing, both relatively and absolutely. Virtually every study on free trade predicts positive consequences for income and employment opportunities. On the employment side, women could well gain more than men because of the concentration of female employment in services industries, where the bulk of job growth is expected to occur.

Women have a demonstrated capacity to adjust to, and even profit from, changes in the workplace. While there will be some job losses, they are likely to occur predominantly in industries in which the major competitive threat comes not from the United States but from newly industrializing countries in Asia and elsewhere. Labour mobility and skills-upgrading programs can assist women to adjust to the new trading environment.

A careful reading of the Free Trade Agreement reveals that it poses no threat to existing social policies and institutions. In the child-care area, for example, Canadian governments are free to maintain or increase quality standards, and can, if they wish, deny access to U.S. child-care enterprises. The Agreement also does not prohibit future policy initiatives directed at women. Pay equity, for example, is fully consistent with the provisions of the Agreement. Social services such as health, education, and welfare are not included in the Agreement. Female jobs in these industries, therefore, are under no threat, and Canadians are ensured continued access to the high-quality services to which they are accustomed.

Are women being manipulated by those who view the Agreement as a means to attract attention to other objectives? The answer is probably yes. To the extent that it calls attention to the circumstances and concerns of Canadian women, however, the debate over free trade and women can serve a useful purpose. In searching for solutions to inequalities in income and opportunity in our society, Canadians should focus on those elements truly detrimental to women's interests. The Canada-U.S. Free Trade Agreement does not fall into that category.

"Women in the Maquiladoras"
Saskatchewan, 1991[19]

"She stares down at the conveyor as a shiny black chassis slides into place. She grasps an electric air gun, presses a switch, and spins a tiny metal bolt into place. She repeats this operation every nine seconds. At this rate, she will spin 3,480 bolts by the end of the day."

This excerpt from an American journal describes the work of a woman in a maquiladora factory in Mexico, along the border with the United States. The maquiladora program is designed to allow transnational companies (mainly based in the United States) to import parts for assembly, and export the finished product with a low value-added export tax. The maquiladora program is a pillar of the export-led growth strategy of Mexican President Salinas.

Free trade, as exemplified by the maquiladora program and the talks on a North American Free Trade Agreement, is part of a larger strategy of restructuring the Mexican economy. However, this restructuring has many victims, mainly Mexican women and their children.

Cutbacks, layoffs, tax hikes, privatization and removal of subsidies on basic items are the results of an Economic Stability Pact imposed by Salinas, under the direction of the International Monetary Fund. During the first six months of 1990, the price of a day's ration of beans, rice, tortillas and milk rose threefold, even though the daily minimum wage had been frozen at 10,800 pesos (U.S. $3.75).

U.S. companies have been using the maquiladora program, and are pushing for a North American trade pact, in order to take advantage of the desperate plight of unemployed Mexicans. They are cashing in on the low production costs gained from minimal wage and benefit expenditures, saving U.S. $20,000 to $30,000 per year per worker...

The vast majority of maquiladora workers are young women. Employers say they prefer to hire women for a number of reasons: they have "more nimble fingers" and are "more adaptable to repetitive jobs."

However, Latin American Connections newsletter reports that the real reason is that most workers are young, single, mothers with no previous trade union experience, who can't afford to organize for better conditions for fear of losing their jobs. There are no promotions or raises, pension plans, seniority rights, or overtime pay. There are frequent pregnancy tests, which the women must "pass" in order to keep their

19. Vicki J. Northcott [Victoria Jean Weatherspoon], *Briarpatch* 20, no. 7 (September 1991), 29–31.

Some Facts About Women in Mexico

* 30 percent of women of childbearing age have been sterilized, many without their knowledge or consent, or as a requirement to receive government services or aid.
* 5 percent are receiving Depo-Provera injections, a cancer causing contraceptive that has been banned in the U.S. and Canada.
* For every 100 women sterilized, only 11 men are sterilized or use condoms.
* Cervical-uterine cancer is the fifth most common cause of death among Mexican women.
* Resources provide for only 20 percent of women over 25 years of age to have periodic pap smears.
* AIDS is transmitted to women mainly through transfusions during ob-gynaecological operations, many of which are unnecessary.
- from The Guardian

---

jobs, and there is sexual harassment and unsafe conditions for health and safety.

"In one plant," said Maude Barlow of her trip to a maquiladora zone, "we all experienced headaches and nausea from spending an hour on the assembly line. We saw young girls working beside open vats of toxic waste with no protective face covering. We saw factories full of teenage girls, some as young as 14, working at eye damaging, numbingly repetitive work for $3.25 a day, well below what is required for even a minimal standard of living."

The dangerous jobs are sent to the young women in the maquiladora factories: work with insecticides, fungicides, herbicides and dangerous chemicals.

At a Sanyo plant in Tijuana, 300 workers quit the plant each month, out of a total work-force of 2,500. Turnover rates in the maquiladora factories can reach 240 percent a year, which translates into a complete turnover every five months. This is costly to the plant owners, but not too costly. For everyone that leaves, there is another to take her place. Training takes a day and the pay is only 56 cents per hour.

The American progressive newspaper, The Guardian, reports that women change plants frequently to try to escape sore hands from silicone, anemia from acetone, and bloodshot eyes from welding under microscopes. There is no protection from the union, invariably affiliated with the Confederation of Mexican Workers (CTM).

Living conditions for the workers around the maquila factories are just as bad as the working conditions on the factory floor. Each day, factory managers drive across the border from the United States, through the cardboard camps of their workers, and into the manicured grounds of the factories ...

Hourly Labour Costs, 1989 Production Workers in Manufacturing	
Canada	$14.72
United States	14.31
Mexico	2.32
Maquiladora Zones	0.98

Source: U.S. Department of Labour

NAFTA and Women's Plan of Action
Valle de Bravo, Toluca, Mexico, February 8, 1992[20]

Over one hundred women from Mexico, Canada and the U.S. participated in the First Tri-national Working Women's Conference on Economic Integration and Free Trade. The conference, organized by Mujer a Mujer (Woman to Woman) and Mujeres en Accion Sindical (Women in Union Action), took place in Valle de Bravo, Toluca, Mexico, February 5 through 9, 1992. Participants represented unions, women's and community groups, church and justice organizations, research and policy institutes, as well as national coalitions and networks. They brought experience from a wide range of sectors, education, health, clothing and textiles, telecommunications, banks and service, and border maquila industries. The conference concluded with unanimous agreement on the following statement and plan of action.

Because economic integration is based explicitly on women's exploitation in the paid labour force, we — women of Mexico, Canada and the United States — demand that our respective governments guarantee basic rights to adequate education, health care, food, nutrition, housing, stability of employment, living salaries and training, voluntary maternity, and peace (that is the ability to live free from violence) within any tri-lateral agreement.

Women are prepared to participate actively, to be protagonists in the dramatic processes of change currently taking place throughout the continent, and globally. Thus we demand also that women's interests and organizations be represented in discussions and negotiations of any tri-lateral trade agreement between our countries.

New and creative collective organizing initiatives and solidarity are essential to ensure that women are not left to bear the brunt of governments' and corporations' actions to restructure our economies. We call

---

20. "Women's Plan of Action," a statement endorsed by 100 women from Central America, Canada and the United States at the First Trinational Working Women's Conference on Economic Integration and Free Trade, 8 February 1992, and circulated by Mujer a Mujer (Woman to Woman). In the possession of Marjorie Cohen.

on women's organizations, popular groups, unions, and other progressive forces committed to women's equality to take steps to:

1 Organize the unorganized and unemployed, using new strategies that take into account women's needs — in their families, communities and workplaces;

2 Strengthen existing unions, fighting for democracy and to make them more responsive to women's needs and lives;

3 Promote women's research, education and action networks, campaigns and coalitions at provincial (state), national, and tri-national levels;

4 Create tri-national links among women and women's organizations in order to exchange information, experiences and materials. Networks of union women across and within sectors are particularly crucial.

Women's coordinated action will not end with the conference closing. Those present committed ourselves to the following.

1 Use the conference Plan of Action in our organizations and networks to promote discussion, education and action around Free Trade and continental integration.

2 Organize an international fact finding tour to different areas in Mexico in order to deepen our understanding of the dramatic impact economic restructuring and continental integration has already had on the lives of Mexican women.

3 Coordinate the sharing (through print and other media) experiences of innovative local initiatives to organize women in communities affected by restructuring.

4 Mexican participants are exploring the possibility of establishing a Women's Action Network on Continental Integration to promote further analysis, discussion and education, and to link with similar efforts in Canada and the U.S.

Canadian women committed themselves to deepen the international and solidarity perspective within the National Action Committee on the Status of Women (NAC), in its campaigns and activities, and to working towards a stronger gender analysis within existing anti-free trade coalitions.

5 Over the next year, the feasibility of a second working women's conference will be assessed ...

Budget and Taxation Issues

"Why the GST will be Harmful to Women"
Vancouver, December 1989[21]

Imagine a government which told people it was redesigning the tax system to make it less fair. This was going to increase the proportion of

---

21. Marjorie Cohen, *Feminist Action* 4, no. 2 (December 1989). Note: This article was written before the proposed tax was lowered to 7 per cent.

income paid in taxes for low and middle income groups, but was reducing it for the already privileged. Saying this would be political suicide, leading to certain electoral defeat and perhaps even rioting and revolution.

In trying to sell the proposed Goods and Services Tax the federal government is sugar-coating a bitter pill. By insisting that the imposition of this tax will make the whole tax system fairer, the government is relying on a known propaganda method. That is, if something, no matter how outrageous, is repeated often enough, people will begin to believe it.

Women are not accepting these attempts to be brainwashed. The GST is not simply the replacement of one tax for another, as the government would like everyone to believe. It is a dramatic shift in principles in taxation. The GST is inherently unfair because it is a tax on consumption. Lower and middle income groups tend to spend their entire incomes on current consumption, while wealthy Canadians save and invest large portions of their income. This means less advantaged groups of people will be paying a much larger portion of their income in tax than will those which are financially privileged.

Women are vehemently opposed to this tax. We will be particularly hurt by price increases. The broad nature of the GST means that virtually everything we buy will be taxed, even those items which are essential for raising children. Most countries which have sales taxes at least exempt children's clothing, as do provincial sales taxes which we now have in Canada. With the GST we'll be paying 9% more for children's clothing, shoes, books, and even diapers.

Daycare Will Cost More

We'll also be paying more for daycare. Daycare, like health care, housing, and education, is in a category called "tax exempt." But this is not the same as tax free. While parents do not see the 9% added to their daycare bill, daycare prices will nevertheless increase. This is because daycare providers will have to pay taxes on supplies and services and will undoubtedly pass these added costs on to parents. Parents whose children are in daycare centres which receive 50% of their funding from government will get some relief because these centres will be able to get tax rebates on half of the sales taxes they pay. Yet, even here half the increased taxes will have to be passed on to parents.

The issue of food is extremely important. Under the design of the sales tax currently being examined basic groceries will be tax free. However, take-out foods and restaurant meals well be taxed. This will place an added tax burden on women who are not in a position to always cook at home. This means women who work outside the home will be penalized for doing whatever they can to make the double burden of housework and paid work lighter. Also, it is extremely punishing to people who are forced by circumstances — such as poor people who don't have kitchens — to eat out.

The very clever political manoeuvring of the government now makes it likely that even basic food will be taxed. This will be hard on low income groups. As household expenditure statistics show, poorer households spend a much higher proportion of their income on food than do wealthy households. In contrast, households with incomes over $50,000 a year spend less than 7% on food. Taxing food will be extraordinarily cruel.

Women are grossly over-represented in the low income groups. Over 40% of the adult women in this country have no income at all. The average earnings for all women who work (including those who work part-time and full-time) is about $15,000 a year; therefore, at least 74% of these earnings will be spent on taxable items. If food is included, virtually the entire income will be spent on taxable items. Families with incomes over $50,000 spend only about 56% of their income in current consumption with about 7% on food. It is easy to see that the GST will mean a greater tax burden on lower income individuals.

Lower Consumer Spending = Less Jobs For Women

The GST will have a depressing effect on the economy and consequently, unemployment will increase. Women are particularly vulnerable to downturns in the economy and tend to be the first fired when things begin to go wrong. A drop in consumer spending of about $5 billion will mean a loss of 180,000 jobs in the service sector alone. Since women account for 55% of all services occupations, at least 100,000 women's jobs will be lost. In addition, women's jobs in manufacturing are likely to be affected. Demand for goods in manufacturing industries where women's work is concentrated (textiles, clothing, footwear) will be considerably affected by the sales tax, since the products from these industries are not currently taxed. The result will be lower consumer demand for these items and consequently, lower levels of employment in these industries.

The government's trick, in trying to sell the tax, is to make people believe that "there is no alternative," or TINA. TINA is an absurd defense which indicates a paucity of imagination on the part of the government.

There Are Alternatives

We could fix tax loopholes which enable thousands of wealthy corporations to escape payment of taxes. We could re-introduce the higher income bracket for those earning over $60,000 a year. We could restore the corporate tax level to what is was in 1984. The alternative are many, but it is clear that replacing a bad tax with an even worse one is no solution.

Women Protest GST on Sanitary Products
Sarnia, Ontario, 1991[22]

March 5, 1991

Dear Editor:

We are now entering the third month of the G.S.T., and most Canadians have become resigned to it; recognizing at the same time that regardless of the party in power after the next federal election, the G.S.T. is here to stay.

Canadians were told that basic needs, such as groceries would not be a subject to this tax. Amazingly, one can purchase a frozen pizza or a cake and these items are not taxed as they are considered groceries. However, the purchase of feminine sanitary products, such as tampons or napkins are G.S.T. taxable! This is infuriating to women. Although this is a sensitive subject, through our recent contact with the public we have found that people are very angry about it and although most do not choose to become vocal, they will certainly express their disgust by signing our petition. We have collected almost 3000 signatures asking the federal government to make these products exempt. Support for our effort has been extremely strong.

Hopefully, with the aid of your readers, others will join us by circulating petitions in the farthest reaches of Canada. Should you like to help, please send your name, address and phone # and we will send you a copy of the petition. Your help will be greatly appreciated. How often have you thought to yourself, 'Someone should do something about this?' This is an opportunity to be that 'someone'. Every signature counts!

Sincerely,

Jacqueline Burnett and

Sheridan Glenn

"Does Your Child Tax Credit Belong to You?"
Ottawa, 1979[23]

Québec

The provincial government is saving money with the Refundable Child Tax Credit and welfare recipients are struggling. Normally welfare recipients would receive the cost of living increase in January in accordance with the Québec Pension Board, which for this year is 9%. However, due to the Child Tax Credit (whereby a family whose yearly income is $18,000 or less will be eligible to receive $200 per child per year from the federal government), welfare recipients are not receiving this expected increase.

---

22. Jacqueline Burnett and Sheridan Glenn, Open Letter sent to 160 publications in Ontario, March 5, 1991. Copy in possession of Marjorie Cohen.
23. *Upstream* 3, no. 4 (March/April 1979), 5.

What in fact is happening is that welfare families are receiving less than a 9% in their welfare — how much less depending on the number of children they have. For example, one adult with one child is receiving $145.56 less this year; one adult with two children, $255.35 less, and one adult with three children, $277.00 less. In other words, the more children you have, the more you lose.

The PQ government is — we were all lead to believe — the government of the people. At this point we would like to know which people.

(Reprinted from Montréal Women's Information and Referral Centre Bulletin.)

Manitoba

Winnipeg Women for Welfare won two victories recently when they stopped the Winnipeg Housing Authority and city welfare from taking part of their child tax credits.

But, now they have to take on the province of Manitoba, which is attempting to do the same.

In response to a letter from R.V. O'Malley, general manager of the Winnipeg Housing Authority, the Women for Welfare group wrote to Mayor Bob Steen:

"Mr. O'Malley informs us that he is making appointments with each of us 'at which time arrangements will be completed whereby an Assignment of your (Child Tax Credit) Income Tax Rebate will be made to the Winnipeg Housing Authority.'

"He does not feel it is an unreasonable demand, 'as this money would appear to be a windfall to the parent concerned.' We would like to point out that Family Allowance money is designated for use for our children. It is not for bills or luxuries, but for our children. We are already getting $8 a month less on our monthly cheques per child. The $200 Child Tax Credit per child is money owing to us."

In another letter to Manitoba Premier Sterling Lyon, Women for Welfare said: "Raising children and doing housework is a job; the only wage many of us get is our Family Allowance. Some of us get the welfare cheque. If we manage to find a paying job outside of our home, we are faced with the fact of inadequate and costly childcare facilities and very few lunch hour and after school programs for our kids. Then we have to deal with a double workload, meagre wages outside the home and almost no wages for the work we still must do inside the home.

"Most of the other provinces have promised that they will not be deducting the Tax Credit from other monies paid to women; we want to know what the government of Manitoba plans to do."

"What's Wrong with Tax Deductions for Daycare?"
Toronto, 1982[24]

Several months ago, one of the workers in our daycare centre asked me to sign a petition in favour of larger deductions of child care expenses from taxable income. After we talked for a while, I decided not to sign. I wasn't convinced that tax deductions was the right policy to support; I had a feeling something was wrong with it.

Now, the Metro Toronto Department of Community Services and Housing has convinced me that tax deductions will not solve daycare's financial problems. Their report, "Day Care Affordability" was reviewed in last month's newsletter. The report argues in favour of full deductibility of actual child care costs from taxable income (removing the present limitation of $1000 per child). Their arguments have convinced me to stand against increased deductions. Let me explain why.

The Community Services report was based on, and gave the results of a major survey of full fee-paying parents in Metro. The survey concluded that many fee-paying parents are near the breaking point. If per diem daycare fees rise by much, many parents will have to take their children out. In fact, 80% of full-fee parents would leave group centre if wages of daycare workers were to rise to the levels common in municipal-run centres ($14,000 per year). This wage level is still far below average salaries in the work force as a whole. The Community Services' report believes wages will move to these levels over the next few years. Their report is directed to finding a solution to the financial crisis they predict will surely come (some of it is here already, of course).

The tax deduction scheme sounds like a good answer to the problem. Give fee-paying parents more money and they can afford to stay in daycare. Wages can rise and fees will still be affordable; many more parents may be attracted to daycare with these tax incentives.

Will it work that way? Come look at the fine print with me; perhaps we're being sold a pig in a poke.

Take for example the middle income families in the survey. They earn between $28,000 and $40,000 total. The present average fee for these families is $60 a week, says the survey, and it will rise to $98 a week if daycare wages are as predicted. Most parents can't afford that; in fact, the majority will pull out of daycare if the fees rise by $10 a week.

So, how much relief will full tax deductibility provide? Would it keep these families in daycare? Tax deductibility would save them between $20 and $30 a week more than it does now (the exact amount depends on their marginal tax rate, which depends on their income level). That would still leave them with from $8 a week to $18 a week more to pay in higher fees. In other words, most middle-income families would still remove their children from daycare according to Community Services and Housing.

How is that possible? The tax deduction scheme sounds generous; in fact, the Community Services' report estimates that it would cost the government $350 million a year in lost taxes in Ontario alone. Why isn't that enough?

It turns out that the tax deduction plan is a very inefficient way of getting extra money to parents who have children in daycare. Even the present partial deduction is inefficient. In 1979 (latest figures available) government lost $55 million in potential tax revenue through the deduction. That deduction was claimed on behalf of 500,000 children, according to the Tax Department. No more than 100,000 of those children would be full or part-time daycare children not receiving subsidy. So, only about one-fifth of the children who benefitted from the tax deduction were in organized daycare.

Most of the $350 million per year in Ontario would not go to daycare at all. If it did, it would more than solve the immediate financing problem. If this extra money were distributed over the approximately 40,000 full daycare spaces in Ontario, it would amount to a subsidy of over $8,000 per child per year. Of course, close to half of the present spaces are already subsidized as the new subsidy would amount to nearly $16,000 per child presently in an unsubsidized space. The figure would be less but still very high if we included part-time spaces.

I'm sure most full fee-paying parents would be satisfied with less than $16,000 per child as a subsidy!

There are many other arguments against the tax deduction scheme. One thing that is clear to me now, thanks to Community Services' report, is that tax deductions are a very wasteful, inefficient way of solving a financial crisis in daycare centres. Direct funding is a much better way to do the job.

"Nanny's Salary Valid Deduction, Court Rules"
Toronto, May 1989[25]

A Toronto woman has won her challenge to income tax regulations that disallow the salary she pays a nanny as a legitimate business expense.

A decision released yesterday by the Federal Court of Canada orders the Minister of National Revenue to accept lawyer Elizabeth Symes' claim of her nanny's full salary as an income tax deduction ...

Revenue Canada initially accepted the deductions for the tax years 1982 and 1983, but later disallowed them. The department ruled that the nanny's salary represented "personal and living expenses," not expenses incurred for the purpose of gaining income from a business.

In her testimony, Ms Symes had said that without a nanny she would not have been able to work as a lawyer. She was seeking to deduct the

---

25. Deborah Wilson, *The Globe and Mail*, 12 May 1989, A13.

nanny's salary of $10,075 in 1982, $11,200 in 1983, $13,173 in 1984, and $13,359 in 1985.

The 'basic child-care deduction permitted over these four years ranged from $1,000 to $4,000 annually and covered only a fraction of Ms Symes' costs. Currently, the basic deduction is $4,000 for children under the age of 6, and $2,000 for older children. Ms Symes has two children.

John Power, counsel for the federal Justice Department, had told the court that the nanny was not a necessity because Ms Symes made a free choice to practice law.

Ms Symes heads the Ontario Pay Equity Hearings Tribunal.

"Child Support Payments: Sexist Tax Strikes Again" Vancouver, October 1992[26]

A Quebec woman's challenge of a sexist taxation policy has been overturned by a Quebec Tax Court. Suzanne Thibodeau, a single mother, took Revenue Canada to court for discriminating against her because her child support payments were taxed [See *Kinesis*, April 1992].

The Revenue Canada policy taxes those who receive child support payments — usually women — and gives tax benefits to those who make the payments — usually men.

Thibodeau, who was asked to pay $4,260 in unpaid taxes on $14,490 in child support payments made by her former partner in 1989, argued that the child support payments were for her children and not for herself. As such, she should not have to include them as part of her taxable income.

Thibodeau also argued that, since it is mostly women who receive child support payments, the current law is a violation against the Charter of Rights and Freedoms which protects against sexual discrimination.

In making his ruling, Judge Alban Garon said that because the court that set the amount of child support payments took into consideration the taxation impact of the payments on Thibodeau, she did not "suffer prejudice." The judge also ruled that Revenue Canada does not discriminate against women or any recipients of child support payments.

A tax system which allows one parent to deduct the support payments they make from their taxable income and insists that the parent receiving the money include it in theirs is not discriminatory, the judge ruled.

However, the judge said, if the court had not taken the impact of taxes on payments into account at the time of settling amounts, "the party concerned should exercise their right of appeal to correct the situation."

On the heels of this decision, a BC woman has launched a challenge against the discriminatory tax laws in a case representative of most single mothers who receive child support payments. The case is set to be heard by the Tax Court of Canada later this month or early in November.

26. Mijin Kim, *Kinesis*, October 1992, 3–4.

Brenda Shaft, a single mother of two children living in Vancouver, is appealing Revenue Canada's order to pay taxes on child support payments she received in 1990. It was the first year since leaving her husband that she had been employed fulltime. However, at the time of setting support payments at $300 a month, Shaft had been on social assistance. Social assistance is not taxable so the tax implications of the settlement were never taken into account.

When Shaft declared the child support payments on her annual tax return that year, Revenue Canada demanded she pay taxes on the payments in the amount of just under $100 on the $300 a month she receives.

Shaft appealed Revenue Canada's demands, but lost initially. She tried several legal service lawyers before getting involved with the Society for Children's Rights to Adequate Parental Support (SCRAPS). She was then referred to Jeanne Watchuk of the law firm Bull, Housser and Tupper. Watchuk says she was interested in the case and agreed to take it over pro-bono because Shaft's case is typical of many single mothers. Most women go on social assistance after marital break-ups and so tax implications are rarely taken into account when determining support payments ...

Shaft is currently vice-president of SCRAPS and a strong advocate for changes in the tax law. She says research shows Canada to be the only country in the world that taxes child support payments, which, says Shaft, "is inhumane to its children."

Shaft also points out that 98 percent of the time it is women who receive child support payments, so the laws are discriminatory on the basis of gender. "Canada has a horrendous enforcement record and groups such as SCRAPS want women's groups to be more vocal," says Shaft. Public awareness campaigns and increased pressure on government to change unfair laws are key elements in resolving the issue, she says.

"Women Meet Michael Wilson"
Edmonton, Alberta, March 1985[27]

On Feb. 6, 1985, six national women's groups met, at his request, with Michael Wilson, federal Minister of Finance, to advise him on women's economic concerns in relation to the up-coming federal budget.

The National Action Committee on the Status of Women, the Canadian Advisory Council on the Status of Women, the National Council of Women, the National Council of Jewish Women, and two Québec Women's Federations comprised the six groups.

We met together for five hours before we met with Mr. Wilson and during this preparatory meeting we were all thrilled with the knowledge, expertise and competence of women. Our long years of work were very much in evidence. And most amazingly of all, these six groups who had never met before, reached consensus on all the major economic issues.

27. *Alberta Status of Women Action Committee Newsletter* 6, no. 2 (March 1985), 8–9.

It was with strength that we walked over to Confederation Hall to meet with Mr. Wilson.

We spent two hours with the Minister of Finance and covered specific topics. We took the position that he was there to listen and so we introduced topic areas and put forth our united positions.

1. ECONOMY OF CANADA

We gave a short overview of our position on the economy, stressing that we were not at all convinced that the deficit was the overriding economic reality. We focused on the tax system and emphasized the need to increase taxation revenues by eliminating tax exemptions for the rich, rather than accepting the need for a reduction in government spending especially in the provision of services. We made it quite clear that we opposed the Reagan model of economic management.

2. CHILD BENEFITS

The complicated area of child benefits was succinctly presented.

We support universality of benefits; we oppose any reductions in child allowances; we want the child tax exemption eliminated; and we are prepared to discuss the child tax credit with a preference that is of benefit to lower income families. The clear principal enunciated was that we are prepared to accept no changes which threaten the family allowance payments or which reduce them in any way. And we pointed out to Mr. Wilson that it is the only bit of direct, public economic recognition women receive for our work in child-rearing.

3. UIC AND MATERNITY LEAVE

While none of us liked the fact that maternity leave is connected both psychologically and administratively with unemployment — as if child-bearing is not work — we were loathe to have it tampered with, e.g.: paid out of general tax revenues instead of through Employment and Immigration. We have worked too hard to achieve even the bit of entrenchment of CEIC to risk losing maternity leave benefits. So our position was, leave it where it is until a better plan is put forth. However, do not increase premiums, decrease payments, or increase weeks for eligibility.

4. JOB CREATION

On this issue we presented a demand for no reductions in public sector jobs — both because women then receive reduced and inadequate services. We also put forth a demand for training and re-training programs. Further to the whole area of job creation, we opposed Mr. Wilson's position of reducing public sector jobs in order to create jobs in the private sector. The whole issue of jobless growth was put before him, as was the need for the government to implement equal pay provisions and compliance legislation.

5. PENSIONS

This area is a complex one and rather than get into convoluted arguments we put forth very specific positions:

a) that the federal government extend CPP/QPP to home-makers.

b) that the federal government increase the CPP/QPP so that this publicly-administered pension provide an increased percentage of replaceable income. This, of course, goes counter to the government's present position of encouraging the increase of private pensions — a position we oppose because so few women actually benefit from private pension plans.

c) mandatory splitting of all pensions upon divorce and at age 65.

d) indexing of pensions to the cost of living.

e) extending the present "widow's/widower's" pension to all people 60-64 years of age.

f) increasing OAP and GIS up to and above the poverty line.

6. FEDERAL-PROVINCIAL COST-SHARING AGREEMENTS

This particular issue is the key to the entire economy of Canada especially in areas of health care, social services and post-secondary education. We put forth the following positions:

a) that the government of Canada initiate a cross-country consultation process in 1986 prior to the renegotiation of the Established Programs Financing Act, and that this consultation ensure access for all women's groups to present their experience of health care and post-secondary systems and services.

b) that no cutbacks occur in post-secondary education programs, social services and health care.

c) that the federal government exercise its enforcement mechanisms, e.g.: penalties, to the full vis-à-vis those provinces in violation of the Canada Health Act.

7. CONSULTATIVE PROCESS

We asked/demanded that Mr. Wilson continue his consultation with us prior to the April (now May) budget and afterwards.

Mr. Wilson's response was predictable. He reiterated his positions on budget matters and continually raised the spectre of the deficit. His commitment to reducing government expenditures as a way of creating confidence in the private sector, is less an economic theory and more of a religious belief. The logic of our positions did not dissuade him from his religious fervour about the role of the private sector in bringing in wealth and economic fulfilment to all Canadians. While giving verbal acknowledgement to women's economic needs, he continued on his preordained course of reducing the deficit by cutting public sector spending ...

While the meeting was important, it was less for what influence we had on Mr. Wilson, and more for the united and competent front we presented ...

"Get the Budget on Track!"
Toronto, May 24, 1989[28]

Dear Friends,

Today, we invite you to participate with us in a national campaign to "get the budget on track."

The campaign is initiated by the National Action Committee on the Status of Women and is being carried out in collaboration with the Pro-Canada Network and the Canadian Brotherhood of Railway Workers (CBRTGW).

Beginning June 4, representatives of the campaign will board trains, departing from points West and East, arriving in Ottawa June 12. Along the routes, campaign representatives will stop at major centres to join protest events against the budget and meet with local committees and coalitions. We suggest that participants wear a green ribbon as a unifying gesture.

Sincerely,

Lynn Kaye,	Tony Clarke,	Tom McGrath,
NAC	Pro-Canada Network	CBRTGW

"Nurses Fight Ottawa Over Trade, Budget"
Edmonton, Alberta, August 1989[29]

Canadian nurses' unions are squaring off against two federal heavyweights: the budget and the free trade agreement with the United States.

Delegates to the National Federation of Nurses' Unions convention agreed last week to endorse the Pro-Canada Network anti-free trade statement, Breaking the Social Contract.

The umbrella group for 26,000 nurses will also monitor the impact of the agreement and subsidy negotiations on social programs, said president Kathleen Connors, who was acclaimed for another two-year term.

"It's very important that we be involved because of the concern of privatization," she said following three days of meetings in Edmonton. "Nurses are truly the patients' advocates, looking at the broader issues that affect their health care."

The national nurses' union opposes the federal budget because it would continue to reduce transfer payments to the provinces for health

28. Letter from Lynn Kaye, Tony Clarke and Tom McGrath, in the Flyer announcing the "Get the Budget on Track" campaign and the arrival times of the train in Western, Eastern and Atlantic Canada, June 1989.
29. The Canadian Press, in *The Toronto Star*, 6 August 1989.

care by $1.9 billion in 1989-90, said Connors. It also attacks unemployment insurance and requires those earning more than $50,000 a year to pay back their family allowance payments and old-age security, she said.

Nurses are being asked to show their support for a cross-Canada train tour to protest the budget, which organizers say uses the deficit as a smokescreen to advance a free trade agenda.

Connors also said the Alberta government's silence over federal health-care cuts may mean the province is considering privatizing health services.

She said the cuts in federal transfer payments give Alberta and other provinces leverage to argue Canadians should start to pay for their own health care.

"It makes me wonder if they are going to press for changes to the Canada Health Act so that privatization of health care can gain a toe-hold in our public system," she told the conference.

The Canada Health Act protects universal access to health care and bans hospital user fees and extra-billing by doctors.

"Liberals Condemn Women to Greater Inequality"
Toronto, February 1994[30]

The Federal Budget furthers the inequality, unemployment and poverty of women in Canada. The political direction set by Mr. Martin maintains the inequality which is the goal of the new-conservative agenda. Dangling a carrot in front of women, the use of the stick hits us even harder than the Tory budget of last year. While cuts in defence spending are a positive step, and nominal sums of money are allocated to a new centre of excellence for women's health, a prenatal nutrition program, a Law Reform Commission on Race Relations, and the reinstatement of the Court Challenges Program, these programs will not be able to end the growing economic inequality of women and children.

This budget means:

* Even before the social policy review begins, spending on social programs is frozen at 1994 levels. Therefore, no matter what the outcome of the review, and irrespective of economic growth, spending on social programs is already determined. The freeze means more cuts, and makes a mockery of the 'consultations' the Liberals have promised us.

* There is no money whatsoever allocated for a campaign to end violence against women, despite campaign promises. Instead, 5% funding cuts to women's groups will continue to undermine the work of women's groups to end male violence against women and children.

* Major cuts were made to Unemployment Insurance, reducing benefits to 55% from 57%, increasing the number of work weeks required

30. National Action Committee on the Status of Women, Flyer, February 1994.

for eligibility, and reducing the length of U.I. claims. This further punishes the unemployed.

* Many of the unemployed are single mothers, and only the very poorest will be eligible for the increase in benefit to 60%. However, to get that slight increase, they will have to open their lives to regulation by UIC administrators. While the increase is welcome, the use of single mothers to introduce a two tier system for U.I. eligibility is a deplorable ploy.

* Salary freezes for federal government employees continue. The lowest paid civil servants, a disproportionate number of whom are women, will be hit hardest. More government jobs will be cut to save $1.5 billion by 1996. Public service unions predict it is women's jobs which will be cut. Conversely, the $6 billion to be spent on infrastructure will create jobs mainly in traditionally male occupations.

*Though money is allotted for the creation of new childcare spaces in 1995-96 and 1996-97, the continuing freeze on transfer payments to provinces will affect the childcare program. The creation of new spaces depends on shared funding, and if the provinces cannot provide their share, the program will be jeopardized.

* Funding to women's groups will be cut by 5% in 1994-95, and there may be no funding for women's groups in 1995-96. These cuts come on top of previous Tory cuts, threatening the continued existence of women's group. Women's groups are essential if we are to have a voice in a society in which we are marginalized, excluded from power, and economically unequal.

Women's Report: The Budget
Ottawa, April 28, 1989[31]

Dear Friends:
As I write this special edition of the Women's Report, the House of Commons is grappling, not only with a budget leak of unprecedented proportion, but with a budget which will devastate many Canadians and their families.

A number of national women's groups came together today for a press conference, but their voices were nearly drowned in the discussion of the budget leak. At the press conference, my colleague Margaret Mitchell, M.P. (Vancouver East) and I expressed our outrage at the government's implementation of such severe and irrational cutbacks and tax hikes. This is clearly an attack on women, children and the poor.

---

31. Member of Parliament Dawn Black, Letter to women.

The burden of deficit reduction lies with those who can least afford it. We must pay more taxes and receive fewer services, while thousands of profitable corporations continue to pay no taxes. And unfortunately, as with no other budget in Canadian history, it actively and deliberately attacks progressive programs which serve to promote and benefit women and children.

Le Réseau National d'Action Education Femmes stated in its budget press release: "The promotion of equality is obviously a low priority in this government." The National Organization of Immigrant and Visible Minority Women of Canada wrote: "It is ironic and devastating that these cuts come at a time when immigrant and Visible Minority women have only just begun to make their case to establish the kinds of structures that are crucial to their search for equity in Canadian society."

I am angered by this budget. The Minister of Finance has slashed child care, funding for women's groups, and transfers to the provinces for health and education. The Minister of Finance has made his cutbacks — they are cuts on the backs of children and women ...

In sisterhood,
Dawn Black, M.P.
New Westminster-Burnaby
NDP critic for women

"Co-opting the Guaranteed Annual Income" Vancouver, 1986[32]

Since the early '60's low income people have worked for a guaranteed annual income (GAI). We thought it would provide enough money for a decent life above the poverty line. We thought it would be given with dignity and no hassle. We also thought that if we were able to work outside the home, decent jobs at decent wages would be available.

Recently, quite a few big business groups have jumped on the GAI bandwagon — groups not know for supporting low-income people. They include the Fraser Institute representing over 400 large corporations; the Canadian Manufacturers Association (CMA), a lobby group for Canada's largest manufacturers; the Macdonald commission, a $20 million Royal Commission on the economy set up by the Liberal Government; and the Financial Post, a weekly newspaper which represents business thinking in Canada.

But business doesn't want the same kind of GAI that low income people want. They don't want a GAI that will end poverty. They want a GAI that will guarantee poverty for people who can't work and help pull down wages for people who do work. Big business wants a GAI which helps build a pool of cheap labour so that people on GAI compete for low paying jobs.

32. Jean Swanson, *Kinesis*, September 1986, 14.

There are four parts to the business version of GAI:

1. Abolish what we have: The Financial Post calls our existing system a "morass of conflicting and confusing social programs" and notes (disapprovingly) the $60 billion annual cost. The Macdonald Commission lists the programs on the chopping block: family allowance, child tax credit, Guaranteed Income Supplement for seniors (this is the program that is responsible for almost getting seniors out of poverty), social housing, married and child tax exemptions, the federal share of welfare payments to provinces (about half of the money paid by provinces on these services), and unemployment insurance.

Business thinks these programs cost too much and contribute to the deficit. In fact, Canada's social spending is already way below the average of industrial countries. As well, many economists say that the deficit is not too high, and if it was, it could be contained by reducing handouts to private corporations.

2. Low incomes for people who don't or can't work: The Macdonald Commission suggests $2750 per year in one option and $3825 in another. This would, presumably be topped up at the whim of provincial governments. For comparison, the poverty line is around $9,000 to $10,000 per person per year.

The Canadian Manufacturers Association (CMA) provides another clue to the level of income that business thinks people outside the paid labour force should have. They say the GAI should ensure that "recipients will be better off working and earning income."

Why doesn't business want GAI rates above the poverty line? According to one report (GATTfly, May, 1986) some business leaders fear that people receiving adequate welfare or GAI will not work at "unsafe, low-paying jobs unless wages and working conditions are improved. Such improvements at the bottom of the employment ladder would push up the whole wage and working conditions scale."

3. Keep what you earn: The Financial Post, the Macdonald Commmission, and Fraser Institute argue that taking away earned income from people who receive the GAI or even welfare creates a "poverty trap" and destroys "incentives to work." This sounds exactly like what low income people have been saying for a long time too. We have wanted to be able to keep much more of what we earn without having it deducted from our monthly welfare payment.

But there is another part of the big business version of GAI that makes a high earning exemption dangerous for low income people, as the following explains.

4. No increase in the minimum wage: The Fraser Institute is famous for calling an end to minimum wage (in BC $3.65 per hour for adults, $3.00

per hour for people under 18). The CMA told the Macdonald Commission the same: the government should loosen up on laws such as minimum wage laws.

Business doesn't like minimum wages because, like welfare payments, they push up the bottom of the wage scale ladder, putting more money into workers' hands than business profits.

What would the effect of a GAI with these four ingredients be? Before considering this, remember that most poor people work in the paid labour force. They're poor because their wages are too low and/or their hours too few.

Imagine that big business gets its way. Their GAI is in place and you're a single mom with two kids. You'll be getting a GAI that is way below the poverty line. Your provincial government will hesitate to add much to it because it won't be getting any money from the federal government for this. You'll have no chance of getting into co-op or non profit housing. Those programs will be gone. Likewise, you won't get a child tax credit or family allowance. Funding for childcare will be drastically cut back too, as the federal government will no longer pay half of costs.

But, because the GAI is so low, you're desperate to feed your kids. And, with the new GAI you can keep what you earn. You scrounge around for a friend or relative to take care of the kids. McDonald's has an opening for $3.65 an hour and you take it. You can't afford not to — even though you know you're worth more than that. So you struggle along, still below the poverty line, feeling guilty that you have to depend on another woman to care for your kids, exhausted at the end of the day. Ask yourself: is this new GAI really better than the old welfare?

For you, the answer is no. But for McDonald's, and other low wage employers, the GAI will be better than the old welfare. Without legislation boosting minimum wages, and with hundreds of thousands of more people forced to compete for low wage work by the GAI rates employers will have no trouble keeping wages low. The money that they paid for wages in the past can now go into acquiring more assets and more control over the economy. Much of the extra profit for multinational companies could even flow out of the country ...

In short, this business version of the GAI is a scheme that lets business appear that it cares for the poor, but at the same time helps create a system that will, over the long term, reduce all wages and make more people poorer, whether they're in the paid labour force or not.

Probably there's no single word or phrase that will end poverty. If there was, business would hire pollsters and public relations experts to take over that word or phrase and put their meaning to it, like they're taking over Guaranteed Annual Income.

We need to be sure that whatever phrase is used, the results will end poverty, not increase it. Anti-poverty groups are beginning to realize that our anti-poverty agenda should include a package of measures.

We need:
- decent jobs at decent wages
- income above the poverty line for people who can't work
- decent minimum wages
- imported insurance programs (UI, WCB CPP)
- maintenance and improvement of universal programs such as education and medicare, and family allowances
- universal childcare
- a tax system based on ability to pay which redistributes income from the rich to the poor.

And, with these conditions, we need an increased earnings exemptions for people receiving welfare or GAI.

Those of us working to end poverty have a big education job ahead of us. We must ensure that voters see the big business GAI for what it is: a way to reverse the decades old tendency for decent welfare rates to push up low wages; and a way to deceive low income people into supporting a scheme that will increase rather than reduce poverty.

"While Some Progress is Being Made ..." Alberta, October 1985[33]

...Generally the view from Alberta is gloomy, with privatization of government services becoming a major issue. A private member's bill has been introduced in the legislature to give civil servants the right to establish private companies providing government services for a profit. The practice is already being considered in the social services department, Richardson says, where the government is considering privatizing services such as adoption home studies. "It is so prevalent now and coming up in the most absurd places that it's difficult to monitor," Richardson reports. She says the provision of services is so bad that "one group on our side," the society of injured workers, wants the workers compensation board privatized in order to improve service.

Richardson says response to a recent report by the right-wing Fraser Institute, which shows that Alberta is the highest taxed province in the country, illustrates the political climate. The government dismissed the report, calling the Fraser Institute "socialist." The Tory leadership race now underway is not expected to change things, Richardson says. "All three candidates are terrible," although, she says, they have voiced support for equal pay for work of equal value and limited support for affirmative action.

---

33. Trudy Richardson, Alberta/Northwest Territories rep, "While Some Progress is Being Made in Alberta, Privatization is a Looming Problem," *Feminist Action News*, October 1985, 11.

"Postal Petition in B.C."
Agassiz, B.C., June 1987[34]

In Agassiz, post office closures became a very important issue for the public in late December 1986. It was inconceivable that Canada Post would do such a thing until one of our staff stepped out from behind the counter to the public space and said, "Really! There is to be a meeting, January 31, about this issue. Really!" The next day at a smaller post office nearby, we loudly voiced objections to closures and a person there in a firm voice said, "Well, if you feel so strongly about it — you'd better hurry up and get your act in gear; the public better DO something." So our tiny group, with no post office connections and varying political persuasions agreed: we'd better get our act in gear. Blank petitions were copied; a box of envelopes was donated; typewriter borrowed, all of which resulted in our first mailing to mayors of villages in B.C. The names were obtained from a list available at our municipal hall. Several petitions were returned causing enough encouragement for us to mark townsites with pins on the B.C. map. Our major mailing was to smaller communities listed on the side of the map. These packets, containing petitions, newspaper clippings and our opinions, were mailed to the postmaster directly in the expressed hope that if she or he was not able to collect petitions someone else could be found. Hugh Clark sent us a dear bouquet and both Parliament postal critic's offices were most positive about it and pleased to receive returned petitions ...

[14,007 signatures] is a tremendous number of signatures to come from rural areas. Little Fort was way ahead. Little Fort Women's Institute had already sent their own petition to M. Côté and were already fighting postal closures. 100% of their population has signed their petition! 150 Mile House, in our minds, is one of the great communities. Their response was rapid, the percentage of population signing their names was high, and the concern of their people, extraordinary. Greenwood, population of 760, provided 563 signatures which is 74% of their town; but "100% of Greenwood's townspeople are determined to keep the building open. After 72 years of service it would be a crying shame to close ..."

As many elderly live in rural areas, the Old Age Pensioners have joined the outcry and are sending their petitions directly to Ottawa. Debbie Cliffe, our Agassiz Postmaster, as an especially coherent appraiser of the national scene, encouraged our effort every step of the way. She recognized the post office in the rural economy, and noted it's part in being the heart of the community, and noted the centralization versus diversification concepts; thereby motivating us to reach out to other provinces. Postmasters signed their names on the return envelope or jotted a helpful note. Along the way it was noted that 82% of rural postmasters are women! That is a very interesting bit of information;

34. Mary Otto Grieshaber and Margaret McRae, Agassiz, B.C. In the possession of Marjorie Cohen.

especially to many of us who sense a different mode in Canada Post's attack ...

CANADA POST

It's easier to take post offices away,
If you've reassured rural people it'll pay.
Whether it's true,
It's quite up to you,
Do they mean what they think they don't say?

We must hope that our news will get through to M. André as well as to those who make decisions at Canada Post. All of us can make a strong effort to send Ottawa petitions, to generate awareness of the postal problem in our own community and support the efforts of others like Rural Dignity who are committed to the same road. Hats off to all those special people who examined the issue and then signed their name.

"The Problem is Still Jobs ... Not Unemployment Insurance" Toronto, August 1989[35]

...In 1986, NAC presented a brief to the Forget Commission where our essential argument was that **continuing high levels of unemployment, and not the Unemployment Insurance system, constitute a fundamental economic problem in Canada.** Since 1982, unprecedentedly large numbers of Canadians have found themselves dependent on unemployment insurance ...

However, with improved economic conditions and a modest fall in the unemployment rate, the UI fund began to run surpluses as early as 1985. The approximately $1 billion annual surpluses in the UI fund present the opportunity to:

- lower premium contributions;
- retain a "savings" account for the periodic recessions in our economy and the mass unemployment which results;
- improve benefits.

Together with other government initiatives to develop a full employment and job market strategy, this would represent a positive forward-looking approach to Canada's employment policies. Instead, the government is proposing a major restructuring of our unemployment insurance program, making it more difficult for the unemployed to draw benefits. It also proposes to withdraw the federal contribution to the UI fund and, furthermore, to divert as much as 15% of employer-employee contributions to labour market programs, which do not constitute proper unemployment insurance usage of funds.

---

35. Laurell Ritchie, "A Brief to the Legislative Committee on Bill C-21: An Act to amend the Unemployment Insurance Act and the Employment and Immigration Department and Commission Act," presented by the National Action Committee on the Status of Women, SUMMARY.

In our opinion, it is rejecting the traditional role of unemployment insurance which is to insure income maintenance during a temporary interruption of work. It is also abandoning the role of unemployment insurance as an economic stabilizer and moving even further away from any commitment to insuring that Canadians from all regions who want to work, men and women, young and old, can find a decent job at a living wage. We also fear that these measures represent the first steps toward the privatization of the Employment and Immigration Commission and the Canada Employment Centres. With the withdrawal of federal government funding, we fear that the next step is the abandonment of a national UI program which insures the same benefits to all Canadians, wherever they live. A national program means that the costs and consequences of unemployment are shared by all Canadians.

We believe that, in adopting this strategy, the government is willing to sacrifice the interests of Canadian workers partly in order to appease the American government and its conception of what constitutes fair labour market practices and partly in response to pressure from Canadian business to undercut social programs in order to reduce their operating costs. We believe that women, in particular, will be hurt most by these cuts as they are still the last hired and the first fired and, in the present economic climate, the most vulnerable to layoffs due to technological change and the restructuring which will result from the Free Trade Agreement with the United States.

The National Action Committee on the Status of Women is firmly opposed to any cutbacks to the Unemployment Insurance program and to the withdrawal of federal funding from this program. Along with the authors of the de Grandpré Report, we believe that "an emphasis on employment promotion measures on the part of both the private sector and governments would eventually lead to a decrease in UI expenditures, as claimants would become far fewer."[36]

NAC supports training programs, particularly for women, However, these programs should be financed from general revenues, must be administered by boards on which unions or other employee representatives have veto and must be integrated into a full employment strategy which insures that jobs will be waiting for retrained workers.

What's wrong with Bill C-21 and the existing UI Act!

The Federal government is trying to put the cart before the horse. Rather than providing the unemployed with adequate skills and productive employment at a liveable wage, it seeks to punish the victims of a disease

---

36. *Adjusting to Win*, Report of the Advisory Council on Adjustment (de Grandpré Report), Minister of Supply and Services Canada, March 1989, p. 47. The Council specifically recommends no "major reorientation of the Unemployment Insurance (UI) program" and recognized how important the safety net is in regions where unemployment remains unacceptably high. While we do not necessarily endorse all the recommendations of the de Grandpré Report, we do find their remarks concerning the interaction of income security measures and retraining programs insightful.

of the economic system for which they are not responsible. This "punishment" is to take many forms:
- making it harder to become eligible for UI;
- shorter benefit periods;
- vary harsh penalties for voluntary quits, losing a job by reason of misconduct, refusing "suitable" employment or disobeying a directive.

In addition, **there are already a number of punitive measures in the existing Unemployment Insurance Act to which the National Action Committee has expressed its opposition in the past.** These include:
- the exclusion from coverage of large numbers of part-time workers, mainly women;
- harsher eligibility requirements for "new entrants" or "re-entrants", most of whom are women;
- stricter eligibility requirements for parental and illness benefits than for regular benefits;
- the two-week waiting period which especially makes no sense in the case of parental and illness benefits;
- benefit levels at only 60% of former earnings; we would like to see replacement at the 95% level, particularly in the case of pregnancy, child care and illness;
- the deduction of various forms of severance pay, vacation pay and pension income from the UI benefits;
- the clawback of UI benefits paid to workers with high income which is an attack on the principle of a universal social insurance;
- the fact that claimants employed on job creation projects are not considered to be employed and are not covered by general labour legislation, the CPP/QPP or UI.

Non-discrimination

Over the years a number of court cases have reinforced the principle of **non-discrimination** set out in the Canadian Charter of Rights. NAC takes positive note of the fact the Bill C-21 proposes to correct some existing anomalies:
- the full inclusion of persons working for companies owned completely or in large part by their spouses; most of these people are women.
- the end of discrimination on the basis of age so that workers over 65 will now be covered by the UI program.

However, additional measures must be taken to improve public pension programs so that at 65 all Canadian workers can take retirement with sufficient income if that is their choice. Additional measures are also needed for older unemployed workers before age 65.

Parental and other special benefits

The Canadian Unemployment Insurance Program also provides for temporary income protection in certain "special" circumstances, notably pregnancy, adoption, child care and illness. In line with our general concerns about the Unemployment Insurance program, **NAC is concerned that the withdrawal of federal funding and the possible privatization of some or all of the functions of the Employment and Immigration Commission will threaten the existence of a national program of parental benefits** and lead to the kind of balkanization found in the United States. **We also object to the fact that the improvements in parental leave are being financed by cutbacks in other areas when the UI fund is running a surplus.**

NAC recognized the progress made by the introduction of 10 weeks of child-care benefits in addition to pregnancy leave. However, **we fail to understand why the duration of UI benefits will continue to be inferior to the needs recognized and granted by the Canada Labour Code: 15 weeks for pregnancy, 24 weeks for child care plus payment of benefits during the 2-week waiting period to be appended to either pregnancy or child care leave.**

We are especially angry at the cutback of leave for adoptive parents from 15 weeks to 10 weeks when we well know that the majority of adoptions are of older children who have special problems and that most adoptive agencies require a parent to stay at home at least 6 months. UI benefits for 26 weeks of child care leave as granted by the Canada Labour Code would allow parents to adopt a child without undue financial hardship.

The relaxation of restrictions requiring that pregnancy or illness leave be taken only during the initial benefit period and that combinations of the two be limited to 15 weeks is also a positive step as is the new rule which will allow people to claim special benefits during a strike or lockout under certain circumstances. However, we feel that there should be no limits on combinations of pregnancy, parental and illness benefits. The 30-week limit is discriminatory with respect to women, because it can never apply to men. In addition the UI program should guarantee a minimum number of additional weeks of regular benefits in the case that a person is unemployed after taking special leave.

We also see no reason for placing any restriction at all on the right to take pregnancy, parental and illness benefits during a strike or lockout.

NAC also recommends:

- the introduction for each dependent child and for each parent of 10 days per year (20 days for sole-custody parents) of parental responsibility benefits;

- the application of the parental leave provisions of the Canada Labour Code to all employees under federal jurisdiction, including the armed forces and public service employees not covered by a collective agreement.

- regulations defining who may take child-care benefits in the case of common-law marriages and recognition of the parental role for both members of homosexual couples.

- the amendment of provincial labour standards codes so as to be at least as generous as the Canada Labour Code in granting pregnancy and parental leave; federal-provincial negotiations on this question should be a priority.

Chapter 5

Global Issues

Ruth Roach Pierson

The Canadian women's movement has operated on local community, municipal, provincial, and federal levels. But its concerns have also vaulted the boundaries of the Canadian state. This chapter will look at ways in which Canadian women's activism and theorizing have taken the larger view and engaged with issues of international and global dimension. The terms "international" and "global" are not synonymous, and Canadian women's internationalism has sometimes been Eurocentric in scope. Yet, despite the contradictions and difficulties inherent in attempts by women of a "developed" society in the North to take a global perspective, many Canadian women have contributed to global feminist initiatives.

International Women's Year 1975

One international decision that would have an impact on Canadian women was the vote of the General Assembly of the United Nations, on December 18, 1972, to proclaim 1975 International Women's Year. For Canadian women, the timing of the declaration was propitious, because it coincided with the resurgence of grassroots feminism in Canada, with the beginnings of women's renewed mass organizing to address the many areas of sex inequality targeted by the Royal Commission on the Status of Women, and with steps being taken, however haltingly, by federal and provincial governments to respond to the Commission's recommendations.[1] It was a woman highly placed within the United Nations who was key to getting the UN to declare 1975 International Women's Year (IWY) — Helvi Sipila of Finland, who served as UN Secretary-General for IWY.[2] Similarly, it was a woman highly placed in the Canadian federal government — Sue Findlay, the founder and chairwoman of the Secretary of State's Women's Programme — who secured $2.5 million for her department to spend on IWY.

CREDIT: Branch for the Advancement of Women, Centre for Social Development and Humanitarian Affairs, United Nations (Vienna)

International Women's Year

Année internationale de la femme

Año Internacional de la Mujer

This was the official emblem adopted to celebrate International Women's Year in 1975 and the United Nations Decade for Women, 1976-1985. The dove symbolizes peace and progress; the mathematical sign, equality; and the biological sign, women.

Unfortunately, the federal government's involvement in IWY got off to a rocky start.[3] First, an IWY Secretariat was created, which was separate from the Secretary of State, and given a budget of $2.5 million. It promptly earmarked $1 million for salaries, $1 million for a series of five conferences, and $500,000 for an advertising campaign for IWY. The contract for the ad campaign was then awarded to the only company in the competition with no women on its creative team. Women's groups across Canada were offended by the contract award (the Secretariat's defence was that the all-male group's "presentation was the best — the Secretariat didn't want to take sex into consideration!!??").[4] Women were equally appalled by the seemingly silly if not offensive ad slogan that the all-male group[5] had come up with — "Why Not?"

Second, two months before the beginning of International Women's Year, the federal government attempted to replace Sue Findlay, who had done so much to organize the Secretary of State's participation in IWY and who, in the process, had won widespread respect by consulting with women's groups in every province and territory. Findlay's job was reclassified upwards from chairperson to director of the Women's Programme, and Findlay lost out in the competition to a more senior female bureaucrat.[6] The action was seen to call "into question the sincerity of the government's commitment to women."[7]

But in the face of the outcry from women's groups, the federal government backed down and reinstated Findlay as head of the Women's Programme in the position of director. And despite doubt from grassroots sceptics as to the wisdom of such state-down initiatives, International Women's Year activities were successfuly organized throughout Canada. The *International Women's Year/Année internationale de la femme Newsletter/Bulletin (1975 IWY/AIF)* provided a record of many of these events. Published and distributed monthly by the IWY Secretariat, *1975 IWY/AIF* took on the look of a grassroots women's movement newsletter, as its pages were filled with short news items about women's movement activities in various parts of Canada and about IWY events being planned in other countries.

The proclamation of 1975 as International Women's Year encouraged women's initiatives in many fields. The Ontario Women and the Law Association was founded in 1975.[8] It was also in 1975 that, in British Columbia, the Service, Office and Retail Workers Union of Canada (SORWUC) was established to organize the least organized, lowest-paid sectors of the labour force where women predominate.[9] Many women took advantage of the possibilities of new funding opened up by IWY to press for increased representation of women and women's perspectives in education and the arts. Buoyed by the stated UN objectives for 1975, Kathleen Shannon petitioned the National Film Board of Canada for funding to support women filmmakers making films about women, an application which eventually led to the creation of NFB's "Studio D."[10] In September 1975, the University of Guelph hosted a three-day Nellie McClung Conference at which there was a performance of *What Glorious Times They Had,* a play by Diane Grant about Nellie McClung and the Manitoba suffragists and performed by the Redlight Theatre, "Canada's professional women's theatre"; a keynote address by historian Veronica Strong-Boag; a bus tour to McClung's birthplace; and six action workshops on topics dear to McClung's heart — women and politics, women and alcohol, women and prisons, sports opportunities for women, opportunities for girls in technical subjects, and pensions, benefits and insurance for women.[11]

Looking back at the year's activities, Canadian women had mixed feelings.[12] Even the most jaundiced, however, had to concede that declaring 1975 International Women's Year had succeeded in educating public opinion and women, in particular, to a wide range of women's accomplishments, grievances, and just demands and in legitimating women's place on the social agenda. In her November 1975 editorial on how International Women's Year affected women, Lorna Marsden, then president of the National Action Committee on the Status of Women (NAC), wrote that "1975 was only one year in a long and slow process of social change. But in sum, I believe it has helped."

> Women who always denied that they had ever been discriminated against, who argued that women just didn't "go out and fight" for their rights, or who classified us as "loud-mouthed" and "angry" are now aware that there are issues [in the priorities of the women's movement] of real importance for the direction which this society will take.[13]

In retrospect, International Women's Year seemed to have served to raise mainstream Canadian women's awareness more of women's issues close to home than of women's issues around the world.

International Women's Day

Even before International Women's Year, and separate in origin from it, International Women's Day (IWD) began to be reclaimed by feminists in the early 1970s "as a day of protest, solidarity, and celebration." Setting aside a particular day each year on which to celebrate women and focus on working women's struggles was a custom introduced before the First World War by European social democrats of the Marxist Second International. Specifically, Clara Zetkin, of the German Social Democratic Party, proposed to the Second International Conference of Socialist Women, held in Copenhagen in August 1910, that a day be observed each year in honour of women's efforts for peace and social progress.[14] March 8th was eventually chosen as the day, in remembrance of the women garment workers on the Lower East Side of New York City who went out on strike on March 8, 1909, to demand shorter working hours, better working conditions, laws against child labour, and women's right to vote. The song "Bread and Roses,"[15] lustily sung on International Women's Day, was inspired by the courage of the 14,000 women textile workers in Lawrence, Massachusetts, who stayed out on strike for three months in 1912 and whose cry was "Better to starve fighting than starve working." Commemorating women's struggles internationally for improved quality of life as well as working conditions, March 8th became part of the women's movement and "Bread and Roses" its anthem.

In their revivals of International Women's Day, Canadian women organized rallies, demonstrations and marches, gave workshops, and held women-only dances. Given its Marxist socialist genealogy, it is not surprising that reclaiming International Women's Day had particular significance for feminists on the left. Starting in the 1970s, feminists in various Canadian cities began holding IWD celebrations; a photo of six women singing into a microphone before Toronto City Hall with a March 8th International Women's Day poster affixed to the podium appeared in the April-May 1973 issue of the Canadian feminist periodical *The Other Woman*.[16] Records of the organization of these early celebrations are scarce. According to one surviving document from Toronto, 1975, it was "a group of women who have worked on women's issues in trade unions, community groups, political organizations, and in other ways" who sent out a general letter to other interested women, inviting them to attend the second general planning meeting to be held at OISE in mid-February. The themes they proposed for that year's IWD were "equality of women in the work force, and equality of women in the family or social sphere."[17] "In the fall of 1977 a number of women in the Revolutionary Workers' League decided to approach other feminists about the possibility of organizing" the 1978 IWD celebration in Toronto.[18] In the process, the socialist feminist International Women's Day Committee (IWDC) was formed, and henceforward took a leading role in initiating and organizing Toronto's IWD celebrations in conjunction with the

In their revival of IWD, Canadian women from all political perspectives began organizing rallies, marches and discussion panels. "The rising of the women, means the rising of the race" is one of the slogans of the socialist feminist movement.

March 8th Coalition, which was composed of a range of feminist and pro-feminist groups. The issues highlighted for Toronto's IWD in 1978 were control of our bodies; childcare; cutbacks in social services and education; employment; lesbian rights; Native, immigrant and Black women; and violence against women.[19]

By 1978, as the flyer announcing Toronto's International Women's Day 1978 Demonstration/Celebration indicated, similar actions were being organized in British Columbia, Edmonton, Winnipeg, and Montreal. The flyer also proudly announced that these events were "being organized simultaneously with women in every major European country, women who are building for a co-ordinated continent-wide mobilization."[20] The internationalism of these early IWD celebrations sometimes did not extend beyond Europe and other parts of North America. The prevailing assumption at the time was that the various forms of women's oppression were universal and that one joined an international sisterhood of women combatting these oppressions when one worked to combat them locally. Often it was women of white European background who held these views. Other women, particularly women whose provenance was outside white northern Europe, had a more global perspective and struggled to bring this into the Canadian International Women's Day celebrations. *The Other Woman*'s special 1976 issue on March 8th made a concerted effort to be international in the global sense.[21] By 1981, there was a slowly growing recognition that racism as well as homophobia were forms of oppression affecting many women. Action Daycare member Sue Colley's 1981 IWD address in Toronto touched on women's demands for childcare, economic independence, equal pay for work of equal value, lesbian rights, and an end to violence against women. She also spoke of "immigrant women ... organizing to fight racism and discrimination" while clearly indicating her conviction that "the struggle against conservative, racist and misogynist groups" must be "the struggle of all women."[22] By 1983, recognition was growing that racism, imperialism, and militarism were at the core of the oppression of women in colonized and brutally militarized parts of the world. When Toronto's March 8th Coalition leaflet for 1983 declared that "women aound the world are preparing to share their struggles, defeats and victories with their fellow sisters," it referred to "Women in Africa, the Philippines, Central and South America, and Palestine ... fighting for their liberation and the liberation of their peoples."[23]

Still there was resistance to having women's global struggles against racism, imperialism, and militarism share the spotlight with women's local struggles against discrimination in jobs, unequal pay, inadequate provision of childcare, and violence against women. Issues of *Broadside* in 1983 carried a raging debate, in articles and letters to the editor, over whether the focus of International Women's Day, indeed of the Canadian women's movement, should or should not be on the problems women face here at home in Canada. On one side were feminists who perceived an emphasis on women in national liberation struggles — in El Salvador, Nicaragua, South Africa, Palestine, for example — as a subversion of the "gender"[24] agenda by male-dominated, left-wing politics. On the other side were feminists, indeed often on the left politically, who saw the necessity of making the connections between women's oppression globally and the politics of imperialist, neo-colonialist, and militarist regimes from which Western economies benefited. In the exchange between Lois Lowenberger and the Toronto International Women's Day Committee (IWDC), the very definition of what it means to be a feminist was at issue.

Clearly most disturbing to Lowenberger was the attention given to the Palestinian cause in the absence of any countervailing Israeli perspective. But Lowenberger would have preferred that even those national liberation movements, which she regarded as feminist, "should not occupy such a large part of the program" of International Women's Day.[25] What should have been front and centre were issues affecting working-class women in Canada who are "interested in such issues as equal pay for work of equal value, equal opportunities, ... affirmative action, daycare"; single mothers who are concerned with "better welfare benefits, personal dignity, decent housing, nutrition and education"; and immigrant women who are concerned with English language classes, education, an end to wife battering, a more enlightened immigration policy, decent jobs, and freedom from harassment. Moreover, "groups of women who are particularly oppressed within Canadian society" should have received more than a passing reference, "groups like black women, Native women, Inuit women, immigrant women in general, Jewish women, and lesbian women."[26]

The IWDC respondents did not disagree with the importance of either the issues or the oppressed groups named by Lowenberger. However, they did disagree with her claiming as feminist only that "perspective" that "sees war, oppression, expansionism, imperialism, the nuclear arms race and other evils as products of the universal patriarchal system, not of 'capitalism,' 'imperialism,' 'zionism' or even 'communism.'"[27] In Lowenberger's analysis, the concept of "patriarchy" has not only been ahistorically and transculturally universalized but also inflated into a uni-causal explanation for all evil. The IWDC respondents also strongly object to Lowenberger's assertion of "no necessary relationship between feminism and anti-imperialism." They point out, as Third World women were insisting and have continued to insist, that feminism and anti-imperialism are "bound up so closely together as to be inseparable in [Third World women's] lives and in their politics."[28]

The United Nations Decade for Women: World Conferences

International Women's Year gave rise to a series of ongoing World Conferences on Women, held every five years and sponsored by the United Nations. The first was held in Mexico City from 19 June to 2 July 1975. The themes of the conference were "Equality, Development and Peace." The eleven-member Canadian delegation consisted of nine women and two men, all drawn from federal or provincial posts directly involved in women's programs or world development and external affairs.[29] While women outnumbered men as delegates by about five to one, the conference was presided over by a man, the male head of Mexico's delegation, "despite many protests by numerous delegates that a conference concerning women should be headed by a woman."[30] Moreover, "a number of 'first ladies' — wives of presidents or prime ministers" — were called upon to address the conference, although they enjoyed no official capacity in their own right but rather only the status of appendage to a man in high office. Nevertheless, Helvi Sipila spoke out forcefully in the opening session on the necessity "to acknowledge that the denial of women's rights and opportunities is at the very root of our development problems and socio-economic ills," and the conference did agree on a Ten-Year World Plan of Action to address many of the debilitating inequalities afflicting women worldwide, including illiteracy, mass poverty, and degrading imagery.[31] And in recognition of the fact that a single year was too little time to address the monumental problems facing women, the 30th Session of the UN General Assembly declared 1976 to 1985 the United Nations Decade for Women.

Running simultaneously with the government conference in Mexico was the Women's Tribune, a parallel conference organized by women representing non-governmental organizations (NGOs). "It had been the women of the non-governmental organizations with Consultative Status at the Economic and Social Council (CONGO) — who had been most active in promoting the idea of International Women's Year."[32] While there were 2,000 delegates to the government conference in Mexico, 6,000 women from NGOs attended the Tribune. They "talked, explored their needs and disagreed at times," creating "a momentum which could not be stopped." For the NGO women, other issues were of equal importance to "Equality, Development and Peace" and demanded attention. These included education, health, and employment. Afterwards, some of the women from the NGOs who had gone to Mexico stayed in touch with one another, gaining a sense of their own power as well as knowledge of the plight of women in various parts of the world. According to Dame Nita Barrow, the Tribune helped create the sense that the women's movement was worldwide.[33]

At the Decade for Women's mid-point, in July 1980, the UN organized the United Nations Decade for Women Conference in Copenhagen around the themes "Employment, Education and Health." As in Mexico in 1975, in Copenhagen in 1980 NGO women held a parallel conference, the Mid-Decade Forum of Non-Governmental Organizations, and, what was new, an arts festival. Twenty-eight NGO delegates attended from Canada. For Marion Berling of the Women in Focus Gallery in Vancouver, the only delegate from B.C., both the NGO Forum and the Festival of Women Artists provided her with a platform from which to present works by Canadian feminist artists to an international audience. Sexuality issues, in particular pornography and sexual harassment, were the focus of a number of her presentations, in keeping with one of the major concerns of mainstream Canadian feminism at the time.

Berling's audiences were mainly North American and European. The responses she got from the few African and Chinese women who attended made her realize that of prime importance for them was "exploring the reality of living as part of a Third World country that has been colonized and oppressed."[34] Berling learned from African women that they were offended by North American women taking interest in the issue of infibulation from outside the culture. Her experience in Copenhagen brought Berling to the threshold of an awareness that women's oppression is culturally specific, but resisting this insight, she assigned the label "ethnocentricity" to the "difference" of the African and Chinese women. At the same time, apparently unaware of her own ethnocentricity, she posited "the belief that we have a common bond as women throughout the world"[35] as a universal truth. This assumption of the homogeneity of women throughout the world as oppressed, as "powerless," as "exploited," as "sexually harassed" was the construction of "women" taking form in white Western feminist discourse at the time. As Mohanty and others have pointed out, this construction universalizes a white, Western, middle-class analysis that contributes to the colonization of Third World women by "othering" them, by suppressing the myriad historical, material, and cultural differences among women, and by preserving Western women's centrality.[36] According to Dame Nita Barrow, women in Copenhagen "began to realize ... societal and other differences ... made universal solutions impossible," but "this realization was by no means complete."[37]

The NGO Forum held in conjunction with the UN End of the Decade Conference in Nairobi, Kenya, in 1985, represented a definite shift away from a Eurocentric perspective. Women from almost all of the 150 states that sent delegates to the official women's conference were in attendance at the Nairobi Forum, 13,503 in all. Many of these women "registered as individuals," though they "had organizational affiliations."[38] For the first time, women from the South — women from Third World countries — vastly outnumbered women from the North — North American and European women. And also for the first time, Third World women were involved in setting the agenda and in taking up leadership roles during the Forum.[39] And therefore, for the first time, "[i]ssues like imperialism, racism, migrants, refugees" got a great deal of attention. For Canadian women of colour who attended Forum '85, it was powerfully self-affirming to be in the overwhelming majority for a change; it was also wonderfully liberating to be out from under the daily grind of white racism. Ravida Din, who went as a youth delegate, recalls Nairobi as a turning point for her. First, about 40 per cent of the Canadian delegation were women of colour. Second, there was the exhilaration of:

Arriving in Nairobi ... WOW! Not only was it my birthplace but here were 13,000 women and two-thirds were women of colour. Nairobi was a coming home for me in more ways than one. Many white women have said feminism or the women's movement is "coming home." I was amongst women who thought and felt just like I did. There were finally names for all those feelings of being "other," of being "separate" and most of those feelings had to do with acknowledging the fact that racism existed in the women's movement.[40]

Mutriba Din remembers calling herself a woman of colour for the first time after her sister, Ravida, returned from Nairobi.[41]

For white, middle-class Canadian feminists, such as Emma Kivisild, Nairobi brought home the realization that "the international women's movement is primarily a movement of Third World women."[42] It also brought home the realization that Third World feminism was not a Western import but indigenous. The vocal and visible presence of Third World lesbians was eye opening, "refuting the myth that lesbianism is one of the products of decadent capitalist societies."[43] But Kivisild also noted "several glaring omissions" in the Nairobi program, "among them any real discussion of indigenous peoples' issues, or the inclusion of disabled women on the platform at 'progressive' events like the unity rally."[44] Janet Laidlaw attended Forum '85 as a delegate of the "Women in Development" Working Group of the Canadian Council for International Co-operation (CCIC).[45] She, too, reported on how the "unofficial" conference brought white, Western delegates, such as herself, face to face with the limitations of dominant white Western feminism's belief that "women's" issues can be separated from issues of racism, national struggle, war.

Before I left Vancouver, I attended a "briefing" at which women from the Jewish Council, the YWCA, and the Status of Women stressed how important it was that the Nairobi conference stick to "women's" issues and not get sidetracked into discussions of "male" issues such as the Palestinian question, apartheid, the Iran-Iraq war, etc.[46]

The thousands of women in Nairobi, from South Africa, the Middle East, and Central America, swiftly disabused Western women of the notion that "women's" issues could be isolated from the politics of international and intranational struggle. "Throughout the conference the fallacy of this view was underlined." How can we "press for 'equality,'" Black South African and Palestinian women asked, "amid racial discrimination?"[47] Kivisild's diary entry for July 15, 1985, noted:

> For all the talk about "unnecessary politicization" of the agenda (the argument that was supposed to keep apartheid, the PLO and Central America off the schedule) the most unifying bond here is an understanding that there must be support for women in liberation struggles, especially Black women fighting in South Africa.[48]

As this book goes to press, preparations are being made for the Fourth World Conference on Women to be held in Beijing, China, September 4 to 15, 1995, focusing on "Action for Equality, Development and Peace." At the same time, women grassroots activists from all over the world are preparing for the concurrent NGO Forum that will take place August 30 to September 8. As in the past, the parallel women's conference in Beijing will provide an opportunity for women from non-governmental organizations to come together to share strategies, to discuss ideas, and to network. The Beijing gathering is expected to be larger than any of the three previous World Conferences on women.

From *Women* and Development to *Gender* and Development

At the same time that many women in the grassroots Canadian women's movement were struggling with the effort of making international and global connections, Canadian women involved in "development" work in so-called "underdeveloped" or "developing" "Third World" countries were struggling to bring a feminist perspective to international aid and development projects. Two Canadian women, Dr. Norma E. Walmsley and Suzanne Johnson, returned from attending the Women's Tribune in Mexico in 1975, inspired to find ways for women in the North to provide material and moral support to women in the South who were fighting oppression.[49] They found their enthusiasm shared by other Canadian women active in the international development area who felt frustrated with the "little or no acknowledgement of women's vital role in the survival and development of their communities."[50] The result was the founding of MATCH in 1976, Canada's only non-governmental international development agency run by women for women. The organization's name refers to the founders' intent to "match" the needs and resources of women in Canada to the needs and resources of women in the South.[51]

When it first opened its doors in 1976, MATCH occupied but a cubby hole in someone else's office. As of 1994 the MATCH International Centre in Ottawa has expanded into its own offices and has survived into its eighteenth year. Its financial survival is based on the arrangement negotiated by its founders with the Canadian International Development Agency (CIDA) to match at a ratio of 1:3 any funds MATCH raises from the public "to an annual maximum of $300,000."[52] With an annual budget over $100,000, a quarterly newsletter (the *MATCH News*), and a host of publications in three languages (Spanish, English and French), MATCH continues to create a North/South dialogue and "is committed, with our Southern sisters, to a feminist vision of development."[53]

MATCH operates on two major fronts. On one, the monetary aid front, it provides funds for women's projects, in response to initiatives taken and priorities set by women in the Third World. On the second, the educational/communications front, it seeks to "facilitate the sharing of information" so that Canadian women's groups and Third World women's groups can learn from one another "and strategize together for change."[54] MATCH assumes that issues of concern to Canadian women, such as "violence against women, child care, employment, new reproductive technologies, access to health care, abortion, birth control," also demand the attention of women elsewhere in the world.[55] At the same time MATCH has come to recognize that the configuration of these issues can be very different in the Third World from their configuration in Canada.

MATCH's programs on both fronts are many and diverse. On the monetary aid front, it extends support to "community-based projects designed and managed by women" in Africa, Asia, the Caribbean, and Latin America. The first requirement is that the project be designed and managed by women from the South. The second major criterion of eligibility is that the project aim "to change the practices and attitudes which discriminate against them." According to MATCH's Annual Report 1991–92, regional projects ranged from support for the publication in Senegal of *Yewwu-Yewwi* (for women's liberation), a periodical dedicated to raising women's status in Francophone Africa, to support for La Voz de la Mujer in Lima, Peru, which "has opened one of the few shelters for battered women in Latin America" and which provides literacy and skills training to marginalized Peruvian women.[56]

On the networking and communication front, MATCH has originated a number of effective programs. Launched in the late 1980s, Words of Women (WOW) has been one of the most important. According to former MATCH programme officer Beth Woroniuk, WOW's roots lay in Caribbean women's expression of interest "in having more access to women's writing from around the world" and in making Caribbean women's words more accessible to the rest of the world, including Canada. The Caribbean women "see their writing as a political activity."[57] Praising the Words of Women project in 1989, Honor Ford-Smith, then artistic director of the Sistren Theatre Collective of Jamaica, made the point that the concept of "development" should not be limited to building dams, but rather should be expanded to include "a whole lump of stuff which gets called 'culture.'"[58] At its Words of Women consultation in Toronto in December 1988, MATCH heard from Stephanie Martin that Sister Vision Press had been created in 1984 in order to overcome the exclusion by white Canadian feminist and other progressive presses of Black women and women of colour.[59] One of WOW's first projects was to provide assistance to the Caribbean Association for Feminist Research and Action (CAFRA) and the Canadian-based Sister Vision Press to publish an anthology of poems by Caribbean women entitled *Creation Fire*, edited by Ramabai Espinet.[60] This project exemplifies WOW's underlying belief in the importance of women's writing for legitimizing and sharing women's experiences. The book has been widely used in workshops and readings with women's groups in the Caribbean and in Canadian Black communities.

Over time, MATCH has kept up with the key changes in thinking about women in relation to development and underdevelopment. In the early 1970s, linking women and development was a major step, as women were not seen as relevant to development until germinal works, like Ester Boserup's *Woman's Role in Economic Development*,[61] documented that not only were "modernization" projects not benefiting women, they were in many cases leaving women worse off than before. First the concept of "Women in Development" (WID) was advanced to stimulate efforts to integrate women into development. But the WID approach began to be questioned in the 1980s when it was often found to lead merely "to small women's components being ... grafted onto existing plans." Not only did this approach usually fail to produce an improvement in women's status, it frequently resulted in a further lengthening of women's already over-long workdays. The replacement of "Women in Development" by "Gender and Development" has meant embracing the notion that women's status is relational and that it is therefore crucial to look at the relations between men and women, in particular the sexual division of labour in the workplace and in the home and the implications of this division for control over property and for decision-making in the home and in the community. To the "Gender and Development" analysis, MATCH has tried to add a global feminism approach in the sense of promoting the importance of women's "organizing and mobilizing at a global level."[62]

Under the rubric of global feminism, MATCH made combating violence against women on a global scale a priority in 1988. In October 1989, MATCH organized a multiracial, multinational team of facilitators to tour Quebec, Ontario, Manitoba, and the Northwest Territories and hold workshops on violence against women.[63] Convinced that "women's organizations all over the world consider violence against women to be the most pervasive problem facing women today,"[64] MATCH produced the resource kit *Linking Women's Global Struggles to End Violence* in 1990.[65] And in March 1991, MATCH brought together twenty-six participants from around the world in a "consultative and planning meeting on the issues of violence against women."[66] A major goal was to put violence against women on the development agenda. As one participant stated, "We cannot continue to speak of international development without taking into account the major obstacle to women's participation which is violence."[67] The topics touched on, indicating MATCH's openness to a broad definition to violence, included:

> "[r]ape, beatings, incest, illegal abortion, forced prostitution, the lack of contraception, the links between violence against women and AIDS, medical violence, poverty, torture, mental cruelty, militarism, sex tourism, female infanticide, traditional customs harmful to women (early marriage, force-feeding, food rationing, sexual mutilation), work in free trade zones, devaluation, traffic in women, dowry murders ... [68]

The phenomena of anorexia and bulimia in the developed world and female circumcision in Africa are both seen, by MATCH staff member Annette Pypops, as examples of women's having "internalized their subordination to the point of doing violence to themselves in order to be accepted."[69] These official MATCH accounts did not analyse the possible imperialist and colonializing effects of involvement by women from the so-called developed world in struggles against "traditional customs" considered violent to women in the so-called developing world. The analysis of violence against women had not yet expanded from a focus on patriarchy to one which includes racism and imperialism.[70]

In 1990, MATCH began an agonizing reappraisal of its "internal structure and the ways in which we replicate exploitative global structures." MATCH's "predominantly white, middle-class character became suddenly and quite shockingly obvious" as one of the ways in which "the racism that exists in Canadian society [had] been reflected in [MATCH's] own organization."[71] The organization's stated purpose shifted from promoting "equality, cooperation, communication and solidarity among women throughout the world"[72] to promoting "the eradication of all forms of injustice, particularly the exploitation and marginalization of women."[73] By 1992, articles in *MATCH News* were reflecting the growing awareness of the crucial importance of global economic and financial structures to the oppression of women in the Third World and of the complicity in that oppression of the political economies of developed countries like Canada. The Fall 1992 issue of *MATCH News* carried a lead article by Ana Isla, a Latin American economist living in Canada, on the devastating effects the foreign debt crisis has had on the poor of Latin America: "It is the latest and most severe reminder of the unequal terms of trade imposed by the International Monetary Fund, the World Bank and the General Agreement on Tariffs and Trade (GATT)," that is, of the dominance of the North over the South.[74]

Women's Rights Are Human Rights

In the early 1990s, MATCH joined other Canadian NGOs and NGOs from around the world in an effort, spearheaded by Charlotte Bunch and her USA-based Centre for Women's Global Leadership, to have women's rights included on the agenda of the UN World Conference on Human Rights slated for June 1993 in Vienna, Austria. During the first part of the campaign, a petition was drawn up asking the World Conference to incorporate women's rights into all its deliberations: first, by considering women in relation to all the other topics, and, second, by addressing the question of violence against women. The petition was circulated in over 120 countries and garnered over 250,000 signatures.[75]

During the second part of the campaign, an NGO parallel conference, the Global Tribunal on Violations of Women's Human Rights, was held on June 15, 1993, the second day of the World Conference. Organized by women's groups from around the world, including Canada's MATCH and National YWCA, the Global Tribunal sought to illustrate through real-life cases and testimonies how human rights mechanisms and laws, such as the Universal Declaration of Human Rights, fail to protect and promote women's human rights. The Global Tribunal took quite literally Article 10 of the Universal Declaration of Human Rights, which guarantees the right in full equality to a fair and public hearing by an independent and impartial tribunal. Organizers broadened the definition of violations of women's human rights, beyond the violent abuse of women in the family, to include four additional areas: the violation of women's right to political participation; the violation of the social and economic rights of women; crimes against women in times of conflict and war; and the violation of women's bodily integrity. Women from around the world who had suffered violations in one of the five areas testified at the Tribunal.[76] In the "Vienna Declaration and Programme of Action," a text agreed to by nearly 150 governments representing a wide range of social, cultural, and political systems and adopted by the UN World Conference on June 25, 1993, women's rights are dispersed throughout. In addition, paragraph 18 contains a gender-specific description of the rights of women and the girl-child, a statement that they form an inalienable, integral and indivisible part of universal human rights, and a call to all "governments, institutions, intergovernmental and non-governmental organizations to intensify their efforts for the protection and promotion of the human rights of women and the girl-child." Having women's rights recognized as human rights was the international lobbying and organizational success story of the June 1993 UN World Conference on Human Rights.[77]

Women, Development, and the Environment

In 1990, when MATCH was beginning to examine its own internal racism and to address Canada's complicity in imperialism, WEED (Women, Environment, Education, Development), a Canadian foundation based in Toronto that focuses on issues of women and the environment, was in the process of globalizing its perspective. In that year, WEED board members, staff, and volunteers began "working with grassroots groups in Canada and in countries of the South to heighten awareness" of the links between environmental and development policies and practices on the one hand and women's health and well-being on the other. WEED mounted the effective "Stop the Whitewash Campaign" to educate the public on the detrimental health and environmental effects of chlorine in general and, in particular, as found in women's sanitary products and in so-called disposable diapers.[78] A spur to WEED's endeavours was the calling of the "Earth Summit," the United Nations Conference on Environment and Development, held in Rio de Janeiro in June 1992. In preparation for the Rio conference, the World Women's Congress for a Healthy Planet was held in Miami in November 1991. Approximately 1,500 women from 83 countries, including Canada, attended and put together a statement of their principles in *Women's Action Agenda 21*. Also in preparation for the "Earth Summit," WEED brought together a group of Southern and Northern women from seven countries to draw the connections between the North/South power imbalance and poverty, population policies, and environmental degradation. The results of this collaboration were published as the book *Power, Population and the Environment: Women Speak*, which was ready for distribution at the "Earth Summit" in Rio. Excerpts from key contributions to the volume were reprinted in a 1993 special issue of *Women & Environments*. A number of contributors forcefully disputed the identification of population growth in the Third World "as a primary cause of environmental destruction."[79] This false causal analysis has led, other contributors pointed out, to the implementation of coercive population control policies, such as widespread sterilization of women in Brazil, which are in violation of women's basic human rights.[80] The real threat to the environment, contributors agreed, is posed by the North's wasteful lifestyles and patterns of consumption and its environmentally unsound practices of resource extraction and industrial production. Joining their voices to Ana Isla's indictment of the debt crisis, Mira and Vandana Shiva blame environmental devastation in the South on the "structural adjustment" programs forced on the debt-ridden Southern countries by the monetary and resource plundering policies of the North.[81]

Women have long been aware of the dangers nuclear power and nuclear war pose to human survival. In 1981, women protested in Vancouver as part of the International Day of Anti-Nuclear Protest demanding that B.C. be a nuclear-free zone.

Women and Peace and Anti-Militarism

Some would date the onset of the second wave of feminism, not with the appointment in 1967 of the Royal Commission on the Status of Women in Canada but with the founding of the Voice of Women (VOW) in 1960,[82] one of the national women's organizations whose members were active in calling for a Royal Commission.[83] The women who flocked to the Voice of Women (its membership swelled from less than one hundred in September 1960 to 2,000 across Canada five months later and to 5,000 by the fall of 1961) came with a global perspective. Many of the grassroots women who joined did so from a sense of frustration and powerlessness as stay-at-home moms. They dared to leave their kitchens, sometimes in defiance of the objections of husbands, because they felt they had as much of a right as the government decision-makers to voice an opinion on issues of concern to all human beings.[84] The paramount global issues for them were the threat of annihilation from nuclear war and from the proliferation of nuclear arms and the hazards to health of nuclear arms testing. But from the beginning "VOW was not simply a Ban the Bomb group";[85] it was also proto-feminist, anti-imperialist and anti-racist. In fact, its global concern for social justice distanced VOW members from the young, white women's liberationists on university campuses in the late 1960s who were, from the point of view of VOW, too narrowly "occupied in discovering themselves and the facts of their oppression."[86]

VOW made connections between war and the oppression of women, recognizing "that a peaceful world would not be achieved in a society where women were oppressed and ignored" (hence its support for the Royal Commission and for the removal of birth control and abortion from the Criminal Code).[87] Indeed VOW was premised on the belief, and operated on the assumption, that women's historic distance from official power and women's common involvement in child rearing gave women a particular outlook on issues of war and peace. As Kay Macpherson, past president of both NAC and the Voice of Women, explained in an interview in 1985:

> Many women are involved in peace organizations and do a lot of work within them, but it's important for women to have a separate voice for peace, to make the connections between inequality, violence and militarization.[88]

In its first decade, VOW opposed the placement of Bomarc missiles on Canadian soil, joined women from other NATO countries to protest NATO's proposed Multi-Lateral Nuclear Force (MLF),[89] condemned the war in Vietnam and Canada's role in it, and denounced the international sale of arms and Canadians' profit from it. VOW Nova Scotia raised as a basic human rights issue the discrimination against Canadian Blacks practised by employers in the province;[90] Quebec VOW spoke out against the James Bay Project's violation of Native rights; prairie VOWs focused attention on the pollution of Native resources from uranium mining; and British Columbia VOWs alerted the public to the radiation hazards of nuclear power plants on the coast and of nuclear arms testing in the Pacific.[91] Many of these concerns persisted into the 1970s, '80s and '90s.[92] For its 1963 campaign to end the atmospheric testing of nuclear weaponry, VOW organized a nation-wide gathering of baby teeth. Each tooth collected was sent to the University of Toronto Faculty of Dentistry for their survey of teeth to determine the amount of radioactive strontium-90 from nuclear fallout travelling through the food chain and deposited in young human bodies.[93] These and similar efforts by Women Strike for Peace in the United States deserve a large measure of credit for the partial[94] Test Ban Treaty of 1963.

VOW members have made use of a great variety of modes of operation. They have prepared and distributed booklets, briefs, and fact sheets. They have arranged letter-writing campaigns and held film and slide shows. They have organized conferences at local, national, and international levels, such as "Women's Alternatives for Negotiating Peace," their third international conference which brought 350 women from thirty-three countries together in Halifax in early June 1985.[95] They have sent delegations to interview prime ministers, cabinet ministers, premiers, mayors, members of Parliament and provincial legislatures, and even heads of state of other countries.[96]

The patient strength and perseverence of VOW women have been impressive. They are in "for the long haul," as one younger admirer of her VOW "elders" put it.[97] These women have also brought a range of strong views to VOW's agenda of anti-militarism and peace activism. In the view of Dr. Ursula Franklin, University of Toronto professor of engineering and adherent to a philosophy of compromise and non-violence,

> militarism [is] a symptom of a much larger form of social organization [that] to me signifies the threat system. Militarism, when you forget about the hardware, is a way of saying, "Do what I say, or else." And to me the essence of feminism and women's experience is that it integrates diversity, enhances cooperation and respects difference.[98]

Halifax activist Muriel Duckworth, VOW national president from 1967 to 1971,[99] takes a phrase from the poet Adrienne Rich to express her conviction that it will be "the people with no extraordinary power who will reconstitute the world, if it is going to be saved."[100] Solanges Vincent, long-time La Voix des Femmes member in Montreal, has used her powers of political and economic analysis to expose "the human costs of the war economy,"[101] and in particular the "impacts of growing militarization on women in the Third World."[102]

Long before ecology became politically popular, VOW members were inveighing against the nuclear industry for creating damage to the environment and hazards to human health. Taking part in such protest could itself prove dangerous, as the following case demonstrates. Starting in 1975, multinational energy corporations, like Gulf, Shell, Esso, Noranda, and Union Carbide, began moving into Nova Scotia to explore for uranium. One "hot" find was just eighteen miles from the rural home in the Annapolis Valley of Dr. Donna Smyth, an Acadia University professor, writer, anti-nuclear activist and VOW member. Together with other concerned citizens, she helped found the community-based organization Citizen Action to Protect the Environment (CAPE). Its goal was to pressure "the provincial government to follow BC's lead and declare a moratorium on uranium exploration and mining."[103] In January 1982, a Dr. Leo Yaffe, McGill University professor and president of the Chemical Institute of Canada, toured the Maritime Provinces, lecturing on the topic "The Health Hazards of Not Going Nuclear." In February 1982, Smyth published an op-ed (an article on the opposite editorial page) in the Halifax *Chronicle-Herald* that challenged the scientific objectivity of Dr. Yaffe.[104] Smyth received letters from Yaffe and his lawyers in March and April 1982, threatening a libel action. But not until January 1983, "two weeks before the statute of limitations would have expired," was the libel suit against Smyth launched. A Nuclear Critics Defence Committee was formed in March 1983 to provide Smyth and other nuclear critics with moral and financial support against "harassment or intimidation for their views."[105] Finally, in mid-January 1985, a jury trial before the Nova Scotia Supreme Court acquitted Smyth. But the acquittal came at great expense — to Smyth herself and to the Nova Scotia environmental movement; for during the three-year period from March 1982 to mid-January 1985, although Smyth's informed and articulate opposition to the nuclear industry was not silenced, others were effectively intimidated and her energies as well as those of her friends and supporters were diverted from work for peace and environmentalism to legal defence.[106]

Another VOW member, Dr. Rosalie Bertell, has won international recognition for her crusade against the hazards to health and environment of low-level radiation.[107] Biometrician and Roman Catholic nun, co-founder of and director of research for the Toronto-based International Institute of Concern for Public Health (IICPH), and author of *No Immediate Danger? Prognosis for a Radioactive Earth*,[108] Dr. Bertell won the highly regarded Right Livelihood Award in 1986, the "alternative Nobel Prize,"[109] presented in the Swedish Parliament for her work in promoting environmental health. As her official biographical sketch states, Dr. Bertell "works by preference on behalf of indigenous peoples and citizen groups most severely affected by militarism and pollution." In keeping with this preference, Dr. Bertell has carried out a birth defect study among the Navajo Indians exposed to nuclear testing and uranium mining in Nevada and "an assessment of cancer risk and probable genetic damage to offspring of Japanese nuclear workers."[110] In January 1988, she gave scientific testimony on behalf of Chinese minority workers in Malaysia bringing a case against the multinational company Asian Rare Earth (35 per cent owned by Mitsubishi) for radioactive contamination of their community.[111] She has helped develop a program of medical assistance for the Micronesian people of the Marshall Islands who have been subjected to staggering levels of radioactive contamination as a result of both the U.S. military's testing of nuclear bombs in the Bikini atoll between 1946 and 1958 and the U.S. military's continued use of other atolls in the archipelago for nuclear missile testing.[112] And Dr. Bertell has been one of the most intrepid reporters of the catastrophic dimensions of the Chernobyl disaster.[113] If the nuclear industry had a hit list, Dr. Bertell and the International Institute of Concern for Public Health would be on it. According to a leaked Atomic Energy of Cnada Ltd. (AECL) document dated 12 January 1988, "[t]he IICPH is a threat to AECL because Dr. Bertell's work 'receives media prominence, reinforcing negatives associated with the nuclear industry.'" While the AECL had a record of attacking Dr. Bertell's scientific credibility in public, the secret document acknowledged her to be "a world-renowned researcher in the field of leukemia and other cancer risks caused by

In the winter of 1983/84, these women placed this message on the Saskatchewan border of the Cold Lake Air Weapons Range to protest the testing of Cruise missiles over Northern Saskatchewan.

nuclear power plants."[114] The document also conceded that the International Institute of Concern for Public Health would be very difficult to infiltrate.[115]

The actions that women have taken, and the groups they have formed,[116] to protest militarization and environmental pollution have been many and imaginative. The decision of women to encamp outside Greenham Common U.S. Air Force Base in England in September 1982 created in its train a chain of women's peace camps throughout much of the developed world. Within a few years, there were women's peace camps located in the United States, Italy, the Netherlands, Scotland, West Germany, Australia, and Canada. Canadian women visited Greenham Common; Canadian women participated in the Seneca Women's Peace Encampment for a Future of Peace and Justice in upstate New York; and Canadian women built their own camps, such as the Women's Peace Camp at Cole Bay, Saskatchewan. The women who set up camp at Cole Bay in August 1983 wanted to remind the world that the testing of Cruise missiles and the leakage of radioactive waters from uranium mines posed a serious danger to the Native inhabitants of "uninhabited" Northern Saskatchewan.[117] The not merely non-hierarchical but often totally structureless organization of the women's peace camps, the webs of brightly coloured yarn the women wove, their casual, mismatched clothing, their hand-to-mouth, improvised means of existence — all this "vibrant ... creative anarchism"[118] — represented a stark symbolic contrast to the "massive impersonal [and] mechanical images of military power"

The Grannies performing at an International Women's Day rally in Vancouver, 1992.

opposite to which they camped. As the historian Dorothy Thompson noted about the peace camp at Greenham Common,

> these women are an international source of inspiration. They represent hope in the face of a mad abstraction which seeks to protect life by obliteration. Greenham is theatre. It is the poetic symbolism of resistance. As such it is art; and art has impact where an appeal to the isolated intellect fails.[119]

Street theatre and performance have been effectively used by women's peace groups, none more so than the Raging Grannies. Formed by a group of Victoria-based women aged forty-eight to seventy-one, the Grannies "were sick of protests that don't work, so we decided to poke fun."[120] The women deck themselves out in flower print outfits, sunbonnets and "grannie" glasses, brandish goofy props, and sing corny songs like:

> Oh we're just a gaggle of grannies
> Urging you off your fannies
> We're telling you boys
> We're sick of your toys
> We want no more Cruise.[121]

For their first "official" appearance in February 1987 at an anti-uranium rally before the Legislature Buildings in Victoria, B.C., the Grannies introduced into the flurry of position papers "their own 'briefs' — a clothesline of men and women's undies."[122] Through their street performances, for the entertainment of people lined up before the cinemas on cheap movie night, for instance, the Grannies have acquired a reputation for trying "to reach people who wouldn't go to a traditional protest."[123] Inspired themselves by such peace and anti-nuclear advocates as novelist Margaret Laurence, who devoted the last years of her life to saving the planet, the Grannies have in turn inspired others. Granny groups have sprung up on a number of the Gulf Islands, on the Sunshine Coast, in Vancouver, and as far away as Edmonton, Toronto, and Montreal.

Women have also organized, and participated in, a range of non-violent, civil disobedience actions.[124] A group of Ontario women formed Women's Action for Peace after a Women and Militarism conference at Grindstone Island in 1982. One of its first initiatives was to organize a women's contingent for the big October 30, 1982, Refuse the Cruise demonstration in Ottawa.[125] In November 1983, Women's Action for Peace called upon women to observe Remembrance Day as a day on which to remember not the veterans and the fallen of past wars but "the victims of countless years of patriarchy" and to resist a system that

- In the name of peace builds weapons of mass destruction.
- In the name of freedom denies women, minorities and peoples of the third world their right to self-determination.
- In the name of progress poisons and rapes our Mother Earth.[126]

Members of Women's Action for Peace themselves planned a demonstration leading up to a political act of non-violent civil disobedience at Litton Systems, the producers of the guidance systems for the Cruise missile. On November 14, two hundred women from Guelph, Montreal, Ottawa, Toronto, and upstate New York marched to the gates of Litton's management building in Rexdale, Ontario, some splattered with their own blood, and sang, danced, recited poetry and read out the indictment of the Litton executives. The protest culminated in the attempt, by twenty-nine women who broke through the police cordon and scaled the fence, to make a citizen's arrest of Litton's corporate officers for violating the Criminal Code of Canada. Instead, the twenty-nine themselves were arrested by the police, "charged under the Ontario Provincial Trespass to Property Act and faced a maximum penalty of $1000 fine and two-year probation."[127] At their trial in late February–early March 1984, the defendants elected to have a collective defence counsel. They were provided with a unique forum for their views when, unaccountably, they were instructed to "restrict [!] their testimony to the motivation and beliefs which led them to participate in the action at Litton."[128] In the end the judge gave all but three of the women suspended sentences[129] and placed all on six months' probation. One defendant, Ruth McMurchy, responded to the verdict:

Members of Women's Action for Peace tie ribbons on the fence of Litton Systems in Rexdale, Ontario, at the non-violent civil disobedience action in November 1983. The ribbons symbolize the hope and beauty of life as compared to the death and destruction of the Cruise missile.

The value of the action stands alone no matter what the judgement. It's always an educational experience for the person who goes through it, for the people around them, for the reporters and the people in the courtroom who are exposed to what we are doing and why we are doing it. But even if all that didn't happen, it would be important for me to keep doing it.[130]

For Innu women, however, acts of civil disobedience have been less an educational experience than a matter of life and death. Until the Second World War, the Innu were spared the genocide which had earlier decimated the cultures and peoples of other First Nations on the North American continent. After the war, the Innu land of Nitassinan on the northern Quebec/Labrador peninsula was wanted principally for its natural resources, particularly as a source of hydroelectric power. Then, starting in 1979, the military resumed a keen interest, inviting NATO to conduct low-level jet training flights out of Canadian Forces Base (CFB) Goose Bay.[131] These flights, which in a split second produce a "roaring, tearing howl [that] builds from nowhere to a hellish pitch,"[132] take place at heights of only 30 metres and at speeds of over 1,200 kilometres per hour.[133] During the practice bombing runs of fighter jets, 500-kilo cement blocks have been dropped. Currently, there are upwards of 7,500 of these high-speed, low-level test flights a season (April to October), many of them directly over Innu camps. Despite the end of the Cold War, the Canadian military and its NATO allies have continued to negotiate escalating the training flights out of CFB Goose Bay up to 40,000 yearly. For more than thirty years, the Innu protest of the ever-increasing state and military incursion into their land went unheard.

Starting in the late 1980s, the Innu turned in desperation to acts, from the Canadian state's point of view, of civil disobedience. In September 1988 several Innu set up a protest camp on one of the testing ranges south of Goose Bay. Soon after Innu began to sit or lie down on the runway of the base at Goose Bay, seeking with their bodies to block the takeoff of military jets. From the Innu point of view, there is no crime involved, as no treaty exists giving the Canadian state a right to Nitass-inan. Indeed, in the first trial of protesters, an Innu judge found them not guilty as "they held an honestbelief that the land on which the base is located belongs to the Innu and therefore they committed no wrong."[134] Since then, there have been many convictions on the charge of illegal trepass or public mischief and many jail sentences. Innu women, mothers and grandmothers, have been at the forefront of these protest actions. And, wrenched away from their children and grandchildren, they have spent months incarcerated in Canadian prisons. In December 1989, Marthy Hurley, who had been in the Stephenville Penitentiary of Newfoundland since the beginning of September of that year, sent out the following message:

> We will continue our struggle as long as we are not assured that our children and grandchildren will ever have to hear again those monsters in the sky. Although the road of our struggle is not easy, we will continue to fight.[135]

When Rose Gregoire, Elizabeth Penashue, and Kathleen Nuna traveled out from Nitassinan to attend NAC's Annual General Meeting in Ottawa in 1989,[136] they explained that their fight for their people "is not a women's issue but an Innu issue and we have welcomed any Innu person who will fight alongside us to create a free and healthy world for our children and grandchildren."[137] These Innu women are struggling for the survival of their identity as a distinct hunting people in their own land. It was not hyperbole when Michele Landsberg, in a recent column, called the Canadian state's treatment of the Innu "our version of ethnic cleansing."[138]

The novelist and poet Lee Maracle has spoken and written powerfully about peace from the perspective of a Native person. She reminds her audience that Métis and First Nations peoples have intimate knowledge, from the present as well as from the past, of the exercise of organized violence against them. She speaks of the absence of peace in a Canada where golfers want to trample on the graves of Mohawk grandmothers in Oka and where corporate logging companies wind up their chainsaws to clear-cut the mountainsides of B.C. And drawing on the belief in the sacredness of creation inherent in the value systems of Native peoples, Maracle calls herself "a caretaker." She believes that the struggle for peace is not just a struggle against violence but also a struggle for protection of the environment and for personal freedom from the internalization of "someone else's perception of you."[139]

nd Pacifism

ve been in sympathy with the women's peace and
vities outlined above. There has no more been an
nsus on the issue of women and peace than there has
er issue. As the American politial scientist Berenice
ed, women = peace is a false equation, as is also femi-
.[140] Clearly women have not always been a force for
all feminisms been pacifist. History is rife with exam-
cting, if not as warriors, certainly as military enthusiasts,
he sidelines as the men in uniform march off to battle,
en not in uniform as cowards. But like the maternalism
inism's first wave, so there developed a strain in second-
wave white feminism, sometimes called "cultural" feminism, that has located a predilection for peace in women's reproductive capacity, or at least in women's mothering practices.[141] Traces of this tendency to contrast women as producers of life with men as destroyers of life (the "boys with the toys") are to be found in some of the slogans and pronouncements of Canadian women's peace and anti-militarist activism. A danger inherent in celebrating women's specificity as life giving and hence life preserving is to cast men as irredeemably violent, aggressive, and murderous.

The radical feminist authors of the 1984 *Broadside* article "Pure but Powerless: The Women's Peace Movement" singled out precisely this danger as one of the reasons why feminism should dissociate itself from pacifism: appealing to women's special peaceloving qualities only served to reinforce the gender differences feminism was supposed to eradicate.[142] Trapped in a third false equation identified by Berenice Carroll, namely that pacifism = passivity and purity,[143] the authors are most exercised by the fear that the women's peace movement will perpetuate the disempowering stereotype of women as pure and passive. Jo Vellacott sought to lay this false association to rest when she wrote that peacemaking is not a task for "a well-behaved woman, wholly passive, passively holy." Instead, those who stand up for peace often have to be troublemakers

> on whom it is laid to rock the boat, challenge the system — perhaps accepting in return unpopularity, false witness and various kinds of danger or unpleasantness.[144]

While Native women were largely absent from this debate, developing their own views on peace and environmentalism, Maracle, in agreement with Vellacott, has declared: "I don't confuse peace with passsive."[145] Later developments in Canadian feminism, however, would bear out the radical feminists' criticism of those white feminist peace advocates who laid claim both to the moral high ground and to a status as victims of oppression that gave them "a special affinity with other oppressed people."[146] As we saw in Volume I and as the authors of "Pure but Powerless" suggest in their 1984 article, a white, Western women's peace movement, which combines a victim mentality with the claim that women as mothers are nurturing and benevolent, escapes its responsibility for, and complicity in, Western racism and imperialism.

But by denying any connection between feminism and pacifism or anti-militarism, the three "Pure but Powerless" authors belittled the feminist analyses of the connections between patriarchal structures and war making, patriarchal constructions of masculinity/femininity and militarism. As Beth McAuley pointed out in one of the many letters to the editor that poured into *Broadside* in response to the "Pure but Powerless" article, the authors also overlooked the fact that there were and are many women in the peace movement "who do not base our anti-militarist position on motherhood."[147] They thus failed to see that feminists could argue, as Virginia Woolf did in *Three Guineas* (one of the reclaimed classics of white feminism), both patriarchy's intimate affiliation with belligerence and military systems *and* women's complicity in war and militarism.[148]

It has been up to feminist theorists and activists to uncover the gendered organization that patriarchal ideologies and structures give to militaries and wars, for until feminist analyses, the literature on war and peace ignored this important dimension of inter- and intranational conflict. Some feminist anti-militarist analyses have erred on the side of overemphasizing or single-mindedly focusing on patriarchy to the exclusion of capitalism, racism, imperialism, and colonialism.[149] Some have made men appear to be the major culprits.[150] But the best have insisted on the intertwining of patriarchal systems of male domination and female subordination with systems of class, race, imperial and colonial domination and subordination.[151]

Pacifists and anti-militarists have been appalled by the ferocity and brutality of the inter-ethnic, nationalist conflicts raging between and among the peoples of former Yugoslavia. But few observers except feminists have considered the gender dimension. An exception is the writer/commentator Michael Ignatief who was struck by his observation that a masculinity construed as domineering and intimidating lures male youths on all sides of the conflict into swaggering, automatic rifle-toting, murderous roles.[152] But it has been feminists who have raised the issue of rape as a vicious weapon of war. Despite the common occurrence of rape during war, "it has traditionally been underplayed or glossed over."[153] Many have shrugged it off "as a part of the spoils of war," an unfortunate but unavoidable "byproduct of conflict." Feminists have laboured long and hard to discredit the notion that rape "is the expression of pent-up sexual desire and thus is apolitical in nature, a 'private crime'." Such attitudes misrepresent rape, keeping it from being seen for what it is, "a brutal show of power and aggression" against women.[154] Furthermore, in wars involving patriarchical, nationalist/racist societies in which women figure symbolically as the property of men and the carriers of the race, the rape and torture of women function as a way for the victorious men to assert their racial superiority and to further humiliate and show contempt for the men they have vanquished.

For the first time in the history of war coverage, the rape of Croatian, Muslim, and Serb women in the war ravaging Bosnia-Herzegovina has been both widely reported *and* condemned. Indeed efforts are being made to have rape formally recognized as a war crime. According to the executive director of the U.S. Helsinki Watch Committee,

> This unprecedented attention to rape may also reflect a change in the public perception of rape, thanks to an international women's movement that has mobilized around the issue.[155]

Canadian women have been active in this international women's movement. A first step has been to get the information out. According to information gathered by Heather Menzies and Ivana Filice of the Women's Health Project in Ottawa, estimates of the number of women and girls raped have reached as high as 60,000. While reports have indicated that "all religious and ethnic groups are guilty of rape," they also "recognize that most of the rapes have been perpetrated by Serbian forces against Muslim women and girls."[156] Observers have identified three patterns of rape.[157] First, rapes are intrinsic to the "ethnic cleansing" strategy of terrorizing people in a particular town or village into fleeing their homes. Second, rapes, including gang rapes, are committed in detention camps. Third, "rape camps" are set up in which women are kept and subjected to multiple rapes over extended periods. Countless women have become pregnant from these rapes, maybe as many as 12,000. It is also "feared that many of the women are dead, either killed due to the violence of the rape or murdered."[158]

A second form of action is to bear witness to the horror "individually, and collectively to refuse the complicity associated with doing nothing at all."[159] Women in various cities in Europe, the U.S.A., and Canada have been holding vigils in solidarity with the women of Bosnia, a practice initiated by the Serbian "Women in Black" with vigils in Belgrade. Nova Scotia Voice of Women organized ongoing, weekly vigils in the late winter and early spring of 1993 every Wednesday at noon outside the Halifax Public Library.[160] They were joined by members of the local Muslim community and refugees from former Yugoslavia. Women associated with the Women's Health Project held a vigil in Ottawa on March 7, 1994.

A third form of action is to offer direct support and assistance to the women survivors of the war-inflicted pain and suffering. On Valentine's

Day 1993, the Women's Multifaith Coalition in Toronto brought together women from the Bosnian Muslim, Serb, and Croatian communities to talk about the rape and killing of women in their homeland. Shortly thereafter, at a conference on "Jewish Women's Voices: Past and Present,"[161] Dorothy Goldin Rosenberg and Anne Adelson led a workshop on the question "As Jews, Can We Remain Silent?"[162] A resulting group of Jewish women joined with the Women's Multifaith Coalition in seeking something concrete to do. Mariam Bhaba, a Muslim member who had been to Bosnia as a representative of the Bosnian-Canadian Relief Association, reported that what was needed was counselling for the women traumatized by rape and other violent acts of the war, and humanitarian aid. The non-partisan project "Women to Women" was born. The call went out to collect items of personal hygiene for women and children in the Bosnian detention camps. The long list included:

> soap, shampoo, sanitary napkins, combs, brushes, toothpaste, toothbrushes, underwear, diapers, wet wipes, warm tights, nylon socks, water sterilization tablets, multi-vitamins, antibiotics, disinfectants, bandages, towels, face cloths, deodorant, vasoline, laundry soap, face cream, nail scissors, toilet paper.

The project received local and national news coverage and "Women to Women" projects were organized in other Canadian cities. Women felt it was a relief to be able to do something. In Toronto, Laurie Buchanan offered her apartment and a room in the basement of her apartment house as the depository for the items collected. Volunteers filled two thousand hand-sewn bags with one of every item and packed the bags in containers. Merhamet, a Muslim charitable society, the International Orthodox Christian Charities, and Caritas, a Roman Catholic charitable organization, oversaw the delivery of the containers to cities in Bosnia and, from there, distribution of the bags to women and children, Muslim, Croate, and Serb, in the detention camps.[163] And in Ottawa, the Women's Health Project is working closely with Dr. Fersada Bajramovic, founder of the Bosnia-Herzegovina Medical Relief Fund, to channel "basic medical supplies to her former homeland," and with St. Catharines-based Fatima Basic, the Bosnian representative of the Canadian Red Cross, to raise funds to open rape crisis centres and orphanages in Bosnia.[164]

Women Refugees

One of the most tragic consequences of the bloodshed and racist "ethnic cleansing" in former Yugoslavia has been to turn millions of people, most of whom are women and children, into refugees.[165] Their numbers swell the world's already rapidly growing refugee population. According to Elizabeth G. Ferris, "virtually all of the international political and economic trends seem to point to an increase in the forced migration of people in the years ahead," as a result of worsening population pressures, economic scarcity, environmental degradation, war, and persecution.[166] Although the term refugee often brings the image of a man to mind, in fact, of the "over 20 million refugees in the world today, and 20 million displaced within the borders of their own countries,"[167] a disproportionate number are women and children. According to the United Nations High Commission for Refugees (UNHCR), about 80 per cent of the uprooted people in the world are women and children, "many of whom live in women-headed households."[168]

Women in Canada and elsewhere in the world have laboured hard to have the gendered nature of the refugee experience taken into account.[169] The agonies refugee women have lived through are literally unimaginable to those with secure national identities and safe homes. As Helene Moussa has movingly shown in her study of Eritrean and Ethiopian women refugees admitted to Canada,[170] there are many stages in the complex journey toward becoming a refugee: the decision to flee one's home country; the flight from one's country of origin; detention in refugee camps in the country or countries of first asylum; application for admission to a country of resettlement; readjustment to one's adopted country and to living in exile. Beyond the anguish of separating oneself from family, friends, and one's formative culture, women are exposed to gender-specific risks of violence and sexual exploitation at almost every stage in this process. According to Susan Martin Forbes,

> During flight, refugee and displaced women and girls have been victimized by pirates, border guards, army and resistance units, male refugees, and others with whom they come in contact.[171]

Reaching a country of asylum does not necessarily guarantee an end to risk of violence. Over-crowded refugee camps frequently offer inadequate protection and women and girls detained in them are vulnerable to rape from within and to rape, armed attack, and abduction from without. Even in countries in which refugees are allowed to live outside camps, the absence of proper documentation brings with it the anxiety of existing in a state of "statelessness" and exposes refugee and displaced women to sexual harassment and abuse from unscrupulous officials, employers, and landlords, among others.

Without admission to a country offering the possibility of starting life anew, women and children can be left to languish indefinitely in the often prison-like conditions of the detention centres. To be able to move on, one has to gain refugee status, in the eyes of the UNHCR and often additionally in the eyes of the potential host country. Almost insurmountable obstacles stand in the way of women who are trying to obtain refugee status. First, although the United Nations Convention Regarding the Status of Refugees recognizes as grounds for granting a person refugee status a well-founded fear of being persecuted for reasons of race, religion, nationality, political opinion, or membership of a particular social group, it does not recognize "a well-founded fear of gender-related persecution." But even when their basis for a well-founded fear of persecution clearly falls into one of the recognized categories, women face special problems and find it difficult if not impossible to discuss rape or sexual torture with a stranger, particularly if the person is male.

Second, an equally insurmountable set of obstacles faces the woman who seeks to obtain recognition of her refugee status from a particular country, such as Canada, for the purposes of immigration to that country. Let us consider the example of Africa with its over five million refugees,[172] at least 80 per cent of whom are women and their dependents. Throughout the continent, there are only five Canadian visa offices with full-time staff equipped to define (a) refugee eligibility and (b) admissibility to Canada according to immigration criteria.[173] Approximately twelve other centres provide occasional refugee status determination and immigration processing, once or twice or up to a maximum of six times a year, when staff from the major visa centres make unannounced visits of undetermined duration. It is almost impossibly difficult for a single woman and even more difficult for a woman with dependent children to travel the hundreds if not thousands of miles from her refugee camp to one of the five major centres. It is equally difficult to find out where these centres are located or when the traveling staff might visit a marginally closer site.

Canadian women involved with refugee women at various levels have been active from the start in the International NGO Working Group on Refugee Women (IWGRW), established in 1986 following the "End of the UN Decade for Women" meeting in Nairobi in 1985. IWGRW convened the first International Consultation on Refugee Women in Geneva in November 1988.[174] Over the eight years of its existence, IWGRW has lobbied hard to raise the profile of refugee women and to provide them greater assistance and protection. One of its most notable achievements, as a result of its persistent advocacy of such a position within UNHCR, has been the appointment of a senior co-ordinator for refugee women.[175]

Groups of Canadian women have also worked hard to increase knowledge about the world's women refugees, to assist and protect them in the camps, and to help them with the settlement process in Canada. One of these is the Working Group on Refugee Women's Issues, Toronto, once a part of the Canadian Council for Refugees (CCR). Co-ordinator Elsa Musa, in an address to CCR Calgary in November 1993, spoke of the impediments to women refugees' admission to Canada. "Between 1986 and 1991, women comprised only 23 percent of the refugees landed."[176] The Canadian government puts persons applying from overseas for refugee status through a process that is especially disadvantageous for women. First, persons already recognized by the UNHCR as refugees must nonetheless also meet Canada's eligibility criteria for

Nurjehan Mawani, chairperson of the Immigration and Refugee Board, issued IRB Guidelines on gender persecution on International Women's Day, 1993. The guidelines, she argued, would raise awareness that sexual violations are forms of persecution.

refugee status and so have to submit to the interview process again. "For women refugees," as Musa explains,

> who have been traumatized and who may, after many years in camps, finally be starting their healing process, a second interview that makes them relive their trauma is too much to bear.[177]

Second, persons applying for refugee status from overseas must also meet Canada's immigrant admissibility criteria, which put a premium on education, skills, and employability. This requirement is in general in contradiction to the allegedly humanitarian purpose of the refugee process. But in the case of women refugees, having to meet immigration admissibility standards often erects an insuperable barrier. For, as Musa persuasively argues, the Canadian immigration system does not "take into consideration the skills, non-formal education, wisdom, [and] re-sourcefulness of refugee women in deciding whether or not a woman will establish successfully."[178]

Persons also seek admission to Canada as refugees by arriving at the Canadian border or a Canadian airport and asking for asylum.[179] In 1989 the Immigration and Refugee Board (IRB) was created to process these

"Refugee Claimants." According to Musa, "1992 saw a rise in the number of women making refugee claims [at Canada's borders] based on gender persecution."[180] Groups specializing in the problems of women refugees were gratified that the media attention accorded some of these cases prompted national women's organizations, in particular the National Action Committee on the Status of Women (NAC), to move the issue of women refugees to a higher place on the agenda.[181] Prompted by NAC executive members such as Hari Dimitrakopoulou-Ashton during Judy Rebick's presidency, NAC joined its considerable voice with the lobbying efforts of such groups as the Working Group on Refugee Women's Issues, Toronto, to have gender persecution recognized as a category for refugee determination. Their efforts have met with a large measure of success. On International Women's Day, 1993, Nurjehan Mawani, the chairperson of the Immigration and Refugee Board, officially issued the IRB Guidelines on "Women Refugee Claimants Fearing Gender-Related Persecution."[182]

As Chairperson Mawani has explained, the Gender Guidelines do not change the UN Convention definition by creating a new ground for determining refugee status. Instead, working within the current Convention definition, the Guidelines seek to make interpretation of the existing grounds more flexible. In Mawani's words, the Guidelines "stress that, although women may fear persecution for the same reasons as men, they also may experience the persecution differently because of their gender."[183] According to Mawani, the Guidelines will cover

> Women who fear persecution because they have experienced severe discrimination owing to their gender or because they have been victims of violence by public authorities or at the hands of private citizens, from whose actions the state is unwilling or unable to adequately protect them ... [184]

She sees the "membership in a particular social group ground" as especially capable of a gender-related interpretation. For instance, the ground can be interpreted to cover the case of a woman who is perceived relationally, not in her own right, and has a political opinion imputed to her because of the political activities of a husband, or brother, or father, of which the woman herself may know little or nothing. Women who fear harsh or inhuman treatment because they have failed to conform to or have transgressed the social mores or religious laws of their country may also "be considered as a 'particular social group' within the Convention definition."[185] Indeed, Mawani sees the following all as examples of women who could seek "refugee status in Canada on the basis of their membership in a particular social group":

> A woman fleeing from an African village to avoid genital mutilation, ... ; a woman from Turkey who was sexually assaulted while

in police custody to obtain a confession; or an indigenous woman from the mountain areas of Ecuador who was abused by her husband and was unable to receive any effective protection from the law or from the police ... [186]

Mawani is justified in feeling excitement over the development in the interpretation of the UN Convention definition of refugee that the Guidelines that she issued is stimulating. Canada is the first country in the world to take such formal action with respect to gender persecution. But women active in refugee and anti-racism work in Canada are worried that the media and public opinion will "focus on women's persecution, state sanctioned or otherwise, in Muslim countries" and thus fan the growing anti-Muslim feeling in the West and divert "attention from persecution of women in many other non-Islamic countries."[187] Mawani, herself an Ismaili Muslim, agrees. At the same time, she counters the criticism that the IRB's Gender Guidelines impose Western standards on non-Western countries by claiming that they are instead "a matter of respecting internationally-accepted human rights standards."[188]

* * * *

The contributions Canadian women have made to bringing the problems women face globally to local, national, and world attention are, as we have seen, many and impressive. At the same time, this noble work is forever shadowed by the risk of further inscribing the racism and imperialism of the West on the world. Feminist movement[189] in Canada has evolved from a preoccupation with women's issues narrowly and parochially defined to a growing recognition that all issues are women's issues — repressive regimes, water scarcity, racism, debt crisis. At the same time Canadian feminists are as committed as ever to the proposition that all issues must be examined from a feminist perspective. For that reason, some Canadian feminists have been active in the struggle to have women's rights recognized as human rights. Finally, global feminist perspectives show the interconnection of the local with the global and the intertwinement of the global issues of poverty, environmental degradation, militarism, imperialism, neo-colonialism, racism, and sexism. As this book goes to press, many Canadian women look forward to Beijing in 1995 and the possibilities of examining these interconnections with women from all over the world.

NOTES

1. Lorna Marsden, "Why Now? The Mirage of Equality," *Canadian Forum*, September 1975, 12.

2. Helvi Sipila of Finland held the high office of United Nations Assistant Secretary-General for Social Development and Humanitarian Affairs at the time. Sandra Hillmer, "Prelude to IWY," *Branching Out*, November/December 1974, 26.

3. See editorial in *Branching Out*, January/February 1975. See also Terry Padgham, "International Women's Year Morning Commentary on CFYK-CBC MacKenzie Network, January 3, 1975," *Status of Women News* 1, no.5 (February 1975), 6-7, reprinted in the documents section of this chapter.

4. Open letter from Mary Hassard-Lepage of the Women's Information Centre, Toronto, for Sandy Stienecker, of the YWCA, late October 1974, reprinted in the documents section of this chapter. Women's Educational Resource Centre, OISE (hereafter WERC): file International Women's Year.

5. The advertising agency was Ronalds-Reynolds. Ibid.

6. Patricia Bell, "Several Groups Voice Concern to Ottawa over International Women's Year Planning," *The Globe and Mail*, 21 October 1974, 13.

7. Open letter from Mary Hassard-Lepage of the Women's Information Centre, Toronto, for Sandy Stienecker, of the YWCA, late October 1974, reprinted in the documents section of this chapter.

8. *1975 IWY/AIF* 2, NO. 4 (May 1975), 6.

9. *1975 IWY/AIF* 2, no. 6 (August 1975), 4.

10. Kathleen Shannon, lst application for special funding, revised 1 April 1974. Canadian Women's Movement Archives (hereafter CWMA): file "National Film Board."

11. "Nellie McClung Conference," 1975. WERC: file "International Women's Year."

12. See "What Did You Think of IWY?," *Branching Out*, November/December 1975, 8-11, reprinted in the documents section of this chapter.

13. Lorna Marsden, Editorial, *Status of Women News* 2, no. 3 (November 1975), 2.

14. Ursula Herrmann, "Social Democratic Women in Germany and the Struggle for Peace Before and During the First World War," in Ruth Roach Pierson, ed., *Women and Peace: Theoretical, Historical and Practical Perspectives* (London: Croom Helm, 1987), 92.

15. For the words to "Bread and Roses," see the documents section of Marjorie Griffin Cohen, "The Canadian Women's Movement," chap. 1 of Ruth Roach Pierson, Marjorie Griffin Cohen, Paula Bourne, and Philinda Masters, "Canadian Women's Issues," Vol. I: *Strong Voices* (Toronto: James Lorimer, 1993), 97.

16. In Nancy Adamson, Linda Briskin, and Margaret McPhail, *Feminist Organizing for Change: The Contemporary Women's Movement in Canada* (Oxford University Press, 1988), 72, the first mention made of International Women's Day celebrations in Toronto is in reference to 1978. According to Philinda Masters, women associated with Toronto's Women's Place and other feminist activists started organizing IWD celebrations in the early 1970s.

17. See the letter dated 27 January 1975 to "Friends" from Kay Macpherson, Lesley Towers, Alice Bhyat, Debra Lewis, and Gail Posen under International Women's Day Committee Sponsorship, reprinted in the documents section of this chapter.

18. Nancy Adamson and Kathy Arnup, "A Committee For All Seasons," *Broadside* 3, no. 5 (March 1982), 4.

19. "International Women's Day 1978 Demonstration/Celebration," flyer, International Women's Day Committee, 1978, reprinted in the documents section of this chapter. CWMA: file "March 8 coalition 1978 Toronto - General File."

20. Ibid.

21. The issue contained articles on French prostitutes organizing, on the new Family Code in Cuba, on Chinese women creating and operating a scrap metal factory, on Indian women fighting oppression, on media and women in Latin America, on lesbians in Rome, on Indonesian women, on the feminist movment in Switzerland, as well as excerpts from a panel discussion with three Canadian immigrant women, Himani Banarjee (East Indian), Clara Costa (Italian), and Sybil Clarke (West Indian).

22. Sue Colley, "Women Stood United/ Women Stand United/...The Wind Will Not Subside," 1981. CWMA: file "March 8th Coalition, #1."

23. Draft leaflet '83. CWMA: file "March 8 Coalition, Toronto, 1983, #2."

24. This was to conceive of gender as if it were a category separable from and not enmeshed with other social categories, such as those of race, ethnicity, class, mental and

physical strength. See Ruth Roach Pierson, "The Mainstream Women's Movement and the Politics of Difference," chap. 3 of Pierson, Cohen, Bourne, and Masters, *Canadian Women's Issues*, Vol. I: *Strong Voices*, 188.
25. Lois Lowenberger, "IWD: Lip Service to Feminism," *Broadside* 4, no. 6 (April 1993), 14, excerpted in the documents section of this chapter.
26. Ibid.
27. Ibid.
28. Letter to the Editor, International Women's Day Committee, Toronto, *Broadside* 4, no. 7 (May 1983), 2, excerpted in the documents section of this chapter.
29. Members included Head Coline Campbell, M.P., Parliamentary Secretary to the Minister Responsible for the Status of Women; Deputy Head Sylva Gelber, Director of the Women's Bureau, Canada Department of Labour; Laurette Robillard, President, Québec Council on the Status of Women; Freda Paltiel, Special Advisor, Status of Women, Department of National Health and Welfare; Ethel McLellan, Executive Co-ordinator, Women's Programs, Ontario Ministry of Labour; Gene Errington, Office of Planning Advisor to Cabinet, Government of British Columbia; Richard Burkart, Department of External Affairs; Hylda Bateman, Liaison Officer, Canadian International Development Agency; Yvette Rousseau, Vice-Chairperson, Advisory Council on the Status of Women; D.R. Whelan, Vice-Consul, Canadian Embassy in Mexico; Mary McLaughlin, Special Assistant to the Minister Responsible for the Status of Women. *1975 IWY/AIF* 2, no. 8 (October-November 1975), 2–3.
30. See "Mexico — Special Report," *1975 IWY/AIF* 2, no. 8 (October-November 1975), 3, excerpted in the documents section of this chapter.
31. Ibid.
32. Nita Barrow, "Reflections on the Women's Decade 1976–85," *Women's Education des Femmes* 4, no. 2 (Winter/Hiver 1985), 17.
33. Ibid.
34. Elaine Aurebach, "Vancouver Feminist Went to Copenhagen for UN Conference," *Kinesis*, September/October 1980, 6, excerpted in the documents section of this chapter.
35. Ibid., 7.
36. Chandra Talpade Mohanty, "Under Western Eyes: Feminist Scholarship and Colonial Discourses," in Chandra Talpade Mohanty, Ann Russo, and Lourdes Torres, eds., *Third World Women and the Politics of Feminism* (Bloomington and Indianapolis: Indiana University Press, 1991), 51–80.
37. Barrow, "Reflections on the Women's Decade 1976–1985."
38. Ibid., 19.
39. Emma Kivisild, "Nairobi Conference: A Decade of Women," *Kinesis*, September 1985, 10, reprinted in the documents section of this chapter.
40. Mutriba Din and Ravida Din, "Sisters in the Movement," *Awakening Thunder: Asian Canadian Women*, special issue of *Fireweed: A Feminist Quarterly*, Issue 30 (1990), 35–39, excerpted in the documents section of Ruth Roach Pierson, "The Mainstream Women's Movement and the Politics of Difference," chap. 3 of Pierson, Cohen, Bourne, and Masters, *Canadian Women's Issues*, Volume I: *Strong Voices,* 251–254.
41. Ibid.
42. Kivisild, "Nairobi Conference: A Decade of Women," reprinted in the documents section of this chapter.
43. Ibid., 11.
44. Ibid.
45. "CCIC, founded in 1968, is a national coalition of more than 100 Canadian non-governmental organizations working for international development overseas and development education in Canada." Janet Laidlaw's "expertise as a woman farmer derives from her experience as the owner-operator of a 400-head livestock (Angora goats) operation in Caribo, British Columbia." Bio for Janet Laidlaw, "The 'Unofficial' Conference," *Canadian Woman Studies/les cahiers de la femme* 7, nos. 1 & 2 (Spring/printemps-Sumer/été 1986), 10.
46. Janet Laidlaw, "The 'Unofficial' Conference," 9.
47. Ibid.
48. Kivisild, "Nairobi Conference: A Decade of Women," reprinted in the documents section of this chapter. For another assessment of the Decade for Women, see Gayle McGee, "Anderson-Manley Redefines Power and Development," *Kinesis*, May 1985, 8.
49. Madonna Larbi, Executive Director of MATCH International Centre, telephone conversation with author, 21 February 1994.
50. Carla Marcelis, "Matching Women's Needs and Resources," *Communiqu'ELLES* 15, no. 2 (March 1988), 21.
51. Madonna Larbi, telephone conversation with author, 22 April 1994.

52. Carla Marcelis, "MATCH Has 10th Anniversary," *Healthsharing* 9, no. 1 (Winter 1987), 9.
53. Statement of principle and purpose appearing on p. 2 of issues of *MATCH News*.
54. Ibid.
55. Carla Marcelis, "Matching Women's Needs and Resources," *Communiqu'ELLES* 15, no. 2 (March 1988), 21.
56. See the excerpt from MATCH International Centre, "Annual Report 1991–92," edited by Marlene Bogert, 5–6, reprinted in the documents section of this chapter. See also "Programmes for 1993 — 1994," *MATCH News* 17, no. 1 (Summer 1993), 5–7, also excerpted in the documents section of this chapter.
57. Beth Woroniuk, "Words of Women: Women of Words," *MATCH News* 12, no. 4 (February/March 1989), 1, 4, excerpted in the documents section of this chapter.
58. Honor Ford-Smith, "Words of Women," *MATCH News* 12, no. 4 (February/March 1989), 4.
59. "For example, in the first 15 years of their existence the Women's Press did not publish one black woman or woman of colour." Stephanie Martin, "Sister Vision: Black Women and Women of Colour Press," *MATCH News* 12, no. 4 (February/March 1989), 5.
60. Ramabai Espinet, ed., *Creation Fire: A CAFRA Anthology of Caribbean Women's Poetry* (Toronto: Sister Vision; Tunapuna, Trinidad and Tobago: CAFRA, 1990).
61. Ester Boserup, *Woman's Role in Economic Development* (New York: St. Martin's Press, 1970).
62. See, *inter alia*, Beth Woroniuk and Josée Lafrenière, "What Do You Mean — 'It Doesn't Affect Women'? Feminists Redefining Development," *MATCH News* 13, no. 2 (September/October 1989), 1, 7, reprinted in the documents section of this chapter. See also, *inter alia*, E.A. (Nora) Cebotarev, "Rural Women in Developing Societies," *Resources for Feminist Research/documentation sur la recherche féministe* 11, no. 1 (March 1982), 28–32; and Susan Prentice, "Demanding a Different Voice: Development with Women," *Women and Environments* 9, no. 2 (Spring 1987), 10–11.
63. Nandipha Ngcobo, "Violence Against Women," *MATCH News* 13, no. 4 (January/February/March 1990), 3–4.
64. MATCH International Centre, "Annual Report 1989–90," 4.
65. *Linking Women's Global Struggles to End Violence* (Ottawa: MATCH International Centre, June 1990), $15.00 Canadian, free to Third World women's groups. The kit included: "a collection of materials examining the global dimension of violence," "international statistics on violence," "women's personal accounts, profiles of groups around the world strategizing to end violence," "poetry and art: women's cultural expression," "bumper sticker: '*Real Men Don't Abuse Women*'," and "a short list of recent readings and audio-visual materials."
66. Participants included activists from Malaysia, El Salvador, Peru, Canada, Cameroon, South Africa, Jamaica and India, as well as immigrant and aboriginal women from Canada. Annette Pypops, "MATCH Links Feminist Efforts to Create World Without Violence," *MATCH News* 15, no. 1 (Summer 1991), 1.
67. Ibid.
68. Ibid.
69. Ibid., 3.
70. An exception was the 1990 article by MATCH staff member Fatima Ameen, which extended the category violence against women to include use of Depo Provera and compared the success of Canadian women's groups in preventing its use in Canada with Depo Provera's promotion as a cheap contraceptive in government-operated clinics for Black and Asian but not white women in South Africa. Fatima Ameen, "Breaking Our Bondage — Ending Violence Against Women," *MATCH News* 13, no. 4 (January/February/March 1990), 7.
71. Cynthia King and Rita Parikh, "New Programmes Propel MATCH into Global Feminism," *MATCH News* 14, no. 2 (Winter 1990), 4.
72. Statement of purpose in *MATCH News* 11, no. 2 (Fall 1987), 2.
73. Statement of purpose, *MATCH News* 14, no. 2 (Winter 1990), 2.
74. Ana Isla, "The Debt Crisis in Latin America: An Example of Unsustainable Development," *MATCH News* 16, no. 2 (Fall 1992), 1, 3–4, reprinted in the documents section of this chapter.
75. "Women's Rights as Human Rights: An International Lobbying Success Story," *Human Rights Tribune des droits humains* (Ottawa) 2, no. 1 (June 1993), 29–32.
76. "Global Tribunal on Violations of Women's Human Rights: Existing Practices Provide Inadequate Protection," *Libertas* (Newsletter of the International Centre for Human Rights and Democratic Development, Montreal) 3, no. 3 (June 1993), 2–3.

77. Jan Bauer, Appendix II of "Vienna Declaration and Programme of Action, 25 June 1993, Vienna, Austria," in "Report on United National World Conference on Human Rights," June 14–25, 1993, Vienna, Austria, Prepared for Article 19 (U.K.) and Canadian Network on International Human Rights, Ottawa, 31 October 1993, 147–164, the full text of paragraph 18 (p. 150) is reproduced in the documents section of this chapter.

78. Dorothy Goldin Rosenberg, telephone conversation with author, 30 March 1994. See Liz Armstrong and Adrienne Scott, *Whitewash: Exposing the Health and Environmental Dangers of Women's Sanitary Products and Disposable Diapers — What You Can Do About It* (Toronto: HarperCollins, 1992).

79. Mira and Vandana Shiva, "Population and Environment: An Indian Perspective," *Women & Environments* 13, nos. 3/4 (Winter/Spring 1993), 20, excerpted in the documents section of this chapter

80. Thais Corral, "Myth and Fact," *Women & Environments* 13, nos. 3/4 (Winter/Spring 1993), 24.

81. Mira and Vandana Shiva, "Population and Environment: An Indian Perspective," 21; Ana Isla, "The Debt Crisis in Latin America: An Example of Unsustainable Development," both excerpted in the documents section of this chapter.

82. For a detailed account of the first two years of the Voice of Women, see Christine M.M. Ball, "The Early Years of the Voice of Women/La voix des femmes" (Ph.D. thesis, University of Toronto, 1994).

83. Kay Macpherson and Meg Sears, "The Voice of Women: A History," in Gwen Matheson, ed., *Women in the Canadian Mosaic* (Toronto: Peter Martin Associates Limited, 1976), 81.

84. See *The Voice of Women: The First Thirty Years,* produced and directed by Margo Pineau and Cathy Reeves, 50 min., 1992.

85. Macpherson and Sears, "The Voice of Women: A History," 72.

86. Ibid., 83.

87. Ibid., 81.

88. Susan McCrae Vander Vogt, "Interview," *Women's Education des Femmes* 3, no. 4 (Summer 1985), 22.

89. "(whereby each NATO country was going to be able to press the nuclear button.)" Kay Macpherson, "Thérèse Casgrain: A Voice for Women," *Broadside* 3, no. 3 (December 1981/January 1982), 6, excerpted in the documents section of this chapter.

90. The VOW focused on the employment practices of department stores and metro libraries in the area. Muriel Duckworth remembers calling a department store in Halifax in the early 1960s to ask whether they employed Blacks and being told "yes." When she countered that she had never seen a Black person on the floor, the representative of management, explaining the store's policy of not hiring Blacks as sales people, exclaimed: "Well, you wouldn't want to buy a hat from a Black woman?" Other VOW women got similar answers from libraries, i.e., the public (assumed to be all white) wouldn't feel comfortable being served by someone Black. Muriel Duckworth, telephone conversations with author, March 8 and 10, 1994. See also, Christine M. M. Ball, "The Early Years of the Voice of Women/La voix des femmes," 361–363.

91. Macpherson and Sears, "The Voice of Women: A History," 86–87.

92. See, for example, Isabelle George (Voice of Women), "Action Alert on Uranium Mining in Saskatchewan," *Feminist Action* 3, no. 4 (May/June 1988), 8.

93. See "Voice of Women," in Beth Light and Ruth Roach Pierson eds., *No Easy Road: Women in Canada 1920s to 1960s* (Toronto: New Hogtown Press, 1990), 388–389.

94. Partial in the sense that above-ground testing was banned, but not testing under ground. The latter persists to this day.

95. For accounts of this conference, see Luanne Armstrong, "Women Negotiating for Peace," *Herizons* 3, no. 6 (September 1985), 9; and Ann Denholm Crosby, "The Urgency for True Security: Women's Alernatives for Negotiating Peace — A Report on the 1985 International Women's Peace Conference," *Canadian Woman Studies* 6, no. 3 (Summer/Fall 1985), 95–97. See the "Conference Statement" published in the "Summary Report" of the WOMEN'S ALTERNATIVES FOR NEGOTIATING PEACE Conference, 9 June 1985, reprinted in the documents section of this chapter. The resolutions were taken by the Canadian delegation to Nairobi for the End of the Decade conference. Copy in the possession of Ruth Roach Pierson.

96. See the discussion of Voice of Women in "Anti-Nuclear Resistance," *Kinesis* 7, no. 4 (April 1978), 21; and Kay Macpherson, "Thérèse Casgrain: A Voice for Women," *Broadside* 3, no. 3 (December 1981/January 1982), 6, excerpted in the documents section of this chapter.

97. Dorothy Kidd, "Our Elders' Voices Singing Out For Peace," *Kinesis*, September 1985, 26.

98. Dr. Ursula Franklin, speaking in *Speaking Our Peace,* Terri Nash and Bonnie Klein (producers), Studio D, National Film Board of Canada, 1987.

99. See "Muriel Duckworth, Peace Worker: An Interview with Christine Ball," *Canadian Woman Studies/les cahiers de la femme* 9, no. 1 (Spring 1988), 42–45.

100. Muriel Duckworth, speaking in *Speaking Our Peace.*

101. See the pamphlet by Solanges Vincent, *The Human Costs of the War Economy* (Montreal: Anlo Inc. for Westmount Initiative for Peace, 1986).

102. Solanges Vincent, "Impacts of Growing Militarization on Women in the Third World," n.d. (ca. 1985/1986), in the possession of Ruth Roach Pierson.

103. Donna E. Smyth, "Radon Daughters," *Broadside* 2, no. 10 (August 1981), 5.

104. Donna Smyth, "That Desperate Attempt to Sell Us 'Nuclear'," *The Chronicle-Herald* (Halifax, N.S.), 15 February 1982, reprinted in the documents section of this chapter.

105. Eleanor O'Donnell Maclean, "Challenging the Nuclear Experts," *Herizons* 3, no. 6 (September 1985), 34.

106. Donna Smyth, telephone conversation with author, 7 March 1994. For a semi-fictionalized account of her experiences as an anti-nuclear activist, see Donna E. Smyth, *Subversive Elements* (Toronto: Women's Press, 1986). A selection of documents from the case is reproduced at the end of the book. For an appreciative and respectful critique of the novel, see Thelma McCormack's review in *Atlantis: A Women's Studies Journal* 13, no. 1 (Fall 1987), 191–193.

107. See Marrianne van Loon, "Rosalie Bertell: Surviving Nuclear Threats," *Kinesis,* June 1986, 17, reprinted in the documents section of this chapter.

108. London: The Women's Press, 1985. *No Immediate Danger?* was also published in 1985 by The Women's Press of Toronto and by The Women's Press of Australia and New Zealand. The book has been translated into Swedish, German, and French.

109. Presented "for vision and work forming an essential contribution to making life more whole, healing our planet and uplifting humanity." Dr. Bertell, reading from her Award in a telephone conversation with Ruth Roach Pierson, 7 March 1994. Swedish millionaire Jakob von Uexkull created the foundation for The Right Livelihood Award (which is structured in the same way as the Nobel prizes, with an international research committee to screen nominees) in order to counteract the bias inherent in the Nobel prizes for scientific research. Their "high tech" requirement effectively rules out Third World recipients and the rigidity of the disciplinary categories effectively rules out mixed-discipline research.

110. "BIOGRAPHICAL SKETCH: DR. ROSALIE BERTELL," n.d. (ca. 1985), in the possession of Ruth Roach Pierson.

111. "Bertell Defends Minority Workers Exposed to Radiation," *Health 2000* (Newsletter of the International Institute of Concern for Public Health) 1, no. 1 (March 1988), 1, 3. According to a telephone conversation with Dr. Bertell on 7 March 1994, the case was eventually won in the Supreme Court of Perak.

112. Rosalie Bertell, "Early War Crimes of WWIII," *Canadian Woman Studies/les cahiers de la femme* 9, no. 1 (Spring/printemps 1988), 7. See also Brigitte Sutherland, "Rosalie Bertell: Can We Survive Our Nuclear Heritage?," *Herizons* 4, no. 4 (June 1986), 21–23, 33.

113. "Notes by Rosalie Bertell, 8 August 1989," on "Side trip to Chernobyl, 26 April 1989," and "Two meetings with All-Union Scientific Centre of Radiation Medicine, Kiev, 28 and 29 April 1989," in possession of Ruth Roach Pierson.

114. Christie McLaren, "Secret AECL Report Analyzes Opposition," *The Globe & Mail,* 20 July 1988, A5.

115. Dr. Rosalie Bertell, telephone conversation with author, 7 March 1994.

116. For instance, in the 1980s, groups of nurses in Edmonton, Vancouver, Toronto, and Ottawa organized "to promote nuclear disarmament as an important health issue for nursing." "Nurses for Social Responsibility," *Healthsharing* 7, no. 1 (Winter 1985), 6.

117. Nicole Laurendeau, "Women's Peace Camp," *Communiqu'ELLES* 10, no. 2 (March 1984), 9.

118. Andrea Doremus, "The Seneca Women's Peace Encampment: Past, Present and Future," *Communiqu'ELLES* 11, no. 2 (March 1985), 10.

119. Paraphrased in the account of the "Women and Education for Peace and Non-Violence Conference," organized by Ruth Roach Pierson and sponsored by the OISE Centre for Women's Studies in Education, September 1984, by Amanda Hale, "Evaluating the Peace Process," *Broadside* 6, no. 2 (November 1984), 6.

120. Quoted in Joni Miller, "Just a gaggle of Grannies," *Kinesis,* September 1988, 5.

121. Ibid.

122. Ibid.

123. Ibid.

124. For an account of participation in one such action by a "middle-aged woman," see Alison Acker, "Webs of Bright Wool: Women in the Peace Movement," *This Magazine* 18, no. 2 (June 1984), 11–13, excerpted in the documents section of this chapter.

125. Margaret Hancock, "Feminist Strategies and Actions for a Non-Militaristic World," New College, University of Toronto, unpublished paper, October 10, 1984, 3-4, in the possession of the author.

126. "Women! Remember and Resist, November 14, 1993," flyer distributed by Women's Action for Peace, Alliance for Non-Violent Action, and Cruise Missile Conversion Project, in the possession of Beth McAuley.

127. Janice Williamson, "A Day of Resistance — November 14, 1983," *Broadside* 5, no. 6 (April 1984), 4.

128. Among the expert witnesses called in their defence were Dr. Ursula Franklin, Sister Rosalie Bertell, and OISE sociologist Dr. Dorothy Smith. Williamson, "A Day of Resistance — November 14, 1983," 4. For an example of these testimonies, see Janice Williamson, "One Final Argument," reproduced in *Broadside* 5, no. 6 (April 1984), 5, reprinted in the documents section of this chapter.

129. These three had been arrested twice during the week of resistance to Litton.

130. Quoted in Williamson, "A Day of Resistance — November 14, 1983," 11.

131. See Marie Wadden, *Nitassinan: The Innu Struggle to Reclaim Their Homeland* (Vancouver/Toronto: Douglas & McIntyre, 1991).

132. Camille Fouillard, "Invasion of Innu Homeland: Nitassinan Under Siege," *The Womanist* 1, no. 3 (February/March 1989), 27.

133. Millions of Germans in the Federal Republic of Germany raised objections to the military jets screaming over their homes, and those jets flew at 75 metres above ground and at speeds up to only 835 kilometres per hour. Marion Mathieson, "Innu Women Imprisoned Again," *News from the National Action Committee on the Status of Women* 4, no. 2 (December 1989), 3.

134. Introductory remarks to Rose Gregorie and Elizabeth Penashue, "Innu People Stand Fast," *Kinesis*, June 1989, 7.

135. Quoted in Marion Mathieson, "Innu Women Imprisoned Again," 3.

136. See Ruth Roach Pierson, "The Mainstream Women's Movement and the Politics of Difference," chap. 3 of Pierson, Cohen, Bourne, and Masters, *Canadian Women's Issues*, Vol. I: *Strong Voices*, 201.

137. Rose Gregoire and Elizabeth Penashue, "Innu People Stand Fast," *Kinesis* (June 1989), 7, excerpted in the documents section of this chapter. They have also welcomed any and all non-Innu supporters. VOW has been very active in support of the Innu cause, especially VOW Nova Scotia.

138. Michele Landsberg, "Innu Abuse — Our Version of Ethnic Cleansing," *The Toronto Star*, 5 March 1994, K1.

139. Lee Maracle, "Peace," *The Womanist* 2, no. 2 (Fall 1990), 9–10, reprinted in the documents section of this chapter.

140. Berenice A. Carroll, "Feminism and Pacifism: Historical and Theoretical Connections," in Ruth Roach Pierson, ed., *Women and Peace: Theoretical, Historical, and Practical Perspectives* (London: Croom Helm, 1987), 2–28.

141. Sara Ruddick, "Maternal Thinking: Toward a Politics of Peace" (New York: Ballantine Books, 1989).

142. Terry Mehlman, Debbie Swanner and Midge Quandt, "Pure but Powerless: The Women's Peace Movement," *Broadside* 5, no. 9 (July 1984), 6–7, excerpted in the documents section of this chapter.

143. Carroll, "Feminism and Pacifism: Historical and Theoretical Connections."

144. Jo Vellacott, "Women, Peace & Power," in Pam McAllister, ed., *Reweaving The Web of Life: Feminism and Nonviolence* (Philadelphia, PA: New Society Publishers, 1982), 37.

145. Maracle, "Peace," 9.

146. Mehlman, Swanner and Quandt, "Pure but Powerless: The Women's Peace Movement," 6, excerpted in the documents section of this chapter.

147. Beth McAuley, Letter to the Editor, *Broadside* 5, no. 10 (August/September 1984), 2, 10, reprinted in the documents section of this chapter.

148. Virginia Woolf, *Three Guineas* (London: The Hogarth Press, 1938).

149. Betty A. Reardon, *Sexism and the War System* (New York and London: Teachers College Press, 1985).

150. See, for example, Micheline de Sève, "Feminism and Pacifism, or, the Art of Tranquilly Playing Russian Roulette," in Pierson, ed., *Women and Peace: Theoretical, Historical, and Practical Perspectives*, 44–49.

151. Cynthia Enloe, *Does Khaki Become You? The Militarisation of Women's Lives* (London: Pluto Press; Boston: South End Press, 1983).
152. He would not have been so surprised had he been familiar with Virginia Woolf's *Three Guineas*.
153. Jeri Laber, "Bosnia: Questions About Rape," *The New York Review of Books*, 25 March 1993, 4.
154. Ibid.   ◆
155. Ibid.
156. Menzies and Filice, "Genocide in Former Yugoslavia: Rape of Women and Children Continues," *The Varsity* (University of Toronto), 8 March 1994, 1. See Amina Adams, "The *Kosmar* of Bosnia-Herzegovina," *The Varsity* (University of Toronto), 8 March 1994, 7, reprinted in the documents section of this chapter.
157. For this Menzies and Filice draw on Jeri Laber, "Bosnia: Questions About Rape," 4.
158. Menzies and Filice, "Genocide in Former Yugoslavia," 1.
159. Ibid., 5.
160. Gillian Thomas, Hants County, Nova Scotia, telephone conversation with author, 29 March 1994.
160. Ibid.
161. "Jewish Women's Voices: Past and Present: A Weekend of Culture, Scholarship & Celebration," organized by a committee headed by Frieda Forman through the OISE Women's Educationalal Resource Centre and held at OISE 19–21 February 1993.
162. For the resolution passed unanimously at the plenary session of the Conference, see the documents section of this chapter.
163. Dorothy Goldin Rosenberg, telephone conversation with author, 30 March 1994.
164. Menzies and Filice, "Genocide in Former Yugoslavia," 5.
165. Because many of the people driven from their homes reside in detention camps within the borders of former Yugoslavia, the United Nations High Commission for Refugees has expanded its humanitarian services to include persons internally dislocated by this war.
166. Elizabeth G. Ferris, *Beyond Borders: Refugees; Migrants and Human Rights in the Post-Cold War Era* (Geneva: World Council of Churches Publications, 1993), xii.
167. Ann Brazeau (Senior Co-ordinator for Refugee Women at UNHCR), "Introduction" to Susan Forbes Martin, *Refugee Women* (London: Zed Books Ltd., 1991), ix.
168. Susan Forbes Martin, *Refugee Women*, 1.
169. See, for example, Lucia Ann McSpadden and Helene Moussa, "I Have a Name: The Gender Dynamics in Asylum and in Resettlement of Ethiopian and Eritrean Refugees in North America," *Journal of Refugee Studies* 6, no. 3 (1993), 203–225.
170. Helene Moussa, *Storm & Sanctuary: The Journey of Ethiopian and Eritrean Women Refugees* (Dundas, Ontario: Artemis Enterprises, 1993).
171. Martin, *Refugee Women*, 17.
172. Ferris, *Beyond Borders: Refugees, Migrants and Human Rights in the Post-Cold War Era*, 136.
173. The five Canadian visa offices in Africa are located in: 1) Cairo, Egypt; 2) Tunis, Tunesia; 3) Abijan, Ivory Coast; 4) Nairobi, Kenya; and 5) Johannesburg, South Africa.
174. In her keynote address on cultural adjustment to the one hundred and fifty (mostly) women from forty countries, Helene Moussa of Canada spoke eloquently of the refugee women's vulnerability on the one side but courage and strength to survive on the other. Kathleen Ptolemy, "First International Consultation on Refugee Women: Geneva (November 1988)," *Canadian Woman Studies/les cahiers de la femme* 10, no. 1 (Spring 1989), 21–24.
175. See "Actions of the International NGO Working Group on Refugee Women 1991–93," prepared by Elsa Tesfay Musa. Copy at the Refugee Desk, Anglican Church of Canada.
176. Elsa Tesfay Musa, "The Gender Issue and Refugees' Overseas Program" (paper presented at CCR Calgary, November 1993). See also, Elsa Tesfay Musa, "Refugee Claims Based on Gender Persecution: The Canadian Experience" (paper presented at the "Consultation on Women Refugees" meeting of the Lutheran Immigration and Refugee Service of New York, New York City, 27 July 1993), excerpted in the documents section of this chapter. Copies of both papers are at the Refugee Desk, Anglican Church of Canada.
177. Musa, "The Gender Issue and Refugees' Overseas Program."
178. Ibid.
179. For a succinct exposition of the two refugee processes as well as of the UNHCR "Women at Risk" program, see Appendix 1 of Helene Moussa, *Storm & Sanctuary*, 264–265.

180. Musa, "Refugee Claims Based On Gender Persecution: The Canadian Experience," excerpted in the documents section of this chapter.

181. See NAC resolutions on refugee women, reprinted in the documents section of this chapter.

182. "*Women Refugee Claimants Fearing Gender-Related Persecution: Guidelines Issued by the Chairperson Pursuant to Section 65(3) of the Immigration Act*" (Ottawa: Immigration and Refugee Board, 9 March 1993).

183. Nurjehan Mawani, "The Convention Definition and Gender-Related Persecution — The IRB Perspective," a presentation for the Conference "Gender Issues and Refugees: Development Implication," sponsored by The Centre for Refugee Studies/The Centre for Feminist Research, York University, held at the OISE Auditorium, 10 May 1993, reprinted in the published proceedings of the Conference, Wenona Giles, Helene Moussa, and Penny Van Esterik, eds., *Gender Issues and Refugees: Development Implications*, Vol. II, forthcoming.

184. Ibid.

185. Ibid.

186. Ibid.

187. Musa, "Refugee Claims Based on Gender Persecution: The Canadian Experience," 6, 2.

188. Mawani, "The Convention Definition and Gender-Related Persecution -The IRB Perspective."

189. bell hooks prefers the openness of the term "feminist movement" over the formulation "the feminist movement," which implies there is only one, unitary movement. bell hooks, *Talking Back: Thinking Feminist, Thinking Black* (Toronto: Between the Lines Press, 1988).

Documents: Chapter 5

International Women's Year 1975

Our Northern Voice
Yellowknife N.W.T., January 1975[1]

Good morning, as you no doubt know 1975 is International Women's Year. Just what does that mean to the individual Canadian woman? By the looks of it — not too much.

The United Nations has proclaimed IWY with great fanfare — in much the same way it sponsored Inter. Geophysical Year or Inter. Cooperation Year. It sounds like that for one year we are on a par with earthquake detection or international peacekeeping. Maybe the men in government see us as a potentially violent force like tidal waves or tribal wars that must be detected or deflected, probably with the same degree of success the UN usually achieves.

On the other hand, consider the value of an International Men's Year — just to put things in a different perspective. I suggested this to one man, who really knows where it's at and he answered "No, we are too busy running the world, but it's a good idea for women to keep busy on committees."

Well, the Government of Canada has a program for IWY cunningly designed to do just that. The government is going to send us to conferences where we can sit around and discuss with each other — not with the people in power — all the problems we already know about.

As well, Canada will sponsor an International seminar to show other countries how they can do the same thing.

Since the Royal Commission on the Status of Women presented its recommendations to parliament in 1970, only a handful of the recommendations have been followed. To cover up its lack of action the government set up an advisory Council on the Status of Women in 1973, with most of the appointed members more noteworthy for their political affiliation than their feminist dedication. In spite of a handsome budget, a paid research staff and $100/day for appointees while attending meetings, the Council has been resoundingly silent.

Now another grand gesture — the government has allotted $5 million for International Women's Year in Canada — about the cost of a well-equipped executive jet plane.

1. Terry Padgham, "International Women's Year Morning Commentary on CFYK-CBC MacKenzie Network, January 3, 1975," *Status of Women News* 1, no. 5 (February 1975), 6–7.

The first step naturally was to set up a bureaucracy of twelve people, directed by a woman whose previous experience was in postage stamps. She has been charged with organizing a series of conferences, expected to cost over $1 million. Canadian women have been violently opposed to this expenditure. In Ottawa at a planning meeting in October last year women, from across the country objected saying, "No more conferences, we don't want conferences, we want action". But, no, with all the logic of a bulldozer, they were told, it's too late to change now. The women wanted the money given to women's groups who could better spend it tackling the problems they already know about. But of course, we all know women can't really handle money, anyway.

However, the director wants to reach men and women who haven't been reached before, those she refers to as "the unwashed". So if you want to go to a conference, forget to take a bath — not too difficult in the NWT anyway, since so many homes don't have plumbing. But don't expect *that* problem to be solved at a conference.

Now just to make sure we all know about International Women's Year, half a million dollars has been given to an advertising agency in Toronto to tell us about it. This agency, of the four that bid on the contract, was the only one that has no women on its creative staff.

About $2 million was allotted to the women's programme of the Secretary of State to set up small seminars, cultural and educational programs. These projects were in jeopardy because the government fired (and has on appeal — just re-hired) the woman who had conceived the program, and had worked well with women's groups.

So all in all, a few of us will get to conferences where we can discuss the problems we already know about — lack of education and job-training, lack of childcare facilities, education and job-stereotyping, lack of political power and professional advancement, etc. We may even discover a few new ones.

With any luck some women's groups will get what funds are left over — to run on the cheap, for one year, some service that should have been provided all along anyhow. And if it's any good we'll probably need it for more than a year.

In the meantime, our world where men and women live, is faced with inflation, unemployment, food shortages, housing crises, resources depletion, wars and international strife. But nowhere in the IWY seminars are we expected to discuss these problems. After all, they aren't women's business, are they? Let's leave it to the men to find the solutions — they are so much better at it.

If IWY means anything to women, it means that if we are to achieve equal rights and responsibility in the world, where we are 51% of the population — we are going to have to get together and work together, for a lot longer than one year. We have the skill, some of the opportunities and legislation now. Slowly women, who bear and raise the children to live in this world are beginning to influence what kind of world we give our children to live in. Maybe when we are 51% of the politicians and decision makers, we will have a better chance to create a safe and happy world for all. And that's something my daughter will probably be working on, long after I'm gone.

Secretary of State and International Women's Year
Toronto, 1974[2]

DEAR SISTERS:

We're two of the 76 delegates who attended the Secretary of State International Women's Year consultation in Ottawa Oct. 19 & 20. The Secretary of State wanted to communicate the objectives of their programme and to discuss our priorities for IWY. So, we're sending out this information to give you an idea of what their programmes are and what kind of money is available for women's groups — also, to let you know about the good and bad things that happened.

First the good things. The native women's groups are hoping to sponsor a conference of the visible minorities in Canada as part of IWY and received the support for their plans from all the delegates.

The Women's Centres that were represented are trying to start a loosely-knit coalition of Women's Centres across Canada to help increase communications and to provide support for centres when needed (witness Otto Lang's interference with the Saskatoon Women's Centre grant on account of their abortion counselling & referral service). A meeting is planned for Mar. 1 & 2 in Thunder Bay, Ont. The Ottawa Women's Centre is writing the proposal to get IWY money for the meeting and the St. John's Centre is gathering information on interest in the idea. If you're interested and a Women's Centre (your definition) write to Celia Griffiths, Women's Centre, Box 6072, St. John's, Newfoundland.

Now for the bad news. Two major problems arose. First the Secretary of State: Sue Findlay, the founder and chairwoman of the Women's Programme is being replaced just in time for IWY! It was Sue who got the Secretary of State the $2.5 million for IWY. Her job was reclassified upwards, a competition for the job held, and she lost the competition. This action jeopardizes the whole IWY programme (S of S's) and calls into question the sincerity of the government's commitment to women. The job contracts of the women working for Sue will run out around the end of November. If they're replaced too, the IWY programme will be in bad shape.

The second problem is the way the IWY Secretariat plans to spend its $2.5 million (totally separate from S of S): $1 million on salaries etc., $1 million on a series of 5 conferences ($200,000 each??) and to top it off $500,000 on an ad campaign for IWY, awarded to the only ad group

2. Open letter from Mary Hassard-Lepage of the Women's Information Centre, Toronto, for Sandy Stienecker, of the YWCA, late October 1974. Women's Educational Resource Centre, OISE (hereafter WERC): file International Women's Year.

(Ronalds-Reynolds) without any women on its creative team. Their ad slogan "Why Not?" is offensive & useless. The IWY Secretarait defended giving the campaign to a male group by saying their presentation was the best — the Secretariat didn't want to take sex into consideration!!?? Who better to run an ad campaign promoting women than women? Who is it who defines a silly slogan like "Why Not?" as best?

Sample letters & the names & addresses of people to write to are included in this package on a separate sheet.

Yours in sisterhood,
Mary Hassard-Lepage
Women's Information Centre
for Sandy Stienecker, Y.W.C.A.

SAMPLE LETTER TO THE SECRETARY OF STATE:

We wish to express our regret and disapproval of the action taken by the Secretary of State to replace Suzanne Findlay, chairperson of the Women's Programme, and organizer of the International Women's Year Programme.

This action represents a serious curtailment of the success of International Women's Year inasmuch as Ms. Findlay, with the help of her staff, has put a lot of energy into the programme and has gained the respect and confidence of women across Canada. It is our hope that Ms. Findlay be allowed to continue her good work at this time. To dismiss her now would be a retrogressive act counter to fulfilling women's equal status in Canada. Furthermore, her removal indicates a lack of sincerity on the part of the government in dealing with women's issues.

We feel we deserve an explanation for this decision, and further, we hope you see a way to reverse it.

SAMPLE LETTER TO THE IWY SECRETARIAT:

We would like to voice our concern over the government's failure to respond to the expressed priorities of women and we disapprove of the allocation of funds to ineffectual programmes of the IWY Secretariat.

Specifically, we oppose the spending of $1 million on a programme of five conferences which representatives of women's groups have strongly indicated they do not want in their present form.

In addition, we strongly object to the expenditure of $500,000 on an ad campaign which we find both ineffectual and offensive. We feel that women who are definitely representative of Canadian women's groups must be involved in the planning of this campaign. An all-male creative team is unlikely to be as responsive to the interests of women as women themselves. Indeed, this seems to be the case.

The government has shown its lack of concern for what women want in failing to consult women at all levels of planning the IWY programs. It is our hope that the responsible parties will see fit to instigate some revisions in accordance with the wishes of Canadian women.

"What Did You Think of IWY?"
November/December 1975[3]

Branching Out wanted to find out how Canadian women felt about IWY. We invited readers to send us their comments; some of them are printed in this article. Sue McMaster interviewed women on the street in Ottawa, and Vivian Frankel photographed them as they responded to the question, "What did you think about IWY?"

IWY was a rather paternalistic gesture — like handing a woman $50 to go have a good time with the girls because she's been such a good wife/mother ... it would have made more sense to at least let her decide what she'd like to spend the money on.

Jean Jorgenson, Edmonton

I think it's great. I don't think IWY will accomplish much as a special year, I don't think it'll make much difference ... maybe the schools could push it a bit. But I think it's seeping in slowly — when the woman out west lost her farm when she got her divorce — the Irene Murdoch case — things like that really make women think.

Mrs. Vanderwood — Timekeeper, Spencerville, Ontario

...

The real goal of women must be to continue their efforts past IWY and not accept the year as a token gesture.

Gloria Heller, Toronto

This has been a year of participation. Countless festivals, conferences, and meetings have been attended by women on local, regional and national levels. This direct experience together with increased media coverage of women's issues has affected and expressed a permanent alteration in women's awareness. As 1967 had the cumulative effect of raising the level of our national consciousness, 1975 will be seen to have altered our identity as women. After IWY is over, its ongoing effect will continue, because every woman who has participated will remain as an agent of change in this society.

Pat Oliver, Toronto

A 'Career Explorations' course! Why not? I had no idea what I was looking for, but all the way through school I had wanted to find a career or interesting job. At first I felt like I was going through a late stage of adolescence. The one thing I learned was that I hardly knew myself. I had never tried to answer questions before like: Who am I? What are my values? What are my needs? What does security, independence or recognition mean to me? My interview lasted two minutes and I was to

3. *Branching Out*, November/December 1975, 8–11.

be given equal opportunity when being considered ... however, the classes were filled, and anyhow someone else would have been accepted because they are only accepting people who are — etc., etc. I am back where I started from, only more confused and unsettled. After all those plans it is hard to face my household routine again ... How do I feel about Women's Year? Right now very bitter and very frustrated. It all seems such a farce and I feel like a fool to have thought Why Not? I'm also mad because I let myself become so disillusioned and let my aspirations run away with me. As I told my friend, I may not do anything right now, but maybe after Christmas, when I feel that I am back to normal, I may take an upholstery course or do some volunteer work. Women's Year might not have provided me with changes, but it has made me more aware of me.

Jean Brown, Burnaby, BC

...

There was a festival in Hull with about 800 women last summer — it was very good. They spoke about work and everything, the women should work outside and be independent, because we need money now, the cost of living is so high. Women are coming to know they're women, they have something now — not only to put the baby in wool and to do housework, no — they can do something else. Like the ex-Mayor, Whitton — she's something. Not too many women like that.

Laure Renfret — Filing Clerk, Ottawa

IWY should have made a greater impact, but then the women were not given the top jobs, so they at least were not to blame for the mediocre publicity, direction and planning.

Katherine Farstad, Vancouver

...

IWY has been exhilarating, interesting, a little frustrating ... most importantly, it has confirmed for most women something we have always felt but weren't too sure we should — we are strong and very much needed in the world.

Mary Tremblay, Timmins

Looking back now, I am very grateful to the United Nations for dedicating this year to all women around the world. It is sad that more emphasis was not placed on rewriting discriminatory school texts and breaking the barriers that prevent women from working at 'men's jobs', but I'm sure that much has been accomplished.

Debbie Dittrick, Deadwood, Alberta

From what I have read and researched, it seems a lot was expected of the year, but nothing of known value materialized for Canadian women.

The $5 million seems to have been frittered away on conferences, symposiums, information mobiles — none of which are lasting and can help women of today in their struggle. I feel, as do others I have spoken to, that the money could have been more productively spent on establishing day care centres, producing non-sexist literature, funding the existing women's centres and beginning new ones. Those would seem more true to the theme of IWY than producing conferences to educate those who are already educated, or those who really do not care ... IWY did not reach me. I am a woman and a writer. Just because 1975 was labelled 'International Women's Year' it has not changed anything.

Noelle Boughton, Winnipeg

...

On a personal level, IWY had no specific effect. I feel sad that a Women's Year should be necessary and I have mixed feelings on this whole business ... we must get the message across, once and for all, that we are a serious group of this population, that we are not riding a 'bandwagon' during 1975, that most of our work began long before 1975 and will continue long after 1975.

Marian Atkinson, St. John's, Newfoundland

En général, les conférences de l'A.I.F. ont été avantageuses, puisque ici, dans les provinces de l'Atlantique les centres de femmes n'en sont qu'à leur début d'existence ... l'année aura mis la lumière sur certains points qui avaient toujours demeurés obscurs. Je pense que c'est un commencement. Il ne faut pas lâcher! Les années à venir nous permettront de réaliser des projets d'envergure, du moins nous l'espérons. Je ne crois pas que cette année soit une faillite. Des femmes ont pris conscience de leur corps, de leur vie comme individu, de leur rôle dans la société. Elles se sont aussi donné la main et cette solidarité demeurera au fond d'elles-mêmes pour toujours.

Les Fam, Moncton, New Brunswick

...

Here in Moosomin, our Mayor declared March 8th as IWY Day and ran a proclamation in the local paper, the World Spectator. The Masonic Lodge #7 picked up the idea and sponsored a tea to honour all ladies of the community. The ladies were reported receiving the royal treatment from the Masonic Lodge ... What 1976 and the future hold is up to all women, not just the 40- and-over group who are now enthusiastic, but the young women who must become more involved. They have not met the problems seen so clearly by older women and somehow they must be made aware of their positions. Only a few of them are striving very hard to change attitudes and legislation. The media and the public will drop IWY once the year is over unless we, as men and women together, unite to keep issues before the public and strive for peace, equality and development.

Jean Smith, Moosomin, Saskatchewan

L'A.I.F. ne doit pas se terminer à la fin de 1975, au contraire: les femmes doivent s'intéresser d'avantage à leurs problèmes si elles veulent atteindre leur but. De ma part je veux continuer d'en discuter dans les groupes des différentes organisations dont je fais partie puisque je me rend compte que la femme ne fait que commencer à chercher à s'épanouir, à sentir qu'elle est quelqu'un. Le monde ne changera que dans lamesure que chacune de nous fera un premier pas. Je suis d'accord avec Jacqueline Lemay du thème de son chant sur l'Année Internationale de la Femme, 'La Moitié du Monde est une Femme'.

Azade McGraw, Sheila, New Brunswick

...

I believe seeds were planted this year. Not in a well-thought-out garden patch, unfortunately, but seeds were scattered. And those seeds that fell on fertile soil, during the right season ... they will take root.

Doreen Gingras, Fort McMurray

International Women's Day

International Women's Day Committee Sponsorship
Toronto, January 1975[4]

Monday, January 27, 1975
Dear Friends:
We are a group of women who have worked on women's issues in trade unions, community groups, political organizations, and in other ways. We are writing to you as members of organizations that may have some interest in the significance of International Women's Day.

As the result of the militant action of women in industry during the early 1900s, and specifically a strike by women in the New York garment industry, March 8 was declared International Women's Day ... The United Nations declaration of 1975 as International Women's Year makes the upcoming celebration of March 8 especially important.

Fifty people attended a January 15 planning meeting, representing some 31 organizations, trade unions, etc. It was probably the widest kind of representation planning a women's event has seen in this city for some time.

Our basic format for March 8 includes morning and afternoon panel sessions followed by more specific workshops; a possible mid-day demonstration, and wind-up plenary. In the evening, we hope to schedule

---

4. Letter from Kay Macpherson, Lesley Towers, Alice Bhyat, Debra Lewis, and Gail Posen, International Women's Day Committee Sponsorship, 27 January 1975.

cultural activities — and perhaps a dance. To facilitate the greatest possible organizational contacts, we would like to see groups set up information tables between sessions.

The Canadian Congress of Women had won a tentative agreement with the previous city administration for use of city hall facilities. We are pursuing this possibility with the new council.

The program committee is organizing its work around two general themes: equality of women in the work force, and equality of women in the family or social sphere. Since the Metro Toronto Labour Council's weekend seminar is on March 8 this year, and is also on women, we plan to focus our discussion of women in the workforce around organizing the unorganized; probably discussing various sectors of the work force where women predominate, as well as some discussion on domestic labour. Equality in the family and social sphere would include topics like day care, family property law, birth control and abortion.

It is also crucial to involve as wide a segment of immigrant women as possible; at all levels of the conference — planning, programming, and of course, attendance at the event itself. To give an international perspective, there will be some discussion of women in national liberation struggles around the world.

We need the participation from many different kinds of women from all walks of life; from as many kinds of organizations and activities as we can bring together. This would provide an opportunity for women from, for example, labour groups to meet their sisters who have been active in many of the same causes and demands. We may establish ties for future work.

To this end, we invite your support and your organization's involvement. First, may we add your organizations name to our list of sponsors? Would anyone in your group be interested in working on programming, publicity etc. for the conference? Third, are your financial resources such that you could help defray costs with a small donation? And fourth, we hope that you will alert your membership to this event and encourage their participation.

Please let us know as soon as possible about possible sponsorship etc. The next general planning meeting will be on February 13, at OISE, 252 Bloor St. W. — room to be announced and posted.

International Women's Day Sponsorship Committee
Kay Macpherson
Lesley Towers
Alice Bhyat

Program committee contact:
Debra Lewis
Gail Posen

"International Women's Day 1978 Demonstration/Celebration" Toronto, 1978[5]

Since 1910, International Women's Day has commemorated through protest and celebrations the struggles of women in the workplace, in the home and in society the world over. It is a day of activity for English Canadian and Quebecois women, and an opportunity to renew our solidarity with women all over the world in their struggles against sexism, political, economic and social oppression.

In Toronto, there will be a demonstration/celebration organized by the International Women's Day Committee on Saturday, March 11th. Saturday was chosen because we felt that more working women could come on a weekend than during a work day. Similar actions are now being organized in British Columbia, Edmonton, Winnipeg and Montreal, creating the possibility for the first real cross-country International Women's Day ever. Other Toronto activities include a feminist feast, rally and parade at 4:00 pm on the afternoon of March the 8th, organized by Women Against Violence Against Women, and a concert at Convocation Hall organized by Sappho Sound in the evening. All these events are being organized simultaneously with women in every major European country, women who are building for a co-ordinated continent-wide mobilization.

Why we are organizing on International Women's Day 1978.

No matter what area of our experience we examine, the evidence points to the need for women to take action. While control of our bodies has always been an essential feminist demand, we do not yet have safe and effective birth control, and antiquated abortion laws are used to deny many women access to safe abortion. In the past few months we have become increasingly aware of another abuse of our bodies — rape and wife-battering. Though child rearing has always been considered 'women's work', our needs as mothers have been almost wholly ignored. We still have no quality childcare, the schools will not heed our demands for non-sexist education and because of the economic situation it is becoming increasingly impossible for many working women and welfare recipients even to have the children we want to have.

Indeed, the economic crisis is making all of our problems more severe. Life in the workforce is deteriorating. We are being hit extraordinarily hard by unemployment, the wage gap between men and women is widening, the Anti-Inflation Board rolls back hard won equal pay increases. Job ghettoization is still the order of the day. Of course, native, immigrant and black women suffer an even greater burden.

Our bodies, our children, our work — our rights to all three are being eroded and attacked. Many of us have been working to strengthen and

5. Flyer, International Women's Day Committee, 1978. CWMA: file "March 8 Coalition 1978 Toronto — General File."

extend these rights for many years. We are organizing around the issues which follow. They are issues basic to the women's movement, they range through all aspects of women's experience, and they have been brought into sharp relief by the economic crisis.

Issues

1 <u>Control of our Bodies</u>: We must have the right to make decisions about our reproduction. We need safe, reliable, available contraception, abortions freely available to all who need them, an end to all forced sterilizations and a guarantee that the full cost of abortions will be covered by government health services. Prostitution must be decriminalized.

2 <u>Childcare</u>: In 1975, one-third of all Canadian children under 15 had working mothers, but there were childcare spaces for only 3.2% of children under three, and 8.18% for those between 3 and 5 years. In spite of this, provincial and municipal governments are planning serious cutbacks in childcare spending, which will result in the closing of many centres. The quality of existing childcare is also being threatened by government moves to increase family home care and private profit centres. This coupled with the failure of the government to expand services in order to meet real needs, continues to ensure that women, especially those who work shifts, do not have adequate childcare. Governments must fund quality, community daycare for all those who need and want it.

3 <u>Cutbacks in Social Services and Education</u>: When social services are cut back it is women who have to pick up the burden dropped by institutions and agencies. We need an end to cutbacks in social services and an extension of these services to meet real needs. Childcare centres, old age homes and hospitals, for example, are crucial to us, but it is also important that government fund the many new and necessary services pioneered by women — from pre- and post-natal care for single mothers to crisis centres to good mental health facilities.

The value of the contribution made by women in the home must be recognized. Women have already protested and overturned the Family Allowance freeze, and we oppose any future "baby bonus" cuts. We protest the fact that welfare payments and old-age pensions are far below official poverty levels.

4 <u>Employment</u>: Forty per cent of all Canadian women over 14 work for wages. They do not work for luxuries, but because they have to support themselves and their families. Sixty per cent of single parent families are headed by women. And yet, as things get tougher, a propaganda campaign is being launched to tell us that women are taking jobs away from men, and that our demands for equal pay are contributing to the crisis. We all need the right to work and the right to a living wage. The ghettoization of women in jobs which are undervalued and underpaid must end. <u>We need equal</u> pay for work of equal value, and an end to restrictive quotas on jobs and training programs of all sorts. Because

wage controls based on percentage increases widen the absolute wage differential between men and women, wage controls must end.

5 Lesbian Rights: We must all be free to express ourselves sexually and not be harassed or discriminated against for a lesbian orientation. Lesbian women need basic legal protection in the Human Rights Code. We demand an end to harassment and forced concealment on the job, in housing and in the courts. Lesbian mothers must have the right to legal custody of children. We refuse to be penalized for our lesbianism by forced separation from our children, and by being denied the right to adopt children.

6 Native, Immigrant and Black Women: Minority women encounter many severe problems. They are almost completely unorganized, have the worst working conditions and wages, and often face the worst sexual assault on the job. It is hard for them to fight back lest they bring on heavy reprisals from employers and governments who are ready to fire and even deport at the drop of a hat. We need full native rights for native women, regardless of their marital status. Bill C-24, with its discriminatory clauses against women, must be repealed. The deportation of Jamaican women must stop. Immigrant women must have full social, trade union and political rights.

7 Violence against Women: Because of the deeply embedded anti-woman sentiment in society, violence against women pervades all areas of life. While the many faces of this violence cannot be eradicated overnight, there are important measures that can be taken to help the women who are its victims. We need government funded hostels and transition houses, such as Nellie's, as well as more rape crisis centres. We need an end to rape laws which put the woman on trial and subject her to humiliating procedures in and out of court. We strongly object to the fact that many women, especially poor women, become special victims of the system through forced confinement in psychiatric hospitals and prisons, where they are further victimized and oppressed. And finally, we demand an end to police harassment and victimization of prostitutes, strippers, body-rub parlour workers and topless waitresses.

****

These are the basic issues around which the Committee is organizing. However, amendment and ordering are still open to discussion within the committee. Other issues which will be discussed include: family law reform, nuclear power, the position of Francophone and Quebecois women. A schedule of the general meetings is included. In addition, many subcommittees are working to make this week, and the demonstration, the largest action of the women's movement to date. We need your help, in the discussions, in the activities and at the demonstration.

"IWD: Lip Service to Feminism"
Toronto, 1983[6]

I want to express my dismay at the handling of this year's International Women's Day march in Toronto. IWD is usually a high point in the year for me; this year I was left feeling frustrated and angry.

The choice and execution of this year's themes (with the exception of freedom of choice), ignored many issues of crucial importance to women. It was divisive and insensitive. In brief, it was far too oriented towards the male left, and paid only lip service to feminism.

The workshop on the theme of "woman's right to peace," held on March 3, was entitled: "Women's Liberation, Disarmament and Anti-Imperialism." On the panel was a woman from "Women for Peace," a woman from Eritrea, a woman from the League of Arab Democrats, and a woman from the Philippines, who also spoke about Nicaragua and El Salvador. These speeches were accompanied by much shouting of revolutionary slogans. The pre-march activities at Convocation Hall put much emphasis on South American and Palestinian liberation movements, again accompanied by the shouting of revolutionary slogans.

There are some movements I support as a feminist, because they have articulated feminist goals, and seem committed to attaining them, such as those in Greece and Nicaragua. There are some movements which I support as a leftist even though they have no particular focus on women, but are working towards a better society where life will perhaps be better for everyone, such as those in El Salvador, Honduras, Guatemala, South Africa and Cuba. Finally, there are movements which are purely nationalist, and with whom I may have some sympathy but who do not have developed social goals, such as the Palestinian Liberation Organization and the Irish Republican Army.

Movements in the first category are relevant to International Women's Day; movements in the second category are marginally relevant; and movements in the last category have no place at all in International Women's Day. I make these distinctions not because I do not support most of these movements, but because I feel that International Women's Day should focus on issues particular to women and on struggles particular to women. By supporting all national liberation movements with equal fervour, we diminish the real achievements of those few which are committed to the liberation of women.

I see no necessary relationship between feminism and anti-imperialism, anti-zionism or national liberation. The mere fact that national liberation movements allow women to fight and die in them is an insufficient reason for feminists to embrace them. The Iranian and Algerian revolutions are examples of movements where women were in the forefront and are now severely repressed.

6. Lois Lowenberger, *Broadside* 4, no. 6 (April 1983), 14.

The failure of the March 8 Coalition to make such distinctions is a crucial error. In particular, it led to the decision to express support for the Palestinian liberation movements and to castigate Israel. That this decision was made is clear from the fact that woman from the League of Arab Democrats was asked to speak, but an Israeli woman was not. It was also made clear by the pre-march activities where we were exhorted to support Palestinian women, but Israeli women were not mentioned. This decision was terribly wrong ...

A lack of feminist analysis led to the focus on national liberation movements preferred by the male left, rather than on women's oppression. The lack of feminist analysis also obfuscated the larger questions. Surely feminists have a unique perspective on war, peace, and disarmament, which should not be ignored in favour of approving certain nationalist struggles. This perspective sees war, oppression, expansionism, imperialism, the nuclear arms race and other evils as products of the universal patriarchal system, not of "capitalism," "imperialism," "zionism" or even "communism."

Even those national liberation movements with whom we quite rightly express solidarity on International Women's Day should not occupy such a large part of the program. This includes both movements which can be classed as pro-feminist, such as Nicaragua, and ones which should ultimately help women along with everyone else, such as El Salvador, although I would have preferred to see more about Nicaragua and less about the other movements. The question we should ask is, are these movements directly relevant to women?

The March 8 Coalition claims to be focussed on "working class women" and "oppressed women." My suspicion is that there are many such women in Canada and internationally who either find national liberation movements irrelevant, or who in fact may oppose some or all of them.

Many working class women are not very interested in South America. They are interested in issues such as equal pay for work of equal value, equal opportunities, the double burden, affirmative action, day care, technological change, decent pensions and sexual harassment. Single mothers are concerned about things like better welfare benefits, personal dignity, decent housing, nutrition and education. And many women are concerned about issues like reproductive freedom, pornography, violence against women and discrimination.

Liberation movements are not even directly relevant to the lives of all immigrant women in Canada. Many immigrant women, even from the areas of armed struggle, have not had any direct involvement with the national liberation movements. Many immigrant women are conservative, may even be right-wing, and may not agree with the liberation movements. Should we ignore them? The immediate concerns of immigrant women are matters such as English language classes, education, wife battering, immigration policy, decent jobs and freedom from harassment.

The women's movement in general, and International Women's Day in particular, should be careful not to unnecessarily alienate women who support us by focussing on issues which are, at best, peripherally relevant to feminism, to the exclusion of more universal problems. Because feminism embraces all classes and all political persuasions, it is unique. We should not assume that what is supported by the left as "progressive" is necessarily good for women. Further, we should listen to women on all points of the political spectrum, even if we ultimately disagree with them on some issues. There is a time for debate on partisan and political matters which divide us, such as the Arab-Israeli dispute, a time to forge a compromise or to decide to go our separate ways. International Women's Day is not such a time; it a time for unity.

Finally, the International Women's Day celebration largely ignored, or made only passing reference to, groups of women who are particularly oppressed within Canadian society, groups like black women, Native women, Inuit women, Immigrant women in general, Jewish women, and lesbian women ...

There is a place for coalition among feminists and groups oriented towards progressive, as opposed to feminist, goals. However, I think we should be careful about coalition. It is far too easy for these other groups to persuade women that "their" concerns are primary and that, once again, we should wait for the revolution to do anything about women. Further, I do not believe that most men can fully understand feminism, or can fight with real commitment for feminist goals, even where they are supportive. As a non-Native, for example, I cannot possibly fully understand the position of Native women, as Native, even though I am supportive of their struggles: I accept this gap and the need for Native women to work separately as well as in coalition with the broader women's movement.

Finally, I believe that feminism is the most revolutionary movement of our time, and that nothing else can be changed in a fundamental way unless feminism achieves its goals. Therefore I, and many women like me, choose to focus my energy on feminism as opposed to other worthy causes, and I think that this choice should be respected. Therefore I feel that when men and progressive movements participate in International Women's Day, they should participate only in a way that demonstrates support for our struggles as women.

International Women's Day should be, first and foremost, a celebration of *women* together. It is tragic that the March 8 Coalition has lost sight of this in its eagerness to submerge feminism into left politics.

International Women's Day Committee Responds
Toronto, 1983[7]

Broadside:

We are writing in response to the letter written by Mary O'Brien and Frieda Forman, and to Lois Lowenberger's opinion piece, "IWD: Lip Service to Feminism," both of which appeared in the April, 1983 issue of *Broadside* ...

In our view, the central question that both the letter and the opinion piece raise is nothing less than: what is a feminist perspective? As feminists, what should be our concerns, our issues, our goals as a movement? All three writers feel that a feminist perspective was not part of Toronto's IWD this year. "In brief," Lowenberger writes, "it was far too oriented towards the male left, and paid only lip service to feminism." Some of us, when we first read these words, or heard similar sentiments in various discussions, thought: "Oh, for Chrissake, you must be joking." We thought: how could someone honestly believe that this day, planned and carried out by an army of hard-working, thoroughly committed feminist women, was male-dominated and unfeminist? However, once we'd set aside these initial impressions, we began to consider this question: just what is this feminist perspective that is alleged to have flown out the window this past International Women's Day?

Let us lay our cards on the table. The International Women's Day Committee (we are not here speaking for the March 8th Coalition), as a socialist-feminist organization, is necessarily committed to the struggle against all forms of oppression, whether based on class, sex or race ... As socialist-feminists, we acknowledge that women's oppression well pre-dated capitalism; we also acknowledge that women's subordination has not ceased to exist in socialist countries. But this does not mean therefore that women's oppression transcends all barriers of class, race and nation and that we all exist in a blessed state of international sisterhood. We believe that while women's subordination is a fact throughout most of human history and in most parts of the world, it takes very different forms and is conditioned by many different factors. And that is the first reason why we raised the question of imperialism: for many women in the world, it is a key structure of their oppression *as women*.

Therefore, we must take exception to Lowenberger's statement that there is no necessary relationship between feminism and anti-imperialism, for the fact is that, for many Third World women, the two are bound up so closely together as to be inseparable in their lives and in their politics. That is why we cannot agree with her position that "a lack of feminist analysis led to the focus on national liberation movements preferred by the male left, rather than on women's oppression" precisely because it perpetuates either/or thinking on questions of international feminism. We also have real problems with Lowenberger's argument

7. Letter to the Editor, International Women's Day Committee, *Broadside* 4, no. 7 (May 1983), 2–3.

that we should abandon issues peripheral to feminism in favour of "more universal problems." But the whole difficulty is, who is to decide what is peripheral and what is relevant? What is peripheral vs. what is universal is a matter of continual debate in the women's movement. Let us remind ourselves that lesbian rights and the critique of heterosexism started out as the peripheral issue *par excellence* in the women's movement. ("Why, lesbianism concerns only one in ten women anyway — surely there is no direct link between feminism and lesbianism. Why alienate a lot of women who have more 'universal' concerns?") We hope you take the point. "Universal issues" can very easily become the issues of the dominant group. As women, we should know this ...

So yes, we believe there *are* real links between feminism and anti-imperialism. Let's get more specific. Lowenberger writes that: "Liberation movements are not even directly relevant to the lives of all immigrant women in Canada. Many women, even those from the areas of armed struggle, have not had any direct involvement with the national liberation movements. Many immigrant women are conservative, may even be right-wing, and may not agree with the liberation movements. Should we ignore them? The immediate concerns of immigrant women are matters such as English language classes, education, wife battering, immigration policy, decent jobs and freedom from harassment." We are not about to deny for one moment that these are central concerns for immigrant women living in Canada today. That is why the Coalition raised these issues in the pamphlet prepared for IWD and why we'll continue to raise these concerns. But what mystifies us is how Lowenberger could think that the question of imperialism (and therefore the significance of contemporary national liberation struggles) is *unrelated* to these very concerns. Two fast examples. One: surely one key root of the racial and ethnic discrimination that we see every day in Canada is a heritage from colonialism and imperialism? And can we talk about immigration policy without referring to the imperialist underdevelopment of many nations — which forces people to come to Canada? Two: surely we cannot talk about decent jobs for all without talking about the role of imperialism in securing a high standard of living for some and a living hell for the rest of the world? As Maria Teresa Larrain of Women Working with Immigrant Women has said on numerous occasions, immigrant women in Canada live a two-fold reality because they do not abandon their identities and political traditions the moment they set foot on Canadian soil. The fact is that many immigrant women active in solidarity groups organized around particular national liberation struggles are the same woen working for the rights of immigrant women in the areas of labour, health and so on. For them, the links between the two political struggles are crucial ...

Many of the links we've developed with women in the anti-imperialist and peace movements are new; we're really just beginning to know one another and we want the space to develop those links without feeling compelled to agree with one another on every issue before the feminist movement — or the socialist movement either, for that matter. We realize that one of the mistakes we made at the meeting was not allowing enough time for a fuller discussion. (We planned for this, but as often happens, some speakers went over their time limit.) Despite the fact that we are clearly at opposite ends of the spectrum in many respects, we are also encouraged that women take these issues seriously enough to debate them in *Broadside*. Our goal was to stimulate such a debate at the forum. Now we've got it. Let's continue.

International Women's Day Committee
Toronto

United Nations Decade for Women: World Conferences

"Mexico — Special Report"
Mexico City, June-July 1975[8]

...In attendance at the World Conference were representatives of 133 countries, 23 United Nations agencies, 8 liberation movements, and 113 non-government organizations. Women delegates outnumbered men by about five to one. Pedro Ojeda Paullada, Attorney-General of Mexico was president of the Conference. U.N. protocol requires that the president be chosen from the host country; since Mexico's delegation was headed by Senor Ojeda, he presided over the Conference, despite many protests by numerous delegates that a conference concerning women should be headed by a woman.

The Conference was addressed by President Luis Echeverria of Mexico, Prime Minister Sirimavo Bandaranaika of Sri Lanka and Prime Minister Olaf Palme of Sweden as well as a number of "first ladies" — wives of presidents or prime ministers. Simultaneous to the Conference were a U.N.-sanctioned Tribune, a more informal international gathering organized by a committee appointed by the Conference of Non-Governmental Organizations, and a Journalists Encounter, organized by the Center for Economic and Social Information of the U.N. Office of Public Information.

Helvi Sipila, U.N. Assistant Secretary-General for Social and Humanitarian Affairs, addressed the opening session with hard-hitting remarks. She said it was "high time to acknowledge that the denial of women's rights and opportunities is at the very root of our development problems and socio-economic ills — including illiteracy, malnutrition, mass poverty and unchecked rates of population growth." What is

8. *International Women's Year 1975/Année internationale de la femme Newsletter/Bulletin* 2, no. 8 (October-November 1975), 3–4.

needed, she said, is "to translate into action the principles already agreed upon" over the last 30 years concerning the equality of women.

A Ten-Year World Plan of Action was the major outcome of the Conference. Its minimum target is a 14-point objective which governments are urged to implement in the first five years to 1980. These include: marked decreased illiteracy among women; extension of vocational, agricultural and other forms of primary education to women; increased employment opportunities for women; enactment of equal opportunity (political, labour force) legislation; increased health-education services; parity of civil, social and political rights; and recognition of the value of women's work in the home and in non-remunerated voluntary activities.

The Plan, in a section dealing with the mass media pointed out that the media "could exercise a significant influence in helping to remove prejudice and stereotypes." At present it stated that "the media tend to reinforce traditional attitudes, often portraying an image of women that is degrading and humiliating, and fail to reflect the changing roles of the sexes." The Plan urged that those in control of the media project "a more dynamic image of women and to take into account the diversity of women's roles and their actual and potential contribution to society."

The Canadian delegation reports that the conference focused primarily on the problems of the third-world countries whose economies differ greatly from our own. They reported: "In this respect, Canada was able to announce that the Canadian International Development Agency had now established status of women as a priority area in its development strategy and that subject to the agreement of the host country Canada would view favourably projects and programs designed to improve the condition of women in the developing countries."

"Canada was able to take the initiative in co-sponsoring a resolution designed to increase the percentage of professional women in all United Nations organizations. Canada also co-sponsored a resolution to eliminate discrimination against women and to enhance the status of women in the communications media field. A resolution concerning measures for the integration of women in development was also co-sponsored by Cabinet."

With respect to the World Plan of Action, the delegation reported that "In many instances social questions ... do not have the same pressing urgency and priority accorded problems of malnutrition, industrialization and state security particularly in the developing countries. For this reason, it is appreciated that some elements of the World Plan of Action are not as applicable to Canada as to many other countries, particularly developing countries. Nevertheless, the document as a whole has great value for Canada, and much of it is very relevant to the work being carried out by all levels of government and by many organizations to improve the position of women."

The report concludes: "Many of the current economic and political issues which are before the United Nations itself were treated by the "professional" representatives of many countries as matters of higher priority than that of the status of women. The influence of these "professionals" was reflected in the offices established for the Conference. Neither the President of the Conference, nor any other elected office, with the exception of the chairman of one committee, was held by women. In spite of these obstacles, the Canadian delegation was impressed with the ability of the Conference to reach consensus on a number of matters which were highly relevant to the subject matter of the conference and which it was expected might have been highly contentious. In addition, the press provided world-wide coverage which brought the issue of the status of women before a world-wide audience.
...

"Nairobi Conference: A Decade of Women"[9]
Nairobi, July 10, 1985

It is impossible to describe my feelings on this, the opening day of the Non-Governmental Organizations (NGO) Forum. There are so many women from so many different places and walks of life. As someone from Canada's largely white middle-class feminist community, one thing does stand out however: the international women's movement is primarily a movement of Third World women. I notice that women from Western countries keep saying how good it feels to be in the midst of so many black and brown faces.

This morning I woke up at six to get to the Keyatta Conference Centre on time. The hall's seating capacity is only 3,000; 13,000 women have registered. Sure enough, the aisles are soon overflowing and thousands of women are forced to hear the proceedings over loudspeakers in the plaza.

The opening address is given by Edda Gachukia, head of the Kenya NGO Organizing Committee, who stresses the significance of this conference being held in a Third World country. "It is imperative that we draw attention to the situation of millions of women in Africa and other Third World countries whose daily toil is directed towards fulfillment of basic human needs," she says. "We must ask what can be done to improve the lot of these women who contribute to the wealth of all mankind (sic). Unless this issue is addressed at the Forum, all the other issues will sound academic and trivial."

Dame Nita Barrow, convenor of Forum '85, points out that at the mid-decade conference held in Copenhagen in 1980, "the international political climate was much less reactionary and confrontational than it is today." Along with Dr. Gachukia, she stresses that despite the predictable differences and arguments that will arise during the Forum, the most important thing is the opportunity for dialogue.

(Later in the day, back at the University of Nairobi where the Forum's proceedings will take place, Dame Barrow orders lesbians distributing leaflets on the lawn to stop, saying that the distribution of literature is not permitted. So much for dialogue.) ...

July 15

... For all the talk about "unnecessary politicization" of the agenda (the argument that was supposed to keep apartheid, the PLO and Central America off the schedule) the most unifying bond here is an understanding that there must be support for women in liberation struggles, especially Black women fighting in South Africa. African National Congress (ANC) and SWAPO (Southwest African People's Organization, Namibia) workshops have been overflowing, even after they have been moved to larger rooms.

T-shirts proclaim 'Free Albertian Sisubu'. Buttons read 'Smash Apartheid'. Clearly, the impact of the heightening struggle against the Botha regime is felt everywhere. ANC and SWAPO women are being encouraged and strengthened by the overwhelming show of support from conference participants.

This show of support is an indication of something that sets Nairobi apart from Mexico City in 1975 and Copenhagen in 1980 — the involvement of Third World women in setting the agenda, and the leadership roles taken up by Third World women during the Forum. Issues like imperialism, racism, migrants, refugees, are getting a great deal of attention here. A coalition of Third World women — (Development Alternatives with Women for a New Era) — is presenting a workshop series on development. White Western women have been, as one delegate puts it, "very well behaved".

The biggest controversy in Nairobi is, without a doubt, Zionism and Palestinian rights, the issues that caused major divisions in Mexico City and Copenhagen. The Peace Tent dialogue and subsequent workshop here drew 500 women representing every possible position. Although the dialogues have been well mediated by collaborative anti-Zionist Israelis and Palestinian women, they have frequently degenerated into shouting matches.

Forum '85, the conference's daily paper, is swamped with letters to the editor. Most Forum participants, it appears, are supportive of the Palestinian struggle for self-determination. But of course it is difficult to imagine any real resolution of differences.

July 19

After dark, women gather around a stage set up on the University lawn, singing and dancing to Kenyan drumming. Two giant balloons, one red and one blue, float above the crowd, bounce off outstretched hands, and then float into the lights. The closing cultural celebration is almost over, and no woman here wants it to end.

The political summary of Forum '85 happened during yesterdays lunch hour with an improvized sound system and a table for a stage. The event was the "unauthorized" Unity rally; "unauthorized" because the organizers absolved themselves of any responsibility for rallies and demonstrations. In fact one group of women was asked to remove their Forum badges if they intended to participate in the march.

But rallies have been happening anyway. Women here have demonstrated against the Marcos dictatorship in the Philippines, U.S. intervention in Nacaragua, and apartheid. The Unity rally, spearheaded by the U.S. based International Council of African Women, heard speakers from Egypt, India, the USSR, France, the U.S., Kenya, Namibia, Zimbabwe, Nicaragua, and Japan.

These women demanded an end to apartheid and U.S. intervention and called for a nuclear freeze as well as another World Conference in five years. All speakers stressed the need for justice in the Third World as an essential step toward women's equality.

Andree McClachlan of the International Research Council for Women of African descent called for a World Conference of African women, and a decade for women of colour from 1990-2000. "There is no doubt the predominance of Third World Women has contributed largely to the success of this Forum," she said. "Black American women will never be the same, Kenyan women will never be the same. All of us will never be the same." ...

Black lesbians in turn were responsible for making sure that documents included discussion of sexual orientation and homophobia. Third World lesbians at the Forum were vocal and visible, refuting the myth that lesbianism is one of the products of decadent capitalist societies.

Despite legitimate fears prior to the conference that lesbians would be silenced or removed, the presence of lesbian women in Nairobi was very strong. After the first day, lesbian literature returned to the lawn when all the groups began to set up tables. It became the centre of daily public education on lesbians and lesbian lifestyles. Daily lesbian caucuses, an afternoon of informal discussion, a women's dance, a press conference and a day of workshops, built networks and established international lesbian organizing as something that won't disappear after the Forum.

Upon reflection, Forum '85 was exciting, educational and it facilitated valuable international networks. But it was also frustrating. There were several glaring omissions, among them any real discussion of indigenous peoples' issues, or the inclusion of disabled women on the platform at 'progressive' events like the unity rally.

There were also organizational problems that went beyond hassles of accommodation — heavy handed political control by convenors and the government served to increase the fragmentation of such a mammoth and diverse event ...

Women were not able to emerge from Forum '85 with strategies or resolutions. What we did achieve was building invaluable networks, both regional and global. It is these networks that will solidify our gains — most importantly, the development of a much more international and inter-racial focus for our movement.

From Women and Development to Gender and Development

Match International Centre Programmes — I
Ottawa, 1992[10]

Regional Programmes

An integral part of MATCH's programming is the support of community-based projects designed and managed by women from the south in order to change the practices and attitudes which discriminate against them ...

Senegal

Yewwu-Yewwi-for women's liberation: Through FIPPU, a prominent periodical in Africa, Yewwu-Yewwi aims to change ideas and attitudes toward gender relations and to raise women's status in Francophone Africa ...

Regional Africa

Educating Traditional Birth Attendants: The Inter-African Committee organizes campaigns to educate traditional birth attendants and raise public awareness about the harmful effects of female genital mutilation, thereby altering traditional practices that harmfully affect women and girls.

Asia

Pakistan

Home Schools: The Home School Teacher's Welfare Organization (HSTWO) runs informal schools for poor girls, thereby providing an access to education that is denied them by customary practice ...

Phillippines

...

Women and Militarization: Using participatory research, GABRIELA-Negros documents the effects of militarization on women, with particular attention to health, economic condition, relationship with

10. MATCH International Centre, "Annual Report 1991–92," edited by Marlene Bogert, 5–6.

families and communities and involvement with grassroots organizations.

Sri Lanka

The Rural Women's Organization Network, an umbrella organization in southern Sri Lanka, facilitates information and skills exchanges among rural women; offers leadership training; works to raise the consciousness of the community about issues of women's oppression and equality and offers childcare workshops.

Caribbean

Jamaica

Women's Media Watch monitors the image of women as portrayed in the media; conducts rural school workshops linking violence and disrespect for women with media portrayals and acts as a women's national advocacy group with media and government.

Grenada

Through workshops and training sessions, the **Agency for Rural Transformation** assists women to deal with the violence in their lives through becoming economically independent, more assertive and self-confident ...

Latin America

Chile

Women's Social and Political Participation in Conchali: To prepare for municipal elections in the re-emerging democracy, CESOC provides political leadership training, thereby enhancing women's capacity to defend their interests and rights and bring a gender perspective to municipal issues.

Nicaragua

Sexuality and Reproduction Workshops: Through a series of workshops, the Sandinista Workers Central (CST) is educating women leaders about women's health, sexuality, reproduction, gender roles and violence against women ...

Peru

...

Shelter for Battered Women: In a poor neighbourhood of Lima, La Voz de la Mujer has opened one of the few shelters for battered women in Latin America. They consider literacy and skill development training as essential to the promotion and protection of women's economic and legal rights in marginalized sectors of Peruvian society.

Match International Centre Programmes — II
Ottawa, 1993[11]

African Programmes

MATCH is assisting with a nationwide campaign to help women work within the transition period between apartheid and democracy, towards becoming full and effective participants in the development process. The focus has been on skills transfer and empowerment because the majority of Blacks in apartheid South Africa have only ever had access to an inferior education system. In this highly patriarchal society, an education was often out of reach for the average woman ...

Women's National Coalition (South Africa)

MATCH is supporting the new **Women's National Coalition** which is an umbrella group working with virtually every women's organization in South Africa — both urban and rural. The primary purpose of the coalition is to prepare a Charter to ensure the elimination of women's oppression, a prerequisite for the creation of a democratic society. The process of designing the Charter is to be a participatory one, and will not only raise consciousness but will provide an education in democratic processes.

ALVF (Cameroon)

MATCH continues to support the highly effective work of **l'Association de lutte contre les violences faites aux femmes.** The association raises awareness of women's issues through public events, a publication and an information centre. They also provide a shelter for abused women with access to medical, legal, financial and psychological help. Plans are in the works to expand these services by opening two branches — one in Douala and the other in Bafoussam.

Inter-African Committee (Ethiopia)

MATCH is assisting with the cost of trainers to develop four sets of workshops to provide intensive and meaningful health education with the help of visual aids. The subjects cover female circumcision, childhood marriage, human reproduction, pregnancy, childbirth, breast feeding, hygiene and nutritional taboos. The structure of these workshops ensures continuity as trainers are being identified and equipped to develop their own workshops ...

11. "Programmes for 1993–1994," *MATCH News* 17, no. 1 (Summer 1993), 5–7.

Southern African Women's Initiative Phase IV (Tanzania, Zimbabwe, Zambia)

MATCH is a partner in this initiative to strengthen indigenous African women's ability to do research and to encourage local publishing of women writers.

Caribbean Programmes

Economically, socially and legally, women in Caribbean societies have far fewer rights than men. Although violence against women has been recognized as an issue, there is little information available about the extent of the problem nor are there appropriate social and legal services for victims of violence ...

Nucleo de Apoyo (Dominican Republic)

MATCH supports this group which provides psychological and legal assistance to women who have been victims of violence ...

Disabled Women's Association (Trinidad and Tobago)

MATCH has been working with this Association which is holding poetry workshops for disabled women. This initiative is intended to increase visibility of disabled people and their issues.

Latin American Programmes

In recent years the women's movement has begun to raise an awareness of the issues of violence against women. However a great deal of work is still needed to sensitize the public to the issue ...

Movimiento Manuela Ramos and Casa de La Mujer (Peru)

MATCH is supporting two organizations which are working towards ensuring women have the same rights as men in Peruvian society. **Movimiento Manuela Ramos** has taken a leading role in countering violence against women. Their scope now includes violence against children as well. **Casa de La Mujer** has been very effective in sensitizing the population around issues of violence against women and gender equality.

Asian Programmes

One of the major barriers to progress in the women's movement in Asia is poor communications. By having access to research and background as well as examples and successes in other areas, much more could be accomplished. MATCH is assisting by providing both networking opportunities and modern communications tools ...

KARMIKA (India)

MATCH is assisting a partner **KARMIKA** to review laws and identify aspects which have a negative impact on women. The intention is to eliminate discrimination at a policy level.

PLRC (Philippines)

Women in the Philippines are consistently discriminated against through legislation and attitudes which have patriarchal biases. MATCH has supported the delivery of a program to offer paralegal training to women in the Philippines. These women will be equipped to address the issues of violence against women, to educate other women about their rights, entitlements and legal procedures so that they can effectively participate on development processes and to provide support for women's organizing activities.

Women Living Under Muslim Laws — WLUML (Pakistan)

MATCH is undertaking communications support for Muslim women recognizing that their ability to control their destiny lies in their ability to change the laws that shape their lives and oppress them throughout the Muslim world ...

"Words of Women: Women of Words"
Ottawa, 1989 [12]

The last fifteen years have seen an explosion of women's words — both in Canada and around the world. Women are using poetry, research, fiction, theory, prose and popular theatre to understand ourselves, initiate change, communicate with others, hammer out theoretical perspectives, document women's day-to-day lives, explore our commonalities and work through our differences. And more and more, we are writing to spread our words.

In Canada we have seen the formation and growth of women's journals, bookstores, presses and newspapers. Yet these organizations do not face an easy task. Most are underfunded and wage a daily struggle just to keep their doors open. They have been the scene of internal discussion, critiques and challenges as issues such as class and racism in the women's movement are debated. Not all have been strong enough to survive these challenges.

The growth in Southern women's writing was clearly demonstrated by the active and vocal presence of Third World women at the International Feminist Bookfair held in Montreal last June. Women from Asia, Latin America, Africa and the Caribbean participated as authors and publishers. These women, and others, are fighting to tell their own stories in their own words.

---

12. Beth Woroniuk, *MATCH News* 12, no. 4 (February/March 1989), 1, 4.

At MATCH, we believe that the Canadian women's movement can benefit from increased exchanges with women writers from the Third World. As a member of Press Gang publishers said at a recent Words of Women consultation, "We need to begin to look at issues outside of white feminist publishing. It is time to move outwards."

People involved in international development could also learn from a greater exposure to women's writing. Writing has an important role in the South-North and North-South flow of ideas and information. Just as a picture is worth a thousand words, a poem is more effective than a chart of numbers in portraying the impact of economic cutbacks imposed by institutions such as the International Monetary Fund on many underdeveloped coutries. A short story can convey the reality of a woman's everyday life in a way that's understandable to readers everywhere. If "development" involves mutual learning, then women's writing can be an important tool in this process.

MATCH is developing a programme called Words of Women (WOW) in order to promote a greater exchange between the women's movement in Canada, the international development community and the Third World women's movement.

The roots of MATCH's Words of Women programme go back several years. Women and women's organizations in the Caribbean expressed interest in having more access to women's writing from around the world. Women's books were scarce and, when available, very expensive.

Women in Caribbean territories were exploring and developing different forms of women's writing: documentation of oral history and the writing of herstory; poetry, short stories and novels; research; news reporting and feature writing; popular booklets and pamphlets. Sistren, the women's theatre collective in Jamaica, conducts research on women and publishes a magazine. The Women and Development Unit of the University of the West Indies (WAND) has spearheaded research and promoted work by women throughout the region. Caribbean Association for Feminist Research and Action (CAFRA) has co-ordinated different initiatives, including a women's history project and an anthology of poems by Caribbean women called *Creation Fire* (soon to be published in Canada, by Sister Vision Press).

Like many of their Canadian counterparts, these women see their writing as a political activity. For them, writing is a tool for organizing and a way of understanding women's oppression and strengths.

In Canada, the MATCH-coordinated Words for Women committee began to make contact and build relations with women's bookstores, publishers, periodicals and magazines through the spring and summer ...

Following a series of consultations, in Canada and the Caribbean, we are now defining the next stages of the Words of Women programme. In the Caribbean, MATCH will be working with CAFRA. Across Canada, a network of women's bookstores, publications and presses will be coordinating a number of exchange activities, beginning with the launching of *Creation Fire* in the late spring.

With the Words of Women programme, MATCH will bring a global perspective to the Canadian women's movement and introduce women's writing as an important aspect in the process of development.

Feminists Redefining Development
Ottawa, 1989 [13]

Women were first recognized as a development issue in the early 1970s. Both activists and researchers began to point out that not only were women not benefitting from the attempts at "modernization", but in many cases women were left worse off.

The "Women in Development" (WID) perspective and programmes were developed to rectify this situation.

The WID perspective, although innovative in the 1970s, primarily focused on the integration of women into development. Its proponents argued that women had been "left out" of development plans and projects, and so had to be brought into these activities.

The WID approach often led to small women's components being tacked on to larger projects; many project planners simply looked at how women could be grafted onto existing plans.

Although WID programmes brought attention to the role of women in the Third World, they often failed to improve women's position and produced few changes in women's subordinate status. Moreover, in many cases, women felt pressured to participate in projects and development activities which stretched their already long workdays.

In the 1980s, women researchers and activists expanded on and developed a critique of the WID perspective and of development practices in general. They pointed out that mainstream development planners had ignored women, overlooking the value of their work and failing to recognize their specific needs. Women the world over began to question the traditional vision of development and to argue for new perspectives and approaches.

MATCH is attempting to bring together two of these alternative approaches: *gender and development* and *global feminism* — drawing on both to develop an analysis and strategies for action.

The Gender and Development approach was formulated by women working in the area of general development. It seeks to provide planners and development workers with concrete tools and frameworks for use in development programmes and plans (primarily at the local and national levels). It focuses on the relationships between men and women and the socially-created definitions of male and female, or gender roles. It uses the concept of the sexual division of labour (in the workplace

13. Beth Woroniuk and Josée Lafrenière, "What Do You Mean — 'It Doesn't Affect Women'? Feminists Redefining Development," *MATCH News* 13, no. 2 (September/October 1989), 1, 7.

and the home) and points out that in almost all cases, this division of labour is biased against women.

Those using a gender and development approach argue that all development activities affect women and that all plans and programmes must take women's situation and needs into consideration. They believe that women's inequality will not be changed by adding a women's component onto a major project, but that the entire project has to be reconceived. For example, it was often felt that large-scale projects, such as dam-building or reforestation, had no impact on women. A gender and development approach argues that these projects, like any project, do have a significant impact on women and should be conceived, implemented and evaluated with the specific needs and interests of women in mind.

MATCH is attempting to add the strengths of another approach, known as *global feminism* to the gender and development analysis. This approach focuses on women's organizing and mobilizing at a global level. It highlights the importance of strengthening women's organizations and the solidarity that women world-wide can offer each other. Proponents stress that all issues are women's issues and should be seen through feminist eyes. It adds a broader political dimension that is often lacking in a gender and development approach.

Building on the experience of the past 20 years and the ongoing discussions of women around the world, MATCH is trying to contribute to a global women's movement and a feminist vision of development. In the international development community, this means strengthening the commitment to a gender and development approach and redefining issues from a feminist perspective. In the women's movement, this means constantly introducing the international component and the links between women's struggles world-wide.

"The Debt Crisis in Latin America: An Example of Unsustainable Development" Ottawa, 1992[14]

The dominant world order today is one of exploitation and accumulation, determined by the demands of profit for a privileged few, rather than by the needs of all the people. In this process, both people and nature are used, and abused. It is a model of development that tends to eliminate social and political organizations, ways of life and living forms on the planet that are incompatible with its demands.

For Latin American countries, foreign debt is the most recent and devastating mechanism of exploitation by the North. It is the latest and most severe reminder of the unequal terms of trade imposed by the International Monetary Fund, the World Bank and the General Agreement on Tariffs and Trade (GATT).

14. Ana Isla, *MATCH News* 16, no. 2 (Fall 1992), 1, 3–4.

As a result of the conditions imposed by these international institutions, there is a net transfer of wealth from the South to the North. This transfer takes the form not only of money, but of taking over national industries, banks and other assets as interest payment.

What is the debt?

By 1981, Latin American countries had borrowed $100.7 billion from commercial banks and the IMF. Between 1982 and 1991, they repaid $240 billion in net financial transfers but still owe $450 billion due to the US manipulation of exchange and interest rates.

In 1982, the US government tried to attract money from the rest of the world to bolster its failing economy, escalating interest rates from 2% to 16.6%. As other countries engaged in a desperate competition to keep needed capital at home, their interest rates rose in tandem. Interest on debt contracted at 2% rose to 15%, costing Latin American people billions of dollars. After 1982, most of the new loans were contracted to repay interest alone. The demand for capital in the US created a vacuum. Encouraged by high interest rates, Latin American elites sent their money abroad in ever increasing amounts. This capital, which left Latin America, continues to appear on the commercial bank's books as loans on which interest is due. Latin American people are repaying debt on money which banks are using to make even more profits.

The impact of the debt shows a depressing picture throughout the world: capital flight, impoverishment and environmental destruction. It is felt everywhere because of the policies imposed by the IMF and the World Bank through Structural Adjustment Programmes.

IMF aid has always come with a considerable number of strings dictating to nations spending priorities. Typically, they include the following elements:

- reduction in government expenditures on social programmes such as health and education
- restrictive labour policies, involving wage reductions and layoffs
- elimination of price controls for basic foodstuffs
- tax reform to give tax breaks to the rich (presumably to give them incentives to invest in the national economy).

Consequences

During the 1980s, Latin American countries were forced to produce for export only, a policy known as "export or perish". This is done primarily through agricultural products such as bananas, coffee, pineapples, etc., sold in the markets of the North. Most of these revenues are used to pay interest on debt. In addition to export production, governments had to eliminate food subsidies, often with dire consequences for the poor. In Peru, Bolivia and Brazil, people are reduced to eating food not fit for human consumption such as fish-meal used for fattening chicken and wet newspaper, not because the country does not produce food but because they are forced to sell it to the North.

Social Costs

Health care and basic education are now much less accessible to the general population. All social service provisions and needs of the people have been subordinated to debt repayment. Countries are forced to pay interest before health, education and other development concerns.

Inflation caused by the Adjustment Programme has reduced the value of local currencies. As a consequence, in the 1980s, several countries' unemployment rate rose to 70%. According to a United Nations survey, half of Peru's population subsists on 10 cents per day.

The crushing debt trap has produced millions of street children, many who are deliberately and systematically assassinated in Brazil, Columbia and Guatemala.

Environmental Degradation

Structural Adjustment Programmes are not only a human tragedy, they are a fundamental economic error. Many Latin American countries, faced with debilitating foreign debt, rising interest rates, adverse terms and trade, interrupted financial flows, are using up their resources and ignoring environmental degradation. Large landowners and transnational corporations are rapidly destroying the Amazon, replacing ordinary farmers with huge grain farms and exotic plants for exportation, to repay the external debt.

Many countries have become the dumping ground for nuclear, industrial and human waste from the richer countries. Supported by the World Bank, industrialized countries in the North barter debt for toxic waste dump sites. Venezuela receives Italy's garbage, Argentina accepts France's garbage, Peru accepts garbage from the US.

Massive deforestation is changing the global weather system, turning storms, floods and droughts into major disasters. Soil and water contamination make it dangerous for people to grow food. Concerns for the environment cannot be separated from international debt.

Resistance to Payment of Debt

All Latin American countries are paying interest on debt despite their desperate internal situation. However, there have been attempts to resist the terms imposed by the IMF and the World Bank. In 1985, Peru declared that it would pay no more than 10% of the value of its export revenue on servicing the external debt. At that time, it was paying 60% of the value of exports revenues. International financial institutions swiftly declared Peru ineligible for further loans. Commercial banks threatened to seize and embargo Peru's assets abroad and destroy foreign trade potential by withdrawing Peru's trade credits, causing further degradation to its already low living standards. Peru had no choice but to comply.

Latin American Women's Network on External Debt

The Latin American Women's Network on External Debt was formed in 1991 in Miami at the World Women's Congress for a Healthy Planet. The Network is opposed to the conditions imposed by the IMF on Latin American people. It is working to mobilize support for the cancellation of the external debt and changes in the terms of trade.

The network is a member of Toronto Women for a Just and Healthy Planet. Women for a Just and Healthy Planet deals with a range of environmental issues from a feminist perspective. Its members work from the perspective that sustainable development is not possible unless people living in the South are allowed to live in dignity. For this it is necessary to make the links between worldwide poverty, Western capitalism and consumerism.

Women's Rights Are Human Rights

"Vienna Declaration and Programme of Action"
Vienna, Austria, June 25, 1993[15]

> 18. The human rights of women and of the girl-child are an inalienable, integral and indivisible part of universal human rights. The full and equal participation of women in political, civil, economic, social and cultural life, at the national, regional and international levels, and the eradication of all forms of discrimination on grounds of sex are priority objectives of the international community.

Gender-based violence and all forms of sexual harassment and exploitation, including those resulting from cultural prejudice and international trafficking, are incompatible with the dignity and worth of the human person, and must be eliminated. This can be achieved by legal measures and through national action and international cooperation in such fields as economic and social development, education, safe maternity and health care, and social support.

The human rights of women should form an integral part of the United Nations human rights activities, including the promotion of all human rights instruments relating to women.

The World Conference on Human Rights urges Governments, institutions, intergovernmental and non-governmental organizations to inten-

---

15. Jan Bauer, Appendix II of the "Vienna Declaration and Programme of Action, 25 June 1993, Vienna, Austria," in "Report on United National World Conference on Human Rights," 14–25 June 1993, Vienna, Austria, Prepared for Article 19 (U.K.) and Canadian Network on International Human Rights, Ottawa, 31 October 1993, p. 150.

sify their efforts for the protection and promotion of human rights of women and the girl-child.

Women, Development, and the Environment

"Population and Environment: An Indian Perspective" Toronto, 1993[16]

Is Population Growth the Primary Cause of Environmental Problems?

Population growth in the Third World is being increasingly and falsely identified as a primary cause of environmental destruction. There are four main reasons why this is not the case. First it should be recognized that poor people in the Third World cannot afford access to many of the resources whose use is environmentally destructive.

Second, the large numbers of poor people use insignificant fractions of the resources used by the North and the elites of the South. An average American citizen uses 250 times as much energy as an average Nigerian. Wealthy lifestyles contribute disproportionately to the pressure on resources.

Third, many production processes that have emerged from the Northern industrialized countries are inherently destructive of the environment, and this capacity for destruction is independent of population growth. According to Barry Commoner, environmental destruction is a function of the resource-destroying capacity of technologies of production and the goods produced or consumed per capita (i.e., total pollution = pollution per unit of economic goods produced x goods consumed per capita x population).

The North contributes disproportionately to the first two factors, both in terms of transfer of resource intensive technologies and in terms of high consumption of resource intensive products.

Finally, population growth should not be viewed as the primary cause of the environmental crisis but as one aspect of it. Both are related to resource alienation and to destruction of livelihoods, first by colonialism and then by Northern imposed models of development ...

The focus on population as the cause of environmental destruction is erroneous in other ways. First, it blames the victims. Second, by failing to address economic insecurity it denies the right to survival that underlies population growth ...

After many decades of failed "population control" it might well be more fruitful to directly address the roots of the problem — economic insecurity. Giving people rights and access to resources so that they can generate sustainable livelihoods is the only solution to environmental destruction and the population growth which accompanies it ...

16. Mira and Vandana Shiva, *Women & Environments* 13, nos. 3/4 (Winter/Spring 1993), 20–21.

Development at Whose Cost?

Country after debt-ridden country in the Third World has been forced into structural readjustment programs, which will only increase disparities and indebtedness in the long term. We are seeing horrifying statistics of rising infant and maternal mortality, an increase in the number of street children, and uncontrolled urbanization. Throughout history, countries in Africa, Asia or Latin America have suffered a brutal plunder of their people and natural resources to further the economies of their colonial masters. Today, an increase in population is being blamed for environmental degradation. However, it is economic reasons that result in the Sarawak forests being cleared and their natives left homeless in their own land to provide Japan its supply of disposable chopsticks; Indonesian forests are felled for toilet paper and tissue napkins; and Amazon forests are burnt down for cattle farms to provide hamburgers for the rich North.

The plunder of such countries continues under unjust world trade practices, unjust terms of loan servicing and unrealistic interest rates on debts. As poverty increases and with it, social insecurity, the poor and the illiterate will tend to look for security in numbers, and national governments will have to apply increasingly coercive population control measures to meet the conditionality of foreign aid.

Today, when social action needs to be redefined, the population issue is increasingly becoming a human rights issue. It is no longer possible to ensure that the basic needs of our people will be met when all major developmental policies are decided elsewhere. To compound the problem, an unprecedented flow of resources is being made available for the implementation of those programs and policies that suit the philosophy of the North. It is difficult to say how much foreign aid has benefited the managers of the aid givers and the aid receivers.

As country after country in the Third World is being forced into "structural adjustment" programs, the new economic order based on foreign loans will only highlight disparities and indebtedness and result in cuts in welfare budgets, in health and education and in increasing privatisation of such services ...

Women and Peace and Anti-Militarism

"THERESE CASGRAIN: A Voice for Women"
Toronto, 1981 [17]

Thérèse Casgrain died on November 3, 1981, at her home in Montreal. She was 85. Her career as a fighter for women's rights, for the vote, for Family Allowances to be sent to the woman of a household, for native women and for human rights had been well documented and recorded.

17. Kay Macpherson, *Broadside* 3, no. 3 (December 1981/January 1982), 6.

Her often repeated statement, "I want peace and I've been fighting for it all my life," was her well-known theme song.

Her connection with the Voice of Women is seldom mentioned in the accolades. Since I was one of the women outside Quebec who saw a good deal of her during those years, I would like to recall some of those occasions.

Thérèse took over as President of Voice of Women in September 1962, when Helen Tucker moved on to organize a Women's International Committee for International Co-operation Year. Thérèse had organized La Voix des Femmes, the Quebec branch of VOW, so when she became National President, the office moved to Montreal. Soon after, the Women's Peace Train to Ottawa was organized. Seven hundred Quebec women were joined by a bus load from Ontario, and together we all walked up Parliament Hill carrying with us a laundry basket filled with telegrams from all over the country demanding "NO NUCLEAR WEAPONS IN CANADA." We were addressing the Diefenbaker government which was undecided about Canada acquiring nuclear weapons. An English-speaking cabinet minister was sent in to hear from the women, who were insulted, and said so quite forcefully until a French-speaking minister was hastily substituted ...

Thérèse arrived in Paris late in 1964 having attended a women's conference in Israel. I had been at a conference organized by Helen Tucker in the UNESCO building ...

Thérèse and I joined a group of women from NATO countries who, as a follow-up to their meeting in The Hague six months earlier, were protesting the proposed NATO Multi-Lateral Nuclear Force (whereby each NATO country was going to be able to press the nuclear button). We arranged with the authorities that we would present a statement from the NATO women to the Secretary General of NATO and we agreed to send only one woman from each country (one English- and one French-speaking from Canada) so that we did not appear to be a demonstration. The French police were very nervous. There were other peace groups protesting NATO's actions and the streets around the NATO building were filled with police cruisers and baton-brandishing gendarmes. We walked quietly in twos and threes up to the building and after some parleying were told that only one woman could enter. This wasn't good enough. We wanted a minimum of two, preferably more. There were women present from the US, France, Belgium, Britain, Germany and the Scandinavian countries. While we were talking to the guards an enormous uniformed monster reminiscent of Hermann Goering stumped out, swept us all up in a gesture, and ordered that we be arrested.

We were hustled into a police paddy wagon and I shall never forget the delighted look on Thérèse's face as she was rudely pushed up the steps. There was a wonderful cartoon later in Montreal's *Le Devoir*, "Thérèse Casgrain à Paris," where she is stepping daintily into the paddy wagon brandishing a peace sign. We were driven half way across Paris and taken to what later turned out to be a police barracks or training college. There, a group of (I think) police recruits were ordered to search and record these dangerous criminals. The two French women in the group had by this time been hustled off to some unknown fate. We were the foreign agitators. So our handbags were searched for dangerous weapons. They took my scissors and pocket mirror and when I asked why, the official vividly demonstrated how I could break the mirror in two and cut my throat with it. That idea had never occurred to me. All this was much too exciting and we were already plotting, first, how much of a nuisance we could make of ourselves and then, more important, what we could do with the press. Besides Thérèse, there were two or three women who were experts at getting publicity for their cause.

We were finally escorted under heavy guard to a large cell with wire netting for walls. Thérèse dubbed it a salad shaker. There was a bench round the sides, so we sat down and planned strategy. The Belgian woman had an appointment with her ambassador which she raised the roof about missing. One by one we asked to visit the washroom — a primitive place if ever I saw one — and this meant an individual escort across two courtyards, with doors to be locked and unlocked, police time to be wasted. Then to our delight we discovered that one of our women was pregnant. How could those brutal police treat a "femme enceinte" in such a callous way, we asked. It was very cold in our unheated salad bowl ...

Finally, after about five hours during which our demands to see our ambassadors never ceased, we were visited by an important-looking group of officials. They read us a severe lecture and explained in threatening tones that we would be released if we promised never to demonstrate or march, nor to do several other things on pain of never being permitted to enter France again — or was it instant deportation; I forget. (The next time I was in a demonstration in Paris was about five years later. I wasn't deported.)

Off we went to make the most of our experience with the press and our embassies. Voice of Women and its "two distinguished representatives" (I liked that) were on the front page of *The Globe and Mail* and the Quebec papers for three days. Official notes were sent ... More important, when all the fun and games were out of the way, the real reason for our protest did get through. We were opposing this highly dangerous escalation of nuclear force by NATO. (It sounds familiar, doesn't it?) Months later, NATO dropped its plan for the MLF. We will take credit for some of that, although it was probably due to all kinds of other reasons ...

"Women's Alternatives for Negotiating Peace"
Halifax, 1985[18]

Conference Statement

* We 350 women of the world community, from 33 countries, meeting at the Women's International Peace Conference in Halifax, Canada, June 5-9, 1985, affirm the overwhelming need and desperate urgency for peace, which we believe is both the process we live and the goal for which we work.

* At this conference, women from diverse racial, cultural, ethnic and political backgrounds representing different sides of conflict areas, came together as a living example of women negotiating peace. Some of us compromised our own safety to make this commitment.

* Although women's voices have not been heard and women have not participated equally in peace negotiations or in formulation of the institutions and the cultural fabric in which we live, we are more than half the world's population; we do have power; and we are shaping it for peaceful living.

* We reject a world order based on domination, exploitation, patriarchy, racism and sexism. We demand a new order based on justice and the equitable distribution of the world's resources.

* We condemn militarism. Militarism is an addiction that distorts human development, causing world-wide poverty, starvation, pollution, repression, torture and death. Feeding this habit robs all the world's children and future generations of their inheritance.

* We all live in the shadow of the threat of nuclear war. We demand an end to research, testing, development, and deployment of all weapons of mass destruction, to the militarization of space and to all forms of violence. As a first step, we call for a comprehensive test ban treaty.

* We support the rights and the efforts of all peoples to self-determination and to freedom from military and economic intervention. As an example, we cite Nicaragua as a new kind of society, and as a symbol of hope which must be allowed to live.

* We will continue to communicate and join with women all over the world in our struggle for peace. As a result of this conference, we are developing a world-wide women's peace network. Our first act has been to pledge our vigilance in monitoring the ongoing safety of our sisters who are at risk as a result of attending this conference.

* We are committed to acting globally, nationally, locally and individually for peace. We will not compromise our commitment to the survival and healing of this planet.

* We affirm the right of every human being to live with dignity, equality, justice and joy.

---

18. "Summary Report," June 9, 1985, 1.

"That Desperate Attempt to Sell Us 'Nuclear'"
Halifax, 1982[19]

There is a form of hysteria which results from the suppression of threatening or disturbing knowledge. Having read William March's coverage in The Chronicle-Herald of Dr. Leo Yaffe's recent lecture on nuclear power, I can only assume Dr. Yaffe, president of the Chemical Institute of Canada, suffers from the complaint he purports to correct — the hysteria, as he calls it, of the anti-nuclear lobby.

Dr. Yaffe's stand on this issue is political rather than scientific; it is obvious that he is neither objective nor impartial. He is only one of many "experts" the nuclear industry will parade in front of us in their desperate attempt to sell "nuclear" to Nova Scotia.

The energy corporations are desperate because nuclear power has proven to be not only unsafe but very expensive. A recent study prepared for the Ontario Royal Commission on Electric Power Planning (1980) estimates that nuclear powered electricity is more than twice as expensive as heating with imported oil or natural gas. What Dr. Yaffe and nuclear proponents always leave out of their economic analyses are the hidden costs of nuclear power: tax breaks, limited liability nuclear insurance with the tab being picked up by the taxpayer; direct and indirect government subsidies; decommissioning of nuclear reactors (average life of 25-30 years) and subsequent management of these forever-radioactive sites; long-term surveillance and management of uranium mine tailings and high-level reactor wastes; long-term degradation of the immediate environment, including hundreds of acres of land used for dumping uranium mine wastes and tailings; long-term degradation of worker and public health.

Apart from these hidden costs at home, the only way to sell Candu abroad is to bribe developing countries with unprecedented offers of direct aid, credit lines and reduced interest rates. While some of us cannot afford to renegotiate our house mortgages, Canada is offering Mexico a 7.5 per cent interest rate to buy Canadian nuclear ... Nuclear power is so capital-intensive that only the wealthy countries can afford to generate it and then they have to dump it on developing countries in order to pay for it at home.

The developing countries who fall for the nuclear line often have a double purpose in mind. In 1951, Canada sold a small research reactor to India. In 1974, India exploded its first nuclear bomb with plutonium produced from that reactor. Canada sold a reactor to Argentina. Recently Dr. Miguel Usher, an assistant to the president of Argentina, "admitted that nuclear power in Argentina is much more expensive than alternate energy sources; however, he indicated that the military potential of the nuclear program made it a worthwhile investment." (Press release, Canadian Coalition for Nuclear Responsibility.) ...

19. Donna E. Smyth, *The Chronicle-Herald*, 15 February 1982.

Nuclear proliferation is a nightmare nobody wants to wake up to. Yet proponents of nuclear power, such as Dr. Yaffe, shrug off this weapons connection. Another symptom of hysteria?

Dr. Yaffe would have us believe we have no alternatives. He speaks as though we have only a black and white choice between coal and nuclear. Alternative technologies, such as solar, and alternative sources, such as tidal, are summarily dismissed. Coal becomes nuclear's whipping boy. We are told how dangerous it is. We hear how even hydroelectric dams break and cause deaths by drowning ...

Dr. Yaffe dismisses the problems of nuclear waste management with a wave of his hand. Yet there is documented evidence of actual and potential health hazards and environmental contamination at every uranium mining development site in Canada. Even on a purely common sense level, no community wants radioactive waste dumped in its backyard. Witness the trouble the Atomic Energy Control Board of Canada had last summer in finding a dump for the radioactive materials discovered in several Toronto suburban yards.

Dr. Yaffe also underestimates, again at the expense of coal, the occupational hazards of uranium mining. The latest study by the National Institute of Occupational Safety and Health, U.S., June 30, 1980, questions the existing maximum permissible radiation exposure doses for uranium miners and states: "There is no margin of safety associated with the present standard ... miners of uranium-bearing ores are at higher risk of cancer than other individuals occupationally exposed to radiation ... "

Finally, Dr. Yaffe spends a lot of time whitewashing the accident at Three Mile Island. He says no one was killed. This is a standard nuclear industry argument and a logical red herring to distract us from the main problems. Immediate deaths are not the point.

The latency-induction period for most cancers is 10-30 years. In this situation, people die later — after industry liability has run out. Accompanying problems are depression of the general immune system leading to lower disease resistance, pre-mature aging, increased incidences of still births and abortions. Also of concern and still a matter of scientific debate are possible mutagenetic defects — irreversible damage to the human gene pool ...

The extraordinary claims Dr. Yaffe makes for nuclear power do not constitute a basis for serious and impartial discussion.

Nova Scotians may have to accept the fact that "experts" not already committed on this issue are hard to find. And we are the ones who will have to live with the results of the decision about uranium development.

We must make sure that we are part of the decision-making process and that we represent, not only ourselves, but the interests of our children and grandchildren for generations.

It would be ironic if, 50 years down the road, people said: Nova Scotia is a "have" province — it has all the radioactive waste nobody else wants.

"Rosalie Bertell: Surviving Nuclear Threats" Vancouver, 1986[20]

Rosalie Bertell recalls the end of World War II with the bombing of Hiroshima and Nagasaki. Although her family was happy that the war was over, there was no celebration in her house. She remembers her mother saying "they shouldn't have done it, they shouldn't have done it."

But Bertell did not become active in the peace movement until she had a heart attack in 1972. She stopped teaching and devoted more time to researching the environmental and hereditary factors influencing leukemia.

"As I learned more I became more and more involved." When she was invited to testify on the effects of low-level radiation at a nuclear plant licencing hearing, she started asking "Where did they get permission to give everyone radiation exposure? And who said it was ok?"

Still, she left the peace aspect to others until two events forced it into her consciousness. Eight years ago she was invited to speak in commemoration of Hiroshima and Nagasaki in Japan. She spoke with survivors, living examples of what she had been researching. Then she went to a Strategic Arms Limitation Treaty II (SALT II) briefing — a whole day describing the weapons of war. During the question period she asked "How many people die every year in the production of these bombs?" Finally Paul Wainke, a key American SALT II negotiator, said quietly into the microphone, "That's not our department."

Said Bertell "that really hit me because I knew the military didn't count the cost in money but it was so obvious that they didn't count the cost in lives either."

For Bertell, there has been no turning back ...

Kinesis spoke with Bertell in February as she passed through Vancouver on her way home from the Marshall Islands.

Kinesis: Does your perspective have anything to do with being a woman?

Bertell: Oh yes, it certainly does. This is a caricature but I think it's fairly accurate. Men somehow or other consider that their part of life is economics, how much it costs, what's the political clout, who's in charge, who has the most power. They judge activities on maximizing the economics and the political clout. This is behind their planning.

Strategic planners have economists and political scientists, physicists and engineers. They don't hire biologists, or medical doctors, geneticists or pediatricians. They consider the other part of life — human life — not their business.

20. Marrianne van Loon, Interview with Rosalie Bertell, *Kinesis*, June 1986, 17.

I think it stems from the fact that somebody has fed them and clothed them and nourished them and they've never worried about that part of life. It's rather astonishing to hear strategic planners talk about the possibility of nuclear war out in the Pacific Ocean without anyone saying "what about our food?" That's the fish supply for the people of the world. That doesn't enter into the equation.

There's very little feeling for the fact that the earth is alive, the earth recycles everything in the water and the food, and the air. We need the trees and the insects and the animals and the birds in order to live ourselves. There's also no feeling for the longterm effects on the human race. If you damage the gene pool (the effect of low-level radiation), you produce children who are damaged.

Those children are physically less able to cope, and then you give them a more hazardous world to cope with. You can't keep doing it. It's a snowballing disaster undermining survivability of the human race. And the strategic planners don't think about that, it's not in the equation.

Kinesis: What do women have to offer?

Bertell: I think women are going to have to do something about this one. The women are the ones who have been cleaning up for years, and this one they can't actually clean up, so they'd better stop the whole thing.

It's going to have to come from someone *outside* this system because this system can't solve its own problems. There's no economic and political solution. It's not going to come from the people in political power because their *basis* of power is war. As the threat of war increases, so does the power of the leaders, so they're not likely to do away with the spiral ...

Kinesis: What is the prognosis for life on this planet, even if there is no nuclear war?

Bertell: We're already into a slow death syndrome, but it's going to soon become very obvious. We're probably now seeing the third generation of the nuclear age. I suspect that by the fifth generation everyone will know what's happened, but by then it becomes more difficult to stop it because you've got genetically damaged people and a genetically damaged earth. We're damaging people.

Quality of life is going to have to be the value we choose. If we don't have life, and strength and health, it's going to become harder and harder to get anything else. Civilization is a sham, it's getting rotten from the inside out.

Kinesis: How do you say stop?

Bertell: Non-cooperation is the basis. We have to find more ways in which we cooperate to stop the escalation. I don't think you can do it alone, you need to belong to a community where you keep questioning "how am I helping, how am I cooperating, how can I withdraw my money and my labour from this insanity and how can I make my non-cooperation visible?"

I would expect the peace movement to eventually say "on Friday between one and three o'clock nobody is going to work. We're giving you a message that we don't approve." If this doesn't work we do it on Wednesday and Friday and so on until the message gets across that we're serious, we're not just out here parading once a year saying we want peace, and meanwhile the rest of the time helping you prepare for war. The message has got to get across loud and clear that business is just not going to be done.

I would expect women will take the lead. Women have always been the change agents in society, while men's traditional role has been maintaining the status quo. Major change movements have been initiated by women.

Kinesis: Is there hope?

Bertell: People give up, but I guess because of my medical background — I don't. If somebody has had polio or a disastrous automobile accident, you don't say "oh well, this person is going to be harmed for life so to heck with it." You don't give up. I feel that way about the earth. We've hurt ourselves as a people, the earth, but you don't just give up and say "what the heck, we might as well just blow the whole thing up." You try to say "ok, yes, we did do that, let's stop doing it in the future and let's maximize what health is left on the earth and have a decent existence."

I can't understand giving up. Every individual has to die at some point, and that doesn't mean you don't ever live. You don't say "well, I'm doomed to die therefore I never will live." I don't understand that attitude at all. There is hope, there's hope that we can live and there's no reason to roll up in the corner and die just because we've done what we've done to ourselves. Life belongs to the survivors.

"Webs of Bright Wool: Women in the Peace Movement" Ottawa, 1984[21]

I AM A MIDDLE-AGED WOMAN sitting in the middle of the road, waiting to be arrested. Six feet in front of me, a green delivery truck stops, its driver staring down. Beside me, Mary and Tina sit comfortably, cross-legged, holding hands. I hunch clumsily, clasping my knees, conscious of mud on my black pants, wondering what my mother would say. Do Mary and Tina have such anxieties?

Behind me, a radio crackles, car doors slam. Then absolute silence, so that I can hear the early morning birds singing in the trees by the Ottawa river, across from the target of our blockage, the Department of External Affairs. Out of the corner of my eye I can see police on the roof of the National Research Office across the way, and riot police lining the sidewalk. Then a scuffle of boots, and two men take my arms, not ungently, pulling me up and dragging me to the police car. My first arrest for civil disobedience ...

21. Alison Acker, *This Magazine* 18, no. 2 (June 1984), 11–13.

Arrest itself is, of course, frightening. Being in jail is a humiliating experience. Every woman I have met in protest actions worries about the reactions of family, employers, neighbours. But getting arrested on purpose is like calling a government's bluff, and finding the emperor has no clothes.

When I sat down on my slatted bunk in the new Ottawa jail (walls painted strawberry ice cream pink and blessed by Princess Diana herself in 1983) I felt like Alice at the final trial scene, when she cries out, 'Why, you're nothing but a pack of cards!' and the King and Queen and officers of the court fly up into the air, mere cardboard. They can hold me briefly, inconvenience me, fine me, lecture me, but they cannot stop me.

Arrest not only liberated me from fear of overt authority. It freed me from years of subtle conditioning ...

Our civil disobedience that day was a very small one — sixteen people blockading the Ministry of External Affairs to protest Canada's continuing complicity with U.S. intervention in Central America ...

With five other women and nine men from Guelph, Kingston, Toronto, Vancouver, Ottawa and Prince Edward Island, we walked through early morning Ottawa, carrying a fake coffin topped by baby dolls ... We set down the coffin in front of the police outside the Deparament of External Affairs, poured blood over the dolls to symbolize Canadian guilt and the slaughter of the innocents, and sat down in the road. (The blood was donated by supporters in Ottawa, and taken just like Red Cross donations. It felt marvellously sticky and mysteriously powerful, so that pouring it was almost like a mass.)

Arrest was like a slowed-down movie, almost choreographed, with no words spoken. And jail itself was anti-climatic. Nobody handcuffed me, and the policewoman who searched me merely patted my body.

The women were distributed into the row of pink cells, each with slatted bed and toilet, watched by TV cameras. It is hard to use the toilet knowing you are on TV. We told stories — fantasies about islands where nobody makes war and nobody dictates. We sang round songs, about women and water that wears through the rock. Police and guards came and went ...

Then, five hours later, we were told we were all being charged with mischief and would be released on our own recognizance. The pressure of authority became bureaucracy, with surely archaic measures such as asking us to write out the alphabet in small and capital letters, presumably in case we wrote threatening letters to the prime minister! Fingerprinting is messy. Two officers struggled for an hour with ink pads that smudged their uniforms. We were 'mugged,' had our height and weight recorded and entered in the archives as more grist for Ottawa's records.

At the beginning of April we returned to court — one of many appearances for some of my women friends, but the first time for me. We were sentenced to seven days in jail or a fifty dollar fine. My friends will be going the same route many more times. I may or may not join them, having too much at stake in the respectable world to make civil disobedience a way of live ...

But any time I feel it necessary, I shall be back, sitting in the middle of that road, along with thousands of others across the world. I will protest where I want, when I want, for my own reasons, and take the consequences, knowing I am right and that those who would stop me are wrong, because they represent destruction of life, and are ultimately powerless, because they cannot stop me.

When they arrested me, they set me free.

"One Final Argument"
Toronto, April 1984[22]

I will speak to our common law defence of necessity which reads in one of its most rigorous definitions as follows:

> We believed on reasonable and probable grounds that serious harm would befall ourselves or some other persons.
> The situation was one of clear and imminent peril such that no other course of conduct was reasonably possible. The offence committed gave rise to less harm than that sought to be prevented.

The impassioned testimony which the defendants have submitted to the court for the last five days attests to the honesty and sincerity of our beliefs. And, the expert witnesses who have spoken to the court have provided expert evidence supporting the "reasonable and probable grounds" for our beliefs that "serious harm would befall ourselves or some other person." The nature of this "serious harm" has become gruesomely apparent during the proceeds of this trial.

Secondly, we have proven to the court in a variety of ways that our actions on November 14 and 18, 1983, were taken because "no other course of conduct was reasonably possible." A number of the defendants repeatedly spoke of their exclusion from access to power and of how masculinist institutions controlled us economically as well as controlling weapons and technology. Sociologist Dr. Dorothy Smith gave expert testimony as to the minimal role women play in the decision making of our society. She also pointed to the *qualitative* difference this exclusion makes in our culture. While military strategists speak statistically of the projected number of dead in a nuclear war, women have been socialized to relate to the individual body as a sister, as brother, as mother, friend, lover, father, child — not as an empty cypher in an endless column of numbers.

As well as this institutional exclusion and lack of a representative woman's perspective, we know that women are less capable in economic terms to affect social change. Women make up the majority of the poor

22. Janice Williamson, *Broadside* 5, no. 6 (April 1984), 5.

in Canada and while the number of poor children in Ontario increases by 20 percent a year, the Canadian Defence Budget of over $7 billion in 1982-83 also increases by 20 percent a year. You have heard testimony on the economics of the arms race from these women who make up the majority of the poor in Canada. You've heard from women who have struggled to raise seven children on their own, and from women of ethnic minorities who remain underrepresented politically in Canada.

These and other women have expressed to this court how they have exhausted all available alternatives in their attempt to stop the production of the guidance system of the cruise missile at Litton and the testing of the cruise missile in Canada. They have spoken to workers at Litton factory through pamphlets and organized meetings. They have attempted to reach the Canadian government, which supports Litton's activity with over $48 million in research funds through, as Martha Waldon describes, "signing petitions, writing letters, and publicly demonstrating with hundreds of thousands of other Canadians." The government has not responded. Litton Systems has not responded. We have conducted educational sessions for the public, and in the case of seventeen-year-old Maria Louladakis, provided workshops for fellow high school students. Seventeen-year-old Nancy Jane Prescott testified that after pamphleting and demonstrating she had "not only a right, but a duty to go to Litton" and express to the public her fears and feelings.

Our expert witness, Dr. Ursula Franklin, testified that "the arsenal of civic action that the citizen has is limited because of the nature of nuclear war. We have to look for preventative techniques that take into account that afterwards there will be no one left to hang." Defendant Vicki Miller testified about why she went to Litton: "Silence is complicity. I cannot be a part of those who commit the sins of commission. I felt I had to be there. I didn't have a choice."

The situation we confront is clearly one of 'imminent peril.' You heard Susan Milwid express her fears for the present and future of her two small sons. And as Marlene Tadman pointed out, the business of military defence wears cruel disguises when a subsidiary of Litton is found to be in the process of constructing camps in Honduras to train mercenaries for the invasion of Nicaragua and El Salvador. The peril is here. You've heard testimony as to the cynical imbalance world military production places on its citizens. One half of the world's population, that is, 2 billion people, live on an income equivalent to world military expenditures.

How do we know the peril is imminent? Defendant Martha Waldon reported on the latest American military policy developed to take advantage of the new capabilities of the cruise missiles. She spoke of their first strike strategy, to strike "early and deep," and not necessarily at military targets. What is the imminent danger? Waldon reported on the figures provided by the Cambridge Study Group on Nuclear Disarmament, where 3,707 false alarms of a nuclear attack were recorded in an eighteen month period from January 1979 to June 1980. Dr. Ursula Franklin described the cruise missile as "different in kind, unmanned, undetectable since it travels at a low altitude, and it is cheap as weapons go at two million dollars." Franklin clarified the significance of the guidance system constructed by Litton. "The cruise can be launched from air, sea and ground ... Its delivery system can be as commonplace as an ordinary truck." And while the cruise missile has been around since World War II, the guidance system is key to the new political and military conditions which have developed with the cruise. According to the Litton Systems (Canada) product catalogue, the system they produce "does more than provide guidance." It also, in their words, "Issues the warhead arming command." In other words, the cruise missile guidance system *triggers* and targets its nuclear warhead. And the blast power of the average nuclear warhead expected to be carried by the cruise causes six times the destruction of the Hiroshima holocaust.

The Mewett and Manning *Criminal Law* textbook published in 1978 cites the Morgentaler case and defines the following as the task of the court in response to the common law defence of necessity:

> It is not the absolute certainty of the projected harm that is required but the accused's belief based upon reasonable and probable grounds that the harm will occur.

In this court yesterday, Sister Rosalie Bertell testified, and more than satisfied this requirement of the court by pointing to the gruesome reality that 16 million people have already been damaged by nuclear production since it began in 1945. She continued, "The casualties have already begun in World War III and continue at the rate of 200 per day. We know that in the case of nuclear war, to prove the "absolute certainty" of the projected harm would be an abject horror too terrifying for any of us to speak. It is enough to know that every year from 38,000 to 78,000 workers and others die from the effects of radiation in the production of materials for nuclear weapons ...

On November 14 and 18, all of the women defendants before this court put themselves at personal risk in the service of their deeply held beliefs. On the witness stand we heard the women over and over again testify that they acted out of a conviction as individuals morally responsible to act in opposition to the war preparations which go on every day in Rexdale (home of Litton Systems), an ordinary suburb where many citizens live their lives oblivious to the danger in their midst. Marlene Tadman said, "There is *no* contradiction between non-violence and action. We are morally committed to act." And her daughter Pamela testified, "We have had to go beyond ourselves and our own daily needs of work, of home, of eating and sleeping. We can run and hide or we can take full responsibility for our actions." And, why do we act? Wendy Moore said yesterday, "It's almost impossible for anyone to hold in their minds what is going on in this world." We hold in our minds this madness that is a world bent on self-annihilation. Dr. Franklin testified that the increased tensions of the cold war in the escalated production of nuclear weapons has two psychological effects on human beings. First, it creates feelings of helplessness, and second, feelings of fear and apprehensiveness. On November 14, these feelings were experienced by more than the women involved in the non-violent civil-disobedience. I spoke with the desk sergeant on my release from 23 Division in Rexdale. He said, "Technology is out of control. There is nothing that we can do. I fought in a war and I'm terrified."

On November 14 and 18, we took hold of our terror to motivate us to act. The women and men who accompanied us to Litton and the 29 defendants before this court today refuse resignation, refuse passivity, refuse inaction, refuse denial in the face of this terror that is World War III.

We went to Litton as sisters and we have prepared and presented our defence collectively, as, in your own words your honour, "a sorority" — a deeply political and ethically engaged sorority. We have invited international experts on the sociology and status of women in our society, on the cruise missile and the effects of advanced technology on our lives, and an international expert on the tragically ongoing effects of radiation on our population. We, the defendants, have also presented our own testimony in good faith and often accompanied by fears of impassioned rage and sorrow.

Our strength lies in our collective representation of the concerns of hundreds of thousands, of millions of citizens. In this country and around the world who have demonstrated their opposition to the cruise missile.

Pam Millar said, "In the history of social change, it is always people who take personal risk that change the course of history." We ask that this court address our ethical, political and moral concerns, and not resort to the technical language of the prosecution as to where the fence is, how high is the fence, how high did we jump.

We present ourselves to the court not as criminals to be convicted, to be punished, but as a community of women who choose life over death, creative politics over the politics of exterminism, non-violent action over sleep, silence and complicity.

We are charged in this provincial court with petty trespass. When you balance this charge on the scales of justice with the knowledge of Litton's production of components for the guidance system, a system which is part of war preparations for a war we cannot even speak of, a war that is already claiming lives, it is evident that the offence we committed "gave rise to less harm than that sought to be prevented" according to our defence of necessity. It is the moral imperative and justice of this court to acquit us.

"Innu People Stand Fast"
Ottawa, May 1989[23]

When we were young girls, the Innu Villages of Sheshatshit, Utshimassit, Pukutshipit, Unemeinshipit and Nutashkuan did not exist. We lived all year in our tents travelling across our own country, Nitassinan. Our mothers and fathers fed us with the animals they killed.

The true life of the Innu People as nomads and hunters is not an easy one. Sometimes we were hungry. But we never felt hopelessness or that we had lost control of our lives or that we did not know who we were. And we always knew, as we know now, that Nitassinan, our country, was our home and belonged to us the Innu People of the Labrador-Quebec peninsula ...

Although we had no police, we never needed any. We did not know what crime was. All the Innu had a purpose in their lives and responsibility in their lives. None of our people ever tried to kill themselves, children were all properly cared for, brought up and educated as Innu, and they knew and were proud of who and what they were.

In the 1950's, Europeans began to move into Nitassinan in large numbers ...

In a few short years we have been completely robbed of our land and freedom. We have seen control of our country, the land that gave us birth as a People thousands of years ago, taken from us. And now we are treated as if were were invisible, as if we do not exist. We are a hunting People. To keep us in one place, in a village, has meant that they have tried to separate us from everything that gives our life as a People meaning. It has also meant that we have been changed in only a few years from one of the most self-reliant and independent Peoples in the world to one of the most dependent.

We think they thought, the Europeans, that because they gave us money to keep us alive, that we would stay silent forever and die off quietly as a distinct People, while they helped themselves to our land and our water.

The settlers often point out that what are supposed to be the organizations that are defending Innu rights receive, and have in the past received, large amounts of money from the European government. This is true but we know that these organizations were introduced among us in the 1970's to try and control us by making it impossible for us to fight back except in ways and places where the rules of the game were set by the European. And if we did something they didn't like, they threatened to cut off money and sometimes did. So even here, in our ways of expressing our anger and sadness and resistance, we were dependent.

These organizations, including the Band Councils, were imposed on us. They are not Innu things and do not work in the way our society works ...

23. Rose Gregorie and Elizabeth Penashue, *Kinesis*, June 1989, 7.

So in our new resistance against what is being done to our People it has almost been easier for us Innu women to fight back because we were never really part of that system which has been imposed on us, and which was paid for and controlled by foreign rulers.

Our fight for our People is not a fight just for women but for all our People. It is not a women's issue but an Innu issue and we have welcomed any Innu person who will fight alongside us to create a free and healthy world for our children and grandchildren ...

... The one thing that has stopped our complete breakdown as a People has been the months we still live away from the villages in our tents in the country.

For the families who now have houses in Sheshatshit, we find ourselves right alongside what Canada wants to make into a NATO base. Even with no base, each year the military grows bigger there and the number of low level flights grows bigger. There is now one bombing range and many, many targets where they do not yet drop anything but use for practice attacks. Most of these are on or near lakes where the Innu go in the Spring and Fall. We feel that we have been shoved to the edge of a cliff in the last 25 years. Now they want to push us over.

Nitassinan is our land. We never gave it to them. How do they feel they can come in and take it and treat us as if we were not human beings, as if we were invisible to them? ...

... We are fighting for our land and for our rights and identity as a distinct hunting people in our own land, Nitassinan. We are not going to jail, becoming separated from our children just to get rich land claims. Our fight is not about land claims, which is only another thing being used against us to get us to surrender what we will never, ever give up, that is our ownership of Nitassinan and our Innu identity.

"Peace"
Ottawa, 1990[24]

Peace. "Tranquility, freedom from strife, freedom from warring conditions, freedom of the mind from annoyance." We have not had peace for some 28,614 days since Columbus first came here. Worse, our homeland has not experienced peace since this country's inception.

Violence: "organized, unwarranted, unjust exertion of force." We know what that is, beginning in the grand banks of Newfoundland with the slaughter of the cod fish and the Beothucks, to the great lakes and the slaughter of the salmon, sturgeon — the main source of food for the Six Nations people — and the reduction of the Huron to a small band in Ontario; the massacre of millions of beaver, mink, and Anishnawbeg people from Sudbury to Winnipeg, the slaughter of the buffalo and the death of the Cree Nation to the war against the Manitoba Nation and the dispersal of the Métis and Native people throughout the northern prairies, to the burning of our great forests in B.C. and the contamination of

24. Lee Maracle, *The Womanist* 2, no. 2 (Fall 1990), 9.

our rivers with toxic waste from pulp mills, saw mills and the very recent cutting of our forests — we know about organized violence ...

Struggle: strenuous and resolute effort. We know what that is too. It took great effort to live the way we did centuries ago, it took emotional effort, physical effort and spiritual effort. To discipline the self to live within the laws of "waste not want not" took huge efforts on our part. The struggle to survive the death of the earth and the disease plagues brought here by such an heroic people as the Hudson Bay Company. Huge efforts on our part, in fact; for a while it looked like we would not make it.

Thousands of citizens have decried violence in the resistance struggle of our people. Violence. "Organized, unjust and unwarranted attacks." We have never organized ourselves to attack anyone, unjustly or otherwise. Ours is a peaceful struggle, but it is not a passive one ...

There is no peace in this country. We are absolutely opposed to a bunch of cowboys in a D-9 Cat running hi-diddle-diddle over the hill, playing texax chainsaw massacre with our tree relatives. Creation is not passive, but it is sacred ...

Violence: to distort basic meaning and understanding. To call upon us to submit to the organized violence of golfers, corporate logging companies, multinational oil corporations or any other such truck who seeks to strip mine, clear-cut or play games on the graves of our ancestors is to distort the meaning of violence. We are being asked to sacrifice our sacred creation, our children, our lineage. We **cannot** do that.

Peaceful struggle is all about expending great strenuous effort to life free from strife, free from war, free from conditions which annoy the mind. It annoys my mind to think about clear-cutting. It annoys my mind to consider the invasion and death of the people of Oka, it annoys my mind to imagine golfers tromping on the graves of Mohawk grandmothers. So I struggle to put a stop to it. I walk, I picket, I block roads. I cannot watch a people die.

I am a caretaker. Every single indigenous person here is a caretaker. Take care. Take care of creation. Creation is not complacent, not inactive. To take care of creation is an active process, an imaginative process, a process full of wonderment. It means strenuous effort, it means healing ourselves of amber-elbow disease. It cannot be done by complacent people who are intoxicated, seeking the pleasure of parties. It cannot be done by disempowered people. It cannot be done by people who cannot imagine a different world, dream of a life of peace and harmony in which all creation is respected and cared for.

It cannot be done by people who have a hierarchy in their minds. All things, all life is sacred. There is no human life, animal life, plant life, more sacred than the next ...

The struggle is struggle for peace, not just one against violence. Peace: harmony. Peace: freedom. Peace: tranquility. Rage is not tranquil. Bitterness is not harmonious. Being locked to someone else's perception of you is not freedom. Freedom is a state of mind. You are free to choose. You may choose to be complacent, you may choose to watch a people die, or you may choose to stop the slaughter. Freedom is personal and significant. Freedom and peace require a deep sense of justice and great love. Harmony ...

If we are all dead we cannot have peace. If we are allowed to die because the good citizens of this country did nothing, they will be left with their violence. They will be left with the memory not of resolute struggle, great effort for peace, but with the memory of unspirited, unemotional, uncaring inactivity in the face of our genocide. My spirit is not passive. Injustice annoys my mind and disturbs my spirit. I will be that way for all eternity. We have done all the unjust dying a people should have to do. This land has done all the unjust dying she should have to do. Don't be a passive soldier for corporate murder. With peace and harmony in your heart go out and spend great effort, strenuous effort to change the story of Canada. Be active, be resolute, be caring and we shall have peace.

Feminism and Pacifism

"Pure but Powerless: The Women's Peace Movement" Toronto, July 1984[25]

From Greenham Common, Seneca, NY, Cold Lake, Alberta, and from many other places and perspectives, large numbers of women are massing together to oppose the weaponry and ideology of a system which many claim is based on the masculine values of violence and aggression. The threat of nuclear annihilation is, according to them, as much a feminist issue as rape or abortion. Some groups even contend that the peace movement should take top priority in women's organizing.

Two points are at issue here for radical feminists. First, the women's peace movement claims that women have a special interest *as women* in preserving the life of the earth and in ensuring the future for the benefit of their children. Secondly, it claims that women are specially suited for this task by virtue of their nurturing and sensitive awareness of life. We are supposedly more peace-loving by nature than men are.

We believe that a substantive critique of these two points is important, since they relate directly to the notion of biological determinism, which states that women's nature is defined by innate biological features. We also intend to address the strategies for change employed by the women's peace movement, their effectiveness, and their implications.

---

25. Terry Mehlman, Debbie Swanner, and Midge Quandt, *Broadside* 5, no. 9 (July 1984), 6–7. The authors are members of the Radical Feminist Organizing Committee, a group with both Canadian and American members. This critique is largely of the American women's peace movement.

In Whose Interest?

How can women have a "special" interest in nuclear war? A nuclear disaster would be the most equal event in the history of the world. Bombs don't discriminate. (An exception would be the neutron bomb which will leave buildings intact.) Women would be neither more nor less affected than any other group. The real point of this argument is the premise that women are somehow responsible for life on earth: since women possess the capacity to bear children, the continued existence of the world and the fate of its inhabitants are of a greater concern to these producers of life, these women, than to men. Whether this argument is used to glorify women's power to affect world events or to pin the responsibility for world events upon us, the basic idea is the same. Simply stated, women's fate and women's interest is defined by the capacity and duty to bear children.

As radical feminists, we reject the notion that women are defined by their reproductive capacity, a notion that was one of the basic tenets of the early women's liberation movement. As Ti-Grace Atkinson has pointed out, the ability to bear children is a capacity which individual women may or *may not* choose to exercise. Radical feminists should object to the equating of motherhood with womanhood. Women as human beings share an interest with other human beings (men) in the preservation of life on earth. Setting women and men in opposition over an issue of human concern only reinforces the artificial constructs of gender which form the basis of women's oppression ...

Are Women Better Than Men?

A prevalent defence of the women's peace movement lies in the appeal to the superior quality of women's "nature." An understanding of the reliance on and celebration of women's "special qualities" is important to any critique of the women's peace movement, since so much of its theory and strategy rests on this way of thinking. Qualities such as nurturing, sensitivity and peacefulness are said to belong, either inherently or as a result of social conditioning, primarily to women — if only men would give up their aggressive, violent, "masculine" values, injustice would disappear and peace would reign.

The notion that "women's qualities" are somehow better than "men's qualities" is in basic opposition to the theory of feminism. Feminist theory states that the potential for all qualities — from aggressiveness to nurturing — exists within each person. But under a system of male supremacy, certain traits are deemed "masculine" and others "feminine." Since gender is not innate but is socially constructed, the goal of feminism is to eradicate the categories of "masculine" and "feminine." An appeal to women's distinctive characteristics only reinforces these categories. Moreover, this position does nothing to change the essential conditions between women and men; it merely seeks to reverse the qualities that dominate. The inability to effect basic change which characterizes the ideology of the women's peace movement stems in part from an excessive preoccupation with psychological factors. Focussing as it does on men's and women's character traits, the movement ignores the structural aspects of male supremacy.[26] ...

Women And Imperialism

The women in the peace movement claim a special affinity with other oppressed people. It is their view that, as victims of everyday male violence, they have special insight into its manifestations all over the world ... But violence against women is not the same as imperialism, and direct, constant, everyday oppression is not the same as the fear of possible nuclear disaster ...

If the women's peace movement were seriously concerned with the imperialism of the government, it would be working to change or overthrow that government. Instead it chooses to identify itself with the victims of imperialism and thus escape its inherent responsibility for it.

The Tactics of Persuasion

The women's peace movement often presents the view that men are inherently, some say biologically, motivated towards violence ... However, after espousing the view that men are inherently violent and evil, it bases its entire campaign for peace on a heavily symbolic appeal to men's "better nature." Surely, if men are as base as all that they can hardly be expected to change their violent ways by being exposed to a group of women protesting in loving harmony. Making such an appeal to the oppressor is a move rooted in hopelessness and despair. It says, in effect, that men hold complete power, that men will always hold complete power, so that the best women can do is ask for concessions. But we refuse to accept this assessment of the situation. The dominance of men over women is not absolute or inevitable; it derives not from biology but from a system of male supremacy ...

Feminism Does Not Equal Pacifism

In contrast to the women's peace movement, we would argue that pacifism is not integral to feminism. One can be a feminist without being a pacifist. One's opposition to war should be based on political and personal reasons which have nothing to do with being a woman.

---

26. In a recent essay, Alice Echols discusses this theoretical weakness with regard to cultural feminism, whose most prominent proponents are Mary Daly, Andrea Dworkin, Robin Morgan, and Adrienne Rich. She also analyzes cultural feminists' belief in the essentially different natures of men and women. As opposed to radical feminists, cultural feminists think that the liberation of women, as well as the solution to many of the world's problems, will come through the growth and spread of female values. Alice Echols, "The New Feminism of Yin and Yang," in Ann Snitow, Christine Stanselle, and Sharon Thompson, eds., *Powers of Desire: The Politics of Sexuality* (New York, 1983), pp. 439–59.

Let's keep the issue of violence in perspective. Women have had no choice but to be non-violent. And men have always counted on the fact that women don't fight back with physical force. Although violence is used by men to exert power over women, violence is not inherently male. It is a tool that can also be used by women against women, women against men, and men against each other. Moreover, women have sometimes been actively involved in warfare. A current example is the women of Nicaragua ... To label women's relative lack of participation in recent wars as the result of an essentially peace-loving nature makes about as much sense as attributing women's relative lack of participation in the work force in the 1905s to an essentially home-loving nature. Women serve willingly in the armed forces of many nations.

We do not believe that feminism equals pacifism or that war is the bedrock of male supremacy. Male supremacy is about the relationship of power between men and women. We could have complete peace and men would still oppress women in countless ways ...

How the Women's Peace Movement Hurts Feminism

It is hard to blame new women coming into the movement for joining the women's peace movement. They are eager to do something, there are not many groups which are vigorously working for women's liberation on a broad front. The women's peace movement fills a vacuum; the peace marches and encampments give women a group to identify with and a place to belong.

Although it would be nice to say that the women in the peace movement should go ahead and do their own thing while we do ours, feminists do not have that luxury. Every year, the basic tenets of women's liberation become more and more diluted. We have been asked to subordinate our struggle to more "pressing" concerns, such as fighting imperialism. This has diverted our energies and hurt us as a movement. There has also grown up within the women's movement the notion that there is a women's perspective on everything. According to this view, feminists should work on a wide range of issues in order to humanize society; they should bring women's values to bear on a variety of social problems at home and abroad. This approach to feminism has diverted us from the goal of women's liberation — the ending of male supremacy. Not only that, it has also diluted the meaning of feminism. If everything is feminist, as the women's peace movement and other elements in the women's movement would have us believe, then nothing is feminist ...

The legacy of altruism and moral superiority hurts us as women and as a movement. One of the ways it harms us is in our relationship to men as a group. What do men feel when they see hundreds of women marching for peace as mothers, lesbians, or feminists? They don't seem to feel threatened: we have not noticed any liberal men complaining about these all-women gatherings. In fact, men would prefer us to focus on the military rather than on their behavior. Certainly men would rather see women climbing fences than disturbing male privilege.

As radical feminists, we question both the assumptions and the consequences of the women's peace movement. It has encouraged women to celebrate the very features that mark our oppression. Exalting the qualities which men have assigned to us and which keep us in our place in no way weakens male supremacy or brings our own liberation closer. Let us return to the principles of women's liberation as they apply to women in the 1980s. It is time we put ourselves first. No one else will.

Response to "Pure but Powerless" Toronto, August/September 1984[27]

I am writing in response to "Pure but Powerless: The Women's Peace Movement" (July 1984) written by the Radical Feminist Organizing Committee (RFOC). While there are interesting criticisms in the article, there is much with which I disagree as a feminist activist.

There are many of us in the movement who do not base our anti-militaristic position on motherhood. But is it fair of us to invalidate the concerns of women for whom motherhood is an important role? Is not their response to the threat of war historically informed? Women, as we know, have been socialized to be mothers, have watched the menfolk (often unwillingly) go off to the slaughter, and have been left with the responsibility of the dead, the rubble and the living. I agree that it is up to all of us, whether we be woman or man, to preserve life. We are not intending to establish an opposition to men nor take full responsibility for nurturing — we too think men are capable of this. Rather, we are criticizing the structure that the dominant male class has constructed over these many centuries — particularly their war machine. We are angry women who value our lives and as feminists we see male supremacy sustained by the patriarchal-military organization.

Militarization and nuclear war, contrary to the opinion of the authors, are special interests because they do oppress us; because if we do not speak out against them they will destroy us through their many reprehensible ways. Let me point out that: nuclear missiles back up the imperialist war machine and will potentially be used against national liberation struggles; the testing of the cruise missile over Alberta denies legitimacy to native land claims; microchip manufacturing, an integral part of the nuclear industry, threatens the health of and exploits Asian women; nuclear testing in the South Pacific has displaced women and their communities, destroyed entire islands and caused radioactive poisoning of entire populations that has resulted in genetic mutations; nuclear reactors spill radioactive waste into our water systems while a million gallons of nuclear waste are yet to be buried; the uranium plants expose workers to unacceptable levels of radiation ...

27. Beth McAuley, Letter to the Editor, *Broadside* 5, no. 10 (August/September 1984), 2, 10.

Militarism, in its sexist and racist forms, is an integral part of the patriarchal-capitalist system: it will take strength, courage and ingenuity to crack it. Our opposition is made concrete and visible through mass non-violent actions, which require that we step out of our passive, acquiescent roles and speak out against male authority. The women's actions at Litton Systems, Toronto (producers of the guidance system for the cruise missile), the peace camps at Cold Lake, Alberta; Seneca, New York; Comiso, Italy; and Greenham Common, England, are actions which publicly identify nuclear war production and deployment. More significantly, the actions place us in an audible position to openly criticize and call into question the oppressive policies that maintain male privilege and male superiority. Our analysis points out that this position is maintained by military power, and that that power has multiple effects on our lives. For instance, consider the military and: pornography, rape and prostitution; militaristic language, media imagery and fashion; war toys; multi-million profits and global economic control; social cutbacks, hunger, disease, death; legal protection of military property and industry; aggressive male attitudes, especially towards women ...

I think it is a mistake to belittle the efforts and advances the women's peace movement is making. It is an even more serious mistake to suggest a redirection of strategy that would diffuse it. The momentum of the women's liberation movement depends on us exerting pressure at all levels. Opposing militarism is but one way of criticizing male violence and initiating alternatives. It is equally important as establishing rape crisis centres and abortion clinics. Perhaps our work doesn't lead to immediate results, but understanding militarism's structure prepares us for the very real struggle involved in dismantling it, and in turn, bringing an end to patriarchal control.

We need to be critical of our strategies and we are certainly open to constructive suggestions; it's too bad the authors did not offer us any to consider. But we still need to work in solidarity with each other's efforts, and we cannot and will not turn a blind eye to patriarchy's war machine. Our resistance is growing stronger — maybe it's just more dynamic in the women's peace movement.

Beth McAuley
Toronto

"The *Kosmar* of Bosnia-Herzegovina"
Ottawa, March 1994[28]

There are many things that should never have been permitted to happen. We [Bosnians] believed the world would provide protection and never allow the Serbs to attack. Yet the world remained silent during the summer, and once the effects of the war finally reached the West — the

---

28. Amina Adams, *The Varsity* (University of Toronto), 8 March 1994, 7. *Kosmar* is Bosnian for "nightmare."

ethnic cleansing and the mass rape of Muslim women — there was an outcry. Yet still, little is being done.

In early April 1992, I called my mother and father who live in Sarajevo with my sister. I begged them to get out. They thought I was over-reacting.

"This is Sarajevo," they said. "We have lived in peace with the Serbs for years. The world will not allow war."

My family, like many others, were so sure. But they misjudged the situation. They thought the world would not allow war to happen. But the world let the Serbs do this. What else must the Serbs do to Muslims before there is action?

I am a Muslim. I was not brought up to hate others. Unfortunately, it has come to this point now because the world refuses to see that this is a war where Christians are killing Muslims. And as I sit here today, I still believe that not all Christians are "bad", and that not all Serbs are "bad". This is difficult for me to say. Those who have hands dirty with the blood of my people have been brought to believe a lie. They have committed crimes and must be brought to justice.

The war is horrible. Our dear ones are suffering. Many have witnessed their mothers being raped in front of them, their sisters and brothers in danger. Rape is being used to humiliate and torture women. Mutiliation — so many atrocities. It is difficult to elevate yourself from what is happening to the women and children in Bosnia. This is the shame of the world ...

Today, I identify myself as Bosnian. I used to be Yugoslave; I was proud to say I was Yugoslave. It feels so far away now. The war has taken my identity and even my language. I used to speak "Serbo-Croatian". Today, I speak "Bosnian". It is the same language, but a new identity. We are European, just like the French, Italian and Swiss. We have come to realize that we are Muslims to others. I never thought we would suffer because of our religion.

In Bosnia, being Muslim was not a religious identity, as it is in some Muslim countries. To say "I am Muslim" often was an indication of our national identity. Muslim women in Bosnia-Herzegovina have not worn the veil since the beginning of this century. Being Muslim means something different in all countries with Muslim populations. And so it is different in Bosnia also. But the world does not see our differences. The war has been permitted to continue because the world is largely uninformed and people do not understand the complexity of the situation. The media unfortunately has not helped.

The flow and increase of the numbers of refugees to parts of Europe has resulted in economic hardships and xenophobia. Yet there are millions of Muslims living in various parts of Europe who have lived in peace with others for many years. The West has contributed to stereotypes of Muslims and has done little to help. Many European leaders have taken little or no action to assist Bosnian Muslims and many

European citizens, with whom I am in contact, say that they are ashamed of their leaders because of this.

Even if the war stopped today, the refugees of Bosnia would not be able to go back to their homes. Most homes have either been burned down, destroyed or taken over by Serbs. Ethnic cleansing has resulted in hundreds of Muslims forcibly being moved to other locations. Imagine someone walking into your home and saying you do not live here anymore. You have to leave ...

Many Muslims in Bosnia have Serbian blood in their families. This will be the case with the children born out of the horrible rape of Muslim women by Serbian soldiers. They are 50 per cent Muslim and 50 per cent Serb. I would like to believe the children will be embraced and taken care of, but it will be difficult for the women to feel this way. Many have lost their own children and families in the war. The children borne are the future of Bosnia ... Serbian soldiers were given orders to rape Muslim women so the babies would bear Serbian pride and not Muslim/Turkish "filth." So many women have been hurt because of hatred. So many injustices have brought pain to the women of Bosnia-Herzegovina ...

Canada has accepted 500 refugees from Bosnia ...

I am concerned about the women who will come ... And of the women who have been raped, violated, mutilated and hurt, they will experience many hardships. Our value system will not allow them to talk about what has happened. We do not talk of the problem as now known ...

Recognizing the difficulty in persuading women to identify themselves for the purposes of treatment and counselling, we are exploring the possibility of an information campaign to publicize the services available, possibly including regional hotlines using Bosnian women. In addition to the obvious aim of spreading information, a matter-of-fact approach could also contribute to de-dramatising the rape for the victim, her family and her community.

"Jewish Women's Voices: Past & Present"
Toronto, February 1993[29]

Resolution unanimously approved by the Plenary of the Conference: Jewish Women's Voices, Past and Present, Feb. 21, 1993, at the Ontario Institute for Studies in Education (OISE), Toronto, Canada.

Deeply disturbed by the mass rapes and other war crimes against women and children in ex-Yugoslavia,

Cognizant and aware of the need for action to stop the rape and save the lives of women and children there until the war is over and

Conscious of our mutual obligation to extend our desperately needed assistance

29. Flyer, "Jewish Women's Voices Past & Present: A Weekend of Culture, Scholarship & Celebration," February 19–21, 1993, Toronto.

The 450 women assembled at the Conference: Jewish Women's Voices, Past and Present in Toronto call for the establishment in ex-Yugoslavia of a SAFE HAVEN run by women for women and children, both survivors of atrocities and those who find themselves at risk, protected and defended by a UN funded and maintained peacekeeping force. A similar sanctuary proposal has already been circulated by Europeans to negotiators David Own and Cyrus Vance.

The rape camps currently in existence must be CLOSED DOWN IMMEDIATELY, and their prisoners enabled through the offices of the aforementioned peace keeping force to arrive safely at the SAFE HAVEN where they will be able to start to rebuild their lives.

Such a SAFE HAVEN — the location to be determined by women's support groups in ex-Yugoslavia — must be geographically and logistically able to provide physically safe and human accommodations and services to the estimated 30 to 50,000 victims of rape and any woman or child who considers themselves at risk of rape and battering. Such services must also include: physical, medical and psychological rehabilitation to be provided by women.

We are calling for the immediate convening of a conference to develop a plan for the logistical implementation of this SAFE HAVEN PLAN. Participants are to include women's groups, politicians, doctors, and technicians to rebuild the communal infrastructure.

We call for at least half of all positions of negotiators and policy makers to be held by women. We believe if this were the case, women and children being raped and killed would be a priority.

We will express our outrage by immediately phoning or faxing our politicians, particularly given that this is an election year in Canada, lobbying for the changing of Canadian Refugee policy and the support of organizations organizing vigils and demonstrations.

Women Refugees

"Refugee Claims Based on Gender Persecution: The Canadian Experience" July 1993[30]

Nurjehan Mawani, the Chairperson of the Canadian Immigration and Refugee Board, chose March 8, International Women's Day, to officially issue the IRB Guidelines on Gender Persecution. The guidelines had been in the works for several months. The draft paper was circulated to some organizations and individuals for their comments. We sent in suggestions for change which, in the end, were not incorporated in the guidelines. However, when we met with Ms. Mawani recently, she said that she remains open to any suggestions. We have therefore not given

30. Elsa Tesfay Musa, paper presented at the "Consultation on Women Refugees" meeting of the Lutheran Immigration and Refugee Service of New York, New York City, 27 July 1993.

up hope in seeing further changes to the guidelines. Thus, the Working Group on Refugee Women's Issues has now embarked on a project to find out whether the guidelines are making any difference and to identify gaps and problems ...

We consider the guidelines a first step in our efforts to have our government pay attention to the protection needs of refugee women. Because the guidelines are not legally binding, meaning that Refugee Board members can ignore them as long as they give a written report explaining why, our long-term plan is to push for amendments to Canadian Immigration Law to have the support of some politicians and national women's groups ...

1992 saw a rise in the number of women making refugee claims based on gender persecution. But it was Nada's case that grabbed the most media attention and finally forced Bernard Valcourt, the minister of immigration, to announce that guidelines were being formulated and that he was willing to hold national consultations on refugee women's issues. Nada is a woman from Saudi Arabia who said she was persecuted because she had been rejected and a deportation order was issued. Nada decided to go into hiding while her lawyer, the Working Group on Refugee Women's Issues, the Centre for Human Rights, the National Action Committee on the Status of Women, the media and many other refugee groups and individuals put pressure on the minister to use his discretionary power to allow her to remain in Canada.

Valcourt had publicly refused to reconsider the decision to deport Nada, saying that Canada should not impose its values on other countries. Speaking in Toronto at the Law Society of Upper Canada, Valcourt firmly stated that Canada would not recognize gender persecution saying that doing so would open the "flood gate". His statements ... were reported by the media on January 16, 1993. It is interesting to note that a few days later, Valcourt made a major turnaround and announced that Nada would be allowed to stay and that he would hold consultations on gender persecution.

Why the change? We believe it was because Nada's cause was taken up by a strong "mainline" national women's organization as a woman's issue. Her case was also taken up as a human rights issue by a respected human rights organization headed by the former leader of the National Democratic Party. Refugee women's concerns had now moved beyond being the concern of new immigrants, minority groups and refugee workers only. It had finally become the concern of "mainline" national groups with lots of political clout, influence and voting power. Also the media had taken up Nada's cause with almost daily news coverage and commentary on the issue. At the same time, the Canadian government was pushing to have violence against women recognized as a human rights issue at the June Human Rights Conference in Vienna.

The focus on Nada's case as an example of gender persecution raises a serious concern for the Working Group on Refugee Women's Issues.

We noticed that the media's coverage of women claiming gender persecution and the examples of gender persecution being cited by the government and even those involved in refugee work tend to focus on Muslim countries. At a time when the Western world is looking for a new evil and when Muslim bashing has become the trend, there seems to be an element of racism in focusing on problems of women in Islamic countries. This also diverts attention from persecution of women in many other non-Islamic countries.

The media or the public does not seem to pay much attention to the stories of women who have suffered or who fear forced sterilization, wife abuse, forced circumcision, dowry death, et cetera. Any coverage given to these issues tends to be very negative, raising questions as to why Canada should accept women making such claims, since "this would open the floodgates and our country would be faced with millions of women coming here". "After all," some say, "there are many women in Canada who are also abused by their partners, but they do not run away to another country. They remain here and look to the courts for protection, which is what refugee women coming here and making such claims should be doing in their own countries." ...

[With respect to the gender guidelines, the Working Group on Refugee Women's Issues] ... agreed that we could still maintain two positions. One is to lobby to have a much wider interpretation of the existing definition and the other to lobby for the recognition of gender persecution using the experience of the women's movement on wife assault and other forms of violence against women ...

Our short-term plan was to comment on the Refugee Board Guidelines and monitor its application. The long-term plan was to lobby the government to include gender in our refugee definition ...

As pointed out earlier, the guidelines are a step forward. Yet there are many problems with the guidelines as well as the refugee determination system as a whole, within which the guidelines operate ...

The guidelines alone cannot address the probelm of refugee women's dual oppression: being refugees and being women. There is a third oppression for refugee women of colour, that of racism. Reflecting on her experience of the Canadian refugee system, Nada said that immigration people laughed at her when she said she had problems because she was a woman. Of the Refugee Board members who heard her case and rejected her claim, Nada says, "They were conservative, one 60 years old, one maybe 50 — maybe they practice the same thing at home, maybe they treat their women as objects."

Problems also exist with the selection of interpreters, the intimidating nature of the hearing room and the board members who appear as judges, lawyers who have not even heard about the guidelines, inefficient lawyers and more. Board members, interpreters, immigration officers and even the clients' lawyers themselves come with their own biases. Interpreters can jeopardize a woman's claim based on gender persecution and whether or not the claim is credible by what they choose to interpret, what they choose not to interpret, by the tone of their voice and their body language ...

National Action Committee's Resolutions on Gender Persecution
Toronto, 1993[31]

10. **BE IT RESOLVED THAT NAC** make the following demands: that the Minister for Employment and Immigration grant amnesty to all 14 women who are currently facing deportation, whose cases have been profiled by the National Action Committee; that there be a moratorium on all deportations of women who face death and physical danger if they are returned to their country of origin until such time as the laws concerning grounds for seeking refugee status are changed; that Canada lead the way in recognizing social and political prosecution of women who strive for equality as grounds for seeking asylum and refugee status; that women whose sponsorship is withdrawn by an abusive partner not be deported and be given all opportunities to make a new life for themselves in Canada; that the Court Challenges Program be reinstituted so that women facing deportation can appeal the process; that Canada establish bilateral relations with all countries, so that children who are abducted by a vengeful and abusive husband can be returned to their mother.

Submitted by the South Asian Women's Violence Committee.
Passed by a majority.

VIOLENCE

11. **BE IT RESOLVED THAT NAC** support a change to the Immigration Act to include gender persecution as a ground for refugee status and that gender persecution include domestic violence in cases where the country of origin is unwilling or unable to protect the woman.

   BE IT FURTHER RESOLVED THAT NAC support a change to the Immigration Act to include persecution on the grounds of sexual orientation as a ground for refugee status.

Submitted by the NAC Committee Against Male Violence
Passed by a majority as amended on the floor.

12. **BE IT RESOLVED THAT NAC** lobby the Immigration Refugee Board and the government to establish a monitoring mechanism and make public information on how the IRB is applying the guidelines on gender persecution and sexual orientation.

   BE IT FURTHER RESOLVED THAT the Minister of Immigration use the guidelines on gender persecution in deciding on humanitar-

31. The resolutions were passed at the National Action Committee's Annual General Meeting, 1993.

ian grounds for the granting of immigration status, and that guidelines on persecution on the basis of sexual orientation be developed and applied in the same manner.

Submitted by the NAC Committee Against Male Violence
Passed by a majority as amended on the floor.

List of Acronyms

A

l'AFEAS l'Association féminine d'éducation et de l'action social au Québec

AUCE The Association of University and College Employees

C

CACSW Canadian Advisory Council on the Status of Women

CAFRA Caribbean Association for Feminist Research and Action

CAHM Canadian Alliance for Home Managers

CAPE Citizen Action to Protect the Environment

CARAL Canadian Abortion Rights Action League

CCIC Canadian Council for International Co-operation

CCLOW/
CCPEF Canadian Congress for Learning Opportunities for Women/Congrés canadien pour la promotion des études chez la femme

CCR Canadian Council for Refugees

CIDA Canadian International Development Agency

CLC Canadian Labour Congress

CORP Canadian Organization for the Rights of Prostitutes

CR Consciousness Raising Group

CRIAW Canadian Research Institute for the Advancement of Women

CRTC Canadian Radio-television and Telecommunications Commission

CTCU Canadian Textile and Chemical Union

CUPE Canadian Union of Public Employees

CWMA Canadian Women's Movement Archives

D

DAWN DisAbled Women's Network

E

EGALE Equality for Gays and Lesbians Everywhere

F

FFQ   Fédération des femmes du Québec
FWTAO   Federation of Women Teachers' Association of Ontario

G

GSS   General Social Survey

I

IICPH   International Institute of Concern for Public Health
INTERCEDE   International Coalition to End Domestics'
  Exploitation
IRB   Immigration and Refugee Board
IWD   International Women's Day
IWDC   International Women's Day Committee
IWGRW   International NGO Working Group on Refugee Women
IWY   International Women's Year
IWY/AIF   International Women's Year/Année internationale de la
  femme Newsletter/Bulletin (1975)

L

LEAF   Women's Legal Education and Action Fund
LOOT   Lesbian Organization of Toronto

M

MAW   Mothers are Women
METRAC   Metro Toronto Action Committee on Violence Against
  Women and Children
MNCW   Métis National Council of Women

N

NAC   National Action Committee on the Status of Women
NAWL   National Association of Women and the Law
NDP   New Democratic Party
NFB   National Film Board of Canada
NGO   Non-governmental Organization
NOIVM   National Organization of Immigrant and Visible Minority
  Women
NRTs   New Reproductive Technologies
NSWC   Newfoundland Status of Women's Council
NWAC   Native Women's Association of Canada

O

OCAC   Ontario Coalition for Abortion Clinics
ONWA   Ontario Native Women's Association
OWN   Older Women's Network

R

RCSW   Royal Commission on the Status of Women
REAL   Real Equal and Active for Life
RFR/DRF   Resources for Feminist Research/Documentation sur la recherche féministe

S

SAWAN   South Asian Women's Network
SORWUC   Service, Office and Retail Workers Union of Canada
SWAG   Status of Women Action Group

U

UN   United Nations
UNA   United Nurses of Alberta
UNHCR   United National High Commission for Refugees

V

VOW   Voice of Women
VSW   Vancouver Status of Women

W

WAVAW   Women Against Violence Against Women
WEED   Women, Environment, Education, Development
WERC   Women's Educational Resource Centre, OISE
WISE   Women Interested in Successful Employment
WOW   Words of Women

Permissions

Every effort has been made to trace the ownership of all copyrighted documents and illustrations reprinted or reproduced in this book. We regret any errors and will be pleased to make any necessary corrections in future editions.

Grateful acknowledgement is made to the following people for permission to reprint their documents:

ALISON ACKER & *THIS MAGAZINE*, "Webs of Bright Wool."

NANCY ADAMSON & *RESOURCES FOR FEMINIST RESEARCH*, "Lesbian issues in women's studies courses."

ELLEN ADELBERG & *BREAKING THE SILENCE, "Sexual Harassment: We've Only Just Begun" ; "Danger to Women: Free Trade Ahead."*

ELLEN AGGER, "Lesbians Fight to Keep Kids"; Letter on behalf of the Waitresses' Action Committee.

ALBERTA STATUS OF WOMEN ACTION COMMITTEE, "Women Meet Michael Wilson."

ALVARINE ALDRIDGE & THE NATIONAL ORGANIZATION OF IMMIGRANT AND VISIBLE MINORITY WOMEN OF CANADA, "The Free Trade Agreement and the Garment Industry."

ANTAGONISH WOMEN'S RESOURCE CENTRE, Responses to NAC Free Trade Questionnaire, May 15, 1989.

PAT ARMSTRONG & *WOMEN'S EDUCATION DES FEMMES*, "Good Jobs, Bad Jobs, NO Jobs: A Not-So-Trivial Pursuit."

SYLVIA ASH, HELEN KING, DOROTHY ROBBINS, GLADYS WATSON & *WOMEN'S EDUCATION DES FEMMES*, "Women Interested in Successful Employment: Perspectives on a Bridging Program."

ASSOCIATION OF UNIVERSITIES AND COLLEGES OF CANADA, "Despite Gains, Women Still Under-Represented in Engineering and Applied Sciences."

LAURA BARRY, "The Mouths of Babes."

DAWN BLACK, Letter concerning the federal budget and its negative impact on women, April 18, 1989.

PAMELA BLACKSTONE, Letter to Mel Couvelier, June 17, 1981.

ROSEMARY BROWN, Letter to Robert Buckner, June 19, 1980.

JACKIE BURNETT, Letter protesting the GST, March 5, 1991.

NADYA BURTON & *WOMEN'S EDUCATION DES FEMMES*,
"Tools not Rules: Challenging Traditional Power Dynamics as
Assault Prevention."
THE CANADIAN PRESS, "Women's wages edging up, but real gains
still not seen"; "Sex exploitation claimed."; "Nurses fight Ottawa
over trade, budget."
LINDA CLIPPINGDALE, Announcement of NEW CRIAW
RESEARCH PROJECT.
MARCY COHEN, MARGARET WHITE, & THE WOMEN AND
WORK RESEARCH AND EDUCATION SOCIETY, Introduction
of *Playing with Our Health: Hazards in the Automated Office.*
COMMUNIQU'ELLES, "Household Workers Demand Protection
Under the Law."
MELANIE CONN & *WORKER CO-OPS*, "Women's worker co-op-
eratives needed, Vancouver organizer says."
MARILYN CORBEIL, Letter to Marjorie Cohen, May 4, 1989.
CATHY CROWE & ROGER HOLLANDER, "Free Trade: Its Effects
Upon Women, the HealthCare System, and the Arms Industry."
JULIET CUENCO, "Domestic Workers in Canada."
DAWN TORONTO, DAWN Toronto Fact sheet on Employment.
KATHLEEN DONOVAN, "Feminist economics a fantasy."
DEBBIE DOUGLAS & *RESOURCES FOR FEMINIST RESEARCH*,
"Young Black Women Speak!"
FRANCES EARLY, "Anglophone Coordinator's Report."
DIANA ELLIS & SHARON MCGOWAN, "Women and Economic
Development."
KATHY ENGLISH & *HOMEMAKER'S*, "Who's Home."
RICHARD FIDLER & *SOCIALIST VOICE*, "Women in railway
trades? Why not?"
JEAN FRANCES & *UPSTREAM*, "Kids — pro and con."
PATRICIA FRANGOS, "All Training and No Jobs: Women Trained
for Hibernia Project Denied Placements."
V. GALT & *THE GLOBE AND MAIL*, "Attendants Complain"; "$375
Jacket."
MONICA GOULET, "Moving Towards an Anti-Racist Feminism";
"President's Letter of Resignation."
JUDITH GRANT & *WOMEN'S EDUCATION DES FEMMES*, "The
Women's Studies Programme at the University of New Brunswick."
ROSE GREGORIE, ELIZABETH PENSSHUE, & *KINESIS*, "Innu
people stand fast."
MARY OTTO GRIESHABER & MARGARET MCRAE, Letter de-
scribing the Postal Petition in B.C., June 1987.
EDWARD HARVEY & *UNIVERSITY AFFAIRS*, "Accessibility to
postsecondary education" — some gains, some losses."
CARMEN HENRY & *THE WOMANIST*, "Racism in Women's
Studies."

BARBARA HERRING & *WOMEN'S EDUCATION DES FEMMES*, "The Status of Women Teachers in Ontario High Schools."
NOREEN HOWES [SHANAHAN] & *KINESIS*, "Lesbians Win Spousal Benefits."
INTERCEDE, "Domestic Workers Need Your Support!"
INTERNATIONAL WOMEN'S DAY SPONSORSHIP COMMITTEE, Letter, January 21, 1975.
INTERNATIONAL WOMEN'S DAY COMMITTEE, TORONTO, Letter to the Editor, *Broadsides*, May 1983.
ANA ISLA & *MATCH NEWS*, "The Debt Crisis In Latin America."
HELGA JACOBSON, "Organizing Women's Studies at the University of British Columbia."
PRABHA KHOLSA, "Profiles of Working Class East Indian Women."
MIJIN KIM & *KINESIS*, "Sexist tax strikes again."
EMMA KIVISILD & *KINESIS*, "Nairobi Conference: A decade of women."
SHEILA LARMOUR & *MATCH NEWS*, "Canada Leaves Third World Domestic Workers Out in the Cold."
PAT LESLIE, "Hands Off the Family Allowance"; "Union Run by Women."
ALBERTHA LEWIS, "Houseworkers"; "Fisheries Workers."
LOIS LOWENBERGER, "IWD: Lip Service to Feminism."
MEG LUXTON, "Housework."
KATIE MACMILLAN & *THE MONITOR*, "Women and Free Trade."
KAY MACPHERSON, "Thérèse Casgrain: A Voice for Women."
LEE MARACLE & *THE WOMANIST*, "Peace."
LORNA MARSDEN & *ONTARIO EDUCATION DIMENSIONS*, "Landmark Conference on Sex."
KATHERINE MARSHALL, "Employed Parents and the Division of Housework,"*Perspectives on Labour and Income.* Reproduced by authority of the Minister of Industry, 1994.
PHILINDA MASTERS, "Feminist Credit Unions."
MATCH NEWS, "Regional Programmes"; Excerpts from Programmes, summer 1993; "What Do You Mean — 'It Doesn't Affect Women'?"
MARCIA MCVEA, Letter from Mary Hassard and Marcia McVea for the Metro Toronto Women's Credit Union Limited.
TERRY MEHLMAN, DEBBIE SWANNER, MIDGE QUANDT & *BROADSIDE*, "Pure but Powerless — The Women's Peace Movement."
HEATHER MENZIES, "Women's Work is Nearly Done."
MINISTER OF EMPLOYMENT AND IMMIGRATION, Excerpts from Bill C-62, first reading 1985.
A. MITCHELL & *THE GLOBE AND MAIL*, "June-Cleaver Style Moms."
ANNE MOLGAT, "Do You Know A Lesbian?"
MUJER A MUJER (MAM) TORONTO, "Women's Plan of Action."

472 Canadian Women's Issues

ELSA MUSA, "Refugee Claims Based on Gender Persecution: The Canadian Experience."

MARTHA MUZYCHKA, KAY ANONSEN AND WENDY WILLIAMS, "A Response to a Strategic Economic Plan for Newfoundland and Labrador."

LESLEE NICHOLSON & OPSEU, "A Powerful Statement on Workplace Sexism."

ONTARIO COALITION FOR BETTER CHILD CARE, "What's Wrong With Tax Deductions for Day Care?"

MIRA & VANDANA SHIVA & *WOMEN AND ENVIRONMENTS*, "Population and Environment: An Indian Perspective."

MAKEDA SILVERA, "Savitri."

DONNA SMYTH, "That desperate attempt to sell us 'nuclear'."

STATISTICS CANADA, Tables 2-1, 2-2, 2-3, 2-4, 2-5 in Chapter 2, "Paid Work." Reproduced by authority of the Minister of Industry, 1994.

NOREEN STEVENS, Cartoon, "Professor Manley's Girls" series.

SANDY STIENECKER, Letter.

JEAN SWANSON & *KINESIS*, "Co-opting the Guaranteed Annual Income."

AISLA THOMSON & *WOMEN'S EDUCATION DES FEMMES*, "Training for Whom?"

ESMERALDA THORNHILL & *THE WOMANIST*, "Black Women's Studies in Teaching Related to Women: Help or Hinderance to Universal Sisterhood?"; "Black Women: The Missing Pages from Canadian Women's Studies."

CHRISTA VAN DAELE & *BRANCHING OUT*, "Time for a Grass Roots Revival."

MARRIANNE VAN LOON & *KINESIS*, "Surviving nuclear threats."

JUDY WASYLYCIA LEIS, "Wages for Housework: An Obstacle to Equality"; "Occupational Health Standards."

GERDA WEKERLE & *STATUS OF WOMEN NEWS*, "Urban Planning: Making it Work for Women."

BETH WESTFALL [DAVIES], "The University, Women's Studies, and Rural Women: Some Thoughts on Feminist Pedagogy and Rural Outreach."

NETTIE WIEBE & *THE WOMANIST*, "What happened in agriculture in the last ten years?"

JANICE WILLIAMSON & *BROADSIDE*, "One Final Argument," from "A Day of Resistance — November 14, 1983."

DEBORAH WILSON & *THE GLOBE AND MAIL*, "Nanny's salary valid deduction, court rules."

VICTORIA JEAN WOTHERSPOON [NORTHCOTT] & *BRIARPATCH*, "Women in the Maquiladoras."

VICKI WRIGHT, "Statistics."

G. YORK & *THE GLOBE AND MAIL*, "Child-care Pay."

Bibliography

Books: Monographs & Anthologies

Aaron, Dorothy. *About Face: Towards a Positive Image of Women in Advertising*. Toronto: The Ontario Status of Women Council, 1975.

Abella, Judge Rosalie Silberman. *Equality in Employment: A Royal Commission Report*. Toronto: Commission on Equality in Employment, 1985.

Acker, Sandra. *Gendered Education: Sociological Reflections on Women, Teaching and Feminism*. Buckingham, UK: Open University Press; Toronto: OISE Press, 1994.

Adamson, Nancy, Linda Briskin, and Margaret McPhail. *Feminists Organizing for Change: The Contemporary Women's Movement in Canada*. Toronto: Oxford University Press, 1988.

Amato, Sheila and Pat Staton. *Making Choices! Women in Non-Traditional Jobs*. Toronto: Green Dragon Press, 1987.

Anderson, Doris. *The Unfinished Revolution: The Status of Women in Twelve Countries*. Toronto: Doubleday Canada Ltd., 1991.

Andrew, Caroline, ed. *Getting the Word Out: Communicating Feminist Research*. Ottawa: University of Ottawa Press for Social Science Federation of Canada, 1989.

Andrew, Caroline and Beth Moore Milroy, eds. *Life Spaces: Gender, Household, Employment*. Vancouver: University of British Columbia Press, 1988.

Armstrong, Liz and Adrienne Scott. *Whitewash: Exposing the Health and Environmental Dangers of Women's Sanitary Products and Disposable Diapers—What You Can Do About It*. Toronto: HarperCollins, 1992.

Armstrong, Pat. *Labour Pains: Women's Work in Crisis*. Toronto: Women's Press, 1984.

Armstrong, Pat and Hugh Armstrong. *The Double Ghetto: Canadian Women & Their Segregated Work*. 3rd ed. Toronto: McClelland & Stewart, 1994.

Arnopoulos, Sheila McLeod. *Problems of Immigrant Women in the Labour Force*. Ottawa: CACSW, 1979.

Backhouse, Constance and Leah Cohen. *The Secret Oppression: Sexual Harassment of Working Women.* Toronto: Macmillan, 1978.

Backhouse, Constance and David H. Flaherty, eds. *Challenging Times: The Women's Movement in Canada and the United States.* Montreal and Kingston: McGill-Queen's, 1992.

Bannerji, Himani, Linda Carty, Kari Dehli, Susan Heald, and Kate McKenna. *Unsettling Relations: The University as a Site of Feminist Struggles.* Toronto: The Women's Press, 1991.

Bannerji, Himani, ed. *Returning the Gaze: Essays on Racism, Feminism and Politics.* Toronto: Sister Vision Press, 1993.

Basen, Gwynne, Margrit Eichler, and Abby Lippman, eds. Misconceptions: The Social Construction of Choice and the New Reproductive and Genetic Technologies. Vol. I. Hull: Voyageur Publishing, 1994.

Bashevkin, Sylvia B. *Toeing the Lines: Women and Party Politics in English Canada.* 2nd ed. Toronto: Oxford University Press, 1993.

Baxter, Sheila. *No Way to Live: Poor Women Speak Out.* Vancouver: New Star Books Ltd., 1988.

Bell, Laurie, ed. *Good Girls/Bad Girls: Sex Trade Workers and Feminists Face to Face.* Toronto: The Women's Press, 1987.

Bertell, Rosalie. *No Immediate Danger? Prognosis for a Radioactive Earth.* London and Toronto: The Women's Press, 1985.

Block, W.E. and M.A. Walker, eds. *Discrimination, Affirmative Action and Equal Opportunities.* Vancouver: The Fraser Institute, 1982.

Bodnar, Ana and Marilee Reimer. *The Organization of Social Services and its Implications for the Mental Health of Immigrant Women.* Toronto: Working Women Community Centre, 1979.

Bourne, Paula. *Women in Canadian Society.* Toronto: Ontario Institute for Studies in Education, 1976.

Bourne, Paula, ed. *Paid and Unpaid Work.* Toronto: New Hogtown Press, 1985.

Brand, Dionne. *No Language Is Neutral.* Toronto: Coach House Press, 1990.

———. *Sans Souci and Other Stories.* Stratford, Ontario: Williams-Wallace, 1988.

Brand, Dionne and Krisantha Sri Bhaggiyadatta. *Rivers Have Sources, Trees Have Roots: Speaking of Racism.* Toronto: Cross Cultural Communication Centre, 1986.

Brand, Dionne with the assistance of Lois De Shield and the Immigrant Women's Job Placement Centre. *No Burden to*

Carry: Narratives of Black Working Women in Ontario 1920s to 1950s. Toronto: The Women's Press, 1991.

Briskin, Linda. *Feminist Pedagogy: Teaching and Learning Liberation.* Feminist Perspectives, no. 19. Ottawa: Canadian Research Institute for the Advancement of Women, 1990.

Briskin, Linda and Lynda Yanz, eds. *Union Sisters: Women in the Labour Movement.* Toronto: The Women's Press, 1983.

Briskin, Linda and Patricia McDermott, eds. *Women Challenging Unions: Feminism, Democracy, and Militancy.* Toronto: University of Toronto Press, 1993.

Bristow, Peggy, co-ordinator. *'We're Rooted Here and They Can't Pull Us Up': Essays in African Canadian Women's History.* Toronto: University of Toronto Press, 1994.

Brodie, Janine. *Women and Politics in Canada.* Toronto: McGraw-Hill Ryerson Ltd., 1985.

Brodie, Janine, Shelley A.M. Gavigan and Jane Jenson. *The Politics of Abortion.* Toronto: University of Toronto Press, 1992.

Brodsky, Gwen and Shelagh Day. *Canadian Charter Equality Rights for Women: One Step Forward or Two Steps Back?* Ottawa: Canadian Advisory Council on the Status of Women, 1989.

Brookes, Anne-Louise. *Feminist Pedagogy: An Autobiographical Approach.* Halifax, NS: Fernwood Publishing, 1992.

Brown, Catrina and Karin Jasper, eds. *Consuming Passions: Feminist Approaches to Eating Disorders and Weight Preoccupation.* Toronto: Second Story Press, 1993.

Burnet, Jean, ed. *Looking in My Sister's Eyes: An Exploration in Women's History.* Toronto: The Multicultural History Society of Ontario, 1986.

Burstyn, Varda, ed. *Women Against Censorship.* Vancouver and Toronto: Douglas & McIntyre, 1985.

Burt, Sandra, Lorraine Code, and Lindsay Dorney, eds. *Changing Patterns: Women in Canada.* 2nd ed. Toronto: McClelland & Stewart, 1993.

Camper, Carol, ed. *Miscegenation Blues: Voices of Mixed Race Women.* Toronto: Sister Vision Press, 1994.

Caplan, Paula. *Don't Blame Mother: Mending the Mother-Daughter Relationship.* New York: Harper & Row, 1989.

———. *The Myth of Women's Masochism.* New York: E.P. Dutton, 1985.

Carty, Linda E., ed. *And Still We Rise: Feminist Political Mobilizing in Contemporary Canada.* Toronto: The Women's Press, 1993.

Cavanaugh, Catherine A. and Randi R. Warne, eds. *Standing on New Ground: Women in Alberta*. Edmonton: The University of Alberta Press, 1993.

Clark, Lorenne and Debra Lewis. *Rape: The Price of Coercive Sexuality*. Toronto: The Women's Press, 1977.

Clarke, Susan. *Supervised Private Home Day Care: One Option for Child Care in Canada*. Toronto: CWSE, OISE, 1984.

The Clio Collective. *Quebec Women: A History*. Trans. by Roger Gannon and Rosalind Gill. Toronto: The Women's Press, 1987. Chaps. 14 and 15.

Cohen, Leah. *Small Expectations: Society's Betrayal of Older Women*. Toronto: McClelland and Stewart, 1984.

Cohen, Marcy and Margaret White. *Playing with our Health: Hazards in the Automated Office*. Burnaby, B.C.: Women & Work, 1986.

————. *Taking Control of Our Future: Clerical Workers and the New Technology*. Vancouver: Women's Skill Development Society, 1987.

Cohen, Marjorie Griffin. *Free Trade and the Future of Women's Work: Manufacturing and Service Industries*. Toronto and Ottawa: Garamond Press and the Canadian Centre for Policy Alternatives, 1987.

————. *Women and Economic Structures: A Feminist Perspective on the Canadian Economy*. Ottawa: Canadian Centre for Policy Alternatives, 1991.

Cole, Susan G. *Pornography and the Sex Crisis*. Toronto: Amanita Enterprises, 1989.

Comack, Elizabeth. *Feminist Engagement with the Law: The Legal Recognition of the Battered Woman Syndrome*. The CRIAW Papers, no. 31. Ottawa: Canadian Research Institute for the Advancement of Women, 1993.

Connelly, M. Patricia. *Last Hired, First Fired: Women and the Canadian Work Force*. Intro. by Margaret Benston. Toronto: The Women's Press, 1978.

Connelly, M. Patricia and Pat Armstrong, eds. *Feminism in Action: Studies in Political Economy*. Toronto: Canadian Scholars' Press, 1992.

Conway, John. *The Canadian Family in Crisis*. Rev. ed. Toronto: James Lorimer & Company Ltd., Publishers, 1993.

Cook, Gail C.A., ed. *Opportunity for Choice: A Goal for Women in Canada*. Ottawa: Statistics Canada in association with the C.D. Howe Research Institute, 1976.

Cornish, Mary and Lynn Spink, with the assistance of Susan Ursel, Harriet Simand & Laurell Ritchie. *Organizing Unions*. Toronto: Second Story Press, 1994.

Courtney, Alice E. and Thomas W. Whipple. *Canadian Perspectives on Sex Stereotyping in Advertising.* Ottawa: Advisory Council on the Status of Women, 1978.

Crean, Susan. *In the Name of the Fathers: The Story Behind Child Custody.* Toronto: Amanita Enterprises, 1988.

———. *Newsworthy: The Lives of Media Women.* Toronto: Stoddart, 1985.

Crean, Susan, ed. *Twist and Shout: A Decade of Feminist Writing in* This *Magazine.* Toronto: Second Story Press, 1992.

Crnkovich, Mary, ed. *"Gossip": A Spoken History of Women in the North.* Ottawa: Canadia Arctic Resources Committee, 1990.

Davy, Shirley, ed. *Women Work and Worship in the United Church of Canada.* Toronto: The United Church of Canada, 1983.

Dawson, T. Bettel, ed. *Relating to Law: A Chronology of Women and Law in Canada.* Toronto: York University Captus Press, 1990.

Day, Shelagh and Stan Persky, eds. *The Supreme Court of Canada Decision on Abortion.* Vancouver: New Star Books, 1988.

Department of Health and Welfare. *Atlantic Consultation Women: Alcohol and Other Drugs.* Halifax: Nova Scotia, 1977.

Devereaux, M. S. and Edith Rechnitzer. *Higher Education—Hired?* Ottawa: Statistics Canada, 1980.

Dodd, Dianne and Deborah Gorham, eds. *Caring and Curing: Historical Perspectives on Women and Healing in Canada.* Ottawa: University of Ottawa Press, 1994.

Dranoff, Linda Silver. *Women in Canadian Law.* Toronto: Fitzhenry & Whiteside, 1977.

Dua, Enakshi, Maureen FitzGerald, Linda Gardner, Heather Green, Shahnaz Stri, Darien Taylor and Lisa Wyndels, eds. *Women Healthsharing.* Toronto: The Women's Press, 1994.

Dubinsky, Karen. *Lament for a "Patriarchy Lost"? Anti-Feminism, Anti-Abortion, and R.E.A.L. Women in Canada.* CRIAW/ICREF *Feminist Perspectives Féministe* No. 1. Ottawa: ICREF/CRIAW, 1985.

Duffy, Ann, Nancy Mandell, and Norene Pupo. *Few Choices: Women, Work and Family.* Toronto: Garamond, 1989.

Dulude, Louise. *Pension Reforms with Women in Mind.* Ottawa: Canadian Advisory Council on the Status of Women, 1981.

Dulude, Louise with update by Ruth Browne. *Statement on Matrimonial Laws in Canada.* Ottawa: Canadian Advisory Council on the Status of Women, 1979.

Dybikowski, Ann et al., eds. *In the feminine: women and words, les femmes et les mots.* Edmonton: Longspoon Press, 1983.

Eichler, Margrit. *The Double Standard: A Feminist Critique of Feminist Social Science.* London: Croom Helm, 1980.

————. *Families in Canada Today: Recent Changes and their Policy Consequences.* 2nd ed. Toronto: Gage, 1988.

————. *Nonsexist Research Methods: A Practical Guide.* Boston: Allen & Unwin, 1988.

————. *The Pro-Family Movement: Are They For or Against Families?* ICREF/CRIAW *Feminist Perspectives féministes* no. 4a. Ottawa: CRIAW/ICREF, 1985.

Enough is Enough: Aboriginal Women Speak Out. As Told to Janet Silman. Toronto: The Women's Press, 1987.

Espinet, Ramabai, ed. *Creation Fire: A CAFRA Anthology of Caribbean Women's Poetry.* Toronto: Sister Vision; Tunapuna, Trinidad and Tobago: CAFRA, 1990.

Faith, Karlene. *Unruly Women: The Politics of Confinement and Resistance.* Vancouver: Press Gang Publishers, 1994.

findlay, barbara. *With All of Who We Are: A Discussion of Oppression and Dominance.* Vancouver: Lazara Press, 1991.

Finn, Geraldine, ed. *Limited Edition: Voices of Women, Voices of Feminism.* Halifax: Fernwood, 1993.

Fitzgerald, Maureen, Connie Guberman, and Margie Wolfe, eds. *Still Ain't Satisfied! Canadian Feminism Today.* Toronto: The Women's Press, 1982.

Forman, Frieda with Caoran Sowton, eds. *Taking Our Time: Feminist Perspectives on Temporality.* Oxford and New York: Pergamon Press, 1989.

Forman, Frieda, Mary O'Brien, Jane Haddad, Dianne Hallman, and Philinda Masters, eds. *Feminism and Education: A Canadian Perspective.* Toronto: Centre for Women's Studies in Education, Ontario Institute for Studies in Education, 1990.

Fox, Bonnie, ed. *Hidden in the Household: Women's Domestic Labour Under Capitalism.* Toronto: The Women's Press, 1980.

Fraser, Sylvia. *My Father's House: A Memoir of Incest and of Healing.* Toronto: Doubleday Canada Ltd., 1987.

Fudge, Judy and Patricia McDermott, eds. *Just Wages: A Feminist Assessment of Pay Equity.* Toronto: University of Toronto Press, 1991.

Fulford, Margaret, ed. *The Canadian Women's Movement, 1960–1990: A Guide to Archival Resources.* Toronto: ECW Press, 1992.

Galana, Laurel and Gina Covina. *The New Lesbians: Interviews with Women Across the U.S. and Canada.* Berkeley, CA: Moon Books, 1977.

Gallino, Kevin. *Women and Pensions.* Ottawa: The Canadian Council on Social Development, 1978.

Galloway, Priscilla. *What's wrong with high school English?...It's sexist—un-Canadian—outdated.* Toronto: OISE Press, 1980.

Gaskell, Jane. *Gender Matters from School to Work.* Intro. by
Sandra Acker. Toronto: OISE Press, 1992.
Gaskell, Jane, Arlene McLaren, and Mira Novogrodsky. *Claiming
an Education: Feminism and Canadian Schools.* Toronto: Our
Schools/Ourselves Education Foundation, 1989.
Gaskell, Jane and Arlene McLaren, eds. *Women and Education: A
Canadian Perspective.* Calgary, Alberta: Detselig Enterprises
Ltd., 1987.
Gee, Ellen M. and Meredith M. Kimball. *Women and Aging.*
Toronto and Vancouver: Butterworths, 1987.
Gender Equality in the Courts. Manitoba: Manitoba Association of
Women and the Law, 1988.
Gerson, Miryam and Rosemary Byrne-Hunter. *A Book About
Menopause.* Montréal: Montréal Health Press, 1988.
Goldenberg, Naomi R. *Changing of the Gods: Feminism and the
End of Traditional Religions.* Toronto: Fitzhenry & Whiteside,
1979.
Guberman, Connie and Margie Wolfe, eds. *No Safe Place:
Violence Against Women.* Toronto: The Women's Press, 1985.
Gunderson, Morley and Leon Muszynski, with Jennifer Keck.
Women and Labour Market Poverty. Ottawa: Canadian
Advisory Council on the Status of Women, 1990.
Gunn, Rita and Candice Minch. *Sexual Assault: The Dilemma of
Disclosure, the Question of Conviction.* Winnipeg: University of
Manitoba Press, 1988.
Harman, Lesley D. *When A Hostel Becomes A Home: Experiences
of Women.* Toronto: Garamond Press, 1989.
Harris, Pamela. *Faces of Feminism: A Photo Documentation.*
Toronto: Second Story Press, 1992.
Herring, Barbara and Helen LaFountaine. *Decade of Promise: An
Assessment of Canadian Women's Status in Education, Training
and Employment 1976-1985.* Toronto: Canadian Congress for
Learning Opportunities for Women, 1986.
Hynes, Maureen. *Letters from China.* Toronto: The Women's
Press, 1981.
Ireland, Gisele. *The Farmer Takes a Wife*: A Study of Concerned
Farm Women. Chesley: Concerned Farm Women, 1983.
Jamieson, Kathleen. *Indian Women and the Law in Canada:
Citizens Minus.* Ottawa: Advisory Council on the Status of
Women/Indian Rights for Indian Women, April 1978.
Johnson, Laura C. *The Seam Allowance: Industrial Home Sewing
in Canada.* Toronto: Women's Educational Press, 1982.
Kaski, Susan E. *The Employment Practices of Farm Women.*
Saskatoon: National Farmers Union, 1983.
Khayatt, Madiha Didi. *Lesbian Teachers: An Invisible Presence.*
Albany: State University of New York Press, 1992.

Kome, Penney. *The Taking of Twenty-Eight: Women Challenge the Constitution*. Toronto: The Women's Press, 1983.
————. *Women of Influence: Canadian Women and Politics*. Toronto: Doubleday Canada, 1985.
Kostash, Myrna. *Long Way From Home: The Story of the Sixties Generation in Canada* Toronto: James Lorimer and Company, Publishers, 1980.
————. *No Kidding: Inside the World of Teenage Girls*. Toronto: McClelland & Stewart, 1987.
Kerr, Richard. *An Economic Model to Assist in the Determination of Spousal Support*. Ottawa: Prepared for the Department of Justice and Status of Women Canada, 1992.
Kirby, Sandra, Danya Daniels, Kate McKenna, Michèle Pujol, and Michele Valiquette, eds. *Women Changing Academe: Les femmes changent l'académie*. Winnipeg: Soroal Publishing, 1991.
Lee, Enid. *Letters to Marcia: A Teacher's Guide to Anti-Racist Education*. Toronto: Cross Cultural Communication Centre, 1985.
Lee, Sky. *Disappearing Moon Cafe*. Vancouver and Toronto: Douglas & McIntyre, 1990.
Leger, Hugette and Judy Rebick. *The NAC Voters' Guide*. Hull: Voyageur, 1993.
Lenskyj, Helen. *Out of Bounds: Women, Sport & Sexuality*. Toronto: The Women's Press, 1986.
Lewis, Debra J. *Just Give Us the Money: A Discussion of Wage Discrimination and Pay Equity*. Vancouver: Women's Research Centre, 1988.
Lewis, Magda Gere. *Without A Word: Teaching Beyond Women's Silence*. New York and London: Routledge, 1993.
Lind, Loren and Susan Prentice. *Their Rightful Place: An Essay On Children, Families and Childcare in Canada*. Toronto: Our Schools/Our Selves.
Luxton, Meg. *More Than a Labour of Love: Three Generations of Women's Work in the Home*. Toronto: The Women's Press, 1980.
Luxton, Meg and Harriet Rosenberg. *Through the Kitchen Window: The Politics of Home and Family*. Toronto: Garamond Press, 1986.
Luxton, Meg, Harriet Rosenberg, and Sedef Arat-Koc. *Through the Kitchen Window: The Politics of Home and Family*. 2nd ed. Toronto: Garamond, 1990.
Macdonald, Barbara, with Cynthia Rich. *Look Me in the Eye: Old Women, Aging and Ageism*. San Francisco: Spinsters, Ink, 1983.
MacDonald, Ingrid. *Catherine, Catherine: Lesbian Short Stories*. Toronto: The Women's Press, 1991.

MacLeod, Linda. *Wife Battering in Canada: The Vicious Circle.*
Ottawa: Canadian Advisory Council on the Status of Women,
1980.
———. *Battered But Not Beaten: Preventing Wife Battering in
Canada.* Ottawa: CACSW, 1987.
Macpherson, Kay. *When in Doubt, Do Both: The Times of My
Life.* Toronto: University of Toronto Press, 1994.
Malette, Louise and Marie Chalouh, eds. *The Montreal Massacre.*
Trans. by Marlene Wildeman. Charlottetown, PEI: Gynergy
Books, 1991.
Maloney, Maureen. *Women and Income Tax Reform.* Ottawa:
Canadian Advisory Council on the Status of Women, 1987.
Maracle, Lee. *Sojourner's Truth & Other Stories.* Vancouver:
Press Gang Publishers, 1990.
———. *Sundogs.* Penticton, B.C.: Theytus Books Ltd., 1992.
Marlatt, Daphne. *Ana Historical: A Novel.* Toronto: Coach House
Press, 1988.
Maroney, Heather Jon and Meg Luxton, eds. *Feminism and
Political Economy: Women's Work, Women's Struggles.*
Toronto: Methuen, 1987.
Marshall, Doris. *Silver Threads: Critical Reflections on Growing
Old.* Toronto: Between The Lines, 1987.
Martin, Sheila L. and Kathleen E. Mahoney, eds. *Equality and
Judicial Neutrality.* Toronto: Carswell, 1987.
Matheson, Gwen, ed. *Women in the Canadian Mosaic.* Toronto:
Peter Martin Associates Limited, 1976.
Matthews, Gwyneth Ferguson. *Voices from the Shadows: Women
with Disabilities Speak Out.* Toronto: Women's Educational
Press, 1983.
McCormack, Thelma. *Politics and the Hidden Injuries of Gender:
Feminism and the Making of the Welfare State.* Ottawa:
Canadian Research Institute for the Advancement of Women,
1991.
McDonnell, Kathleen. *Adverse Effects: Women and the
Pharmaceutical Industry.* Toronto: The Women's Press, 1986.
———. *Not an Easy Choice: A Feminist Re-examines Abortion.*
Toronto: The Women's Press, 1984.
McDonnell, Kathleen and Mariana Valverde, eds. *The
Healthsharing Book: Resources for Canadian Women.* Toronto:
Women's Press, 1985.
McLaren, Angus and Arlene Tigar McLaren. *The Bedroom and
the State: The Changing Practices and Politics of
Contraception and Abortion in Canada, 1880-1980.* Toronto:
McClelland & Stewart, 1986.
McQuaig, Linda. *The Quick and the Dead: Brian Mulroney, Big
Business and the Seduction of Canada.* Toronto: Viking, 1991.

Megyery, Kathy, ed. *Royal Commission on Electoral Reform and Party Financing*. Vol. 6: *Women in Canadian Politics: Toward Equality in Representation*. Toronto: Dundum, 1991.

Menzies, Heather. *Fast Forward and Out of Control*. Toronto: McClelland & Stewart, 1989.

————. *Women and the Chip: Case Studies of the Effects of Informatics on Employment in Canada*. Montreal: The Institute for Research on Public Policy, 1981.

Miles, Angela R. and Geraldine Finn, eds. *Feminism in Canada: From Pressure to Politics*. Montreal: Black Rose Books, 1982; rev. ed., 1989.

Mouré, Erin. *Domestic Fuel*. Toronto: House of Anansi Press, 1985.

Moussa, Helene. *Storm & Sanctuary: The Journey of Ethiopian and Eritrean Women Refugees*. Dundas, Ontario: Artemis Enterprises, 1993.

Mukherjee, Arun, ed. *Sharing Our Experience*. Ottawa: Canadian Advisory Council on the Status of Women, 1993.

Muzychka, Martha. *A Report on the Effectiveness of the Support Enforcement Agency in Newfoundland and Labrador*. St. John's: Provincial Advisory Council on the Status of Women, Newfoundland and Labrador, 1992.

National Council of Welfare. *Women and Poverty*. Ottawa: National Council of Welfare, 1979.

Nemiroff, Greta Hofmann, ed. *Women and Men: Interdisciplinary Readings on Gender*. Montreal: Fitzhenry & Whiteside, 1987.

Ng, Roxana. *The Politics of Community Services: Immigrant Women, Class and State*. Toronto: Garamond, 1988.

Nickerson, Betty, ed. *Girls Will Be Women/Femmes de Demain*. Ottawa: All About Us/Nous Autres, Inc., 1975.

Norman, H.D. and A. Micco. *A History of the Women's Movement in Prince George*. Prince George, B.C.: Women's Resource Centre, 1985.

O'Brien, Mary. *The Politics of Reproduction*. London and Boston: Routledge & Kegan Paul, 1981.

————. Reproducing the World: Essays in Feminist Theory. Boulder: Westview Press, 1989.

Oikawa, Mona, Dionne Falconer, Rosamund Elwin, and Ann Decter, eds., *Out Rage: Dykes and Bis Resist Homophobia*. Toronto: The Women's Press, 1993.

Oikawa, Mona, Dionne Falconer, and Ann Decter, eds., *Resist!: Essays Against a Homophobic Culture*. Toronto: The Women's Press, 1994.

Overall, Christine. *Ethics of Human Reproduction: A Feminist Analysis*. Boston: Allen & Unwin, 1987.

Overall, Christine, ed. *The Future of Human Reproduction*. Toronto: The Women's Press, 1989.

Pedersen, Diana. *Women and Health: An Annotated Bibliography of Articles in Selected Canadian Medical Periodicals 1970-1979*. Ottawa: ICREF/CRIAW, 1979.

Penny, Jennifer, ed. *Hard Earned Wages: Women Fighting for Better Work*. Toronto: The Women's Press, 1983.

Philip, M. Nourbese. *Frontiers: Essays and Writings on Racism and Culture*. Stratford, Ontario: The Mercury Press, 1992.

Phillips, Paul and Erin Phillips. *Women and Work: Inequality in the Labour Market*. Toronto: James Lorimer and Company, Publishers, 1983; revised edition, 1993.

Prentice, Alison, Paula Bourne, Gail Cuthbert Brandt, Beth Light, Wendy Mitchinson, and Naomi Black. *Canadian Women: A History*. Toronto: Harcourt Brace Jovanovich, 1988.

Prentice, Susan, ed. *Sex In Schools*. Toronto: Our Schools/Our Selves, 1994.

Priest, Lisa. *Conspiracy of Silence*. Toronto: McClelland & Stewart, 1990.

Proulx, Monique. *Women and Work: Five Million Women: A Study of the Canadian Housewife*. Ottawa: Advisory Council on the Status of Women, 1978.

Razack, Sherene. *Canadian Feminism and the Law: The Women's Legal Education and Action Fund and the Pursuit of Equality*. Toronto: Second Story Press, 1991.

Rees, Ruth. *Women and Men in Education: A National Survey of Gender Distribution in School Systems*. Toronto: Canadian Education Association, 1990.

Rochon Ford, Anne. *A Path Not Strewn With Roses: One Hundred Years of Women at the University of Toronto*. Toronto: University of Toronto Press, 1985.

Romalis, Shelley. *Childbirth: Alternatives to Medical Control*. Austin: The University of Texas Press, 1982.

Ross, Kathleen Gallagher, ed. *Good Day Care: Fighting for It, Getting It, Keeping It*. Toronto: The Women's Press, 1978.

Rossiter, Amy. *From Private to Public: A Feminist Exploration of Early Mothering*. Toronto: The Women's Press, 1988.

Royce, Marion. *Continuing Education for Women in Canada: Trend and Opportunities*. Monographs in Adult Education, No. 4. Toronto: The Ontario Institute for Studies in Education, 1969.

Rudd, Andrea and Darien Taylor, eds. *Positive Women: Voices of Women Living with Aids*. Toronto: Second Story Press, 1992.

Sadlier, Rosemary. *Leading the Way: Black Women in Canada*. Toronto: Umbrella Press, 1994.

Scheier, Libby, Sarah Sheard and Eleanor Wachtel, eds.

—*Language in Her Eye: Writing and Gender—Views by Canadian Women Writing in English*. Toronto: Coach House Press, 1990.

Sheehy, Elizabeth A. *Personal Autonomy and the Criminal Law: Emerging Issues for Women*. Ottawa: Canadian Advisory Council on the Status of Women, 1987.

Silvera, Makeda. *Her Head a Village and Other Stories*. Vancouver: Press Gang Publishers, 1994.

————. *Silenced*. Toronto: Williams-Wallace Publishers Inc., 1983; 2nd ed. with New Intro. Toronto: Sister Vision, 1989.

Silvera, Makeda, ed. *Piece of My Heart: A Lesbian of Colour Anthology*. Toronto: Sister Vision Press, 1991.

Smith, Dorothy E. *Feminism & Marxism—A Place to Begin, A Way to Go*. Vancouver: New Star Books, 1977.

Smith, Dorothy E. and Sara J. David, eds. *Women Look at Psychiatry*. Vancouver: Press Gang Publishers, 1975.

Smyth, Donna E. *Subversive Elements*. Toronto: The Women's Press, 1986.

Special Committee on Pornography and Prostitution. *Pornography and Prostitution: Issues Paper*. Ottawa: Department of Justice, Communication and Public Affairs, 1983.

Steed, Judy. *Our Little Secret: Confronting Child Sexual Abuse in Canada*. Toronto: Random House of Canada, 1994.

Stephenson, Marylee, ed. *Women in Canada*. Toronto: New Press, 1973; Rev. ed. Don Mills, Ontario: General Publishing, 1977.

Stone, Sharon Dale, ed. *Lesbians in Canada*. Toronto: Between the Lines, 1990.

Storrie, Kathleen, ed. *Women: Isolation and Bonding*. Toronto: Methuen, 1987.

Struthers, Betsy. *Running out of Time*. Toronto: Wolsak and Wynn, 1993.

Székely, Éva. *Never Too Thin*. Toronto: The Women's Press, 1988.

Tancred-Sheriff, Peta, ed. *Feminist Research: Prospect and Retrospect*. Kingston and Montreal: McGill-Queen's University Press, 1988.

The Telling It Book Collective, ed. *Telling It: Women and Language Across Cultures*. Vancouver: Press Gang Publishers, 1990.

Turner, Joan, ed. *Living the Changes*. Winnipeg: University of Manitoba Press, 1990.

Turner, Joan and Lois Emery, eds. *Perspectives on Women in the 1980s*. Winnipeg: The University of Manitoba Press, 1983, 1989.

Tynes, Maxine. *Woman Talking Woman*. Lawrencetown Beach, Nova Scotia: Pottersfield Press, 1990.

Valverde, Mariana. *Sex, Power and Pleasure*. Toronto: The Women's Press, 1985.

Vickers, Jill, Pauline Rankin, and Christine Apelle. *Politics as if Women Mattered: A Political Analysis of the National Action Committee on the Status of Women.* Toronto: University of Toronto Press, 1993.

Vincent, Solanges. *The Human Cost of the War Economy.* Montreal: Anlo Inc. for Westmount Initiative for Peace, 1986.

Vorst, Jesse et al., eds. *Race, Class, Gender: Bonds and Barriers.* Toronto: Between the Lines; Winnipeg: The Society for Socialist Studies/Société d'études socialistes, 1989.

Wachtel, Eleanor. *Report on Feminist Periodicals.* Ottawa: Women's Programme, Secretary of State, 1982.

Wachtel, Eleanor. *Update on Feminist Periodicals.* Ottawa: Women's Programme, Secretary of State, 1985.

Wadden, Marie. *Nitassinan: The Innu Struggle to Reclaim Their Homeland.* Vancouver/Toronto: Douglas & McIntyre, 1991.

Warland, Betsy, ed. *Inversions: Writing by Dykes, Queers & Lesbians.* Vancouver: Press Gang Publishers, 1991.

What You See: Drawings by Gail Geltner. Intro. by Linda Hutcheon. Toronto: Second Story Press, 1992.

White, Jerry P. *Hospital Strike: Women, Unions and Public Sector Conflict.* Toronto: Thompson Educational Publishing, 1990.

White, Julie. *Mail & Female: Women and the Canadian Union of Postal Workers.* Toronto: Thompson Educational Publishing, Inc., 1990.

———. *Sisters & Solidarity: Women and Unions in Canada.* Toronto: Thompson Educational Publishing, 1993.

———. *Women and Part-Time Work.* Ottawa: The Canadian Advisory Council on the Status of Women, 1983.

———. *Women and Unions.* Ottawa: Canadian Advisory Council on the Status of Women, 1980.

Williamson, Janice. *Sounding Differences: Conversations with Seventeen Canadian Women Writers.* Toronto: University of Toronto Press, 1993.

Williamson, Janice and Deborah Gorham, eds. —Up and Doing: Canadian Women and Peace. Toronto: The Women's Press, 1989.

Wilson, Lois. *Turning the World Upside Down: A Memoir.* Toronto: Doubleday Canada.

Wine, Jeri Dawn and Janice L. Ristock, eds. *Women and Social Change: Feminist Activism in Canada.* Toronto: James Lorimer and Company, Publishers, 1991.

Women Unite! An Anthology of the Canadian Women's Movement. Toronto: Canadian Women's Educational Press, 1972.

Women's Self-Help Network. *Working Collectively.* Campbell River, B.C.: Ptarmigan Press, 1984.

Zuker, Marvin A. and June Callwood. *The Law is NOT for Women: A Legal Handbook for Women.* Toronto: Pitman Publishing, 1976.

Articles in Journals & Anthologies

Achilles, Rona. "Desperately Seeking Babies: New Technologies of Hope and Despair." In Katherine Arnup, Andrée Lévesque, and Ruth Roach Pierson, eds. *Delivering Motherhood: Maternal Ideologies and Practices in the 19th and 20th Centuries.* London and New York: Routledge, 1990. 284-312.

Acker, Sandra and Keith Oatley. "Gender Issues in Education for Science and Technology: Current Situation and Prospects for Change." *Canadian Journal of Education* 18, no. 3 (Summer 1993), 255-272.

Arat-Koc, Sedef. "In the Privacy of our own Home: Foreign Domestic Workers as Solution to the Crisis in the Domestic Sphere in Canada." *Studies in Political Economy* 29 (Spring 1989), 33-58.

Bashevkin, Sylvia. "Free Trade and Canadian Feminism: The Case of the National Action Committee on the Status of Women." *Canadian Public Policy* 15, no. 4 (1989), 353-375.

Benston, Margaret. "The Political Economy of Women's Liberation." *Monthly Review* 21 (September 1969).

Bertell, Rosalie. "Early War Crimes of WWIII." *Canadian Woman Studies/les cahiers de la femme* 9, no. 1 (Spring/printemps 1988).

Bogdan, Deanne. "When Is A Singing (Not) A Chorus? The Emancipatory Agenda in Feminist Pedagogy and Literature Education." In Lynda Stone, with the assistance of Gail Masuchika Boldt, eds. *The Education Feminism Reader.* New York and London: Routledge, 1994.

Briskin, Linda and Rebecca Priegert Coulter. "Introduction—Feminist Pedagogy: Challenging the Normative." *Canadian Journal of Education* 17, no. 3 (Summer 1992), 247-263.

Bryson, Mary and Suzanne de Castell. "Queer Pedagogy: Praxis Makes Im/Perfect." *Canadian Journal of Education* 18, no. 3 (Summer 1993), 285-305.

Calliste, Agnes. "Canada's Immigration Policy and Domestics from the Caribbean: The Second Domestic Scheme." In Jesse Vorst et al., eds. *Race, Class, Gender: Bonds and Barriers.* Toronto: Between the Lines; Winnipeg: The Society for Socialist Studies/Société d'études socialistes, 1989. 133-165.

Carty, Linda. "Women's Studies in Canada: A Discourse and Praxis of Exclusion." *Resources for Feminist Research/*

Documentation sur la recherche féministe 20, nos. 3/4
(Fall/Winter 1991), 12-18.

Carty, Linda and Dionne Brand. "'Visible Minority' Women—A
Creation of the Canadian State." *RFR/DRF* 17, no. 3 (December
1988), 39-42.

Castel, Jacqueline R. "Discerning Justice for Battered Women
Who Kill." *University of Toronto Faculty of Law Review* 48
(Spring 1990), 229-258.

Clark, Susan and Andrew S. Harvey. "The Sexual Division of
Labour: The Use of Time." *Atlantis: A Women's Studies
Journal* 2, no. 1 (Fall 1976).

Cohen, Marjorie Griffin. "Americanizing Services." in Ed Fin, ed.
The Facts on Free Trade. Toronto: James Lorimer & Company
Ltd., Publishers, 1988.

———. "The Implications of Economic Restructuring for Women:
The Canadian Situation." In Isa Bakker, ed. *Engendering
Macroeconomic Policy Reform.* London: Zed, 1994.

———. "Women and Free Trade." In Duncan Cameron, ed. *The
Free Trade Debates.* Toronto: James Lorimer & Company Ltd.,
Publishers, 1986.

Cox, Sue. "Strategies for the Present, Strategies for the Future:
Feminist Resistance to New Reproductive Technologies."
Canadian Woman Studies/les cahiers de la femme 13, no. 2
(1993), 86-90.

Currie, Dawn H. "Subject-ivity in the Classrooom: Feminism
Meets Academe." *Canadian Journal of Education* 17, no. 3
(Summer 1992), 341-364.

Debate on Laurie Bell, ed., *Good Girls/Bad Girls* in *Broadside* 9,
3 (December 1987/January 1988) and 9, 4 (February 1988).

Dulude, Louise. "Taxation of the Spouses: A Comparison of
Canadian, American, British, French and Swedish Law."
Osgoode Hall Law Journal 23, no. 1 (Spring 1985), 67-129.

Eichler, Margrit. "The Unfinished Transformation: Women and
Feminist Approaches in Sociology and Anthropology." In W.K.
Carroll, L. Christiansen-Ruffman, R.F. Currie, and D. Harrison,
eds. *Fragile Truths: Twenty-Five Years of Sociology and
Anthropology in Canada.* Ottawa: Carleton University Press, 1992.

Erickson, Lynda. "Canada." In Joni Lovenduski and Pippa Norris,
eds. *Gender and Party Politics.* London: Sage, 1994.

Eyre, Linda. "Compulsory Heterosexuality in a University
Classroom." *Canadian Journal of Education* 18, no. 3 (Summer
1993), 273-284.

Henry, Annette. "African Canadian Women Teachers' Activism:
Recreating Communities of Caring and Resistance." *Journal of
Negro Education* 61, no. 3 (1992), 392-404.

Henry, Annette. "Missing: Black Self-Representations in Canadian Educational Research." *Canadian Journal of Education* 18, no. 3 (Summer 1993), 206-222.

Hoodfar, Homa. "Feminist Anthropology and Critical Pedagogy: The Anthropology of Classrooms' Excluded Voices." *Canadian Journal of Education* 17, no. 3 (Summer 1992), 303-320.

Kornberg, Mona. "Employment Equity: The Quiet Revolution?" *Canadian Woman Studies/les cahiers de la femme* 6, no. 4 (Winter 1985).

Leach, Belinda. "Flexible Work, Precarious Future: Some Lessons from the Canadian Clothing Industry." *Canadian Review of Sociology and Anthropology* 30, no. 1 (1993), 64-77.

Leah, Ronnie. "Linking the Struggles: Racism, Feminism and the Union Movement." In Jesse Vorst et al., eds. *Race, Class, Gender: Bonds and Barriers*. Toronto: Between the Lines; Winnipeg: The Society for Socialist Studies/Société d'études socialistes, 1989. 166-195.

Lensky, Helen. "'Beyond Plumbing and Prevention': Feminist Approaches to Sex Education." *Gender and Education* 2, no. 2 (1990), 217-230.

———. "Going Too Far? Sexual Orientation(s) in the Sex Education Curriculum." In Lorna Erwin and David MacLennan, eds. *Sociology of Education in Canada*. Toronto: Copp Clark Longman, 1994. 278-289.

Litner, Bluma, Amy Rossiter, and Marilyn Taylor. "The Equitable Inclusion of Women in Higher Education: Some Consequences for Teaching." *Canadian Journal of Education* 17, no. 3 (Summer 1992), 286-302.

Macdonald, Martha. "Economics and Feminism: The Dismal Science." *Studies in Political Economy* 15 (Fall 1984).

Macdonald, Martha and Patricia Connelly. "Class and Gender in Fishing Communities in Nova Scotia." *Studies in Political Economy* 30 (Autumn 1989), 61-87.

Mackenzie, Suzanne. "Neglected Spaces in Peripheral Places: Homeworkers and the Creation of a New Economic Centre." *Cahiers de Geographie du Québec* 31, no. 83 (1987).

Macpherson, Kay and Meg Sears. "The Voice of Women: A History." In Gwen Matheson, ed. *Women in the Canadian Mosaic*. Toronto: Peter Martin Associates, 1976. 71-89.

Manicom, Ann. "Feminist Pedagogy: Transformations, Standpoints, and Politics." *Canadian Journal of Education* 17, no. 3 (Summer 1992), 365-389.

Marsden, Lorna. "The Importance of Studying Affirmative Action." *Canadian Woman Studies/les cahiers de la femme* 6, no. 4 (Winter 1985).

Marsden, Lorna. "The Role of the National Action Committee on the Status of Women in Facilitating Equal Pay Policy in Canada." In Ronnie Steinberg Ratner, ed. *Equal Employment Policy for Women: Strategies for Implementation in the United States, Canada, and Western Europe.* Philadelphia: Temple University Press, 1980.

Martindale, Kathleen. "Theorizing Autobiography and Materialist Feminist Pedagogy." *Canadian Journal of Education* 17. no. 3 (Summer 1992), 321-340.

Miles, Angela. "Margaret Benston's 'Political Economy of Women's Liberation.'" *Canadian Woman Studies/les cahiers de la femme* 13, no. 2 (Winter 1993), 31-35.

Morgan, Kathryn Pauly. "The Perils and Paradoxes of Feminist Pedagogy." *RFR/DRF* 16, no. 3 (September 1987), 49-52.

Morris, Cerise. "Determination and Thoroughness: The Movement for a Royal Commission on the Status of Women in Canada." *Atlantis: A Women's Studies Journal* 5, no. 2 (Spring 1980), 1-21.

Ng, Roxana. "'A Woman out of Control': Deconstructing Sexism and Racism in the University." *Canadian Journal of Education* 18, no. 3 (Summer 1993), 189-205.

Novak, Sylvia. "Not Seen, Not Heard: Women and Housing Policy." *Canadian Woman Studies/les cahiers de la femme* 11, no. 2 (Fall 1990), 53-57.

Pierson, Ruth Roach. "Colonization and Canadian Women's History." *Journal of Women's History* 4, no. 2 (Fall 1992), 134-156.

—————. "Experience, Difference, Dominance, and Voice in the Writing of Canadian Women's History." In Karen Offen, Jane Rendall, and R. R. Pierson, eds. *Writing Women's History: International Perspectives.* London: Macmillan; Bloomington and Urbana: Indiana University Press, 1991. 79-106.

Prentice, Susan. "The 'Mainstreaming' of Daycare." *RFR/DRF* 17, 3 (September 1988), 59-63.

Ptolemy, Kathleen. "First International Consultation on Refugee Women: Geneve (November 1988)." *Canadian Woman Studies/les cahiers de la femme* 10, no. 1 (Spring/printemps 1989), 21-24.

Ramirez, Judith. "Domestic Workers Organize." *Canadian Woman Studies/les cahiers de la femme* 4, no. 2 (Winter 1982).

Razack, Sherene. "Issues of Difference in Women's Studies: A Personal Reflection." *RFR/DFR* 20, nos. 3/4 (Fall/Winter 1991), 45-46.

—————. "Story-telling for Social Change." *Gender and Education* 5, no. 1 (1993), 55-69.

—————. "Using Law for Social Change: Historical Perspectives." *Queen's Law Journal* 17, no. 1 (Spring 1992), 31-53.

"Reports of the Canadian Women's Studies Project." *Atlantis: A Women's Studies Journal* 16, no. 1 (Fall 1990).

Ritchie, Laurell. "So Many Unorganized." *RFR/DRF* 10, no. 2 (July 1981), 13-14.

Schultz, Erma. "Organizing the Unorganized Farmworkers in Ontario." In Robert Argle, Charlene Gannage, and D.W. Livingstone, eds. *Working People and Hard Times*. Toronto: Garamond, 1987.

Shea, Catherine. "Changes in Women's Occupations." *Social Trends*. Ottawa: Statistics Canada, Autumn 1990.

Sky, Laura. "Commercial Interests in New Reproductive Technologies." *Canadian Woman Studies/les cahiers de la femme* 14, no. 3 (Summer/été 1994), 105-109.

Smith, Dorothy. "A Sociology for Women." In Julia Sherman and Evelyn Torton Beck, eds. *The Prism of Sex: Essays in the Sociology of Knowledge*. Madison: University of Wisconsin Press, 1979. 135-187.

Taylor, Jane. "'What Do You Do At the Women's Centre?': A Study of Some Canadian Women's Centres." Ottawa: Women's Programme, Secretary of State, 1974.

Thakur, Usha. "Combatting Family Violence: The South Asian Experience in Canada." *Canadian Woman Studies/les cahiers de la femme* 13, no. 1 (Fall 1992), 30-32.

Thobani, Sunera. "Making the Links: South Asian Women and the Struggle for Reproductive Rights." *Canadian Woman Studies/les cahiers de la femme* 13, no. 1 (Fall 1992), 19-22.

Thornhill, Esmeralda. "Focus on Black Women!" In Jesse Vorst et al., eds. *Race, Class, Gender: Bonds and Barriers*. Toronto: Between the Lines; Winnipeg: The Society for Socialist Studies/Société d'études socialistes, 1989.

Tite, Rosonna with the assistance of Margaret Malone. "Our Universities' Best-Kept Secret: Women's Studies in Canada." *Atlantis: A Women's Studies Journal* 16, no. 1 (Fall 1990), 25-39.

Vellacott, Jo. "Women, Peace & Power." In Pam McAllister, ed. *Reweaving the Web of Life: Feminism and Nonviolence*. Philadelphia, PA: New Society Publishers, 1982.

Weir, Lorna. "Anti-Racist Feminist Pedagogy, Self-Observed." *RFR/DRF* 20, no. 3/4 (Fall/Winter 1991), 19-26.

Wekerle, Gerda. "Responding to Diversity: Housing Developed by and for Women." In Helalata C. Dandekar, ed. *Shelter, Women and Development: First and Third World Perspectives*. Ann Arbor, Michigan: George Wahr Publishing Co., 1993.

Index